GERMAN IDEALISM

Frederick C. Beiser

German Idealism
The Struggle against Subjectivism,
1781–1801

HARVARD UNIVERSITY PRESS
Cambridge, Massachusetts, London, England

First Harvard University Press paperback edition, 2008

Library of Congress Cataloging-in-Publication Data

Beiser, Frederick C., 1949–
    German idealism : the struggle against subjectivism, 1781–1801 / Frederick C. Beiser.
      p.   cm.
    Includes bibliographical references and index.
    ISBN 978-0-674-00769-7 (cloth: alk. paper)
    ISBN 978-0-674-02717-6 (pbk.)
    1. Idealism, German—History—18th century.   2. Subjectivity—History—18th century.
  3. Philosophy, German—18th century.   I. Title.

  B2745 .B47   2002
  141'.0943'09033—dc21   2002017186

For Julia

Preface

"German idealism" is a common phrase in literary, historical, and philosophical circles. Broadly, it designates the philosophical doctrines initiated by Kant and then continued by Fichte, Schelling, and Hegel. But, beyond this very general definition, it is difficult to give the phrase a more precise meaning. That is not very surprising. What idealism means in Kant, Fichte, Schelling, and Hegel has been a matter of discussion and dispute for centuries.

The present study continues that discussion and dispute. Its chief task is to explain the meaning of idealism in Kant, Fichte, Schelling, and the young romantics (Hölderlin, Novalis, and Friedrich Schlegel). My chief excuse for doing so is that, at least in the case of Fichte, Schelling, and the romantics, though less so in the case of Kant and Hegel, the meaning of German idealism has remained comparatively underexplored in the English-speaking world. There have been many studies of Kant's transcendental idealism and a few of Hegel's absolute idealism; but there has been very little in English about German idealism as a whole. The greatest student of German idealism in the Anglo-American world was Josiah Royce, whose *Spirit of Modern Philosophy* and *Lectures on Modern Idealism* have influenced generations of students. Yet I hope to show that, for all its merits, Royce's interpretation has been profoundly misleading; in any case, Royce wrote without the benefit of much of the material available today.

There are good reasons for rethinking the meaning of German idealism. Since the 1960s there has been a remarkable resurgence of interest in the subject. *Prima facie* this is puzzling, since so much contemporary philosophy—whether in the pragmatic, existentialist, or analytic tradition—has its roots in the reaction against German idealism. There is indeed no going back to the age when the absolute once ruled the philosophical firmament. Yet, paradoxically, the very reasons for the obsolescence of German idealism have also been the reasons for its revival. These modern traditions understand themselves only when they appreciate what they grew out of and reacted against. If pragmatists, existentialists, and analytic philosophers wish to recover their roots, they must eventually grapple with German idealism itself.

The renewed interest in German idealism has as much to do with its abiding philosophical relevance as its vast historical significance. Recent epistemology still struggles to find some middle path between the extremes of skeptical subjectivism and naive realism, foundationalism and relativism, materialism and dualism, Platonism and historicism. But these were essentially the concerns of the German idealists themselves, whose attempts to find that middle path were subtle and sophisticated. Contemporary philosophers seeking to avoid these dilemmas can still find a rich source of inspiration in German idealism.

After centuries of intensive scholarship, no work on German idealism can claim great originality or novelty. Of course, this study is no exception. My debts to previous scholarship, which I have tried to acknowledge in many footnotes, are wide and deep. It is probably worthwhile, however, to point out a few respects in which this study differs from past work, especially the grand surveys of the subject in the German tradition. First, I have not attempted to do justice to the full scope of German idealism, its contributions to the fields of aesthetics, morals, and metaphysics, as well as to epistemology. This study is much more limited in focus. It concentrates on one specific theme: the meaning of idealism itself, and more specifically the reaction against subjectivism. I have focused upon this specific theme because it has been fateful for the reception of German idealism, which has so often been dismissed as a grandiose form of subjectivism. My central thesis is that, from its very inception, German idealism was a reaction against subjectivism, an attempt to prove the reality of the external world and to break out of the egocentric predicament. Second, I have made the young romantics—Hölderlin, Schlegel, Novalis—into crucial figures in the development of German idealism. The romantics have usually been placed either outside the idealist tradition entirely or inside it as mere transitional figures. But neither view is correct: the early romantics were the true founders of absolute idealism. Third, this study of German idealism omits Hegel, and it is indeed a reaction against the Hegelian legacy. Hegel's history of the period, which interprets it as a progression culminating in his own system, is tendentious philosophically and anachronistic historically. Fourth, there is no teleology to my history. I do not see German idealism either as a progression toward Hegel or as a decline from Kant. If we impartially and thoroughly examine each thinker in his own terms, it is unlikely that the results will show simple progress or decline. Each thinker is more likely to have his unique strengths and weaknesses—a gain here is a loss there—so that the end result is an *aporia* or invitation to eclecticism. Fifth and finally, I have attempted to integrate Kant's *Opus postumum* into the general history of German idealism; Kant's final years mark such an important development in his thought that they cannot be ignored.

My methodology has been essentially historical and hermeneutical. As far as possible, my aim has been to reconstruct an author's work in its individuality according to his original intention and context. Since they can be tendentious and anachronistic in application to historical material, I have bracketed contemporary philosophical concerns and concepts. I have also given primacy to textual exegesis over philosophical criticism, partly because the interpretation of the texts is so controversial, and partly because the most fair and accurate criticism has to come from the most thorough and sympathetic interpretation.

In this work, unlike my previous studies of classical German philosophy, I have not attempted to interpret a text in its cultural and political context. Although I regard cultural and political interpretation as essential, I do not think that the time is ripe for it in the case of German idealism. The problem is that the basic philosophical content of the texts is still too indeterminate and controversial. No one who approaches them can afford to ignore the fraught history of their interpretation. Without, however, an understanding of their content, any cultural or political interpretation is a hazardous business. A scholar who fails to appreciate the precise status of Fichte's absolute ego, for example, cannot appraise its political and cultural significance.

This study does *not* pretend to be a contribution to what the Germans call "*Konstellationsarbeit*," that is, detailed research into the context and interactions of German philosophers in Jena in the 1790s. While such research is invaluable, and indeed a necessary basis for work like my own, I have not been able to undertake it in any detailed or concerted manner here. Much of my work has rested on the more detailed research of Dieter Henrich, Manfred Frank, Michael Franz, Violetta Waibel, and others. Given the general state of knowledge of German idealism in the English-speaking world, it is impossible to presuppose acquaintance with this context, still less philosophical interest in it.

Some of the best scholarship on Kant and German idealism was written prior to World War I, and it has been the foundation for much of my own work. I have profound debts to the German historical tradition, especially to the work of Erich Adickes, Benno Erdmann, Wilhelm Dilthey, Rudolf Haym, and Ernst Cassirer, which, I believe, provides a far superior paradigm for doing history of philosophy than the analytic tradition. Regarding more contemporary scholarship, my chief debts have been to Paul Guyer and Henry Allison in Kant studies, and to Dieter Henrich and Manfred Frank in post-Kantian philosophy. Although I often take issue with these scholars, that is in direct proportion to my debts to them.

The first drafts for this study were written in 1995, but my work on German idealism ultimately goes back to 1975 when I first began my Oxford D.Phil. dissertation on the origins of Hegel's *Phänomenologie des Geistes*. The immediate stimulus for this study came from the philosophy department at Indiana University, Bloomington, which became a hotbed for German idealism in 1995. For their stimulus and encouragement, I am especially indebted to my colleagues there, Michael Friedman, Paul Franks, and Graciela DePierris. Large parts of the draft of this work were read by Michael Friedman, Paul Franks, Frederick Neuhouser, Robert Richards, Allen Wood, Eric Watkins, Andrew Janiak, and Karl Ameriks; their criticisms and suggestions have greatly improved the whole. Many of my views grew out of discussions over the years with graduate students, especially Stephen Cho, Hess Chung, Andrew Janiak, Michah Gottlieb, Joshua Shaw, Rondo Keele, and Christian Johnson. Sadly, the happy and heady days of German idealism in Bloomington have come to an end. This book is my tribute to them.

Finally, my greatest debts are to my wife and daughter, Matilde and Julia, whose love and patience sustained all.

Bloomington Indiana
April 2001

Contents

GERMAN IDEALISM

Introduction

1. Realism in German Idealism

There has been in the history of philosophy a remarkably popular and persistent interpretation of German idealism that, much scholarship notwithstanding, continues to find adherents to this day.[1] Both detractors and defenders of German idealism endorse this interpretation; for the detractors it is a compelling reason to spurn the idealist tradition, for the defenders a persuasive reason to embrace it.

According to this interpretation, German idealism is essentially the culmination of the Cartesian tradition. It accepts some of the central assumptions of this tradition: that epistemology is *philosophia prima;* that only self-knowledge is certain; that the immediate objects of knowledge are ideas; and that knowledge consists in contemplation rather than action. But it goes even further than Descartes because it takes these assumptions to their ultimate bitter conclusion—namely, *subjectivism,* the doctrine that the subject has an immediate knowledge only of its own ideas, so that it has no knowledge beyond its circle of consciousness. Supposedly, rather than struggling against subjectivism, the German idealists welcomed it, seeing it as the result of a deep epistemological truth: that it is impossible to get outside our representations to compare them with reality itself. To be sure, the German idealists reject solipsism, the theory that I know the contents only of my own *empirical* or *individual* mind; nevertheless, they still insist that all knowledge is a function of some *transcendental* or *universal* mind, which somehow exists within all empirical and individual ones. Hence the circle of consciousness is never really broken; rather it is only widened to embrace everyone.

This interpretation usually goes along with a seductively simple narrative about the history of German idealism. This narrative is essentially a story about the gradual and inevitable completion of Kant's "Copernican Revolution." The story begins with Kant's Copernican doctrine that truth consists not in the conformity of concepts to objects (transcendental realism) but in the conformity of objects to concepts (transcendental idealism). The drama then unfolds when Kant suffers a loss of nerve, failing to take his revolution to its final conclusions. Fatefully, Kant clung to his belief in things-in-themselves, things independent of the conditions of our knowing them; and he insisted upon a dualism between understanding and sensibility, so that the transcendental subject is the source of only the form but not the matter of experience. It was then the task of Kant's great successors—Fichte, Schelling, and Hegel—to remove these recidivistic inconsistencies and to complete Kant's revolution. They achieved their grand ambition first by purging dogmatic residues from Kant's system (the thing-in-itself, the given manifold), and then by extending its underlying principle (the creative powers of the subject). The story ends with the triumph of the subject, which is now expanded to cosmic dimensions so that it becomes the source of *all* reality. This subject is no longer the meager and pale Kantian transcendental 'I,' which is only the formal condition of experience; rather, it is the rich and mighty absolute 'I,' which is the origin of both the form and content of experience. In essence, then, the development of German idealism is a tale about the *expansion, aggrandizement,* or *inflation* of the transcendental subject.

Despite its attractive simplicity, this interpretation of the history of German idealism is deeply problematic. In fundamental respects it is more accurate to say the exact opposite: that the development of German idealism is not the *culmination* but the *nemesis* of the Cartesian tradition. Explicitly and emphatically, the German idealists criticized some of the central assumptions of that tradition: that self-consciousness is certain and given; that we know ourselves with more certainty than objects in space; that knowledge is the result of contemplation rather than action; that the bearers of meaning are ideas; and, at least after Kant, that we know ourselves apart from and prior to others. This critique of the Cartesian legacy begins with the early Kant; it grows in intensity with the first *Kritik;* and it comes to a climax with Fichte, Schelling, and Hegel.

Rather than consisting in the progressive triumph of subjectivism, in the gradual expansion of the circle of consciousness, the development of German idealism is more the story about the growing reaction against subjectivism, about the increasingly intense effort to break out of that circle. Since the 1760s there had been a reaction in Germany against "the way of ideas" inspired by the Scottish philosophy of common sense.[2] It was widely believed that this tradition, by imposing ideas between the perceiving subject and external reality, ends in the abyss of Humean skepticism. Hence there had been a long history of attempts to refute "egoism" or "nihilism," the doctrines that we know only our own representations. After the 1760s in Germany, the critique of idealism had become a favorite theme of metaphysical treatises and university lectures.[3]

German idealism only continued and developed the earlier reaction against the way of ideas. The refutation of idealism, the proof of the reality of the external world, became a fundamental desideratum and preoccupation of post-Kantian idealism. Within this tradition there were different, even conflicting, accounts of the nature of this reality, of what constitutes its independence or externality. It could be the universal and necessary structure of space, the thing-in-itself, the single universal substance, or the eternal archetypes. But, whatever form it took, external reality had to exist independent of the consciousness of the empirical and individual subject; and it had to be as certain as self-knowledge itself.

The critique of subjectivism, the attempt to establish a satisfactory form of realism, was indeed the driving impulse behind the development of German idealism. One form of idealism succeeded another when a previous form was found to provide too weak a foundation for realism. Kant rejected Leibniz's and Berkeley's empirical idealism because it had made the existence of objects in space a mere illusion; Fichte became disappointed with Kant's transcendental idealism because he had not provided a sufficient basis for his empirical realism; Hölderlin, Schlegel, Novalis, and Schelling broke with Fichte's ethical idealism because it still trapped the ego inside the circle of consciousness.

Hence the development of German idealism consists not in an increasing subjectivism but in the very opposite: a growing realism and naturalism.[4] This movement toward a greater realism and naturalism already begins with Kant and Fichte, whose "critical" or "formal" idealism upholds the empirical reality of objects in space, limits the role of the understanding to providing the form of experience, and postulates some independent reality to the matter of experience, whether it is a thing-in-itself or some "check" or "obstacle" (*Anstoß*). But Kant's and Fichte's critical idealism proved insufficient for the absolute idealists—Hölderlin, Novalis, Schlegel, Schelling, and Hegel—who advocated a "higher realism," which postulates the existence of the absolute or the infinite reality of nature. Rather than making nature the product of the transcendental subject, the absolute idealists did the very opposite, deriving the transcendental subject from its place within nature. The rationality of the Kantian-Fichtean subject now became nothing more than the highest manifestation and realization of the powers of nature.

2. Exorcising the Spirit

The central theme behind the subjectivist interpretation of German idealism has been "the infinite self," "the universal spirit," or "absolute ego." This theme has been regarded as "the thread . . . through the labyrinth of German speculation," the key to unlock the temple holding the mysteries of post-Kantian philosophy.[5] Accordingly, German idealism has been interpreted as a story about the gradual discovery of this ego, as a tale about the progressive path toward absolute self-awareness. Thus the account Fichte, Schelling, and Hegel once gave of the history of self-consciousness is applied to German idealism itself.

The drama of absolute self-awareness is a subplot within the grander tale about the completion of the Copernican Revolution. The subplot begins with Kant's doctrine of the unity of apperception, the 'I' of the 'I think,' which signifies only my possible self-awareness throughout a succession of sensations. The action then proceeds when Fichte, Schelling, and Hegel progressively uncover the deeper metaphysical meaning underlying this meager and abstract 'I.' In several bold steps, they removed all the restraints and restrictions Kant had so carefully placed upon his transcendental self. First, they purged the Kantian 'I' of all empirical and individual connotations, arguing that, as condition of experience and individuality, it could not be individuated within experience itself. Second, contrary to Kant's strictures in the Paralogisms, they maintained that the 'I' gives us knowledge of some noumenal activity or entity underlying all reality. Third, after removing the thing-in-itself as the cause of experience, they made the Kantian transcendental self the source of not only the form but also the content of experience, so that it creates not only the general forms of the understanding (the categories) and sensibility (space and time), but also the specific content of experience itself. Hence the Kantian transcendental self, which was essentially only a construct to explain the possibility of a single objective experience, gradually became converted into a metaphysical principle, the single universal self that is the source of all of nature and history. On this account, German idealism becomes something like a transcendental revival of Christianity, theology through philosophical means.[6]

Sadly, despite its narrative charm, this story too is more fantasy than reality. The problem is that its hero hardly ever appeared on stage. The truth be told: the absolute subject, the infinite ego, or universal spirit, *understood as a metaphysical principle or noumenal reality*, never had much of a role to play in German idealism. If it appeared at all, it was only very briefly, confined to a short phase of Schelling's philosophical development, the few months he adhered to the doctrines espoused in his early *Vom Ich als Prinzip der Philosophie* (1796); but Schelling quickly moved away from this position, and even during this period he equivocated whether he meant to commit himself to the existence of the absolute subject. The first to postulate the idea of an absolute subject was Fichte in his 1794 *Grundlage der gesamten Wissenschaftslehre;* but he stressed the regulative status of this idea, and firmly rejected the thesis of 'dogmatic idealism' that the absolute subject creates the entire world. After Fichte, the early romantics heavily criticized the concept of an absolute ego. Hölderlin, Schlegel, Novalis, Schelling, and Hegel all disputed the thesis that the absolute can be described as something subjective, as something mental rather than physical. The absolute, they argued, must be interpreted as something impersonal, neutral, or indifferent, whether it be pure being, life, or the indifference point; to construe it as the ego is to hypostatize and anthropomorphize it, dragging it down into the realm of finite experience.

Another serious problem with this story is that it ignores the underlying logic behind one central concept of post-Kantian idealism: the concept of the absolute.[7] The post-Kantian idealists understood the absolute in transcendental terms as the fundamental condition of the possibility of experience; as such, they refused to define it as either subjective or objective; rather, they argued that both subjectivity and objectivity fall within experience, so that these concepts cannot be applied to the absolute except on pain of circularity. The champions of the subjectivist interpretation saw that the self of German idealism cannot be interpreted in empirical or individual terms; but they never fully recognized that, even if its empirical and individual dimensions are removed, it is still impossible to apply the concept of the self to the absolute.[8] The very logic of the concept of the absolute excludes its description as either subjective or objective, since such terms limit what is meant to be unlimited. To be sure, the realm of spirit, the subjective, could be the highest *manifestation, expression,* or *embodiment* of the absolute; even so, however, it had to remain only one of its appearances.

The basic error behind the subplot, and the subjectivist interpretation in general, has been its failure to distinguish between two very different versions or forms of idealism. The conflation is understandable, given that the idealists themselves sometimes failed to disentangle them. The two versions of idealism correspond to two senses of the term "ideal": the ideal can be the mental in contrast to the physical, the spiritual rather than the material; or it can be the archetypical in contrast to the ectypical, the normative rather than the substantive. Idealism in the former sense is the doctrine that all reality depends upon some self-conscious subject; idealism in the latter sense is the doctrine that everything is a manifestation of the ideal, an appearance of reason. This second sense is perfectly compatible with the equal and independent reality of the mental and physical; and it has no difficulty in ascribing reality to a physical world. The problem with the subjectivist interpretation is that it stretches the mental and the subjective to do the work of the ideal or the intelligible, so that it becomes the reality of the entire world; but then the concept of the subjective is in danger of losing all meaning.

Once we admit this distinction we get a very different account of the history of German idealism from the subjectivisit interpretation. Here again that interpretation proves itself to be the very opposite of the truth. Rather than a story about the triumph of the subject, German idealism becomes a story about the progressive *de-subjectivization* of the Kantian legacy, the growing recognition that the ideal realm consists not in personality and subjectivity but in the normative, the archetypical, and the intelligible. The subjective played a diminishing role in German idealism as the post-Kantian idealists realized that the Kantian transcendental subject plays a residual role in the constitution of experience, whose objectivity ultimately depends upon its universal and necessary normative structure. The history of German idealism is therefore more the story about the progressive unfolding of neo-Platonism. Ironically, its ultimate heirs were the Marburg neo-Kantians Hermann Cohen, Paul Natorp, and Ernst Cassirer.[9]

3. The Critique of Foundationalism

Another cardinal tenet of the subjectivist interpretation is that German idealism was a radical renewal of Cartesian foundationalism.[10] Its supposed ambition was to restore and finally realize the Cartesian program of beginning with some self-evident first principle, and then deriving from it, in a series of deductive steps, all our fundamental beliefs about the world. Like Descartes, Kant and Fichte found this principle in self-awareness, in some variant of *cogito ergo sum.*

Though it has some plausibility, this thesis conceals the complexity and variety of German idealism. It applies only with the greatest difficulty to Kant. One can interpret the Transcendental Deduction of the first *Kritik* as a form of foundationalism, since it *appears* to begin with the self-evidence of the 'I think' and then to derive the application of the categories to experience. Yet this interpretation has been hotly contested;[11] and even if it were vindicated, it is false that the Transcendental Deduction is part of a general foundationalist program. As early as his 1755 *Nova dilucidatio* Kant explicitly rejected the rationalist program of deriving all philosophy from a single self-evident first principle; and he always stressed the need for a separation of our faculties, deliberately thwarting any attempt to reduce them to a single source and function. Last but not least, the first *Kritik* demotes the privileged place of the Cartesian subject by arguing that self-consciousness is no more certain than the awareness of objects in space outside me.

The interpretation of German idealism as a revival of foundationalism has most plausibility in application to K. L. Reinhold's *Elementarphilosophie,* whose purpose was to systematize and deduce all the fundamental results of the critical philosophy by deriving them from a single self-evident first principle. Reinhold's program was indeed very influential. It was endorsed by Fichte and the young Schelling, even though they rejected his specific proposal about what should be the the first principle. Following Reinhold, their strategy was to begin with some self-evident first principle about self-awareness, and then to derive from it the systematic order of the Kantian categories and the most general laws of experience. Reinhold's foundationalism was indeed so influential that it was even endorsed by some of his severest critics, among them the neo-Humean skeptic G. E. Schulze, who saw it as a necessary ideal of reason.

Despite these points, it would be a serious mistake to generalize Reinhold's influence, as if it held sway over the entire period, and as if his foundationalism were the methodological ideal for all the German idealists.[12] There are several difficulties with such a generalization. First, it applies only with the greatest difficulty to Fichte and Hegel, though they are held to be its most important heirs. Although Fichte had once expounded a radical foundationalist program, he soon placed severe constraints upon it, insisting that the first principles of philosophy would have to be regulative postulates. More important, Fichte's solution to the problem of skepticism is essentially pragmatic rather than foundationalist, for he taught that the problem of knowledge could be resolved only in the realm of practice. For his part, Hegel had explictly criticized Reinhold's program in his *Differenzschrift*, rejecting any attempt to begin philosophy with self-evident first principles. Though Hegel endorsed the systematic ideal, he forswore any attempt to base it upon the geometric method. If Hegel was a foundationalist at all, it was only by subverting the foundationalism of the Cartesian tradition.[13] Second, such a generalization would not apply at all to Schlegel, Novalis, and Hölderlin, who were were sharp critics of Reinhold's foundationalist program from the very beginning. They denied that there were any self-evident first principles in philosophy, disputed the possibility of constructing a complete and perfect system, and extended skepticism to the principles and procedures of transcendental philosophy itself. Third, Reinhold's influence was limited to a very short period, which did not extend beyond 1795, and it found only a few adherents. In fact, the followers of Reinhold's program were a small minority, heavily outnumbered by its critics. When Fichte arrived at Jena in 1794 his foundationalist program was already seen as outmoded and untenable.

The common picture of German idealism as neofoundationalism breaks down entirely as soon as we consider the general intellectual context of philosophy in Jena, the small university town that gave birth to so much of German idealism. One of the most interesting and important features of that context was its pervasive *critique* of foundationalism. Recent scholarship has revealed the profound extent to which the early students of Reinhold— J. B. Erhard, C. I. Diez, F. Weißhuhn, C. C. Schmid, F. C. Forberg, J. P. A. Feuerbach, and F. I. Niethammer—were extremely skeptical of any form of foundationalism.[14] They doubted the possibility of establishing a single self-evident first principle from which one could derive, in a manner immune to skeptical doubt, our most basic beliefs about the world. They also criticized the possibility of creating the single perfect system of knowledge, a system that would provide the only valid structure for all possible knowledge. They saw such a first principle, and indeed the system derived from it, as a regulative ideal, a goal that could be approached but never attained in the infinite progress of enquiry.

This *Grundsatzkritik* had an immediate and profound effect on the development of German idealism. Despite his early avowal of the Reinholdian program, it made its mark on Fichte, who soon reinterpreted his first principles as regulative ideas. It then became central to the philosophy of the early romantics—to Hölderlin, Schlegel, and Novalis—who, in one form or another, were closely connected with the circle surrounding Reinhold. They too soon embraced its skepticism about first principles and systems, and made that skepticism an integral part of their own *Weltanschauung*.

To an extraordinary degree contemporary philosophers regard antifoundationalism as a unique characteristic and singular accomplishment of their own postmodernist age. But this is sheer complacency, arising from ignorance of the past. The rich legacy of German idealism will only be fully understood and appreciated when contemporary philosophers see the profound extent to which it has not merely anticipated but transcended their own postmodernist agenda. The German idealists not only foresaw but lived through and responded to the collapse of foundationalism; their subtle and sophisticated response to this crisis makes them of abiding relevance today.

4. The Troublesome Hegelian Legacy

Ultimately, the subjectivist interpretation of German idealism must trace its origins back to Hegel's history of philosophy. It was Hegel who saw his own system as the culmination of German idealism and who made the self-consciousness of spirit the end of history itself. Although Hegel himself was no subjectivist, it must be said that he unwittingly gave enormous impetus to the subjectivist interpretation of German idealism. If Hegel's absolute is interpreted as an infinite mind, and if one accepts that his system is the culmination of German idealism, then it seems as if the idea of the absolute or infinite subject must be the final purpose of German idealism itself. This simple but seductive view has had a deep impact upon the historiography of German idealism, if only because so much of its history has been written from a Hegelian standpoint.[15]

Prima facie the subjectivist interpretation has some plausibility in application to Hegel's later system. There is a sense in which the more mature Hegel went back to Fichte by recasting the absolute in more subjective terms. After the dissolution of his alliance with Schelling in 1804, Hegel began to criticize Schelling's idea of the absolute for its excessive naturalism, for not providing sufficient place for the realm of spirit that consists in society, the state, and history. This led him to conceive of the absolute less as nature and more as spirit. On these grounds some scholars see spirit rather than nature as the fundamental concept of Hegel's system, as if his fundamental loyalty were to Kant and Fichte rather than to Spinoza and Schelling.[16] But such an interpretation is very one-sided, exaggerating Hegel's attempt to correct the one-sidedness of Spinoza and Schelling. No less than Schelling and his romantic forebears, Hegel too saw the absolute as the idea—the infinite formal-final cause—that manifests itself in the realms of both nature and spirit. To be sure, Hegel gave a greater weight to spirit than Schelling, who gave pride of place to nature over spirit, and who never gave the realms of society and history a significant role in his *Identitätssystem*. Nevertheless, Hegel still saw the realm of spirit as one manifestation of the absolute, as one part of his system, whose culmination was really the idea itself.

Whatever the proper interpretation of Hegel, his history of philosophy has now lost its grip over research on German idealism. Scholars now investigate the earlier idealists for their own sake and in their own terms, without considering them as stepping stones on the triumphal path toward Hegel's grand system. But it is important to see precisely what is wrong with Hegel's history. It is not that Hegel had a bad methodology; like any good historicist he insisted that each philosophy should be interpreted from within and taken on its own terms. Rather, the problem is that Hegel did not follow his own method, he did not practice what he preached. Instead, he *expropriated* the past, exaggerating his own originality and individuality. What Hegel portrayed as his own characteristic doctrine, what he regarded as his unique achievement, was all too often said years before him. There is not a single Hegelian theme that cannot be traced back to his predecessors in Jena, to many earlier thinkers whom Hegel and the Hegelian school either belittled or ignored. The fathers of absolute idealism were Hölderlin, Schlegel, and Schelling—though the first would find no mention in Hegel's history, the second would be trivialized and dismissed, and the third treated as a mere footstool. So many ideas that are seen as uniquely Hegelian—the dialectic, immanent critique, the synthesis of Fichte and Spinoza, the absolute as the identity of identity and nonidentity, the importance of history within philosophy, self-positing spirit, alienation, the unity of community and individual liberty—were all commonplaces in Jena before Hegel came there in 1801.

To say this is not to belittle Hegel's achievement: in unsurpassed fashion he summarized and integrated into one system all the themes his less scholastic and organized contemporaries had left in fragments or notebooks. Nevertheless, to say this is to put Hegel in proper historical perspective: he was not the creative and original thinker that his history suggests or that his disciples imply. Hegel's strength lay in his synthetic and systematic powers, in rationalizing and organizing the wealth of ideas created by his contemporaries. In truth, Hegel was just as his friends in the *Stift* once portrayed him: *der alte Mann*, who ambled along on crutches. He was a tortoise among hares; and, when all the hares had squandered or consumed their energies, he alone trudged, slowly but surely, over the finish line. Like all victors, he then rewrote history from his point of view, as the tale of his own triumph.

5. The Taxonomy of German Idealism

It should come as no surprise to any student of German philosophy in its great classical period from Kant to Hegel that the term "German idealism" is not univocal. Such is the diversity and complexity of the period that there is not a single doctrine to which all thinkers adhere, and which could be described for the same reasons as 'idealism.' There are rather a number of doctrines that are often in conflict with one another, and that at best bear some very general similarity to one another.

The absence of univocity does not imply, however, that it is impossible to make generalizations, still less that the term should be altogether abandoned. It is one of the main results of this study that there were essentially two fundamental forms of German idealism from 1781 to 1801. There was first of all the "subjective" or "formal" idealism of Kant and Fichte, according to which the transcendental subject is the source of the form but not the matter of experience. Contrary to it, there was the "objective" or "absolute" idealism of the romantics (Hölderlin, Novalis, Schlegel, Schelling, and the young Hegel), according to which the forms of experience are self-subsistent and transcend both the subject and object. The basic difference between these forms is simple and straightforward. While subjective idealism *attaches* the forms of experience to the transcendental subject, which is their source and precondition, objective idealism *detaches* them from that subject, making them hold for the realm of pure being as such.

Both subjective and objective idealism can be understood as idealism in a broad sense because they both claim that reality depends upon the ideal or the rational. But they give very different meanings to the ideal or rational corresponding to the two senses noted above (section 3). In subjective idealism the ideal or the rational is the subjective, mental, or spiritual; in objective idealism it is the archetypical, intelligible, and structural. Very crudely,

Kant's and Fichte's subjective idealism maintains that the form of experience derives from the transcendental subject, even though the matter of experience is given. Conversely, the romantics' objective idealism holds that everything is a manifestation of the archetypical or rational form. Obviously, these are distinct doctrines. Unlike subjective idealism, objective idealism does not privilege the subject over the object. Rather, both the subjective and objective are equal instances of the archtypical; in other words, both the mental and the material conform to rational necessity.

If this distinction is simple and straightforward, it has also been persistently confused. The source of this confusion came from the idealist tradition itself. Both Leibniz and Kant had understood the *mundus intelligibilis* not only as the archtypical or nomological but also as the mental or spiritual. It is only much later in the history of German philosophy—more specifically, in the mid-1790s—that these meanings become finally disentangled. It was one of the achievements of the romantic generation to distinguish them and to develop a new form of objective idealism on the basis of this distinction. The distinction came to its fullest and clearest expression only in 1801 in Hegel's *Differenzschrift*.[17]

Although the ideal has a different meaning in subjective and objective idealism, it would be artificial to draw too rigid a distinction between these forms of idealism. This is first and foremost because objective idealism grew out of subjective idealism by developing objective strands of thought already implicit within it. Objective idealism took its starting point from the analysis of experience in subjective idealism. Both Kant and Fichte had claimed that the very possibility of self-consciousness depends upon the universal and necessary forms of experience. The subject could know itself, attribute ideas and actions to itself, and perceive an objective world only by virtue of these forms. Where objective idealism departed from subjective idealism was in its insistence that the subjective is possible only *within* experience itself. The subject could not be the source and precondition of these forms when its very identity already depended on them. So rather than having priority over these forms, the subject became subsumed under them. According to the objective idealists, the subject and object are both manifestations or instances of these forms, which constitute the absolute or the realm of pure being itself.

Another reason for not drawing too sharp a distinction between subjective and objective idealism is that the objective idealists to some extent restored the central role of subjectivity within the absolute. Without exception, they held that the transcendental subject is the highest organization and development of all the powers of nature or history.[18] To be sure, the subject would be only a manifestation, embodiment, or appearance of the absolute; but it would still be given pride of place as the very culmination of nature and history. The central role of subjectivity was reinstated as the *end* or *purpose*, though not as the foundation or starting point, of nature and history. For just this reason, it is necessary to be extremely cautious in claiming that absolute idealism permits the absolute to exist independent of the knowing subject. Schelling, Hegel, Schlegel, Hölderlin, and Novalis all held that the absolute comes to its fullest realization, organization, and development only in the self-awareness of the knowing subject. They were utterly opposed to any view that would permit a dualism between the subject's knowing the absolute and the absolute itself. In their view, the subject's awareness of the absolute is the self-knowledge of the absolute through the subject.

What unites these forms of idealism—what makes them belong to a single tradition—is their similar approach to some common philosophical problems. Since Kant, philosophers had become preoccupied with two distinct but closely related issues: how to explain the possibility of knowledge, and how to account for the reality of the external world. The entangling of these problems created a paradoxical and apparently irresolvable predicament for Kant and the entire generation after him. The predicament made it impossible to solve one problem without undermining the solution to the other. To explain the possibility of knowledge requires demonstrating that there is some kind of *identity* between the subject and object; for if the subject and object are completely distinct from one another, they will not be able to interact or correspond with one another to produce knowledge. Hence all the German idealists after Kant, and essentially under his influence, developed what they call the principle of *subject–object identity*, which, very crudely, means that there must be some point of identity between the subject and object of knowledge for there to be some correspondence and interaction between them. But this principle seems to come unstuck in the face of the need to explain the reality of the external world. For, to account for this reality, it is necessary to establish some kind of *dualism* between the subject and object, given that it is just a fact of our experience that the object appears given to us and independent of our conscious control. Hence the general problem of German idealism was how to find a principle of subject–object identity that could surmount but also explain the subject–object dualism of ordinary experience. Paradoxically, such a principle had to both over-come dualism yet also demonstrate its necessity. Hegel put the whole problem in a nutshell when he famously stated that the task of philosophy is to find the "identity of identity and nonidentity." Though this formula seems mystical and metaphysical, it states perfectly well the main epistemological predicament facing all the German idealists: How is it possible to explain the possibility of knowledge according to idealist principles and yet to account for the reality of the external world?

The following chapters explore how the German idealists attempted to resolve this paradoxical predicament. Each of them examines one respect in which the German idealists—from Kant to Schelling—attempted to explain the reality of the external world on the basis of idealist principles. German idealism thus turns out to be a search for that elusive but necessary ideal: the identity of identity and nonidentity. Let us now examine in some detail the history of that quest.

PART I

Kant's Critique of Idealism

Introduction:
Kant and the Problem
of Subjectivism

1. The Clash of Interpretations

In the more than two hundred years since the publication of the *Kritik der reinen Vernunft* in May 1781 there have been countless interpretations of Kant's transcendental idealism. These interpretations vary greatly, and they often flatly contradict one another. But, whatever their differences, all have to define themselves in terms of two antithetical extremes. At one extreme there is the *subjectivist* interpretation, which maintains that Kant's transcendental idealism is a species of subjective idealism;[1] at the other extreme there is the *objectivist* interpretation, which states that transcendental idealism is, if only implicitly, a primitive form of objective or absolute idealism.[2]

According to the subjectivist interpretation, Kant's transcendental idealism is the epitome of the way of ideas inaugurated by Descartes, and then developed by Locke, Berkeley, and Hume. Supposedly, transcendental idealism is based upon the fundamental principle behind this tradition: that the immediate objects of perception are the ideas of the perceiving subject. But it takes this principle to its ultimate skeptical conclusion: that we have no direct knowledge of reality in itself; rather, all that we know are our own representations, from which we must infer the existence of an independent reality. The fundamental premise behind this interpretation is its account of Kant's concept of an appearance. On this account, appearances are not aspects or extrinsic properties of things-in-themselves but simply representations. Since Kant often states that appearances are nothing more than representations, and since he also insists that we know nothing more than appearances, it follows that all we know is our own representations. Hence transcendental idealism proves to be a form of subjectivism or skeptical solipsism, a doctrine limiting knowledge to the contents of our individual minds.

Prima facie the subjectivist interpretation seems to be wildly implausible, riding roughshod over the realistic aspects of Kant's transcendental idealism. More specifically, it appears to ignore not only Kant's belief in the reality of things-in-themselves but also his empirical realism, his doctrine that the existence of objects in space is given in perception. But the subjectivists are perfectly aware of these realistic aspects of Kant's system; they argue, however, that they are incompatible with his more fundamental principles. Hence they stress the subjectivist premise behind Kant's empirical realism: the identification of material objects with representations; and they point out that Kant's belief in the reality of things-in-themselves is inconsistent with his critical teaching that we cannot know anything beyond experience. If Kant were only consistent, the subjectivists contend, there would be very little difference between his idealism and Berkeley's. Ultimately, the only difference between their idealisms is Kant's greater rationalism: transcendental idealism is simply Berkeley's idealism without its empiricism.

According to the objectivist interpretation, transcendental idealism is not the apotheosis of, but the antidote to, the Cartesian way of ideas. Nowhere is this antidote more apparent than in the Transcendental Deduction of the first *Kritik,* where Kant shows how the ideas of the knowing subject are determined by the intersubjective order of the a priori concepts of the understanding. There Kant turns subjectivism upside down, for he demonstrates that the intersubjective public world constituted by these concepts is not constructed from the ideas of the individual mind; rather, it is the necessary condition of even having such ideas. The knowing subject therefore loses its primacy, because it is not the first condition of experience but simply another element within experience itself. The fundamental mistake of the subjectivists, the objectivists further contend, is that they construe Kant's forms of understanding and intuition as psychological faculties, as if they were only the subject's ways of conceiving and perceiving the world. But this hypostatizes these forms, treating them again as objects within experience when they are instead the conditions for its possibility. These forms cannot be conceived as either subjective or objective because they lay down the conditions under which anything can be identified as either subjective or objective.

Prima facie the objectivist interpretation seems to be as implausible as the subjectivist one. Most conspicuously, it appears to ignore or eliminate the

Kantian version of the Cartesian *cogito*, the 'I' of the unity of apperception, which is the source of all the categories. But it is precisely with regard to the unity of apperception that the objectivist interpretation shows its true colors. The objectivists insist that 'I' does not designate any subject at all, whether pure and universal or empirical and individual. Following Kant's suggestion in the Paralogisms, they note that 'I' designates nothing more than an impersonal 'it.' This 'it' is either the activity of pure thinking—the mere exercise of a cognitive function—or it is the unifying principle behind the totality of experience, that which makes the forms of understanding and sensibility into a systematic whole.[3]

Whether implicitly or explicitly, unwittingly or intentionally, the objectivist interpretation brings Kant's transcendental idealism very close to the absolute idealism of Schelling and Hegel.[4] The central thesis of absolute idealism is that everything is an appearance of the idea, where the idea is not something in the individual conscious mind but the form, archetype, or structure of reality in general. Since it is a normative order that makes possible both subjectivity and objectivity, this idea is neither subjective nor objective itself; rather, it transcends both the subject and object and yet manifests itself in both. Because they provide the conditions under which the subject and object, the appearances of inner and outer sense, become objects of experience, Kant's a priori forms are the prototypes for such a normative order.

2. Method and Results

Prima facie it seems absurd that Kant's transcendental idealism can be interpreted in such antithetical ways. Yet Kant's texts are so rich and dense that advocates of both interpretations have been able to find evidence for them. Both parties concede that there are some passages that count against their interpretation; but they insist that these do not represent the *spirit, intention,* or *ultimate direction* behind Kant's thought. For them, it is not so much a question of what Kant *did say* but of what he *ought to have said* according to his fundamental principles.

How is it possible for the Kant scholar to determine the strengths and weaknesses of these interpretations? How can he find his way through the textual labyrinth, which seems to support both readings? The most simple and straightforward approach is historical: to investigate Kant's philosophical development, and more specifically Kant's own reaction to subjective and objective idealism. It is still an underappreciated fact that, for decades,

Kant himself had been a sharp critic of all forms of idealism. From his 1755 *Nova dilucidatio* to his 1797–1800 *Opus postumum*, he had opposed both extremes of the idealist tradition. He had criticized Descartes' subjective idealism because it doubted the reality of the external world; and he had attacked Leibniz's objective idealism because it affirmed only the reality of the noumenal world. After the formulation of his own idealist doctrine in the 1770 Inaugural Dissertation, Kant struggled to distinguish his idealism from other variants, especially Leibniz's Platonic idealism. This concern only intensified after the publication of the first *Kritik*, when Kant became especially troubled by the charge of Berkeleyianism. Finally, in both the first and second editions of the *Kritik*, and in the *Reflexionen* of the 1790s, Kant devoted much energy to the refutation of Descartes' skeptical idealism. It is safe to conclude that, throughout his development, Kant conceived his transcendental idealism as the middle path between the extremes of subjective and objective idealism. It is as if he already foresaw—and forcefully rejected—both the subjective and objective interpretations of his transcendental idealism.

Since the historical approach promises to shed the most light on the difficult interpretative issues, Part I provides a close study of Kant's reaction toward idealism. I focus especially on the development of Kant's views, begining with the 1755 *Nova dilucidatio* and closing with the *Opus postumum*. The first chapter considers Kant's attitude toward idealism in the precritical years; the second, third, and fourth chapters examine his refutation of dogmatic and skeptical idealism in the first edition of the *Kritik*. Chapters 5 and 6 are devoted to Kant's critique of idealism in the *Prolegomena* and the second edition of the *Kritik*, while chapters 7–9 evaluate the objectivist interpretation of Kant's idealism. The final chapter examines the development of Kant's transcendental idealism in the *Opus postumum*. The main result of my investigation is that Kant's transcendental idealism is not entirely or exclusively either subjective or objective idealism; rather, it is a relatively coherent synthesis of both forms, which preserves and negates elements from each.

If transcendental idealism is such a synthesis, the business of Kant scholarship is to determine exactly its place between the extremes of subjectivism and objectivism. Its task is to specify the respects in which this synthesis is both subjectivist and objectivist. In attempting to fulfill this task, I have come to the following conclusions:

1. Kant's transcendental idealism is objectivist insofar as (1) the intersubjective forms of experience are not ideas but the necessary conditions of

having ideas, and (2) these forms are the necessary conditions of subjectivity and objectivity, the representations of both inner and outer sense (7.2, 7.3).

2. Kant's transcendental idealism is subjectivist insofar as (1) it attaches all appearances to a transcendental subject, which is their source, and insofar as (2) this subject is ineliminable, that is, it is not only consistent with but necessary to the transcendental conditions of experience (8.2–8.5). This subject cannot be simply an impersonal 'it' because Kant is justified in attributing to it two of the necessary conditions of subjectivity: self-awareness and spontaneity.

3. Kant has an ambivalent position vis-à-vis the way of ideas. On the one hand, he denies some of the fundamental tenets of this tradition: that ideas are given, self-evident, and resemble their objects (7.2–7.5). On the other hand, he sometimes reaffirms its basic principle: that the immediate objects of awareness are ideas. For Kant, no less than Berkeley, an idea resembles nothing but an idea.

4. Kant's ambivalence vis-à-vis the way of ideas is also apparent from the new meaning he gives to this principle. Kant both radicalizes and neutralizes it. He radicalizes it insofar as he extends it to outer as well as inner experience; outer experience, the perception of objects in space, consists in the immediate awareness of my own ideas no less than inner experience, self-awareness in time. Hence the existence of objects in space is not the result of mere inference (3.1–3.2; 8.1). Nevertheless, by radicalizing this principle Kant also neutralizes it, because it is no longer the basis for a doctrine of privileged access, as if I knew only myself with certainty and had to infer the existence of the external world. Kant's extension of this principle means that I know myself not only as much as, but also as little as, objects in space. If I know both myself and outer objects directly and immediately, I also know them only as appearances and never as they are in themselves (7.6).

5. Kant's transcendental idealism is irresolvably ambiguous, its meaning varying according to how Kant uses the term "appearance." Kant both attaches appearances to, and detaches them from, things-in-themselves. He attaches them insofar as appearances are aspects or extrinsic properties of things-in-themselves; and he detaches them insofar as they are only representations within the consciousness of the perceiving subject. The source of this ambiguity lay not in equivocation, and still less in the systematically misleading "language of appearance." Rather, it rested in Kant's complex polemical context. Kant detached appearances from things-in-themselves when arguing against transcendental realism and Descartes' skeptical ideal-

ism; but he attached appearances to things-in-themselves when distinguishing his idealism from Berkeley's more metaphysical idealism (3.4–3.5).

6. Although Kant gives appearances a double sense, this does not mean that his transcendental idealism is incoherent or contradictory, since from a transcendental perspective it is possible, and indeed necessary, to regard appearances as both representations and properties of things-in-themselves (3.4–3.5).

7. The dispute between two-worlds and two-aspect theories concerning the status of appearances–whether they are only representations or aspects of things-in-themselves–is sterile and irresolvable, insofar as the texts give evidence for both readings and insofar as Kant used "appearance" in different senses depending on his polemical context.

8. Kant's transcendental idealism is both epistemological and psychological. Its psychological dimension is irreducible and necessary insofar as Kant connects the questions of what we know with how we know. To discount its psychological dimension is also to undermine its response to skeptical problems.

9. Kant's most important idealist opponents were Descartes and Leibniz, not Berkeley or Hume. While Kant did not regard Hume as an idealist at all (1.6), he interpreted Berkeley's idealism in essentially Leibnizian or Platonic terms (5.5). Throughout his career Kant was especially troubled by Leibniz's idealism, which he criticized to an extent that has still not been fully appreciated. There are criticisms of Leibniz's idealism in the Transcendental Aesthetic and Second Antinomy of the first *Kritik* (4.1–4.4), in the *Nova dilucidatio* (1.2), in the metaphysics lectures, in the Inaugural Dissertation (1.4), and in the 1766 *Träume eines Geistersehers* (1.3). Some of the essential doctrines of Kant's transcendental idealism–the distinction between reason and sensibility, the empirical reality of space and time, and the limitation of knowledge to appearances–were forged from Kant's critique of Leibniz's Platonic idealism.

10. The foundations of Kant's transcendental idealism were laid in the 1770 Inaugural Dissertation; and Kant stuck by its fundamental principles even in the *Opus postumum*. The *Opus postumum* marks no fundamental break with the transcendental idealism of the first *Kritik*. Kant still retains the thing-in-itself, and he rejects the radical subjective idealism of Fichte as well as the new absolute idealism of Schelling. The *Opus postumum* is an evolution and expansion of Kant's earlier transcendental idealism, since he now en-

riches and enlarges his conception of the a priori to accomodate his new dynamics.

11. Kant's critique of idealism remains essentially the same throughout his philosophical development. The most important shift appears in the 1760s when Kant's growing skepticism prompted him to doubt his early refutations of idealism. The changes in the refutation of idealism from the first to the second edition of the *Kritik* were more in exposition than in substance (2.2–2.3; 6.2–6.5).

3. Contemporary Kant Scholarship

All work on Kant has to define itself in relation to the rich history of Kant interpretation. Whether explicitly or implicitly, one is following or departing from other scholars, past and present. While my work has many debts, it also takes issue with several recent trends in Kant scholarship, specifically the tendency among many scholars to take extreme positions on issues surrounding transcendental idealism.

One of these issues concerns the relationship of transcendental idealism to skepticism. While some scholars prize Kant's response to skepticism but belittle his transcendental idealism, others value his transcendental idealism but play down his response to skepticism.[5] One of my tasks in the following chapters is to show that both these positions are unsatisfactory. I reject both for the simple reason that Kant's transcendental idealism and his response to skepticism are inseparable.[6] As we shall see in Chapters 2 and 3, Kant saw transcendental idealism as the only possible guarantee of empirical realism, which alone could secure philosophy against skepticism. It is only by placing Kant's refutations of idealism within the context of his transcendental idealism, I shall argue, that we save it from obvious and fatal objections.[7]

Another issue provoking extreme interpretations concerns Kant's relation to skepticism, and more specifically whether his transcendental project was fundamentally antiskeptical. The traditional interpretation, which has been renewed by Strawson, Bennett, and Wolff, stressed the importance of Kant's reply to skepticism. It assumed that Kant's intention in the Transcendental Deduction and Refutation of Idealism was to combat Hume's and Descartes' skepticism about the external world and the principle of causality. Recently, however, this interpretation has been subject to much criticism on the grounds that it was never Kant's intention—either in the Deduction or the

Refutation—to take issue with Hume's or Descartes' skepticism.[8] According to this new "modest" reading, the main purpose of the Transcendental Deduction was to provide a regressive analysis of our ordinary beliefs; and it is a complete misreading of Kant's project to see it as a form of foundationalism on the Cartesian model.

On this issue too I have attempted to steer a middle path. While it is indeed correct that Kant's project was not foundationalist, and while it is also true that it does not attempt to prove the existence of the external world in the strong transcendental sense, it does not follow that Kant was not troubled by skepticism. In the Fourth Paralogism of the first edition of the *Kritik*, and in the Refutation of Idealism of the second edition, Kant's fundamental aim was to prove the *empirical reality* of the external world. Though this was indeed a modest goal, it also involved refuting Cartesian skepticism, which doubts the empirical reality of our experience on the grounds that it has no foundation in transcendental reality. It was just this doubt that Kant believed he could remove on the basis of his transcendental idealism.

Finally, there is the issue surrounding the extent of Kant's subjectivism, which I have discussed above. Here too scholars have taken extreme positions. Some stress that Kant's transcendental idealism is essentially subjectivist, little more than a rationalist version of Berkeley, while others insist that it is radically antisubjectivist, fundamentally opposed to Berkeley's central principles and indeed the whole way of ideas.[9] Not surprisingly, these opposing intepretations are the basis for conflicting assessments of transcendental idealism. If the former party dismisses transcendental idealism on the grounds that it is too close to subjectivism, the latter party defends it on the grounds that it is far from subjectivism.

Ironically, the problem with this dispute is not that it has been too extreme, but that it has not been extreme enough. It is a striking weakness of the antisubjectivist interpretation that it has been formulated without reference to the traditional objectivist reading of Kant's transcendental idealism.[10] It is as if Schelling's and Hegel's absolute idealism, and Marburg neo-Kantianism, never existed. This has had two troublesome consequences. First, some antisubjectivists unwittingly accept elements of the subjectivist reading; for example, they endorse the subjectivist view of the Kantian categories as subjective.[11] Second, some also fail to take a stand on some of the most basic issues; they have ignored, for example, such questions as the status of the categories and the eliminability of the transcendental subject

What has motivated the recent intense debate about Kant's subjectivism has been the underlying assumption that if one recognizes *both* the subjectivist and objectivist elements of Kant's transcendental idealism one must also admit its incoherence. There is some basis for this implicit assumption, however, since the traditional third alternative to subjectivism and antisubjectivism have been patchwork theories, according to which Kant's transcendental idealism is an incoherent mixture of doctrines from different stages in his development.[12] Hence Kant scholarship faces a dilemma: transcendental idealism is either an incoherent patchwork or an implausible extreme, whether that is subjective or objective idealism.

The following chapters are an attempt to avoid this dilemma. They have been written from two fundamental convictions. First, that from the very beginning Kant's transcendental idealism was an attempt to find a middle path between the extremes of subjective and objective idealism. Second, that the synthesis of subjectivism and objectivism in transcendental idealism is not incoherent. This is not to say that Kant's transcendental idealism is entirely unproblematic; but it is at least to say that it is not a patchwork, and very far from a botch.

CHAPTER 1

Idealism in the Precritical Years

1. The Idealist Challenge

There is a widespread belief that Kant did not concern himself with the problem of idealism until the 1780s.[1] Supposedly, the issues of how to refute idealism, and of how to distinguish his idealism from other forms, became important for Kant only after the first reviews of the *Kritik*. It is as if Kant developed his own system only in reaction against realism or materialism, and as if there were no problem with idealism, which was after all his own doctrine.

But such a belief is very far from the truth. A close examination of Kant's precritical writings reveals that he had been doing battle with idealism for decades. Kant's struggle with idealism began early, starting in the 1750s and continuing well into the 1770s. There are refutations of idealism in the 1755 *Nova dilucidatio* and in the 1770 Inaugural Dissertation; there are discussions of idealism in the metaphysics lectures from the 1760s and 1770s; and there is an exposé of the motives behind idealism in the 1766 *Träume eines Geistersehers*. Rather than identifying his views with idealism, Kant was eager to distance them from it. His damning remark on idealism in the 1790s—that it is "a kind of cancer in metaphysics"—had been his sentiment since the 1750s.

Kant's early concern with idealism was far from idiosyncratic. To a large extent he was following his contemporaries, who regarded idealism and materialism as the two dangerous extremes of metaphysics. After the 1760s in Germany the critique of idealism had become a favorite theme of metaphysical treatises and university lectures.[2] It became a virtual *Ehrensache* for an aspiring professor to refute idealism. Berkeley's idealism and Hume's skepticism were well known in Germany, and both were perceived as a threat.[3]

Many *Popularphilosophen* had heeded the Scottish philosophers of common sense—Thomas Reid, James Oswald, and James Beattie—who had warned that the skepticism of Hume was inherent in the way of ideas of Descartes and Locke.[4]

For all its orthodoxy, there was something unique to the young Kant's concern with idealism. With his discovery of the subjectivity of space and time in the late 1760s, Kant himself had developed a doctrine akin to idealism, and so he had to distinguish it from the idealism he had once spurned and refuted. Kant's eagerness to determine the *differentia specifica* of his idealism is already evident in the early 1770s, and it was not therefore merely a reaction to the first reviews of the *Kritik*. In the 1770 Inaugural Dissertation the germs of some of his later strategy are already apparent. Here Kant attempts to distinguish his idealism from competing variants by stressing the empirical reality of space and time. The need to find the *differentia specifica* became even more pressing later in the 1770s when Kant affirmed some of the central tenets of the subjectivist tradition: that the immediate objects of consciousness are ideas and that all inferences to the existence of external objects are uncertain (see below, 1.1.4). As a result of this subjectivist turn, Kant's strategy against idealism changes course from his first efforts in the 1750s and 1760s. Rather than trying to prove the reality of objects distinct from all consciousness, he insists upon the role of coherence, the universal and necessary structure of consciousness itself.

For Kant, as indeed for his contemporaries, the cancer of idealism took many forms. It could be the "dogmatic idealism" of Leibniz, Plato, and the Eleatic tradition, which maintains that only reason gives knowledge of reality in itself, and which dismisses all sense perception as illusory or confused. It could also be the "skeptical idealism" of Descartes, which doubts the possibility of knowledge of the external world on the grounds that all causal inferences are uncertain. Or, finally, it could be the "egoism" of Spinozism,[5] a solipsism that either doubts or denies the reality of everything beyond my own consciousness.

Kant was careful to distinguish between idealism and kindred doctrines, and then between the many versions of idealism itself. In his lectures on metaphysics he distinguishes sharply between *idealism* and *egoism:* idealism maintains that all that exists is immaterial, or at least all that I *know* to exist is immaterial, while egoism holds that only I myself exist, or at least all that I *know* to exist is my own self. Accordingly, there was both a *problematic* and *dogmatic* version of both idealism and egoism: in their problematic forms they *doubt* the existence of all other things (egoism) or material things (idealism); in their dogmatic forms they *deny* either that any other substance exists or that any material substance exists. While Kant thought that problematic idealism performed a valuable role in showing the limits of sense knowledge and in provoking enquiry, he believed that dogmatic idealism should be banished from philosophy as a danger to morality and religion.[6] Though Kant sharply distinguished between idealism and egoism, he also held that idealism quickly degenerates into egoism because the skeptical problems in demonstrating the reality of matter easily apply to the reality of other spiritual beings.[7]

Of all these forms of idealism, the most important for Kant was the dogmatic idealism of Leibniz and the Platonic tradition.[8] While the young Kant did not neglect other forms of idealism, it was the criticism of Leibniz's Platonic idealism that became especially fruitful for his philosophical development. This is indeed just what we should expect, given Kant's schooling in the Leibnizian-Wolffian tradition and his long struggle to free himself from its legacy. The importance of Platonic idealism becomes especially apparent later when Kant virtually defined all idealism in Platonic terms. Ignoring his earlier more subtle taxonomy, he stated in the *Prolegomena* that "the dictum of all genuine idealists" is that "All knowledge through the senses and experience is nothing but illusion and only in the ideas of the understanding and reason is there truth"(IV, 374). Such was the preeminence of Platonic idealism in Kant's mind that he even interpreted Berkeley's idealism in such terms.

There are at least four respects in which Kant's early reaction to idealism was crucial for the development of transcendental idealism. First, Kant's early system of mental–physical interaction, some elements of which will later play a crucial role in the Refutation of Idealism in the first *Kritik*, partly grew out of his concern to avoid the apparent solipsistic consequences of Leibniz's dogmatic idealism. Second, Kant's doctrine of the parity of inner and outer sense, his claim that both provide an immediate knowledge of things, came from his response to Descartes' problematic idealism in the 1770s. Third, Kant's attempt to develop a *critical* idealism that observes the limits of human knowledge, and that finds its place in the "bathos of experience," stemmed from his response to the visionary idealism of Swedenborg. Fourth, Kant formed his pivotal distinction between empirical reality and transcendental ideality—a distinction crucial for transcendental idealism— in reaction against the idealism of Leibniz and the Platonic tradition.

2. The First Refutation of Idealism

Kant's first refutation of idealism appeared in his first systematic metaphysical work, his 1755 *Nova dilucidatio*. The refutation takes place in the context of his general metaphysics, which consists in two fundamental propositions, the *principle of succession* and the *principle of coexistence*. Each principle requires some comment.

The principle of succession states: "No change can happen to substances except insofar as they are connected with other substances, whose reciprocal dependence determines their mutual change of state" (I, 410). In other words, no substance has the power to effect change in itself, and every change in it must be the effect of some other substance acting upon it; hence if a substance were completely separated from all others, it would remain unchanged. This principle is for Kant a generalization of the law of inertia, which states that a body remains at rest, or in motion at a constant speed, unless acted upon by some other body. Significantly, Kant extends this principle so that it applies not only to all physical bodies but to all substances whatsoever, whether they be mental or physical. So generalized, Kant's principle takes issue with one of the fundamental doctrines of Leibniz's metaphysics: that all change in a substance must arise from within it alone.

The principle of coexistence declares: "Finite substances do not, in virtue of their existence alone, stand in relationship with one another, nor are they linked together by any interaction at all, except insofar as the common principle of their existence, namely the divine understanding, maintains them in a state of harmony in their reciprocal relations" (I, 412–413). This principle means that substances are independent of one another in their sheer existence, but that they are dependent upon one another in their relative properties; as Kant also puts the distinction, substances are independent of one another in their *intrinsic* determinations but dependent on one another in their *extrinsic* ones.[9] Since substances do not interact with one another in virtue of their existence and intrinsic properties, they are made to do so, Kant maintains, only by an extra act of creation that relates them through their extrinsic or relational properties.

If these principles seem abstract and arid, there was also some urgency behind them: the need to resolve the mind–body problem, one of the most burning issues of German philosophy in the mid-eighteenth century.[10] Kant wanted a theory of mental–physical interaction that would do justice to the separate existence of the mind and body while also explaining the interaction between them.[11] His principles were designed to fill just these require-ments. The principle of coexistence ensures the distinct existence of mind and body, because they are separate substances that, despite interaction, re-main the same in their existence or inner determinations. The principle of succession, however, provides for some interaction between them, for changes in the mind and the body can come only from outside them, not from within.

Kant developed his theory to avoid the chief problems of competing theo-ries. There were three predominant theories of mental–physical interaction in mid-eighteenth-century Germany: occasionalism, preestablished har-mony, and physical influx. The chief problem with occasionalism and the preestablished harmony is that they could not explain the apparent interac-tion between substances, which seemed to be not only a fact of experience but also a requirement of Newton's physics. The difficulty with the physical influx theory is that it seemed to demand something as strong as the "trans-fer of reality" between the mind and the body, some change in their *inner* determinations, which seemed impossible given the differences in kind be-tween them.[12]

By forbidding interaction between *intrinsic* properties, and by limiting it to *extrinsic* ones, Kant believed that he had avoided the main problems of both theories. He argued that his theory avoids materialism because, although it connects mind and body into a system of mutual interaction, it does so only in virtue of their *extrinsic* characteristics (Prop. XII, Scholion; I, 412). The mind still retains its distinctive status as something representative, for, even though all changes in its representations derive from something outside it, its intrinsic properties remain the same. He also contended that his theory escapes idealism because all changes in representations derive from some *external* cause and cannot arise from the mind alone (Prop. XII, Usus. 1; I, 411–412).

Kant's refutation of idealism appears as a corollary to his exposition of the principle of succession (Prop. XII, Usus. 1; I, 411–412). Formulated syllogis-tically, his argument consists in two stages. The first stage consists in the fol-lowing premises. (1) The soul is subject to inner changes (fact of inner expe-rience). (2) These changes cannot arise from the soul itself (the principle of succession). Therefore, (3) they must arise from something outside the soul with which it stands in a necessary connection. But this conclusion is not sufficient to refute the skeptical idealist, who might admit that his represen-tations have some external cause but still doubt that they correspond with their object; after all, it is still possible that all representations are caused by some malicious demon.

Perhaps to avoid just such a skeptical scenario, Kant adds a few more lines to his argument propounding something like a causal theory of perception. These lines constitute the second stage of the argument, which now takes the following form. (1) A representation is true if it corresponds to its object (definition of truth). (2) A representation corresponds to its object *if* it arises from it (causal theory of perception). (3) Representations *must* arise from external objects (the principle of succession). Therefore, (4) our representations of the external world correspond to their objects, and so are true.

Even if this were a good argument against skeptical idealism, it does not work against dogmatic idealism. While it shows at best that there must be some *external* cause of my representations, so that I am not the only thing that exists, it does not show that this external cause must be some *material* object, something extended in space. It could be that it is some other mind, or an idea in the mind of God.[13] This is no quibble since an idealist like Berkeley does not deny that representations have external causes; he simply maintains that these causes are immaterial.

Kant does have a response to this difficulty, however. Since, prior to 1768, he maintains that space is a *phenomenon bene fundata*, arising of necessity from the interactions between substances,[14] it follows that the objects that are interacting with one another will be in space. Yet this destroys the evil of idealism only by running the risk of materialism.[15] For if substances that interact with one another are in space, then it would seem that the mind and body interact only if the mind too is somehow in space. While Kant admits some *apparent* materialism, even stating that the mind must be necessarily connected with the body, he still firmly denies that his theory is materialist (Prop. XII, Scholion; I, 412). All such interaction concerns only the *extrinsic* properties of the mind, he argues, so that if it were removed from all interaction with other substances, it would still retain its character as a thinking being. In other words, even if all its representations have external causes, they will still retain their *sui generis* character as representations.

Whatever the strengths and weaknesses of Kant's argument, the question remains who, if anyone, was the target of his refutation. Kant mentions no one, and perhaps he had no specific historical figure in mind. Nevertheless, his description of idealism excludes some figures and implicates others. Berkeley, the usual suspect, can be ruled out, since he does not deny that representations have external causes, as Kant portrays the idealist here. Another more plausible culprit is Descartes, who indeed doubts whether our representations have external causes. Still, Descartes did not deny, as the idealist does here, that there is interaction between distinct substances. The most likely target of Kant's polemic is staring the reader in the face. This is the philosopher Kant criticizes most frequently in the *Nova dilucidatio:* Leibniz. It was Leibniz who maintained that the representations of the soul arise completely from within and that they cannot have external causes. This is just the view Kant criticizes here. Although Kant often portrays Leibniz in the *Nova dilucidatio* as the author of the preestablished harmony, he also regards him as an idealist—and indeed as an egoist—because this doctrine leads directly to a kind of solipsism. One common objection against the preestablished harmony was that it ultimately leads to idealism, for all the changes of perception in a monad arise from within itself and cannot have any external cause.[16] Indeed, Leibniz himself admitted that the mind could have all its perceptions even if there were no body to act upon it, and even if it were the only finite substance;[17] hence the external world, and even other minds, become superfluous. It is indeed telling that, in his later lectures on metaphysics, Kant not only described Leibniz as an idealist but also endorsed this common objection against him.[18] This suggests that one of the main reasons for the young Kant's opposition to the preestablished harmony was its solipsistic implications.

Whoever the target of Kant's refutation, it is clear that the argument of the *Nova dilucidatio* is the forerunner of Kant's later Refutation of Idealism in the second edition of the first *Kritik.* To be sure, Kant will later drop the metaphysical claim that his system of interaction applies to things-in-themselves; and still less will he make an explicit appeal to interaction as a premise of his Refutation. Nevertheless, the system of interaction still plays an implicit role in Kant's argument, which intends to establish the reality of a representation by showing how it conforms to the general laws of experience, more specifically, the mutual attraction and repulsion of substances as defined in the Third Analogy. Thus the critical Kant will continue to hold, just as he once did in the *Nova dilucidatio,* that the reality of a representation depends upon its being part of a system of appearances following laws of mutual attraction and repulsion.

3. Idealist Dreams and Visions

Undoubtedly, the most interesting and puzzling work regarding Kant's early attitude toward idealism is his 1766 *Träume eines Geistersehers.* The main purpose of this fascinating tract is to determine the aims and limits of metaphysics by exposing the fabulous claims of the Swedish mystic Immanuel Swedenborg. *Prima facie* Kant's general views on metaphysics, and his criticism of Swedenborg's mysticism, have little direct relevance to idealism, which Kant mentions only once and then merely parenthetically (II, 364). Yet Kant's single reference to "idealism," when placed in context, reveals that it is a central, if implicit, theme of the entire work.

In his parenthetical sentence Kant describes Swedenborg's metaphysics as "idealism" because it holds that corporeal beings have no substance of their own, and that they exist only by virtue of the spirit world (II, 364). There can be no better term for his metaphysics, Kant says, because Swedenborg thinks material things have only an *outer* significance among themselves, while their deeper *inner* significance comes from designating the forces of the spirit world, which are their ultimate causes. The analogy of Swedenborg's doctrine with Leibniz is striking, and it is indeed no accident, given that Swedenborg had been schooled on Leibnizian-Wolffian metaphysics and had written several tracts in its defense.[19] The analogy is especially noteworthy since it helps to explain one of the more baffling and troubling features of Kant's tract: its conflation of metaphysics with spirit-seeing. What the metaphysician tries to demonstrate through pure reason, the mystic tries to establish through a special kind of experience. The metaphysician and the mystic might indeed have different methods; but they still come to similar conclusions about the nature of reality itself. Both see the spiritual world as more real than the physical world, and they attempt to demonstrate its greater reality by some special kind of insight—whether purely discursive or intuitive—that transcends our ordinary experience. That Swedenborg was a mystic never made him less of a metaphysician, for Kant always said that mysticism is a hallmark of the Platonic and Eleatic tradition.[20]

Idealism plays a central role in the *Träume* as Kant's paradigm for the false hopes and illusory claims of metaphysics. Like all metaphysicians, the idealist wants to support religious belief, especially belief in immortality, and so he attempts to prove the existence of the spirit world, whether through discursive or mystical means. The idealist is an extreme case of this aspiration, however, because he thinks that the spirit world has more reality than the empirical world. What the idealist fails to see is that the ultimate basis for religious beliefs has to be moral and practical rather than metaphysical and speculative.

What was Kant's criticism of idealism in *Träume eines Geistersehers?* This is the most skeptical of all Kant's writings, and its stance toward idealism reflects this skepticism. In the first part of the work Kant argues that it is impossible either to demonstrate or refute the existence of spirits, which lie beyond the boundaries of experience. Since the main premise of idealism is the existence of spirit, it follows that idealism too will be indemonstrable by theoretical means.

The heart of Kant's argument against idealism consists in three steps. (1) It is possible to prove the existence of something only through experience. (2) We have an experience of something only insofar as it is in some space, or insofar as it is impenetrable and resists our activity to move it. (3) Spirits are penetrable and do not fill space. Therefore, it follows that (4) we cannot prove the existence of spirits (II, 321–323, 368). Of course, Swedenborg would contest this conclusion because he thinks that we can have a special mystical experience of the presence of spirits, which is not limited to the conditions of our material senses. Yet Kant replies that it is in just this respect that Swedenborg deludes himself and his readers. All Swedenborg's reports of his visions hypostatize spirits, confirming the impossibility of conceiving spirits in any but a material sense. Thus Swedenborg himself admits that a spirit recently released from its body might perceive heaven as if it were the old material world; and he even confesses that, because the spirit world is so like the material world, he had to take one spirit to its own funeral service to convince it that it had departed from the material world![21]

For Kant, the fundamental problem with the metaphysics of idealism is not that it is false but that it is speculative, going beyond the limits of our cognitive powers. All idealism—whether it is the mystical variety of Swedenborg or the rationalist variety of Leibniz—suffers from a common failing: it transcends the limits of human sense experience, which must be the source of all our knowledge. The Leibnizian ignores sense experience by constructing a priori demonstrations; the Swedenborgian flaunts it by claiming some kind of special mystical experience. By ignoring these limits both speak a kind of nonsense, which is especially evident in the case of Swedenborg's mystical fantasies.

Kant thinks that the remedy for this malady is for metaphysics to become a science of the limits of human reason (II, 367–368). Such a science will limit reason to the sphere of experience, so that it acquires knowledge of benefit to life. It will also recognize that the source of metaphysics—especially its idealist form—has been the practical concern to establish human immortality. It will stress, however, that this concern cannot be addressed by hypostatizing the immaterial, as if it were the very structure and essence of things; and it will further emphasize that this concern arises from moral interests whose validity ultimately does not depend upon any kind of speculation.

When Kant wrote the *Träume* in late 1765 he was still several years away from developing his own transcendental idealism. Yet this early tract shows us clearly the mistakes of past idealism and what form a transcendental idealism would have to take: it would have to be essentially a *critical* idealism; in other words, an idealism that observes the limits of human experience, and that avoids all speculation about the existence of spiritual substance. It is no accident that Kant will later stress these aspects of his transcendental idealism as some of its distinguishing features from the metaphysical idealism of Berkeley and the Eleatic tradition.

4. The Critique of Idealism in the Inaugural Dissertation

The importance of Kant's struggle against idealism for his general philosophical development becomes even more apparent from his 1770 Inaugural Dissertation. In §§11–12 of this work Kant attempts to distinguish his doctrine from what he calls simply "idealism." Although Kant does not identify any specific form of idealism, he almost certainly has in mind the "dogmatic idealism" of Plato and the Eleatic school. According to Kant's later description of that school in the *Prolegomena*, its fundamental dictum is that "All knowledge through the senses and experience is nothing but illusion and only in the ideas of the understanding and reason is there truth" (IV, 374). This is just the doctrine that Kant wishes to discuss in §§11–12. It is no accident that at the close of §12 he makes a critical reference to "those who drew their inspiration from the Eleatic school." In general, Kant traced all idealism, even that of Berkeley, back to the Eleatic school (IV, 374).

A closer look at the context of Kant's remarks in §§11–12 shows that he is again fighting against his old rationalist opponent: Leibniz. In his lectures on metaphysics Kant had frequently placed Leibniz in the Eleatic tradition, seeing him as an adherent of Plato.[22] The Platonic dimension of Leibniz's doctrine is apparent in two respects: from its attitude toward the senses, which are described as only a confused mode of knowledge; and from its analysis of the monads, which are regarded as purely intellectual entities. Although Kant already criticized Leibniz's idealism in the *Nova dilucidatio*, he now specifically targets the Platonic aspect of his idealism, which he did not consider in the earlier work.

Seeing that Kant's target in §§11–12 is *dogmatic* idealism is important, not least because it corrects the common interpretation of these sections as a rehearsal for the later Refutation of Idealism in the first *Kritik*. In these sections Kant does not attempt to refute skeptical or problematic idealism, as he will later do in the Refutation of Idealism. The points made in §§11–12 are better viewed as an anticipation of the argument in the Appendix to the *Prolegomena*, where Kant attempts to distinguish his idealism from Berkeley, whom he also places in the Eleatic tradition.

The anti-idealist polemic of the Inaugural Dissertation has often been overlooked because of its Platonic metaphysics. While Kant's criticism of some aspects of the Platonic tradition is implicit, his endorsement of other aspects is much more explicit. There are indeed good reasons for describing the Inaugural Dissertation as Platonic: Kant makes a firm distinction between the noumenal and the phenomenal; he warns us against confusing the sensible and the intellectual; and he thinks that it is possible for reason alone to give us insight into the noumenal realm.

Yet all these affinities with the Platonic tradition should not obscure Kant's criticisms of it. In three fundamental respects Kant takes issue with Leibniz and the Platonic tradition. First, Kant maintains that mathematics does not give us knowledge of the noumenal but only of the phenomenal world, because geometry and arithmetic are dependent upon the forms of intuition of space and time, which determine the structure of the phenomenal world alone (§12). The Eleatic tradition had seen mathematics as the paradigm of purely rational knowledge, citing it as proof of the power of reason to grasp noumena. Second, Kant denies the possibility of an intellectual intuition on the grounds that, for human beings, all intellectual cognition is symbolic or discursive, and the objects of knowledge must be given to intuition (§10). Intellectual intuition played a crucial role in the Platonic tradition: it was that form of insight transcending all discursive thinking where the intellect had a pure vision of the forms themselves. Third, and most important, Kant steps forward as a defender of sensible knowledge, contending that knowledge through the senses is neither illusory nor confused but amounts to a distinct form of knowledge in its own right. Sensible and intellectual cognition are completely distinct from one another, he maintains, because each has its own subject matter and "principle of order" (§§3–7). While the subject matter of sensible cognition is phenomena or appearances, that of intellectual cognition is things-in-themselves; and whereas the principles of order of sensible cognition are space and time, those of intellectual cognition are the ideas of reason. It is wrong for Leibniz to dismiss sensible knowledge as only a confused form of intellectual knowledge, Kant then argues, because sensible knowledge can be distinct while intellectual knowledge can be confused (§7). Similarly, Kant implies that Plato goes astray in regarding sensible knowledge as only illusory, as if all real knowledge were only in the intellect (§11).

Thus the main aim of Kant's critique of Leibniz and the Platonic tradition is to vindicate knowledge through the senses. His chief concern in §11 is to show that we do have knowledge of appearances, and that the idealist is mistaken in thinking that all knowledge of sensible things is only illusory. He explains that even though knowledge of phenomena does not give us knowledge of "the internal and absolute quality of objects," and even though it gives us knowledge only of the appearance of things and not of ideas in the Platonic sense, it still amounts to a form of knowledge in its own right. Kant gives two reasons why this is so. First, appearances are the appearances *of* objects, or they are the effects of their acting upon us, so that they at least testify to the existence of objects. In this respect Kant explicitly declares that his doctrine is "opposed to idealism"(II, 397).[23] Second, it is still possible to make true judgments about appearances because truth consists in the agreement of a predicate with a subject, and both subject and predicate arise from the common laws of the phenomenal world. Kant makes a point here that he will later repeat in the Aesthetic: that all empirical judgments maintain their truth value even though they are true only of appearances (A 27–28/B 43–44). In the Appendix to the *Prolegomena* Kant will later revive both of these points to distinguish his idealism from Berkeley.

The first argument has been dismissed as an obvious *non sequitur.* Simply because appearances must be appearances of objects does not mean that we know these objects exist, given that we need to know with what right we describe them as appearances in the first place.[24] But, again, this is to misunderstand Kant's target. In §11 Kant is not criticizing the skeptical idealist for doubting the reality of the external world, but the dogmatic idealist for confusing appearances with illusion. He is only pointing out against the dogmatic idealist that appearances are not complete illusions because we can make perfectly true judgments about how objects appear relative to our senses.

Although Kant's argument against the dogmatic idealist is explicit only in §11 of Section Two, it also resurfaces unmistakably in §§14.6 and 15E of

Section Three. In these later sections Kant maintains that even though space and time are not something objective and real, and even though they are only subjective and ideal as pure a priori intuitions, they still provide us with a certain knowledge of things in the spatial and temporal world. He gives two reasons why this is so. First, he states that these forms of intuition coordinate our sensations according to fixed laws, and so prevent arbitrariness and chaos. Second, and more important, he declares explicitly that they are necessary conditions under which anything appears to the senses at all. In other words, as Kant will later put it, space and time are transcendental conditions of the possibility of experience.

Anticipating another argument of his later work, Kant takes his case against the idealist a step further by arguing that his doctrine alone explains how the axioms of geometry are necessarily true of the objects of experience (II, 404–405). Since all objects of experience must conform to the form of space, and since the axioms of geometry describe this form, it follows that all objects of experience must also conform to the axioms of geometry. The Leibnizian idealist, however, treats the concept of space as a mere abstraction from the distances between things in experience, and so deprives geometrical theorems of their universality and necessity.[25] Hence Kant thinks that, unlike the Leibnizian idealist, he can establish the empirical reality of space because he alone can show how all Euclid's axioms must be true of it.

Sections §§14.6 and 15E are plainly a full dress rehearsal for Kant's later argument for the empirical reality of space and time in the Aesthetic of the first *Kritik*. Though the concepts of *empirical reality* and *transcendental ideality* appear only in the first *Kritik*, they are still already implicit in the Inaugural Dissertation. This is significant because it shows that, as early as 1770, Kant already had in place those arguments against idealism that he would later pit against Berkeley in the *Prolegomena*. These arguments therefore cannot be regarded as later polemical modifications or reformulations of Kant's original doctrines. Insofar as Kant placed Berkeley in the Eleatic tradition, he had every reason to be offended at the later charge of Berkeleyianism, which completely ignored how he had developed his views in reaction against that very tradition.

In the early 1770s Kant had not only developed his response to idealism, but he had also already heard many of the charges of idealism that would later be made against him. Shortly after the Inaugural Dissertation appeared, J. H. Lambert and Moses Mendelssohn objected against Kant's doctrine of the subjectivity of time on the grounds that it seemed to make time illusory.[26] Lambert put the objection succinctly: "If changes are real, so is time too, whatever it may be. If time is not real, then no changes are also real." Both Lambert and Mendelssohn made the point that even the idealist had to admit that the changes of his representations were real, so that time itself had to be so too.

In his February 21, 1772, letter to Marcus Herz, Kant responded to this objection, which he felt to be very natural and important (X, 34–35). "It has made me reflect considerably," Kant confessed to Herz. The essence of Kant's reply, which resurfaces in §7 of the second edition of the Aesthetic, is that he fully admits the reality of the changes of our representations, and indeed the changes of things in space. He resists the inference, however, that these changes apply to things-in-themselves, which are not in time. In effect, Kant is happy to make the admission because it only underscores his point that time is not illusory but has reality for all objects of the senses. "Why do people make this objection against the ideality of time but not that of space?" Kant asks. His explanation is that they unwittingly accept a central premise of skeptical idealism: that while we have to infer the reality of objects in space from our representations, the changes of our representations are immediately given. Kant's response is that space and time have equal reality because both are ultimately only forms of representation of the empirical world, so that we no more have to infer the reality of objects in space than we have to infer the reality of changes in our own representations. This point, so central to Kant's refutation of problematic idealism in the Fourth Paralogism of the first edition of the *Kritik*, is already explicit in his 1772 letter to Herz.

5. Skeptical Ambivalence

Kant's early attitude toward idealism is not simply a history of his attempts to refute it. Some of the lectures of the 1760s and 1770s reveal a much more ambivalent skeptical attitude. If during these decades Kant continued in his efforts to refute idealism, attempting new tactics in his struggle against his old foe, he also sometimes insisted that it is impossible to refute either idealism or egoism on theoretical grounds, stressing instead that they had to be rejected simply on moral ones. For example, in the *Metaphysik Herder*, which consists in Herder's notes on Kant's metaphysics lectures from 1762–1764, Kant actually defended Berkeley against common objections, and then concluded that it is impossible to refute him on logical grounds (XXVIII, 42–43). The main problem with idealism, he implied, is that it so quickly degenerates into egoism, which is dangerous for natural theology. In the Metaphysik L1, which is based on lectures given from the mid-1770s, Kant stated that it is impossible to refute egoism because the same effect does not necessarily always have the same cause, so that our representations might arise as much from our imagination as external objects (XXVIII, 206).[27]

It is striking that in both lecture series Kant in effect declares his demonstrations in the *Nova dilucidatio* and Inaugural Dissertation to be misconceived in principle. It is as if his refutations were worthless because they transcend the limits of reason. Though Kant never entirely abandoned any of his refutations, which reappear in a critical guise in the 1780s and 1790s, he sometimes had clear reservations about them. On further reflection, however, Kant's more skeptical attitude toward the refutation of idealism is not really that surprising because it reflects his changing views regarding the powers of reason itself. The *Nova dilucidatio* and the Inaugural Dissertation were the two most rationalist works of Kant's development, and the refutations of idealism in them reflect that rationalism. But first in the mid-1760s, and then again in the mid-1770s, Kant's confidence in the powers of reason began to wane, so that a refutation of idealism began to seem pretentious and preposterous.

By the time Kant wrote the *Träume eines Geistersehers* in 1766 he had come to two general conclusions about the limits of reason. First, it is impossible to establish the existence of anything without the evidence of experience.[28] Reason is only a power of inference by which we determine the logical relations between propositions; by itself it does not determine whether anything exists. Second, it is necessary to distinguish between the logical and real grounds of things.[29] While a logical ground is determined simply by the analysis of a subject to see whether it entails the predicate, a real ground has to be determined by experience because the cause of an event is logically distinct from its effect.

Both points had important implications for the refutation of idealism. The first means that it is impossible to disprove idealism because, as Kant argued in the lectures, the question of the truth of idealism is not one that can be determined by experience (XXIX, 207). Anyone who examines the dispute between idealism and realism, he contends, will see that there is no disagreement between them regarding the content of our experience. The second point implies that it is impossible to demonstrate a priori that our representations must have some external or material cause because, as Kant also held in the lectures, it is always possible to affirm the effect and to deny the cause without contradiction. The argument in the Inaugural Dissertation that appearances give witness to the existence of their objects therefore must be abandoned.

Since the critical Kant reaffirmed his earlier views about the limits of reason, the question arises how he could return to the refutation of idealism. Surely, if reason cannot prove the existence of anything, as Kant continued to preach after 1766, then *a fortiori* it cannot prove the existence of external objects against the idealist. The inconsistency is only apparent, however, and seeing why it is so proves instructive. The tension disappears once we consider that Kant's early reservations about a refutation of idealism were directed against dogmatic attempts to prove the reality of things-in-themselves. The later refutations of idealism attempt to work within a more critical or transcendental framework: they do not attempt to prove the existence of objects distinct from all consciousness but they try to show only how one form of experience involves another.[30] Hence those who interpret the later refutations in a stronger sense[31]—as attempts to prove the existence of things-in-themselves—cannot so easily avoid the inconsistency. At the very least they ignore Kant's scruples about the possibility of such arguments.

For all his skepticism of the 1760s and 1770s, Kant did not abandon his attempts to refute idealism. The *Reflexionen* of the late 1760s and 1770s show Kant attempting to develop a new refutation more in accord with his critical scruples. Starting in the late 1760s Kant began to sketch an argument against Descartes' problematic idealism that he would later repeat in the *Prolegomena* and the second edition of the *Kritik*. This argument does not attempt to prove the reality of things-in-themselves but stresses the significance of the coherence of our representations, their conformity to universal and necessary laws. By the late 1760s Kant had already abandoned any form of direct realism, affirming instead that the representations of objects are really only a representation of our own inner states (R 3929, XVII, 351). Anticipating the Fourth Paralogism of the first edition of the *Kritik*, Kant then worried about the skeptical objection that we cannot know objects in themselves because all causal inferences from our own representations are uncertain (R 4536, XVII, 586). His response to such an objection is that the criterion of truth is essentially formal: the idealist has to be refuted by the coherence of our representations among themselves.[32] We will later note the important role of this argument in the development of the Refutation of Idealism in the second edition of the *Kritik*.

6. David Hume, Transcendental Realist

Prima facie the main idealist challenge to Kant in the pre-critical years came from Hume's skepticism. In the preface to the *Prolegomena* Kant famously confessed that it was the recollection of Hume that had aroused him from his "dogmatic slumber," and he explained that the main problem of the critical philosophy arose from Hume's challenge to the principle of causality (IV, 260). Surely, it seems, this problem must have arisen from Hume's skeptical idealism, which questions whether all our ideas, the idea of necessary connection among them, corresponds with anything objective in nature. Furthermore, Hume seems to be a "problematic" or "skeptical idealist" in the strict Kantian sense, for he doubts, though he does not deny, that our perceptions correspond to some object existing independently of them. So, given the role of Hume in Kant's development, it is tempting to read the entire "silent decade" as one long struggle against Hume's skeptical idealism. This would indeed seem to be the most important chapter in Kant's long early struggle with idealism.

However seductive, such a conclusion confronts insurmountable difficulties. These become apparent as soon as we raise one question: why does Kant never refer to Hume as a skeptical or problematic idealist? Remarkably, it is always Descartes and never Hume who serves as his example of such an idealist.[33] Why? The answer is strange but simple: Kant does *not* think that Hume is a skeptical idealist, or indeed an idealist of any kind. There are at least three reasons why this is so.

The first comes from Kant's account of skeptical idealism, which, upon closer inspection, does not apply to Hume after all. According to the Fourth Paralogism and Refutation of Idealism, the skeptical idealist is someone who doubts whether our representations correspond with their objects because all inferences from cause to effect are doubtful (A 372, B 276). Since it is always possible that the cause of our representation is not the object itself but only our own imagination, the skeptical idealist argues, we have reason to mistrust all our sense perceptions. As Kant portrays him, then, the skeptical idealist does not doubt the principle of causality in general, but simply whether we can infer from that principle that our sense perceptions are true.

This explains why Kant always makes Descartes rather than Hume his example of skeptical idealism. In the Third Meditation Descartes indeed questions the inferences from this principle, but not the principle itself.[34] For Kant, however, Hume's skepticism was of a different order: its role was to question the principle of causality in general, not its application to objects of perception.

The second reason is that Kant thinks of Hume as a transcendental realist, who naively or implicitly equates appearances with things-in-themselves, and not as a skeptical idealist, who doubts whether appearances correspond with things-in-themselves. This is an odd interpretation of Hume, to say the least, but it appears unmistakably in Kant's alternative—and usually neglected—account of his awakening by Hume: the Transcendental Deduction of the *Kritik der praktischen Vernunft.* In the context of explaining his differences with Hume, Kant categorically states that "Hume took the objects of experience as things-in-themselves (as is almost always done)" (IV, 53).

Of course, Kant's regarding Hume as a transcendental realist is not incompatible with him also thinking of Hume as an empirical idealist. Kant indeed argued in the first edition of the first *Kritik* that empirical idealism presupposes transcendental realism because the empirical idealist accepts the transcendental realist's standard of truth as the correspondence of appearances with things-in-themselves, and then doubts whether it is possible to satisfy such a standard (A 369, 372). Kant makes just this point again in the second *Kritik* when he says that Hume's doubts about the principle of causality presuppose his transcendental realism (V, 51–54).[35] It is important to see, however, that Kant thinks of Hume as a transcendental realist who could become, despite himself, a skeptical idealist; he does not say the converse: that he is an empirical idealist who presupposes transcendental realism. In general, Kant maintains that empirical idealists *presuppose* a transcendental realist standard of truth; but he does not equate them with transcendental realists *simpliciter,* as he does with Hume in the second *Kritik.*

The third reason is Kant's limited reading of Hume's skepticism. In the preface to the *Prolegomena* and in the Deduction of the second *Kritik,* Kant writes as if Hume's skepticism were essentially restricted to his doubts about the principle of causality. According to Kant, Hume rightly saw that this principle cannot be justified from experience or the principle of contradiction. What he did not realize, however, is that the same argument applies to other synthetic a priori principles, such as the categories of substance and reciprocity. Kant thought it was *his* special contribution to generalize Hume's problem and to show how it infects all the synthetic a priori principles of the understanding. Such a narrow reading of Hume's skepticism fits hand-in-glove with Kant's interpretation of Hume as a transcendental realist, because such a narrow skepticism concerns only whether there are necessary connections between things in experience, not whether these things exist independent of our experience.

Kant's interpretation of Hume appears preposterous if we consider Hume's earlier *Treatise of human Nature,* which advances a very radical Pyrrhonism and which contains several chapters devoted to "skepticism regarding the senses."[36] It appears perfectly plausible, however, if we consider Hume's later *Enquiry concerning human Understanding,* which retreats to a more moderate skepticism, and which focuses its doubts upon the principle of causality. To be sure, Section 12, Part 1, of the *Enquiry* does summarize the skeptical arguments against the senses in the *Treatise;* but Kant would have had good reason for not identifying these arguments with Hume, who distances himself from them in his later work. While Hume still thinks that these arguments are irrefutable, he also maintains that they cannot produce conviction and that they are useless in practice.

The oddity of Kant's interpretation of Hume disappears, then, if we assume that Kant knew the *Enquiry* but not the *Treatise.* There are good historical reasons for thinking that this was indeed the case. That Kant read the *Enquiry* seems certain, and it has never been in dispute. He probably read the work when the Sulzer edition of Hume's *Vermischte Schriften* first appeared around 1756.[37] Kant indeed cited this work in his 1763 *Beobachtungen* (II, 253), and he recommended Hume's *Enquiries* in his *Vorlesungsnachricht* of 1765–66 (II, 311). That Kant did not read the *Treatise* is also very probable. Since the *Treatise* was not translated into German until 1793, and since Kant could not read English,[38] at least not with much fluency, it is unlikely that Kant could have known it at first hand. Of course, it is possible that he knew some of the contents of the work from other sources, such as writings citing Hume or conversations with friends. There was a German translation of James Beattie's *Essay on Truth,* which contains lengthy extracts from the *Treatise;*[39] and two of Kant's friends, Hamann and Christian Kraus, knew the *Treatise.*[40] Still, even if we consider these alternative sources, Kant almost certainly did not know the main doctrines of the work.

That Kant was ignorant of these doctrines simply follows from his own interpretation of Hume. There are three features of Kant's interpretation that are at odds with Hume's doctrines in the *Treatise.* First, Kant's assumption that Hume is a transcendental realist flies in the face of those chapters from the *Treatise* where Hume defends a skepticism regarding the senses. Second,

Kant's claim that Hume's skepticism was limited to the principle of causality ignores the basic fact that Hume had indeed extended his skepticism to other concepts as well, especially the concept of substance. Third, Kant states that Hume was prevented from generalizing his skepticism because he believed that mathematics is analytic a priori.[41] While this is indeed the case for the Hume of the *Enquiry*, it is false for the Hume of the *Treatise*, who maintains that geometry is derived from experience, and who doubts the application of mathematical principles to the sensible world.[42] All these features of Kant's interpretation would have been quickly corrected by even a cursory knowledge of the contents of the *Treatise*, whether that came from primary or secondary sources.

For all these reasons it has been the conventional wisdom for decades that Kant did not know the *Treatise*. There would be no point rearguing the case were it not for some recent developments in Kant scholarship. Some scholars have recently argued that Kant most likely knew one part of the *Treatise* after all: the final chapter of Book I.[43] They point out that Hamann translated this text and published it in July 1771 as an appendix to the *Königsbergischen gelehrten und politischen Zeitung*, a newspaper he edited. The article was entitled *Nachtgedanken eines Zweiflers*, and it appeared anonymously, with no note of the original author or source.[44] It has been argued that Kant must have known the translation, whether from the published version or from an earlier draft that circulated in the late 1760s.[45] If this is the case, then perhaps Kant knew of, and was indeed battling against, Hume's skeptical idealism after all. For does not the final chapter of Book I contain a summary of Hume's skepticism? Does it not end with Hume's famous confession of failure, his rejection of a philosophy that limits our knowledge to nothing more than our passing impressions?

Great claims have been made for this translation. It has been argued that it was the source of Kant's recollection of Hume; and, since Hume writes in it about the necessary contradictions of the understanding, it has also been seen as the stimulus for Kant's discovery of the antinomies. Thus the translation seems to bring together the two crucial moments that gave birth to the critical philosophy: the recollection of Hume and the discovery of the antinomies.[46]

All these claims, however, are but castles built on sand. There is no concrete evidence that Kant ever read this article.[47] And, if he did, it is highly unlikely that he learned anything from it. For one cannot learn much about Hume's skepticism from the final section of Book I, whose melancholy conclusions are intelligible only to a reader who has followed the many chapters leading up to them. If Kant read this article closely, he would have perhaps surmised that the author—whoever he was—was no transcendental realist, and that he had generalized his skepticism beyond the principle of causality. Still, judging from his interpretation of Hume, Kant learned nothing of the kind.

In any case, Kant could have discovered nothing about the antinomies from this extract. Although the final section of Book I does refer to some contradictions in the understanding, they become intelligible only in the light of Hume's earlier arguments. More significantly, when placed in context, they have almost nothing to do with the antinomies later discovered by Kant. Hume finds a contradiction in the fact that the principle of causality is the source of our belief in the existence of the external world *and* of our knowledge that all our perceptions must come from ourselves.[48] This has little to do with the structure of the Kantian antinomies, which concern how a series both must and cannot have a beginning.

In general, it is necessary to conclude that those who have argued the case for the influence of Hume's *Treatise* on Kant have forgotten some of the general features of Kant's interpretation of Hume, which are blatantly at odds with the doctrines of the *Treatise*. Before indulging in detailed speculations about what we do not know, it is wise to consider whether its central assumptions fit with what we do know. That this is not the case should be clear from the above.

Recognizing the peculiar features of Kant's interpretation of Hume has some important consequences for our reading of the first *Kritik*. The strategy of many scholars has been to interpret the Transcendental Deduction as a response to Hume's skepticism.[49] While this approach has been questioned,[50] it is important to note that *if* there is any struggle with Hume in the Transcendental Deduction at all, it cannot be with a skeptical idealist but must be with an empiricist and transcendental realist. All Hume's skepticism about the application of the categories to experience, Kant argues in the second *Kritik*, arose from his empiricism and transcendental realism, not from any general doubts about the correspondence of our representations with an external world. Kant's battle against skeptical idealism takes place not in the Transcendental Deduction but elsewhere in the *Kritik*—in the Aesthetic, in the Dialectic (first edition), or in the final chapters of the Analytic (second edition)—and its target is not Hume but Descartes.[51]

CHAPTER 2

Transcendental Idealism and Empirical Realism

1. The Case for Subjectivism

For all its intensity and duration, Kant's early battle against idealism had been in vain. Despite his early critique of idealism and his painstaking efforts to distinguish his idealism from traditional forms, his critics continued to regard his philosophy merely as the latest form of subjectivism. During the first decade after the publication of the *Kritik der reinen Vernunft* in May 1781, the most common criticism of Kant's philosophy was that it ends in a skeptical idealism. If Kant were only consistent, his early critics charged, he would have to doubt not only the existence of God and the soul, but also the existence of the external world and other minds. In their view, Kant's philosophy was simply the culmination of the way of ideas of Descartes, Locke, Berkeley, and Hume. Kant had reaffirmed some of the fundamental tenets of that tradition—that the immediate objects of awareness are ideas, and that nothing resembles an idea but another idea—and so he had to admit the consequences: that we must doubt the existence of any reality beyond our own immediate consciousness.

This criticism of Kant's transcendental idealism was virtually universal, shared by philosophers of every school. It was the *leitmotiv* of the empiricist *Popularphilosophen* (Christian Garve, J. G. Feder, Adam Weishaupt, and H. A. Pistorius), of the rationalist metaphysicians of the Leibnizian-Wolffian school (Moses Mendelssohn, J. A. Eberhard, and J. G. Maass), of the *Glaubensphilosophen* (J. G. Hamann, F. H. Jacobi), and of the later generation of "objective" or "absolute idealists" (Hölderlin, Schlegel, Novalis, Schelling, and Hegel).[1] To all these critics, it seemed as if Kant had trapped us inside the circle of our own consciousness, so that the entire world appeared to be a dream or illusion.

But was Kant really guilty of subjectivism? Given his intellectual history, it seems that we should immediately reject such a charge, which seems to ignore Kant's intentions and all his attempts to refute idealism. Still, there are strong reasons why we should not be so hasty. For, even if Kant is not a subjectivist *by intention*, the question remains whether he is one *by implication*. In other words, even if Kant wanted to avoid subjectivism, it is still possible that it is the consequence of his principles. This was indeed just the view of Kant's early critics, who were deaf to Kant's protests that he had been misunderstood.

Despite its apparent crudity and naivité, the subjectivist interpretation has some textual foundation. Its basis is the many passages of the first *Kritik* where Kant seems to equate appearances with representations.[2] Since Kant often explicitly states that appearances are only representations, and since he also expressly insists that we know only appearances, it follows that all we know are only representations. This alone seems to be sufficient to ascribe some form of skeptical idealism to Kant.

The first objection one is likely to make against such an interpretation is that it ignores those many other passages of the *Kritik*—in both the first and second editions—where Kant insists that appearances have objects, or that they are appearances *of* something, namely, things-in-themselves.[3] When we consider these passages, it appears as if Kant does *not* adhere to the subjectivist principle that the immediate objects of perception are only ideas. For what we now perceive are things that exist independent of us; its just that we do not perceive them as they are in themselves but only as they appear to us. The distinction between appearances and things-in-themselves is then not between distinct kinds of entity—mind-dependent ideas and mind-independent things—but between distinct aspects of the same entity. Appearances refer to that thing insofar as we know it, or insofar as it conforms to the conditions of our experience of it; and the thing-in-itself refers to that thing insofar as we do not know it, as it exists independent of these conditions.[4]

It is important to see, however, that Kant's early critics had a reply to this objection. They were perfectly aware of those passages where Kant refers to appearances of things-in-themselves; but they still insisted all the same that they could not represent his ultimate position. If Kant were only consistent, they argued, he would have to identify appearances with representations alone. The problem is that Kant's own critical limits gave him no grounds to claim knowledge of the existence of the thing-in-itself. Given that knowledge is limited to possible experience, and given that the thing-in-itself cannot be given in possible experience, how is it possible to know that things-in-themselves exist? But if they cannot be known to exist, how is it possible to say that we know appearances of things-in-themselves? So these critics concluded that even if Kant were not a subjectivist by intention, he was still one by implication.

2. The First Edition Definitions of Transcendental Idealism

The subjectivist interpretation seems confirmed when we consider Kant's own definitions of transcendental idealism in the first edition of the *Kritik*. Some scholars maintain that these definitions are entirely subjectivist, and that the charges of subjectivism leveled against them led Kant to revise his account of transcendental idealism in the second edition.[5] In their view, there is a fundamental tension between transcendental idealism in the first and second edition: while the first edition doctrine is indeed subjectivist, the second edition doctrine is antisubjectivist, or at least more realistic. To assess this thesis, it is necessary to consider Kant's definitions in a little detail.

In the first edition Kant gave two explicit definitions of transcendental idealism. Significantly, both were either altered or deleted in the second edition. The first definition, which appears in the Critique of the Fourth Paralogism, a section entirely deleted from the second edition, states: "By the *transcendental idealism* of all appearances I understand the doctrine according to which we regard all appearances as mere representations and not things in themselves, and space and time as only sensible forms of our intuition, but not given determinations or conditions of objects as things in themselves" (A 369). Immediately after giving this definition, Kant goes on to explain that the transcendental idealist does not deny or doubt the existence of matter. Rather, he has no difficulty in admitting its reality for the simple reason that matter is for him "only a species of representation." Matter is a kind of *external* representation because it relates perceptions to things that appear in space, though this space is again only a representation within us. Kant then restates his earlier definition by emphasizing that the transcendental idealist holds the following doctrine: "Now external objects (bodies) are mere appearances, and consequently nothing but a species of my representations, whose objects are something only through these representations but nothing at all separated from them" (A 370).

The second definition comes from a passage in Section Six of the Antinomy of Pure Reason, which Kant retained but qualified in a footnote to

the second edition (B 518–519).[6] Kant now states that transcendental idealism is the doctrine that "everything intuited in space or time, and therefore
all objects of any experience possible to us, are nothing but appearances,
that is, mere representations, which, in the manner in which they are represented, as extended beings, or as series of alterations, have no independent
existence outside our thoughts" (A 490–491)[7] He then emphasizes that this
doctrine holds that "[s]pace itself . . . and all appearances are not *things*, but
rather nothing but representations, which cannot exist at all outside our
mind" (A 492).

It is striking that in both his definitions Kant plainly identifies appearances
with representations, and not with aspects of, or perspectives on, an object
in itself. He does not refer to appearances *of* things-in-themselves, as if appearances were simply how an independent reality manifests itself under
the conditions of human sensibility. Rather, Kant writes about appearances
as if they were distinct entities, as if they were representations detached
from objects in themselves, and as if their existence and essence depends
entirely upon the perceiver. As such, then, these definitions provide no evidence for the dual aspect interpretation.

Some advocates of the dual aspect interpretation attempt to explain away
the language of Kant's definitions by distinguishing between the transcendental and empirical levels of his discourse, that is, between the philosopher's second-order analysis of our commonsense standpoint and that
standpoint itself. They maintain that the the distinction between appearances and things-in-themselves as kinds of entity is valid on the empirical
level; but on the transcendental or philosophical level, it is only between different perspectives or aspects of the same object, depending on whether we
consider it as dependent on or independent of the subjective conditions of
human sensibility (space or time).[8] Although this distinction is indeed important, and often confused, it is difficult to see its relevance in the present
context. Kant's definitions are clearly valid on the philosophical plane; and
they are unambiguous in their identification of appearances with representations themselves.[9]

Kant's definitions appear slightly less subjectivist, however, in the light of
his distinction between transcendental idealism and transcendental realism
(A 369, 490–491). According to this distinction, *transcendental realism* maintains that how objects appear to us in our experience *is* how they are in
themselves; that is, even independent of our perceiving them, objects have
the properties they are perceived to have. *Transcendental idealism*, however,

holds that how objects appear to us in our experience is *not* how they are in themselves; that is, independent of our perceiving them, objects do *not* have the properties they are perceived to have. In other words, transcendental idealism *distinguishes* between appearances and things-in-themselves while transcendental realism *identifies* appearances with things-in-themselves. Hence the transcendental realist affirms, while the transcendental idealist denies, that appearances give us knowledge of things-in-themselves.

Seen from this perspective, Kant's definitions seem less subjectivist because transcendental idealism appears to involve some commitment to the existence of things-in-themselves. Although the transcendental idealist does not claim that appearances are of things-in-themselves, he does distinguish them from things-in-themselves, and so he seems to admit the reality of something besides mere representations. Yet, on closer examination, the definition does not commit the transcendental idealist to the *existence* of things-in-themselves. It gives them only a hypothetical status: *if* they exist, we cannot assume that we know them through appearances. Hence it seems that Kant at best can distinguish his transcendental idealism from a dogmatic idealism that denies the existence of things-in-themselves; the definitions do not exclude, however, a skeptical idealism that doubts their existence.

So far, then, Kant seems guilty of subjectivism. At least the first edition definitions of transcendental idealism seem to imply a kind of subjectivism, or more precisely, skeptical idealism. But does the subjectivism of these definitions warrent the conclusion that transcendental idealism in general, as conceived in the first edition of the *Kritik*, is subjectivist?

3. Transcendental versus Empirical Idealism

That this is not the case becomes clear when we consider the wider context of the first edition definitions. This shows that Kant is not endorsing but criticizing subjectivism. The main point behind his account of transcendental idealism in the Critique of the Fourth Paralogism and the Antinomy of Pure Reason is to distinguish it from forms of idealism in the subjectivist tradition. So, even if we remain within the first edition of the *Kritik*, there is something to be said against the charge of subjectivism. This is indeed just what we should expect, given Kant's long struggle with idealism in the precritical decades.

In defining transcendental idealism in these texts Kant is careful to distinguish it from *empirical* or *material* idealism. Indeed, Kant defines such idealism in subjectivist terms. According to the empirical or material idealist, the existence of objects in space outside us is either (a) doubtful and indemonstrable or (b) false and impossible (A 377, 491). Kant calls the first position *skeptical,* the second *dogmatic* idealism. He chooses the term "empirical idealism" not because these positions advance empiricist principles, but because they doubt or deny the reality of the empirical world. In the first edition of the *Kritik,* Kant made Descartes his paradigm of skeptical idealism; though he cites no historical figure, his chief example of dogmatic idealism was Leibniz.[10] In the second edition, however, Berkeley alone is mentioned as the example of dogmatic idealism (B 71, 274).

To understand how transcendental idealism differs from empirical or material idealism, it is important to recognize Kant's distinction between two senses in which an object exists *outside us (außer uns)*. There is the *transcendental* sense in which it exists outside us as a thing-in-itself, that is, its existence and nature are independent of all consciousness of it. There is also the *empirical* sense in which the object belongs to *outer* appearance or to *"things which are to be found in space"* (A 373).[11] In this sense the object is outside me simply because it is in a different place from my body in space;[12] hence Kant states in the Aesthetic that to refer sensations to something "outside me" means that they must be "in another region of space from that in which I find myself" (A 23).[13]

The fundamental distinction between transcendental idealism and empirical idealism, Kant argues, is that the transcendental idealist affirms, while the empirical idealist doubts or denies, the existence of objects outside us *in the empirical sense*. In other words, material idealism holds that the empirical world either could be or is an illusion; but transcendental idealism affirms that it is real. Or, in more Kantian terms, the transcendental idealist maintains that these objects are appearances (*Erscheinungen*); but the empirical idealist holds that they are, or at least could be, an illusion (*Schein*).[14] Thus the main advantage of transcendental idealism over empirical idealism is that it is an *empirical realism* that affirms the reality of the empirical world or the existence of objects in space outside us.

Kant's doctrine of the empirical reality of space is meant to exclude three rival theories. The central thesis of his empirical realism is that I *know* that there are three-dimensional objects outside me in space *in an empirical sense*. Such a thesis excludes three positions. First, the claim that it is only an *illusion,* or that it *is* false, that we see things in space. This is the position of dogmatic idealism. Second, the claim that it only *seems* or *appears* to be the case, or that it *could be* false or an illusion, that what we see is in space. This is the standpoint of problematic idealism, and indeed that of traditional sense data theories or phenomenalism.[15] Third, the claim that I know that there is an object outside me in space *in the transcendental sense.* This is the position of transcendental realism. Although transcendental idealism and transcendental realism both claim that I know of the existence of objects in space outside me, Kant argues that transcendental realism cannot provide sufficient support for this claim because it conflates empirical with transcendental externality and then demands the impossible: proof of transcendental externality. Thus each of the alternatives to transcendental idealism—dogmatic idealism, skeptical idealism, and transcendental realism—either explicitly denies or implicitly undermines the central thesis of empirical realism.

It has been argued that the central thesis of Kant's empirical realism is incompatible with his doctrine that we know things only as appearances. To say that we know things only as appearances—this objection goes—must mean that we know things only as they appear or seem to us; for we deprive the distinction between reality and appearance of all meaning if reality becomes conflated with how things appear to us.[16] But this argument fails to see that the ordinary and commonsense distinctions between reality and illusion, between how things are in themselves and how they simply appear to us, can be perfectly accommodated within Kant's realm of appearances.[17] It is possible to distinguish between reality and illusion, between objects themselves and how they seem to us, within the realm of appearances by distinguishing between those perceptions that are abnormal, disjointed, and, idiosyncratic and those that are normal, interconnected, and intersubjective. Indeed, Kant himself was very careful to distinguish between appearances in the transcendental and empirical sense.[18]

Why does Kant think that the empirical idealist has to doubt or deny, *even in the empirical sense,* the existence of objects outside us? He explains that this is because the empirical idealist shares a fatal premise with the transcendental realist: that to know something in space outside us we must know whether our representations correspond with things-in-themselves (A 369, 372). If we accept such a standard of knowledge, Kant argues, then it becomes necessary to doubt or deny the existence of objects outside us, for the simple reason that we cannot get outside our own representations to compare them with reality in itself. Such a standard of knowledge demands the impossible, Kant argues, because to represent the object as outside us it would be necessary to represent it in space, which is again only the form of representation (A 376). Since, however, the empirical idealist presupposes this standard of knowledge, and since he also recognizes that it is impossible to satisfy it, he doubts the reality of all things in space. What he sees will be, for all he knows, only an illusion. Hence the empirical idealist conflates the transcendental and empirical reality of an object. Since he cannot know the object outside us in the transcendental sense, he assumes that we also cannot know it in the empirical sense. It is just this inference, however, that Kant intends to block with his distinction between transcendental and empirical reality.

The underlying problem with empirical idealism, then, is that it accepts the same standard of knowledge as transcendental realism. Hence, just as Kant aligns transcendental idealism with empirical realism, he pairs transcendental realism with empirical idealism. If transcendental idealism provides a basis for empirical realism, transcendental realism unwittingly establishes a foundation for empirical idealism. The transcendental realist is eventually compelled to "play the part" of the empirical idealist, Kant argues, because he cannot satisfy his own criterion of knowledge: the conformity of representations with a thing-in-itself. Like the empirical idealist, he is then forced to doubt whether we have knowledge of an external world (A 369, 372). There is indeed much truth in Kant's contention about the role of transcendental realism in empirical idealism, given that Descartes had used its standard of knowledge to come to his skeptical conclusions.[19]

4. Empirical Realism in the Aesthetic

Since Kant thinks that the great strength of transcendental idealism lies in its empirical realism, the case for transcendental idealism must ultimately involve determining the precise meaning of empirical realism. This makes it necessary to take a close look at the Transcendental Aesthetic of the first *Kritik*, for it is here that Kant provides his most detailed account of empirical realism. The arguments for empirical realism in the Critique of the Fourth Paralogism and the Antinomy of Pure Reason have to be read in the context of this earlier section.

In the Transcendental Aesthetic Kant provides several accounts of the empirical reality of space. These appear in the context of his attempt to explain why the ideality of space does not undermine its empirical reality, or what he calls its "objective validity." Since most of these explanations are already fully apparent in the first edition, and since they indeed go back to the Inaugural Dissertation, they belong to Kant's original conception of transcendental idealism. They are not, therefore, polemical adaptions or later modifications. The second edition does make some important clarifications, but adds nothing substantially new.[20]

Kant's first and chief explanation for the empirical reality of space is *transcendental,* pointing out the transcendental status of the representation of space.[21] This account is the most basic of the three, because the other two presuppose or elaborate it. Kant stresses the transcendental status of the representation of space when he claims that it is *a necessary condition of experience,* and more specifically the necessary condition under which anything appears to the external senses, sight or touch. To say that space is a necessary condition of the external senses means that if we see or touch anything we *must* perceive it as somewhere in space. According to this explanation, then, the empirical reality of space means that appearing in space is a *universal* and *necessary* property of all objects of the external senses. Such an explanation excludes two possibilities: the empiricist view that space is simply an abstraction from experience, having at best only an accidental or contingent validity; and the rationalist view that space is only a fiction of the understanding or an illusion of the imagination.

Kant's second explanation of the empirical reality of space is *second-order* or *logical.*[22] This account determines the conditions under which *judgments* about space in general, or specific things in space, are true. Kant explains that the objective validity of space means that the judgment 'All things are next to one another in space' is true of all appearances or objects of sensible intuition. If we exactly specify the subject of a judgment, he says, the judgment is universally valid (A 28). Thus the proposition 'All things are in space' is true under the limitation that these things are objects of sensible intuition or appearances. If, however, we remove this restriction—if we assert the proposition of things in general or in themselves—then it is false. So, according to this account, the empirical reality of space simply means that the proposition 'All things are in space' is universally true, where it is understood that these things are appearances.

Kant's point here becomes clearer when we consider one of his later remarks: that the transcendental ideality of space preserves the truth of all empirical judgements about particular things in space. "This [ideality] of space and time," Kant argues, "leaves the certainty of empirical knowledge unaffected" (A 39). The empirical reality of space therefore means that all empirical judgments about specific things in space retain their truth regardless of the transcendental ideality of space. As we shall soon see (1.3.2), this point is crucial for Kant's reply to the Cartesian skeptic.

Kant's third and final account of the empirical reality of space is *mathematical* or *geometrical*. According to this explanation, space has empirical reality because transcendental idealism shows that the axioms and theorems of geometry are necessarily true of appearances. If propositions such as 'Only one straight line lies between two points' and 'Within two straight lines no space can be enclosed' are universally and necessarily true, then what appears in space cannot be an arbitrary or private perception, still less an illusion of the imagination. Rather, these appearances will be real in virtue of their universal and necessary structure.

Kant's argument in the Aesthetic for the applicability of geometry to things in space ultimately goes back to the Inaugural Dissertation (§15E, II, 404). The argument consists in the following steps: (1) space in general is a necessary condition of anything appearing to the senses; (2) the axioms and theorems of geometry determine the properties of space in general; therefore (3) anything appearing to the senses must conform to the axioms and theorems of geometry (A 48). This argument is much stronger in its claims for transcendental idealism than the logical one, for it holds that the ideality of space is not only a *sufficient* condition for empirical truths (synthetic a posteriori) about things in space but also a *necessary* condition for geometrical truths (synthetic a priori) about things in space. More specifically, Kant maintains that transcendental idealism alone guarantees the empirical reality of space because only it ensures that the axioms and theorems of geometry apply to all things in space.

Kant's transcendental and mathematical accounts of the reality of space amount to his own transcendental version of the traditional distinction between primary and secondary qualities.[23] This distinction surfaces in the Aesthetic when Kant states that the spatial properties of appearances really do belong to them, unlike such properties as warmth, color, and taste, which consist in nothing more than "effects accidentally added by the particular constitution of our sense organs" (A 28–29). To be sure, in the *Prolegomena* Kant rejects the traditional distinction, claiming that such primary qualities as impenetrability and shape are also appearances and not properties belonging to the object in itself (IV, 289). There is not, however, any inconsistency between these standpoints. For Kant still maintains the traditional distinction *within the realm of experience* itself; even though spatial appearances are not properties of things-in-themselves, they are still distinct from such qualities as heat, color, and taste. Unlike these qualities, the spatial characteristics of an object are locatable in the intersubjective structure of a single universal space, and hence they really do belong to an object. So while Kant accepts the traditional distinction, he refuses to draw the usual inferences from it: that primary qualities are true of the object in itself.

Kant's endorsement of the traditional distinction is also qualified by his attempt to give a new rationale for it. In Locke, the basis for the distinction is purely empirical: some sense qualities, such as size, shape, and weight, are the objects of several senses, and they seem less dependent upon physiology and perspective than others, such as color, taste, and warmth. No less than Berkeley, however, Kant thinks that it is impossible to draw such a distinction in empirical terms alone; hence in the *Prolegomena* he endorses Berkeley's argument that the appearance of size, shape, and weight do depend upon perspective and physiology (IV, 289). Unlike Berkeley, however, Kant thinks that it is possible to salvage something of the traditional distinction provided that we recognize the transcendental status of space. What makes primary qualities objective is not their empirical component, but that they, unlike secondary qualities, conform to the universal and necessary structure of space in general.

5. Empirical Realism and Empirical Dualism

So far we have explained Kant's empirical realism essentially in terms of his argument for the empirical reality of space in the Transcendental Aesthetic. This argument consists in Kant's contention that space is a universal and necessary form of experience, a form sufficient to preserve the truth of all empirical judgments about space and necessary to maintain the truth of all mathematical judgements about space. According to this reading, then, the empirical reality of things is basically a *formal* rather than *material* characteristic: it means the conformity of appearances to the universal and necessary *structure* of space; it does not mean that these things have an *existence* apart from the consciousness that intuits them in space. To equate empirical reality with such a material characteristic seems to be a relapse into transcendental realism.

There is, however, a competing reading of Kant's empirical realism that attempts to give a stronger material or ontological meaning to empirical reality without lapsing into transcendental realism. This is the interpretation

propounded by the adherents of the theory of double affection, most notably by Hans Vaihinger, Erich Adickes, and Norman Kemp Smith.[24] According to this theory, there are two levels of affection in transcendental idealism: the transcendental ego is affected by things-in-themselves, while the
empirical ego is affected by empirical objects. Although empirical objects are
given to the consciousness of the empirical ego, they are *created* by the transcendental ego in its interaction with the thing-in-itself. Since these objects
are *entirely* given to the empirical ego, which plays no role in their constitution, they exist apart from its consciousness. Hence the empirical reality of
an object is not only formal but also material: it means not only that the object conforms to the universal and necessary structure of experience, but
also that it exists completely independently of empirical consciousness. Supposedly, this is the meaning of Kant's *empirical dualism,* and the implication
of his statement that empirical objects can be treated as things-in-themselves.

There are two serious problems with this interpretation.[25] First, Kant's
teaching in the Aesthetic implies that the object in space cannot exist apart
from *empirical* consciousness. Space is a form of sensibility, and sensibility is
an essentially empirical faculty because it is "the capacity to acquire representations through the manner in which we are affected by objects" (A 19).
While space and time are indeed *forms* of sensibility, and so independent of
specific empirical content, they are still connected to the subject's empirical
nature, and more specifically to its power to be affected by objects. If, then,
there were no sensibility or empirical consciousness, there would be no object in space. Second, there is a curious replication of appearances: the appearance of the object for empirical consciousness becomes the appearance
of the appearance of the object for the transcendental subject.[26] The whole
problem of knowledge then arises all over again for the empirical subject: for
how does it know that its consciousness is truly of the appearance for the
transcendental subject?

Whatever the logical difficulties, the texts usually cited in behalf of the
theory do not really support it. When Kant writes of *"empirical dualism"* in
the Critique of the Fourth Paralogism, he does not commit himself to the
distinct *existence* of appearances apart from the empirical subject. Rather, all
that empirical dualism means for Kant is that (1) there are objects outside
me, that is, in a different space from my body (A 370), and (2) there is a *heterogeneity* between the representations of inner and outer sense, because
what is within me cannot be represented as outside me and what is repre-

sented as outside me cannot be within me (A 379). Kant insists, however, that such an empirical dualism, which holds only for appearances, provides no grounds for a *transcendental dualism* that would conceive the appearances of inner sense as properties of some independently existing mind, and the appearances of outer sense as properties of some independently existing material object (A 389, 391). All that we are allowed to affirm is that the appearances of inner and outer sense are very different from one another, but not that they are properties of independently existing substances. Although Kant sometimes describes appearances as things-in-themselves,[27] this does not mean that he gives them an existence independent of empirical consciousness; rather, it means only that, from the standpoint of empirical consciousness, we can speak or think of them *as if* they were things-in-themselves.

CHAPTER 3

The First Edition Refutation
of Skeptical Idealism

1. The Priority of Skeptical Idealism

In the first edition of the *Kritik,* Kant did battle against all forms of empirical idealism, whether it was the skeptical idealism of Descartes or the dogmatic idealism of Leibniz. It was the dispute with skeptical or problematic idealism, however, to which Kant himself gave greatest priority. In one passage in the Critique of the Fourth Paralogism he virtually equated idealism as such with its skeptical variant, questioning whether the dogmatic idealist really deserves the title of idealist at all. "As an idealist," Kant wrote, "one should understand not he who denies the existence of the external objects of the senses, but only he who does not admit that it is known through immediate perception, and who concludes from this that their reality can never be completely certain through all possible experience" (A 368–369).[1] The reason for this curious definition appears only a few pages later when Kant compares the dogmatic idealist unfavorably to the skeptical idealist, who is "a benefactor of human reason" because he warns us against "taking for granted what we perhaps obtain only surreptitiously" (A 377). The dogmatic idealist does not benefit human reason, Kant implies, because his claims to knowledge transcend its proper limits.

But Kant did not always give such precedence to skeptical idealism. Sometimes he would do just the opposite, bestowing priority upon dogmatic idealism. Hence, in the *Prolegomena,* he defined idealism in general in dogmatic terms, claiming that "the dictum of all genuine idealists" is that "All knowledge through the senses and experience is nothing but pure illusion, and only in the ideas of understanding and reason is truth" (IV, 374). The truth of the matter is that Kant's definitions of idealism, and the priority he gave one form of idealism over another, very much depend upon his polemical context. In the first edition of the *Kritik* he was eager to distinguish his transcendental idealism from Descartes skeptical idealism; in the *Prolegomena* he was desperate to dissociate it from Berkeley's dogmatic idealism.

While Kant's demotion of dogmatic idealism should not blind us to the real importance it had for him,[2] we must also take seriously the extra weight he sometimes gave to skeptical idealism. This was no passing fancy of the first edition of the *Kritik*, since Kant reaffirmed the point in the second edition. Thus, in the Refutation of Idealism, he again declared that skeptical idealism alone is "rational and appropriate for a thorough philosophical manner of thought" because it prohibits "decisive judgment until a sufficient proof has been found" (B 274–275). For Kant, the great value of skeptical idealism is that it demands some proof or reason for our ordinary beliefs. Such a demand is completely irrevocable. Philosophy cannot begin with our ordinary beliefs, as if they were unproblematic; and still less can it appeal to common sense, as if it were a datum. Rather, it has to justify ordinary belief from some self-evident basis, providing a rationale for it acceptable to the skeptic himself. Anything less is indeed "a scandal," "the euthanasia of philosophy."[3]

Kant's reasons for demoting dogmatic vis-à-vis skeptical idealism has much to do with his dislike for its mysticism. Referring to Berkeley's dogmatic idealism in the *Prolegomena*, Kant stated that it "always had a mystical intention and cannot have any other" (IV, 375n). In a similar vein, Kant claimed that mysticism was one of the distinguishing features of the Platonic tradition, the main source of dogmatic idealism.[4] Kant disliked mysticism chiefly because of its dogmatism. Mysticism would attempt to justify certain ontological claims—the existence of archetypes or spirits—by appealing to an esoteric intellectual intuition, which could be had only by an elite. Virtually by definition, skeptical idealism was not guilty of such dogmatism. Rather than going beyond the limits of reason by appealing to a special intuition, it demands only that we have sufficient reasons for our beliefs.

2. The Critique of the Fourth Paralogism

Kant's refutation of skeptical idealism in the first edition of the *Kritik* takes place chiefly in the Critique of the Fourth Paralogism (A 367–380), a text completely omitted from the second edition, where Kant replaced it with the Refutation of Idealism. Yet Kant's dissatisfaction with the text arose from its exposition rather than substance.[5] The first edition version remains of great importance for the interpretation of his transcendental idealism, not least because the subjectivist interpretation has been largely based upon it.

Kant's account of skeptical idealism in the first edition version of the Critique of the Fourth Paralogism is entirely Cartesian. While there is no trace of Hume anywhere in Kant's exposition, he explicitly mentions Descartes (A 367). Kant's chief concern is to refute the Cartesian doctrine that we have immediate knowledge only of our own inner states, and that our knowledge of the external world is only by inference.

Kant expounds skeptical idealism in the form of a tidy and compressed syllogism, which he calls 'The Fourth Paralogism of the Ideality of Outer Relation.' The syllogism consists in three steps: (1) that whose existence can be inferred only as a cause of given perceptions has only a doubtful existence; (2) the existence of outer appearances cannot be immediately perceived, but can be inferred only as the cause of given perceptions; therefore, (3) the existence of all objects of outer sense is doubtful (A 367).

The context behind this reasoning came straight from Descartes' *Meditations.*[6] The central thesis behind the argument, as Kant explains, is the Cartesian doctrine that I immediately perceive only what is inside myself, so that I know with certainty only my own existence and representations. Since it is always possible to doubt the existence of anything beside myself, it is necessary *to infer* the existence of external objects, which therefore cannot be given directly in perception itself. The inference from a perception to the existence of its object is very uncertain, however, because this is an inference from effect to cause, and all such inferences are questionable when the same effect can have more than one cause. It is therefore possible that all my perceptions arise from an internal rather than external cause, so that they turn out to be nothing more than "a mere play of our inner sense" (A 368).

Kant's diagnosis of the paralogisms is that they are a case of *sophisma figurae dictionis,* the fallacy of ambiguous middle. Both premises of the argument are correct; but they reach their conclusion only by virtue of an ambiguity in the middle term. The ambiguity arises from a confusion between the transcendental and empirical use of a concept (A 402–403). With some accuracy,[7] this analysis applies to the Fourth Paralogism. The ambiguous term of the syllogism is the concept of outer appearance (*äußere Erscheinung*), which is construed both in an empirical and a transcendental sense (A 373). In the empirical sense the concept designates nothing more than the object in space, or that which appears outside me in a different place than my body; in the transcendental sense it refers to something independent of all consciousness, the thing-in-itself. When these two senses are conflated it seems impossible to know whether we have perceptions of external objects in space *even in the empirical sense*. Because the inference from our perceptions to a thing-in-itself is uncertain, it seems as if the perception of something outside us in space must be equally uncertain. Since we cannot get outside our perceptions to see if they correspond with things-in-themselves, it seems impossible to know whether we perceive objects in space.

Kant does not content himself simply with exposing the equivocation behind the paralogism; he also subjects each premise to a searching examination. He is willing to accept the first premise of the syllogism. He admits that inferences to the causes of our perceptions are uncertain, in both the empirical and the transcendental sense. In the empirical sense the cause of a given perception would be nothing more than other perceptions acting according to natural laws; and since any effect can have more than one cause, there is no guarantee that we make certain inferences about the causes of given perceptions. It is indeed precisely this that explains the possibility of illusion, Kant notes (A 376). In the transcendental sense the cause of a given perception would be some thing-in-itself. Here again Kant concedes that we cannot make reliable inferences to the causes of our perceptions; but now the reason is very different. While the empirical cause of perceptions is in principle knowable, their transcendental cause would be nothing less than a thing-in-itself, which is in principle unknowable (A 372).

If Kant accepts the first premise of the syllogism, he questions its second premise, because it is precisely here that the fundamental equivocation occurs. The concept of an outer appearance is interpreted in both the transcendental and empirical sense. The premise is true in the transcendental sense because it is clear that things-in-themselves are not immediately perceived; but it is false in the empirical sense because, following the Transcendental Aesthetic, objects in space are not something apart from, and prior to, our representations of them. Since their reality is given within the perceptions themselves, we do not have to rely on inferences to their causes.

According to Kant's diagnosis, then, the fatal underlying assumption behind the Fourth Paralogism is nothing less than transcendental realism, the doctrine that appearances are things-in-themselves, or that the object that appears in space exists apart from and prior to our perception of it. This assumption condemns us to skepticism, Kant argues, for the simple reason that it is impossible for us to get outside our representations to compare them with an object in itself (A 376, 378). It is just this assumption, however, that Kant believes he has already undermined in the Transcendental Aesthetic. There he had argued that outer appearances—what appears to us in space and time—are not things-in-themselves but only representations.[8] If this is the case, then there will be no need to base the reality of outer appearances upon uncertain inferences to their causes; rather, the reality of outer appearances will be given with the representations themselves. Hence Kant thinks that his own transcendental idealism provides an indubitable basis for proving the reality of outer appearances. If these appearances are distinct from things-in-themselves—if they amount to nothing more than "a species of representations . . . which are called external"—then we can know of their existence simply by having representations of them.

3. The Proof of the External World

After dissecting the fallacy behind the Fourth Paralogism, Kant proceeds to formulate an argument for the existence of the external world according to the principles of his transcendental idealism. This argument, which appears in three compressed sentences at A 370–371, amounts to the first edition version of the Refutation of Idealism. Each sentence serves as a premise of the argument. (1) It is certain that I have representations. (2) External objects, or things in space, consist only in representations. Therefore, (3) it is certain that external objects, or things in space, exist. These points show, Kant concludes, that the existence of external things is based on "the immediate testimony of my self-consciousness" (A 371). The only difference between my self-awareness and that of external things, he further explains, is that the former is based on inner sense while the latter is founded on outer sense; but I do not have to infer the existence of the object of outer sense anymore than the existence of the object of inner sense. *Pace* Descartes, then, self-consciousness of my inner states is not privileged, because what I know through outer sense is just as certain as what I know through inner sense. The existence of external objects in space is given to my representations as well as my own representations and existence.

As Kant first expounds his argument, it seems as if he is claiming that *all* our representations of objects in space are certain. Hence he states that the existence of objects in space is based on "the immediate testimony of self-consciousness"; and he even declares that the mere having of representations of external objects is "a sufficient proof of their reality" (A 371). But this is problematic for the simple reason that we can suffer illusions, having the awareness of external objects when none are really there. This is a point that Kant would later recognize in the second edition of the *Kritik*, and it was one of the central reasons for the reformulation of his argument in the Refutation of Idealism (see below, 1.7.2). It is important to recognize, however, that Kant already saw the point in the first edition. It is a simple fact that sometimes our representations are deceptive, he noted, because they do not correspond to an object or do not have an external cause (A 376). The source of such deception, he explained, can be a false judgment (as in sensory illusions) or a delusion of imagination (as in dreams). To avoid such deceptions, he advised, we should determine whether the representation conforms with others according to empirical laws (A 376). Here we must proceed according to the rule: "*Whatever is connected with a perception according to empirical laws is actual*" (A 376).

Kant tacitly admitted, therefore, the skeptical idealist's point that the perception of external objects is not immediate, and that we have to determine the validity of perceptions through inferences or by determining their causes. Yet it is important to see that this concession is still not fatal to Kant's general critique of skeptical idealism in the first edition of the *Kritik*. For Kant is still in a position to claim that the transcendental idealist alone can establish the truth of our perceptions. Since the transcendental idealist identifies outer appearances with perceptions, he seeks the cause of any perception among other perceptions; he then determines the validity of a perception simply by a formal criterion, by ascertaining the connection of perceptions among one another. While it is possible that we cannot in practice complete the procedures of verification, it is still possible in principle, because we do not have to get outside the order of our perceptions. The transcendental realist, however, is compelled to verify perceptions by seeing whether they have a transcendental cause; it is not sufficient for him to determine their validity simply by checking the order of perceptions among themselves. It is also necessary for him to know *per impossible* whether these perceptions correspond with a transcendental object. Hence the transcendental idealist can, while the transcendental realist cannot, provide verification in principle. This point is already implicit in the first edition of the *Kritik;* but it will become even more explicit in the second edition.[9]

4. A Cartesian Reply

As it is presented in the first edition of the *Kritik*, Kant's argument against skeptical idealism is vulnerable to an obvious Cartesian objection. The Cartesian will reply that the argument indeed shows that we have *representations* of objects in space, but he will immediately add that this is not really in question. What the argument does not show, he will insist, is that there are three-dimensional objects existing *independent* of those representations. Kant's conflation move—the identification of objects in space with representations—appears to prove the empirical reality of objects in space only by forfeiting the independent reality of the object to be known.

If we follow the spirit of Kant's arguments in the first edition, it is not difficult to reconstruct his first line of reply to this kind of objection. Kant would point out that the Cartesian demand for some independent reality rests upon a false presupposition: that knowledge consists in the conformity of a representation with a thing-in-itself. Kant admits that *if* this must be the standard of knowledge, then the Cartesian skeptic is indeed correct in doubting all our representations, for it is an inescapable fact that we cannot get outside our representations to compare them with things as they are in themselves (A 105, 376, 378).[10] Still, he thinks that it is possible to avoid this skeptical conclusion because he denies that it is *necessary* to hold this standard of knowledge in the first place. Instead, he maintains that it is possible to make the distinction between reality and illusion completely within the realm of appearances themselves.[11] His criterion of knowledge will be purely formal: conformity of representations with the universal and necessary forms of experience (A 376–377). If such a criterion is *sufficient* to explain the distinction between reality and illusion, then it is not necessary to fulfill the impossible standards of knowledge required by the skeptic. There will be no need, then, to doubt the empirical reality of things outside us in space.

Of course, this reply will not satisfy the Cartesian skeptic. He insists that our ordinary conception of truth involves something more than internal coherence, namely, the notion of correspondence, the conformity of representations with some independent reality. He will then point out that it is just this notion that Kant cannot capture with his formal criterion of knowledge. For even if the forms of experience are universal and necessary, that still leaves the question of their truth. It is still possible that the entire structure of experience—no matter how coherent—is illusory because it does not correspond with independent reality. After all, if we follow through with the method of radical doubt, it is possible to imagine that this structure is nothing more than an elaborate dream or the cruel deception of a malicious demon.[12]

There is a sense, of course, in which Kant concedes this very point to the Cartesian. He admits that we cannot assume that the whole framework of our experience has *transcendental* reality, that is, that it corresponds to things as they are in themselves. Still, Kant has another strategy up his sleeve to stymie wholesale Cartesian doubt. Namely, he blocks one crucial Cartesian inference: that if the framework of our experience does not have *transcendental* reality then nothing within it can have *empirical* reality. Simply because the structure itself does not correspond with things-in-themselves does not mean that all propositions affirmed within it are false. On the contrary, as Kant argued in the Aesthetic (see below, 1.2.4), their truth can remain the same whether the framework has transcendental reality or ideality. As long as the structure or organization of the whole web of belief remains the same, there will be no discernible difference between truth and falsity. So, ultimately, Cartesian doubt does not really matter.

What continues to drive Cartesian doubt against the Kantian is the fact that its transcendental realism seems to capture something about our ordinary conception of truth, namely, the notion that an idea must correspond with some independent reality. Kant attempts to undermine this very motivation, however, insofar as he claims that his transcendental idealism accommodates our *ordinary* conception of the truth. Transcendental idealism does not dispute the commonsense notion that truth consists in the correspondence of a representation with an independent reality; rather, it questions only the *philosophical doctrine* that explains or justifies this notion, namely, transcendental realism. Transcendental realism attempts to explain this notion in terms of correspondence with a thing-in-itself; transcendental idealism accounts for it in terms of the connection or order among representations themselves.[13] According to transcendental idealism, to say that a representation corresponds with its object means that it is a necessary part of a synthesis of representations; here the object is not a thing-in-itself but the unity or whole imposed by a norm or rule.

Thus the ultimate basis of Kant's strategy against the Cartesian is his general distinction between the transcendental and empirical, which he thinks the Cartesian is guilty of confusing. This distinction can be viewed *inter alia* as a distinction between two distinct logical levels: between that which is a necessary condition of something and that of and for which it is such a condition. While the transcendental deals with the framework of experience itself, the empirical concerns specific objects *within* that framework.[14]

Now it is in terms of this broader distinction that Kant attempts to establish his distinction between the transcendental ideality and empirical reality of space, and ultimately to defeat Cartesian skeptical idealism. Judgments about things within space can have empirical truth because transcendental questions about the truth of the framework itself do not affect our answer to empirical questions about specific things within it. When the Cartesian persists in doubting our *empirical* knowledge because we cannot establish whether it corresponds to things-in-themselves, Kant would reply that this is a confusion between two quite distinct levels of discourse, the transcendental and empirical. The transcendental question whether the framework itself corresponds to things-in-themselves does not affect the truth value of any empirical judgements made within it.

5. Appearances and Spatiality

This is not the end of Kant's problems, however. For the fundamental difficulty of establishing empirical realism on the basis of transcendental idealism still persists. Namely, how is it possible for transcendental idealism to explain the empirical reality of things in space if it identifies these things with representations, which cannot be three-dimensional? If spatial objects are not illusory, then they must be three-dimensional. It seems, however, that Kant cannot cross the great divide between the Cartesian *res cogitans* and *res extensa* because things in space are three-dimensional, whereas ideas or representations have no length, breadth, or depth. Indeed, Kant himself insists that all ideas belong to inner sense, and that the objects of inner sense cannot be in space (A 23, 357). Must we then conclude that spatiality is an illusion after all?[15]

The basic question here is this: What is spatial or three dimensional according to transcendental idealism? Or to what does Kant ascribe spatiality? It cannot be material objects which exist independent of all consciousness, for to say that only these objects are spatial is transcendental realism; but it also cannot be representations or ideas, because these are not spatial or three-dimensional. Yet if it cannot be material objects or mental representations, what can it be?

It seems as if the difficulty disappears if we distinguish between two aspects of representation: the *state* of representing, which is the mental act of representing, and the *object* of representation, which is what is represented. Although it is surely nonsense to say that the *mental act* is spatial, because a mental act cannot have a size, shape, or weight, it is not absurd to say that *its object* is spatial. It is no more problematic to say that a nonspatial mental act can represent something spatial than it is to say that a two-dimensional picture can represent a three-dimensional object.

Yet this distinction does not fully solve the problem. It still leaves the hoary and horrible question of intentionality: What is the *object* of representation? What kind of ontological status does it have? If it is only mental, then it too cannot be three dimensional; and if it is something more than that, the actual thing represented, it would seem to be material, so that we are again back to transcendental realism. Kant, it seems, still cannot escape the dilemma of transcendental realism or empirical idealism.

Another apparent solution to the difficulty is to distinguish between two senses of appearance corresponding to the two levels of Kant's discourse, the transcendental and the empirical.[16] When Kant writes about appearances as if they were three-dimensional spatial objects he is speaking about their empirical status, in which they are a specific kind of object of experience, namely, an object of outer sense compared to one of inner sense. When, however, he refers to them as representations or ideas, he is describing their transcendental status, in which they do not oppose any specific kind of thing in experience but the thing-in-itself that lies beyond all possible experience. This solution too is problematic, however, because it does not explain what gives Kant a right to think of empirical objects as three-dimensional when they are really only representations when viewed transcendentally.

The problem seems to disappear only when we recognize and appreciate the other meaning of appearance within transcendental philosophy. This is the sense in which appearances are not simply representations but aspects of things insofar as they are perceived according to the conditions of human sensibility. In this sense, appearances are not a kind of entity opposed to things-in-themselves, and still less are they monadic properties of either the perceiver or the thing-in-itself alone. Rather, they essentially involve a *relation* between perceivers and an independent reality; and, more specifically, they are *how* things-in-themselves appear to perceivers endowed with a human sensibility. We cannot reduce such appearances to entities or monadic properties of the perceiver or the thing-in-itself—the mistake of empirical idealism and transcendental realism (respectively)—because if we remove either term of the relation there simply cannot be appearances. According to this sense of appearance, it is simply a false dilemma to say that spatial objects must be material or mental, because this would be to treat appearances as if they were some kind of entity or monadic property. What is spatial, then, are the appearances *of* things-in-themselves, their manner of appearing to a human sensibility, or how they are perceived by it. The answer to the question "What is three-dimensional in transcendental idealism?" is then simply "Things *insofar* as they are perceived by beings with a human sensibility."

There is more than sufficient textual warrent in the first edition of the *Kritik* for reading the concept of appearance in this second sense. In the Aesthetic Kant is clear that spatial appearances are *of* things-in-themselves (A 38). In Phenomena and Noumena he argues that the very concept of an appearance implies that it is the appearance of some reality, and he explains that all the teaching of the Aesthetic led to the conclusion that sensibility deals with the *mode* in which things-in-themselves appear to our human sensibility (A 251–252). Finally, in the Paralogisms he states that the unknown substratum of matter affects our senses, producing in us the intuition of something extended (A 359).[17] All these passages go back to the Inaugural Dissertation, where Kant wrote of phenomena as "aspects of things" (*rerum species*) to distinguish his position from idealism (II, 397). For reasons we shall soon consider, Kant explicitly reaffirmed this doctrine in the *Prolegomena* (§13, Anm II, IV, 289).

The problem still remains how idealism can explain the origin and necessity of spatial representation. In other words, why does our human sensibility represent things-in-themselves as spatial? How is it that things-in-themselves interact with our sensibility so that spatial perception results? In the Concluding Observation to the Paralogisms in the first edition, Kant admits that idealism faces a difficulty here (A 387); but he also insists that the problem is irresolvable if transcendental philosophy remains within its self-imposed limits of possible experience. Thus Kant raises the question "How is outer intuition . . . possible at all in a thinking subject?" (A 393), only to reply that this question cannot be answered because we know nothing about the transcendental object that is the cause of this species of representation. In the end, then, Kant was willing to leave the problem of spatial perception a mystery.

6. The Ambiguity of Transcendental Idealism

Assuming that Kant can explain three-dimensionality by attaching appearances to things-in-themselves, there is still an additional difficulty for him to ponder: that he would again be making himself vulnerable to Cartesian skepticism. The Cartesian skeptic doubts that there is any reality beyond his own representations, and so he questions whether they are appearances of things-in-themselves. So it now seems that Kant is caught in a dilemma: if he attaches appearances to things-in-themselves, he falls victim to skepticism; but if he detaches appearances from things-in-themselves, he cannot explain their three-dimensionality.

This dilemma reflects a deeper tension with Kant's empirical realism: it is caught within, yet pushes beyond, the realm of experience. It is caught within experience because, to reply to the Cartesian skeptic, Kant has to explain the distinction between truth and illusion entirely within the realm of experience itself. Yet it also pushes beyond experience because, to explain the three-dimensionality of space, Kant has to attach appearances to things-in-themselves. The account of empirical reality in the first edition of the *Kritik* reveals just this tension. Kant sometimes defines empirical reality strictly in *formal* terms, as if it consists in nothing more than the structure of experience; but at other times he understands empirical reality in *material* terms, because he states that appearances are *of* things-in-themselves.[18]

Despite this ambivalence, it is striking that the *definition of transcendental idealism* in the earlier edition involves a strictly formal account of empirical reality. When Kant attempts to distinguish his transcendental idealism from the empirical idealism of Descartes he stresses that it, unlike empirical idealism, affirms the certainty of our knowledge of things in space outside us, where these things are defined strictly in formal rather than material terms. They are equated simply with representations conforming to a structure of laws, where these representations are understood as mental states rather than appearances of things. This formal account of appearances is perfectly understandable from the context: Kant's aim is to reply to the Cartesian skeptic, and any reference to appearances of things-in-themselves would be vulnerable to the very skeptical doubt he intends to refute.

It is important to see, however, that in the *Prolegomena* and the second edition of the *Kritik* Kant will develop a new and different strategy for distinguishing his transcendental idealism from empirical idealism.[19] He will now begin to stress a material as well as a formal account of empirical reality. He will become more explicit and emphatic in insisting upon a doctrine only implicit and inchoate in the first edition of the *Kritik:* that appearances are not merely representations in us but representations of things-in-themselves. In other words, appearances will now consist not only in a formal structure but also in a material substrate. This shift in emphasis arises from Kant's new context: the need to distinguish his doctrine from Berkeley's dogmatic idealism.

The result of this shift is nothing less than a new definition of transcendental idealism. After 1781 Kant resolves to drop the term 'transcendental idealism' and instead defines his doctrine as *formal* idealism, which he now contrasts with *material* idealism.[20] Somewhat misleadingly, he chooses the term 'formal' in reference to the transcendental *ideality* of appearances to stress the point that only the form of things depends upon us, while their existence must be given independent of us. While the material idealist doubts or denies even the *existence* of objects outside us, the formal idealist affirms the existence of such objects and claims that only their essence or form depends upon us.

7. The Coherence of Transcendental Idealism

But if transcendental idealism is ambiguous, is it incoherent? Since its ambiguity stems from the two senses of appearance, everything hinges on whether Kant can use that concept in both its senses. Is it possible for him to say both that appearances are representations and that they are aspects of things-in-themselves?

The eternal dispute between subjectivism and antisubjectivism suggests otherwise. It seems that an appearance cannot be both a mere representation, a monadic property of the perceiving subject, and an aspect of things-in-themselves, a relation between a subject and an object. Yet there is an implicit assumption underlying this dispute: that it is possible to decide this question within Kant's own limits of knowledge. The very opposite is the case. In several passages of the second edition of the *Kritik* the purport of Kant's argument is that all we can do is *think* of appearances as aspects of things-in-themselves; as transcendental philosophers we cannot claim to *know* this without transcending the limits of possible experience.[21]

Recognizing this limitation on transcendental knowledge provides the solution to Kant's dilemma. As long as he is speaking transcendentally or epistemically rather than metaphysically or ontologically, Kant can regard appearances *both* as representations and as aspects of things-in-themselves. If, however, we speak metaphysically or ontologically, then we claim that appearances *exist* as either representations in the mind or as aspects of things; in this case we have to make a choice between one view or the other, given that nothing can exist at the same time as both an idea in the mind and as an aspect of things. That contradiction disappears, however, if we speak transcendentally or epistemically, for then our main concern is only with the conditions of knowledge of objects and not objects themselves. Speaking transcendentally or epistemically means recognizing the limits of knowledge and admitting an agnosticism about the ontology of appearances. We then say that, *as far as we know,* appearances might be only representations, because we cannot know whether they are aspects of things-in-themselves that exist independent of us. Nevertheless, *again as far as we know*, it is still possible for these appearances to be aspects of things-in-themselves, for in thinking this we do not contradict ourselves or transcend the limits of experience.

At first blush this account seems very unsatisfying because it amounts to admitting an *aporeia*, to conceding that the issue is irresolvable. Yet Kant's critical doctrine, let alone the ambiguity of his texts, permits nothing more. If we are to remain true to the limits Kant imposes upon transcendental discourse, we have no choice but to permit him to talk about appearances in both senses, provided, of course, that this is understood in a hypothetical or problematic sense.[22] Ultimately, then, the ambiguity of transendental idealism is not accidental or equivocal; rather, it is systematic and deliberate.[23] It is the result not only of Kant's polemical context, but also of his own teachings about the limits of knowledge.

CHAPTER 4

The First Edition Refutation
of Dogmatic Idealism

1. The Missing Refutation

So far we have considered Kant's refutation of *problematic* or *skeptical* idealism, which *doubts* the reality of the external world. Kant's case against empirical idealism could be complete, however, only if he also had a rebuttal of *dogmatic* idealism, which *denies* the reality of the external world. Kant's critique of problematic idealism in the first edition of the *Kritik* appears mainly in the Critique of the Fourth Paralogism. Where, though, does Kant deal with dogmatic idealism?

That question raises something of a mystery. For, strangely, Kant does not seem to discuss dogmatic idealism in the first edition of the *Kritik*. He makes a promise to do so, when, in the Critique of the Fourth Paralogism, he implies that he will deal with dogmatic idealism in the Antinomies (A 377). Yet Kant never does that, at least not in any explicit way. In the Antinomies he makes a brief reference to empirical idealism; but he mentions it only *en passent* to say that it should not be confused with his own position (A 491). It is not surprising, therefore, that some scholars have concluded that there is no refutation of dogmatic idealism in the first edition of the *Kritik*.[1] They maintain that Kant engaged in such a refutation only in the second edition, and that he did so only when he added a section to the Aesthetic which deals with Berkeley's idealism (§8, III).

Some of those scholars who deny that there is a refutation of dogmatic idealism in the first edition of the *Kritik* have a theory to explain the omission. They assume that Kant *equates* dogmatic idealism with Berkeley's idealism because, in both the *Prolegomena* and the second edition of the *Kritik*, he calls Berkeley, and no one else, a dogmatic idealist. They then argue that

Kant could not refute dogmatic idealism in the first edition because he had used some of Berkeley's central arguments to refute Descartes' problematic idealism in the Critique of the Fourth Paralogism. Hence Kant could not refute dogmatic idealism without refuting himself!

But this theory rests on two false assumptions. First, it assumes that Berkeley was the only dogmatic idealist for Kant, though Leibniz and Swedenborg had already played that role for him. Second, it supposes that Kant's reasoning in the Paralogisms is essentially Berkeleyian, thus overlooking the fundamental differences between the Kant's and Berkeley's arguments, which we will consider below (1.5.3).

There is another possible explanation for why Kant did not refute dogmatic idealism in the first edition of the *Kritik*. This explanation stresses the passage from the Critique of the Fourth Paralogism where Kant defines idealism in general in terms of skeptical idealism alone (A 368). This passage virtually defines dogmatic idealism out of existence, so that it is no wonder that Kant did not care to refute dogmatic idealism in the first edition. There was really nothing to refute!

It would be unwise, however, to place too much weight on this passage. For if Kant banishes dogmatic idealism in some passages, he reinstates it in others. This is clear even from the Critique of the Fourth Paralogism, where Kant carefully distinguishes between two versions of empirical idealism, the skeptical and the dogmatic (A 377). Furthermore, even if Kant does not have that high an opinion of dogmatic idealism, he still takes its claims seriously enough to promise to examine them in the Antinomies (A 377). So, unless we are to burden Kant with gross inconsistency, it is necessary to assume that the equation of idealism in general with skeptical idealism is more rhetorical or forensic than philosophical or substantive. Its point was not to dismiss dogmatic idealism entirely, as if it were unworthy of refutation, but simply to stress the importance of the subject of discussion, which was skeptical idealism.

Whatever Kant's rationale for not making an *explicit* refutation of dogmatic idealism in the first edition of the *Kritik*, we create more mysteries than we solve if we assume he refutes dogmatic idealism only in the second edition. For then why should Kant promise in the first edition to deal with dogmatic idealism in the Antinomies? Granted that he nowhere explicitly kept that promise, it is less odd to assume that he kept it implicitly than that he made it glibly, for the simple reason that Kant had to refute dogmatic as well as problematic idealism to secure his own transcendental idealism. Furthermore, if Berkeley is the paradigm of the dogmatic idealist, why does Kant describe the dogmatic idealist as someone who admits the reality of space but denies the reality of bodies within it (A 491/B 519)? That is not a description of Berkeley's dogmatic idealism, not even according to Kant himself, who maintains explicitly that Berkeley denies the reality of space (B 71, 274). These apparent mysteries disappear, however, as soon as we assume that Kant refuted, if only implicitly, some other dogmatic idealist in the first edition of the *Kritik*.

That it would be very odd for Kant to ignore dogmatic idealism in the first edition of the *Kritik* is especially clear from his philosophical development. The path toward transcendental idealism consisted in no small part in Kant's struggle with dogmatic idealism. Some of the fundamental tenets of transcendental idealism—such as the distinction between transcendental and empirical reality, or that between the forms of sensibility and understanding—arose from that conflict. It should come as no surprise, therefore, that Kant's defense of these tenets in the *Kritik* rehearses, if only implicitly, former quarrels. And, indeed, it takes but little scratching under the surface to see Kant's old battles in the first edition of the *Kritik*. Those disputes take place especially in the Aesthetic, but they are also evident in the Amphiboly and Antinomies. For the most part, just as we should expect, they are basically a critique of Kant's old idealist foe: Leibniz.[2]

Although Kant never explicitly refers to Leibniz as an idealist in the first *Kritik*, there can be little doubt that he regarded him as such even in this work, quite apart from the testimony of the lectures.[3] For, in his concluding chapter, he places Leibniz in the Platonic tradition,[4] which he characterizes as holding "that in the senses there is nothing but illusion and that only the understanding knows that which is true" (A 854). That fits exactly Kant's later definition of idealism in the *Prolegomena*: "the doctrine that in the senses there is only illusion and in the intellect alone truth" (IV, 374).

Prima facie this is a rather weak concept of idealism, because it seems to be entirely *epistemological*; it does not seem to be *ontological*, involving some claim about the spiritual or intelligible nature of things. In the Amphiboly, however, Kant's description of Leibniz's idealism becomes much richer, making it an idealism not only in the epistemological but also in the ontological sense. Thus on several occasions Kant states that Leibniz could understand the inner properties of his monads only in mental, spiritual, or noumenal terms (A 266, 276, 283).

If we assume that Leibniz is the dogmatic idealist of the first edition of the

Kritik, the mystery also disappears in Kant's apparently odd account of the empirical idealist as someone who admits the reality of space but denies the existence of bodies within it (A 491). While this description scarcely applies to Berkeley, it does fit Leibniz, at least according to Kant's interpretation of him. Although Leibniz rejects the idea of an *absolute* space as a mere fiction, he still thinks that space has reality as "the order of co-existence of things" or "the order of things possible at the same time."[5] In the Amphiboly Kant himself takes note of this aspect of Leibniz's doctrine when he states that Leibniz saw space as "a certain order in the community of substances" (A 275), or as "the intelligible form of the connection of things" (A 276).[6] According to Kant's interpretation, then, Leibniz is committed to the reality of space, because (a) Leibniz thinks that space has an intelligible structure, and (b) he also hold that things-in-themselves are intellectual or noumenal. Yet if Leibniz admitted the reality of space, he denied the existence of bodies within it, Kant believes, because he held that matter has no independent reality but consists solely in the confused aggregation by the senses of more simple and real units, the monads.

There seems to be one insuperable obstacle to making Leibniz the chief dogmatic idealist of the first *Kritik.* Namely, in an important passage in the Amphiboly Kant implies that Leibniz is a transcendental realist because he "took appearances for things-in-themselves" (A 260/B 320). *Prima facie* it seems impossible for Leibniz to be both a transcendental realist and a dogmatic idealist. The inconsistency is only apparent, however, arising from the persistent habit of construing idealism solely in subjectivist terms. Leibniz's idealism is not the Berkeleyian doctrine that the sole reality consists in ideas in some individual mind but the more Platonic doctrine that all reality conforms to some intelligible structure, the archetypes or forms of things. These archetypes or forms exist independent of my own individual mind, whether they are perceived or not. It is indeed for just this reason that Kant can hold that Leibniz is both a dogmatic idealist and a trancendental realist. When Leibniz took appearances for things-in-themselves he assumed that they represent—even if in a very confused way—some reality independent of them that is purely intelligible in nature. Of course, this is not the transcendental realism of the naive empiricist, who equates sensible qualities with things-in-themselves; but it is transcendental realism all the same, insofar as it assumes that our sense perceptions have an underlying intellectual structure that give us some awareness of independent intellectual reality.

2. Kant's Interpretation of Leibniz

Although Kant promises to deal with dogmatic idealism in the Antinomies, his chief dispute with dogmatic idealism in the first *Kritik* takes place primarily in the Aesthetic. Commentators have always recognized that there is a critique of dogmatic idealism in the Aesthetic, though they usually limit it to Kant's critique of Berkeley in the second edition. But Kant's debate with dogmatic idealism in the first *Kritik,* which appears equally in the first and second editions, was directed chiefly against Leibniz. That Kant is conducting a dispute with Leibniz in the Aesthetic is obvious because he stresses that his whole teaching about the ideality of space and time would be "entirely misunderstood" if it were conflated with Leibniz's doctrine that space is only a confused representation of the understanding (A 43). It is less obvious, however, that Kant's debate with Leibniz is essentially a quarrel with his idealism.[7] Yet Kant's definition of idealism, and his interpretation of Leibniz, show that this must be the case. According to Kant's interpretation, Leibniz is committed to the idealist doctrine that "in the senses there is nothing but illusion and in the intellect alone there is truth."[8] The specific version of this doctrine to which Kant responds in the Aesthetic is Leibniz's claim that the representation of bodies in space is nothing more than a confused representation of the understanding. For Kant, such a claim is tantamount to saying, with all dogmatic idealism, that the perception of bodies in space is an illusion. This was the flat antithesis of Kant's own empirical realism.

Prima facie Kant's interpretation of Leibniz is a gross misrepresentation. For Leibniz never states explicitly that the representation of bodies in space is *illusory.* To be sure, he often states that the idea of space is a mere "fiction," "an ideal thing," or "something imaginary";[9] but then he has in mind not the perception of bodies in space but only the idea of mathematical or absolute space, which arises by abstracting from all the particular relations between things. Leibniz's considered position is that the bodies in space are *phenomena bene fundata,* which are not mere illusions but the necessary sensible manifestations of monads.[10] Such phenomena have an objective dimension because they arise of necessity from the intrinsic properties of monads, and so "express" or "represent" them, at least to some degree. Furthermore, Leibniz makes the distinction between reality and illusion *within* the realm of phenomena, so that not *all* phenomena can be illusory.[11]

So far is Leibniz from regarding the perception of space as an illusion—

one could further argue—that he criticizes Berkeley's view that it is entirely subjective.[12] *Prima facie* Leibniz's doctrine of spatial perception is reminiscent of Berkeley's critique of the distinction between primary and secondary qualities, because, like Berkeley, Leibniz maintains that spatial qualities also depend upon the perceiver. It is important to see, however, that Leibniz rejects Berkeley's conclusion that spatial qualities amount to nothing more than ideas in the mind. Unlike Berkeley, Leibniz maintains that *all* our sensory perceptions are representative, so that there is no distinction to be made between primary and secondary qualities as far as sense perception alone is concerned.[13]

All this makes it seem as if Kant's interpretation of Leibniz is inaccurate, so that Kant seems to be criticizing a target of his own imagination.[14] But Kant's interpretation is perfectly defensible once we consider the precise target of his criticism. Kant is not attributing to Leibniz the doctrine that sense perception is *entirely* illusory. If he were, then half his criticism of Leibniz would be pointless, for he also reproaches Leibniz for thinking that sense perception is representative in giving us a kind of knowledge of things-in-themselves. Rather, the specific target of his criticism is Leibniz's doctrine that sense perception is illusory *insofar as it is sensory.* It is Leibniz's attitude toward the senses that troubles Kant, who wishes to vindicate the *sui generis* sensory element of cognition. Kant wants to maintain that the senses give us a distinct knowledge of phenomena and not simply a confused knowledge of noumena.

And in this regard Kant did not misinterpret his illustrious predecessor. For Leibniz does expressly state that the confusion of sense perception arises entirely from its *sensible* component, and that its representative or objective dimension comes completely from its underlying *intellectual* component.[15] Leibniz is indeed explicit that the essential function of the senses is to distort and confuse what would be truly and distinctly conceived by the intellect. He maintains that the sense perception of spatial qualities, such as size, shape and distance, is confused because it arises from compounding or aggregating a multitude of things that are intrinsically simple, and whose structure and identity are unknown to us.[16] In his terminology, the ideas of size, shape, and distance are clear, but indistinct and therefore "confused," because they do not perceive the simple elements of which they are composed.[17] If, *per impossibile*, we could completely analyze the sense quality into its elements, its sensible component would vanish entirely and we would be left with a purely intellectual perception of reality itself.[18] In this case, the spatial qualities of the object would disappear completely and we would perceive nothing less than the monads, which are extensionless points. All this means that our sense perception is illusory after all, not in the sense that it consists in an hallucination or mirage, but in the sense that it naturally gives rise to false judgments about reality itself. If we were to judge reality itself on the basis of the senses alone, we would make false judgments, because the senses perceive as one and extended what is many and extensionless.

3. The Dispute in the Aesthetic

Whatever the accuracy of Kant's interpretation of Leibniz, his critique of Leibniz's idealism in the Aesthetic plays a crucial role in his case for transcendental idealism. Kant's defense of the empirical reality of space, which is the characteristic teaching of his transcendental idealism, is essentially directed against Leibniz's claim that the perception of bodies in space consists in only a confused perception of the understanding. Against this claim, Kant reaffirms the thesis of the Inaugural Dissertation that sensibility is not a lesser form of the understanding but a distinctive faculty in its own right. To perceive things in space is not to have a confused intellectual perception of something noumenal but a clear sensible perception of something phenomenal. The representation of things in space has empirical reality, then, insofar as it consists in a clear perception of the phenomenal.

Kant's case against Leibniz's idealism therefore ultimately rests upon his general distinction between understanding and sensibility, and thus his attempt to establish the autonomy of sensibility vis-à-vis the understanding. To justify the independence of sensibility from understanding, Kant attempts to prove two propositions. First, that sensibility has its own distinctive *structure* or *form*, that is, that the representation of space is not reducible to concepts of the understanding. Second, that sensibility has its own characteristic *subject matter*, that is, its objects are not noumena but phenomena. Kant had already argued for both propositions in the Dissertation; he reaffirms both in the first *Kritik*.

Kant's main defense of the first proposition consists in his argument that the representation of space is intuitive rather than discursive, so that it belongs to sensibility, a faculty of intuitions, rather than understanding, a faculty of concepts (A 24–25).[19] According to Kant, intuition is a singular representation of something particular, and so it stands in an *immediate* relation to its object; by contrast, a concept is a general representation of something universal, and so it stands in a *mediate* relation to its object because it is a single representation of many singular representations of objects.[20] The representation of space is an intuition in this sense, Kant argues, since it is a representation of something unique, singular, or individual. Space is a unique indivisible whole that *precedes* all its parts (points, lines, places), each of which is possible only through it. This is because we can conceive a point, line, or place only *within* some space; but they do not precede the idea of space, as if it were only abstracted from them. The representation of space cannot be a concept, then, because a concept is an abstraction from its particular instances, each of which precede it and make it possible.[21]

Kant's argument for the distinctive structure of sensibility vis-à-vis the understanding ultimately presupposes his contrast between two kinds of whole–part relations, which is only implicit in the Aesthetic but much more explicit elsewhere.[22] According to this contrast, there is a singular whole or *totum* that is prior to its parts, each of which is possible only within it; or there is a universal whole or *compositum* that abstracts from its parts, each of which it presupposes. In other words, in a *totum* the whole precedes its parts, whereas in a *compositum* the parts precede the whole. Kant maintains that space is a *totum* rather than *compositum* because each particular space is conceivable only as a limit of a single universal space. The particular instances of a concept, however, exist prior to the universal term, which is abstracted from them.

Although it is not explicit, Kant's argument for the distinctive structure of sensibility is anti-Leibnizian, probably by intention and certainly by implication. It is directed against Leibniz's claim that the idea of space arises from the idea of a place, which is only an abstraction from all the particular distances between things.[23] In Kantian terms, Leibniz holds that the idea of space is general rather than singular, a concept rather than intuition, because we know of space only by abstraction from particular distances, each of which precede that idea and make it possible. Against Leibniz, Kant countered that even these distances were conceivable only within the single space of which they were only parts. As a marginal note of the first edition puts it: "Space is not a concept of external relations, as Leibniz supposed, but that which grounds the possibility of external relations" (XXIII, 22).

Kant's two arguments for the second proposition—that sensibility has its distinctive subject matter—are more explicit in the Dissertation and Amphiboly than in the Aesthetic. The first argument is from incongruous counterparts, that is, two objects that are exactly alike except they cannot be enclosed in the same space, for example, the right and left hand, two drops of water, helices winding in opposite ways (§15, II, 402–403; A 263–264).[24] The central thrust of the argument is that there are purely spatial differences between such objects that are not expressible in concepts of the understanding. Kant sees such objects as a violation of Leibniz's principle of the identity of indiscernibles, according to which two objects are the same if, and only if, they have the same inner determinations or properties. Since these properties are universal, they are concepts of the understanding in Kantian terms, so that the identity of indiscernibles identifies or distinguishes objects strictly according to their conceptual structure. While Kant concedes that this principle is true for noumena, objects of the understanding, he insists that it is false for phenomena, objects of the senses (A 264). For two phenomena can be distinct from one another simply by virtue of occupying distinct places and even if all their sensible properties are the same. A part of space can be completely identical with another part in intrinsic terms, yet they are still different from one another because they are in different places in space (A 264). It does not help Leibniz here to maintain that spatial differences are also expressible in terms of general properties—'east of Tucson,' 'right at the stop light'—because such differences would be purely extrinsic for Leibniz, who insists that differences cannot be entirely extrinsic but must be based upon their intrinsic properties.[25] Kant's point, however, is precisely that there are extrinsic differences not based on intrinsic ones.

Kant's second argument is much stronger than the first. It maintains not only that phenomena have extrinsic characteristics not reducible to intrinsic ones, but that phenomena consist entirely in extrinsic characteristics. Alternatively, the intrinsic properties of phenomena consist solely in relations, so that phenomenal substance is "entirely a sum total of mere relations" (A 265–266). Kant's argument for this view consists in three steps. (1) We know of things in space only through the forces they exert, whether by resisting other bodies entering their place (repulsion) or by drawing other bodies to it (attraction). (2) Such forces of attraction and repulsion consist entirely in relations. (3) Phenomena are constituted by the properties we know of them. Hence it follows that phenomena or objects in space consist entirely in their relations. We have no reason to assume that objects in space have any inner determinations in addition to these purely relational characteristics, Kant argues, because such inner determinations would have to be nonphysical or spiritual, given that all relational properties are physical properties (A 265–266). The only evidence for ascribing spiritual characteristics to an object must come from experience; and we know of the existence of things from experience only by noting their physical characteristics, for example, whether they are impenetrable and resist other things from entering their space.[26]

One of the most striking results of Kant's polemic against Leibniz's idealism in the Aesthetic and Amphiboly is that, contrary to the *weaker* dual-aspect interpretation,[27] appearances cannot be determinations or aspects of things-in-themselves. Kant could make his case against Leibniz's idealism only if appearances were aspects of *phenomenal* substances rather than aspects of things-in-themselves or noumenal substances. If sensibility were to consist in clear perceptions of its own objects rather than confused representations of things-in-themselves, then these objects would have to be distinct from thing-in-themselves. Sensibility is not illusory for Kant precisely because its spatial qualities are truly predicable of phenomena but falsely predicable of noumena. Hence, in arguing against Leibniz, Kant reaffirms the doctrine of the Inaugural Dissertation that understanding and sensibility differ not only in form but also in content or subject matter (A 44, 265–266, 284, 285). This distinction resurfaces very explicitly in the following passage from the Aesthetic:

> [T]hrough sensibility we do not cognize the constitution of things-in-themselves merely indistinctly, but rather not at all, and, as soon as we take away our subjective constitution, the *object* with the properties that sensible intuition attributes to it is nowhere to be encountered. (A 44; my emphasis)

The same result appears even more explicitly in the Amphiboly. Here Kant attacks Leibniz's theory that the *substrata* of appearances are things-in-themselves, and contends instead that such substrata must be phenomena (A 284–285). It is an error of the understanding, he argues, to assume that the relations of space must be based upon the inner properties of things-in-themselves. Such an inference would hold only in the realm of the pure understanding, when abstraction has been made from all the conditions of the sensible world. In the realm of sensibility, however, no such inference is permissible. All that it is possible to say in this realm is that appearances inhere in *phenomenal* substances, whose reality consists entirely in their relations. "It is certainly startling to hear that a thing should consist entirely of relations," Kant reassures us, "but such a thing is also mere appearance" (A 285). Here Kant draws a sharp distinction between noumenal substances having inner determinations and phenomenal substances whose reality consists entirely in relations or extrinsic determinations. We must not confuse these ontological orders, Kant warns us, as if properties of one were attributable to the other. If we attribute appearances to a noumenal substance, then we are guilty of an amphiboly: we confuse the faculties of understanding and sensibility, assuming that the inner determinations of the noumenal world are the basis for the phenomenal world.

4. Dogmatic Idealism in the Antinomies

The Antinomies have always been seen as crucial for Kant's discovery and defense of transcendental idealism. It is less well appreciated, however, that they also involve a critique of idealism. It is easy to overlook this critique, given that Kant's single critical remark on idealism in the Antinomies is parenthetical and simply repeats a point already made in the Critique of the Fourth Paralogism (A 491). If we dig a little deeper, however, it is clear that Kant is also criticizing Leibniz's idealism. Although it is not explicit in the Proofs themselves, many of Kant's explanatory remarks reveal that the Thesis of the Second Antinomy represents the dogmatic idealism of Leibniz.

Prima facie the Thesis and Proof of the Second Antinomy have nothing to do with idealism. The Thesis states that every composite substance consists of simple parts, and that nothing exists except the simple and what is composed of it (A 434). The Proof is a *reductio ad absurdam* of the antithesis: if composites were infinitely divisible, then there would really be nothing to divide, so that even composites would be impossible (A 435). As stated, the argument is so general that it seems to concern the existence of *any kind* of simple substance, whether material or immaterial, be it an atom or a soul. Hence it seems as if the Thesis could represent materialism or idealism, or at least that it is neutral between them.

However, Kant's comments on the Thesis make it evident that it represents idealism alone.[28] There are three comments that show simple substance cannot be the atom of the materialist but only the monad of the idealist. First, in his Remark on the Thesis, Kant explicitly rejects labeling the Thesis "transcendental atomistic" on the grounds that "this word already has been used to indicate a special way of explaining *corporeal* appearances"; he insists instead on calling it "monadology" (A 442). Second, in the Third Section and Remark on the Antithesis, Kant interprets the substance of the Thesis to have the simplicity of the thinking self (A 443, 466). Third, again in the Third Section, Kant sees the opposition between the Thesis and Antithe-

sis as a conflict between Platonism and Epicureanism (A 471), which is later
described as a battle between idealists and empiricists, or between those
who maintain that only the objects of reason are real and those who assert
that only the objects of the senses are real (A 853–854).[29]

When in the Critique of the Fourth Paralogism Kant first makes his promise to deal with dogmatic idealism, he describes the dogmatic idealist as
someone who holds that "he can find contradictions in the possibility of
matter" (A 377). It is possible to interpret the Proofs of the Second Antinomy in just this light. The spokesmen for both the Thesis and Antithesis find
the very idea of material substance to be self-contradictory because matter
involves extension, which consists in aggregation or divisibility, whereas
substance implies the existence of something simple and indivisible.

Once we take into account that the Thesis of the Second Antinomy represents dogmatic idealism, the conflict between Thesis and Antithesis turns
into a dispute about the existence of *immaterial* substance. It is a general assumption behind the proofs of both the Thesis and the Antithesis that the
very idea of *material* substance is impossible. Both Thesis and Antithesis
define substance as simple, and identify matter with something extended,
which is a form of aggregation. Hence they assume that *if* there are substances, they cannot be material. The main point at dispute between them is
simply whether there are such substances. The Thesis asserts their existence
on the grounds that infinite divisibility is impossible, while the Antithesis
contests their existence on the grounds that infinite divisibility is necessary.

Kant's critique of Leibniz's idealism in the Second Antinomy, which appears chiefly in the Proof and Remark on the Antithesis, repeats a central
theme of the Amphiboly: that Leibniz creates a castle in the air, a purely intellectual system of the universe (A 270). However true his arguments for
the existence of monads might be for the realm of the understanding, they
cannot apply to the domain of sensibility, which has its own distinctive
structure, subject matter, and origin. Kant concedes that it is perhaps the
case that a whole thought through the understanding alone does consist in
simples (A 439–441);[30] but this is completely false, he insists, when it comes
to the realm of appearances, or the objects of the senses. For phenomena
are essentially infinitely divisible. After all, these entities consist in nothing
more than relations of space and time, which are infinitely divisible. Kant
insists that it is a basic truth of mathematics, which has been proven countless times, that space, and whatever appears in it, is infinitely divisible (A
439). The Leibnizians attempt to escape this conclusion by a desperate strat-

agem: they distinguish between the objects within space and space itself, and then claim that the mathematical truths hold only for space, which is a mere abstraction. But, against this ploy, Kant cites the central thesis of the Aesthetic: that space is the necessary condition for anything to appear to the senses, so that all the mathematical proofs describing this space must apply to all things within it (A 442). At this point, then, the argument against idealism in the Antinomies presupposes that in the Aesthetic.

Ultimately, the chief problem of the dogmatic idealist is the same as that of all the positions in the Antinomies: transcendental realism. Of course, the Leibnizian is not a naive transcendental realist who simply equates appearances with things-in-themselves; rather, he insists that things-in-themselves do not exist just as they appear to the senses. Nevertheless, he does hold, as Kant himself describes him in the Amphiboly, that spatial aggregates are appearances *of* things-in-themselves (A 270–271). They are appearances of things-in-themselves because they are composites of simple substances, whose activity and structure somehow produces them. For Kant, however, this assumption becomes unstuck because of the argument of the Antithesis, which he accepts for appearances though not for things-in-themselves. If it is indeed the case that the appearances of things in space are infinitely divisible, it becomes difficult to understand how they are appearances of things-in-themselves, which are indivisible. Here again, then, as in the Aesthetic, we see how Kant detaches appearances from things-in-themselves in his polemic against dogmatic idealism (see above, 1.3.5).

CHAPTER 5

Kant and Berkeley

1. The Göttingen Review

The first review of the *Kritik der reinen Vernunft* to raise the charge of subjectivism against Kant was also the most notorious, and indeed the most influential. This was the so-called Göttingen Review, which appeared anonymously in early 1782 in the *Zugabe zu den Göttinger gelehrte Anzeigen*.[1] Though the full story behind its composition and authorship is complex and controversial,[2] the main facts are simple and straightforward. In the summer of 1781 Christian Garve, a leading Berlin *Aufklärer*, was traveling through Göttingen where he had been enjoying the hospitality of J. G. Feder and C. G. Heyne, the editors of the *Göttinger gelehrte Anzeige*. To repay his generous hosts, he volunteered to write a review for their journal and chose Kant's recently published work. Garve made his offer expecting a short and popular work, something like Kant's *Träume eines Geistersehers*, which he had enjoyed many years ago. So he was shocked by the length and depth of the tome handed to him. No book in the world, he later complained, had cost him so much trouble.

At first Garve wrote a very long review, some twelve sheets long, which he then reduced by half. Since even this was too long, the manuscript was heavily edited by Feder, who deleted some sentences, compressed others, and then finally added a few sentences and phrases all his own. Garve later disowned the review, which he said bore little resemblance to the original,[3] though it also must be said that he greatly exaggerated the degree of the editing.[4] Nearly two-thirds of the published review came from Garve's original, at least in meaning if not entirely in style. It was indeed Feder, however, who added some of the most controversial sentences of the review, and who is mainly responsible for the interpretation of Kant's idealism.[5]

Whoever the authors, the review epitomized the subjectivist interpretation. It was essentially a hostile polemic that judged the *Kritik* from the standpoint of the philosophy of common sense. The reviewers summed up Kant's work as "a system of higher or transcendental idealism" that transforms the world and ourselves into mere representations. The central principle of Kant's idealism was said to be the same as Berkeley's: that what we perceive are only ideas, which are only "modifications of ourselves." Although the reviewers noted Kant's insistence that things are real in space and time, they countered that this ultimately means very little, given that Kant also stresses that space and time are only "subjective laws of our faculty of representation." Kant's distinction between appearance and reality was then criticized on the grounds that dreams and visions also appear in space and time and occur in their own order. The reviewers also recognized that Kant wanted to distinguish his transcendental idealism from empirical idealism; but they saw this as another distinction without a difference, for Kant had demonstrated the reality of things in space simply by equating them with representations. What indeed is the point in talking about a higher transcendental idealism, Garve and Feder asked, when it still affirms the fundamental principle behind all idealism: the identification of the objects of consciousness with ideas?

2. Kant's Reaction

What was Kant's reaction to the Göttingen Review? How did he reformulate or defend his philosophy against the charge of subjectivism?

That Kant was angered by the review would be an understament. He was distressed and dismayed, and indeed provoked. He dispatched a bitter reply, which appeared in the spring of 1783 as the Appendix to his *Prolegomena*. Here Kant held up the review as an egregious example of sloppy and careless method and ignorant and biased judgment. Rather than considering the central problem behind the *Kritik*—the possibility of metaphysics—the reviewers simply condemned the work according to their own metaphysical system. They saw transcendental idealism as another system of metaphysics, and so failed to grasp that its central purpose is to solve a problem on which the very fate of metaphysics depends: namely, 'How are synthetic a priori judgments possible?' Not once had the reviewers wrestled with the Transcendental Deduction, though this was really the core of the book. The judgments cast in the review were so superficial that it was as if Euclid were blamed for subtle and long-winded reasoning about something everyone could see with their own eyes! Kant then challenged the author to emerge from behind his anonymity and to debate in public.

Mortified, Garve duly revealed himself and begged apology.[6] Though he admitted responsibility for the review, he assured Kant he would be inconsolable if it were entirely from his own hand.[7] The sad irony was that Kant greatly respected Garve, whom he had once called "one of the great analysts of the age."[8]

Not surprisingly, Kant vehemently rejected Garve's and Feder's interpretation of his transcendental idealism, dismissing it as a deliberate distortion and caricature. In seeing his transcendental idealism as a system of metaphysics, they had ignored its central critical intentions, which placed severe contraints on all metaphysics, especially idealism. What particularly bothered Kant, however, was the equation of his idealism with Berkeley's. He feared that such an insinuation could completely undermine the reception of the *Kritik*. Given the general reputation of Berkeley's philosophy in late-eighteenth-century Germany,[9] this could serve as a cheap and popular *reductio ad absurdam* of his entire work. Transcendental idealism would be dismissed as a radical solipsism or *Egoismus* that doubts or denies the existence of everything except one's own self.

Kant was so disturbed by the imputation of Berkeleyianism that, throughout the 1780s and 1790s, he made repeated attempts to distinguish his idealism from that of Berkeley. The Appendix to the *Prolegomena* was only the beginning. In several other sections of the main body of this work Kant went to considerable pains to distinguish his position from Berkeley's.[10] Then, in the second edition of the *Kritik*, he added some passages to prevent any confusion of his idealism with that of the Bishop of Cloyne.[11]

The new importance of Berkeley for Kant's thinking is apparent from the stature he now accords his idealism. In the first edition of the *Kritik* Kant never mentions Berkeley, and he is explicit that only Descartes' doubt about the existence of the external world deserves to be called 'idealism' in the proper sense (A 368–369). In the second edition, however, Berkeley becomes Kant's explicit example of dogmatic idealism (B 274). Furthermore, in the *Prolegomena* Kant defines idealism in terms that align it much more with Berkeley than Descartes. Thus he states that idealism is no longer *doubt* about the existence of the external world but the dogmatic claim that "there are none but thinking beings" (IV, 288–289). While Kant is still intent on a refutation of Descartes' problematic idealism, he now conceives of his idealism as "the proper antidote" to that of Berkeley (IV, 293–294).

The new significance Kant gave to Berkeley altered his conception of dogmatic idealism in the *Kritik*. The dogmatic idealist of the first edition assumes the proper reality of space but denies the existence of bodies within it (A 491). The dogmatic idealist of the second edition, however, holds almost the opposite view: that because the idea of absolute space is absurd, matter or all things within it are illusory (B 70–71, 274). Both forms of dogmatic idealism deny the reality of objects in space; but they give different reasons for such a conclusion. Leibniz denies their reality because of contradictions inherent in the very idea of matter, while Berkeley does so, at least according to Kant, because of the absurdity of absolute space. As a result of these differences, Kant shifts the locus of his refutation. In the first edition of the *Kritik* he implies that the refutation of dogmatic idealism will take place in the Antinomies (A 377); but in the second edition he declares that it has been already achieved in the Aesthetic (B 274).

For all the new importance Kant gave to Berkeley after the Göttingen Review, it would be wrong to conclude that Berkeley was now his paradigm of dogmatic idealism.[12] Such a conclusion is unwarranted not only because Kant continues in the second edition to see Leibniz as a dogmatic idealist, but also because he characterizes Berkeley virtually in Leibnizian terms. Thus he places Berkeley in the same Platonic tradition as Leibniz, which claims that all sense perception is illusory while there is truth only in the ideas of reason (IV, 374). Surely, only someone preoccupied with Leibnizian rationalism could cast Berkeley in such terms! It is not surprising, therefore, that Kant adds no new refutation of dogmatic idealism in the second edition of the *Kritik* but simply assumes that his arguments against Leibniz in the Aesthetic apply to Berkeley. Even after the Göttingen Review Kant never ceased to patronize "*der gute Berkeley*," whose idealism he could not take seriously but saw only as a paradox to stimulate thinking.[13]

Whatever the stature of Berkeley in Kant's thinking, it was chiefly, if not entirely,[14] the charge of Berkeleyianism that made Kant become aware of and respond to the subjectivist interpretation of his transcendental idealism. To understand Kant's reaction to this interpretation, then, it is necessary to consider first and foremost his response to this accusation. This raises some hoary questions: How did Kant attempt to distinguish his idealism from Berkeley's? And did he succeed? Were his differences with Berkeley real or only apparent?

The issue is complex for several reasons. First, Kant himself ignores or understates some of his underlying affinities with and differences from Berkeley. Second, some of Kant's apparent differences with Berkeley rest on doctrines that appear to be inconsistent with, or unnecessary to, the critical philosophy as a whole. It seems that if Kant were completely consistent and rigorous, ridding his philosophy of all superfluous and troublesome assumptions, such as the thing-in-itself, then his position would indeed be much closer to Berkeley's after all. Third, Kant's interpretation of Berkeley is peculiar, resting on an apparent misunderstanding of his doctrines. While Kant's philosophy is indeed distinct from the imagined Berkeley, it still seems perilously close to the real historical Berkeley.

For these reasons, the issue also has been very controversial. There are those who argue that Kant's idealism, if it were only consistent, would be essentially the same as Berkeley's,[15] while there are those who contend that Kant's idealism is in its central principles at odds with Berkeley's.[16] Some adopt a middle position: that Kant's idealism was essentially Berkeleyian in the first edition of the *Kritik* but that it became much more realistic in the second edition and *Opus postumum*.[17] In this and the next chapter I will defend anew the case for Kant's anti-Berkeleyianism. While Kant himself did not make the best case for the distinctive status of transcendental idealism, it is in some of its fundamental principles opposed to the idealism of Berkeley, and it was so from its original conception in the first edition of the *Kritik*.

3. Berkeleyianism in the First Edition of the *Kritik*

The case for the Berkeleyian interpretation of Kant's idealism mainly rests on the Critique of the Fourth Paralogism in the first edition of the *Kritik* (A 367–380). Here Kant's definition of transcendental idealism—"the doctrine that appearances are to be regarded as being, one and all, representations only, not things-in-themselves" (A 369)—seems to be perfectly Berkeleyian. Furthermore, in lines that could have been virtually lifted from Berkeley, Kant maintains that matter and external bodies are "only a species of ideas" (A 370).

But the analogy with Berkeley does not stop here. The Critique of the Fourth Paralogism seems to show that Kant is struggling with the same problem as Berkeley, and that he has the same solution to it.[18] The problem is the skeptical consequences of Cartesian dualism. Both Kant and Berkeley think that the inevitable result of Descartes' standard of knowledge—the correspondence of a representation with a thing-in-itself—is complete skepticism because it is impossible to get outside our representations to compare them with things-in-themselves.[19] Both also argue that the only solution to this problem is idealism, more specifically the identification of the objects of experience with representations or ideas. Like Berkeley, Kant argues that if these objects consist in representations, then merely having the representations is sufficient to prove their reality (A 370, 371, 374–375).

It is essentially for these reasons that Kant's transcendental idealism has been, and continues to be, equated with Berkeley's. It has indeed been said that in this section Kant uses Berkeley to refute Descartes.[20] Even more radically, it has been argued that Kant was influenced by Berkeley when he wrote this section of the *Kritik*, and that, if he later repudiated Berkeley, it was only to conceal his debt to him.[21] What are we to make of these arguments?

Surely, there is something to be said for a Berkeleyian reading of the Fourth Paralogism. It is indeed the case that Kant is struggling with a problem similar to Berkeley, because he too is concerned to avoid the skeptical consequences of dualism. It is also the case that Kant has a similar solution, because he too avoids skepticism only by identifying the objects of experience with their representations. Like Berkeley, Kant thinks that the only way to avoid skepticism is to place the criterion of reality within the realm of consciousness itself, so that the distinguishing characteristic of reality is not correspondence with a thing but coherence among representations. To be sure, Kant has a much stronger conception of the coherence necessary for reality, because he thinks that it involves universality and necessity, not simply association and frequency; but, in the present context, this appears to be only a minor difference. For Berkeley and Kant agree that the criterion of reality must be within the realm of consciousness itself.

The affinity with Berkeley stops here, however, for Kant does not share Berkeley's metaphysical agenda and refuses to draw his grander metaphysical conclusions from their common epistemological context. If, like Berkeley, Kant identifies the objects of experience with representations, at least in the Fourth Paralogism, this does not mean that he endorses Berkeley's *esse est percipi* principle. On the contrary, Kant denies this principle, holding that it goes beyond the limits of human experience. There are two respects in which Berkeley's principle transcends these limits: first, it assumes that what is true of objects of experience (appearances) is true of objects in general; and, second, it assumes that objects of experience are only representations, when, for all we know, they could be aspects of things-in-themselves.

Kant's differences with Berkeley on this score become especially evident when we consider that Kant, unlike Berkeley, never doubts or denies the existence of things-in-themselves. This difference is not basic, as Kant himself sometimes portrays it, but follows from their very different agendas. Kant's essentially epistemological intentions mean that he only wishes to know the conditions of the possibility of a priori knowledge. If such limits mean that he cannot go so far as to affirm the reality of things-in-them-selves, they also entail that he cannot deny it. Indeed, on several occasions in the Critique of the Fourth Paralogism, he refers to a *transcendental object* that might exist as the ground of our representations (A 372, 379–380). For Berkeley, such an assumption, even if it is only hypothetical, is as absurd as it is superfluous. This reveals all the more plainly, however, the difference between Kant's and Berkeley's arguments against skepticism: Berkeley affirms and Kant denies that it is necessary to eliminate things-in-themselves to combat skeptical doubt. It is indeed just because Berkeley goes beyond the limits of knowledge in denying the existence of things-in-themselves that Kant dubs his idealism 'dogmatic.'

So, *suma sumarum,* while Kant engages in Berkeleyian reasoning to resolve a Berkeleyian problem, he does this essentially for non-Berkeleyian ends, for an epistemological rather than metaphysical agenda. Kant's aim is not to determine the meaning of existence, the essence of being, but simply to determine the conditions for the possibility of objective knowledge. It is solely for this end that Kant makes use of Berkeley's point that ideas resemble nothing but ideas. While, for Berkeley, this is a metaphysical principle about the heterogeneity of the mental and physical, for Kant it is simply an epistemological principle about the ultimate conditions of the possibility of knowledge.

Whatever the similarities between Kant and Berkeley in the Fourth Paralogism, the indisputable differences between them show that the first edition of the *Kritik* had its own antisubjectivist dimension. If Kant used Berkeleyian weapons to criticize Descartes, that was not because he endorsed the general metaphysical principles behind Berkeley's idealism. Still, the apparent affinity with Berkeley was enough reason for others to conflate transcendenal with empirical idealism, and so enough reason for Kant to delete the text in the second edition. Hence the changes of the second edition were not the result of any change in Kant's principles. Rather, they were, as Kant himself insisted, merely the result of a tireless effort to avoid misunderstanding (B xxxvi).

4. The Argument of the *Prolegomena*

How did Kant himself attempt to distinguish his idealism from Berkeley's? To answer this question we need to take a close look at his arguments in the *Prolegomena.* Here, in various scattered passages, Kant makes three fundamental distinctions between his transcendental idealism and Berkeley's doctrine.

Metaphysical versus Critical Idealism

First, Kant maintains that transcendental idealism attempts to determine only the necessary conditions of knowledge, whereas Berkeley's idealism claims to have knowledge of reality in itself. Hence in Remark III to §13 Kant stresses that his idealism concerns "not the existence of things" but simply "the sensible representation of things" (IV, 293). Kant concedes, however, that his term 'transcendental' has given rise to a serious misunderstanding. He originally chose this term because it does not refer to "our cognition of things" but only to "our faculty of cognition."[22] Since, however, this term has inexpungable associations with things beyond experience, it appeared to his reviewers as if his transcendental philosophy were a new system of metaphysics. To avoid any further confusion, Kant now resolves to withdraw the term and to call his idealism 'critical' instead. This term has the advantage of stressing the essential concern of his philosophy: the critique of the conditions of knowledge (293–294; 373n; 375).

Following his proscription of metaphysics, Kant further explains in the Appendix that his idealism breaks with the fundamental dictum of all past idealism: "All cognition through the senses and experience is nothing but sheer illusion, and only in the ideas of the understanding and pure reason is there truth" (IV, 374). It adheres to the very opposite principle: "All cognition of things merely from pure understanding or pure reason is nothing but sheer illusion, and only in experience is there truth" (IV, 374). Kant insists that his place is "the fruitful bathos of experience," because his idealism prohibits all purely rational speculation about the nature of reality beyond experience. He again admits that his term 'transcendental' has been the source of misunderstanding. This term does not signify something *beyond* experience, he stresses, but simply that which *precedes* it a priori and makes cognition possible (373n). In this regard he complains that the reviewer has not observed his own distinction between the transcendent (going beyond experience) and the transcendental (preceding experience).

The Role of Things-in-Themselves

Second, Kant remarks that transcendental idealism affirms, while Berkeley's idealism denies, the reality of things-in-themselves. For these reasons, Kant sometimes writes as if he cannot be an idealist at all. He defines idealism as the view that "there are none but thinking beings, and that everything we believe to find outside ourselves in intuition is nothing but representations in some thinking being, to which in fact no object outside them corresponds" (IV, 288–289). Kant points out that, by this definition, he cannot be an idealist, because he holds that there are objects existing outside our representations, which are the causes of them (289). He later qualifies this point, however, claiming that it only makes him a special kind of idealist. Simply by holding that appearances must be appearances *of* something, namely things-in-themselves, his idealism differs from that of Berkeley, which holds that all that exists are thinking spirits and their representations. His idealism is merely *formal* because it states that the mind determines only the form of our experience; it differs therefore from the *material* idealism of Berkeley, which holds that the mind determines not only its form but also its matter.[23]

On this account, then, Kant's postulate of the thing-in-itself is an essential distinguishing feature of his idealism.[24] It could be argued, however, that if Kant were to be consistent he should not postulate the existence of the thing-in-itself, and still less that it is the cause of our experience.[25] So on this score Kant's idealism collapses into Berkeley's after all.

It is important to recognize, though, that Kant himself was aware of this objection, which he regarded as one aspect of his teaching most in need of clarification.[26] In the second *Kritik* he made two points in reply to it.[27] First, although it is indeed impossible *to know* anything beyond the limits of experience, it is still possible *to think* of something beyond it. Second, it is necessary to distinguish between the *categories*, which have to be schematized according to the forms of intuition, and the *concepts of the understanding*, which are valid of objects in general. While the categories are indeed necessary for us to know an object, the pure concepts of the understanding are sufficient for us to think of one. The net effect of this line of reply is to give the thing-in-itself a strictly *problematic* status as a *theoretical* concept; but it at least shows that it is not entirely inconsistent with the critical principles established in the first *Kritik*.[28]

But if Kant avoids the charge of inconsistency, he does not vindicate his stronger claims that the thing-in-itself exists and that it is the cause of our sensations. All that he can say is that this is possible, or that he can think this, but not that he knows it to be the case. For this reason Kant also cannot claim that appearances are *of* things-in-themselves; it is still possible that they are only representations, just as Berkeley maintains. In this regard, then, Kant's differences with Berkeley boil down to little more than a flimsy and pale possibility. Since this possibility is based on Kant's critical principles, the second difference ultimately reduces down to the first.

The Reality of Things in Space

Third, Kant argues that transcendental idealism upholds, while Berkeley's idealism undermines, the reality of objects in space outside us (IV, 290–291, 374–375). That objects in space have empirical reality was a point Kant made against Descartes' problematic idealism in the Fourth Paralogism and against Leibniz's dogmatic idealism in the Aesthetic; he now turns the same point against Berkeley's dogmatic idealism.

Why does Kant think that Berkeley holds the perception of space to be illusory? Since Berkeley never expressly says this, Kant must be attributing to him what he thinks is the proper consequence of his general principles. If we examine Kant's texts carefully, we find two reasons for his attribution of illusionism to Berkeley. First, in the *Prolegomena* Kant reaffirms his view that the distinction between reality and illusion is determined not by the *content* of representations but by their *form*, that is, by whether they conform to universal and necessary rules (IV, 290). Objects in space are real, therefore, because they conform to a universal and necessary structure, the a priori form of space and the categories. Because of his empiricism, however, Berkeley thinks that space is a mere abstraction from experience, and hence it must lack universal and necessary form. Since reality presupposes conformity to universal and necessary rules, and since Berkeley's empiricism provides no basis for such rules, it follows that Berkeley reduces all of experience down to an illusion.[29] Second, Berkeley thinks that the idea of the absolute reality of space is something impossible, so that all the things that appear to be in space must also be illusory (B 56–57, 70–71). Hence in the Aesthetic Kant says that we cannot blame Berkeley for "degrading bodies to mere illusion" because this is a correct conclusion from the absurdities of assuming that space is a property of things-in-themselves (B 70–71).[30]

Prima facie it does not seem fair of Kant to maintain that Berkeley wants to reduce everything in space down to an illusion. There are several reasons for thinking that Berkeley too wants to uphold the *reality* of things in space. First, Berkeley insists that his philosophy alone is able to rescue our ordinary belief in the reality of the senses, and he criticizes materialism precisely because it will make all our ordinary beliefs illusory.[31] Second, like Kant, Berkeley distinguishes between two senses of "external"—a transcendental sense in which it means "absolutely independent of the mind" and another more empirical sense in which it means "externally caused"—and he prohibits the former but permits the latter.[32] Third, Berkeley has his own criterion to distinguish between truth and illusion, which, like Kant's, functions within the realm of experience itself.[33] Thus he attempts to establish a criterion of reality by distinguishing between ideas of sense and of imagination. The ideas of sense are more strong, lively, and distinct than those of the imagination; and they also have greater order, coherence, and regularity.[34] This is a two-fold criterion in terms of *form* and *content:* in *content* ideas of sense are more vivid and distinct, and in *form* they are more coherent and regular.

This is not the end of the story, however. For while Berkeley *intends* to establish the reality of things in space, the question remains whether he can do so on the premises of his philosophy. Kant's point is that Berkeley's premises undermine his intentions. Regarding Berkeley's criterion of reality, Kant would no doubt reply that Berkeley's distinctions are inadequate. The distinction in terms of content does not work since dreams can be stronger and more vivid than reality. The distinction in form also fails because, on empiricist premises, appeals to past experience have no binding validity for the future. The only form of coherence possible will be based on constant conjunction and association; but there is no more connection between events that are constantly conjoined than between those that occur by sheer chance. Hence events that are constantly conjoined will be no more real or illusory than events that appear by chance.[35]

Concerning Berkeley's claim to rescue the reality of the senses, Kant could argue that it is undermined by Berkeley's own account of the perception of space in the *Principles* and *New Essay on Vision*. While Berkeley does indeed insist that he wants to save our commonsense belief in the reality of the senses, he also comes very close to saying that the perception of space, and of things in space, is only an illusion. Thus, in both the *Principles* and *New Essay*, he maintains that, strictly speaking, we do not see things in space, or at a distance from us. He writes in the *Essay:* "In truth and strictness of speech I neither see distance itself, nor anything that I take to be at a distance. I say, neither distance nor things placed at a distance are themselves, or their ideas, truly perceived by sight" (§45). We do not have an *immediate* perception of distance, Berkeley contends, because this idea arises from the habit of coordinating tactual with visual sensations. If we think we see something at a distance from us, that is the result of coordinating what I see with what I would feel within an interval of time if I approached and then touched the body. As Berkeley explains in the *Principles:* "The ideas of sight, when we apprehend them by distance, and things placed at a distance, do not suggest or mark out to us things actually existing at a distance but only admonish us what ideas of touch will be imprinted in our minds at such and such a distance of time, and in consequence of such and such actions"(§44; compare *Essay* §44–46). On these grounds Berkeley seems to be committed to the view that it is indeed an illusion that we see distance or things in space. If an illusion is a mistaken belief about what we see, and if people believe falsely that they see things at a distance or outside themselves, then they indeed suffer from an illusion. In the *Essay* Berkeley virtually admits this point when he claims that it is "a mere delusion" that we see things in space (§126). Indeed, he finds it necessary to correct our common language when we say that we see something a mile away or that we see and touch one and the same object (§§44, 49). Regarding the reality of things in space, Berkeley will have to insist that it is just another one of those things where, though we must indeed speak with the vulgar, we will have to think with the learned.[36]

5. Kant's Interpretation of Berkeley

Kant's interest in, and knowledge of, Berkeley goes back to at least the 1760s. In his lectures on metaphysics from 1762–64 he explicitly criticizes Berkeley's idealism. This was part of his general precritical campaign against dogmatic idealism, which he believed should be banished as useless speculation and as a danger to natural religion.[37] Kant's early understanding of Berkeley is very typical of the early German reception: he attributes egoism, illusionism, and skepticism to Berkeley. Like Wolff and Baumgarten, Kant distinguishes between *idealism,* which affirms the existence of only spiritual beings, and *egoism,* which admits the existence only of my own self.[38] Although Kant recognizes that Berkeley is an idealist rather than egoist, he also thinks that the borderline between idealism and egoism is very fine once the idealist applies his argument against external things to other minds.[39] Kant also interprets Berkeley as a skeptic "who doubted whether there are any bodies at all." Rather than recognizing Berkeley's claim to have saved the reality of the senses from skepticism, Kant interpreted him as saying that everything we perceive is only an illusion. Hence he attributes to Berkeley two standard skeptical arguments: the relativity of sense qualities and the lack of a distinction between dreaming and reality. While Kant eventually dropped the skeptical interpretation of Berkeley, who later became his paradigm of a *dogmatic* idealist, he never ceased to regard Berkeley as an illusionist who denies the reality of sense experience.

It is uncertain whether, in these early years, Kant had actually read Berkeley. Kant owned a German translation of Berkeley's *Dialogues*, but this edition appeared only in 1781.[40] An earlier translation of the *Dialogues* had appeared in 1756 by Johann Christian Eschenbach,[41] but there is little clear evidence that Kant had read it.[42] Some of the views that Kant attributes to Berkeley, especially skepticism and the denial of any distinction between appearance and reality, indicate that he had been influenced by the prevalent German interpretation rather than by any direct reading. Indeed, they suggest that Kant had *not* read Berkeley, for such an interpretation would have been corrected by even the most cursory reading.[43]

It has been suggested that Kant had read *De Motu*, which first appeared in Paris in 1723.[44] But, if so, this work would *not* have acquainted Kant with the principles of Berkeley's idealism, since it concerns only the causes of motion and contains no arguments against the existence of matter. While it does indeed contain some of Berkeley's criticisms of absolute space, Berkeley does not use these arguments to deny the reality of matter, as Kant later portrayed him in the second edition of the *Kritik*.[45]

The only work of Berkeley's to which Kant refers in any of his writings is *Siris*, which had been translated into both French and German.[46] In his notes on Kant's 1762–64 lectures on metaphysics Herder wrote: "Bishop Berklei [*sic*] in his treatise on the use of tarwater, doubted whether there are bodies" (XXVIII, 42). Of course, this does not show that Kant actually read *Siris*, and indeed he only seems to refer to the work to make a joke about Berkeley's solicitude for the body after he questions its very existence. If Kant read Berkeley at all, it was most probably after the Garve-Feder review, which gave him plenty of occasion to examine his philosophy. He was at least interested enough to acquire the edition of Berkely's *Werke* that appeared in 1781.

While there is no clear evidence that Kant read Berkeley, there is also no compelling reasons to think that he did not read him. Although Kant's interpretation of Berkeley as a skeptic suggests that he was ignorant of Berkeley's writings, it hardly proves this because Kant does not maintain that Berkeley *intended to be* a skeptic, but only that skepticism was the *implication* of his principles. However, some scholars, basing their case on Kant's very peculiar interpretation of Berkeley in the second edition of the *Kritik* and the *Prolegomena*, have argued that Kant was completely ignorant of Berkeley.[47] In these texts Kant attributes three doctrines to Berkeley that seem to be not only blatantly inconsistent but also wildly inaccurate. (1) *Illusionism:* Kant accuses Berkeley of "degrading bodies to mere illusion" (B 69), of regarding things in space as "merely imaginary entities"(B 274), and of holding, with all idealists, that sense perception is illusory: (2) *Rationalism.* Kant sees Berkeley as a rationalist because, like all idealists, he is an Eleatic who holds that all sense experience is illusory and that there is truth only in the ideas of reason (IV, 374): (3) *Mysticism.* Kant holds that all idealism has a mystical tendency because it infers from our a priori cognitions a power of intellectual intuition (IV; 293, 375n).

It is not difficult to understand why, given his argument for an a priori standard of reality, Kant attributes illusionism to Berkeley. But it appears impossible to understand how Berkeley can be a rationalist or a mystic, given that he is an empiricist who affirms that the main spring of all our knowledge comes from the senses.[48] Historical accuracy aside, it is also necessary to ask whether Kant even has a coherent interpretation of Berkeley. Upon closer inspection (1) and (2) contradict one another since Kant ascribes illusionism to Berkeley because of his alleged empiricism. So, incoherently, Kant seems to hold that Berkeley is both a rationalist and an empiricist.

After considering these points, it is indeed tempting to dismiss Kant's interpretation on the grounds that he was probably simply ignorant of Berkeley. But such a conclusion would be premature, and indeed anachronistic. To understand Kant's interpretation, we must be careful not to read our modern picture of Berkeley back into the eighteenth century, which had a very different view of him based on works little read today. The modern reading of Berkeley is essentially derived from his earlier works, his *Principles of human Knowledge* (1710) and his *Dialogues between Hylus and Philonous* (1713); but the eighteenth-century reading was very much influenced by Berkeley's later writings, and most notably by his *Siris* (1744). A medical and metaphysical work whose main purpose was to publicize the virtues of tarwater, *Siris* proved to be an immediate sensation and was soon translated into both French and German.[49] While Berkeley's *Principles* and *Dialogues* had been the subject of much controversy shortly after publication,[50] they never reached the popularity of *Siris*, which helped to publicize Berkeley's later views.

If we place Kant's interpretation of Berkeley in this eighteenth-century context, then it makes much more sense, and it is indeed accurate. For while the younger Berkeley was very much an empiricist and nominalist, the elder Berkeley moved toward rationalism, mysticism, and Platonism. In *Siris* Berkeley doubts the knowledge of the senses because it is a fleeting transitory realm, and he stresses that true knowledge comes from reason.[51] He even suggests that, though it is very weak, we have a kind of intellectual intuition of God.[52] Apparently, Berkeley's views underwent some drastic revision in his later years when he had to explain the possibility of our knowledge of the spiritual world. His earlier empiricism made it difficult for him to explain knowledge of spiritual substances, which were not the same as ideas. This led to some of the second edition revisions of the *Principles*, which refer to our *notions* of spiritual things that are not derived simply from the ideas of sense.[53]

In the end, then, the historical evidence is not compelling regarding whether Kant actually read Berkeley. Fortunately, not a lot hangs on this question, which settles nothing about the accuracy of Kant's interpretation of Berkeley, nor anything about the relationship between Kant's and Berkeley's idealism. Still, it does lead to one negative conclusion: that in the absence of any clear evidence that Kant actually read Berkeley, it is groundless to assume, as some have done,[54] that Kant was *directly* influenced by him.

6. The Small but Real Differences?

Now that we have considered Kant's attempt to distinguish himself from Berkeley, what can we conclude about his *real* differences from him? It would seem that these are not as great as Kant wants them to be. For one thing, Kant can at most say that it is *possible* that appearances are of things-in-themselves, so that he also must admit that it is possible that they are only representations. For another thing, Kant's complaint that Berkeley reduces the appearance of objects in space down to an illusion not only ignores Berkeley's own criterion, but it also presupposes the difficult argument that something as strong as universal and necessary rules is required to distinguish reality from illusion. In the absence of such an argument, though, the only difference between Kant and Berkeley seems to be the *kind of structure* necessary to distinguish truth and illusion. For Berkeley, that structure consists in empirically established generalities, whereas for Kant it resides in universal and necessary rules. The differences between Kant and Berkeley now seem to have shrunk down to nothing more than the distinction between an empiricist and rationalist variant of idealism.[55] The formula for Kant's idealism would then seem to be *Transcendental idealism = Berkeley's idealism + rationalism.*

Such a conclusion is still very one-sided, however. If the differences are not everything that Kant wants them to be, the similarities are also not everything that the subjectivist would like either. The most salient difference is *the critical dimension* of Kant's idealism. This makes it necessary for Kant to forbid not only all of Berkeley's speculations about the existence of God and the soul, but even his central dictum *esse est percipi*. This critical agnosticism means that there is some room for the notorious things-in-themselves after all. Although Kant cannot indeed claim knowledge of the existence of things-in-themselves, his critical strictures also prohibit him from denying their existence. Here again Kant differs from Berkeley, who finds the very idea of a thing-in-itself an impossibility.

Still, it could be argued that this difference, though real, is not that considerable. The general formula is now longer but still simple enough: *Kant's transcendental idealism = Berkeley's idealism + rationalism + agnosticism.* The differences are not so great because, granted the young Berkeley would spurn Kant's rationalism and agnosticism, there still *seem to be* deeper underlying affinities between them, based on the apparently indisputable fact that Kant and Berkeley both advocate the central principle of all modern idealism: that the objects of our awareness are nothing but ideas or representations. After all, this was the central contention of the Göttingen Review, and it still remains unscathed by all Kant's polemic in the *Prolegomena*, which, remarkably, never touches this fundamental point. The only differences between Kant and Berkeley seem to be how they qualify this principle or the conclusions they draw from it.

Are we to accept, then, the charge of subjectivism, at least in substance if not in all its details? We shall see in Chapter 7 that this would be a serious mistake. For all Kant's polemics, he failed to state some of his fundamental departures from Berkeley and the entire subjectivist tradition. But before we consider Kant's deeper break with the subjectivist tradition, it is necessary to consider how he revised his refutation of idealism in the second edition of the *Kritik*.

CHAPTER 6

The Second Edition Refutation
of Problematic Idealism

1. The Problem of Interpretation

In the second edition of the *Kritik der reinen Vernunft*, which was published in 1788, Kant added a short section of four pages entitled the Refutation of Idealism. This section is of crucial importance to understand Kant's transcendental idealism. It is here that Kant's break with the subjectivist tradition becomes most explicit and extreme, and it is here that he makes his strongest case yet against the problematic idealism of Descartes. Unfortunately, these few pages have proven to be some of the most intractable and controversial in the entire work. It has rightly been said: "The Refutation of Idealism is Kant's *chef d'oeuvre* of compressed obscurity."[1] His motives, his thesis, and his argument all pose serious problems of interpretation.

If the Refutation still troubles its readers, it also tormented its author. Before the second edition went to press, Kant inserted an elaborate emendation into his new preface, where he completely recast his whole argument (B xxxix–xli). But even this did not completely satisfy him. After the second edition appeared Kant did not cease to revise. From 1788 to 1793 he redrafted his refutation of problematic idealism no less than ten times.[2] The lectures on metaphysics from the early 1790s also show evidence of struggle, for they too contain interesting reformulations of his arguments against problematic idealism.[3]

Ever since its first publication the Refutation of Idealism has been the source of heated controversy in Kant scholarship.[4] One cause of friction has been the role of the Refutation in Kant's system and development. There are those who see it simply as a restatement of Kant's transcendental idealism in the Fourth Paralogism of the first edition; but there are also those who regard it as a fundamental shift in Kant's position, such that it breaks with his earlier transcendental idealism and amounts to a new form of realism.[5] Another source of disagreement concerns the merits of Kant's argument. Some consider the argument a *petitio principi* against the Cartesian skeptic;[6] others view it as the paradigm case of the problems with "transcendental arguments";[7] still others regard it as a source of great insight, though rarely in the terms Kant intended it.[8]

The task of the present chapter is to reexamine some of these old issues. I will argue that the Refutation is, in at least one basic respect, consistent with Kant's transcendental idealism as stated in the first edition of the *Kritik:* it attempts to prove nothing more than the *empirical* reality of objects in space, and not a stronger form of realism that claims the *transcendental* reality of such objects. The Refutation therefore accords with Kant's earlier arguments for empirical reality in the Dissertation, Aesthetic, and Critique of the Fourth Paralogism. However, I will also contend that, in another crucial respect, the Refutation marks an important development in Kant's thinking. While in the first edition of the *Kritik* Kant argued for the *parity* of inner and outer sense, and indeed for the priority of inner sense in schematizing the categories, in the second edition he makes a case for the priority of outer over inner sense. There is still no fundamental inconsistency between these priority claims, however, because Kant gives priority to each sense in different respects. Rather than a simple restatement of his earlier doctrines, and still less a fundamental break with them, the Refutation marks a *progression* in Kant's views, a *reformulation* and *revision* of his position in the Fourth Paralogism.

Any plausible interpretation of the Refutation of Idealism has to avoid a basic dilemma.[9] When Kant attempts to prove the existence of external objects it seems as if these objects can be only of two kinds: appearances or things-in-themselves. While appearances are representations of an object in space outside me, and so have only *empirical* reality, things-in-themselves are objects existing completely independently of representations, and so have *transcendental* reality. If Kant tries to demonstrate only the existence of the former kind of objects, he is consistent with his transcendental idealism; but he begs the question against the Cartesian skeptic, who does not doubt that we have *representations* of objects in space outside us. If, however, he attempts to prove the existence of the latter kind of objects, he does not beg the question against the skeptic; but he does violate the principles of transcendental idealism, which forbid knowledge of things-in-themselves, and which denies the transcendental reality of objects in space. Hence Kant's Refutation is either trivial or inconsistent.

The interpretation sketched here attempts to escape this classic dilemma.

The middle path between its horns, I shall argue, consists in Kant's attempt to prove that we have an *experience* of objects in space. The objects of experience are not things-in-themselves because they do not exist apart from the representations of them; but neither are they appearances in the sense of single perceptions or mere representations. Rather, they are appearances only insofar as they conform to universal and necessary rules of the understanding and the form of outer sense, which is space. Following Kant's analysis of the concept of an object in the Analytic, the object of experience consists in more than any conjunction of mere perceptions or representations, because it also involves (a) their systematic order, lawful unity, or interconnection, and (b) their locatability in a single, universal space. Such an object is indeed distinct from its representations or appearances, though not in an *ontological* sense as an *entity* existing apart from them, but only in a *formal* sense as a whole whose individual perceptions are only its parts. This is to say that the Refutation of Idealism attempts to establish the existence of an object in Kant's own technical sense of existence or actuality: "*Whatever is connected with a perception according to empirical laws is actual (wirklich)*" (A 376).[10] While the Refutation is therefore consistent with the Transcendental Deduction and transcendental idealism as a whole, it also marks an advance over Kant's critique of empirical idealism in the first edition Fourth Paralogism, because there Kant had too simplistically equated appearances with representations themselves, leaving himself open to obvious skeptical objections.

2. Kant's Motives

The first problem in the interpretation of the Refutation concerns Kant's motives in writing it. The Refutation replaces the Critique of the Fourth Paralogism, which had been deleted in the second edition of the *Kritik*. Why did Kant write the new section and delete the old? One common explanation is that it was a response to the Göttingen Review.[11] Supposedly, Kant wanted to distinguish his idealism from that of Berkeley, and he did so by adding the Refutation and deleting the Fourth Paralogism, which contained many incriminating Berkeleyian passages about how objects in space are simply representations.

There is, however, a serious problem with this account. It ignores the simple but basic fact that the explicit target of the Refutation is not Berkeley's dogmatic idealism but Descartes' problematic idealism. Kant explicitly states that the refutation of Berkeley's idealism has already been achieved in the Aesthetic (B 274). Of course, the Refutation can still be read as a refutation of Berkeley's idealism; but that is more by implication than by intention.

For all the importance Kant gave Berkeley after the Göttingen Review, he did not cease to concern himself with Descartes' problematic idealism. Indeed, in the introduction to the Refutation he seems to return to his older more favorable assessment of Descartes in the Fourth Paralogism (A 368–369). Comparing Descartes' and Berkeley's idealism, Kant states explicitly that Descartes' idealism is more "reasonable and in accordance with a thorough and philosophical mode of thought" because it raises the important question of how we can prove the existence of things in space outside us, and because it does not make the dogmatic claims of Berkeley's idealism, such as space, if it exists, must be a thing-in-itself (B 274–275).[12]

The explanation for Kant's addition of the Refutation of Idealism lies more with his new strategy for a rebuttal of Descartes' problematic idealism. In the Fourth Paralogism Kant criticizes Descartes' skepticism essentially on the grounds that it is based on a false standard of truth: the correspondence of a representation with a thing-in-itself. Kant's reply to Descartes consists basically in his identification of the object in space with the representations of it. The argument against the Cartesian is that *simply by having the representation of something in space* it is possible to establish the reality of things in space, because these things are nothing more than the representations of them (A 370–371). Indeed, Kant insists twice that to refute empirical idealism it is sufficient to show merely that I am having a representation of things in space (A 371, 376–377). In making this argument, however, Kant failed to emphasize some of his critical doctrines crucial to his case against Descartes, more specifically his own criterion of empirical truth.[13] Though Kant presupposed this doctrine, and even expressly stated it (A 376), he never stressed it, and so he failed to reveal its central role in his argument. What Kant had come to see, however, is that, as stated, the refutation is very weak. It would not do to refute a Cartesian skeptic simply by identifying things in space with representations, for the Cartesian never doubts that we have *representations* of things in space. What he holds is that these representations might be completely illusory because they do not conform to things-in-themselves. So what Kant needed to show is not only that we have *representations* of things in space but also that we have *knowledge* of things in space. In the footnote to the second preface Kant posed just such a Cartesian objection to his whole argument:

> To this proof it will probably be objected, that I am immediately conscious only of that which is in me, that is, of my *representations* of outer things; and consequently that it must still remain uncertain whether outside me there is anything corresponding to it or not. (B xxxix)

While Kant thinks that this objection is not valid against his new proof, he seems to acknowledge that it is fatal against the initial formulation of his earlier argument in the Fourth Paralogism. It was this very objection, I suggest, that compelled Kant to write a new refutation of idealism for the second edition.

Although Kant's primary concern is with a Cartesian objection, he still wanted to distance himself from Berkeley. The identification of objects with representations already seemed much too Berkeleyian for a thinker who hated to see his position conflated with the Bishop of Cloyne. Still, it was Descartes who Kant wanted to refute in the Fourth Paralogism, and what he now realized was that his earlier identification move was no good for this purpose. In short: the decision to delete the Fourth Paralogism was overdetermined. It not only seemed too Berkeleyian; it was also just a bad argument against Descartes.

Further evidence for this reading of the Refutation appears in several sections of Kant's *Prolegomena*, which were probably written in 1782, before the second edition of the *Kritik* and in response to reviews of the first edition. In §49, Remark 3 of §13, and the Appendix, Kant is especially eager to rebut the charge of idealism made against him by the Göttingen Review. It is noteworthy that this review based its charge upon texts Kant would soon revise or delete: the Aesthetic and the Critique of the Fourth Paralogism. It is also significant that Kant now stresses a point against idealism that he did not make in these earlier texts: that the distinction between reality and illusion resides in the coherence of experience, its conformity to universal and necessary laws.[14] Transcendental idealism provides a sufficient basis to distinguish between reality and dream, Kant argues, because it has a conception of truth as the "connection of appearances in both space and time according to universal laws of experience" (IV, 337, 290). It is enough to refute material idealism, Kant then contends, if we can show that appearances conform to such laws. There is indeed no other criterion available to us, given that we can concern ourselves only with our representations and the existence of things-in-themselves outside them is "nothing to us" (336). While Kant thus continues to affirm the argument of the Fourth Paralogism (337)—that we know things in space with certainty because their reality does not consist in their conformity to things-in-themselves independent of our representations—he now realizes that he must also stress the role of coherence if he is to counter empirical idealism. Stressing the ideal status of single representations alone could not be sufficient, not when the incoherent representations of dreams could claim such status. The truth of our experience cannot be ascertained simply by the *content* of the representations, Kant now argues, because both the empirical idealist and transcendental realist agree about *what* they see; the crucial question concerns the *form* of these representations, whether their content conforms to universal and necessary laws (290). Only transcendental idealism provides a proper formal basis to distinguish between truth and illusion, Kant insists, because it alone shows the possibility of the a priori structure of experience (375), and so does justice to its universal and necessary structure. These passages from the *Prolegomena* anticipate Kant's later argument to such a degree that in §49 Kant even states *in nuce* the central idea behind the Refutation: that we have a proof that something real corresponds to our perceptions if we show "that there is something empirical, ie, some appearance in space outside us," whose objective reality is proven by its "connection according to laws of experience" (336).

Whatever the *fons et origio* of the Refutation, the net result of Kant's thinking about idealism after the first edition of the *Kritik* is that he needed to reformulate his argument against material idealism. Sure enough, in the section introducing the Refutation of Idealism, Kant announces a new strategy against Descartes (B 274–275). He now explains that he will begin with Descartes' own starting point, the apparent self-evidence of my inner experience, the self-consciousness of my existence in time. He will then argue, however, that the condition of such self-consciousness is the consciousness of something permanent in space outside me. This will show, in other words, that inner experience is possible only through outer experience, because an inner experience will be determinable in time only through a spatial framework. The essence of this strategy, as Kant describes it in Remark 1 (B 276–277), is to turn the idealist's game against him. Rather than basing outer experience on uncertain inferences from inner experience, Kant will show that inner experience has to be founded upon outer experience.

This is a new strategy against Descartes because nowhere in the Fourth Paralogism does Kant attempt to connect inner and outer sense, and still less does he argue for the *priority* of outer over inner sense. The argument there treats the senses as separate and equal, contending only that outer sense has *parity* with inner sense because it gives as much certainty about objects outside us as inner sense gives certainty about objects inside us. Now, however, Kant holds that we can know our inner states in time—we can say that we had an experience at a certain moment—only if we can somehow locate them within a single public space. In other words, knowing *when* I had certain experiences somehow involves knowing *where* I had them; and to know where I had them demands the possibility of identifying them in a single universal space shared by everyone alike.

Now that the idealist's game has been turned against himself, there is no mistaking the point that the intersubjective spatial world cannot be subordinated or constructed out of the mere ideas of the individual subject. Rather, the very opposite is the case: that intersubjective order precedes or makes possible the subjective order of my inner consciousness. In short, Kant's break with the subjectivist tradition is final and complete.

3. The Question of Kant's Realism

Another no less serious problem in the interpretation of the Refutation is determining exactly what Kant intends to prove. The central thesis of the Refutation states: "The mere, but empirically determined, consciousness of my own existence proves the existence of objects in space outside me" (B 275). The conclusion reads: "[T]he consciousness of my existence is at the same time an immediate consciousness of the existence of other things outside me" (B 276). What Kant seems to mean in these obscure lines is that I can be self-conscious of myself in time—I can determine when I am having certain perceptions—only if I am also conscious of the existence of things in space outside me. In more Kantian terms, empirical apperception, or my self-consciousness in time, involves outer sense, the awareness of objects in space outside me. But why this should be so, and what it means exactly, is still open to interpretation.

The question immediately arises what Kant means by the phrases "existence of objects in space outside me" or "the existence of other things outside me." What ontological status do these objects have? Are they things-in-themselves? Or are they only appearances? And if they are only appearances, what kind are they? Are they appearances understood as mental states? Or appearances as aspects *of* things-in-themselves? Or even "appearances in themselves," that is, objects that exist independent of the empirical subject though they are indeed posited by the transcendental subject?[15] Strangely, Kant's texts give no unambiguous answer to these questions.

Prima facie there might not seem to be that much of an issue about how to read Kant's phrases, given that Kant himself provides precise instructions in the Critique of the Fourth Paralogism. According to his own explanation, the phrase 'things outside us' (*außer uns*) can have two possible meanings. It can refer to the *transcendental* reality of an object, its existence as a thing-in-itself; or it can allude to its *empirical* reality, its existence as an outer appearance, that is, as an object located in space according to outer sense (A 373). Kant is quite explicit that his transcendental idealism denies the transcendental reality but affirms the empirical reality of the objects given in experience. So, it would seem that Kant must intend to demonstrate the existence of objects in the *empirical* sense, their reality as outer appearances. For if he were to attempt to prove their reality in the *transcendental* sense, he would be patently violating his own strictures about the limits of knowledge, according to which we cannot know anything about things-in-themselves.

Because reading the phrase 'things outside us' in a transcendental sense leads to such a blatant inconsistency, the common interpretation of the Refutation has been to read it as an attempt to prove only the empirical reality of objects.[16] Kant's aim, it is usually argued, is to prove that we know inner appearances in time only through outer appearances in space; but it is not to demonstrate the existence of any kind of objects ontologically distinct from all representation. According to this interpretation, then, the Refutation of Idealism is only a new version of the argument against problematic idealism put forward in the Critique of the Fourth Paralogism. Though there is indeed some change in exposition and argument, there is none in doctrine. After all, this is only in keeping with Kant's own description of the Refutation in the preface to the second edition as one "affecting the method of proof only" (B xxxix).

But understanding Kant's Refutation is not as simple and straightforward as some advocates of the traditional interpretation would have us believe. There are some serious difficulties in squaring the text of the Refutation with Kant's earlier formulation of transcendental idealism in the Critique of the Fourth Paralogism. First, there is the more realistic language of the Refutation, which appears to commit Kant to the existence of objects distinct from *all* representations. Second, there is the even more realistic language of Kant's later refutations of idealism, the *Reflexionen* from the late 1780s and early 1790s, where Kant not only refers to objects that are distinct from representations but to things-in-themselves. Third, Kant deletes the Critique of the Fourth Paralogism in the second edition, so that it is questionable whether it should be used as a guideline about how to interpret that edition.

In any case, the simplistic distinction between transcendental and empirical reality in the Fourth Paralogism invites a dichotomy between mere representations and things-in-themselves that Kant himself had moved beyond in the second edition.

Basing their interpretation upon these later texts, some scholars have stressed the greater realism of the Refutation, and have argued that Kant began to move away from the transcendental idealism of the Fourth Paralogism.[17] They maintain that the objects in space outside me are indeed ontologically or numerically distinct from the conscious subject, existing independently of all actual or possible representations. There is a sharp difference of opinion, however, regarding the precise nature of these objects. Some straightforwardly identify them with things-in-themselves;[18] others with the appearances of things-in-themselves;[19] and still others with appearances in themselves.[20]

Although it is tempting to dismiss the stronger realistic interpretation because of the inconsistency it seems to attribute to Kant, it would be very rash, and indeed naive, to do so. Several more arguments can be made in its defense.

First, it is not so obvious that the more realistic reading is incompatible with Kant's transcendental idealism. Most advocates of this interpretation do not maintain that Kant simply returns to transcendental realism, as if the object, as spatially represented, were the thing-in-itself. They indeed question the basic dilemma behind the conventional reading of the Refutation: Kant reduces appearances to representations or he claims knowledge of things-in-themselves. Some of them hold that empirical objects are appearances in themselves and as such neither things-in-themselves nor representations; others argue that appearances are *of* things-in-themselves, and that Kant's transcendental idealism involves a distinction between *epistemological* and *ontological* independence, which claims that we can know that something exists independently of us without knowing what it is like independently of us.[21]

Second, this interpretation is perfectly in keeping with the direction of Kant's thinking after the Göttingen Review. We have already seen how Kant reformulated his transcendental idealism in a much more realistic manner in the years immediately after the publication of the first edition of the *Kritik*. In the *Prolegomena* and second edition of the *Kritik* he ceased to identify appearances with mere representations, and instead began to stress that they are appearances *of* things-in-themselves. He now began to describe his idealism as only one of the form, but not of the content or matter, of experience. Hence the realistic reading of the Refutation and the *Reflexionen* corresponds fully to the basic direction of Kant's thinking in the 1780s. In line with this development, the objects in space referred to in the Refutation could well be things in themselves as they appear in space. Could it not be that Kant intended to prove the reality of these objects to give a further distinction between his formal idealism and the material idealism of Descartes and Berkeley?

Third, it can also be argued that, even prior to the Göttingen Review, there were deeper realistic tendencies in Kant's thought, which finally emerged in the Refutation of Idealism of the second edition of the *Kritik*. It has been contended, for example, that even in the first edition of the *Kritik*, Kant sometimes saw the object as distinct from our representations.[22] It has also been maintained that the Refutation of Idealism returns to an earlier realism Kant had attempted to formulate in the 1770s.[23]

If the stronger realistic reading cannot be so easily dismissed, then it seems that the problem of interpretation is still unresolved. The only means of settling the dispute about the proper reading of the Refutation is to return to the texts themselves, sifting through the evidence pro and con.

4. Realism in the Refutation

There are three passages in the Refutation of Idealism where Kant uses much stronger realistic language than in the first edition Critique of the Fourth Paralogism. The first passage comes from the conclusion of the Refutation. Here Kant states explicitly that the perception of something permanent is possible "only through a *thing* outside me and not through the mere *representation* of a thing outside me" (B 275). The second passage derives from the second edition preface where Kant deliberately restates the argument in more realistic terms. He writes that the permanent cannot be an intuition in me because everything within me amounts to only representations (B xl). The third passage also comes from the second preface where Kant warns us against confusing the representation of something permanent with a permanent representation, and argues that our representations refer to something permanent though they themselves are transitory (B xli).

Some commentators have been so struck by the marked discrepancy in language between the Refutation and the Fourth Paralogism that they place selected passages in apposition to one another in a manner reminiscent of

Kant's own antinomies.[24] Thus the conclusion of the Refutation states: "Perception of the permanent is possible only through a *thing* outside me and not through the mere *representation* of a thing"; but the thesis of the Fourth Paralogism goes: "Outer objects are mere appearances, and are therefore nothing but a species of my representations, the objects of which are something only through these representations; apart from them they are nothing" (A 370). According to Kemp Smith and Vaihinger, for example, there is a great disparity between the critique of Descartes in the first edition and that in the second edition. Both arguments attempt to establish the immediacy of our perception of objects in space, that is, that we know objects are in space and do not simply infer that they exist. But, they contend, there is a very large difference in *what* they regard as immediately known. In the first edition what is known are representations alone, whereas in the second edition what is known are objects distinct from representations.

Granted that Kant is using stronger language here, the question still remains how to interpret it. What are these objects distinct from my representations of them? There are four possibilities, each with its own problems.

The first possibility is that they are ordinary material objects, which continue to exist when we do not perceive them, and which have independent of us all the properties we perceive them to have. The most obvious problem with this reading is that it attributes transcendental realism to Kant, flatly contrary to his explicit avowal of transcendental idealism. It could be replied, however, that this very contradiction is implicit in Kant's texts, and that it is in just this respect that the second edition marks a retreat from the transcendental idealism of the first edition. But this imputes a blatant contradiction to Kant—it is hard to understand how it could be only implicit—and makes it difficult to understand why Kant reaffirmed transcendental idealism in the second edition.

Leaving that aside, however, there is another more telling rejoinder to this interpretation: that the argument of the Refutation is scarcely plausible if it attempts to prove the existence of material objects in the ordinary sense.[25] Crudely, Kant's argument attempts to show that the awareness of objects in space is a necessary condition for the consciousness of inner states in time. Such an argument will work, however, only if these objects in space are appearances. For if, *per contra*, we assume that they are transcendentally real material things, the argument is vulnerable to skeptical objections, the very kind of objections it was Kant's aim to refute.[26] Simply because we must be aware of objects in space to be self-conscious of representations in time does not show that these objects exist independent of our awareness of them. In more general terms, a necessity of our conceiving or representing X does not prove that X exists independent of our conception or represention; it does so only if the existence of X is a function of how we conceive or represent things; in other words, X must be an appearance.

A second possibility is that the objects are things-in-themselves as they appear in space.[27] Although there is some evidence for this view, as we have just seen, it still suffers from some grave difficulties. The main problem is that the Refutation would still violate Kant's strictures upon the limits of knowledge. Even if the thing-in-itself is identified as the thing that appears, and not as a noumenon completely distinct from phenomena, to attempt to prove its existence still goes beyond the limits of possible experience. This would still amount to a transcendent application of the category of existence. Furthermore, to interpret the thing outside me as a thing-in-itself stretches the text of the Refutation. For Kant always refers to the thing as something permanent in space, a clear allusion to the concept of substance, which is applied to things in experience, and so cannot be a thing-in-itself.

Yet a third possibility is that the objects are appearances in themselves. If this is the case, then they exist independent of our empirical consciousness but are still dependent upon the synthetic activities of the transcendental ego. This proposal has some clear advantages: it does not blatantly violate Kant's teachings about the limits of knowledge, and it does justice to the more realistic language of the Refutation. Most important, it shows how the Refutation is consistent with Kant's transcendental idealism because it shows how objects can exist independent of us but still be created by our knowing activity: namely, they are independent of our *empirical* consciousness but dependent on the activity of our *transcendental* ego. However, this explanation too has some serious disadvantages, which we have already noted above (1.2.5). The chief difficulty concerns the very idea of an appearance in itself, which leads to a paradoxical duplication of appearances: empirical subjects perceive not appearances of the thing-in-itself but only appearances of an appearance. Furthermore, to assume that appearances exist independent of all empirical consciousness not only underestimates the role of sensibility in their production, but it also reinstates the whole problem of knowledge on the level of empirical consciousness.

The fourth and final possibility is that the objects are simply appearances, and more specifically appearances in the empirical sense or what conforms to the a priori forms of space and the categories of the understanding. According to this interpretation, when Kant writes of a thing outside me and distinct from my representations he is using the phrase 'outside me' in a very narrow and specific sense to contrast the appearances of outer sense with those of inner sense.[28] This is only in keeping with the context of the Refutation because Kant is beginning from empirical apperception and starting from the Cartesian premise that all my representations are inner rather than outer, in time alone rather than in space. From this Cartesian perspective objects in space do indeed appear outside me. So when Kant writes about objects outside my representations he contrasts them with something more specific than representations in general: namely, my *inner* representations, which appear to occur according to inner sense alone. This means that when Kant refers to objects outside me he is using the expression 'outside me' strictly in the empirical sense. There is no contradiction, then, between the Refutation, where Kant appears to distinguish representations from their objects, and the Fourth Paralogism, where he identifies objects with representations, because the first usage is empirical while the second is transcendental. While Kant speaks from the standpoint of the transcendental philosopher in the Fourth Paralogism, he writes from the standpoint of empirical consciousness in the Refutation.[29]

This reading has several strong advantages: it does justice to the realistic language of the Refutation; it makes Kant's transcendental argument plausible; and it is consistent with Kant's transcendental idealism as a whole. But it too seems to suffer from a fatal difficulty. If all Kant means by objects outside us are appearances in space, then he has not established much at all, and certainly nothing against the Cartesian, even if he has proven their existence. For the Cartesian does not doubt that we have *representations* of things outside us, though that is all that has been demonstrated on this reading. In the footnote to the second preface Kant indeed restates this very objection and makes it clear that his Refutation is designed as an answer to it (B xxxix). But on this interpretation it is hard to see how the Refutation responds to Descartes' skepticism at all. Kant just has no new strategy against Descartes, or if he does it is an abject failure.

We have now come full circle. After considering all the options it seems as if we have gotten nowhere. The whole strategy against Descartes demands a stronger realistic rendition of the phrase 'things outside us'; but any stronger reading burdens Kant with other paradoxes and inconsistencies. It seems, then, as if Kant is still caught between the dilemma of triviality or inconsistency.

5. The New Strategy

The path out of this morass appears when we recognize that Kant himself thinks that there is something between the mere representation of outer things and things-in-themselves, and that it is not an appearance in itself. This third term is *experience*, the representation of outer things according to universal and necessary principles. 'Experience' (*Erfahrung*) is a technical term for Kant. He defines it as "an empirical cognition, that is, a cognition that determines an object through perception" (B 218). The term almost always means representation *insofar as* it is the product of the synthetic activities of the understanding, or the perception *of an object* arising from these activities.[30] Experience signifies more than single perceptions and contains a reference to their *systematic unity* and *lawful interconnection*. It also implies the idea of a single spatial and temporal system, of which all perceptions, no matter what their content, are only parts. While already clear in the first *Kritik,* this meaning of experience will become even more explicit and emphatic in the *Opus postumum,* where Kant defines it as a systematic whole of perceptions, and insists constantly that there can be but one experience.[31]

Now what Kant wants to demonstrate in the Refutation is that even our inner consciousness involves an *experience* of things in space, and not merely single *representations* or *perceptions* of them. If we have such an experience, then our representation or perception will not be an illusion because it will conform to the universal and necessary principles of experience in general, which serve as the criteria to distinguish between all truth and illusion. Such an argument does not beg the question against the Cartesian because it does not simply identify objects with representations in the manner of the Fourth Paralogism. Rather than stating merely that we have only a *representation* of things in space, it claims that we have a *knowledge* of things in space because our representations of space conform to the universal and necessary conditions of experience.

That Kant's aim in the Refutation is to demonstrate that we have an *experience* of things, and not merely the imagination of them, the texts leave no doubt. Indeed, Kant himself insists on the point. In the introduction to the Proof Kant is explicit that he must show against Descartes "that we have *experience*, and not merely imagination of outer things" (B 275; Kant's emphasis). And in the preface to the second edition he states against the Cartesian objection that we have only *representations* of things in space: "But through inner *experience* I am conscious of *my existence* in time (consequently also of its determinability in time), and this is more than to be conscious merely of my representation" (B xl; again Kant's emphasis).[32]

The context of the Refutation also confirms that this is Kant's intention.[33] The Refutation is situated almost as an appendix to the Postulates of Empirical Thought. In this section Kant's main concern is to show how the categories of modality—possibility, actuality, and necessity—can be understood as transcendental conditions of experience. Kant explains that the possible is that which agrees with the *formal* conditions of experience; the actual is that which also conforms to its *material* conditions, namely sensation; and the necessary is that which *must* comply with these conditions (B 265–266). In discussing the concept of actuality Kant stresses that to determine the actuality of a concept we do not need the immediate perception of it; all that we require are connections with other perceptions according to the analogies of experience (B 272). In other words, the concept of actuality extends beyond objects immediately given in perception to those whose existence can be inferred according to the analogies, the categories of substance, causality, and reciprocity. Kant gives as an example of such an object the magnetic matter pervading all bodies that is inferred from the attraction of iron filings. Though our senses are too crude to perceive such a matter, we can still know that it is real because it is connected with other perceptions according to the principles of experience.

Now it is in just this context that Kant raises the problem posed by skeptical idealism. He explains that he must consider the problem of idealism because it raises objections to proving the existence of anything mediately or by inference from what is given in perception (B 274). Kant provides little further explanation, but the context makes clear the difficulty confronting him. The Cartesian idealist treats the relationship of our inner consciousness to things in space on the same model as the relationship between the iron filings and the magnet. Just as we have to infer the existence of the magnet, which we cannot immediately perceive, so we must infer the existence of things in space, which we also cannot immediately perceive. It then seems as if the existence of things in space can be as uncertain as the existence of the magnetic matter. But, for Kant, the whole analogy is misplaced and misleading. The relationship between inner consciousness and spatial order is not like that between two objects within our experience which are the cause and effect of one another. Rather, spatial order is the *transcendental condition* of inner awareness, and as such *constitutive of* our awareness of ourselves in time. There is no need to infer spatial order from our inner consciousness, then, for the simple reason that it is already a necessary condition of it. In a word, the Cartesian is guilty of *hypostasis*, of treating a transcendental relationship as if it were a causal empirical one.

This provides another formulation for what is wrong with the Cartesian's doubts about the whole objective order of experience, his fears that its entire structure could be an illusion (see also above, 1.3.2–1.3.4). Such suspicions arise in the first place, Kant would say, only because the Cartesian extends his analogy beyond its proper limits. We make inferences according to the principle of causality about specific things or events *within* our experience; but we cannot extend it to the entire realm of experience itself. This is exactly what the Cartesian does, however, when he casts doubts upon our entire experience because the relationship between cause and effect is only an inference. It is always possible, he argues, that all my experience is an illusion because all my perceptions might have their cause from a malicious demon rather than from the spatial order of things. For Kant, however, such doubts amount to a transcendent use of the principle of causality. Rather than using it to determine truth or illusion about specific events within our experience, we extend it to experience as a whole. The problem with such a transcendent use of the category of causality is not that it is meaningless—the categories still have a *formal* significance when not applied in experience—but simply that it cannot have any application or *cognitive* significance. It is impossible to know the existence of any object that is independent of the whole of experience, and so absurd to think that there could be more or less reliable inferences about it.

Hence Kant's final response to Cartesian skepticism is that it is self-defeating, its intelligibility parasitic on the very rules it would question. The Cartesian skeptic attempts to cast doubt on the normal rules of experience because he doubts if we can make a reliable inference from the whole of experience to the thing-in-itself; yet in doubting the truth of the whole of experience he still presupposes the basic rules of its possibility. For to doubt any inference from effect to cause is to apply the category of causality; it is to assume the general norms of evidence for assessing cause–effect relations. This skeptic wants to say that *all* of our experience could be illusory; yet there is no possible case in which this could be so because we determine that something is an illusion only *within* our experience according to its rules. Hence Kant himself remarks in note 3 to the Refutation that "Whether this or that supposed experience is merely imaginary must be checked from its specific determinations and from its conformity with the criteria of all real experience" (B 279).

Here it could be objected against Kant that if we determine the veracity of our perceptions through their coherence, through their causal connections with one another, then we are forced to use inference after all, because such coherence is not given with the content of any particular representation. If, however, we have to use inference, we are stuck again with all the problems of its unreliability. This objection again fails to recognize, however, the important difference between the two kinds of inference. There is a difference between determining the connections between representations within experience and determining the connection between experience as a whole and reality in itself. The former connection is something verifiable in principle; the latter is not, for it involves the impossible task of determining whether our representations conform to things-in-themselves. Kant's recognition of the role of causal inference also involves no inconsistency with his claim that our empirical self-awareness involves an *immediate* awareness of objects in space. For what is mediate or inferential is determining the veracity of a *specific* representation; what is immediate or noninferential is the spatial framework in general, which is a necessary condition of having any representation of ourselves in time.

If, then, we grant that Kant's aim in the Refutation is to prove that we have an *experience* of objects, this begins to shed further light on Kant's more realistic language, the sense in which objects are distinct from mere representations. The objects in space outside us are indeed appearances; but because they also are *objects of experience* they conform to the structure imposed by the a priori forms of space and the categories, and so they are not reducible to individual representations or perceptions. The objects are distinct from their representations not in an *ontological* sense—they are not an entity that exists independent of them—but only in a *formal* sense—they are wholes of which individual perceptions or representations are only parts. To say that a whole is not reducible to its parts does not mean that the whole *exists* apart from its parts—it indeed exists only through them—but that its meaning or identity is more than the conjunction of its parts. In short, the irreducibility refers to its *essence*, not its *existence*.

Kant's conceptual shorthand for the conditions of objectivity is the *transcendental object*, and it is noteworthy that the transcendental object plays an important but implicit role in the Refutation of Idealism.[34] The transcendental object works in the background to provide the necessary formal conditions for the experience of objects in space. It is distinct from specific representations because it is the whole of which they are only parts. This is only in keeping with Kant's analysis of objectivity in the first edition's Deduction and Analogies, where he explains what it means for a representation to correspond to an object. Kant's explanation provides a sense in which the object, though really only a rule imposed by the activity of the understanding, can be distinct from representations. As an a priori rule it precedes all the representations of experience; and as a rule for the synthesis of representation it cannot be reduced simply to the sum of them. Of course, when Kant does refer to an object outside us it is an empirical object in space (*einen Gegenstand ausser uns im Raume*) and not anything so abstract as the transcendental object, which does not appear as such in experience (B 275). But because the transcendental object is applied to every manifold that becomes something objective in consciousness, it should also be involved in empirical objects in space. That Kant had it in mind becomes clear from *Reflexion* 5654, which bears the explicit title *Wieder den Idealism*. Here, in discussing the senses in which an object can be distinct from a representation, Kant writes:

> It is to be observed that every object refers to something distinct from the representation, but which is only in the understanding; hence inner sense itself, which makes ourselves objects of our representations, relates to something distinct from our self (as the transcendental object of apperception).(XVIII, 312)

6. The Argument of the Refutation

This reading of Kant's intentions in the Refutation becomes clear from a detailed examination of the argument itself. Scrutiny of the text shows that Kant's aim was to establish only that our inner consciousness conforms to the conditions for the experience of objects in space, not that we know objects independent of consciousness. While the argument has some plausibility when read in the light of Kant's account of experience in the Analytic, it has none at all if it is interpreted as requiring a stronger realism. The only kind of realism permitted by the argument is that in which the object in space has empirical reality because it conforms to the universal and necessary conditions of experience in general.

Kant's main argument consists in four steps, each of them formulated in a single sentence.[35]

STEP 1: *I am conscious of my own existence as determined in time.*

This is the premise of a classical transcendental argument. It states a self-evident fact that even the skeptic must accept: that I am conscious that I exist at a specific time, or that I am having an experience at such and such a time.[36] Since it is only a statement about myself and inner consciousness, it should be certain in ways that statements about the external world, other minds, and my own body are not.[37]

It is important to recognize that the self-consciousness of my existence in time amounts to my *empirical* self-consciousness, and that it is not simply the formal self-consciousness of the unity of apperception. Kant is clear in the Paralogisms that no substantive conclusions about the existence of things follows from the unity of apperception alone. Indeed, in the preface to the second edition he casts the fallacy of the Cartesian in terms of his confusion between transcendental and empirical apperception (B xl, xli). The argument of the Refutation is not, then, a reformulation of the thesis of the Transcendental Deduction.[38]

STEP 2: *All determination of time presupposes something permanent in perception.*

This is one of the central theses of the First Analogy. There Kant argues that all perception in time requires something permanent, and that this something is substance. Only the first claim seems relevant to the Refutation, since Kant does not refer explicitly to the category of substance in his Proof. Still, Kant does introduce it in both the second Remark (B 278) and in the General Remark to the System of Principles (B 291–292). It is also noteworthy that Kant barely distinguishes substance from the permanent. He writes that the proposition 'substance is permanent' is tautological because permanence is the sole ground for applying the category of substance to appearance (B 227). If, then, we have sufficient warrant for applying the concept of the permanent, we should also *ipso facto* have adequate basis to introduce substance.

It is indeed a serious mistake to jettison the concept of substance from the Refutation.[39] Rather than having no place in the argument, the concept of substance plays the crucial role of providing the objective element of experience. Substance is that analogy of experience that shows our inner consciousness is connected according to the same rules that apply to spatial objects. It serves as the mediating link between my awareness of time and my awareness of things in space, for temporal awareness requires something permanent and the permanent must be in space.

In the First Analogy Kant provides at least three arguments for his claim that all determination of time requires something permanent. First, that all appearances are in time—they are simultaneous or successive—and that the time in which they are represented remains and does not change (B 224–225). The underlying assumption behind this argument is Kant's peculiar identification of the permanent with time itself. He explains that change does not affect time itself but only appearances in time: "Permanence . . . expresses time in general. For change does not affect time itself but only appearances in time" (B 226). Second, our apprehension of the manifold is always changing, and through it we cannot determine whether the object of experience is really coexistent or in sequence. To determine whether the object of experience (as opposed to the manifold of successive representations) is coexistent or successive, we require something abiding and permanent, of which all change and coexistence are only so many determinations or ways in which it exists (B 225–226). Clearly, this argument resurfaces in the Refutation itself. Third, a coming or ceasing to be that is not the determination of something permanent but is purely absolute cannot be an object of perception. If we assume that something begins to be absolutely, we must have a point of time in which it is not; but we cannot attach this point to anything. Since it is an absolute beginning, there is no previous thing in relation to which it is perceived. But an empty time is not an object of perception (B 231).

What Kant is saying in all these arguments is that (a) we cannot determine coexistence or succession except with reference to some framework within which these events appear, and that (b) this framework must be permanent, at least relative to these events themselves. This is to say that the standard or criterion by which we measure change cannot be changing itself, at least with respect to the events it measures.[40] Kant's main point here is that the criterion to determine objective positions in time must be independent of the events themselves, because it is only in virtue of its independence from these events that it provides an objective measurement of them.[41]

Another formulation for the underlying point behind Kant's arguments is to see it as a version of his distinction between the form and matter of experience. While the temporal framework consists in the *relations* between ideas or representations, and so belongs to the form of experience,[42] the events which they measure consist in the contents of the ideas themselves. Now Kant insists that it is necessary to distinguish between the form and matter of experience because the relations in which we order sensations cannot belong to sensation itself (A 20/B 34). But this poses a difficulty for the material idealist. Since these relations are not given in perception itself, and so do not amount to an object of perception, the material idealist cannot claim that their essence consists solely in their perception.[43]

STEP 3: *This permanent cannot be something in me, since it is only through it that my existence in time can be determined.*

The revision in the second preface reads:

But this permanent cannot be an intuition in me. For all grounds of determination of my existence which are to be met with in me are representations; and as representations [they] themselves require a permanent distinct from them, in relation to which their change, and so my existence in the time wherein they change, may be determined.

The point of the revision is to clarify why the permanent cannot be something within me: namely, that what is in me are representations, which are always changing, and that their change must be measured by something permanent. But this very point has been controversial. That the permanent cannot be within me has often been perceived as a sticking point in Kant's proof.[44] It might be admitted that the measurement of all change requires something permanent; but then the question arises why it cannot be within me.

Kant has several reasons for excluding the possibility that the permanent is something within me. First, from the empirical standpoint, all my representations are changing, and so the permanent cannot be found among them. Second, from the transcendental standpoint, the 'I think' cannot provide any evidence for the existence of something permanent within me, as Kant will soon argue in the Paralogisms. Third, the permanent is the *transcendental condition* for the measurement of change, and as such it must be distinct from the very phenomena that it makes possible; it cannot be a representation itself because it is that which measures change among *all* representations. None of these points entails, however, that the permanent must be in space outside me.

STEP 4: *Therefore perception of this permanent is possible only through a thing outside me and not through the mere representation of a thing outside me.*

Kant writes as if this step follows from the previous ones, and it is indeed already the nub of the main conclusion. However, it does not follow from the others if a *thing outside me* means either (a) an appearance in space, (b) an appearance of a thing in itself, or (c) the thing-in-itself. All that does follow is that the permanent must be distinct from my representations in the sense that, as the framework within which the change of my representations is determined, it cannot be one of those representations themselves. It is distinct from the representations themselves only because it provides the transcendental condition under which we determine change within them. This is all that follows from the argument of the First Analogy, which is the basis for step 2.

This is problematic, however, because Kant often writes as if he has demonstrated that the thing outside us is an object in space. The thesis refers to "the existence of objects in space outside me" (B 275), and the conclusion of the Proof mentions "the existence of actual things outside me" (B 276). As it stands, Kant's argument needs another premise about how the meaning of the concept of substance must be specified in outer sense or space.

It is striking that Kant provides just such a premise in the General Note on the System of Principles, which is appended to the Postulates. Here he contends that to demonstrate the objective reality of the categories we need not only intuitions in general but *outer* intuitions specifically. To have something permanent in intuition corresponding to the concept of substance, for example, we require the intuition of space. "For space alone is determined as permanent, while time, and everything in inner sense, is in constant flux" (B 291). Kant then argues that we can represent change in general only through the movement of a point in space, and that we can represent inner change only by drawing a line (B 292). With this simple psychological observation Kant rests his case for the spatial schematization of transcendental principles.

Whatever the precise details of Kant's argument, its general point and structure seem plain. Kant attempts to show that, to know the time in which any of my representations occur, I must be able to locate them within a framework that is permanent relative to them. But this framework must be distinct from the representations themselves because (a) it is that in which their change is measured, and (b) it is permanent while they are changing. Furthermore, this framework must be spatial since we represent all change through space, though a point moving along a line. The net result of the argument is that the change of our subjective experiences is determinable only within the public framework of space.

7. Outer vis-à-vis Inner Sense

Behind the argument of the Refutation there lies a new and fundamental assumption that Kant articulates only in several places in the second edition of the *Kritik:* that inner states must be represented spatially. The dependence of empirical self-knowledge—the awareness of myself in time—on the perception of space stated in the Refutation is only one case in point of a more general argument in the second edition about how the representation of time depends upon space. In the second edition's Deduction and in the General Note to the System of Principles, which were added in the second edition, Kant stresses that we can represent time to ourselves only spatially through the drawing of a line or through the movement of a point in space (B 156, 292). This has important implications for our empirical self-knowledge, given that the a priori form of inner sense, the general form of all self-knowledge, is time. This means that we also must represent all change in ourselves spatially or through motion (B 292). Kant goes so far as to state that "the determinations of inner sense have to be arranged as appearances in time in precisely the same manner in which we arrange those of outer sense in space" (B 156).

One of the most remarkable changes from the first edition of the *Kritik* is the central importance that Kant now gives to space.[45] In the first edition Kant gave primacy to time: inner sense was the form of all appearances whatsoever; and it played the central role in the Schematism in applying the categories to experience. In the second edition, however, space usurps the title once accorded to time. Kant now stresses that space is fundamental to give objective reality to a priori concepts. In the General Note to the System of Principles, for example, Kant argues that to demonstrate the objective reality of the categories we need *outer* intuitions (B 291–292). The concept of the permanent, he explains, requires an intuition of *matter,* and the concept of causality requires an intuition of *motion.* Nowhere is Kant more explicit about the central role of outer sense, however, than in the preface to the second edition where he says that it is from the existence of things outside us that "we derive the whole material of knowledge, even for our inner sense" (B xxix). In a similar vein he writes in passage added to the Aesthetic: "the representations of the *outer senses* constitute the proper material with which we occupy the mind" (B 67–68).

The new role of outer sense in the second edition of the *Kritik* probably originated from Kant's reflections while writing his 1786 work *Metaphysische Anfangsgründe der Naturwissenschaften.*[46] There Kant had stated that metaphysics should derive the meaning of its concepts from the doctrine of physical body, in other words, from external intuition (IV, 478); and he had stressed that a discipline is a science only to the extent that its concepts are capable of mathematical construction in space (470). In the first part of the work, the Metaphysical Principles of Phoronomy, Kant maintains that temporal measurement is made through spatial intuition, or that we should represent units of time through lengths in space (IV, 489). Equal temporal intervals are measured by equal spatial ones, that is, the intervals in which a point traverses equal spatial units. It is indeed possible that it was this point that suggested to Kant the dependence of temporal upon spatial perception that lies at the base of the Refutation.[47]

It is important to see that, for all the new importance Kant gives to outer sense in the second edition of the *Kritik,* he does not completely demote the past role of inner sense. It is not as if he holds that only outer sense is immediate and all inner sense is based on it, as if the converse does not also hold in other respects.[48] Significantly, Kant retains the passages in the second edition that make inner sense the form of all representations, and those that make time central to schematizing the categories. Kant still thinks that inner sense is also the basis for outer sense, insofar as we construct motions outside us on the basis of momentary sensations given inside us. The main shift is that Kant now thinks that both senses are *interdependent:* inner sense depends on outer sense as much as outer sense on inner sense.

8. Kant's Refutations in the *Reflexionen,* 1788–1793

From 1788 to 1793 Kant continued to rethink his refutation of idealism. The *Reflexionen* from these years are filled with long passages having such titles as *Gegen den (materialen) Idealism* (R 5653), *Widerlegung des problematischen Idealismus* (R 6315), and *Wider den Idealism* (R 6316). There are essentially two groups of fragments: *Reflexionen* 5653–5655 (XVIII, 305–316), which were written in October 1788, probably as part of a reply to Eberhard's *Philosophisches Magazin;* and *Reflexionen* 6311–6316 (XVIII, 606–629), which were most probably written in 1790 in conjunction with the visit to Königsberg of J. C. E. Kiesewetter, a student of Kant.[49] In the autumn of 1790, every other day from 11:00 to 12:00, Kant and Kiesewetter would meet to discuss problems of the critical philosophy. Evidently, a major subject of discussion was the refutation of idealism.

These fragments are interesting and important chiefly because they clarify concepts of, and supply missing premises for, the argument in the second edition Refutation. The most important new point is the introduction of the concept of simultaneity to link the concepts of permanence and spatiality, whose connection was left obscure in the earlier proof.[50] It has often been objected against Kant that even if the recognition of change requires something permanent, there is no need that this permanent object be something in space. Kant now addresses this very point with the concept of simultaneity. The nub of his argument is that we can recognize something as permanent only through simultaneity, and that the awareness of simultaneity cannot be reducible to inner sense, the awareness of my representations in time. The main premises of the argument are that (1) we know something to be permanent only if we can recognize it more than once in the order of our perceptions, and that (2) we can do this only if we also can know it to be coexistent or simultaneous with other things (R 6312, 612). How do we recognize things to be simultaneous, Kant asks? He answers: only if it is possible for us to reverse the order of our perceptions, so that we can proceed not only forward from A to C but also backward from C to A. But if we are able to reverse the order of our perceptions, Kant then argues, that cannot be a function merely of inner sense, because all representations of inner sense are only successive.

Besides clarifying some steps of his reasoning, the *Reflexionen* also help to clarify the general intuition underlying Kant's argument. The obscure connection between inner and outer senses becomes much clearer when Kant states that I know myself as a particular person existing at a specific time only through also knowing my place in the world and how I interact with other things. If I only had inner sense, he argues, then I could not recognize my place in the world, and I could not even know the location of the soul in my body (R 6315, XVIII, 619, 5–8; and 620, 16–19). Hence it is only through locating my place in space that I also recognize myself as this particular person at this particular time. This conception of knowing my place in the world, of knowing myself through interaction with other things, will later play a crucial role in the *Opus postumum*.[51]

The *Reflexionen* mark no fundamental change of position from the second edition Refutation. Kant continues to criticize transcendental realism,[52] and he reaffirms the central principles of his transcendental idealism, and more specifically his doctrine of *formal idealism*, according to which the form of an object has transcendental ideality while its existence or reality is something given (R 6316, XVIII, 621–622). The central thesis of the second edition Refutation also remains intact. The *Reflexionen* do not argue for the existence of objects independent of representations in a stronger realistic or transcendental sense, where the objects would be things-in-themselves existing independent of all consciousness. Rather, they attempt to prove the existence of objects in space outside us in the empirical sense, where existence is again taken in the technical Kantian sense: "Whatever is connected with a perception according to empirical laws." The main strategy of the Refutation also reappears: to show that inner sense—my empirical self-consciousness—involves outer sense, the awareness of objects in space. It is sufficient to refute idealism, Kant thinks, if we can demonstrate that inner sense requires outer sense, and that outer sense is *sui generis,* irreducible to the awareness of my own representations through inner sense.[53] The problem with idealism, as Kant sees it, is not that it denies the transcendental reality of objects, but that it does not admit their empirical reality when it reduces all forms of outer to inner sense. While Kant considers the possibility that we could have a representation of space that does not refer to an external object, his response is not that the external object must indeed continue to exist unperceived but only that such deception or illusion could not be universal.[54] The possibility of illusion and deception presupposes that we do have genuine representations of things in space, where these things are perceptions complying with the form of outer sense and the categories.

It has been argued, however, that the *Reflexionen* mark an important shift from the transcendental idealism of both the first and second edition of the *Kritik.* Supposedly, they provide unmistakable evidence for Kant's attempt to establish a much more robust form of realism than the mere existence of objects in space.[55] In attempting to establish the existence of objects distinct from our representations, Kant's aim is to establish their transcendental reality, and more specifically how the representations of outer sense involve appearances of things-in-themselves. This does not mean, of course, that Kant is relapsing into transcendental realism; but it does show him trying to prove one of the central theses of his formal idealism, namely that representations are appearances of things-in-themselves.

The evidence for this reading derives from the stronger realistic language of the *Reflexionen,* which seems to commit Kant to the existence of objects distinct from representations in the ontological or transcendental sense. Hence Kant sometimes uses expressions such as 'something I must represent in another manner than myself,' 'something existing distinct from the subject' (R 5653, 309, 20–21 and 29), and 'the representation in me . . . the object outside of me' (R 6315, 620, 21–23).

When placed in context, however, these phrases imply nothing more than similar ones in the second edition Refutation. Kant is contrasting not consciousness as such with objects in themselves, but the representation of myself as a specific person with that of another object in space that is in a different place from myself. There is a specific representation in question: that of my *empirical* self-consciousness, the representation of myself in time and as having a body. Kant is saying only that the content of this representation is distinct from that of the object in space outside me. It is important to stress that the subject in question here is not the transcendental but the empirical subject, the subject that is aware of itself in time, and that has a physical body. Hence Kant sometimes summarizes the point of his argument by saying that the empirical subject must locate its body in a wider space, whose existence comprises many other objects (R 6315, 619, 5–10, and 620, 17–20). The object would exist independent of the subject in a transcendental sense only if Kant were contrasting it with the transcendental subject, pure self-consciousness; but he makes it clear in many places that this is not the case.

The most plausible passages in the *Reflexionen* in favor of a stronger realist reading are those where Kant refers to the object outside us as existing "*in itself.*" It is not clear from some of these passages, however, whether Kant is using the phrase 'object in itself' in an empirical or transcendental sense (R 6312, 612, 13; R 6323, 643, 19–21). Kant sometimes permits an empirical use of the phrase when he contrasts illusions with appearances; for example, he writes in the Aesthetic of the first *Kritik* that the rain can be considered as a thing-in-itself, and the rainbow as its appearance, even though the rain is only an appearance from the transcendental perspective (B 63). There are indeed other passages, though, where Kant does use the phrase 'in itself' in a transcendental sense (R 6315, 618, 28–29; R 6312, 613, 9–16). In these Kant writes of how outer sense refers to an object outside us "even if we cannot know what it is in itself but only how it appears to us." Still, these passages provide no evidence for the stronger realist reading of the Refutation, for in them Kant is not explicitly arguing for the existence of something external to ourselves but only explaining how the doctrine of inner sense fits with his belief in the existence of things-in-themselves.

Some *Reflexionen* have been interpreted as arguments for the existence of the thing-in-itself.[56] This seems to be especially the case in R 5653 where Kant argues that my perception of a thing outside me in space proves that I am passive and that I am acted on by things outside me. Since the things in question here are interpreted as things-in-themselves, Kant appears to be providing an argument in behalf of affection by things-in-themselves. But there is no reason to assume that the objects affecting me here are things-in-themselves. They could be other empirical objects acting on my body in space. That this is the more plausible reading is confirmed by R 6315, where Kant makes it clear that the dependence of inner upon outer sense means that I can locate my body in space in interaction with other bodies. In any case, such an interpretation goes against Kant's explicit admission around this time that we can only *think* things-in-themselves according to the categories.[57]

CHAPTER 7

Kant and the Way of Ideas

1. The Theory of Ideas

Kant famously said that a philosopher is not always the best interpreter of his own words, and that we can often understand him better than he understands himself (A 314/B 370). That maxim also holds for Kant himself, of course, and especially with regard to his own standing vis-à-vis the subjectivist tradition. In fundamental respects Kant's break with that tradition was truly profound and pervasive; but it was not always fully apparent to himself, and much less so to many of his readers. The problem is that Kant retained much of the language of subjectivism, even when arguing against it.

To fathom the depth of Kant's break with the subjectivist legacy, it is necessary to get beyond the level of his explicit polemics in the *Prolegomena*, which are marred by his misunderstanding of Berkeley and by his own lack of historical perspective. It is important to go back to the very foundation of the subjectivist tradition itself and to consider how Kant departed from some of its most basic assumptions. We have to examine, then, the central doctrine of that tradition, the source of so much of its teaching: the theory of ideas.

The main thesis of the theory of ideas is that the basic objects of awareness consist in ideas. Whatever we are thinking of is an idea, so that ideas are the *objects* of all thought. It was Descartes who inaugurated this usage by defining an idea as "whatever is immediately perceived by the mind" or as "any object of thought."[1] Leibniz, Arnauld, Malebranche, Locke, Berkeley, and Hume would soon follow in his footsteps.[2]

In all these authors there is an ambiguity whether an idea refers to only the object of thinking in a narrow sense, so that it is involved only in conceiving, judging, and reasoning, or whether it is the object of all forms of consciousness, including even dreaming, sensing, and willing. It is the latter more generic sense that eventually became dominant, however, and that is usually associated with "the way of ideas."

According to the way of ideas, ideas are not only objects in consciousness—whatever we are aware of when we are thinking—but they are also essentially representative, standing for or referring to some object beyond themselves. They are understood as the *medium* by which the subject knows the world because he becomes aware of the world *through* them. "We have no knowledge of what is *outside* us except by mediation of the ideas *within* us," as Arnauld put it.³ Hence ideas are often described as the *immediate* objects of perception, because we know them directly and the world indirectly through them. What we know with certainty are ideas, and we must infer the existence of the world from the evidence they provide. Thus arose the infamous "veil of perception" and the skepticism whether we can see beyond it.⁴

There were three pervasive assumptions behind the theory of ideas. First, an assumption about *origins:* that ideas are given to, not constructed by, the mind; this holds whether an idea is innate or acquired from experience. If it is innate, it is only a question of our reflecting upon it; and if it is empirical, it is only a matter of our receiving it. In either case we do not make it. Second, an assumption about *meaning:* that the idea is the basic unit or bearer of meaning. All meaningful terms are either compounds of simple ideas or simple ideas themselves, each of which has a complete, self-sufficient, and unanalyzable meaning. Third, an assumption about *truth:* that ideas represent their objects only by virtue of some kind of similarity with or resemblance to them. This assumption appears in various forms in Descartes, Leibniz, and Locke,⁵ though it was questioned by Berkeley, who maintained that an idea could resemble only another idea.⁶

2. Loyalty and Apostasy

It is important to recognize that, to a considerable extent, Kant himself was an adherent of the theory of ideas. *Prima facie* this might not seem to be the case because, in a notable passage in the Dialectic of the first *Kritik,* he laments the fashionable use of the term 'idea' (*Idee*) to refer to all the forms of mental life, insisting that it should be used to designate only the special objects of reason. Kant then proposes instead the word 'representation' (*Vorstellung*) as the generic term for all forms of consciousness (A 319–320, B

376–377). Representation should designate every kind of mental content, whether it is the ideas of reason, the concepts of the understanding, or the intuitions of sensibility. This term was the jargon of the Leibnizian-Wolffian school, which saw the mind essentially as a *vis representativae*, a faculty or power of representation.[7]

Nevertheless, Kant's preference for the term 'representation' amounts to merely verbal departure from the way of ideas. Indeed, he uses this term in ways remarkably similar to the traditional 'idea.' In many passages of the first edition of the *Kritik* he writes as if representations, like ideas, are the objects of consciousness. His usage of 'representation' is also ambiguous in the same manner as 'idea': a representation not only has the function of standing for something else, but it can also be the object of representation. Kant himself notes this very ambiguity but only to endorse it: "All representations have, as representations, their object, and can themselves in turn become objects of other representations"(A 108).[8] Finally, Kant appears to accept the theory of meaning behind the way of ideas, for he often writes as if representations are basic, as if they are simply given to our sensibility, and as if they are complete in themselves, the fundamental units of all mental synthesis.[9] Indeed, he is sometimes explicit that representations can be given to us without their being subsumed under, or processed by, the rules of the understanding (A 89–90, B 122–123). All this is consistent with, and even follows from, Kant's adoption of the Leibnizian-Wolffian terminology, because Leibniz and Wolff had absorbed many of the elements of the theory of ideas into their account of representation.

Yet, for all his apparent adherence to the theory of ideas, Kant's allegiance was shaky and ambivalent, to say the least. For he also undermines, if only implicitly, each of the central assumptions behind the theory of ideas. First, he questions its assumption about the origin of ideas. For Kant, no idea is simply given, but all are constructed, the products of more basic synthetic activities. While he indeed admits that an idea might be *given to consciousness*, he still insists that its appearing to consciousness is the result of subconscious activities. Representation is never something simple, basic, and given, but it is always something complex, derived, and constructed. According to one line of argument in the Analytic, especially evident in the first edition of the *Kritik*, the very possibility of representation depends on more fundamental activities, such as apprehension, imagination, and apperception (A 98–104).

Second, Kant also contests the assumption about meaning. He denies that ideas have a self-sufficient meaning, as if they somehow represent objects by virtue of their own nature alone. It is one of Kant's central theses in the Analytic that ideas acquire their representative status—their capacity to designate or refer to an object—only if the understanding synthesizes a manifold of sensations according to a rule. This act of synthesis creates a necessary connection between these sensations, such that each plays a necessary role in a whole. The sensation of a red patch becomes the representation of a rose, for example, because it, along with many other sensations, can be subsumed under the concept of a rose in a judgment like 'This is a rose.' Without being combined with other sensations according to rules—without being able to serve as the possible subject of a judgment—a sensation would be "impossible to us" or "nothing to us," that is, it would not *represent* anything at all, and so would have no cognitive significance.

Nowhere is Kant's distance from the theory of ideas more apparent than when he writes in the opening section of the B Deduction that all analysis presupposes synthesis (§15, B 130). Here, by implication if not by intention, Kant denies that there can be any such thing as a simple idea. An idea is not something complete and self-sufficient, he is saying, because it acquires its significance only from the whole of which it is a part. The very idea of a simple idea now shows itself to be a false abstraction from its whole. In these lines Kant rejects the analytical paradigm of explanation of the theory of ideas, which understood something only by analyzing it into its separate components. It is no accident that his own paradigm is more holistic: a system organized around and derived from a single principle (A 654/B 673; A 833–834/B 861–862).

Finally, Kant also criticizes the assumption about truth. He denies that ideas represent their objects by virtue of their similarity to them, insisting instead that they represent their objects only because they are synthesized according to rules.[10] In a nutshell, representation consists not in *resemblance to a thing* but in *conformity to rule*. Such is the purport of Kant's analysis of the object of representation in the first edition version of the Transcendental Deduction (A 104–105). Here Kant raises the central question what is meant by the object of our representations, and more specifically by representations corresponding to something distinct from themselves. He argues that the concept of an object as something completely distinct from all of our representations—a mere something in general = X—is useless because we have to admit that we cannot get outside our representations to compare them to something existing apart from them. Once we admit that we have to deal with nothing more than our own representations, it becomes necessary to account for the concept of the object within the realm of consciousness it-·self. This concept admits of a perfectly adequate analysis within this realm, Kant argues, as that which confers necessity upon our representations, preventing them from being arbitrary and chaotic. What gives them such necessity, he continues, is "the unity of rule" (A 105), the synthesis of representations "through a common function of the mind for combining it in one representation" (A 109).

On this analysis, the object is still something distinct from its representation, and it is still possible to speak about a representation corresponding to its object; but the meaning of this distinctness and correspondence has changed.[11] The object is distinct from its representations not by virtue of its existential or ontological status as a thing-in-itself, but by virtue of its formal or epistemological status as a synthesis of representations. Such a synthesis is not reducible to any of its individual elements because it is that which binds them together and gives each of them their representative status. The representation corresponds to its object not in the sense that it resembles some thing-in-itself, but in the sense that it conforms to a rule and plays a necessary role in a whole.

Though it is central to his philosophy, Kant's concern with the problem of representation is not always apparent in the Analytic of the first *Kritik*. This is chiefly because Kant explains his intentions in terms of the more narrow problem of knowledge rather than the more general problem of representation. Kant often presents his problem in terms of how a priori concepts apply to a manifold of representations, where it seems as if these representations are already complete and given, and as if the only issue is to determine how they acquire objectivity or become knowledge. For this reason Kant's account of the concept of an object is often interpreted in a narrow sense as the object of *knowledge* alone, overlooking its more general sense as the object of *representation*.

Such a restricted reading of Kant's problem ignores, however, some of his most important innovations. There can be little doubt that Kant's enquiry in the Analytic went much further than the problem of knowledge alone. Kant's concern with the more general issue of representation becomes perfectly explicit in the Second Analogy when he poses the striking question: what does it mean for an appearance—a term often synonomous with representation—not only to be an object but to stand for one (A 189–190/B 235; A 108). Now the issue is not only how a manifold of representations can be synthesized to give knowledge of an object, but how even a single representation is possible. What the subjectivist tradition had simply presupposed—that mental states have a meaning, that they represent something—had now become a problem for Kant.[12]

3. The Transcendental versus the Subjective

Despite Kant's break with the theory of ideas, the subjectivist can still defend his interpretation. Although he might concede that Kant denies *simple* ideas, he will still insist that Kant accepts one central thesis of the way of ideas: that ideas are the ultimate bearers of meaning. He will point out that Kant has questioned only the account of *how* ideas establish meanings—as wholes rather than as parts, or through synthesis instead of analysis—but not *that* ideas are the source of meaning. This becomes fully apparent, the subjectivist will contend, when we consider that the categories are themselves merely representations. They too are only ideas, just more abstract and second-order ones.

But such an interpretation of the categories stretches the concept of an idea beyond its already broad boundaries in the subjectivist tradition. It is important to see that the categories cannot be just ideas in the traditional subjectivist sense—whether ideas are taken as conscious states or objects of consciousness—because the categories also lay down the conditions under which we have ideas. They determine the conditions for having conscious states and for these conscious states representing objects. To interpret the categories merely as representations, even the most general kind of representations, is therefore to abstract from their transcendental role in the formation of representations. Rather than seeing the categories as ideas, it is more accurate to interpret them exactly as Kant describes them: as *rules* (*Regeln*) (A 106, 126, 302). As such they cannot be mistaken for just another kind of representation, given that they are norms whose specific task is to form and govern representations.[13]

The fundamental problem of the subjectivist reading of the categories, then, is that it does not recognize their *transcendental* role or *normative* status. This interpretation attempts to reduce all of experience down to the level of the purely subjective, to the individual subject and its ideas, whether actual or possible. But this neglects all of the conditions under which subjects have ideas, and indeed under which we individuate subjects. In beginning with the experience of an individual subject who has ideas, the subjectivist simply presupposes the phenomena that are to be explained: ideas, individuality, and consciousness. That a subject has ideas, that it identifies itself as the subject having them, and even that it is conscious all presuppose the operation of the activities of synthesis and the application of the categories to experience. In short, the subjectivist interpretation of Kant's philosophy fails to recognize the point behind its central and characteristic dimension: the transcendental.

Rather than reducing experience down to the level of individual consciousness, the critical philosophy makes both the subjective and objective—understood as the representations of inner and outer sense—equal and co-ordinate parts of a single intersubjective structure or form. This normative order is neither mental nor physical but transcendental, the necessary condition for the possibility of experience of any rational being equipped with a human sensibility. Its extramental and extraphysical status becomes apparent as soon as we recognize that it is *the condition* under which we identify anything as mental or physical, as an object of either inner or outer sense. In other words, as the norm that governs or regulates the mental and the physical, it cannot be mental or physical itself. Indeed, its normative status remains unaffected whether it governs what is inside me in time or what is outside me in space. Both spatial objects outside me and temporal objects inside me are equal instances or cases of its neutral and inescapable laws.

Recognizing the normative status of the transcendental is crucial if we are to understand Kant's attempt to solve the classical problem of knowledge: How do I know that my representations correspond to things? If the transcendental consists merely in the subjective—the ideas or consciousness of the perceiver—then the question still remains how we know that the subjective corresponds with the objective. This problem cannot be resolved simply by pointing to the order among the ideas of the subject, for on subjectivist premises this order too consists in nothing more than just another set of ideas. Though these ideas are relational and of a higher order, they are still ideas all the same, so that the correspondence of this set of ideas with reality still stands in need of demonstration.

If, however, the transcendental consists in the normative, then both the subjective and objective—the appearances of inner and outer sense—become parts of a single experience.[14] The subject's ideas correspond to its objects because the interaction of these appearances conforms to one universal and necessary structure, one common system of interconnected laws. It is not the subjective status of the mental and the physical—that they are both appearances—that makes their correspondence possible, for Kant still admits the heterogeneity of the representations of inner and outer sense.[15] To guarantee the correspondence between such distinct kinds of appearances there must be, then, some higher intelligible form that governs both. Transcendental idealism is an empirical dualism precisely because the normative status of the transcendental explains the interconnection between the very different appearances of inner and outer sense.

4. The Question of Consistency

Granted that Kant breaks with the theory of ideas, at least in some basic lines of his thinking, the question still remains whether he is consistent in doing so. His critique of the theory of ideas hardly squares with his frequent statements that representations are something given to sensibility, and that they appear independent of the functions of the understanding. How are we to interpret such statements? Is there an inconsistency here, or is there another reading compatible with his antisubjectivism?

To understand Kant's language, it is necessary to place it within the context of his own implicit distinction between two standpoints: the transcendental and the empirical. While the transcendental standpoint holds for the philosopher who investigates the conditions of experience, the empirical viewpoint is valid for ordinary consciousness *within* the framework provided by these conditions.[16] The apparent inconsistency arises from a confusion between these levels, from failing to see that Kant can speak with two voices. When Kant states that representations are given he is speaking—often if not always—from the empirical standpoint as an accommodation to our ordinary ways of thinking; but when he states that they are possible only through the forms of synthesis he is speaking from the transcendental standpoint. Although not developed by Kant himself, such a distinction is already implicit in his own distinction between transcendental ideality and empirical reality.

Admittedly, when writing of representations as given, Kant does not always speak from the empirical standpoint. In the opening chapter of the Transcendental Deduction, for example, he speaks from the standpoint of the philosopher when he explains that the problem of knowledge arises because appearances can be given to us in space and time without their subsumption under the categories (A 89/B 122; A 90/B 123). However, a careful examination of Kant's language reveals that, though he is indeed writing as a philosopher, he is only making a hypothetical assumption for the purposes of argument. To paraphrase, he is saying something like "Since it *seems to be* that the objects of sense are given prior to the application of concepts, we have to raise a question about their justification." In other words, the givenness of the objects of sense is only a problematic thesis whose falsity Kant intends to demonstrate in the course of his argument. Sure enough, shortly after speaking of representations as if they were given, Kant explicitly writes that the transcendental deduction of the concepts of the understanding shows them to be a priori conditions of the possibility of experience, "*whether of intuition or of thought*" (A 94/B 126, my italics).

Seen from the transcendental standpoint, it is Kant's more precise and strict doctrine that the given in experience consists not in representation but sensation (*Empfindung*). It is sensation that constitutes the matter of experience, which is merely given to our sensibility through the action of some object upon it (A 19–20, B 34). Kant explains that sensation is the proper *empirical* element of experience, or that which gives an intuition its specific quality; for example, it is what makes red that color rather than blue, green, or yellow.[17] It is striking and significant that Kant expressly states that, by itself, sensation amounts to only "a modification of the subject," "a mere affection of sensibility" (A 320/B 376), and that it does not involve any reference to an object (A 166–167, B 207–208). Indeed, sensations do not even appear in space or time. Since sensation takes place only at one moment or at each instant, it does not involve *successive* synthesis, and so it has no *extensive* magnitude. Rather, it has only an *intensive* magnitude, which can be measured by the extent to which something affects our senses (A 166–167, B 208–209). Furthermore, by themselves sensations do not even appear to consciousness, and they do so only by virtue of their synthesis according to rules. Kant reserves the term 'perception' (*Wahrnehmung*) for those sensations that are synthesized and finally appear to consciousness (A 166, 168/B 207, 209). So, properly speaking from the transcendental standpoint, what is given independent of the understanding are not representations but simply sensations, which are "blind" by themselves, having no meaning for us until they become representations of something.[18]

5. The Doctrine of Inner Sense

Although much of Kant's language can be reconciled with his critique of the way of ideas, there is still another side to his philosophy that seems to betray its deeper affinity with the subjectivist tradition. This is Kant's trying and troublesome notion of inner sense. One aspect of the earlier version of this theory in the first edition of the *Kritik* seems to place Kant firmly in the Cartesian tradition, for it states that we have an immediate knowledge only of our inner states.

What does Kant mean by inner sense? Kant gives little explicit account of it in the first *Kritik,* most probably because the term had been so widely used in eighteenth-century psychology. Following the lead of Locke's *Essay concerning human Understanding,* such thinkers as J. N. Tetens, Alexander Baumgarten, and Francis Hutcheson developed a theory of inner sense.[19] Locke had suggested that we could call the knowledge the mind acquires from reflection on its own operations *inner sense.* Though he recognized that such a term was purely metaphoric, Locke still thought it was apposite to describe the awareness of our inner states, because such awareness is a form of perception or experience rather than judgment or inference. For Locke, the theory of inner sense was deeply bound up with his allegiance to the Cartesian tradition, for it was through inner sense or reflection that we become aware of those ideas that are the immediate objects of all our thinking. Kant's retention of the concept of inner sense then raises the suspicion that it is a lingering element of subjectivism.

Sure enough, Kant's sketchy account of inner sense seems to follow in Locke's footsteps. In the first *Kritik* he defines inner sense very schematically and almost *en passant* as the *intuition* of ourselves or our inner state (A 22).[20] An intuition is a singular representation of an object, one that stands in a direct or immediate relation to it; a *concept* is a general representation of many particular representations, and so a mediate representation of an object.[21] So, in describing inner sense as an intuition, Kant seems to agree with Locke's thesis that the knowledge of inner states is a form of experience rather than of judgment or reasoning.

What Kant adds to the Lockean theory is his own view of the a priori status of time. Since our inner states are constantly changing, we perceive them in time; and since time, according to the Transcendental Aesthetic, is an a priori form of intuition, we must intuit these states according to such a form. Hence Kant states that time is the a priori form of inner sense (A 23). It is through inner sense, then, that the mind becomes self-conscious of its inner states in time, or that it becomes self-aware of the change in itself.[22]

To understand inner sense, we must distinguish it from other faculties of the mind. First, Kant contrasts *inner* with *outer* sense. If by inner sense we become conscious of states inside ourselves in time, by outer sense we become aware of objects outside ourselves in space. Hence space is the a priori form of outer sense as time is the a priori form of inner sense (A 22–23). Second, Kant also distinguishes inner sense from apperception, with which, he says, it is all too often confused (B 153–154). Both are forms of self-consciousness, but they differ in kind. Through the 'I think' of apperception I express my activity or spontaneity as a knowing subject; but through inner sense I know myself as passive and determined in time.[23] Apperception is an essentially *intellectual* faculty, the source of the application of the categories to experience; inner sense is an intrinsically *sensible* faculty, applying to intuitions the a priori form of time characteristic of human sensibility.

What motivates Kant's doctrine of inner sense is some of the logical peculiarities involved in empirical self-awareness. According to his theory, there are three central characteristics of such self-awareness. First, it is intuitive or experiential rather than intellectual or discursive because it does not involve, at least explicitly and consciously, judgment and reasoning. Hence Kant calls inner sense a form of *sense* (*Sinn*). Second, to know my inner states I do not use one of my outer senses; for example, when I focus my attention upon any of my mental activities, I do not become aware of it through seeing, touching, tasting, hearing, or smelling.[24] This is why my knowledge must be an *inner* rather than *outer* sense. Third, my inner states are temporal but nonspatial. They are temporal because they are constantly changing; but they are not spatial because I cannot assign a size, shape, or weight to them. Hence time rather than space is the form of inner sense.

The Cartesian interpretation of Kant's doctrine of inner sense is suggested by some passages in the Transcendental Aesthetic of the first edition of the *Kritik*. Here, unlike the argument of the Fourth Paralogism, Kant sometimes seems to give inner sense clear priority over outer. He now maintains that time is "the formal a priori condition of *all* appearances whatsoever," whereas space is the a priori condition "*only* of outer appearances" (A 34). The meaning of these lines seems tolerably clear: that we intuit all representations, even those of things in space, as in time, because all of them, as mental states, are changing. But Kant goes a step further. He is explicit that "time is the *immediate* condition of the inner appearances (of our souls), and thereby the *mediate* condition of outer appearances" (A 34). The precise purport of these lines is very unclear. But Kant seems to give epistemic priority to knowledge of our *representations* in time rather than to knowledge of the *objects* of these representations in space. While knowledge of these representations appears immediate and certain, knowledge of the objects of them seems mediate and inferential.

Such is the natural reading of this passage, and one sometimes given.[25] It is, however, a distortion of Kant's real meaning. That this is so becomes clear from the first edition of the Aesthetic itself, where Kant already anticipates the later argument of the Fourth Paralogism (A 38). In the Elucidation to Section II Kant argues that *both* space and time give us *immediate* certainty of their objects, so that we do not have to infer the existence of objects in space outside us (A 38). So, unless we are to attribute a gross inconsistency to Kant within the Aesthetic itself, we have to develop a different interpretation of his statement about the immediacy of inner sense.

We can understand what Kant means only when we consider the problem that arises for his view that the objects of inner sense are not spatial. Kant is clear that we do not see mental states as outside us in space anymore than we see objects in space as inside us in time (A 23, 357). Thus space and time are separated from one another as the respective forms of outer and inner sense. This raises the question: how do we see objects in space as in time? Clearly, Kant has to admit that we see objects in space in time, given such obvious facts as motion. Indeed, he does not deny the point. All that he wants to say is that such facts are constructions and not immediately given. We construct such facts as motion by attributing time to spatial objects according to the categories.

After considering this point, another more plausible reading of the passages in the Transcendental Aesthetic suggests itself. When Kant states that time is the immediate condition of inner appearances and the mediate condition of outer ones, he is not saying that we have *certainty* only about inner states and that we know of outer appearances only through *inference*. Kant is really only making a point about how we *attribute time* to outer appearances rather than about how we *know* outer appearances as such. The claim is that although we immediately perceive our inner states in time, we attribute this time to outer appearances only by virtue of the application of concepts. While the knowledge of spatial objects *throughout time* is constructed, this does not diminish the immediate certainty of knowledge of outer states *at any given moment;* it is only when we also see the outer state as *throughout time* that we must begin to apply the categories to them and the role of mediation or conceptualization begins. How such conceptualization occurs is, of course, a much longer story, shortly to be told in the Analytic and Principles. But the main point to see here is that the contrast between the immediate and mediate is not between *degrees of certainty*—the certain versus the inferred—but between *modes of cognition*—the intuitive versus the conceptual.

The advantage of this reading is that we can reconcile Kant's statement at

A 38 that both space and time give us an immediate certainty of their objects with his claim that time is the immediate condition of inner appearances and the mediate condition of outer. Seen in this light, Kant's theory of inner sense does not endorse but criticizes the subjectivist doctrine that we have an immediate awareness only of our inner states, for, true to the Fourth Paralogism, this theory holds that inner sense and outer sense are on a par in giving us equal knowledge of their objects.

6. Kantian Self-Knowledge and the Cartesian Tradition

There is another aspect to Kant's doctrine of inner sense that appears to be irreducibly and inexpungably subjectivist. This apparently ineliminable subjectivist element becomes plain as soon as we consider one of its immediate consequences: that we know ourselves only as appearances. Such a consequence follows directly from Kant's view that time is the a priori form of inner sense. To know ourselves, we must apply the form of inner sense to ourselves; but this form affects ourselves, so that we cannot know ourselves as we really are prior to such self-affection. Sure enough, Kant draws just this conclusion, and reasons in just this manner, in the second edition version of the Transcendental Aesthetic (B 67–69).

Such a result only seems to reveal Kant's abiding subjectivism, and indeed to carry the subjectivist tradition to its bitter extreme. Like Hume, Kant appears to be saying that we cannot know our real self anymore than things outside us. After all, the subjectivist holds that we know only representations, not even the self that has them.

It is important to see, however, that Kant is not claiming, as the subjectivist implies, that self-knowledge is illusory. Here again he maintains that we have *knowledge* of ourselves as we have of things in space, so that self-knowledge too has *empirical* reality. Kant places both self-knowledge and knowledge of external things on par insofar as they are both forms of knowledge conforming to the universal and necessary structure of experience. Both have *empirical* reality insofar as they conform to the conditions and limits of such a structure; but neither has *transcendental* reality because there is no reason to assume that the frameworks themselves, and indeed anything within them, corresponds with things-in-themselves.

Seen from another angle, Kant's theory of self-knowledge does not radicalize the subjectivist tradition but breaks with it. For not everyone in the subjectivist tradition drew the radical skeptical conclusions of Hume. If we consider Descartes, Leibniz, or Berkeley, we find them maintaining that there is an asymmetry between our self-knowledge and the knowledge of the external world: while we have direct and certain knowledge of ourselves, we know the external world only through indirect and uncertain inferences. Thus Descartes had argued that, though our knowledge of things in space is only of appearances, we have an immediate knowledge of ourselves as thinking things;[26] Berkeley insisted that we know ourselves as substances, though he vascillated about whether we know ourselves immediately or through inference;[27] and Leibniz stated unequivocally that "the existence of intelligible things, particularly of the I who thinks and is called a mind or soul, is incomparably more certain that the existence of sensible things."[28]

Kant's break with the subjectivist tradition consists in his disputing this asymmetry. We have already seen how he undermines this asymmetry in the Critique of the Fourth Paralogism by arguing that knowledge of external things is as certain as knowledge of ourselves. But Kant also rejects this asymmetry for the converse reason: he claims that knowledge of ourselves gives no more insight into reality in itself than knowledge of external things. This is indeed the flip side of the argument in the Critique of the Fourth Paralogism. For this argument has the effect not only of *upgrading* the certainty of our awareness of things in space, but also of *downgrading* self-awareness to the level of appearances. *Both* consciousness of our inner states and consciousness of things in space are certain, to be sure, but they are also only *of* appearances.

Of course, it is at least plausible to argue that, to some extent, Kant reinstates the Cartesian tradition in the first *Kritik* by giving pride of place to self-consciousness as the foundation of knowledge. In the Transcendental Deduction, in both the first and second editions, Kant makes the principle of the unity of apperception the basis for his deduction of the categories. This principle accords a central role to self-knowledge in all my consciousness since it states that my having a representation requires at least the possibility of my self-awareness of it. The Cartesian provenance of this principle becomes apparent from its most common formulation: alluding to Descartes' *cogito*, Kant states his principle in terms of the phrase 'I think' (*Ich denke*) (B 132).

Yet, for the more demanding and discerning Cartesian, Kant's apparent act of homage was a formal and empty gesture. While Kant does give self-consciousness a central role in the Transcendental Deduction, he is explicit and emphatic that such self-consciousness does not amount to the knowledge of my inner self, or to the awareness of some soul or substance. He insists repeatedly that the principle of the unity of apperception is purely formal, the condition under which I know anything in my experience—whether inner and outer—so that it should not be confused with any experience of an object itself (A 341, 343, 355). To assume that the self-knowledge that is the condition of my experience provides me with a knowledge of myself is indeed sheer hypostasis, the central fallacy exposed in the Paralogisms. Indeed, the whole thrust of the Paralogisms was anti-Cartesian: that the 'I think' cannot provide the basis for any doctrine about the substantiality, permanence, or personal identity of the soul.

Though it is a distinctive feature of his transcendental idealism, Kant's demotion of self-knowledge to the level of appearances plays a largely implicit role in the first edition of the *Kritik*. There Kant's aim was to show the parity of outer to inner sense rather than to downgrade the knowledge of both senses to the level of appearances. To be sure, Kant does affirm in the first edition that we can know ourselves only as appearances;[29] but nowhere does he stress its importance for his transcendental idealism.

The doctrine probably would have been left implicit and inchoate if it were not for the objections of H. A. Pistorius, who, in a review of the *Prolegomena*, confessed that he found the whole doctrine that we know ourselves only as appearances paradoxical.[30] If we know ourselves only as appearances, Pistorius argued, then we should know only our representations too as appearances, so that all we really know are appearances of appearances. Pistorius confessed that he did not understand Kant here, and he begged him to explain how appearances are possible if all knowledge of them is also only an appearance.

This request did not fall on deaf ears. In the second edition of the *Kritik* Kant added several sections to dispel the paradox.[31] That we know ourselves only as an appearance, he argued, is the inevitable outcome of any doctrine of inner sense, according to which the mind affects itself in the act of knowing itself. Such self-affection occurs in every act of attention, he explained, whenever the mind seeks out that which lies within itself, thereby determining how it appears to itself (B 68–69, 156–157). Kant admitted, however, that there is indeed something of a paradox to his theory: the self that knows itself is different from the self that is known, raising the question how there is self-knowledge at all. But he stressed, somewhat desperately, that these were problems inherent in any theory of self-knowledge (B 68, 155, 156–157n).

Kant's insistence in the second edition of the *Kritik* that we know ourselves only as appearances seems somewhat ironic in view of his later desperate efforts to distinguish his idealism from that of Berkeley. That Kant had radicalized Berkeley's subjectivism by denying knowledge even of the self was a point made by some of his early critics. The only explanation for the apparent irony must be that Kant did not believe his theory of self-knowledge had the skeptical consequences attributed to it. Kant could indeed maintain that his theory supported rather than undermined the reality of self-knowledge. There are reasons to have doubts about the reality of self-knowledge, Kant could argue, only if we demand that our representations correspond to some soul or substance behind them. Once we admit, however, that such a demand is inappropriate because we can never get outside our own representations, and once we recognize that knowledge of ourselves conforms to the universal and necessary order imposed by inner sense and the categories, then it is possible to accord *empirical* reality to self-knowledge as well as to knowledge of things in space outside us. Such a line of reasoning, though never explicitly developed by Kant, is implied by Kant's general position in the first *Kritik*. It at least explains Kant's readiness to stress that we know ourselves only as appearances amid his general attempt to distinguish his idealism from all forms of subjectivism in the second edition of the *Kritik*.

CHAPTER 8

The Transcendental Subject

1. Persistent Subjectivism

So far, we have examined some respects in which Kant's transcendental idealism is antisubjectivist. Whether by intention or implication, Kant breaks with some of the basic assumptions of the subjectivist tradition: that ideas are simple, given, and resemble objects; that the subject is transparent to itself; and that the subject knows its ideas with more certainty than objects in space, whose reality must be inferred from these ideas. Indeed, in fundamental respects, Kant turns the subjectivist tradition upside down, reversing the priority it once gave the subject over the object. No longer is the public world constructed from the ideas of the individual subject; rather, these ideas acquire their meaning, or represent something, only by virtue of their conformity to universal and necessary norms.

Kant's profound break with the subjectivist tradition raises the inevitable question: Is his transcendental idealism subjectivist at all? It is tempting to conclude, as some have done,[1] that Kant's subjectivism resides only in his retention of the language of the way of ideas, and that, stripped of such nomenclature, his philosophy cannot be properly labeled idealism at all. Yet such a conclusion would be premature. For all Kant's criticisms of the subjectivist tradition, there are still deep subjectivist strands to his philosophy.

One of these strands is Kant's qualified but persistent adherence to the subjectivist principle that the immediate objects of perception are only ideas. Of course, there is an important sense in which Kant breaks with this principle; but there is also another in which he retains, and indeed radicalizes, it. Kant's stance toward this principle is ambivalent, depending on the meaning given to the crucial term 'idea.' If ideas are taken to be the private data of an individual mind, from which the reality of the external world must be inferred or constructed, then Kant denies this principle. If, however, ideas are representations conforming to the intersubjective conditions of experience—the categories and the forms of space and time—then he affirms it. For Kant sometimes identifies the objects of awareness with appearances, which he says are only representations in us.[2]

That Kant reaffirmed the subjectivist principle becomes especially apparent when we consider the strategic use it had for him. This principle was his chief weapon against transcendental realism. When Kant identifies objects in space with representations he is basically making a point against transcendental realism: that appearances, or what we perceive, do not exist as things-in-themselves, because they would disappear without consciousness. In making this point, Kant forms a common cause with the subjectivist, who maintains that the objects of consciousness are not things-in-themselves. Like the subjectivist, Kant rejects direct realism; he too argues that what we perceive depends on the conditions of our perceiving it; hence he warns that we should not hypostatize the object of perception, as if it continues to exist independent of these conditions (A 384–385, 386). So, rather than completely rejecting the subjectivist principle, Kant is in one respect reaffirming it, and indeed generalizing it, so that it applies to the objects of outer sense (things in space) as well as objects of inner sense (things in time). Thus Kant parts company with the empirical idealist not in denying this principle but in extending it to the objects of outer sense; the empiricist idealist wants to restrict it to the objects of inner sense alone, as if these alone were known immediately, and as if the existence of objects of outer sense had to be inferred.[3]

Of course, Kant's agreement with the subjectivist against transcendental realism does not mean that he identifies appearances with representations in the same sense as the empirical idealist. As we have already seen, Kant's representations are not those of the subjectivist tradition: they are not given to consciousness, and they do not correspond to objects by some similarity to them. Rather, his representations are those analyzed in the Transcendental Deduction: they are produced by the synthetic activities of the understanding, and they correspond to objects by their conformity to rules. If we understand representations in this Kantian sense, the argument against transcendental realism still works; but it also does not commit Kant to empirical idealism. On the contrary, Kant is questioning one of the central assumptions of the empirical idealist: that representations are the private data of an individual mind, from which we have to infer or construct the reality of the external public world.

Another persistent strand of subjectivism in Kant's transcendental idealism appears from his analysis of objectivity. In both the first edition Transcendental Deduction and Critique of the Fourth Paralogism Kant argues that it is impossible for us to get outside our own representations to compare them with things-in-themselves (A 104–106).[4] Any comparison of our representations with an object will have to be nothing more than another representation (A 378, 376). The whole argument reaffirms a central premise behind Berkeley's polemic against dualism: that "an idea can be like nothing but an idea."[5] After making this argument, Kant draws a conclusion that the subjectivist too would endorse: that objectivity, the distinction between reality and dreaming, has to be explained within the realm of consciousness itself.

To be sure, Kant's use of this argument does not mean that he completely endorses the subjectivist account of objectivity. For Kant's account does not analyze the concept of an object into actual or possible representations, as if it were nothing more than a construction out of them. Rather, the concept of an object has priority over each particular representation, providing the conditions for its being a representation. According to Kant's analysis, each representation performs its role of representing an object only by virtue of its coherence with other representations according to a rule; it has no power to represent an object by virtue of its own nature alone. With this move Kant turns subjectivism upside down. Since these rules are universal and necessary, the public intersubjective world becomes the condition for the data of the private individual mind.

One way to formulate Kant's ambivalance toward subjectivism is to see it as a partial endorsement of the subjectivist claim about the *existence* of objects of experience, but also as a complete rejection of the subjectivist claim about their *essence*.[6] While the subjectivist is right to maintain that the *existence* of such objects is analyzable into a set of actual and possible representations, he is wrong to claim that their *essence* or *nature* is reducible to, or is only a construction of, particular representations. Clearly, there is a difference between claiming that the *existence* of an object depends on having actual or possible experiences, and claiming that objectivity simply *means* having such experiences. It is a simple distinction, but one often ignored, especially when scholars think that Kant's analysis of objectivity alone implies a rejection of subjectivism or phenomenalism *tout court*.[7]

2. Eliminating the Transcendental Subject

Apart from Kant's qualified endorsement of the subjectivist principle that what we perceive are ideas, there is another even deeper subjectivist dimension to his philosophy. This appears in the fundamental principle of the Transcendental Deduction: the unity of apperception. According to this principle, the 'I' of the 'I think' is inescapable and ineliminable: I cannot abstract from it, or think it away, because the very attempt to do so presupposes it. This 'I' is the necessary condition of all awareness, because a representation of which *I could not be aware* would be impossible, or at least nothing to me (B 131). So important is the principle for Kant that he declares the 'I think' to be "the highest principle of the understanding": it precedes or "accompanies" all representations, while no representation precedes or accompanies it (B 132, 135).

Such a principle has notable subjectivist implications. For Kant insists that the synthetic activity of the 'I' in appropriating the manifold of sensation is the source of all combination, and therefore the form of experience (B 130). This means that the form of experience is created by me, so that all appearances are only appearances *for me*. Of course, the 'I' in question here is not my personal and private self but my impersonal and public self (whoever that is); and these appearances are still intersubjective in the sense that they have a universal and necessary *validity* in conforming to the norms of the understanding, which hold for all human beings. Nevertheless, these appearances are still subjective in the sense that their *existence* depends on the subject who has them. In other words, if there were no subjects, there would be no appearances; so in this respect it would seem that transcendental idealism is properly described as idealism after all, and indeed a form of *subjective* idealism.

Still, there have been those who deny that, even to this limited extent, Kant's transcendental idealism is subjectivist. They maintain that the concept of the transcendental subject is incompatible with Kant's deeper principles, or with the ultimate meaning of his analysis of experience. If we follow these principles to their final conclusion, they argue, it becomes necessary to eliminate the transcendental subject entirely. All that we are then left with is the normative dimension of Kant's idealism. The forms of sensibility and understanding are now self-subsistent, existing independent of the subject who has them.

Advocates of the extreme antisubjectivist reading usually begin by pointing out the very peculiar status of the Kantian transcendental subject. As the referent of the 'I' of the 'I think,' the fundamental condition of experience, this subject cannot be individuated or identified as having a body. Because it is the condition of all such individuation and identification, it cannot be individuated and identified itself. To attempt to individuate or identify it simply presupposes it. But if it is not possible to individuate or identify it, how is it possible to say that it is a subject at all? Kant himself seems aware of this very point when he suggests characterizing the 'I' of the unity of apperception as even an "It" or "thing" that thinks (A 346/B 404). Some have argued that the concept of a subject makes sense only *within* the realm of possible experience, so that it is impossible to describe the condition of possible experience as a subject at all.[8] They contend that to be a subject means to be an individual person who has a determinate body somewhere in space and time; and they further point out that the very concept of subjectivity makes sense only in contrast to objectivity, a contrast that also works only within experience.

On these grounds it has been argued that there should be no subjective dimension to Kant's transcendental idealism. This was indeed one of the most powerful motives behind the formation of objective idealism, which is *inter alia* transcendental idealism without a subject. According to the objective idealists, the subjective falls entirely within the domain of experience, so that the conditions of experience cannot be regarded as subjective themselves (see below, 3.1.3). They ask: What is the point in calling the conditions of experience subjective when both the subjective and objective fall under these conditions and have their meaning only in contrast with one another? In their view, these conditions are better described as completely noumenal or intelligible, as the archetypes, ideas, or forms of things. Although they retain the concept of appearance, they alter its meaning: it is no longer the subjective as opposed to the objective but the phenomenal in contrast to the noumenal, the ectypical rather than the archetypical.

Lately, the subjective dimension of Kant's transcendental idealism has come in for some hard knocks from very different quarters. The recent trend of much Kant scholarship has been to make Kant safe for cognitive science. With that goal in mind, some scholars have been eager to reduce the

Kantian transcendental subject down to the more natural dimensions of its cognitive functions. They maintain that the unity of apperception designates only "the fact that cognitive states are connected to each other through syntheses required for cognition," but not "any awareness of a separate thing . . . or even that cognitive states belong to a separate thing, a self."[9] All that the Kantian subject amounts to, on one reading, is "the global representation, the single representation within which many of the usual denizens of a system of representations are all contained," or "a continuing interdependent system of representations."[10]

Although such an interpretation seems implausible or anachronistic from the perspective of traditional Kant scholarship, there is a sound motivation behind it. These scholars have come to their interpretation in the attempt to resolve a perennial dilemma facing any attempt to explain the Kantian transcendental subject: it is neither a bundle of impressions nor a single numerically identical substance. Their middle path between these extremes is the idea of a cognitive system. Since the units of such a system are "contentually interdependent," it is not simply a bundle of impressions; and since the system does not require a substrate behind it to function, it also is not a substance. The Kantian subject is then best seen as simply the entire functioning of such a system, or as some representation of such a system; in any case, it is not any entity above and beyond it.

Whether objective idealist or cognitive scientist, the aim has been to eliminate the Kantian transcendental subject. If it is banished, transcendental idealism loses every trace of subjectivism. For there simply will be no subject that is the source of the forms of experience, no subject for whom appearances exist. Detached from the subject, these forms have their own *sui generis* status, whether as archetypes or functions.

3. The Criteria of Subjectivity

There is some truth behind these antisubjectivist arguments. It is true that Kant's transcendental subject is no ordinary subject, given that it cannot be individuated or physically identified. Furthermore, because it is neither a substance nor a bundle of impressions, its ontological status remains obscure. Nevertheless, one goes too far in concluding that the subject should play no role in Kant's theory. Oddity alone gives no grounds for elimination. There are indeed important respects in which subjectivity remains an ineliminable feature of Kant's transcendental idealism. Arguably, it is one of its *defining* features, for Kant's transcendental idealism differs from objective idealism—and cognitive science—mainly in retaining a dimension of subjectivity.

Before we explain why subjectivity is irreducible, it is necessary to raise a crucial question: In what sense is Kant's transcendental subject subjective? Why did Kant think himself justified in referring to the transcendental 'I' as a subject? Why did he not always refer to it as "a thing," as he once suggested? This raises the more general question what Kant means by subjectivity or its synonyms: intelligence (*Intelligenz*), reason (*Vernunft*), or personality (*Persönlichkeit*).

Like many of his contemporaries, Kant maintains that one distinguishing characteristic of subjectivity is self-consciousness. The power of a human being to refer to itself as "I," he writes in the *Anthropologie*, is that which elevates it above all other earthly creatures (VII, 127). If self-consciousness is one defining condition of subjectivity, the transcendental subject meets this requirement. For Kant thinks that the 'I think' of the unity of apperception expresses self-consciousness. Of course, this is a very minimal form of self-consciousness—the possibility of recognizing that I have a representation—but it still seems enough to ascribe subjectivity to the transcendental 'I.'

Another distinguishing feature of subjectivity for Kant is freedom. He understands freedom in the very specific sense of autonomy, the power to create and act according to self-given laws. The importance of autonomy for subjectivity becomes very clear in the *Grundlegung zur Metaphysik der Sitten* where Kant states that the distinguishing characteristic of a rational being is its power to act not only according to laws but according to the very *idea* of a law (IV, 412, 427). It is indeed this very power to act according to the idea of a law, he adds, that is characteristic of the will (*Wille*).

Now it is striking that Kant also attributes this feature of subjectivity to the transcendental subject. This emerges from Kant's statement in the B Deduction that the 'I think' of the unity of apperception expresses "the act of determining my existence" or "the spontaneity of my thought" (B 157–158n). It is by virtue of this spontaneity, he says, that "I call myself an *intelligence*." The use of the term 'intelligence' (*Intelligenz*) here is crucial. For Kant, this is a technical term, designating the power of spontaneity and freedom distinctive of a rational being. In the second *Kritik* he explicitly defines *Intelligenz* in terms of autonomy, as "a being that is capable of actions according to the idea of law (a rational being)"(V, 125).

Kant's description of the transcendental subject as spontaneous is remarkable because it explicitly links this subject with the noumenal or intelligible realm. This is to make the 'I' of the 'I think' designate the subject as noumenon or thing-in-itself. *Prima facie* such an interpretation should not be controversial because there are passages in the first *Kritik* where Kant makes just this identification (B 520, 574). But this reading becomes problematic as soon as we consider that there are other passages where Kant expressly states that the 'I think' does *not* give knowledge of the subject as either phenomenon or noumenon (B 157, 423n). It then seems necessary to distinguish the *transcendental* self, which is a mere "logical subject," from the *noumenal* self, which is a thing-in-itself. Such a distinction seems necessary not least because of Kant's arguments in the Paralogisms, which forbid all metaphysical inferences from the 'I think.'

Still, Kant's texts can be made consistent, and the lesson of the Paralogisms observed, provided that we recognize one simple point: that although the 'I' of the 'I think' does indeed designate the noumenal subject, this principle alone does not give us grounds *to know* it. The force of Kant's argument at B 157 and B 423n is only that I cannot *know* myself as a thing-in-itself from the 'I think,' not that the 'I' must designate a special kind of subject, no matter how sparse or formal. Those who invent a third transcendental self in addition to the noumenal and phenomenal selves therefore only multiply entities beyond necessity.

According to this reading, then, the 'I' of the unity of apperception is just the noumenal self in its transcendental role. As far as we know, it designates only "that which experiences," and as such it is only a "logical subject"; but this does not mean that it somehow designates some new kind of subject distinct from the noumenal self. Still less does it mean that the 'I' has no referent, as if it were a purely "formal requirement" of experience, for Kant is perfectly clear that the 'I think' gives me knowledge of my *existence* as a spontaneous self (B 157–158n, 423n).

4. The Subjectivity of the Transcendental

Granted that self-consciousness and spontaneity are the distinguishing traits of subjectivity, the question still remains: What justifies Kant in attributing these characteristics to the transcendental 'I'? The problem has not been resolved but only deepened because, *on Kant's own principles*, it seems impossible to ascribe these very properties to the transcendental subject. Of course, the principle of the unity of apperception expresses one form of self-consciousness; but Kant insists that it is only the self-consciousness *that* I exist, not *how* I exist (B 157–158n). On its own, this principle expresses a merely formal requirement of experience: that all representations have a subject. But it does not tell us anything about the nature of the subject. Indeed, in the Paralogisms, Kant expressly and emphatically argues that the transcendental subject cannot know itself, for, as the condition under which the categories are applied to experience, it cannot in turn become an object of experience (B 422, A 346, 366, 402). Kant's general constraints on knowledge also mean that the subject cannot know itself as a free or spontaneous being. He holds that self-knowledge, like all knowledge, requires the application of the categories; but to apply the categories to myself is to make myself passive and determined, given that anything that falls under the categories is determined according to the principle of sufficient reason.

For these reasons, the transcendental subject appears unknowable, a mysterious entity, which Kant appropriately designates with the symbol 'X.' If, however, the transcendental subject is unknowable, then we cannot attribute self-knowledge or spontaneity to it, which are Kant's own criteria of subjectivity. So, again, we are left with the question: Why is the 'I' not simply "a thing" or "it" that thinks?

Kant does have an answer to this question, though it is not developed systematically and lies buried in a few methodological remarks in the first *Kritik*. He thinks that he has sufficient grounds to ascribe subjectivity to the 'I' simply from its *transcendental* role in grounding experience. This 'I' cannot ascribe personality or substantiality to itself, to be sure, but it can regard itself as subjective because both self-consciousness and spontaneity are necessary conditions of possible experience. If we view these conditions purely transcendentally, as necessary conditions of possible experience, then ascribing them to the subject does not make any transcendent metaphysical claims about noumena.

That self-consciousness is a necessary condition of experience is already clear from the principle of the unity of apperception itself. According to this principle, the subject can have representations, and so experience, only if it is possible for it to be self-conscious of them; if it could not recognize the representations as its own, they could not represent anything at all for it. While such self-consciousness does not give the subject knowledge of its inner properties, it does express one fundamental condition of the possibility of experience. Hence the analysis of possible experience alone gives reason to ascribe self-consciousness to the subject.

That spontaneity is a necessary condition of experience is also evident from the unity of apperception. This principle, Kant says, expresses "an act of spontaneity" (B 132, 157–158n), an act that is the source of the synthetic activity of the understanding, the very activity that creates the form and structure of experience. It is only in virtue of its spontaneity, Kant contends, that the 'I' synthesizes its representations, and so establishes order and connection among them (A 125, B 129). There are places in the A Deduction where Kant maintains that the self somehow *sees* its spontaneity in the act of synthesizing its representations (A 108, 116). This suggests something almost mystical, as if the self knew its spontaneity without qualification. But it is important to keep these passages in context. The subject knows that it is spontaneous not insofar as it is the source of free actions, but solely insofar as it is the source of the forms of experience. Furthermore, it is their source not in the sense that it literally creates or makes them, but only in the sense that it can explicitly bring to self-awareness what is entirely innate within itself. Just as I can excogitate the rules of logic by reflecting on the rules implicit within my reasoning, so I can produce the forms of understanding and intuition by reflecting on the necessary conditions of my experience.

It is a common point that Kant thinks the activity of the 'I' is utterly obscure in its *moral* role. Though perfectly correct, this point is exaggerated, so that it seems as if the activity of this 'I' is completely mysterious in all its roles. This tends to overshadow the fact that Kant assumes just the opposite about the activity of the 'I' in its *transcendental* role: that it is completely transparent to itself. The self-transparency of the subject—one of the hallmarks of the subjectivist tradition—then returns to Kant's philosophy on a metacritical level. This reappearance of the self-transparent subject is especially clear from the prefaces to the *Kritik* where Kant is concerned to explain the possibility of transcendental knowledge. Reason is self-explaining and self-illuminating, he contends, since it knows whatever it creates, and its creative activity is completely apparent to itself (A xx, B xiii, xxviii). "Nothing escapes us, because what reason produces entirely out of itself cannot be concealed, but is brought to light by reason as soon as one has discovered its common principle" (A xx). In the Amphiboly Kant even invents a name for the method by which the subject recreates the forms of its activity and assigns them to their respective source: transcendental reflection (B

316–319, 325, 351). It is through transcendental reflection that the subject knows its own spontaneous activity insofar as it becomes embodied in the forms of experience.[11] There is indeed no mystery how the subject knows itself in its transcendental role, Kant later argues, because here there is not really a distinction between the subject and object at all (B 505). The spontaneous subject knows its own creative activity for the simple reason that, in this singular case, it creates what it knows. To know that I act, I only have to act, and so I create what it is that I know, namely, activity. This is not to ascribe an intellectual intuition to myself because I still do not know myself as an object, but only as that activity that constitutes itself through the forms of experience.

It could be argued, however, that even this minimal form of transcendental self-knowledge goes beyond Kant's own critical limits. Although Kant is careful to say that the 'I think' gives me knowledge not *how* but only *that* I exist as a spontaneous subject, he still makes a transcendent claim for the simple reason that existence too is a category. But Kant is aware of this very problem, duly addressing it in a footnote to the second edition of the Paralogisms. In this case existence does not function in its normal role as a category, he explains, because there is no determinate object in intuition to which it is applied (B 423n). The 'I think' expresses only an "indeterminate empirical intuition" in the sense that it designates "something that in fact exists," even though it is given neither as noumenon nor as phenomenon but only to "thinking in general." Although Kant's reply seems evasive and *ad hoc*, there is a solid rationale behind it. Kant is saying that to know itself in its transcendental role the subject only has *to think* itself according to the categories—there is no need for a specific intuition—because the subject's activity is examined only insofar as it creates and acts according to them. The transcendental subject is purely formal in the sense that its activity is expressed through and constituted by the forms of experience. Since its existence is so limited, such a formal subject can be known purely formally, that is, through unschematized categories. Hence the intuition of its existence will be "indeterminate" and given only to "thinking in general."

Kant himself insisted that the subject's self-knowledge in its transcendental role gave it no basis for self-knowledge in its moral role. It was for this reason that he abandoned the precritical doctrine that apperception provides proof of spontaneity, and it was for this reason that he maintained he had established only the *possibility* of freedom in the first *Kritik*. The proof for spontaneity in the moral sense would have to wait for the second *Kritik*, where the *ratio cognoscendi* of freedom is found in the moral law. Nevertheless, it should be clear that Kant's denial of a proof of freedom in the first *Kritik* did not prevent him from attributing spontaneity to the transcendental subject.[12]

5. Restoring the Transcendental Subject

Granted that Kant has some reason to regard his transcendental 'I' as a subject, why should this subject remain irreducible and ineliminable? This raises two more specific questions that are closely connected. First, why must it be transcendental and not just phenomenal? Second, why should it be more than simply the system of its representations, or more than a special kind of representation?

The most obvious reason the transcendental subject cannot be phenomenal lies with its spontaneity. According to Kant's argument in the Third Antinomy, spontaneity is impossible within the phenomenal realm where every event happens according to the category of causality. Spontaneity involves *unconditioned causality*, the power to begin a causal series without a prior cause; but the category of casuality implies that every event happens of necessity because of other events prior in time (B 476). So, contrary to those critics who think that transcendental-noumenal status is incompatible with subjectivity, Kant insists that such status is not only compatible with, but even necessary to, subjectivity.

Of course, this point has not been lost on Kant's critics. They still maintain, however, that there are overwhelming reasons against granting transcendental status to the Kantian subject. They argue that since Kant makes all kinds of claims about the subject, and since these claims must take place according to the categories, all of whose objects are phenomenal, it follows that the subject also must be something phenomenal.[13] Hence the price of insisting on the transcendental status of the subject would be complete silence, the abandonment of transcendental philosophy itself.

But such an argument rides roughshod over two of Kant's careful distinctions. First, it ignores his distinction between thinking and knowing an object according to the categories, a distinction that makes it possible to think about nonphenomenal objects. Second, it confuses his distinction between the transcendental and the empirical, or between second-order discourse about the conditions of our knowledge of things and first-order discourse about these things themselves. Since transcendental discourse does not deal with objects but with the conditions of our *knowledge* of objects, its subject matter is not some kind of entity, whether that is noumenal or phenomenal.

Rather, its object is nothing less than the pure forms of experience, which we can reconstruct simply by reflecting on the forms inherent in our perception and practices. Insofar as the subject is involved at all, it is only in its transcendental role as that which acts according to these forms.

The other less obvious reason the transcendental subject cannot be phenomenal rests with its self-consciousness. In the Paralogisms, in both the first and second editions, Kant argues that the subject that is the condition of all awareness cannot be—except on pain of circularity—an object of awareness. Any attempt to make the transcendental subject an object of the categories is to reason in a circle, given that it is this very subject that makes it possible for anything to be an object of the categories (B 422, A 346, 366).

Hence the main reason the transcendental subject is an irreducible and ineliminable dimension of Kant's transcendental idealism ultimately rests with its two distinguishing characteristics: spontaneity and self-consciousness.[14] Such a subject cannot be reduced to a system of representations, and still less a special kind of representation, because it is that which can be self-conscious of, and also that which produces, any representation, and indeed the entire system of representations. What is aware of having representations, and what plays a role in producing them, cannot be merely the system of representations, and still less just a special kind of representation. To make any such identification is to fly in the face of a common Kantian argument: that the conditions of experience cannot be given within it.

While these points are sometimes acknowledged, it is still replied that they do not prove the case for irreducibility. It is only necessary to enrich the concept of a cognitive system, it has been argued, to do justice to these features of the Kantian subject. Cognitive systems are not only dynamic, but even self-reflexive, so that there is no need to place spontaneity and self-consciousness in some transcendental realm; rather, they can be directly attributed to the system itself.[15]

Perhaps these are indeed properties of cognitive systems. Whether this is so obviously raises larger questions that cannot be pursued here. Suffice it to say now that this is not a *Kantian* view about them. Such a contention runs up against Kant's constraints on reflective judgment in the third *Kritik*. In §65 and §73 of that work,[16] Kant provides strong reasons for thinking that we cannot ascribe self-awareness and spontaneity to an organism—the eighteenth-century analogue of a cognitive system—in a constitutive sense, and that we can do so only in a regulative one. In other words, we are justified in treating an organism only *as if* it were spontaneous and reflective.

The main thrust of Kant's arguments is that we can ascribe *self*-generation, *self*-organization, and indeed *self*-consciousness to an organism only by analogy with our own selves. We only project these human attributes onto the organism, because it is impossible to acquire sufficient empirical evidence that it really has them.

Assuming, for all these reasons, that the Kantian transcendental subject is irreducible and ineliminable, the problem still remains of accounting for its peculiar status. If it is impossible to reduce the Kantian subject down to a system of representations, it is also incorrect to inflate it into a metaphysical entity. Kant not only rejects Humean empiricism, which would reduce the subject to a collection of impressions, but he also repudiates Wolffian rationalism, which would make the subject into a single permanent substance. What, then, is the middle path between reduction and inflation, phenomenalism and metaphysics? How is it possible to keep the transcendental subject and to forestall inferences about the existence of a single numerically identical substance?

The answer to these questions comes when we identify the transcendental subject with that agent that performs the roles, functions, or tasks necessary for the possibility of experience. On the hand, this subject is not simply reducible to these roles, functions, or tasks, because it is the agent behind them, that which executes them. But, on the other hand, there is no commitment to a single numerically identical and enduring substance behind this agency: there could be many numerically distinct but related selves that perform them. While Kant holds that the 'I' of the unity of apperception is a referring expression, he simply leaves it open to what it refers, and he even admits that it could be nothing more than a series of selves whose experiences are communicated to one another (A 353, 363–364n). Whatever this subject might be in itself, the transcendental philosopher maintains a strict agnosticism about it, claiming to know it only as that X that performs certain functions. He makes no claims about its nature beyond these functions; and indeed he does not even claim that it must have an unknowable nature beyond them. All that he says is that, *as far as I know*, this subject is only what enacts these roles and tasks.

Sometimes, when faced with all the difficulties of making the transcendental subject safe for cognitive science, the cognitive scientists frankly admit that their interpretation is revisionist rather than historical.[17] They concede that their aim is not to reconstruct what Kant said, but what he meant or *ought to* have said. But the crucial question to ask here is: *According to whose principles?* It is tendentious in the extreme for them to say that their interpretation represents what Kant ought to have said according to *his* principles, especially when placing the Kantian subject in the phenomenal world deprives it of its transcendental and moral status.

In general, we must beware of cutting Kant into contemporary shapes and sizes according to what he ought to have said in some modern discipline. This is fine provided that we distinguish sharply between the historical Kant and the contemporary Kant; but this is done too little, and we are too often made to think of Kant as the greatest protocognitive psychologist, as if he not only anticipated cognitive psychology but even superseded it. Alas, those who preach to cognitive psychology about what it has to learn from Kant have really told us more about what Kant should have learned from cognitive psychology.

CHAPTER 9

The Status of the Transcendental

1. The Problematic Status of the Categories

Concerning the objective or subjective nature of Kant's transcendental idealism, there is no more important issue than the status of the categories themselves. We have already seen that the categories are not simply representations but the *rules* or *norms* governing representations (1.7.3). But this is hardly a sufficient account of them. For, granted that the categories are norms, how are we to understand them? Are they mental functions, "laws of thought"? Or is their status independent of all psychology? If so, how are we to interpret their extrapsychological status? Is it logical, epistemological, or metaphysical?

Subjectivists and objectivists have been deeply divided over these questions. Subjectivists have always advocated the psychological interpretation. They stress that the categories are only mental functions or faculties, so that they have no validity apart from our manner of conceiving things. The objectivists have always championed the nonpsychological interpretation; but they have rarely agreed about precisely how to characterize the nonpsychological status of norms. Some give them a purely logical status, so that they are nothing more than fundamental presuppositions of empirical judgment;[1] others regard them as "epistemic conditions," as necessary conditions of our representing things;[2] and still others see them as having a metaphysical status as the ideas, forms, or archetypes of things.[3]

The issue surrounding the status of the categories raises another hoary and tricky question: the relation between psychology and epistemology in Kant's critical philosophy. There can be no doubt that Kant's main concern in the *Kritik* is epistemological, at least in the very vague and general sense that his aim is to determine the *validity* of synthetic a priori judgments. But the question remains: What role does Kant's transcendental psychology play in this epistemological enterprise? Is it a necessary part of his epistemological task? Or is it completely superfluous? Here again scholars are divided. There are those who insist that the psychological dimension of the critique is ineliminable, playing a necessary role in Kant's transcendental idealism;[4] and there are those who insist that it is superfluous, masking or betraying Kant's essential epistemological goals.[5]

The questions concerning the status of the categories raise an even broader issue: What is the transcendental? This is a wider issue since Kant uses the term "transcendental" to refer to *all* the necessary conditions of experience, whether they are the a priori forms of the understanding (the categories) or the a priori forms of sensibility (space and time). What Kant meant by this term is obviously crucial for understanding his *transcendental* idealism. But in his first *Kritik* Kant gives us only the sketchiest account of the meaning of this term. He tells us that the transcendental concerns not objects themselves but the conditions of our *a priori knowledge* of objects (B 25), and that it deals with not the nature of things but the *understanding that judges* about the nature of things (B 26). But how are we to understand these conditions for a priori knowledge? Are they psychological, metaphysical, or logical? In some respects each of these characterizations seems to be accurate; in other respects each seems to be misleading.

2. The Metaphysical Interpretation

One of the most common interpretations of the transcendental understands it in metaphysical terms, so that the categories are the intelligible structures, forms, or archetypes behind experience. This is how Kant's categories were transformed in the late eighteenth century by the objective idealists—by Hölderlin, Schelling, and Hegel—who freed the categories from their subjective moorings and made them into Platonic or Aristotelian forms constitutive of reality itself. The objective idealists argued that the categories could not arise from the knowing subject because, as necessary conditions of experience, they precede and make possible subjectivity itself. Both the subject and the object fall within experience, so that these necessary conditions of experience cannot be conceived as either subjective or objective; rather, they belong to the realm of the intelligible or noumenal, which is neither subjective nor objective though it appears equally in both. This interpretation of Kant has not lacked modern protagonists, since it can be found, more or less, among the Marburg neo-Kantians and the British Hegelians.[6] Perhaps its last major exponent was Norman Kemp Smith.[7]

Because it seems so flatly contrary to Kant's intentions, the metaphysical interpretation appears scarcely plausible. If the categories are forms or archetypes, it seems as if we blatantly violate Kant's express teachings about the limits of knowledge. It appears as if we go beyond the transcendental realm, which is limited to possible experience, and enter into a dangerous transcendent one, which lies beyond experience. Even worse, such an interpretation appears to commit that fallacy that Kant exposed in the Dialectic of the first *Kritik*: hypostasis, the reification of the conditions of experience. If the categories are conditions under which anything becomes an object of experience, they cannot be objects in their own right. Last but not least, this interpretation seems to run counter to Kant's firm distinction between the categories and the ideas: while the categories have a constitutive status because they are necessary conditions of experience, the ideas or archetypes have a purely regulative status because they cannot be schematized in experience itself.

The metaphysical interpretation seems even less plausible when we recall Kant's explicit repudiation of the metaphysical interpretation of his transcendental idealism in the *Prolegomena*. There Kant blasted the interpretation of his philosophy as a form of Platonism, firmly dissociating it from the doctrine that true reality lies in the intelligible realm alone. Clearly and categorically, Kant denied any knowledge of an intelligible realm, insisting instead that the place of his philosophy lay in the "bathos of experience." Indeed, on just these grounds, he revoked the term "transcendental" to describe his idealism because it suggested something lying beyond the realm of the senses. It is more accurate, he stressed, to describe his system as *critical* idealism because its main concern is with the conditions of the knowledge of objects rather than with the objects themselves (IV 293–294, 373–374n).

It is not clear, however, that these apparent problems are decisive. Much still could be said in behalf of the metaphysical interpretation. At least some of the most common objections against it are misconceived. For one thing, it is a mistake to object that it commits a paralogism, as if it hypostatizes the conditions of experience; for the metaphysicians do not understand the categories as objects in the empirical sense, though these are the only objects that presuppose the categories. Rather, they stress that the categories are not entities at all but simply the intelligible form or structure of experience that all entities instantiate or exemplify. This structure does not have a mental or physical status, they further argue, because it consists in the *conditions* under which anything appears to inner and outer sense.

Furthermore, it is also problematic to insist on Kant's distinctions between categories and ideas. For the metaphysicians' point is precisely that this distinction breaks down. They insist that their ideas play the same transcendental role as the categories: they too are necessary conditions of possible experience. And since such conditions are also necessary conditions of the *objects* of experience, the ideas should have the same objective validity as the categories. The whole matter becomes more complicated and compromised for the orthodox Kantian when we consider that Kant himself, in the Appendix to the Transcendendental Dialectic, made principles of reason into necessary conditions of experience and gave them a constitutive status.[8]

The metaphysical interpretation is indeed unsound if its advocates claim that the categories are Platonic archetypes that exist independent of experience. Since Kant insists that the categories are valid only as necessary conditions of experience, this would be to transcend his critical limits. It is not always or necessarily the case, however, that the metaphysician makes such a strong claim. His point is that there is no fundamental distinction between ideas and categories because both are necessary conditions of experience. He would be violating the spirit of Kant's philosophy only if he were to claim some intellectual intuition for the existence of the archetypes; but the metaphysician need not do this. His main defense of the idea is perfectly Kantian because he claims that they too can have their own transcendental deduction when they are necessary conditions of experience.

3. The Psychological Interpretation

According to the subjectivist reading, the categories are nothing more than "laws of thought," the necessary modes of operation of our cognitive constitution. It is precisely the psychological status of the categories, the subjectivist argues, that ensures their subjective status, their limitation to how we conceive of the world. The subjectivist might admit, therefore, that the categories are not simply representations but the rules governing them; nevertheless, he will add that this gives them no extrasubjective status because these rules determine only how we conceive the world.

While there is something to be said for the psychological interpretation, as we shall see below (1.9.5), it still cannot be a *complete* explanation for a very simple reason: it fails to do justice to the specifically normative dimension of the categories. Simply because they are normative, the categories determine the conditions for how someone *ought to think* rather than how they *happen to think,* or even how they *must do so.* Kant himself often stressed this point with regard to the laws of logic, the formal basis of the categories. He insisted in the *Kritik* that logic "draws nothing from psychology"; and in the *Logik* he is even more explicit: "Some logicians presuppose psychological principles in logic; but to bring such principles into logic is as absurd as deriving morals from life" (IX, 14). Similarly, in the third *Kritik* he criticized the psychological interpretation of regulative maxims on the grounds that they do not tell us how we *happen* to judge but how we *ought* to do so (V, 182). For these reasons alone, it is unfair to suspect Kant of the fallacy of psychologism, the attempt to base logic on psychological laws.

It might be countered, however, that the Kantian categories are really not properly speaking normative at all. They could be normative only if they were imperatives; but they are imperatives only if we could somehow fail to comply with them, which is not really the case. We cannot but conform to the categories, for they are necessary to and constitutive of any possible experience. They are not like the laws of logic, which are indeed normative, but only because it is possible for us *not* to comply with them, as, for example, when we commit a fallacy for want of attention to the rules of inference.

Though the categories are indeed necessary conditions of experience, it is also noteworthy that they provide rules of judgment to apply in particular cases. While we necessarily follow them in having experience of the world, it is not necessarily the case that we always heed them in conscious acts of judgment. We can indeed lapse into fallacies—transcendental illusions—if we attempt to extend them as rules of judgment beyond their appropriate domain in possible experience. Hence the categories do have a normative meaning after all, at least when we consider them as rules of judgment rather than as conditions of experience.

There is a more modern psychological reading of the normative that explains it according to the concepts of cognitive science.[9] On this interpretation, the categories are mental *functions* that essentially consist in the forms of mental processing necessary to achieve cognitive tasks. This reading has several strengths. First, in appealing to functions rather than representations, it does justice to Kant's insistence that we understand the categories as rules. Uncannily, Kant himself seems to anticipate the functionalist reading when he describes judgment as a "function of unity"(B 93–94). Second, it explains the psychological dimension of Kant's transcendental discourse without postulating metaphysical causes, or even without referring to psychological processes. A function, we are often told, "transcends its tokens," the specific events that instantiate it. Third, it accounts for the normative because a function involves a task, which involves standards and purposes.

Still, there are reasons to doubt whether this interpretation too provides a *complete* explanation of the normative or transcendental. For one thing, the very concept of a mental function is essentially derivative, depending upon the normative rather than *vice versa*, because we identify a function in terms of the requirements of a task or role. Hence the explanation of the normative in terms of the functional proves to be circular. For another thing, Kant is not especially concerned with the mental processes, or causal conditions, involved in performing tasks or following these roles.[10] Rather, his main interest is in identifying the standards and roles themselves. But if this is the case, the question remains: In what sense is Kant doing psychology at all?

Any psychological account of Kant's transcendental discourse must be careful to avoid burdening it with the fallacy of psychologism. This desideratum is flaunted, however, as soon as we claim that Kant's ultimate response to the *quid juris?* is "We can do no other."[11] If the necessity is only one of psychological constitution—our faculties cannot function otherwise—then it becomes simply a contingent fact about our human nature. But Kant explicitly rejected such a result, and for two very instructive reasons. First, he insisted that the principles of logic, and the categories based on them, are valid for any rational being and not only our human nature. Second, he recognized that all appeals to the subjective necessities of our own nature—whether based on innate ideas or habits of association—could never establish claims to objective validity, for the question remained whether these necessities corresponded to anything in nature itself. Hence psychologism begged the question against the Humean skeptic.[12]

These difficulties of the psychological reading of the categories reveals one of the main shortcomings of the subjectivist interpretation. While this interpretation might be correct in seeing the categories as laws of our cognitive constitution, it does not follow from this that they have only a subjective validity, as if they were only subjective dispositions of our nature. Such an interpretation fails to account for the claims to *objective* validity of the categories, that is, their validity for all rational beings, and their truth for experience itself. To establish the objective validity of the categories—to show that they are not only subjective necessities of our nature but true of objects of experience itself—was precisely the goal of all Kant's labors in the Transcendental Deduction. Of course, it is possible that the Deduction fails, so the subjectivist interpretation is correct after all. But then the subjectivist must first contend with the Deduction itself.

4. The Logical Interpretation

The main danger of both metaphysical and psychological interpretations of the transcendental is that they fail to do full justice to Kant's explicit definition of the transcendental. Though dense and brief, this definition has to be constantly held in view: "I entitle *transcendental* all knowledge which is occupied not so much with objects as with the mode of our knowledge of objects insofar as this mode is to be possible a priori" (B 25). The immediate purport of Kant's statement is that transcendental discourse is essentially *second-order*, dealing not with the world itself but with our knowledge of the world. If we take this statement at its full value, then it means that transcendental philosophy does not deal with any specific kind of entity, whether that be noumenon or phenomenon.[13] Hence we should beware of interpreting the transcendental as if it concerns either archetypes (the metaphysical interpretation) or even the mind itself (the psychological interpretation); for both interpretations fail to consider the second-order status of transcendental discourse.

It is important to recognize, however, that there are different interpretations of the second-order status of Kant's transcendental discourse. We can read this second-order status in *epistemological* terms, so that it deals with *cognition* about the world rather than the world itself; or we can construe it in *logical* terms, so that it is concerned with *judgments* about the world instead of the world itself. It could be argued such second-order status has a strict logical rather than epistemological meaning because the epistemological still deals with faculties and activities, which are still something first-order within the world itself.[14]

There is some good evidence for the strict logical interpretation of the transcendental, which appears confirmed by some of Kant's own statements about the general purpose of transcendental philosophy. One of these statements appears in the preface to the first edition of the *Kritik* where Kant describes the critique of pure reason as a "tribunal" to judge the claims of reason according to "its own eternal laws" (A xi–xii, B 799). To judge the claims of reason is an essentially logical enterprise, involving assessing whether there is sufficient evidence for certain propositions. Another statement emerges in §13 of the Analytic where Kant distinguishes sharply between the *quid juris?* and *quid facti?*, the question of the justification of a principle and the question of its origins (B 126–124). Kant then makes it perfectly clear that his main interest in the Transcendental Deduction is with the *quid juris?* While Kant insists elsewhere that his answer to the *quid facti?* is "of great importance for my chief purpose," he also stresses that "it does not form an essential part of it," and that it is indeed somewhat "hypothetical in character," for his central concern is to determine what the understanding can know apart from experience and not to discover the sources of thinking itself (A xvii).

Both of these passages seem to show that Kant's investigation is second-order in the strict logical sense. They state that what the critique investigates are *claims to knowledge*, and that its central concern is with the *justification* for some of our beliefs. Hence the main issue for Kant seems to be whether we have *sufficient evidence* for some of our fundamental principles, more specifically synthetic a priori ones, which are especially problematic because they cannot be justified by experience or the laws of logic alone. Seen in this light, Kant's chief business is not psychological but logical in a very strict sense. That is to say, his central concern is not with the *activities* of knowing, and still less with the *origins* or *causes* of these activities, but with the *truth or falsity* of judgments, and more specifically synthetic a priori judgments.

If we are to interpret the transcendental in the strict logical sense, then the necessary conditions of experience should determine the *truth-conditions* of our making more specific judgments. Sure enough, Kant sometimes regards a necessary condition of experience as a specific kind of synthetic a priori *principle*, namely one that establishes the general truth-conditions for all specific synthetic judgments, whether a priori or a posteriori. Among these principles are the axioms of intuition ("all intuitions are extensive magnitudes"), the anticipations of perception ("all intutions are intensive magnitudes"), and the analogies of experience ("In all change of appearances substance is permanent," "all changes take place according to the law of cause and effect"). These principles lay down only necessary or minimal conditions for the truth of these judgments in the sense that if they were false, then these specific synthetic judgments would be also false; but if they are true, it does not follow that these judgments are also true. To determine the truth or falsity of specific synthetic judgements it is necessary to consult experience or resort to mathematical construction.

According to this logical reading, then, the transcendental consists in those synthetic a priori principles necessary for the truth of other judgments, principles that cannot themselves be dependent on any higher principles. This is indeed just how Kant explains the a priori in one striking passage: "Principles a priori are so named not merely because they contain in themselves the grounds of other judgments, but also because they are not themselves grounded in higher and more universal cognitions" (B 188). In this sense the transcendental is normative because these principles lay down the minimal *desiderata* or *standards* for making true synthetic judgments.

Further confirmation for the logical reading of the transcendental—a point too often passed over in psychological interpretations—comes from the fact that the model for Kant's transcendental discourse is formal logic. In the preface to the first edition of the *Kritik* Kant is explicit that the critique of pure reason can achieve certainty and completeness because, like logic, it deals with nothing but "reason itself and its pure thinking." "Common logic itself supplies an example," he writes, "how all the simple acts of reason can be enumerated completely and systematically" (A xiv). In the second edition preface Kant further explains that logic is the paradigm of a complete science, because it deals with the pure forms of thought regardless of its content (B ix). Transcendental philosophy has similar hopes of becoming a science because it too deals with synthetic a priori knowledge, which also has its origins entirely in the thinking subject. Like logic, its methodology is essentially one of conceptual analysis. Hence Kant explains that completeness in the critique is perfectly possible because its knowledge is "derived solely from pure concepts" (A xx). In general, he maintains that philosophical knowledge is "knowledge gained by reason from concepts" (B 741).

The primacy of the logical in Kant's transcendental discourse also becomes clear from his few remarks on transcendental method in the first *Kritik:* his account of *transcendental reflection* in the Amphiboly of the Concepts of Reflection (B 316–319). *Prima facie* Kant's account of his method is entirely psychologistic. He explains that the task of transcendental reflection is to determine the specific *faculty* to which a representation belongs. While *logical* reflection does not consider the *origin* of a representation but simply compares it with other representations, *transcendental* reflection not only compares representations among themselves but also considers their *source*, the specific *faculty* to which they belong. Nevertheless, the essentially logical interest behind transcendental reflection finally and fully emerges when Kant states that its aim is to prevent dialectical illusion. We need to determine whether a representation belongs to understanding or sensibility, so that we do not draw conclusions beyond the kind of evidence each faculty warrants. Ultimately, then, Kant's main purpose is to prevent fallacies rather than to understand mental activities. In the final analysis, the logical precedes the psychological because it is logical form or the type of discourse, rather than the origin or genesis, that determines the specific faculty to which a representation belongs. All too often Kant's talk of a faculty is simply a metaphor for a type of discourse or evidence.

5. The Ineliminable Psychological Dimension

Although we have to understand Kant's transcendental discourse in essentially logical terms, and as such concerned with the truth-conditions of judgments, it does not follow that we must explain it *entirely* or *exclusively* in such terms. Indeed, there is good reason to hold that we cannot, and indeed should not, attempt to eliminate the psychological idiom of the critique. It is obvious to any reader of the *Kritik* that Kant's discourse abounds in psychological terms referring to the activities and faculties of the mind. While we have to understand these activities and faculties as essentially normative because they are identified by their roles and tasks, it is obvious that they are not only that. Quite simply, they are also the mental *activities* and *powers* that follow these roles and that fulfill these tasks, so that they cannot be one and the same as them.[15]

It is indeed questionable whether we can understand the normative dimension of Kant's discourse entirely apart from all reference to the psychological. The very idea of a norm is that of a constraint on activity; and the very concept of a rule is that which governs or imposes limits on conduct. So if there were no activity or conduct, there would be no purpose in invoking the idea of a norm or rule in the first place. This means that the transcendental cannot be understood entirely logically, as if the necessary conditions of experience were nothing more than truth-conditions for empirical judgments. We must also interpret the transcendental psychologically, as including the conditions necessary for the actual or hypothetical *perception* and *conception* of the world. In other words, they are not only normative constraints with which the mind *ought to* comply, but conditions with which it *must* comply. The transcendental consists in more than a system of synthetic a priori principles; it also comprises those activities that produce these principles.

Although Kant's concept of a faculty has to be understood as a metaphor for a type of logical discourse, there is still an undeniable *genetic* dimension to transcendental discourse. Kant is explicit that one of his central tasks is to determine the *origins* or *sources* of knowledge; hence he analyzes representations into the a priori and a posteriori according to whether they originate in the spontaneity of the understanding or the passivity of sensibility. Indeed, the very idea of a faculty involves that of a cause or a disposition, even if the cause is not made explicit. This genetic dimension of transcendental discourse is central to Kant's transcendental idealism, because, as we shall soon see (1.9.7), it is the subjective origin of the forms of sensibility and understanding that establishes one of the central conclusions of the *Kritik:* the limitation of knowledge to the realm of appearances alone.

The close connection between the logical and the psychological in Kant's transcendental discourse is also present in that aspect of the *Kritik* apparently most removed from the psychological: the Transcendental Deduction. *Prima facie* Kant's distinction between the *quid juris?* and the *quid facti?* means that the Transcendental Deduction should not deal with the origin or genesis of concepts. According to this reading, the *quid juris?* concerns the *second-order* question about the justification for a belief while the *quid facti?* deals with the *first-order* question about the causes or origins of a belief. Kant's distinction is then between the *epistemic justification* and the *causal explanation* of a belief, where the epistemic justification requires reconstruction in the form of a deductive argument.[16] Such an interpretation does not entirely fit the text, however, because Kant does not completely separate questions of justification from questions of origin. In two respects he thinks that these questions are joined. First, he holds that we can justify empirical concepts by showing their origin. Second, he maintains that we can justify synthetic a priori principles by showing how they originate from some source other than experience. The aim of the Transcendental Deduction is indeed to show that a priori principles have a completely different "certificate of birth" (*Geburtsbrief*) from empirical concepts (B 119). The point of Kant's distinction is not to exclude all genetic questions but simply an *empirical deduction* of synthetic a priori principles. His target is a very specific one: Locke's attempted derivation of a priori concepts from experience. The Transcendental Deduction will inevitably involve genetic considerations since it will attempt to show how synthetic a priori principles arise from a more fundamental faculty of the mind, such as the unity of apperception.[17] It is indeed in just this sense that we must understand Kant's "subjective deduction" in the first edition version of the Transcendental Deduction. The point of the subjective deduction is to show how one kind of mental operation or activity is involved in a more fundamental operation or activity, whose existence and functioning cannot be called into question. While such a subjective deduction does not replace the objective deduction, which is logically deductive in form, it does serve as a supplement to it by showing how the knowledge justified in the objective deduction can be acquired.

The significance of the logical, and the ineliminability of the psychological, aspects of Kant's transcendental discourse mean that, ultimately, it is necessary to combine both the logical and psychological interpretations. There is no reason to assume that these interpretations must be exclusive. We can consider the transcendental as both logical and psychological, as laying down constraints both about how we *ought to* think and about how we *must* do so. There is no fallacy of psychologism in doing so, provided one does not attempt *to base* normative constraints on psychological laws.

6. Problems of Transcendental Psychology

It is important to realize, however, that attempting to preserve the psychological dimension of the *Kritik* also invites serious trouble. It was indeed all the problems of transcendental psychology that made the austere logical interpretation so attractive in the first place. One of these problems arises from the genetic interpretation of Kant's faculties. If we regard a faculty as literally a source or origin of knowledge, then it is in some sense the *cause* of its representations. But then Kant's transcendental enquiry is caught in a vicious circle: to know the causes of some representations presupposes the principle of causality, whose validity it is the very purpose of the critique to investigate.[18] Even worse, it seems as if Kant is guilty of transcendent speculation, applying the category of causality to the conditions of experience when these cannot be given in experience itself.

The reply to this objection is that transcendental psychology does not use the concept of cause in its everyday sense. Kant is not making statements about the causes of specific representations; still less is he speculating about the origins of certain activities or events. Rather, the point of his faculty talk is to identify the specific *function* or *role* of certain kinds of representations in producing knowledge. To postulate a faculty is essentially to identify a distinct kind of function or role, and not to discover a special kind of activity or event taking place somewhere within the mind. The faculty is a cause of knowledge in the sense that it exercises a function or role indispensable to having knowledge. Of course, there is some activity answering to these functions insofar as they explain actual cognition; and furthermore there is some cause of these activities. But while the very idea of a faculty postulates some cause for these activities, it does not designate *which specific cause* this should be. The concept of a cause here serves only as a variable or place holder. This does not involve a transcendent use of the category of cause since there is no determinate claim to knowledge. This is perfectly in keeping with Kant's distinction between thinking and knowing an object according to the categories. For when we *think* of faculties as causes we do not postulate any *determinate* cause of representation but simply assume that there must be some cause without making any specific claims about it.

Another serious problem concerns the ontology of these mental activities and processes. What kind of entities are these? Here we encounter an apparently insurmountable dilemma: they must be either noumena or phenomena.[19] But if they are noumena, discourse about them is transcendent; and if they are phenomena, they fall within the realm of experience whose possibility is to be explained.

The middle path out of this dilemma is to deny that the distinction between transcendental and empirical psychology is a distinction between two different kinds of subject matter, between two kinds of entity, namely noumena and phenomena.[20] Rather, it is more a distinction between different *roles, functions,* or *forms of activity* of one and the same thing.[21] Which role or function is performed simply depends on our perspective and the purpose of our enquiry, whether it is empirical and concerned with the causes of specific mental events, or whether it is transcendental and deals with the necessary conditions of knowledge. There is no need to assume, however, that the mental roles and functions are each instantiated by some special kind of entity; they could instead simply refer to our normal and everyday faculties and activities. It is just that these faculties and activities also perform roles or functions that are not reducible to their empirical and everyday ones. Just because the transcendental and empirical are distinct roles or functions— because the transcendental is not reducible to the empirical—we have no reason to think that each role or function must be assigned to a specific kind of entity.

What makes transcendental psychology different from empirical psychology, then, is ultimately the different kinds of roles and functions assigned to the self in their performance. In its transcendental role it is considered as productive of the necessary conditions of knowledge; and in its empirical role it is considered as the source of certain mental events. But there is no real distinction in subject matter, between the transcendental and empirical self, because there is only one and the same self that performs these very different roles and functions. In its transcendental role and function it is abstracted from its normal and everyday function. To think that there are different selves here is like assuming that MacBeth and Laurence Olivier refer to two distinct persons because they are distinct roles.

7. Transcendental Psychology and Transcendental Idealism

Granted that transcendental psychology is possible, the question remains whether it is necessary. There are strong reasons for thinking that some form of it is indeed inevitable, given any basic and straightforward account of the goals of epistemology. The main purpose of epistemology is to examine the limits of knowledge, or what we can know. But to examine *what* we can know of necessity involves consideration of *how* we know; and to consider how we know is also to investigate the *origins* and *sources* of knowledge. In other words, it seems impossible to provide a justification for a belief without also considering *the sources* of evidence for it. To claim that one knows that *P*, but to refuse to answer the question how we came to know that *P*, is *ipso facto* to cast doubt on the claim.[22]

But if we admit that transcendental psychology is inevitable, we must also accept a result unwelcome to some: that transcendental idealism is an essential part of Kant's epistemology. Though we might question many of Kant's steps along the way, the move from transcendental psychology to transcendental idealism is inescapable. The general reason is obvious: the more we examine how we know, the more we see the contribution of the knowing subject in determining what it is that we know, so that it is difficult to sustain a direct realism according to which the objects of knowledge are simply given.[23]

Kant himself certainly did not think he could separate the central argument of the Deduction from his transcendental idealism. Indeed, he regarded transcendental idealism as the underpinning of his whole argument. As he explains in the Summary Representation of the A Deduction, the synthetic a priori principles of the understanding apply to experience only if the objects of experience are appearances, that is, objects whose existence and form depends on the cognitive activities of the subject perceiving them (A

128–129). If *per contra* these objects were things-in-themselves, there is no guarantee that the categories would apply to them. These concepts are a priori, and so have a universality and necessity that cannot be derived from perception, and that therefore must arise from the understanding itself. But if concepts arise from the understanding, Kant contends, there is no reason to assume—barring some miraculous preestablished harmony—that they apply to thing-in-themselves, which *ex hypothesi* have an existence and essence independent of them. To be certain that concepts apply to such things, they must derive from them; but this would be to forfeit their universal and necessary status. Hence the only guarantee that the categories are necessary conditions of experience is to assume that their objects are appearances.

It has been argued, most notably by P. F. Strawson, that we can separate the central arguments of Kant's Analytic from his transcendental psychology, and indeed from the transcendental idealism that follows from it. The main purpose of the Analytic, Strawson argues, is simply "to investigate what we can conceive of, or make intelligible to ourselves, as a possible general structure of experience," or to determine "the set of ideas which form the limiting framework of all our thought about the world."[24] With all its allusions to "ideas," "thought," and "what we can conceive of," such a description is blatantly psychologistic itself; to be purely logical it would have to be cast in "the formal mode of speech," making only reference to judgments and their logical relations. But, whatever his description of the transcendental enterprise, Strawson insists that it is completely separable from any consideration of the origin of these fundamental ideas. Supposedly, it determines the essential structure of our "conceptual scheme" rather than anything about our "cognitive constitution." To prove his point, Strawson interprets the Deduction so that it makes no reference to the concepts of transcendental psychology, and he duly concludes that transcendental idealism is "superfluous to the essential structure of reasoning, as an extra wheel, zealously but idly turning."[25] According to his interpretation, the Deduction only shows by regressive analysis the necessary conditions for the understanding of experience, namely that experience must be conceptualized, and that it must be so according to the principles of the understanding. Alternatively, it attempts to determine how certain very basic principles of objective order—of universal and necessary connection—are involved in the possibility of ascribing representations to myself over time.[26] In either case, he insists, the success of the argument does not depend on the thesis of transcendental idealism that these principles are valid only of appearances. For showing that certain principles of objective order are necessary conditions of experience does not imply that the objects within experience are only appearances.[27]

Yet such a sparse interpretation of the Deduction really begs the central question it intends to solve. If the fundamental principles of the understanding make a claim to universality and necessity that cannot be derived from experience, how do we know that they apply to it? Or, granted that certain basic principles are necessary to my understanding of experience, or even to my ascribing identity to myself over time, what makes me think that they are anything more than subjective necessities of my understanding? If these principles are simply requirements of our *understanding* experience, the question arises whether that subjective necessity still holds of experience itself. The whole problem of skepticism arises all over again: Why should the subjective necessity of our thought be true of reality itself? There is some rich irony here: since Strawson is content to leave these principles subjective necessities, and since he fails to deal with the *quid juris?*, his interpretation is more psychologistic than anything in Kant.

It is striking that Kant himself envisages, and decisively rejects, an interpretation of this kind. His reasons for dismissing it are telling. Toward the close of the B Deduction (B 167–168) he considers a *preformation system of pure reason*, according to which our principles originate in the understanding but still harmonize with things-in-themselves because of the creator. He rejects this possibility, because it does not ensure that these principles have any "objective validity." They would amount to nothing more than "subjective dispositions of thought" having "an arbitrary subjective necessity" because they do not necessarily conform to their objects, and because their creator could have chosen to create our cognitive constitutions differently. Such a preformation system would concede "just what the skeptic desires," Kant further argues, because we could not say "the effect is connected with the cause in the object" but only that "I am so constituted that I cannot think this representation otherwise than as so connected" (B 168). What, in the end, gives our synthetic a priori principles an objective validity is that they apply to the objects of experience; but the only condition under which we can say this is that these objects are appearances.

Ultimately, the problem with any such anodyne interpretation of the Analytic is that it begs fundamental questions. What validity are we to ascribe to those principles that are necessary conditions of any experience? If they are only subjective necessities, we are left with something like a Humean skepticism. If they are true of objects themselves, then we need to know why that is the case. Simply to dismiss this question is really to beg it. In the end, it is necessary to admit that Kant's Transcendental Deduction—as "phantasmagoric" and "baroque" as it seems—has much more philosophical interest than the sparse interpretation imposed on it.

CHAPTER 10

Kant's Idealism in the
Opus postumum

1. Kant's Peruke

In the spring of 1790 Kant stated bluntly in the preface to the *Kritik der Urtheilskraft:* "With this I end my entire critical undertaking. Without delay I will now proceed to the doctrinal part, so that I snatch from my growing years what time remains favorable to the task" (V, 170). So much had been done, but there was still so much to do. The three *Kritiken* had been written, but now he had to erect the system of philosophy on their foundations. Kant achieved part of this grand task with his *Metaphysik der Sitten,* which constituted the practical part of his system. Yet he never published his long promised system of metaphysics, for which the entire critical philosophy was to be a propadeutic.

Kant's public statement that he was putting his critical labors behind him, and the fact that he published no major metaphysical or epistemological work after the third *Kritik,* has led to one of the most stubborn myths about the history of German idealism: that Kant drops off the philosophical stage in the 1790s. This myth reappears every time we assume that *post*-Kantian philosophy begins in that decade. It is as if Kant were dead when Reinhold, Beck, Fichte, and Schelling wrote their first works. But rumors of Kant's demise, and indeed of his irrelevance, were greatly exaggerated. Kant continued to work throughout the 1790s, and even into the first year of the new century. If his energies were declining, making it difficult for him to execute ambitious projects, his acuity remained perfectly intact.

For three reasons, the myth of Kant's obsolescence is especially misleading. First, some of his most important moral and political works appear only in the 1790s. Almost all his political writings were published in that decade, and they reveal an author eager to participate in all the crucial issues of the day; and, of course, the *Metaphysik der Sitten*, Kant's most systematic work on moral philosophy, appeared only in 1796. Second, to the extent that time and energy permitted, Kant did keep abreast of the latest developments in transcendental philosophy; thus he often responded to, if only in private, the criticisms of Fichte, Beck, Herder, Schulze, and Tiedemann. Since his powers completely failed him only in 1801, and since the absolute idealism of Hölderlin, Schelling, and Hegel was essentially formed by 1800, this means that Kant was a witness to, and indeed participant in, the transformation of German idealism in the 1790s. If he seemed to have exited the philosophical stage in the 1790s, that has more to do with his isolation in Königsberg—far from the literary centers of Jena, Weimar, and Göttingen—than his waning powers as a philosopher. Third, and most important of all, despite his claim in the preface to the third *Kritik*, Kant continued to work on his critical philosophy well into the 1790s, and indeed he began to take it in new and remarkable directions. If Kant *published* little in epistemology and metaphysics in the 1790s, the fact remains that he continued *to think and write* intensively about these topics. This is apparent from his *Opus postumum*, the unedited mass of papers that he left after his death, which only became the subject of commentary—and controversy—in the twentieth century. Most of these papers, which amount to two volumes of the Akademie edition, were written between July 1797 and December 1800. They show that Kant continued to rethink, with remarkable zeal, persistence, and clarity, the fundamentals of his critical philosophy until the beginning of the 1800s. Here we witness Kant's great merit as a philosopher: his tireless readiness to rethink the basics of his position, to find the most precise formulation of his own views, and to explore issues for their own sake.

It is this last development that especially concerns us here, for it raises the question: What happened to Kant's critical idealism after the third *Kritik?* Did he complete or abandon it? Did he remain true to the formal idealism of the 1780s? Or did he abolish his old dualisms and develop a more radical idealism like that of Fichte, Schelling, or Hegel? To put the issues metaphorically: Did Kant doff his peruke in the 1790s or did he simply repowder it?

Since the publication of the Akademie edition of the *Opus postumum* in 1936, and indeed to some extent even before then, these have been disputed questions. There are those who contend that the transcendental idealism of the *Opus postumum* is essentially that of the 1780s. They maintain that Kant kept his basic dualisms, and that he remained true to his formal idealism, holding that the subject determines only the form but not the matter of experience, which remains simply given.[1] But there are also those who insist that Kant overturned his dualisms, at least in principle, and developed a more radical idealism that unifies the form and content of experience in a single fundamental principle.[2]

Attempting to steer a middle path between these extremes, I shall argue in the following sections that Kant indeed continued to wear his wig, but that he also did more than just repowder it: he recurled and indeed refashioned it. While he *reformulated* and *narrowed* some of his fundamental dualisms, he still *retained* them, and so kept his critical distance from the idealism of Fichte and Schelling. Ultimately, Kant remained a formal idealist in 1801 just as he had been in 1781, though formal idealism no longer had the same meaning it had in 1780s. For Kant had redefined the domain of form and extended its sway over the realm of matter, even if he did not abolish the given manifold and the thing-in-itself. There was, however, one respect in which Kant did let his hair down: he gave the idea of the systematic unity of experience a constitutive status, making it a valid principle not only for reflective but determining judgment. Since, however, Kant continued to hold that this principle held only for appearances, he made no plunge into the deep waters of absolute idealism.

2. The Gap in the Critical System

To understand the development of Kant's transcendental idealism in the 1790s, it is necessary to ask why there was such a development at all. Why, contrary to Kant's claims in the third *Kritik*, was the critical philosophy not complete? Why did Kant begin to rethink his system in the 1790s? What problem could be so pressing that it compelled him to return to his intellectual labors?

The source of the problem lay with a "gap" in the critical philosophy that had begun to trouble Kant as early as the 1780s. Kant first revealed his worries about such a gap in his September 21, 1798, letter to Christian Garve, where he complains about suffering "a pain like that of Tantalus" in writing a new work entitled 'Transition from the Metaphysical Foundations of Natural Science to Physics.' This work had to be completed, Kant stressed, "for otherwise there would be a gap in the system of the critical philosophy" (XII, 257). It is likely, however, that Kant's first plans for such a work went back to the Autumn of 1790, for shortly after completing the third *Kritik*, he had announced to his student J. G. Kiesewetter that he had plans to write a new short work that would be "a transition from the metaphysical foundations of natural science to physics."[3]

What, precisely, was this gap, and how did it arise? Since the first *Kritik*, Kant had become very concerned about the apparent discrepancy between the categories of the understanding and specific empirical laws. He held that the categories are very general principles, valid for all objects as such, and that they cannot derive specific empirical laws, which are only contingent for the understanding (B 165, 263, 303). Since they are purely formal principles, the categories are compatible with many possible particular laws, so that it is necessary to consult experience to determine which particular laws are true. In other words, the categories establish only the possibility of law as such; but they do not specify *which* specific laws are true in experience, and *what* the order is among them. Indeed, they cannot even determine *whether* there is any systematic order among them. Since Kant insisted that systematicity is a prerequisite of all scientific knowledge (A 832), this was to leave the possibility of an empirical science of nature still hanging in the balance.

Kant began to treat this problem in earnest only in the third *Kritik*. Yet he was already fully aware of it by the first edition of the first *Kritik*. In the Appendix to the Transcendental Dialectic he explained that the categories did not establish the systematic unity of empirical laws, and he went so far as to concede that if there were no guarantee of systematicity, there could be "no coherent employment of the understanding" and "no sufficient criterion of empirical truth" (B 679). Without systematicity, he added, there would not even be empirical concepts or experience (B 682). Here, then, lay a very serious problem indeed: the transcendental principles of the first *Kritik* did not guarantee the possibility of empirical knowledge after all.[4] Already in the first edition of the *Kritik*, then, Kant had already discovered a serious gap in his philosophy.

The issue that disturbed Kant in the 1790s was a variation of the basic discrepancy he had already discussed in the first *Kritik*. The gap now arose between empirical physics and the metaphysical principles of natural science, which had been the main subject of Kant's 1786 *Metaphysische Anfangsgründe der Naturwissenschaften*. This work had closed some of the gap discovered in the first *Kritik*. Its task was to develop a purely rational physics, a *physica rationalis*, which applies the transcendental principles of the first *Kritik* to physical nature. The metaphysical principles of this science are not as general as the categories, because they are not valid for any kind of object but are applied to one specific kind of object in nature, namely matter. Nevertheless, if the gap had been narrowed, it remained far from closed. For these metaphysical principles are still very general and a priori, determining only the necessary properties of matter as such, so that the laws of empirical physics remain as contingent for them as for the categories. Kant himself stressed this point when he stated that his metaphysical principles were "completely heterogeneous" with empirical ones (IV, 469), and that they could not specify the different kinds of matter. In general, he drew a sharp line between metaphysical questions, which are resolvable a priori, and empirical physics, which must rely on observation and experiment (IV, 517–518, 522–523, 534). Hence the troubling question raised in the 1780s persisted: What ensured the possibility of *empirical* knowledge of nature?

Although Kant struggled to close this gap in the 1780s, all his efforts proved to be problematic. In the first *Kritik* the ideas of reason, and in the third *Kritik* the principles of reflective judgment, had been assigned the task of systematizing the multiplicity of empirical laws. But both these solutions suffered from an underlying ambiguity. Kant often insisted that these ideas and principles have a merely regulative validity, permitting the understanding to proceed in its enquiries only *as if* there is some systematic unity; yet he also seemed uncertain whether such regulative status is sufficient. Hence he sometimes admitted that empirical science requires the stronger constitutive claim that there *is* systematic unity (B 680), stressing that if we do not assume that there is such an order we will lose all motivation or rationale to search for it (B 679, 681–682, 685, 688). The principle of reflective judgment in the third *Kritik* is also far too general to be of use in determining *how* to close the gap between the transcendental principles of the understanding and the multiplicity of empirical laws. It specified only that we should proceed as if there is some systematic order; but it gave no guidelines about what this order could be.

All these unresolved issues of the 1780s finally emerge in the late 1790s in the fourth, seventh, and tenth fascicles of the *Opus postumum*. Kant now formulates the central problem behind his transition program in the simple question 'How is physics possible as a science?' This was not the same question Kant had already asked in the *Prolegomena:* 'How is pure natural science possible?' (IV, 306) For the physics in question in the later work is an essentially empirical discipline, whose main goal is to determine the specific laws of motion, and whose chief activities are observation and experiment. Nevertheless, Kant still insists that, to have the status of a science, empirical physics too must have systematic unity, or that it must have an a priori structure where its laws have universality and necessity. In the *Anfangs-gründe* Kant continued to stress that systematic form, and universality and necessity, are the requisites of any science, and that a mere collection of observations, an aggregate of data, fall far short of such standards (IV, 468–469).

The problem behind the Transition, as Kant now formulates it, is that these high standards are almost impossible to attain. Physics confronts an apparently insurmountable dilemma because it cannot become a science by either purely rational and a priori methods or by strictly empirical and a posteriori ones. It is impossible a posteriori because, as Kant admits and Hume taught, we cannot derive systematic unity, or universality and necessity, from all the data of experience. Experience provides us only with an aggregate of observations and gives no evidence for a universal and necessary connection between events. But it is also impossible a priori because the metaphysical principles of natural science determine only the general laws of motion, and are compatible with all possible kinds of particular laws and not only those confirmed through observation and experiment.[5] Hence there is a gap between the metaphysical principles of natural science, which we know a priori, and the empirical findings of physics, which we know a posteriori through observation and experiment.

3. The Transition Program and Its Implications

What was Kant's response to the apparently insurmountable gap confronting him? His first formulation of a solution appears in the third fascicle of the *Opus postumum*, which he probably wrote between August and September 1798. He explains that, to bridge the gap between the metaphysical principles of natural science and empirical physics, it is necessary for there to be certain fundamental mediating concepts (*Mittelbegriffe, Zwischenbegriffe*) to join these distinct domains. These mediating concepts are nothing less than the specific moving forces of matter—the forces behind such phenomena as cohesion, solidification, electricity magnetism, and chemical affinity—whose interactions explain the specific kinds of matter. These forces were nothing less than the standard forces of "experimental physics" in the eighteenth century.[6] These concepts are especially suited to cross the divide between metaphysics and physics, Kant argues, because they are both a priori and a posteriori (XXI, 289). They are a posteriori because their existence must be given empirically (287);[7] but they are also a priori because their structure and form can be determined according to the table of categories (291, 367). We can organize all the variables of force according to this table, Kant believes, so that each variable is assigned to a specific category. Hence ponderability (quality), coercibility (quantity), cohesion (relation), and exhaustability (modality) each represent one of the categories.[8] Because its *form* is a priori while its *matter* is a posteriori (293, 486), the system of the moving forces of matter—or what Kant calls his "universal doctrine of forces of matter" (*allgemeine Kräftenlehre der Materie*) or "*physiologia naturalis*" (286)—provides the transition science between metaphysics and physics.

Both the problem and the solution of the Transition are analogous to that of the Schematism in the first *Kritik*. The similarity is not only apparent, however, given that Kant himself described the Transition as a Schematism on several occasions (XXI, 168, 362–363; XXII, 487). The central problem of the Schematism was how to apply the a priori concepts of the understanding to the particular appearances of experience (B 177). The solution was "there must be some third thing, which is homogeneous on the one hand with the category, and on the other hand with the appearance, and which thus makes the application of the former to the latter possible" (B 177). The same principle is at work in the Transition, because the moving forces are homogeneous on the one hand with the metaphysical principles (in their systematic form), and on the other hand with the data of empirical physics (in their content). The main difference between the two schematisms is that the earlier one works for inner sense as the later one does for outer sense. Since the variables of moving force describe some form of motion, the moving forces schematize the metaphysical principles according to outer sense, just as Kant had required in the second edition of the *Kritik*.

As Kant first expounds the general idea behind his transition program, it seems perfectly in accord with his earlier critical principles. It seems as if nothing more is involved than schematizing the general principles of natural science, just as Kant had once schematized the categories in the first *Kritik*. Indeed, to an extent, Kant himself wanted to think that the Transition would be business as usual, a matter of expanding his system rather than rethinking it. Yet, in the later execution of his program, Kant began to develop ideas that took him well beyond some of his earlier critical doctrines.[9]

One of the most important changes appears in the fifth and tenth fascicles, which Kant probably wrote between May 1799 and April 1800. Kant now begins to use the system of moving forces to explain not only the specific kinds of matter but also the specific perceptions or qualities of sensation itself. He treats the perceiver as another one of the moving forces of nature, so that its perceptions are the result of the forces acting upon it and its reactions to them. Perceptions are then nothing less than "the moving forces joined together by consciousness" (XXII, 392). Or, as he puts it in the fifth fascicle: "External perceptions necessary to possible experience . . . are themselves nothing more than the effect of agitating forces of matter upon the perceiving subject" (XXI, 557). Now that the perceiver is brought within the general system of moving forces, Kant argues, the content of its perceptions will be amenable to a priori classification and organization. He announces this possibility explicitly in the eleventh fascicle:

> In view of matter and its moving powers of externally affecting the subject, the perceptions themselves are moving powers bound up with the capacity of reaction, so that the understanding *anticipates* perception according to the only possible forms of motion—attraction, repulsion, inclusion and penetration. Thus is revealed the possibility of establishing an a priori system of empirical representations—what would otherwise seem impossible—and to anticipate experience *quod materiale.* (XXII, 502)

Of course, Kant had already developed the idea of a material a priori in the Anticipations of Perception of the first *Kritik,* where he stated that we can anticipate a priori the content of experience by treating sensation as an intensive magnitude (B 207–208). Even then he had noted the apparent oddity of anticipating a priori something that belongs to the sheer matter of experience (209). Nevertheless, Kant's conception of the material a priori in the first *Kritik* was decidedly modest, explicitly leaving out of account the specific qualities of the manifold. There Kant had insisted that *all* we can anticipate is the *intensive magnitude* of a sensation, the degree of intensity with which it strikes our senses (B 218); the *quality* of sensation, however, is "always merely empirical and cannot be represented a priori" (B 217).

The new development in Kant's thinking lies less in the general idea of a material a priori than in the transcendental status he ascribes to the moving forces themselves. Kant describes the moving forces as "principles of the possibility of experience" (XXII, 390) and their whole system as "a material principle of the unity of possible experience" (XXI, 585). Their transcendental status becomes especially apparent when Kant writes in the ninth fascicle that the quantity of matter cannot be measured, or be an object of experience, "except under the presupposition that it has some dynamic quality that must be presupposed a priori" (XXII, 230). In other words, these moving powers are not, like empirical laws, simply *subsumed under* the transcendental conditions provided by the categories; rather, they constitute *more specific* transcendental conditions themselves. Hence the transition science expands the realm of the transcendental and a priori so that it consists in not only the categories of the understanding and the forms of sensibility but also the major variables of interaction between the dynamic powers of matter.[10]

The changes in Kant's concept of the transcendental in the *Opus postumum* become especially apparent from the ether proofs of the second and fourth fascicles, which were written between July 1797 and October 1798. The ether, caloric, or world matter plays a central role in Kant's transition science: it is nothing less than "the highest principle of the transition" (XXI, 600). The ether is the substrate of all the moving forces of nature, the basis for their unity and interconnection (XXI, 563). Although it now seems to be only the quaint relic of bygone physics,[11] the chief role of the ether is not physical or scientific for Kant, who insists that he does not adopt the ether simply as an hypothesis to explain certain phenomena (XXI, 563–564). Rather, Kant's ether is essentially a *transcendental* principle, and more specifically his formulation for the necessary unity of experience. Kant indeed conceives the existence of the ether as the principle of the unity of all experience, as *the fundamental* transcendental condition of possible experience (XXI, 224, 229). Hence the proofs for the existence of the ether are not empirical but transcendental arguments. They contend that the existence of the ether is a necessary condition for the perception of any object in space. Crudely, Kant's argument goes as follows: that we perceive a body in space only if space as a whole is completely filled and constantly in motion; but space is completely filled and constantly in motion only if there exists a universally penetrating, constantly moving, and omnipresent primal matter.

What is so "strange" about the ether proofs, as Kant himself notes, is that they demonstrate the *existence* of an object as a necessary condition of experience (XXI, 221, 226, 230, 538, 562). They do not attempt to prove its existence from experience but a priori, through reasoning from a priori concepts and the law of identity alone. This is "singular" in the critical philosophy, Kant admits, because it is a central doctrine of the first *Kritik* that the existence of objects cannot be derived from concepts alone, and that we confirm the reality of anything only by its agreement with the material and formal conditions of experience. Yet in this single case "it is possible to say *a poße ad esse valet consequentia*" (XXI, 592).

Although the full implications of this singularity are a matter of dispute, there is at the very least here a basic shift in Kant's conception of the conditions of experience, which makes it necessary for him to revise the dualism between the form and matter of experience. The distinction between the two in the first *Kritik* was such that the form of experience comprised only its structure, while its matter consisted in not only specific sense qualities but also the existence of objects. Whether an object existed had to be determined within experience from perception and the laws governing it (B 279–280). Now, however, the conditions of experience consist in not only its form or structure but also its very existence. The conditions of experience are not only formal but something very real. Hence Kant sometimes calls the ether "hypostatized space" (XXI, 224, 228), or a "*material* principle of the unity of possible experience" (XXI, 585).

The ether proofs also raise serious questions about the regulative constraints that Kant imposed on reflective judgment in the third *Kritik*.[12] There Kant had insisted that the idea of the systematic unity of experience is a strictly regulative principle, such that the understanding can proceed only as if all the particular laws of nature have been created according to some rational design. Since, however, the ether proofs demonstrate the existence and objective reality of the ether, and since the ether amounts to nothing less than the systematic unity of nature, it follows that the ether too must have constitutive status, if only as a necessary condition of experience. To be sure, in one respect, the regulative constraints of the third *Kritik* still remain in force, for Kant's main purpose there was to limit the claims of teleology, and more specifically the idea of the purposiveness of nature. Yet, in another respect, Kant also abandons these constraints, since the idea of the systematic unity of nature becomes detached from the idea of purposiveness and is given a constitutive status.

It is important to stress that, since they make no claim about the unity of nature deriving from its purposiveness, the ether proofs do not rehabilitate teleology. The system of dynamic forces of the Transition remain entirely in the inorganic realm, and so can have a constitutive status without violating Kant's strictures on teleology.[13] Throughout the *Opus postumum* Kant adheres to a doctrine he had already emphasized in the *Anfangsgründe:* that matter is dynamic but not organic, that it consists in moving but not living forces. Hence he argues repeatedly that matter is not living because it does not have the power to move itself, and because the idea of a purpose involves some immaterial principle (XXII, 499, 501, 506–507, 547, 548). It is Kant's persistent insistence upon this borderline between the living and nonliving that separates him most sharply from the later more metaphysical doctrines of Schelling and the romantics.

Still, for all its novelty and implications, it would be wrong to think that the ether proofs are transcendent from the standpoint of the Transcendental Dialectic of the first *Kritik*, as if Kant were returning to the metaphysical tradition or moving toward absolute idealism.[14] Kant himself is very keen to avoid any impression that he is committing the fallacy of the ontological argument,[15] and he counters this by insisting that the ether proofs are valid only as *transcendental* arguments; that is, they do not determine the existence of the ether except insofar as it is a necessary condition of possible experience. Concerning the existence of the ether in itself, apart from these conditions, they make no claims whatsoever. Kant is insistent that though the proofs establish the *reality* or *objective* status of the ether, they do so only by establishing its *subjective* necessity as a condition of experience (XXI, 575, 581, 583, 601).[16] As he writes in the fifth fascicle: "Regarding the question of the existence of the caloric, when it must be known a priori, it is not how the object is possible but how the experience of this object . . . is subjectively possible" (XXI, 581).

4. The Transition and Refutation

What significance did Kant's transition program have for his struggle against subjectivism? Some scholars have said none at all. They argue that rather than attempting to continue his battle against subjectivism in the *Opus postumum*, Kant succumbed to a radical "transcendental solipsism" all his own.[17] This is apparent, they contend, chiefly from the growing powers Kant attributes to the transcendental subject, which now creates not only the general form but also the specific matter of experience. This increasing subjectivism is obvious, it is said, from Kant's lack of interest with the refutation of idealism in the *Opus postumum*. Allegedly, Kant now abandoned the Refutation of Idealism.[18]

We shall treat the charge of growing subjectivism later. But there is one question that we must answer now: What is the connection, if any, between the Transition and the Refutation? What role, if any, does the Refutation play in the *Opus postumum*?

It should be said from the outset that Kant did not foresake his attempt to refute idealism in the *Opus postumum*. There are several passages in the seventh and eleventh fascicles where Kant argues explicitly against idealism, and more specifically against the charges of subjectivism hurled against him

by Dietrich Tiedemann in *Theätet* (XXII, 11, 19, 35–36, 445, 447). Tiedemann made two charges against Kant: first, that the Refutation does not really prove the existence of external objects but only the necessity of our nature *to assume* their existence; and, second, that Kant had no right to assume
transcendental affection, given that he had argued in the Fourth Paralogism
of the first edition that all inferences from my inner experience to their external causes are uncertain.[19] Predictably, Kant was no more pleased with
Tiedemann's criticisms than Garve's. He made several attempts to rebut
Tiedemann, sprinkling his texts with caustic comments about "Theatetus."

Kant's concern to refute idealism was not limited to his asides against
Tiedemann. There are other passages in the eleventh fascicle where Kant
reaffirms his empirical realism against empirical idealism by insisting that
transcendental idealism does not undermine the truth of any of our ordinary judgments, whose truth value is entirely preserved: "It is one and the
same in transcendental philosophy whether I make sense representations
into a principle idealistically or realistically. For everything depends not on
the relation of the objects to the subject but their relation to one another"
(XXII, 442–443, 469).

If the *Opus postumum* does not contain the many refutations of idealism of
the *Reflexionen* of the 1790s, that is not because Kant has becomes less realistic in his thinking, and still less because he has become a transcendental solipsist. It has more to do with the immediate goals of the transition project.
To secure the possibility of physics as a science, Kant has to establish some
systematic unity, some form of a priori organization, for the aggregate of empirical data acquired from observation and experiment. But to achieve this
end he does not have to prove that there are objects in space outside him
and that there are moving forces acting on the subject. That point is simply
presupposed. The argument of the Transition is therefore purely hypothetical in form: *if* there are objects in space or moving forces acting on me, they
must have a systematic order or a priori form.

It is noteworthy that Kant himself saw the argument of the Transition in
just these terms. In a note appended to one of the ether proofs he explains
that his proof will begin with the assumption of the existence of objects in
space, and that he will not attempt to prove this assumption. Kant states
baldly that his proof will adopt as its premise "A totality of simultaneously
existing sense objects is given"; he then adds tellingly: "unless one wants
to adopt idealism, whose claim belongs to another branch of philosophy,
which is not the subject here" (XXI, 552).

This makes it seem as if the Transition presupposes the Refutation, but not conversely. Even worse, it appears as if the Refutation were relevant to the Transition in a merely peripheral way, proving a presupposition that the Transition shares with many other parts of the *Kritik*. But this impression is very misleading. If the Transition is not a *reformulation* of, or *replacement* for the Refutation, it is a necessary *supplement* to it, and indeed an *extension* of it. The Transition not only builds on the central conclusion of the Refutation, but it also explains some of its central concepts, justifies some of its hidden premises, and explores some of its deeper implications.

The close connection between the Refutation and Transition becomes clear as soon as we reconsider the origins of both projects. One of the central ideas behind the Refutation is the primacy of outer intuition in giving meaning to the concepts of the understanding. The need to reschematize the basic principles of the understanding through outer sense was, however, also one of the central motivations behind the Transition. In effect, then, the Transition would continue the anti-idealist project of establishing the primacy of outer sense.

The link between the Refutation and Transition becomes further apparent as soon as we recall their central theses. The Refutation intends to show how a necessary condition of my empirical self-consciousness—my awareness of myself in time—is my awareness of the existence of something permanent in space outside me (B 275). The Transition attempts to establish systematic unity among the moving powers of matter by showing how such unity is a necessary condition of my perception of objects in space outside me. Hence the Transition attempts to take the argument of the Refutation a step further by specifying the *conditions* under which I become aware of something permanent in space. Essentially, it contends that to perceive something in space, I must have a physical body that stands in a dynamic interaction with other physical bodies, which must all be parts of a single unified dynamic system of nature. In other words, the Transition builds on and explains the Refutation by stating that my perception of objects in space must be part of a general system of experience, which basically consists in a system of moving forces standing in relations of attraction and repulsion to one another.

Despite his intense and tireless efforts, Kant never succeeded in providing a formal and final argument for the central thesis of the Transition. Elements of the argument appear in his various ether proofs in fascicles II–VI, and in his various comments on the system of moving powers in the seventh, tenth, and eleventh fascicles. If we summarize these texts, the following line of argument emerges:

1. To perceive space, it is necessary to perceive some body in it, because empty space cannot be perceived (XXI, 209, 216, 218, 223, 227, 229, 233–234, 247, 376, 535, 538, 547, 550).

2. To perceive the existence of some body in space, it must affect my senses (XXI, 216, 552).

3. To affect my senses, the body must exercise some force upon them (XXI, 573, 583, 587, 588).

4. To perceive the body acting on me, I must be able to react against its force, such that I repel its motion as it repels my motion; in other words, my body and the body acting on me must stand in relations of mutual attraction and repulsion (XXI, 490; XXII, 326, 502).

5. My body and the body acting on me mutually attract and repel one another only if that body in turn mutually attracts and repels other bodies, which stand in similar relations to still other bodies, and so on. In other words, these bodies must form a continuum of interaction, a system of mutually interacting forces (XXI, 507, 535–536, 552; XXII, 293, 300, 431).

Therefore, my perception of the existence of some body in space is possible only insofar as I have a body that is part of the system of physical bodies in dynamic interaction.

Whatever its precise formulation, the main thrust of this argument supports one of the central premises of Kant's critique of idealism. For it states that my perception of objects in space must take place within the general system of experience, and that means, according to the Postulates of Empirical Thought, that this perception cannot be illusory. That my perception of an object in space is part of the general system of experience was crucial to the argument of the Refutation, because this alone established against the Cartesian skeptic that such a perception cannot be illusory. Though this point was crucial to the argument of the Refutation, Kant implied more than explained it in the first *Kritik*. The Transition now picks up where the Refutation left off. It argues in more detail why the perception of objects in space must take place within the general system of experience. In the *Kritik* the principle of community behind the Third Analogy—that all substances perceived in space are in interaction—played a crucial, if tacit, role in the Postulates and the Refutation of Idealism, because it established that all objective experience of objects in space must take place in a system of interaction. The Transition now completes this argument with its ether proofs, though now the principle of community assumes a decidedly constitutive status.[20]

That Kant himself believed that the argument of the Transition had important implications for the Refutation appears from some of his *obiter dicta* on Tiedemann's *Theätet*. Though Kant does not discuss the detail of any of Tiedemann's arguments, he does suggest on at least two occasions that the Transition serves as a response to his charge of skepticism (XXII, 11, 447; XXI, 440–441). Because the Transition shows that belonging to a general system of moving forces is a necessary condition of our experience of objects in space, it shows their reality in a manner that "cannot even be disputed by a Theatetus."

5. The *Selbstsetzungslehre*

The most important doctrine for the development of Kant's idealism in the *Opus postumum* is that of the self-positing subject, or the so-called *Selbstsetzungslehre*. In the seventh Convolut, which was written between April and December 1800, Kant began to employ a new terminology to describe how the transcendental subject creates its experience. He says that the subject "makes," "posits," "presents," "objectifies" or "constitutes" itself in the act of forming its world. The terms '*sich selbst setzen*,' '*sich selbst machen*,' '*sich selbst darstellen*,' '*sich selbst vorhermachen*,' '*sich selbst constituiren*,' and '*sich selbst zum Object machen*,' appear frequently and almost interchangeably. Although they have slightly different connotations, all these terms stress the activity and spontaneity of the transcendental subject. The most common expression, however, is '*sich selbst setzen*,' and hence the name '*Selbstsetzungslehre*.'

The main purpose behind Kant's *Selbstsetzungslehre* is to rationalize his transition program and to secure the possibility of physics as a science. The fundamental idea behind this doctrine is that the subject creates the world that it knows, or that what it knows is its creation, and indeed a function of its self-consciousness or self-objectification. The basis for this idea is nothing less than the central principle behind Kant's "new way of thought": "that we can know a priori of things only what we put into them" (B xviii). Already in the preface to the second edition of the *Kritik* Kant saw this principle as the explanation for the scientific revolution and the progress of science (B xiv). In the *Opus postumum* he made this principle into the basis for physics itself. Physics too can be an a priori science, Kant argues repeatedly in the tenth Convolut, because what we know of the physical world is ultimately only our creation (XXII, 287, 306, 309–310, 319, 323, 331, 343). We derive knowledge from nature only to the extent that we have created it according to the laws of our own a priori activity.

The language of self-positing sounds very Fichtean, leading some scholars to speculate about the origins of the *Selbstsetzungslehre*. It has been said that Kant was writing under Fichte's influence, deliberately appropriating his terminology to show that the critical philosophy could keep pace with all the new ideas.[21] There is something to be said for this hypothesis. Although Kant himself had used the term 'positing' long before Fichte's heyday,[22] he had not done so systematically or made it a central theme. Kant was indeed worried about his legacy and the growing apostasy of his students;[23] and, furthermore, he was not slow to adopt some of the jargon of his contemporaries in the *Opus postumum*, including that of Fichte.[24] To be sure, Kant was no close reader of Fichte's writings; but he was familiar enough with their contents from reviews.[25] Still, the crucial question remains: Did Kant give the concept of self-positing the same *meaning* as Fichte? And here it is necessary to be very cautious indeed. If Kant adopted Fichte's language, it was for his own ends, and it came from his own principles, on which Fichte himself was deeply dependent.[26]

Although the significance of the *Selbstsetzungslehre* for Kant's idealism has been much disputed,[27] there is an extent to which its implications are obvious. The most striking development of the *Selbstsetzungslehre* is that it gives Kant a general concept to unify the faculties of mind involved in the creation of experience. Understanding and sensibility are no longer static, given, innate, and separate faculties, but expressions or manifestations of a single underlying activity. Both are simply different forms of self-consciousness, different ways in which the self posits or objectifies itself. This shift is most marked when Kant states that the subject posits itself through the a priori forms of time and space (XXII, 70, 73–74, 88, 90, 96, 97, 409). Rather than belonging to sensibility alone, these forms are now integrated with the understanding and subsumed under the same function of self-consciousness. Of course, to some extent, this development was already implicit in the first *Kritik*. In the second edition version of the Transcendental Deduction Kant went to pains to bring the forms of sensibility under the forms of understanding conditioned by the unity of apperception. Even then he had made the self-consciousness involved in the unity of apperception the fundamental principle of experience, and he had also spoken about the transcendental subject positing itself through its act of 'I think' (B 158n). Still, this line of thought had not been fully explicit, and it had been obscured by the separate exposition of the Transcendental Aesthetic. The *Selbstsetzungslehre* now develops the doctrine of the primacy of the unity of apperception in the first *Kritik,* explicitly making not only the understanding but also sensibility forms of self-consciousness. The 'I think' is the highest act not only of understanding, but also of sensibility, denoting a single activity by which the self posits itself not only as *cogitabile* but also as *dabile.*

It is important to see that the *Selbstsetzungslehre* brought together more than understanding and sensibility. It also wedded theoretical and practical reason, the speculative and the moral, under the single concept of the autonomy of reason. Thus unity was achieved not only in the critique of pure reason, but in the system of transcendental philosophy as a whole. Kant had always stressed the unity of theoretical and practical reason, and he had even stated in the preface to the second *Kritik* that the concept of freedom is the "keystone to the whole architechture of pure reason" (V, 4). But here too these statements were never developed into explicit doctrine. The *Selbstsetzungslehre* now gave Kant the conceptual tools he needed to join the various realms of his philosophy. Signs of this move are already apparent in the seventh and tenth fascicles, when Kant describes the subject's self-positing activity in terms of "autonomy" or "self-determination" (*Selbstbestimmung*) (XXII, 11, 73, 82, 85, 404, 406). Apperception is now regarded as "an a priori principle of self-determination" (82), and it is according to "a principle of autonomy" that the subject makes itself into an object. Only in the first Convolut, which was written much later between December 1800 and February 1803, does this development become fully explicit. Kant now makes the concept of autonomy into the fundamental principle of transcendental philosophy itself (XXI, 59, 89, 93, 100, 106–107, 115), and the uniting term of theoretical and practical reason (89, 93, 100). The concept of autonomy is understood in terms of the acts by which the subject determines or posits itself. Transcendental philosophy is now described as a "system of autonomy" where reason constitutes itself or becomes an object to itself (100–101, 107, 115).

The most controversial question about the *Selbstsetzungslehre* still remains, however. Granted that this doctrine involved an *extension, consolidation,* and *development* of Kant's idealism, did it also imply its *transformation* or *revision?* Did Kant abandon his formal idealism through the *Selbstsetzungslehre* and turn, at least in principle, toward the absolute idealism of Schelling and Hegel?[28] There are some good reasons for thinking that this is indeed the case. For the *Selbstsetzungslehre* seems to overthrow some of the fundamental dualisms of Kant's earlier idealism—the very dualisms that distinguish it from Schelling's and Hegel's absolute idealism. Foremost among these dualisms is that between the form and matter of experience. In the first *Kritik*

Kant seemed to uphold this dualism by making the understanding the law-giver of nature in a purely *formal* sense, where it is the source of the categories that are only "concepts of objects in general." In the *Opus postumum,* however, Kant appears to undermine this dualism by making the understanding the source of not only the form but also the content of experience. The system of moving forces is made into a constitutive principle of the possibility of experience, and it explains all perception, even colors, tastes, and sounds, as the product of the relations between forces (XXII, 319, 323, 341, 357). It is indeed striking how Kant, in rationalizing his Transition, insists time and again that we get out of experience only what we have put into it, and that we can know something only insofar as we create it.[29] His favorite slogan becomes '*Forma dat esse rei,*' which seems to imply that the forms of the understanding determine the very essence of perception itself. There are also many passages in the tenth and eleven fascicles where Kant states that the affection of the empirical subject by the moving powers of nature is nothing more than the *self-affection* of the transcendental subject, so that the perception of external objects is nothing more than the transcendental subject's subconscious awareness of its own creations (XXII, 392, 395, 461, 465, 477).[30] Thus it appears as if Kant has so extended the powers of the transcendental subject that he has virtually eliminated the need to postulate the thing-in-itself and the given manifold of sensation.

To what extent did Kant really abandon the dualism between form and matter in the *Opus postumum?* It is indeed the case that Kant expands the domain of form insofar as the system of moving forces is made into a constitutive principle of experience itself. But the border line has only been moved, not abolished. There is still a realm of matter that remains contingent for the dynamic categories. The problem is that the basic categories of the system of forces are still very general, such that they do not determine a priori how any specific object exemplifies them. Of course, for something to be an object of perception, it must illustrate in some manner all the dynamic categories—ponderability (quality), coercibility (quantity), cohesion (relation), and exhaustability (modality)—because these determine *necessary* characteristics of any moving force. But this still leaves room for the realm of the a posteriori, because these categories do not determine the *degree* to which any specific object is ponderable, coerceable, and cohesible. Indeed, Kant himself seems to insist on an irreducible a posteriori dimension to physics when he insists that, though its form is a priori and created, its matter is simply given (XXII, 308, 310–311, 313, 316, 331; XXI, 293, 486, 609).

Nowhere is Kant's retention of his old dualisms more apparent than in his continuing allegiance to the distinction between understanding and sensibility. Although Kant now says that the self-positing subject posits itself through sensibility as well as understanding, this does not mean for him that understanding dominates sensibility, as if sensibility were now only an inchoate or confused form of understanding. Rather, he holds that the subject posits itself through only the *form* of sensibility, while its *matter* is simply given, something that sensibility receives through affection by objects that we know only as appearances (XXII, 115–116). Even if such affection plays a lesser role in the *Opus postumum*, Kant does not deny that sensibility receives its matter through affection by things-in-themselves (XXII, 36).[31] Most important of all, Kant still insists that the a priori forms of sensibility (space and time) are *sui generis*, in principle irreducible to the forms of the understanding. Hence he continues to write, just as he did in the first *Kritik:* "Space and time are not concepts (*conceptus*) but pure sense intuitions (*intuitus*)" (XXII, 12).[32]

Kant's concern about upholding his critical distinctions between form and matter, and understanding and sensibility, appears in a revealing passage from the first fascicle, which was probably written very late (December 1800–February 1803). The note, which seems directed against Fichte, Beck, and all radical idealists, reads like Kant's last will and testament. Writing about the limits of transcendental philosophy, which are transcended when the object ceases to be given and becomes a mere idealistic *Unding*, Kant adds this final cautionary note:

> Here we must remember that we have the *finite* mind before ourselves. The finite mind is that which is active only through passivity, and that reaches the absolute only through limits, [or] only insofar as it receives, acts upon, and shapes matter. Such a mind would therefore combine a drive toward form or the absolute with one toward matter or limits, which are the conditions without which he cannot satisfy or have the first drive. (XXI, 76)[33]

That Kant does not intend to abolish his dualisms is also clear from the transition program itself. If there were no dualism at all between the form and matter of experience, it is difficult to see how there could be a transition problem in the first place. While it is the purpose of the transcendental dynamic to bridge the gap between the transcendental and the empirical, it is important to see that it does so only by preserving that dualism within itself. There can be a science of transition, Kant argues, only if it mediates between the form and matter by containing these elements within itself and doing justice to them both (XXI, 285, 289, 366–367). Thus Kant states time and again that there is a distinction between the form and matter of his dynamic: its form consists in its systematic unity, whereas its matter consists in the aggregate of perceptions given in experience.[34] He then explains that it is only the form of this science that rests on a priori principles, while its matter or content must be established through experience (XXI, 293, 486; XXII, 376). What is capable of a priori classification, he adds, is only the moving powers, while the data in which they are sensed elude in principle all such organization (XXII, 358, 482). Kant also stresses that physics has to consult experience to establish the existence of some of its fundamental objects (XXII, 383, 462), and that the matter or empirical data for the system of physics must be "absolutely given" (XXII, 331). Among these data whose existence has to be established by experience are the moving powers themselves (XXI, 287).

Though it seems perfunctory, Kant's distinction between the two aspects of his transcendental dynamic expresses a central concern of the *Opus postumum*. Kant feared that his extension of the transcendental to the realm of moving forces would blur, or even appear to abolish, his careful distinctions between the a priori and the a posteriori, the transcendental and the empirical, established in the first *Kritik*. Time and again he admits that it is very strange that there can be an a priori system of moving forces, and that it is possible to give a transcendental deduction of the ether.[35] This apparent oddity arose, of course, because it seemed to violate the distinction between the a priori and the a posteriori in the first *Kritik*. Kant's way of removing this air of inconsistency was to distinguish between an a priori and a posteriori dimension of the transcendental dynamic itself. This distinction is his way of saying that although there is indeed an a priori system of the moving forces of matter, it is still necessary to know about the existence of these forces from experience itself. Kant's concern with maintaining the distinction between a priori and a posteriori appears most forcefully in a striking passage from Convolut V where he raises the question why there is need for a transition program at all: Why not just apply the metaphysical principles to experience and be done with it? (XXI, 526) Kant's response is that we must be careful not to confuse the realms of the transcendental and empirical. There is nothing worse for "*Gründlichkeit*," he warns, than when these domains are simply pushed together, for that gives rise to all kinds of fallacies and confusions.

Granted that Kant still wants to retain his dualism between the a priori and the a posteriori, the form and matter of experience, his *Selbstsetz-*

ungslehre seems to undermine two other basic dualisms of the first *Kritik:* the distinctions between the noumenal and phenomenal and the transcendental and empirical. There are two apparent implications of the concept of self-positing that seem to undercut these dualisms and to anticipate Fichte's more radical idealism. First, to say that the subject posits itself is to say that it *makes* itself, that it *constitutes* itself through its creations. Kant himself appears to make this perfectly explicit when he states that "the subject makes itself" (XXI, 85, 94; XXII 82, 353). Second, to say that the subject posits itself is to say that it objectifies itself, that it reveals itself through its productions. Kant himself seems to endorse this implication too by speaking about the subject's "objectifying" and "presenting" itself through its manifestations. Thus Kant's language of self-positing seems to mean both *self-creation* (according to the first implication) and *self-revelation* (according to the second). If self-positing means self-creation and self-revelation, then Kant's dualisms crumble. For if the subject creates and reveals itself through its *phenomenal* manifestations, then in some sense it must become *identified* with them. If the transcendental and noumenal becomes and reveals what it is through the phenomenal, then it must also in some sense *be* phenomenal or empirical. It was indeed on just these grounds that Fichte believed his concept of the self-positing self made it necessary to dispense with an unknowable subject in itself.

Still, despite these apparent implications, Kant does not give the concept of the self-positing subject the same meaning as Fichte. That he does not think that the self-positing subject creates or reveals itself through its phenomenal manifestations becomes clear from his retention of the earlier concept of *self-affection,* which he had put forward in the second edition of the *Kritik.* The concept of self-affection is the ancestor of self-positing, and so much so that the terms 'self-affection' and 'self-positing' (or 'self-objectification') are virtually synonomous (XXII, 326, 358).[36] When Kant writes in the *Opus postumum* of the self "positing," "making," "objectifiying" itself he also means or says that the self "affects" itself. This is crucial because the doctrine of self-affection involves the *negation* of self-creation and self-revelation. Self-affection means that the subject that affects itself knows itself only as an appearance and not as it is in itself (against self-revelation), and that there is a distinction between the self as the subject who affects itself and the self as object who is affected by itself (against self-creation).

To see this, it is only necessary to recall that in the first *Kritik* Kant develops the concept of self-affection to show that self-knowledge is subject to the same restrictions as all knowledge. To know itself the subject must apply the categories and form of inner sense to a given manifold. This means, however, that the subject knows itself only as an appearance, because in affecting itself by applying the categories and inner sense to itself it changes or alters itself, so that it cannot know itself as it exists apart from and prior to the application of the forms of understanding and sensibility. Hence the self knows itself only as it appears for the categories and inner sense. Rather than denying the restriction of self-knowledge to appearances in the *Opus postumum*, Kant reaffirms it repeatedly, making it perfectly explicit that to affect myself implies that I know myself only as an appearance (XXII, 27, 31, 73, 78, 390, 416, 417).

Rather than making self-positing the pivotal concept of the *Opus postumum*, it would be more accurate to stress the concept of self-affection. Though Kant himself often writes of *Selbstaffektion*, he never uses the term '*Selbstsetzung*,' and '*sich setzen*' is only one of the many phrases he uses to express the basic idea of self-affection. The term '*Selbstsetzungslehre*' is indeed only a scholarly anachronism, and it would be more true to Kant's intentions to speak of a *Selbstaffektionslehre*, given that he repeatedly stresses the importance of the concept of self-affection for his transition program (XXII, 366, 387–388, 392, 395, 404, 405).

6. Appearance of Appearance: Continuity with Critical Doctrines

Another new development in Kant's transcendental idealism in the *Opus postumum* is his concept of "appearance of appearance" (*Erscheinung der Erscheinung*). This concept is a central theme of the tenth Convolut, which Kant most probably wrote from August until the end of 1799. The shift from his earlier writings is striking. Kant no longer writes simply of appearances, as he did in the three *Kritiken*, but now distinguishes between degrees or levels of appearances, between appearances and the appearances of them, "appearances of appearances." He also formulates this distinction in terms of *direct* and *indirect* appearances or phenomena,[37] appearances of the first and second order (*Ordnung*) or degree (*Rang*) (XXII, 339, 367), and even experiences of experience (455). To add to the confusion, Kant also distinguishes between appearance in the metaphysical and physiological sense (320, 325), and between *subjective* and *objective* appearances (339, 378).

The concept of appearance of appearance is closely connected to that of the self-positing or self-affecting self. The product of the self-positing self's activity—its self-objectification—is nothing less than appearance of appearance. When the subject affects itself through its own activity, Kant often writes, it does so as appearance of appearance. Hence the distinction between levels of appearance is sometimes formulated in terms of kinds of affection: appearances arise from the affection of our sensibility, whereas appearances of appearances arise from self-affection (XXII, 321, 326, 340, 367, 371, 373).

It has been said that the concept of appearance of appearance is "among the most difficult developed by Kant,"[38] and not least because it shifts greatly in meaning from one passage to another. No less than eighteen features of its meaning have been noted.[39] Since the texts are very involved and confused, it should not be surprising that there is much dispute about its meaning. There has first been some debate about whether the concept involves the retention or elimination of transcendental affection and the thing-in-itself. According to Vaihinger, Adickes, and Kemp Smith, the concept is the ultimate product of Kant's growing empirical realism,[40] the final proof for his allegiance to the doctrine of double affection, which assumes that empirical objects act on the empirical ego as the thing-in-itself acts on the transcendental ego.[41] According to Lehmann, however, the concept expresses the result of Kant's increasingly radical transcendental idealism, which makes the whole realm of perception nothing less than the product of the self-positing self.[42] Rather than a proof of a doctrine of double affection, Lehmann insists that this concept dispenses entirely with the thing-in-itself. There also has been some debate about whether the concept presupposes or abolishes Kant's distinction between the form and matter of experience. According to Vitorrio Mathieu and Kurt Hübner, the concept only makes sense in the context of Kant's distinction between understanding and sensibility; according to Lehmann, however, the concept involves the reduction, if not the abolition, of Kant's original distinction.[43] To find a clear path through this maze, it is best to reconstruct Kant's concept from its original context.

After writing the ether proofs in the second and fifth fascicles, Kant introduces the concept of an appearance of appearance in the tenth fascicle in the context of reexplaining his transition program. Here he asks himself repeatedly a question he had already raised many times in fascicles II–VI: "What is physics?" Time and again he attempts to find the proper formulation for the subject matter of the physics he intends to transform according to the metaphysical principles of natural science. He distinguishes between two forms of physics: that *before* and that *after* the execution of the transition program. Before the transition, physics is essentially an empirical discipline, whose main business is observation and experiment, and whose central goal is to collect an aggregate of observations or mass of data. After the transition, however, physics acquires an a priori form, becoming a single system organized according to a priori principles. Kant sometimes uses other terms to define this distinction: it is that between *Naturbeschreibung* and *Naturerklärung* (XXII, 341), *Naturgeschichte* and *systematische Physiologie* (307), or *System der Natur* in the sense of Linneus and *Systematik der Natur* (501; cf. 482). Whatever the terms, he says that these two kinds of physics relate to one another as matter and form (281, 311, 313, 319). While empirical physics provides the matter, which derives from observation and experiment, a priori physics supplies the form, which consists in systematic unity according to metaphysical principles.

Following this distinction, Kant also distinguishes between the two forms of physics in terms of their subject matter or epistemic elements. The special subject matter of empirical physics is the aggregate of perceptions (*Wahrnehmungen*), while that of a priori physics is experience (*Erfahrung*). Kant defines perception as "empirical representation with consciousness," which consist in the sensations that arise from the affection of sensibility and whose contents are represented in space and time. In contrast, he identifies experience with "a *system* of perceptions" (400), "the thoroughgoing *connection* of perceptions in space and time and both joined together" (346), "a *whole* of perceptions according to the understanding formed under one concept" (361), and "the absolute *unity* of the knowledge of the objects of the senses" (497). What is characteristic of, and essential to, experience, then, is its unity, wholeness, or systematicity. There can be really *only one* experience, Kant insists, and if we speak of many we really only mean *perceptions* within one experience. According to these distinctions, then, a priori physics relates to empirical physics as experience does to perception, that is, as the unity of the manifold to the aggregate of its particular elements.

Though it seems to be purely routine, Kant's distinction between the two forms of physics is especially relevent to his concept of appearance of appearance. For Kant develops this concept especially to designate the distinctive subject matter of a priori physics. While empirical physics deals directly with appearances themselves, a priori physics concerns appearances of appearances. Following the distinction between experience and perception, this means that the realm of appearance of appearance should consist in ex-

perience, whereas the domain of appearance alone should consist in perceptions. This is indeed the case. Kant's distinction between the two levels of
appearance in fascicles X and XI corresponds perfectly to his distinction between experience and perception. Kant almost always uses 'appearance of
appearances' to refer to the *system* of perceptions, their *unity* in a coherent
whole, whereas he applies 'appearances' to designate the *aggregate* of perceptions in space and time.[44] In other words, the realm of appearance consists in the manifold of perceptions, whereas the domain of appearance of
appearance consists in experience. Hence Kant sometimes uses the expression 'object of experience' (*Erfahrungsgegenstand*) as a synonym for appearance of appearance (XXII, 364).

This context gives a perfectly straightfoward account of the sense in which
appearances of appearances are second-order, a function of first-order appearances. Experience is an appearance of appearance because it is formed
by the concepts of the understanding, which synthesize appearances, the
manifold of perceptions given to sensibility. The distinction between levels
of appearance then mirrors Kant's earlier distinction between understanding and sensibility in the first *Kritik*. There Kant maintained that the concepts of the understanding are *mediate* representations—or representations
of representations—because they consist in a universal that represents the
many particular representations of the manifold; those particular representations that relate directly to their object are intuitions given to sensibility
(B 93). Since the realm of experience is formed by concepts of the understanding, representations of representations, it too consists in appearances
of appearances. The distinction between second- and first-order appearances then corresponds to Kant's earlier distinction between understanding
and sensibility in the first *Kritik*.

Rather than destroying the earlier distinction between understanding and
sensibility, the distinction between orders of appearances presupposes it.
Appearances are a function of sensibility because it consists in perceptions,
which arise from the affection of the sense organs by external things; but appearances of appearances are a function of the understanding, which unifies
the manifold of sensibility. In some passages from fascicle X Kant is perfectly
explicit in explaining the distinction in terms of his old dualism between the
a priori and the a posteriori:

The appearance of things in space (and in time) is twofold. 1. Those objects
that consist in what we posit in them (a priori) and is metaphysical. 2.

[Those] that are empirically given (a posteriori) and is physical. The latter is
direct appearance; the first is indirect appearance, ie. appearance of an appearance. (XXII, 340)

Kant returns to the old distinction again when he states that appearances
arise from the forms of intuition of sensibility, whereas appearances of appearances derive from the synthetic activity of the understanding:

The pure intuition of the manifold in space contains the form of the object
in the appearance a priori of the first order, ie. direct. The combination of
the perceptions . . . in the subject for the sake of experience is again the appearance of the so affected subject as it represents itself, and is indirect or of
the second degree, appearance of appearance.(XXII, 367)

The old distinction between understanding and sensibility resurfaces yet
again when Kant states that appearances must be first given to sensibility
before they are combined according to the acts of the understanding, which
create the unity of experience and hence appearances of appearances (XXII,
364, 367, 371, 458).

That Kant intends to distinguish between his layers of appearance according to some form of the distinction between understanding and sensibility is
apparent from his reintroduction in the tenth fascicle of an old theme from
the first *Kritik:* the amphibolies of reflection. The purpose of reflection, Kant
held in the *Kritik,* is to determine the cognitive faculty to which representations belong (B 317–318). It deals not only with the logical form but also the
content of concepts, ascertaining whether they belong to understanding or
sensibility. An amphiboly arises when we confuse these faculties, conflating
a representation of the understanding with an intuition of sensibility or conversely (B 326).

Now it is striking that Kant returns to this theme when he introduces his
concept of the appearance of appearances.[45] He now explains that there are
two kinds of illusion involved in the amphibolies (320). The first occurs
when we mistake the subjective with the objective, or appearances with
things-in-themselves; the second happens when we confuse the empirical
with the transcendental, or when we reify the necessary conditions of experience as if they were some kind of thing within experience itself. The point
behind the concept of an appearance of appearance is to prevent these kinds
of confusion. It draws a distinction between different logical orders so that

we do not confuse the transcendental (appearances of appearances) with the empirical (appearances).

Despite such textual evidence, this interpretation has been dismissed on the grounds that Kant had already abandoned his sharp dualism between understanding and sensibility in the Transcendental Deduction of the first *Kritik*.[46] According to this objection, the drastic dualism between understanding and sensibility, in which sensibility receives representations that are then processed by the understanding, was only provisional and completely undermined by the Deduction, whose central conclusion is that nothing can be given to sensibility unless it is formed through the understanding. This objection has a point: there is indeed something troubling about Kant's simplistic restatement of his earlier dualism, which seems to regress to older abandoned doctrines. Furthermore, such a restatement appears flatly inconsistent with his frequent statements in Convolut X that nothing can be given in perception that we have not put into it (XXII, 287, 306, 309, 319, 323, 331, 343, 361–362).

It is important to see, however, that we can uphold the central conclusion of the Deduction without dropping the form–matter dualism. Kant can continue to think that nothing can be given to sensibility apart from the understanding, and still retain some form of his dualism between understanding and sensibility. There is a simple but crucial distinction to be made here between being *conditioned* by the understanding and being *created* by it. It is possible that the object of perception is completely conditioned by the understanding, so that no aspect of the object as it is presented to consciousness is simply given; nevertheless, there is still an underlying material of sensation that cannot be created by the understanding. *Forma dat esse rei*, of course, but essence does not mean sheer existence and materiality. This is Kant's position in the first *Kritik*—apart from the preliminary exposition in section 1, chapter II, of the Analytic—and it remains his view in the *Opus postumum*.

Applying this distinction to the concept of an appearance of appearance, the distinction between levels of appearance is then a distinction between those appearances that are only *conditioned* by the understanding and those that are entirely *created* by it. While appearances are indeed conditioned by the understanding, since the content of perception has to be formed by the understanding, they are not completely created by it, because they must also be given to sensibility. Appearances of appearances, however, are *created* by the understanding since the form of experience is entirely the product of self-affection and is not given in any manner. While Kant never puts the distinction in just this form, and his language sometimes suggests his pre-Deduction dualism, this *reformulation* saves him from a serious inconsistency.

It would seem, then, that Kant develops the concept of an appearance of appearance to maintain his dualism between understanding and sensibility, and not to express the consequences of abolishing it. The whole point of the concept appears to be to reveal the difference in kind between those representations that are a function of understanding and those that are a function of sensibility; or, to speak more in accord with the result of the Deduction, between those that are *entirely* a function of the understanding and those that are *only partly so* and also a function of sensibility. After all, this is only in keeping with Kant's concern to maintain some form of his dualism within the transition program, which had to observe boundaries as well as bridge them.

7. Appearance of Appearance: Its Novelty

Yet this is not the end of the story. The whole business becomes much more complicated once we realize that the idea of an appearance of appearance also played another role for Kant: to explain and defend the peculiar status of the ether. It is indeed noteworthy that Kant first writes about direct and indirect objects of experience in his remarks on the ether proofs in the section entitled *Übergang* 1–14 (XXI, 543, 576). Furthermore, he seems to have first planned a section on the amphibolies to prevent confusion about the transcendental status of the ether (XXI, 545–546). Kant fears that it is very easy to think of the ether as a kind of hypothesis—a mere fiction or *qualitas occulta*—because it cannot be confirmed by direct experience. The amphibolies remove this confusion between the transcendental and the empirical, because there are two different—but equally legitimate—means of establishing the existence of something that cannot be given in immediate experience: either through conjectures from experience or by showing something to be a necessary condition of the possibility of experience itself.

If the point behind the concept of appearance of appearance is to legitimate the ether, then this concept cannot be simply a variant of the distinction between understanding and sensibility after all. The very opposite would seem to be the case, for, as we have already seen, the ether does not readily or easily follow Kant's normal distinction between the formal and the material, or the transcendental and empirical. This concept has a unique status because it has objective reality and yet also serves as a necessary condition of experience. Kant states that the ether is the *substrate* underlying all moving forces, that it is the *objective basis* for the community of nature, and that it is the *basis* or *matter* of all experience; nevertheless, he also holds that it cannot be found within experience because its existence cannot be confirmed by perception (XXI, 543, 561–562, 574, 576). Now it is striking that the concept of an appearance of appearance has just this peculiar status. The term is especially apt because an appearance of appearance stands on a different logical level from appearances themselves, and so cannot be derived from perception; yet it is still a kind of appearance or experience, even if an indirect or second-order one, because the transcendental conditions of experience enter into the very constitution of experience itself, and so have a kind of reality themselves. What we create is indeed part of what we perceive; the only mistake comes in thinking that it is derived from perception when it is created for it. The whole concept of appearance of appearance then denotes something very like the ether: it is not simply a formal condition of experience on the one hand, but also something that it is not within the content of perception itself on the other hand. It is that which has reality as the whole of experience but cannot be verified in any particular experience.

If we consider all these factors, it is necessary to conclude that the concept of an appearance of appearance plays a new and unique role in Kant's transcendental idealism. On the one hand, it presupposes the distinction between understanding and sensibility because it tells us that the products of the understanding (appearances of appearances) must not be confused with those of sensibility (appearances). Kant could indeed defend the transcendental status of the ether only by maintaining a distinction in kind between these forms of representation. Yet, on the other hand, the concept also bridges that dualism by showing how, at least in the case of the ether, the transcendental condition of experience enters into experience itself. The point in talking about appearances of appearances, of indirect appearances, is to show that the transcendental too appears, entering into the constitution of experience itself, if only indirectly.

In sum, the concept essentially amounts to a *reformulation* or *refinement* of the distinction between the form and matter of experience. It brings out how in some cases the form of experience becomes an element—though only an indirect one—constitutive of experience itself. To an extent, this conclusion was already implicit in the first *Kritik,* because Kant had always insisted in the Transcendental Deduction that the conditions of the possibility of experience are constitutive of experience itself; yet this point did not jibe well with his own sharper distinction between form and matter, understanding and sensibility. The value of the concept of appearance of appearance, then, is that it reformulates Kant's distinction between matter and form so that it is more in accord with the results of the Deduction. Kant now devises the term 'appearance of appearance,' or 'indirect appearances,' to express how the transcendental conditions of experience are an element within experience itself. He was most likely led to such a conclusion through his reflection on the peculiar status of the ether.

It is only necessary to add that this interpretation of the concept of an appearance of appearance differs markedly from that given by some of its foremost exponents. According to Vaihinger, Adickes, Drews, and Kemp Smith,[47] the concept of an appearance of appearance is essentially the result of Kant's growing empirical realism, which began with the Refutation of Idealism in the second edition of the *Kritik*. The point of the concept is to express how, according to Kant's empirical realism, we can treat appearances as if they were things-in-themselves, so that they exist in both matter and form independent of *empirical* consciousness. Empirical realism means that appearances act on empirical consciousness just as if they were physical things, so that the whole distinction between subject and object falls within the realm of appearances. This implies that the empirical ego's representations of physical things are appearances of appearances, given that from a transcendental standpoint its objects are really only appearances. This account of the concept becomes more complicated, however, when these scholars also interpret it along the lines of their doctrine of double affection. According to this doctrine, the distinction between levels of appearance is also a distinction between forms of affection: appearances are the result of the affection of the transcendental self by the thing-in-itself, whereas appearances of appearances are the effect of the affection of the empirical ego by empirical objects.

There are some grains of truth to this interpretation. There is indeed a deeper empirical realism in the *Opus postumum*—even if Vaihinger, Adickes, and Kemp Smith underestimate its presence in the first edition of the *Kritik*—insofar as Kant often writes about appearances as if they were things-in-themselves. Furthermore, Kant does introduce the concept in the context of a discussion about how appearances can be treated as things-in-themselves from the scientific standpoint (XXII, 318–320). Apart from this, however, there is a grave lack of textual evidence for this reading. It is strik-ing that Kant *rarely* uses the phrase 'appearance of appearance' to designate the status of the empirical ego's representations.[48] Most passages show that the very opposite is the case: rather than referring to empirical representa-tions, which are only perceptions and so on the level of appearances them-selves, 'appearance of appearance' denotes the transcendental ego's second-order construction of appearances from empirical representations.[49]

There is also little warrant for reading the concept of appearance of ap-pearances according to the doctrine of double affection. *Prima facie* there seems to be some evidence for this interpretation because, in one central passage, Kant writes of the distinction between appearance and thing-in-it-self as concerning "the manner in which the subject is affected (by the ob-ject) in its form" (XXII, 19–20, 320).[50] Although Kant often refers to the dis-tinction in terms of kind of affection, the kinds of affection he has in mind give no support for the double affection interpretation. What Kant often says is that the affection of sensibility gives rise to perceptions, while the self-affection of the transcendental self creates experience.[51] This is not a dis-tinction between affection by appearances and by things-in-themselves but between self-affection and affection by something else, whether that is ap-pearances or things-in-themselves.

8. The Thing-in-Itself

One of the most interesting—and controversial—aspects of the *Opus postumum* for the interpretation of Kant's transcendental idealism concerns the status of the thing-in-itself. There are many passages in the seventh and tenth fascicles where Kant seems to doubt or deny the existence of the thing-in-itself and where he explicitly assigns it the status of a mere *Gedankending* or *ens rationis*.[52] It is as if Kant finally admits the full conse-quences of his critical principles, realizing that he cannot postulate the exis-tence of something whose nature and reality should be completely unknow-able to him. The implications for his idealism are obvious: if the thing-in-itself is a mere fiction, then transcendental idealism cannot claim to be a kind of formal idealism whose distinguishing characteristic is that it leaves intact the reality of things-in-themselves.

The passages from the seventh and tenth fascicles are intricate and ob-scure, giving different accounts of the thing-in-itself and why it should be understood as an *ens rationis*. Not surprisingly, then, these passages too have been the subject of conflicting interpretations. Some scholars have regarded them as a disavowal of the reality of things-in-themselves, while others see them as simply a restatement of views Kant already held in the 1780s.[53] Since the interpretation of these passages is so controversial, it is necessary to consider them in a little detail.

There is one set of passages where Kant states that the thing-in-itself is not a kind of existing object but only the basic principle for synthetic a priori knowledge. The thing-in-itself is assigned a purely immanent function in establishing the objectivity of our knowledge; but as a transcendent entity it is dismissed as a mere *ens rationis*. Thus Kant writes: "The thing-in-itself is not a given object existing outside our representation, but only the positing (*die Position*) of a thought-entity which is thought of as corresponding to the object" (31). The thing-in-itself is explicitly identified with a principle of synthesis: "The object in itself = X is not a particular object but only the mere principle of synthetic a priori knowledge, which contains the formal element of the unity of this manifold of intuition" (20). In a similar vein Kant states: "The thing-in-itself = X is not an object given to the senses but only the principle of the synthetic a priori knowledge of the manifold of sense intuition in general and the law of its coordination"(33). More simply, Kant says: "the thing-in-itself is not at all an existing thing but is merely a principle" (34).

In another set of complementary passages Kant develops this line of thought by insisting that the thing-in-itself is only the correlate of the self-positing self, the product of its purely rational activity. Hence in referring to the matter of experience he writes: "The material [element of experience]— the thing in itself—is = X [and] is the mere representation of the subject's own activity" (37). A striking passage from fascicle X reads: "The thing in itself is a thought-entity [*Gedankending*] (*ens rationis*) through which the subject constitutes itself for the connection of the whole manifold to unity" (414). Of course, these passages only reinforce those where Kant equates the thing-in-itself with a principle of the unity of experience. They simply add that this principle is the product of the self-positing subject, or that it is nothing more than its self-objectification. On the basis of these passages, it has been argued that Kant wants to eliminate the thing-in-itself as a kind of entity and to ascribe to it a completely *immanent* function in creating objectivity for the manifold of perceptions. The thing-in-itself now becomes nothing more than an expression for the *limitation* of our own self-positing activity, the fact that we are finite and cannot create all of our experience.[54]

Read in context, however, there is little surprising or new in these passages, which simply return to a line of thinking established in the first *Kritik*. They do not necessarily imply that Kant doubts or denies the reality of the thing-in-itself, but only that he thinks it plays no useful role in the explanation of the objectivity of knowledge. The *X* in question here, the formal principle of our experience, is an old friend from the first edition of the first *Kritik:* the transcendental object. In many passages of the *Kritik* Kant had often equated the thing-in-itself with the transcendental object, because it usurped the thing-in-itself's traditional role of providing objectivity to experience (e.g., A 250–251, 277).[55] He had argued against transcendental realism that the concept of the thing-in-itself, interpreted as a transcendent entity that exists apart from and prior to our perception of it, is useless in explaining the objectivity of experience. To ascribe objectivity to our perceptions, we had to understand the thing-in-itself in terms of the *concept* of an object (the transcendental object), which provides objectivity by synthesizing a manifold of perceptions according to a rule.

It is striking that the passages from the *Opus postumum* appear in a similar context, where Kant again attempts to explain the source of the objectivity of our experience. He is again saying—as he already had in 1781—that to explain the objectivity of our experience the thing-in-itself is best interpreted as the transcendental object. It is for this reason—and this alone—that Kant insists in these passages that the thing-in-itself is an *ens rationis*. He is not denying or doubting the existence of things-in-themselves, but only arguing against transcendental realism that they can have no useful role as an explanation of the possibility of experience.

It is in the same context that we should read other passages of the seventh fascicle where Kant seems to make the thing-in-itself a mere idea. He writes, for example, that "the thing-in-itself is not an object existing for itself but only an idea" (28), where this idea is that of a completely determined experience, one in which every property of a perception is made determinate according to some concept of the understanding. When Kant describes the thing-in-itself as a *Gedankending* this means, at least in some contexts, that it is not a mere fiction or illusion but an ideal for the complete knowledge of appearances. Again, Kant is not necessarily doubting or denying the reality of things-in-themselves understood as transcendent entities—their status remains simply problematic—but only explaining how the concept should be used in an immanent sense.

There is another set of passages where Kant states explicitly that the thing-in-itself is not a specific entity but only another perspective on the object that appears (XXII, 26, 42–44, 412, 414). The thing-in-itself now seems to designate only that purely negative standpoint in which we consider the object in abstraction from all features of our sensibility. Kant comes closest to this perspectival reading when he writes: "the thing-in-itself = *X* is not another object but only another [standpoint], namely the negative standpoint from which we consider one and the same object" (42). He also stresses that the thing-in-itself is simply "a relational concept" (*Verhält-nißbegriff*) to consider another relation of the object to our representation of it: "The thing-in-itself *(ens per se)* is not another object but another relation of our representation to the same object" (26). This other relation arises when we consider the same object insofar as it is *not* subject to the transcendental conditions of our experience of it; but we have no right to think of it as a separate entity, Kant insists, because it is a mere "cipher" to designate something problematic (37).

Here again, though, there is little new in these passages, which only restate a position Kant had already developed in the 1780s. Kant simply reaffirms his view—already stated in some passages of the first *Kritik*—that the distinction between appearance and thing-in-itself is not between kinds of entity but only different aspects or relations of one and the same entity.[56] He is not denying or doubting that there are other aspects of these entities besides phenomenal ones; rather, he is only insisting on their problematic status. But that too is hardly a new development. That the concept of a thing-in-itself is purely problematic was already firmly stated in the chapter on 'Noumena and Phenomena' in the first *Kritik* (B 310–311).

The more closely we consider these later passages the more it becomes obvious that Kant cannot be doubting or denying the reality of things-in-themselves. To be sure, he is not affirming their reality; but he is definitely insisting on their possibility. This emphasis on the purely problematic status of the thing-in-itself is only in keeping with his general doctrine about the limits of knowledge, which forbid us to affirm or deny the reality of anything beyond possible experience. Hence Kant cannot be claiming that the concept of a thing-in-itself is a complete fiction in the sense that it does not exist, for that too would be to make a dogmatic claim that violates his strictures about the possibility of knowledge. Of course, it could be argued that Kant does mean to deny their existence because he now finally recognizes that any existence claim has meaning only within the realm of phenomena; but this interpretation flatly contradicts Kant's increasing insistence after

1787 that the categories do have meaning for objects in general, or that we can at least *think* things-in-themselves according to the categories.

A close reading of the seventh and tenth fascicles confirms, then, that Kant was still clinging to his doctrine of the 1780s. While he insists upon the problematic status of things-in-themselves, Kant is still far from denying their reality. Indeed, he continues to reaffirm the doctrine of the second *Kritik* that practical reason gives us reason to believe in their reality, even when it cannot be demonstrated by theoretical reason. Thus in the seventh fascicle Kant repeatedly states that we can affirm the reality of freedom and God only because of the concept of duty, which is prescribed by practical reason (52–53, 58, 60, 62). The explanation for Kant's greater caution in the seventh fascicle most probably lies in his historical context. Pressed hard by his critics and students, he had to show that he was not violating his critical principles.[57] Nevertheless, he remained fully convinced of the essentials of the doctrine he had already established in the three *Kritiken*.[58] In this regard, as in so many others in the *Opus postumum*, Kant kept his peruke firmly attached.

PART II

Fichte's Critique of Subjectivism

Introduction: The Interpretation
of Fichte's Idealism

Since the late eighteenth century, there have been two dominant interpretations of Fichte's early idealism, the so-called Jena *Wissenschaftslehre*
developed by Fichte in his Jena years (1794–1799). According to one interpretation, Fichte's early idealism is essentially a form of "*absolute* idealism"
because it affirms the existence of an absolute ego that posits itself as all reality, and that creates not only the form but also the content of experience.
This absolute idealism is a radical and complete form of Kant's transcendental idealism for two reasons: first, it eliminates the thing-in-itself and the
given manifold; and, second, it universalizes the transcendental subject, so
that there is not one such subject per person but only one infinite subject.
According to the other interpretation, Fichte's early idealism is basically a
form of "*subjective* idealism" because it limits all knowledge down to the representations of the *finite* subject and confers only a regulative status upon
the absolute ego. Such subjective idealism is essentially a form of solipsism,
because it either denies or doubts the reality of anything beyond our own
representations. After trapping the ego inside the circle of its own consciousness, it acknowledges only a *practical* basis for our belief in an external
world. In other words, though it admits we do not *know* there is an external
world, it still insists that we *ought to* believe in one.

The first interpretation, which is still widespread in the English-speaking
world, has been common in standard histories of philosophy.[1] The second
has been less prevalent, but it too has a venerable history. It began with
Jacobi's famous 1799 *Brief an Fichte;* it was then adopted by Schelling and
Hegel; and it is still common in Marxist histories of philosophy.[2]

These interpretations are utterly irreconcilable, at conflict on every point.
The first interpretation *removes* all limits on the transcendental subject, gives
it a *constitutive* status, and *denies* the reality of the thing-in-itself as well as the
given empirical manifold. The second interpretation *retains* all limits on the

217

transcendental subject, grants it only a *regulative* status, and *affirms* the existence of both the thing-in-itself and the empirical manifold.

It seems extraordinary that there can be two such radically opposed readings of any philosopher. But that this is so only demonstrates the difficulty of interpreting Fichte. Each interpretation has its strengths. The first alone seems consistent with Fichte's radical idealist program, which expressly banishes the thing-in-itself, and which explicitly affirms the unity of the intellectual and empirical. The second alone does justice to Fichte's insistence upon the limits of knowledge: that we cannot transcend experience, that we cannot escape the circle of consciousness, and that we are doomed to an infinite striving toward unattainable ideals. But each interpretation also has its weaknesses. The first, by postulating the reality of an absolute subject, makes Fichte's idealism into a transcendent metaphysics, flatly contrary to its teaching about the limits of knowledge. The second, by trapping the ego inside the circle of its own representations, flies in the face of Fichte's empirical realism, his attempt to demonstrate the reality of other minds and the external world.

Obviously, the best reading of Fichte's idealism would combine the strengths, and avoid the weaknesses, of both interpretations. It would show how Fichte evades both solipsism and a transcendent metaphysics; and it would explain his idealist principles *and* his teaching about the limits of human knowledge. The following chapters attempt to do justice to these apparently conflicting demands. I will try to steer a *via media* between the opposing interpretations of Fichte's early idealism.

Against the absolute idealist interpretation, I read Fichte's early philosophy as a system of *pragmatic* idealism.[3] Such a system consists in four fundamental propositions, all of them aspects of Fichte's doctrine of the primacy of practical reason.

- The world, in its present condition, *is* not ideal or rational, but it *ought* to become so through our striving as moral agents. Although what we now know in our experience is indeed posited by our rational activity, there always remains an extent to which the world is simply given, for we as finite beings do not have the power to create all of our experience. We can, however, diminish the given, and increase the created, content of experience as we approach the ideal of complete independence: total power over nature. We approach this ideal through concrete action, through making nature conform to our purposes.

- The absolute ego, which posits all reality, is not a constitutive principle but a regulative ideal. It represents the ideal for moral action of the finite ego: absolute independence, complete causality over nature.
- Knowledge arises from action or practice, not from contemplation or theory. There cannot be any reply to skepticism from a purely contemplative or theoretical standpoint, which only thinks about the world but which does not change it; rather, the problems of skepticism can be resolved only through action, through changing the world and making it conform to the demands of our reason.[4]
- We cannot explain the possibility of experience according to theoretical reason but only according to practical reason. The fundamental principle for the deduction of experience is the self-consciousness of our freedom.

Against the subjective idealist interpretation, I argue that the central purpose of Fichte's Jena *Wissenschaftslehre* was to avoid the charges of subjectivism that had been leveled against Kant's philosophy in the 1780s. For Fichte, no less than Kant, transcendental idealism had to explain empirical reality, the existence of an external world. Throughout the Jena years Fichte developed several refutations of empirical idealism and solipsism, or various deductions of the reality of the external world and other minds. In Chapters 7 and 8 below I attempt to reconstruct Fichte's arguments for the reality of the external world and other minds. Although we shall find serious problems with these arguments, the need to examine them seriously and in detail shows that Jacobi's charge of nihilism fails.

Although Fichte's idealism has often been read as the very epitome of modern subjectivism, the truth of the matter is that Fichte radically broke with this tradition. We shall see in subsequent chapters that he departed from it in three fundamental respects. First, he argued that I am self-conscious only because I am also conscious of an external world. Second, he questioned the privacy of the Cartesian subject by defending the thesis that all self-knowledge is intersubjective, depending on a normative structure of mutual recognition. Third, and most radically, he contended that all knowledge is based on our practical activity, and ultimately on the will; in other words, we acquire knowledge not through contemplation but through action. The subjectivist tradition had made itself vulnerable to skepticism, Fichte charged, because it presupposed a contemplative model of knowledge, according to which we know objects simply by thinking about them.

Fichte is the first philosopher in the modern idealist tradition to attack radically the classical distinction between knowing and doing, thinking and acting.[5]

To be sure, this does not mean that Fichte completely rejected the Cartesian heritage. We still have some reason to place Fichte within this tradition since, like Kant, he continued to affirm that the world is constituted by, and appears according to, the activity by which we know it. He too was an opponent of transcendental realism, the doctrine that the objects of knowledge are thing-in-themselves that continue to exist when we do not perceive them. For this reason, recent accounts of Fichte's idealism, which understand it entirely in terms of his antinaturalism, or his belief in "the autonomy of the normative," are insufficient.[6] The problem with such interpretations is that antinaturalism alone is still compatible with transcendental realism, a doctrine that Fichte decidedly rejects. When Fichte defines his philosophy as 'criticism' in contrast to 'dogmatism' he explicitly opposes it to transcendental realism as well as naturalism (see below, 2.3.2). Hence Spinozism, Fichte's nemesis, represents not only mechanism but a monistic form of transcendental realism, the belief in the reality of the thing-in-itself.

It is indeed one general result of the present reading of Fichte's early idealism that its differences with Kant's transcendental idealism are not as great as commonly assumed. Regarding the limits of knowledge and the sources of experience, some of the main principles of Fichte's *critical* idealism turn out to be very similar to Kant's *formal* idealism. Although Fichte does avow radical idealist principles, which imply the elimination of the thing-in-itself and the given manifold, these principles eventually reveal themselves to be regulative rather than constitutive, prescriptions for action rather than descriptions of reality. In the end, the critical idealism of the Jena *Wissenschaftslehre* does affirm the existence of a thing-in-itself and a given manifold, even if their status is greatly diminished. Like Kant's formal idealism, it maintains that, to some extent, the matter of experience remains given; through the ceaseless striving to gain power over the world we can approach, but never attain, its complete elimination.

This is not to say, of course, that Fichte's idealism is identical with Kant's. We shall find below that there are still fundamental differences, and that these are so great that they undermine Fichte's claim that his system represents nothing but "the spirit of Kant's philosophy." To summarize and anticipate, there are four basic differences. First, Fichte makes practical reason, the root of all reason, the fundamental basis of experience itself. Second,

Fichte understands the transcendental activity by which we form experience not only in a theoretical but also a practical sense; it is not only an intellectual but also a practical operation. Third, Fichte makes the distinction between understanding and sensibility a matter of degree rather than kind. Fourth, Fichte assumes a greater self-awareness of freedom than is possible in the Kantian system: he thinks that I can know not only *that* I am free but also *how* I am so, or in what my activity consists.

The interpretation of Fichte's idealism in the following chapters is based on all the central works of the Jena years. It gives priority, however, to Fichte's own published works rather than the lecture transcripts. It therefore focuses on the 1794 *Grundlage der gesammten Wissenschaftslehre,* the 1795 *Grundriß des Eigenthümlichen der Wissenschaftslehre,* the 1796 *Grundlage des Naturrechts,* and the 1798 *System der Sittenlehre,* which were all published by Fichte himself. This means that I use the *Wissenschaftslehre novo methodo,* which is only based on lecture transcripts, chiefly as a supplement to the published works. This goes contrary to some recent trends in Fichte scholarship, which regard the *Wissenschaftslehre novo methodo* as "the crowning achievement" of the Jena period.[7] However, I think that this is a mistake for two reasons. First, even if we assume that the transcripts are completely faithful and accurate, the most they tell us is how Fichte was thinking only during the two semesters covered by them.[8] Fichte's thinking was in constant development, and he never reached a point where he was satisfied with his exposition. Second, if we compare the contents of the *Wissenschaftslehre novo methodo* with Fichte's major published works of the same years— the 1796–1797 *Grundlage des Naturrechts* and the 1798 *System der Sittenlehre*— there is no comparison between them in terms of providing sustained, detailed, and rigorous technical argument. Any close reader of the *Wissenschaftslehre novo methodo* will soon be frustrated because not only the detail but even the thread of argument is often lost. Time and again issues are raised but not explored, arguments are promised but never delivered. It is a great mistake to regard the 1796 *Grundlage* and the 1798 *Sittenlehre* as simply moral or political works, as if they simply apply the first principles of the *Wissenschaftslehre;* rather, these works reformulate and reargue some of Fichte's fundamental themes and give specific content to the more theoretical works.

CHAPTER 1

Fichte and the Subjectivist Tradition

1. The Challenge of Subjectivism

That the problems of the father are inherited by the son is a maxim true in philosophy no less than in domestic life. The problem of subjectivism that had so troubled Kant in the 1780s began to torment Fichte in the early 1790s. Fichte had been converted to the Kantian philosophy in the summer of 1790, and he had resolved to devote his life to its exposition and defense. But, by 1793, his faith in the critical philosophy had been so deeply shaken that he could no longer trust its very foundations. What had undermined his confidence was his reading of Hume, Jacobi, and the neo-Humean skeptics, especially the writings of Ernst Platner, Gottlieb Schulze, and Solomon Maimon.[1] These thinkers had convinced him that Kant's philosophy was still vulnerable to skeptical objections, and that, at least in its present formulation, it could end in a morass of doubt worse than anything imagined by Hume. Such a skepticism would undermine all reason for belief in the external world, other minds, and even our own selves; it would trap the self inside the circle of its own consciousness, so that it knew nothing more than its representations. In short, Fichte had discovered the horrors of nihilism.[2]

Although Fichte's faith had been shaken, it had not been destroyed. Throughout the 1790s he continued to believe that the spirit—though not the letter—of Kant's philosophy provided the only solution to the problem of nihilism. Kant's philosophy alone, he maintained, could provide a rational basis for our belief in the existence of the external world, other minds, and the self. Still, Fichte was also convinced that the critical philosophy had to be rebuilt on a completely new basis. Hence his chief goal in the 1790s was to place Kant's transcendental idealism on a firmer foundation, one so solid that it could withstand the many skeptical objections against it. We can

223

explain much of Fichte's early intellectual development by seeing it as an attempt to secure Kant's philosophy against neo-Humean objections.[3]

For Fichte, to rebuild Kant's transcendental idealism on a secure foundation meant first and foremost showing how it is immune to the charge of subjectivism. Like Kant, Fichte wanted to show how transcendental idealism could demonstrate the reality of the external world, or how it could provide a basis for an empirical realism and dualism. But Fichte could no longer rest content with Kant's response to the problem of subjectivism. The advent of the 1790s witnessed a new generation of anti-Kantian skeptics who were even more unforgiving than the old. The criticisms of Garve, Feder, and Mendelssohn now gave way to those of Schulze, Jacobi, and Maimon. These later critics gained the aging Kant's attention and, to some extent, even his respect; but they never received a detailed reply.[4] It was the task of the young Kantians to defend the spirit of the critical philosophy against this latest wave of skepticism.

Such was Fichte's concern with the problem of subjectivism in the Jena years that he made its solution nothing less than the central goal of philosophy itself. Like Kant, Fichte saw the task of philosophy in transcendental terms: its main purpose is to demonstrate the possibility of objective knowledge. This conception of the task of philosophy appears time and again in Fichte's Jena writings. The main goal of philosophy, he wrote in his *Streitschrift gegen Schmid*, is to answer the question: "What is the basis for our claim that there is something outside of us which corresponds to our representations?"[5] The purpose of all philosophizing, he said in the *Wissenschaftslehre novo methodo*, is to answer the question: "Why do we believe that there are real things outside our representations?"[6] The central problem of philosophy, he wrote in the *Erste Einleitung in die Wissenschaftslehre*, is to explain why we refer some of our representations to a truth independent of them, and why we believe that they correspond to a reality external to them.[7]

It is important to understand the precise problem subjectivism posed for Fichte.[8] In stressing the need to demonstrate things outside our representations his statements about the task of philosophy make it seem as if his problem is to vindicate some form of transcendental realism against skeptical doubt. But, like Kant, Fichte insists that the ordinary notion of truth as correspondence with an external reality does *not* involve any commitment to the reality of things-in-themselves; the problem is only how *to interpret* this notion in a manner consistent with the principles of transcendental idealism. No less than Kant, Fichte recognizes that knowledge is impossible if it involves demonstrating that our representations correspond with some thing-in-itself. Nevertheless, the skeptical challenge arises for him even within the realm of experience alone, even inside the strictly immanent domain of transcendental idealism itself. The problem is that if the new skeptics are correct, then even *empirical realism* will be unsustainable. For, at the very least, empirical realism demands that our sensations conform to universal and necessary laws; it is these laws that give experience its intersubjective structure, ensuring coherence among perceptions. But it is the very validity of such laws that had been cast in doubt by the neo-Humean skeptics, who insisted that Kant had not succeeded in demonstrating the applicability of the categories to the given manifold of intuition. Self-consciously reviving Hume, they argued that Kant gave us no reason to think that the given manifold consisted in anything more than accidentally associated, contingenty conjoined, impressions. This was just the nihilist scenario that Jacobi loved to dramatize: not only did our representations fail to conform to any external reality; they also had no universal or necessary structure, so that *the* world was ultimately really only *my* world, the arbitrary and accidental rhapsody of my impressions.

Fichte's statements about the task of philosophy show, then, that his concern with nihilism goes back to the early 1790s. This point has not been fully appreciated, however, because Jacobi made his famous charge of nihilism against Fichte only in 1799, so that it then seems as if Fichte became concerned with nihilism only *after* the development of the Jena *Wissenschaftslehre*. It has indeed been argued that Fichte's concern with this problem pushed him away from his earlier doctrines and toward the later versions of the *Wissenschaftslehre*.[9] Still, there can be no doubt that Fichte was troubled by nihilism *before* the development of his early philosophy. His concern with neo-Humean skepticism shows that he knew the substance of the issue; and the notorious term already had currency in Jena before Jacobi, from sources all too familiar to Fichte.[10]

Hence Fichte's later reaction to Jacobi's criticism was perfectly predictable: it was based on a complete misunderstanding of the aims and principles of transcendental idealism.[11] Jacobi failed to see that the task of the *Wissenschaftslehre* is not to undermine but to justify our belief in the independent reality of things. While Jacobi was indeed a perceptive critic of transcendental idealism, there was one aspect of that doctrine he never fully understood: its empirical realism.[12] His charge of nihilism simply confused the transcendental standpoint of the philosopher with the empirical standpoint of ordinary consciousness.[13]

Fichte's involvement with the problem of subjectivism has been obscured for another less apparent reason: his famous statement that idealism and dogmatism are the only systems of philosophy. Since Fichte's 'dogmatism' is a form of transcendental realism, this makes it seem as if the antithesis of Fichte's idealism is transcendental realism alone. This tends to conceal, however, the extent to which Fichte developed his idealism in opposition to *dogmatic* idealism as well as transcendental realism. Like Kant, Fichte contrasted his "critical idealism" not only with transcendental realism but also with "dogmatic idealism," which denies the reality of the external world.[14] He too insisted that the great strength and advantage of transcendental idealism is that it can explain the reality of the external world, and he too stressed that any adequate idealism must involve an empirical realism and dualism.[15] Thus he dismissed the idealism of Berkeley because it could not account for objective reality except by resorting to the transcendent hypothesis of God.[16]

Fichte's rejection of dogmatic or empirical idealism becomes especially apparent in the two versions of the Jena *Wissenschaftslehre*, his 1794 *Grundlage der gesamten Wissenschaftslehre* and his 1798 *Wissenschaftslehre novo methodo*. In these works Fichte makes a distinction between a critical and dogmatic idealism much like Kant's distinction between *transcendental* and *empirical* idealism.[17] The main distinction between a *critical* and a *dogmatic* idealism, he explained, is that critical idealism can account for the limits of our consciousness, the reality of something distinct from ourselves or independent of our consciousness, while a dogmatic idealism sees everything as a product of the ego and reduces everything down to mere representations. What is characteristic of critical idealism is that it recognizes the *interdependence* of both the subject and object, the ego and the non-ego. Hence the slogan of the Jena *Wissenschaftslehre* became 'No subject, no object; no object, no subject.'

Our task in this chapter is to examine one limited aspect of Fichte's early concern with subjectivism: his early break with the subjectivist tradition regarding the foundations of knowledge. We shall consider how this break arose, and its general consequences. We will examine Fichte's reply to the neo-Humean skepticism of Schulze and Maimon in Chapter 2.

2. Early Critique of Reinhold

That the spirit of the critical philosophy is antisubjectivist was one of the formative insights of Fichte's early intellectual development. In the winter of 1793–1794, the crucial and creative phase for the genesis of his *Wissenschafts-*

lehre, Fichte saw clearly that the central thrust of Kant's analysis of experience undermined the whole theory of ideas. He recognized that, according to Kant's principles, ideas or representations cannot be basic and given because they are the products of more fundamental activities. The starting point of our analysis of experience, should not be "facts of consciousness" (*Thatsache*), as Fichte put it, but "activities" (*Thathandlungen*) below the level of consciousness itself.[18]

Fichte came to this conclusion in the course of his examination of K. L. Reinhold's *Elementarphilosophie*, the most influential exposition of Kantian doctrine in the early 1790s. The *Elementarphilosophie* was first and foremost an attempt to systematize and provide a new foundation for the critical philosophy. Its method was to derive all the main results of the critical philosophy from a single self-evident first principle, which would express a fundamental "fact of consciousness." To achieve this end, Reinhold reinterpreted the critical philosophy in a subjectivist manner, attributing to it some of the central theses of the theory of ideas in the Leibnizian-Wolffian tradition. Though scarcely aware of his debt to Wolff, Reinhold closely followed his spirit by making the *vis representativae* the fundamental faculty of the mind. Taking his cue from Kant's statement that all forms of consciousness could be regarded as species of representation (*Vorstellung*), Reinhold maintained that representation is the most basic fact of consciousness, the fundamental datum of which every particular form is only a variant. The first principle of the critical philosophy should therefore consist in the analysis of consciousness in terms of representation. Reinhold called this principle "the proposition of consciousness" (*Satz des Bewusstseins*): "In consciousness, the representation is distinguished from, and related to, the subject and object, by the subject." In other words, all consciousness involves three components—a representation, a subject who represents, and an object represented—and these are distinct from, yet connected to, one another. It is from this fundamental principle alone, Reinhold believed, that it is possible to establish the systematic unity of the critical philosophy. This principle provides the single root for all Kant's separate faculties—knowledge, will, and judgment—which now turn out to be so many forms of representation.

In his *Eigene Meditationen über Elementarphilosophie*, his early notebooks examining the *Elementarphilosophie* written in the winter of 1793–1794, Fichte contested the central role of representation in the critical philosophy (AA, II/3, 26–35). The proposition of consciousness cannot be its first principle, he reasoned, because representation is the product of even more basic activities. This becomes clear from a closer examination of this proposition. We cannot have a representation, the proposition states, if there is not a subject who has it, an object that it represents, a conscious state of representing, and the possible self-awareness of all these facts. In other words, the proposition implies that if the subject were not able to relate itself to, and to distinguish itself from, the object and the state of representing, then it could not have a representation at all. All of these points can be seen as an analysis of the Kantian unity of apperception, the conditions for the self-consciousness of one's representations.

Fichte simply drew the appropriate and inevitable conclusion from such an analysis of representation: that the possibility of representation depends on the *acts* (possible or actual) by which the subject relates itself to, and distinguishes itself from, the conscious state and its object. Since, however, these acts are the condition of any possible representation, they cannot be representations themselves; rather, they are the manner in which the mind produces representations. Hence it was Reinhold's central mistake, Fichte argues, to assume that philosophy must begin from some fact, from something given to consciousness. Although this assumption came from the correct insight that philosophy must begin from some *material* first principle, as opposed to the formal laws of logic, it failed to see that such a material principle should not express a fact *(Tatsache)* but an act *(Tathandlung)*.

3. The Discovery of Desire

Fichte's argument that the first principle of philosophy should express an act rather than a fact marks an important break with the subjectivist tradition, for it questions the simplicity and givenness of representations or ideas, a central premise behind "the way of ideas" so central to that tradition (see 1.7.1). It is important to see, however, that this was only the *beginning* of Fichte's split from this tradition. Even before his examination of Reinhold in the winter of 1793–1794, Fichte had gone further than Kant in questioning another central premise of the subjectivist tradition: the separation of the theoretical and practical, or the distinction between the realms of speculation and action. This separation was always implicit in the Cartesian view of the mind as the mirror of nature, or in its concept of knowledge as contemplation. Fichte began to undermine this view when he traced the source of the activities behind representation to the faculty of desire itself. It is not only that representation is derivative because it is created by activities, but also that these activities have their source in the faculty of volition. These activities are not theoretical or contemplative but practical or moral, because they are ultimately directed and created by the will itself. Hence Fichte replaced Reinhold's faculty of representation with the faculty of desire as the fundamental organizing principle of the mind.

How did Fichte come to such a radical conclusion? It is not easy to reconstruct his reasoning, partly because Fichte himself does not explain it in any detail, and partly because of the sheer lack of documents for the period in question. Here the historian of philosophy can only reconstruct a "likely story."

At least the basic facts are clear and indisputable. Fichte developed his doctrine about the primacy of the faculty of desire at least as early as the spring of 1793 when he rewrote the introduction to the second edition of his *Versuch einer Kritik aller Offenbarung*.[19] The purpose of that introduction was to provide a "theory of the will" (*Theorie des Begehrungsvermögens*) as a basis for his deduction of the concept of religion, though Fichte did not hesitate to make some interesting *obiter dicta* about philosophy in general. Here he stated perfectly explicitly his central conclusion about the first principle of philosophy: that "the final, single universally valid principle of all philosophy" lies in the faculty of desire, and more specifically in the self-consciousness of the will through the moral law (23–24). It is striking, however, that there is one respect in which Fichte fails to anticipate, and indeed contradicts, his later doctrine: he states that the first principle of philosophy is a "fact of consciousness" (23, 118). This means that Fichte had still not identified the will as the source of the subconscious activities underlying consciousness. That crucial step would emerge only after his encounter with Schulze's *Aenesidemus* in November 1793. Still, by the spring of that year, Fichte already had given priority to the faculty of desire over the faculty of representation as the fundamental faculty of the mind, and he saw the self-consciousness of the will as the first principle of philosophy.

In the new introduction of the *Versuch* Fichte announces this conclusion almost *en passant* and provides no justification for it. But a careful reader of the first edition of the *Versuch* would not have been too surprised by Fichte's bold announcement. The first edition, which was published in December 1791, some two years before Kant's *Religion innerhalb der Grenzen der blossen Vernunft*, had already extended Kant's doctrine of the primacy of practical reason in the *Kritik der praktischen Vernunft* (1788) in important and interesting directions not suggested by Kant himself. First, Fichte had argued that all the attributes of God are deducible from practical reason alone (40–41). Second, he contended that the possibility of revelation could not be decided on theoretical grounds but had to be determined by practical reason, which laid down all the criteria for the legitimacy of a revelation (112, 147, 151). Most important of all, though, he had affirmed that the interaction of the realm of freedom and of nature—how free moral actions take place in the causally determined sensible world—could be explained only by attributing sovereignty to practical reason (49). Although he admitted that we are not justified in deriving practical conclusions from theoretical premises, or in inferring how the world ought to be from how the world is, he stressed that the opposite procedure is perfectly legitimate: that we can derive theoretical conclusions from practical premises, or infer how the world *is* from how it *ought* to be. This latter procedure is not only possible but necessary, he argued, for it is only by it that we can explain how free moral action takes place in the sensible world. The primacy of practical reason then means that we can do in the sensible world what we ought to do in the supersensible world, or that the realm of nature, the domain of theoretical reason, can be subordinated to our moral ends, the domain of practical reason. This was, if only *en nuce*, a cardinal tenet of the later *Wissenschaftslehre*.

Fichte's new introduction provides other clues about why he gave priority to the faculty of desire over that of representation. Without attacking it explicitly, Fichte takes issue with the analysis of the will prevalent in the rationalist tradition. According to that tradition, the faculty of desire is consequent to, or simply a function of, the faculty of representation, and more specifically the representation of good or perfection. Fichte criticizes this tradition on at least two grounds. First, the faculty of desire cannot be determined into action by representation alone because it must *determine itself* through the representation (17); in other words, we must first decide or resolve to act according to some representation because simply having it does not determine us to act on it. Second, we cannot explain the lower faculty of desire—that whose object lies in sensation rather than reason—by means of concepts because its determining ground lies in sensation alone, that is, why we desire something lies in the *sui generis* qualities of the sensation, which are not explicable or describable by concepts (19–20).

We can get another perspective on Fichte's reasoning in early 1793 if we consider some of the internal problems of Reinhold's own *Elementarphilosophie*. It is worthwhile to view the *Wissenschaftslehre* as an attempt to resolve one outstanding difficulty of the *Elementarphilosophie:* how to explain the faculty of desire. Reinhold's rationalist single-faculty theory obliged him to explain the faculty of desire as a form of representation. There are, however, two classical difficulties in doing this.[20] First, the faculty of representation attempts to know an object whose existence is already given, whereas the faculty of desire attempts to create an object that does not yet exist. Second, desire is not simply the product of a representation, such as the representation of the good, since it involves the possibility of weakness of will where we know the good but do not act according to it. These problems were especially serious for Reinhold, given his intention to provide a foundation for Kant's philosophy. For in the third *Kritik* Kant himself had stressed the independence of the faculty of desire from the faculty of knowledge; and in the second *Kritik* he had given practical reason primacy over theoretical, and had even suggested that freedom is the "the keystone of the whole architecture of the system of pure reason and even of speculative reason."[21]

All this left Reinhold in a serious dilemma. If he attempted to explain the faculty of desire as a species of representation, he could not pretend to represent the spirit of Kant's philosophy. But if he admitted the independence of the faculty of desire, then he had to abandon the central thesis of the *Elementarphilosophie* that representation is the fundamental faculty of the mind, the single root of knowledge, desire, and judgment. Although he was not fully aware of its consequences, Reinhold swallowed the bitter pill of self-destruction and chose the second alternative. In the concluding section of his *Versuch einer Theorie des menschlichen Vorstellungsvermögens*, the first exposition of his *Elementarphilosophie*, he choose to vitalize representation rather than to intellectualize desire by making the faculty of desire the fundamental faculty of the mind.[22] Thus he states that the faculty of representation provides only the conditions for the *possibility* of representation, while the faculty of desire supplies the conditions for their *existence*. The faculty of desire consists in two drives (*Triebe*) that correspond to the two constituents of representation: the drive for matter or content (*Trieb nach Stoff*) and the drive for form (*Trieb nach Form*). Hence, though Reinhold does not fully admit it, the faculty of desire has virtually become the basis for the faculty of representation by creating the essential constituents of all representation. This daring thesis allows him to maintain his single-faculty theory and to preserve the primacy of practical reason. But it came at a heavy price: the abandonment of the central role of representation itself.

We can reconstruct some of the reasoning that led Fichte to his *Wissenschaftslehre* as an attempt to avoid Reinhold's dilemma. Fichte agreed with

Reinhold about the need to find a single root for Kant's faculties. That search had been encouraged by Kant himself, who had insisted on systematic form in science, and who had suggested that there is a single source of understanding and sensibility, and indeed of both theoretical and practical reason. But it was also clearer to Fichte than it had ever been to Reinhold that this unifying principle could not lie in the faculty of representation. If there must be a single source and root of all our faculties, if representation cannot be that source, and if finally the concept of freedom is the keystone of the critical philosophy, then it seems inevitable that the fundamental faculty of the mind should be desire. Rather than seeing desire as a function of representation we should now regard representation as a function of desire. Such a conclusion involved a complete reversal of classical rationalism, and a total break with the separation of theory and practice in the subjectivist tradition.

4. The Primacy of Practical Reason

Fichte's doctrine of the primacy of practical reason was crucial to his break with the subjectivist tradition, and indeed it was the heart and soul of his Jena *Wissenschaftslehre*. It is of the first importance, therefore, that we know its precise meaning. This is not easy, however, because the doctrine is complex and ambiguous. If we carefully examine Fichte's Jena writings, we find three different—though closely related—senses of the primacy of practical reason. In each of these senses Fichte departs significantly from Kant, who first fathered this doctrine in the *Kritik der praktischen Vernunft*.[23]

In the first sense practical reason has primacy over theoretical because it explains the fundamental presupposition of theoretical reason: that there exists an external world. Fichte defined the primacy of practical reason in just this sense in the *Grundlage der gesamten Wissenschaftslehre* when he wrote that the proof that reason is practical is that it could not be theoretical if it were not practical (I, 264). He explained that the central assumption of theoretical reason—that there exists some object outside myself—is demonstrable only as the condition for the possibility of moral action, or of my striving to change and improve the world (I, 261–262). In his short conspectus of this work Fichte defined more precisely this sense of the primacy of practical reason.[24] The fundamental concept of practical reason—the concept of striving—could answer three questions that could not be answered on the assumptions of theoretical reason alone. (1) Why, given the presence of an affection, must we have representations at all? (2) What justification do we have for referring representations to things outside us as their cause? (3) What justification do we have for even assuming a faculty of representation?

In ascribing primacy to practical reason in this sense, Fichte made the principles of morality nothing less than a transcendental condition of the possibility of experience itself.[25] This means that we can assume that there is an external world—the fundamental presupposition of our experience—only as a condition for moral action. In other words, what justifies belief in the external world is that it is the medium and means for the execution of moral duty. As Fichte summarized this view: "Our world is the sensibilized material of our duty; this is the proper reality in things, the true fundamental content of all appearance."[26]

Though it had no Kantian precedent, Fichte saw such a transcendental deduction of the external world as the very spirit of the critical philosophy. Kant had always insisted that reason is a unity—that theoretical and practical reason are ultimately the same—and that reason must take systematic form.[27] But he failed to explain the source of this unity, leaving it a mystery for the speculation of his successors. Fichte was confident that his transcendental deduction finally revealed the secret unity of the Kantian system. It unified the realms of theoretical and practical reason because it made the main interest of practical reason—moral action—the solution to the central problem of theoretical reason—the explanation of the possibility of experience. The irony is, however, that Fichte's strategy also marks an important break with Kant, who had expressly prohibited any subordination of the understanding to the interests of practical reason. Kant had always insisted that practical reason has no power over the understanding, which has complete independence in laying down the constitution of experience.[28]

According to the second sense, practical reason has primacy because it gives us the warrant or justification to hold certain moral and religious beliefs that we cannot demonstrate or refute through theoretical reason. This sense corresponds closely to the original meaning that Kant gave to the primacy of practical reason in the second *Kritik*. According to Kant, practical reason has primacy over theoretical because it gives us moral grounds to believe in what we cannot demonstrate or refute according to theoretical reason; more specifically, we have a right, indeed a duty, to believe in the existence of God and immortality because, although we cannot prove them, belief in them is a necessary condition of our achieving the highest good. Although Fichte follows Kant in ascribing primacy to practical reason in this sense, his application of the doctrine is much more radical. His use of it differs from Kant's in one fundamental respect: namely, Fichte thinks that we are justified in holding the moral ideas of God, immortality, and providence not as *objects of belief* but only as *goals for action*.[29] The primacy of practical reason does not give us the warrant *to believe* in the existence of entities beyond experience but only the right *to act* for the sake of certain ideals. Though here Fichte was departing from Kant in one respect, he was also following him in another, for he was simply drawing the final conclusions from Kant's analysis of transcendental illusion in the Transcendental Dialectic: that the ideas of pure reason are valid only as *regulative* rather than *constitutive* principles. Applied rigorously to the ideas of God, immortality, and the highest good, this doctrine means that these ideas should consist in only ideals for moral action rather than beliefs in the reality of things.

According to the third sense, practical reason has primacy over theoretical because knowledge is the result of action rather than contemplation. This sense of the doctrine is the direct consequence of Fichte's voluntarist transformation of Kant's epistemology. Fichte endorsed the fundamental principle behind Kant's "new method of thought": that "we can know a priori of things only what we ourselves put into them."[30] Like Kant, he held that the paradigm of knowledge is the self-awareness of our own activity, or that only the activity of the mind is completely transparent to itself, so that the mind knows objects only to the extent that it creates them. Where Fichte went beyond Kant was in seeing such activity not only in intellectual or theoretical but also in practical or moral terms. The activity by which we know objects is ultimately directed by the will itself, and it takes place not in the mind alone but in its deeds and actions in the external world. We know an object, then, only to the extent that we produce or create it, making it conform to the demands of our own moral activity. As Fichte neatly summarized this point in his later *Bestimmung des Menschen:* "We do not act because we know, but we know because we are destined for action; practical reason is the root of all reason."[31]

While Fichte's doctrine of the primacy of practical reason—in all its senses—anticipates many postmodern views about the dependency of knowledge on action and volition, it would be anachronistic to read into it any of the many forms of relativism characteristic of postmodernism.[32] For Fichte never ceased to hold that our creative activity must comply with the norms of reason, which are universal and necessary. Although these norms are not "laws of nature" that are preordained by providence, although they are indeed created by us as autonomous beings, they still have a universal authority because they express the necessary structure of reason. Fichte did not think that standards of rationality are somehow historically conditioned, so that what is rational in one culture is not so another. Rather, he reaffirmed the classical Enlightenment doctrine of the universality of reason, of its uniformity throughout all cultures and epochs of history.[33] Still less did Fichte think that criteria of rationality are determined by nothing more than acts of the will, as if the act of choice alone determines the validity of our ends. Instead, he held that we could determine the rationality of the ends themselves, or that we could appraise the good or evil of acts of choice, by seeing whether they conform to such minimal criteria of rationality as universalizability and consistency.[34] For all his voluntarism, Fichte was much more an heir of the Enlightenment than a forerunner of Schopenhauer or Nietzsche.

5. Fichte's Foundationalism?

Fichte's doctrine of the primacy of practical reason does not seem to square well, however, with his foundationalism, his affirmation of the ideals of first philosophy. While this doctrine claims that knowledge is only the result of action, Fichte's foundationalist program seems to provide knowledge through contemplation alone by an priori deduction from self-evident premises. Whereas the primacy of practical reason means that we cannot demonstrate or refute the existence of the external world, Fichte's foundationalist project promises a demonstration of the existence of the external world and other minds.

There can be no doubt that Fichte was some kind of foundationalist. In some of his methodological writings,[35] he outlines a philosophical program that is essentially Cartesian in inspiration. He explains that the philosopher should begin with some self-evident premise, with something like the Cartesian *cogito*, and more specifically with the indisputable statement "I am"; from this premise he should then derive its necessary conditions; and from these conditions he should derive further conditions, and so on, until "the whole extent of our experience emerges before the eyes of the reader or spectator."[36] Such a strategy will be something like Kant's argument in the transcendendental deduction: it will show that the possibility of self-consciousness requires knowledge of an objective world. But Fichte intends to go even further, and is much more ambitious. He wants to derive not only the categories, but also space and time, and the necessity of the empirical manifold itself. Indeed, Fichte hopes to derive the most general laws of natural science itself, which are properly speaking laws for the observation of nature and not laws learned from experience itself.[37] If such a deductive program could only succeed, Fichte believed, then it would avoid that drastic dualism between the form and content of experience, between understanding and sensibility, which had created so many difficulties for Kant. Rather, the content will be nothing more than "the form in its entirety," and the object will be simply "the sum of all relations as combined by the power of the imagination."[38]

Fichte had envisaged such a rigorous foundationalist program for two closely related, yet distinct, reasons. First, like Descartes, Kant, and Reinhold before him, he saw it as a sheer necessity to refute the skeptic, who would accept only a self-evident premise and rigorous deduction from it. In many of his letters from late 1793 and early 1794, Fichte describes the new skeptical threat to the critical philosophy, and then states that philosophy must become as rigorous and self-evident as geometry if it is to meet it.[39] Second, only such a program would manifest and secure the systematic unity of the critical philosophy, whose necessity Kant had stressed but whose precise nature he never revealed. Kant had not explained the unity of theoretical and practical reason, nor the basis for the deduction of the categories from the forms of judgment, and still less the single source of understanding and sensibility. To establish the unity of the critical philosophy it was necessary to derive all its various facets from a single principle.

Given Fichte's foundationalist and systematic ideals, it is not surprising that his *Wissenschaftslehre* has been interpreted as an attempt to realize the classical ideals of the *philosophia prima*. But if there is much evidence for such a reading, there is also much against it. While Fichte reaffirms the foundationalist program in some respects, he also seems bent on its destruction in others. His critique of the powers of theoretical reason is indeed so severe and thoroughgoing that it seems to undermine the whole program. Consider the following points. First, Fichte admits that philosophy can deduce only the necessity of limitation in general, but that it cannot derive any of the specific properties of this limitation. He insists that all deduction comes to an end in the face of the basic sensible qualities—tastes, colors, and sounds—and that these must be simply given in experience.[40] Second, Fichte sometimes goes even further, not only conceding but even insisting that we cannot derive the necessity of limitation in general. Indeed, in his

Grundlage der gesammten Wissenschaftslehre he explicitly and emphatically argues that the existence of the non-ego is a mere *presupposition* of theoretical reason that it cannot explain.[41] This limitation of theoretical reason becomes especially clear in the first section of the *Grundlage* where Fichte maintains that his first principle, "the ego posits itself absolutely," cannot derive his second principle, "the ego opposits a non-ego to itself," because the act of self-positing and the act of oppositing are completely opposed to one another.[42] Third, it is one of the central contentions of the second and third part of the *Grundlage* that theoretical reason gets caught in contradictions whenever it attempts to explain why the ego is limited by a non-ego outside itself.[43] Any attempt at such an argument fails in the face of the paradox of inner affection: that the ego is purely active, and so it cannot make itself passive by positing a non-ego that opposes it. Fourth, Fichte contends that all deductions of theoretical reason are based on the principle of sufficient reason, which is incompatible with the possibility of freedom. Hence Fichte's remarkable statement that the entire theoretical *Wissenschaftslehre* is nothing but "systematic Spinozism"(I, 122). This means, however, that the first principle of the *Wissenschaftslehre*—human freedom—falls outside the domain of theoretical reason.

How do we explain this contradiction? Why is there such a discrepancy between Fichte's affirmation of foundationalism and his critique of theoretical reason? It is tempting to say that Fichte simply abandoned his foundationalist ideals when he discovered that he could not execute them. However, this easy solution does not work. The problem is that the critique of theoretical reason is most explicit in the 1794 *Grundlage;* yet Fichte reaffirms this foundationalist program on several occasions after that.[44] Indeed, in his 1796 *Rechtslehre* and his 1798 *System der Sittenlehre* he attempts to realize these ideals by developing elaborate arguments for the reality of the external world and other minds.

Why not, then, try the converse strategy: that Fichte abandoned the critique of theoretical reason in the *Grundlage* and then returned to foundationalism? Unfortunately, this too fails, given that Fichte reaffirms his critique of theoretical reason in later works.[45] The scholar has to face the hard fact that time alone cannot heal this tension in Fichte's thought.

The contradiction disappears only if we consider more precisely the object of Fichte's critique of theoretical reason. This critique was not directed against *all* use of reasoning or *any* attempt at a deduction, and its aim was not to abolish transcendental philosophy as such. Rather, it was intended against a *certain* use of reasoning and a *specific kind* of deduction: namely, one whose premises are *constitutive*. Such a constitutive deduction would attempt to derive the existence of the world from the *existence* of the ego; its premises would consist in the description of a purported kind of entity. It was Fichte's firm belief that any such deduction would have to fail, because theoretical reason cannot prove the existence of anything. This applies not only to the existence of God and the soul, Fichte realized, but also to the external world itself. We cannot attempt to demonstrate or refute the reality of the external world, whose existence must be simply given for theoretical reason.

Although Fichte denies that we can prove the existence of the world from constitutive principles, he does think that we can do so from *regulative* ones, that is, from principles that tell us what we ought to do, or whose form is prescriptive rather than descriptive. This is because the true explanation for the existence of the external world is that it is the condition for our moral action, the medium and means for the realization of our moral duties. While we cannot demonstrate the reality of the external world according to theoretical reason, we can do so according to practical reason, which gives us not only the right but the duty to believe in anything that is a condition of our moral action. Hence, as we have seen above, Fichte simply extended Kant's doctrine of the moral postulates to the reality of the external world itself.

This means that there can be a demonstration of the reality of the external world after all. However, such a proof will differ markedly from the traditional one. Its principles and premises will be nothing less than the first principles of morality and natural right, imperatives rather than self-evident axioms. The purpose of transcendental argument will then be to determine the conditions for acting according to such principles in the sensible world. Hence Fichte's transcendental arguments will not consider the truth conditions for some proposition, but the practical conditions for the fulfillment of some imperative.

This interpretation alone is consistent with Fichte's foundationalism and his critique of theoretical reason in the 1794 *Grundlage*. Although Fichte insists that theoretical reason must *presuppose* the reality of the external world, in section 5 of Part III he also attempts to provide an explanation or deduction of the existence of the non-ego after all. But he is explicit that we can do so only on the basis of the *demand* that the ego ought to derive the non-ego. Because theoretical reason cannot derive the non-ego from the ego, and because it cannot unify the ego and non-ego in the absolute ego, we are left with nothing more than a fiat of reason that makes the unity of the ego and non-ego into a regulative ideal.

The most serious problem for this interpretation is that Fichte's first principle appears to make a constitutive claim. What indeed could be more constitutive than the claim 'I am' or 'I exist,' with which Fichte begins the 1794 *Grundlage?* This is certainly misleading, and it is the chief reason the regulative status of Fichte's arguments has not been recognized. But here it is only necessary to insist on a point that Fichte himself stresses: namely, that his first principle is a *postulate*. This is a command or demand that we do something, and it is not a proposition or statement about what is the case. More specifically, this means that the first principle of the *Wissenschaftslehre*—the self-consciousness of my freedom—is not some given state of affairs that I observe or introspect in myself but an action that I am commanded to perform within myself. That his first principle is only a postulate is a point that Fichte himself emphasized in his 1798 *Wissenschaftslehre novo methodo;* furthermore, it was not a later doctrine but an insight that he had recognized as early as 1793 in his *Eigene Meditationen.*[46]

We can now see that the dispute about Fichte's foundationalism is misleading. Fichte was and was not a foundationalist, depending on whether one considers his views on practical or theoretical reason. He rejected foundationalism insofar as its arguments are based on constitutive principles; but he attempted to revive it by basing its arguments on regulative principles. In any case, it should be clear that Fichte was not a naive foundationalist who simply reaffirmed the Cartesian program. He saw all too well that such a program grew out of the metaphysical ambitions of traditional rationalism, and that it could not work in the face of Kant's critical arguments. It was his aim to reestablish this program according to the limits Kant had imposed on theoretical reason, and according to the primacy he had established for practical reason. It should also be clear, however, that Fichte was not an antifoundationalist *simpliciter,* who rejected first principles in favor of internal coherence.[47] Fichte never accepted the Hegelian conception of a system that is somehow self-grounding, and whose internal coherence is the only guarantee of its truth. Rather, he insisted that the only guarantee of the truth of a system is its first principle.[48] To that extent, then, Fichte remained firmly within the foundationalist tradition.

CHAPTER 2

The Battle against Skepticism

1. First Doubts

Fichte began to have his first doubts about Kant's philosophy in early 1793, months before his encounter with Schulze's or Maimon's skepticism. In the draft of a letter to F. V. Reinhard, which was written in February 20 of that year, Fichte wrote that he had always considered the critical system to be "an unassailable fortress," and that he had encountered no objections, even those of Reinhold, which were effective against its central spirit.[1] Recently, however, in a conversation with "an independent thinker" (*Selbstdenker*), he had been struck with doubt about the first principle of the critical philosophy, which threatened to end in "the most soulless skepticism," one which was even worse than Hume's.

What had brought about such a severe and sudden loss of confidence? Unfortunately, all that remains is only part of the draft of Fichte's letter, which does not identify this "independent thinker," nor explain the contents of the conversation. There are good reasons to assume, however, that Fichte's interlocuter was none other than Johann Friedrich Schultz, a *Hofprediger* in Königsberg and a friend of Kant's. Schultz knew Kant's philosophy well: he had written two commentaries on the first *Kritik*,[2] and Kant trusted him so much as to declare him his most accurate expositor.[3] Fichte too was a friend of Schultz, and had been a frequent visitor to the Schultz household, where he often discussed Kant's philosophy. It was during a conversation with Schultz, Fichte later said, that he had first expounded his idea of basing philosophy on the pure I.[4]

Prima facie it seems extraordinary that Schultz, Kant's faithful expositor, should be the first to raise Fichte's doubts about the critical philosophy. Indeed, for just this reason, G. E. Schulze, alias Aenesidemus, is usually seen as

Fichte's first gadfly. Yet, for all his loyalty to Kant, Schultz did not hesitate to criticize him. He wrote an appreciative but critical review of the Inaugural Dissertation;[5] and he was deeply concerned about the adequacy of Kant's response to skepticism in the *Kritik*. His first commentary on Kant stresses the significance of the Transcendental Deduction, and sees Kant's response to skepticism as the crux of the critical philosophy.[6] Indeed, Schultz had grave reservations about the adequacy of Kant's response to skepticism, which nearly fractured his relationship with Kant.[7]

Schultz's doubts about Kant's Transcendental Deduction were voiced in his review of J. A. Ulrich's *Institutiones logicae et metaphysicae*, which appeared in the *Allgemeine Literatur Zeitung* in 1785.[8] Here Schultz's main concern was to defend Kant against the objections of Ulrich, an erstwhile convert to Kant who had now turned into his bitter opponent. In attempting to reply to Ulrich, Schultz stressed the importance of the Transcendental Deduction, but only to concede that it suffered from some serious ambiguities. The aim of the Deduction, Schultz explained, is to show that synthetic a priori concepts are a necessary condition of experience. But Kant equivocates concerning the meaning of 'experience' (*Erfahrung*). If experience consists in *judgments of perception,* which simply report accidental associations regarding the material of sensation (for example, "This stone feels warm when the sun rises"), then Kant's argument is false, because no such judgement implies the universal and necessary connections between sensations attributed by synthetic a priori concepts. If, on the other hand, experience consists in *judgments of experience,* which do imply such connections (for example, "The heat of the sun causes the warmth of the stone"), then Kant's argument is trivial, because it says that such connections involve synthetic a priori concepts, which by definition are universal and necessary. The main skeptical problem, Schultz concluded, still seems unaddressed by the *Kritik:* what right do we have to attribute universal and necessary connections to our perceptions? Although Schultz did not think that his objection was necessarily fatal, he begged Kant for further clarification.[9]

It is probable, though of course far from certain, that Fichte's first doubts about Kant's philosophy go back to Shultz's early review. It raised the important question whether the Transcendental Deduction did resolve Hume's doubts after all. If it were indeed the case that there is no reason to assume that the categories apply to our perceptions, then it would be possible that our experience consists in nothing more than the accidental association of distinct impressions. There would then be no basis for the belief in necessary connection, a synthetic unity of our representation, and so no grounds to assume the possibility of objective knowledge. Hence the nihilist scenario raises its ugly head: everything in our experience could be nothing more than a dream or illusion.

Whether or not Fichte's first misgivings were raised by Schultz's review, there can be no question that he was soon troubled by such neo-Humean doubts. By late 1793, Fichte had read G. E. Schulze, Solomon Maimon, and Ernst Platner, who had all made neo-Humean objections similar to Schultz. According to Schulze, Maimon, and Platner, the entire Transcendental Deduction is a *petitio principi*. Kant had shown that *if* there are to be empirical judgements having universality and necessity, then the categories must apply to experience; but this assumed that there were such judgments, which was the very point Hume had brought into question.[10]

2. The *Aenesidemus* Review

Fichte's first extended encounter with skepticism came with his review of G. E. Schulze's *Aenesidemus,* which he wrote in late 1793. Appearing anonymously in 1792, Schulze's work is essentially a neo-Humean polemic against Kant and K. L. Reinhold's *Elementarphilosophie*. *Aenesidemus* soon achieved rapid notoriety for the acuteness and subtlety of its arguments, whose withering effect proved to be one of the main reasons for the eventual decline of the *Elementarphilosophie* on the Jena literary scene. It is noteworthy that Schulze was intimately associated with Feder's circle in Göttingen,[11] which explains some of the tone and content of his polemic. It should come as no surprise, then, that Schulze revived Feder's charge of Berkeleyian idealism against Kant.

If it was not his conversations with Schultz, Schulze's *Aenesidemus* would surely have awakened Fichte from his critical slumbers. Some of his letters from late 1793 and early 1794 give frank and graphic testimony about its impact on him. Thus he wrote J. F. Flatt in November or December 1793 that he regarded *Aenesidemus* as "one of the most remarkable products of our decade," and he confessed that it had "shaken my own system to its very foundations."[12] *Aenesidemus* had now convinced him that the critical philosophy had to be rebuilt upon a completely new foundation to secure it against skeptical objections.[13]

Clearly, then, Fichte had to meet the challenge posed for him by Schulze's skepticism. As early as May 1793 he accepted the opportunity to review

Schulze's work for the *Allgemeine Literatur Zeitung*. But he could not complete the review promptly because, as he explained to the editor, he had been "thrown into unforeseen labor by Aenesidemus's skepticism."[14] Indeed, Schulze's skepticism proved to be such a challenge that Fichte did not complete the review until January 1794.

Fichte's review of *Aenesidemus* is a seminal text for the development of his later philosophy. It anticipates some of the central themes of the Jena *Wissenschaftslehre*, such as intellectual intuition, infinite striving, and the self-positing ego. The importance of the review has long been recognized,[15] and with good reason, given that Fichte himself said that it "indicates my new viewpoint (as far as possible within the narrow limits of a review)."[16] Our task now will be to reconstruct Fichte's reply to Schulze's skepticism and to show how some of the central themes of the later *Wissenschaftslehre* emerge from it.

One of Schulze's major criticisms of Kant's philosophy is that it ends in a complete subjectivism. He maintains that it is guilty of "formalism" because it reduces all of reality down to nothing more than "an aggregate of forms and effects of the mind."[17] What Garve and Feder once wrote against the first edition of the *Kritik*, Schulze now said against the second. Although he takes note of the Refutation of Idealism, Schulze still thinks that Kant fails to distinguish his idealism from Berkeley's. He argues that the Refutation does not work for two reasons. First, the proof shows only that there are permanent things in space; but that does not mean that they exist independent of our consciousness, given that in the Transcendental Aesthetic Kant had already argued that space is only a form of intuition. Second, if Kant is consistent and rids his philosophy of the thing-in-itself, then it is identical with Berkeley's idealism after all, for it then places all of reality within the realm of consciousness.

Fichte's reply to this objection is that it tacitly presupposes the transcendental realist criterion of truth, and so begs the question against Kant. According to this criterion, truth consists in the correspondence of representations with things-in-themselves. Schulze holds that this criterion is essential to any distinction between truth and reality, and that by rejecting it Kant turns all of our experience into a dream. But Fichte counters that Schulze's allegiance to this standard of truth reveals his own dogmatism and the main weakness of his own skepticism (I, 10, 12). Such a criterion is indeed "the common source of all the objections—skeptical as well as dogmatic—which have been raised against the critical philosophy" (I, 19).

Fichte repudiates this criterion of truth not because it makes a demand impossible to fulfill—that would, of course, only beg the question against the skeptic—but because it involves an absurd presupposition. The criterion presupposes the idea of a thing-in-itself, of something that could exist apart from any possible conception of it. But it is nonsense, Fichte argues, to think of a thing-in-itself that exists apart from how it *must be* conceived according to any rational being. The object of knowledge is "actually constituted in itself in just that way in which it must be thought to be constituted by any conceivable intelligent subject" (I, 20). Hence Leibniz was correct to think that monads consist in their power of representation, Fichte explains, because this contains the correct insight that "the thing would be constituted in itself just as it represented itself to itself" (I, 20). Fichte then announces the general principle, one central to his idealism: "what is logically true for any intellect . . . is at the same time true in reality and there is no other truth than this" (I, 20).

Fichte thinks that this principle provides a sufficient basis to blunt the skeptic's doubts. It means that there is no need to worry that we cannot get outside our representations to see if they correspond with things-in-themselves, for the very idea of a thing-in-itself is nonsense. There is no problem of knowing whether the laws of thinking correspond with things-in-themselves, because the criterion of truth consists in conformity to these laws, which alone provide the basis to distinguish between reality and illusion. Like Kant, then, Fichte thinks that the criterion of truth consists not in correspondence with a thing-in-itself, but in conformity with the universal and necessary laws of understanding. It is important to note, however, that Fichte has already gone much further than Kant in the direction of a complete idealism. By rejecting the very possibility of the thing-in-itself, Fichte refuses to admit Kant's distinction between a formal and material idealism, which was so important for Kant's later attempt to distinguish his idealism from Berkeley's. Ironically, then, Fichte had only provided more fuel for Schulze's charge of Berkeleyianism.

Though the rejection of the thing-in-itself seems to involve a clear break with Kant, Fichte insists that it is perfectly in accord with the *spirit* of the critical philosophy. Indeed, he refuses to admit that Kant even entertained the idea of the thing-in-itself (I, 19–20). He concedes that Kant's language sometimes seems to endorse the idea, when, for example, he makes a distinction between appearances and things-in-themselves, or when he writes of space and time as if they are true only for our human sensibility. But,

Fichte asserts, Kant's language in such passages is only provisional, a concession to our ordinary ways of speaking (I, 19). When Kant refers to a thing-in-itself he speaks from the standpoint of ordinary consciousness, which does not reflect on its knowing activity, and which therefore sees objects as existing independent of it.

It is questionable, however, whether Fichte's interpretation of the thing-in-itself is true to Kant's meaning. The central premise behind his reading is that the thing-in-itself is not only something independent of the forms of sensibility, which are valid only for *human* beings, but also something independent of the forms of the understanding, which are valid for all *intelligent* beings. Such an interpretation makes things-in-themselves not only *imperceptible* but also *inconceivable*, and so it undermines Kant's own distinction between thinking and knowing an object.

Whatever its merits, the charge of subjectivism was only one aspect of Schulze's polemic against Kant. There was another aspect—one that proved no less challenging to Fichte. This is best described as its *meta-critique*, its attempt to show that Kant's restrictions upon first-order knowledge apply to his own second-order transcendental knowledge. *Aenesidemus* contains a whole battery of meta-critical arguments against Kant, but only four points are directly relevant to Fichte's review. (1) Kant's investigation into the faculty of knowledge, or into the origin and conditions of experience, considers not only the content but the genesis of representations, and so it presupposes the principle of causality, which only begs the question against Hume.[18] (2) Because he insists that all of knowledge is limited to appearances, Kant must also assume that we know the faculty of knowledge too only as an appearance and not as it is in itself.[19] (3) Kant's reasoning about the conditions and limits of experience is just as guilty of transcendental illusion as traditional metaphysics. It assumes that because we must *think* of the the mind as the lawgiver of nature, the mind must also *be* the lawgiver of nature; but this is a form of hypostasis because it confuses a necessity of thought with the nature of things-in-themselves.[20] (4) Kant's concept of the transcendental subject is ambiguous, and in whatever sense one interprets it—whether as thing-in-itself, noumenon, or transcendental idea—it is nonsense to think of it as the origin or source of knowledge. If it is the thing-in-itself, we cannot apply the category of causality to it, since that would violate Kant's own teaching about the limits of knowledge. If it is a noumenon, then it is either a purely intelligible entity or the formal unity of experience (the unity of apperception); in the first case, we again apply the category of causality beyond experience; and in the second case, we assume *per impossibile* that a merely formal unity creates the order of experience. If, finally, it is a transcendental idea, then we cannot claim constitutive validity for it; for Kant himself insists that all ideas have only a regulative validity.[21]

Fichte makes one central point against all of Schulze's meta-critical arguments: that they *hypostatize* the Kantian subject, treating it as if it were some kind of entity that exists apart from and prior to our knowledge of it. Here again Schulze's retention of the concept of the thing-in-itself was working its mischief. When Schulze hears the words 'faculty of representation,' Fichte explains, he thinks only of "some sort of thing (round or square?) which exists as a thing in itself, *independently of its being represented,* and indeed exists as a thing which *represents*" (I, 11). If we conceive the transcendental subject in this manner, then Schulze's objections indeed have their point: there is the danger that all representations might not conform to it, that we know it only as an appearance, and that we cannot apply the principle of causality to it, and so on. But, Fichte insists, we need not accept, and indeed we must reject, this whole conception of the transcendental subject. We cannot think of the transcendental subject as something that exists apart from and prior to its knowledge of itself, as something that transcends all its own self-conceptions, because that is to ignore the simple but fundamental point that self-consciousness is essential to, and constitutive of, the very nature of our subjectivity. Who we are depends on what we conceive ourselves to be; a subject which could not be self-conscious would be a thing but not a subject at all. Hence Fichte states as his counter principle: "The faculty of representation exists *for* the faculty of representation and *through* the faculty of representation" (I, 11); or, as he also puts it: "The I is what it is . . . *for* the I" (I, 16).

This principle that 'the I is only *for itself*' will later play a pivotal role in the Jena *Wissenschaftslehre*. The principle has a *methodological,* an *ontological,* and an *ethical* meaning, all of them implicit in the review but never disentangled by Fichte himself. In the methodological sense, the principle implies that any explanation of the mind must be in terms that could be given by the mind itself; in other words, we cannot understand the mind by accounting for it from some third-person standpoint, such as the laws of physics; rather, we must interpret it from within, according to its own *self*-conceptions or *self*-understanding. Fichte alludes to this methodological meaning when he writes "that everything which occurs in the mind can be completely explained and comprehended on the basis of the mind itself" (I, 15). In its ontological sense, the principle means that the ego does not exist, or at least does not fully realize its nature, apart from and prior to its self-conceptions; its very essence and existence is constituted by its self-conceptions. This ontological meaning becomes apparent when Fichte refuses to admit a faculty of representation that "*exists* as a thing in itself *independently of its being represented*" and insists "The faculty of representation *exists* for the faculty of representation and through the faculty of representation" (I, 11; my italics). Finally, in its ethical sense, the principle means that the essence of the ego consists in its activity of self-determination, of autonomy, of making itself what it is; the categorical imperative of the ego is to realize this autonomy, to become completely independent. This ethical meaning emerges when Fichte says that the I is "*self-positing*, absolutely independent and autonomous" (I, 22).

It was this principle, especially its methodological aspect, that provided Fichte with his solution to the meta-critical problem posed by Schulze. The net effect of Schulze's arguments was to pose the question: How does the transcendental philosopher know that his analysis of the faculty of knowledge corresponds with that faculty itself? Fichte was now ready with an answer: the philosopher has a correct explanation or analysis of the faculty of knowledge, or of the subject of consciousness, when it agrees with the *self*-explanation or *self*-analysis of the subject itself. The transcendental philosopher will then know the faculty of knowledge, the subject of experience, when he can account for it in terms by which it would account for itself. We know that this will be the nature of the subject in itself because that subject consists in its *self*-explanations or *self*-conceptions. This was a principle that Fichte soon put into practice in the Jena *Wissenschaftslehre*. An important part of the 1794 *Grundlage*, and almost all of the 1798 *Wissenschaftslehre novo methodo*, consist in a dialectic of consciousness by which the ego comes to recognize for itself what has been postulated and hypothesized by the philosopher.

The general moral and message of the *Aenesidemus* review is that transcendental philosophy must be built on a strictly *immanent* foundation, that is, it has to remain strictly within the limits of possible experience and the reflection on its conditions. This means that transcendental philosophy must fulfill two tasks: first, it must interpret the ego from within according to its own self-conceptions, and not try to explain it according to some naturalistic standpoint; and, second, it must avoid postulating all transcendent entities, such as the thing-in-itself. It was the admission of transcendent entities into the critical philosophy, Fichte argued, that was the source of all the skeptical objections against it. If such entities were permitted, then all of Schulze's meta-critical objections would indeed hold against it. The irony was, of course, that Kant himself was deeply reluctant to apply Fichte's medicine. Indeed, as we shall see (2.8.4), this eventually proved to be one of the main sources of friction between Fichte and his erstwhile teacher.

For all of its importance for Fichte's later philosophy, it is still important to keep the *Aenesidemus* review in proper perspective. Some of the ideas sketched in the review take on a different hue when seen in the context of Fichte's later writings. It would be wrong to interpret the review as the anticipation of a later radical idealism, as the program for a complete idealism that eliminates the thing-in-itself and makes the sole criterion of reality the laws of consciousness alone. Although Fichte appears to reject the thing-in-itself entirely, he in fact does so in only one sense: that which is utterly *unthinkable* or *inconceivable*. And while he also seems to espouse a radical idealism, according to which all external reality is explained in terms of the universal and necessary forms of consciousness, he later qualifies this doctrine, postulating the existence of something like the Kantian thing-in-itself in the form of an irreducible "check" or "limit" to the infinite activity of the ego.

3. Maimon's Skepticism

At the very least, Maimon's skepticism was as important as Schulze's for Fichte's philosophical development. Fichte himself virtually said as much. He happily acknowledged his debts to Maimon, whose acumen he greatly admired. He would often mention Maimon's name along with Schulze's and Hume's as one of the most worthy of modern skeptics,[22] and he even referred to Maimon as "one of the greatest thinkers of our age."[23] It was through reading the new skeptics, "especially the excellent Maimonian writings," he wrote, that he became convinced that philosophy is not yet a science.[24] On several occasions he insisted that any attempt to rebuild the critical philosophy would have to answer Maimon's skepticism.[25] In his March–April 1795 letter to Reinhold Fichte paid very handsome tribute to Maimon:

My respect for Maimon's talents knows no bounds. I firmly believe that he has completely overturned the entire Kantian philosophy as it has been understood by everyone until now, including you, and I am prepared to prove it. No one noticed what he had done; they had looked down on him from their heights. I believe that future centuries will mock us bitterly.[26]

Why was Maimon so important for Fichte? What challenge did he pose, and how did Fichte respond to it? These questions are not so easy to answer, partly because Fichte himself never explains his reaction in any detail, and partly because his few remarks are sketchy and even misleading. The difficulties are compounded by the intricacy and obscurity of Maimon's own thought. To understand Maimon's significance for Fichte requires knowledge not only of Maimon's major writings, such as the *Versuch über die Transcendentalphilosophie* (1790) and the *Versuch einer neuen Logik* (1794), but also of some of the lesser known ones, such as the *Wörterbuch der Philosophie* (1791) and the *Streifereien im Gebiete der Philosophie* (1793).

The heart of Maimon's skepticism, and the main challenge it posed for Fichte, lies in its critique of the Transcendental Deduction. The essence of Maimon's critique is that Kant cannot solve the problem behind the Deduction—'How do a priori concepts apply to experience if they do not derive from it?'—because of his rigid and sharp dualism between understanding and sensibility. According to Kant, knowledge of experience arises from two distinct faculties: the *understanding*, which spontaneously generates universal and necessary concepts; and *sensibility*, which receives particular and contingent intuitions from the senses. While these concepts provide experience with its *form*, the intuitions supply it with its *matter*. Kant stressed that knowledge requires the most intimate interchange between these elements: concepts without intuitions have no content or reference; and intuitions without concepts have no structure or meaning. As he put it in a famous dictum: "Concepts without intuitions are empty, intuitions without concepts are blind" (B 75). Yet the problem of the Transcendental Deduction arose because each of these elements derive from distinct sources. If concepts originate a priori in the understanding, and if intuitions come a posteriori from sensibility, then what guarantee is there that these concepts apply to these intuitions? In short, what makes a priori concepts apply to experience if they do not derive from it?

According to Maimon, the very dualism that was the source of Kant's problem was also the main obstacle to its solution. The gulf between understanding and sensibility—in the absolute terms in which Kant formulated it—is simply unbridgeable, so that the interchange between them necessary for all knowledge is impossible. Maimon gave several reasons why the dualism is insurmountable, and each of them deserves separate explanation.

The most striking problem posed by Kant's dualism, Maimon argued, is that it seems impossible for such heterogeneous faculties as understanding and sensibility to interact with one another.[27] The understanding is a purely intellectual faculty, which is active and beyond space and time; and sensibility is a strictly empirical faculty, which is passive and within space and time. But if these faculties are so unlike, then how do they interact with one another? They *must* interact if there is to be that close cooperation between them necessary for knowledge: the understanding must act on sensibility because it has to organize intuitions according to concepts, making their raw content take on definite shape and form; and sensibility has to act on understanding, providing it with the material to form and synthesize. Yet it also seems that they *cannot* interact because they belong to different realms: understanding to the noumenal world, and sensibility to the phenomenal. To Maimon, the problem here seemed analogous to the Cartesian mind–body problem. It seemed as if Kant had simply replaced Descartes' heterogeneous substances with his own discrete faculties. Thus the mind–body problem, which had so haunted seventeenth-century philosophy, seemed to sneak in through the backdoor of the critical system. The mind and body of Descartes, Spinoza, and Leibniz had simply been replaced by the noumenal understanding and phenomenal sensibility of Kant.

Another problem raised by Kant's dualism is that it seems impossible *to know* when, and indeed whether, the a priori concepts of the understanding apply to the a posteriori intuitions of sensibility. The concepts of the understanding are so abstract and general that they do not necessarily ensure order among the specific intuitions of our actual experience; indeed, they seem to be compatible with the complete absence of order, with that haphazard and arbitrary phantasmagoria that Kant so deeply feared. Maimon made this point clear by arguing that Kant could not provide a *criterion* to determine whether the categories apply to any specific intuitions.[28] The category of causality, for example, is compatible with all kinds of specific empirical laws; it tells us that experience must conform to causal laws, such that there must be a sufficient reason for each event. But it does not tell us *which* events are causes; it is as compatible with smoke being the cause of fire as fire being the cause of smoke. Hence if we want to know which specific events illustrate the category of causality, we must consult experience. But,

Maimon then insisted, experience really cannot help us either. For, as Hume pointed out and Kant conceded, all that experience ever shows is constant conjunction, not universal and necessary connection. This means that, in any specific case, we cannot be sure that the category of causality really does apply to our experience. Even if we see that smoke always follows fire, we cannot infer that smoke is the cause of fire, because all that experience shows is a constant conjunction between fire and smoke. So, even if we know from the Deduction that the category of causality applies to experience, we do not know that it applies in this, or indeed in any, specific case. Even if we know *that* the categories apply, we will never be able to determine when and where they do so. But that leaves the disturbing question: If we cannot know when and where they apply, do we really know that they apply after all?

On these grounds Maimon dismissed the schematism as a plausible solution to the problem of the application of the categories.[29] In the 'Schematism' chapter of the first *Kritik* Kant had addressed this very issue by developing the idea of a schema—a monogram or image—that mediates between the categories of the understanding and the intuitions of sense. What allows us to apply the category to experience, Kant maintains, is the a priori form of inner sense, time. This faculty determines the concept's application by assigning it a temporal significance; for example, the category of cause applies to temporal sequences where the cause is that which precedes and the effect that which follows. Assigned such a schema or temporal significance, the category of causality becomes compatible with only certain sequences, since, for example, fire always precedes smoke in time. But, Maimon retorts, this still does not provide a sufficient criterion. Again, the problem is that all the evidence of my senses does not warrant the application of this category. If I constantly observe fire preceding smoke, this still does not justify applying the category of causality, which attributes a universal and necessary connection between fire and smoke. There is no means, then, of distinguishing cases where there is only a contingent constant conjunction from those where there is a universal and necessary connection. Although Kant is right to think that the application of a category requires knowing its temporal schema, he is wrong to conclude that this is a sufficient condition of its application, since knowing the temporal schema alone does not justify applying the category.

Such, in rough outline, was the challenge Maimon had laid down for Fichte sometime in the early 1790s. It is clear that it poses an even greater threat to Kant's philosophy than the skepticism of Schulze, which had simply presupposed the standard of truth characteristic of transcendental realism. Maimon rightly saw that such a standard of truth simply begged the question against Kant, and he too chastened Schulze for his implicit "dogmatism."[30] Maimon's skepticism poses a deeper danger because it shows that there is still reason to doubt even if we adhere to the standard of truth of the critical philosophy itself. Assuming that truth consists in the conformity of intuitions with rules, the problem still arises of how we know that these rules ever do apply to these intuitions. It is possible that all of our experience is illusory because Kant does not provide sufficient reason to think that it conforms to the categories, which provide the formal conditions of all empirical reality. The nightmare of nihilism—the possibility that our representations represent nothing at all—now recurs even when we accept the Kantian account of representation as the conformity of intuition with rules. Hence Maimon's critique of Kant, unlike Schulze's, is purely internal. Its ultimate—and very dangerous—message is that the critical philosophy cannot solve the problem of knowledge even when it is formulated in its own terms.[31]

Thus the ultimate challenge of Maimon's skepticism—for Fichte, and indeed the whole post-Kantian generation—was how to bridge the gap between understanding and sensibility, noumena and phenomena. If it were not possible to surmount Kant's dualisms, to find some synthesis or middle term between them, then the skeptical problem remained unsolved, so that the whole realm of experience remains an illusion. The whole predicament was perfectly summarized by Maimon himself: "Philosophy has not been able to build a bridge that makes possible the transition from the transcendental to the particular."[32]

4. The Official Response

Fichte's official account of his reply to Maimon appears in some brief and dense passages from two pivotal works of the Jena years, the *Grundlage der gesamten Wissenschaftslehre* and the *Grundriß des Eigenthümlichen der Wissenschaftslehre*.[33] The thrust of his reply is that Maimon too is guilty of his own form of dogmatism. Like Schulze, Maimon assumes that the categories must apply to some object independent of them, though in his case the object is something given in experience rather than a thing-in-itself beyond it. According to Fichte, Maimon ascribes our belief that the categories apply to experience to a mere illusion of the imagination. We have no evidence from reason or experience that the categories do apply to our sense impressions; but because we are so accustomed to associating these impressions, we imagine something corresponding to them in the world outside us. The proper response to this argument, Fichte contends, is to question the premise that the object is given independent of the activity of the imagination. Maimon fails to appreciate the creative power of the imagination, which not only supplies schemata to apply the categories to given objects, as Kant assumes, but which also produces the objects themselves.

Fichte concedes that this is in effect to admit the skeptic's case: that we have no reason to believe that our concepts apply to an object independent of them. But he still insists that we do not have to accept the skeptic's conclusion that all of our experience consists only in an illusion. This is because there is simply no given object to which our concepts have to conform. All of our experience is the work of the imagination, and indeed all reality depends on it, so that there is no criterion of truth outside it to which we can appeal. Illusion must be opposed to truth, and illusion must be avoidable. But the activity of the imagination provides the rule of truth, and its activity is inescapable. We can no more doubt the reality of the productive imagination, Fichte argues, than we can doubt the reality of our existence, because the activity of the imagination is a necessary condition of our own self-consciousness (I, 227).

Fichte's argument against Maimon alludes to, and indeed presupposes, his account of the productive imagination in the *Grundlage* and *Grundriß*. This faculty plays a pivotal role in Fichte's analysis of experience. Imagination unites the two fundamental elements of all experience: form and matter (I, 215–217). It engages in the infinite task of attempting to create order out of chaos, of striving to determine the infinitely determinable matter of sensation. Although no single determination is ever completely adequate to this matter, precisely because it is infinitely determinable, the imagination still attempts to determine it anew, forever creating new forms, and so making experience increasingly more determinate and comprehensible. To the extent that it determines the matter of sensation, making it conform to its a priori forms, the imagination *internalizes* it, making it part of consciousness; but to the extent that it cannot determine this matter, it is "repelled" by it and *externalizes* it, seeing itself as limited by something outside itself. The imagination is "the hovering" (*Schweben*) between these two tendencies: internalizing the matter and making it submit to some form; and externalizing it because it cannot completely dominate and control it.

In the *Grundlage* and *Grundriß* Fichte ascribes enormous powers to the imagination. All reality is produced by it, making possible "all consciousness, all life, and our being for ourselves, that is, our being as ego" (I, 227). It is indeed only because of the imagination that we have an awareness of the external world. In a section of the *Grundlage* entitled 'The Deduction of Representation,' Fichte explains how intuition, or the representation of something outside ourselves, is essentially the product of the imagination (I, 232–233). Fichte thinks that Kant was profoundly correct to suggest the fundamental role of the imagination in the constitution of our experience; he went astray, however, in limiting its role to producing the schemata alone when it also creates the very objects we know.

Prima facie Fichte's reply to Maimon works only by presupposing some rather speculative transcendental psychology and some even more extravagent transcendental idealism. It seems that Fichte intends to defeat Maimon by a more radical idealism that makes the productive imagination responsible for not only the form but also the content of experience. If this is the case, then Fichte has engaged in a very high-risk strategy indeed, since Maimon only has to doubt the fanciful claim that the imagination produces all of reality. Such a claim seems to come to grief in the face of the stubborn events of ordinary experience, which seem to come and go independent of my will and imagination.

Such a counterargument would be much too hasty, however. To be fair to Fichte, it is important to see exactly what role he ascribes to the productive imagination. He is not as extravagent as he first appears. Contrary to one very popular interpretation, Fichte does not hold that the imagination creates *ex nihilo* the entire world, as if nothing exists prior to its act of creation. This would be a metaphysical hypothesis for which Fichte believes he has no warrant. He constantly stresses how we, as finite beings, are limited by a reality external to ourselves, which is simply given to us, and that an idealism is transcendent or dogmatic when it fails to acknowledge such a reality.[34] Fichte is also not claiming that the imagination somehow creates the entire content of experience—that it literally produces the matter of sensation—because he is explicit elsewhere that the feelings or sensations that make up the primitive qualia of experience are given.[35] He assumes that the imagination is limited by something infinite—the infinitely determinable content of sensation—that it cannot entirely control;[36] and it is indeed partly for this reason that it externalizes its object as something outside itself. What the imagination does create for Fichte is the *object of experience*, that is, its universal and necessary form, the structure that makes objective knowledge of experience possible. While Fichte extends this form much further than Kant, so that it comprises not only the categories of understanding and forms of sensibility but also empirical properties of an object, he still does not completely abrogate the given matter of experience, which remains to some degree irreducibly particular and contingent. Although all the determinations of the object of experience can be created by the imagination, the matter of experience, its raw sensations or feelings, remains simply given, recalcitrant to all the efforts of an infinite striving.

According to this more modest reading of Fichte's concept of imagination, then, Fichte's reply to Maimon does not commit him to any extravagent metaphysical assumptions; more specifically, it does not presuppose a cosmic imagination that somehow creates the entire world or the matter of experience. To defeat Maimon, Fichte needs to assume only that *the object of experience* is entirely created by the imagination. If this is the case, then the skeptical problem disappears, because there is nothing to the object of experience that is given prior to synthesis. While the object in itself—the matter of sensation prior to its synthesis—remains unknowable to us, this poses no problem for knowledge within experience itself. Indeed, as we have already seen, Maimon himself admits that the problem of knowledge does not arise from the difficulty of knowing whether our representations conform to things-in-themselves.

Although this interpretation makes Fichte's reply to skepticism more plausible, it nevertheless remains doubtful whether it would satisfy Maimon. For the question still remains: What right do we have to assume that the concept of an object, the universal and necessary forms of the understanding, apply to the given manifold? How do we know that our perceptions conform to the universal and necessary forms of experience? Again, as Hume argued and Maimon reiterated, we cannot appeal to the content of experience itself, to the world as we perceive it, because that only reveals a constant conjunction. What Fichte must establish is that all the empirical characteristics of an object are somehow necessary conditions of self-consciousness; but, clearly, that is a proof of a very tall order, which any skeptic will find plenty of reasons to doubt. Indeed, Fichte himself doubted whether such a transcendental deduction of the more general features of experience is possible.[37]

5. The Final Line of Defense

It would be a serious mistake to leave things here and to accept this conclusion. For Fichte has another strategy, another line of defense against

Maimon's skepticism, which is much more promising and interesting. He began to develop this response in the winter of 1793–1794 in his two notebooks *Eigene Meditationen über Elementarphilosphie* and *Practische Philosophie*, whose themes reappear in the third part of his 1794 *Grundlage der gesamten Wissenschaftslehre*. Although Fichte rarely directly discusses Maimon in these works,[38] he is still grappling with the main problem posed by his skepticism: how can we establish knowledge of an objective world? What is most striking of all, however, is that Fichte's response to skepticism was already clearly anticipated by Maimon himself. It is indeed not implausible to hold that Fichte was influenced by Maimon in this regard, even though the evidence is rather circumstantial, resting entirely on the similarity of some of their ideas. If there is such an influence, though, the irony is rather rich: no one helped Fichte to defeat Maimon more than Maimon himself!

To understand Fichte's final line of reply, it is best to return to Maimon's formulation of the problem of knowledge in one of his lesser known works, his 1791 *Wörterbuch der Philosophie*.[39] Here Maimon summarized the whole dilemma facing the critical philosopher in terms of "a universal antinomy of thought." According to this antinomy, there are two conflicting but necessary requirements of all thinking. On the one hand, thought must have something given, a subject matter or object to think about, because thinking essentially consists in the application of something universal (a rule of the understanding) to something particular (the matter of sensation). On the other hand, though, the perfection of thought demands that nothing is given and that everything be created and pure form. With the first horn of this dilemma, Maimon wished to express the point that our human understanding is finite, that it creates the form but not the content of our experience, which is simply given. With the second horn, he formulated the ideal of knowledge already implicit in Kant: that we know perfectly only that which we create, a noumenon produced by the activity of the understanding alone. The antinomy therefore points out the vast discrepancy between our ideal of knowledge and our *de facto* condition as finite beings: knowledge demands creating an object, making it something purely intelligible or noumenal; but objects are given to us as something empirical or phenomenal. The ideal of knowledge therefore seems reserved for the *intellectus archetypus*, the infinite understanding of God alone.

Rather than advising resignation to this predicament, Maimon demands that we *act* to overcome it. Taking his cue from Kant's theory of ideas, he suggests that we regard the idea of the infinite understanding, the *intellectus archetypus*, as a regulative ideal, the goal of all enquiry. If we only exert the powers of our understanding, he maintains, then we can approach, even if we still cannot attain, this ideal of knowledge. In other words, we can approximate, even if we cannot reach, the status of the *intellectual archetypus*. We can make some progress toward this ideal, Maimon assures us, if we constantly strive to exert our power over nature and make it conform to the laws of our own understanding. The more we gain power over nature, the more its phenomenal content will decrease and the more its noumenal content will increase.

What Maimon is proposing here is a pragmatic solution to his own skepticism. The key to our knowledge of experience, and the resolution of skeptical doubt, now lies in the field of action rather than contemplation. Rather than just thinking about the object in a new way, we must actually make the object conform to the laws of our rational activity. Although Maimon never abandons his argument that the dualism between understanding and sensibility is fatal to the possibility of knowledge, he now suggests that, if we only act, we need not consider this dualism as something absolute and eternal. If we exert our powers over nature, then we can diminish, even if we cannot completely remove it. We will acquire at least some degree of knowledge to the extent that we have gained control over nature and made it conform to the laws of our own activity. Here, more by implication rather than intention, Maimon was proposing some significant alterations to Kant's system. First of all, the dualism between understanding and sensibility was now more a matter of degree rather than of kind. Kant regarded the dualism as eternal and static; but Maimon made it temporary and moving, depending on the extent that we exert our powers over nature. Second, the concept of a noumenon no longer designates a transcendent entity beyond appearances, but it serves as a limiting concept to designate the goal of a complete knowledge of appearances.[40]

Such was Maimon's own solution to the problem of skepticism, to the very challenge he himself had laid down. But it was another of Maimon's many suggestions, another of his many proposals, that neither time nor temperment allowed him to elaborate. Fichte soon developed it on a grand scale, however, making it one of the central themes of the his early 1794 *Wissenschaftslehre*. It is striking that, in Part III of his *Grundlage*, and in the first lecture of his *Bestimmung des Gelehrten*, Fichte considers an antinomy very similar to Maimon's. According to this "fundamental antithesis," we are all finite beings because we are limited by and acted on by a world outside us;

we are divided into reason and sensibility, where our sensibility is purely passive, subject to the influence of nature. It is the fundamental demand of reason, the essence of the categorical imperative, however, that we attain complete autonomy and independence, or that we become only what we posit ourselves to be. We can fulfill this demand—we can achieve such complete independence—only when we attain complete control over all of nature, for only then are we no longer dependent on, or influenced by, an external world. Needless to say, then, such complete independence is the prerogative of the divine understanding, which alone has the power to create all of nature.

According to Fichte, the only solution to this predicament—the only means to overcome the vast discrepancy between the demands of reason and our actual condition as finite beings—is for us *to strive* to realize the ideal of complete independence. Although we cannot ever fully attain this ideal, we can at least approach it through constant struggle and effort. We can approximate this ideal if we exert ourselves to bring nature more and more under our control, and if we try with all our power to make it conform more and more to the demands of our reason. The more nature is under our control, the more our passive sensibility will disappear, and the more our noumenal and rational nature will grow, so that we will become more like the purely rational *intellectus archetypus.*

It should be clear that Fichte's antithesis is very much like Maimon's antinomy, and that his concept of striving plays virtually the same role, and is based on the same idea, as Maimon's concept of the infinite progress of enquiry. The main difference between Fichte and Maimon is that Fichte sees the problem in *moral* terms: we should strive to realize the status of the infinite understanding because the categorical imperative commands it, and because nothing less is at stake than our autonomy or independence. There can be no doubt, however, that Fichte also sees the problem in epistemological terms, and indeed as the main predicament facing the possibility of knowledge. For, no less than Maimon, he thinks that the ideal of knowledge is the *intellectus archetypus,* and that the dualism between thought and its object, or between understanding and sensibility, is the main obstacle to its realization.

All this makes it plain how Fichte's doctrine of the primacy of practical reason serves as his final response to the challenge of skepticism. We have already seen how that doctrine means *inter alia* that knowledge is the result of action rather than contemplation. Applied to the problem of skepticism, this implies that the cure for radical doubt lies not in the field of specula-tion—in building firmer foundations from self-evident principles—but in the realm of action. All the objections of the skeptic are completely unan-swerable, Fichte thinks, as long as we remain captive in the confines of spec-ulation or theory. For if we simply contemplate or reflect upon an object, we do not change it, and so the dualism between subject and object persists; but as long as that dualism remains, we have made no progress toward acquir-ing knowledge. The only means of overcoming the despair of skepticism, then, is through acting, for only in acting on the world do I change it, and so diminish the subject–object dualism. In Fichte's view the chief error of all previous epistemology, and especially that of the subjectivist tradition, is its purely contemplative or speculative paradigm of knowledge, according to which knowledge is possible apart from, and prior to, activity.[41] For Fichte, however, knowledge is only the result of activity, and ultimately the will itself.

Though Fichte's pragmatism marks an important break with the contem-plative model of knowledge characteristic of the subjectivist tradition, it would be absurd to stress its originality. For Fichte is not only borrowing an insight of Maimon's; he is also going back to a tradition of thought as old as Francis Bacon. According to this tradition, knowledge is the product of ac-tion rather than contemplation, of making the world conform to our de-mands rather than trying to mirror its essence through rational theorizing. This was indeed the only possible response to Pyrrhonism, Bacon argued, given that the skeptic could always demolish the subtlest scholastic demon-stration.[42] This allegiance to the Baconian tradition was not, however, un-conscious or unacknowledged. For it was no accident that the motto of Fichte's *Einleitungen in die Wissenschaftslehre*—and, indeed, of Kant's first *Kritik*—came from the *Novum Organum*.

CHAPTER 3

Criticism versus Dogmatism

1. The Transformation of the Kantian Problematic

We have seen how Fichte developed some of the most important principles of his idealism in combating the skepticism of Schulze and Maimon. That things exist only as any rational being must conceive them, that the ego is only for itself, that knowledge is the result of practical activity, and that transcendental philosophy has to be completely immanent—all these central ideas of Fichte's *Wissenschaftslehre* were developed in response to the challenge of skepticism. Still, it should be obvious that we are far from a complete and accurate account of Fichte's idealism. We have only traced the genesis of some of its parts; but we have not considered how they form a whole.

To have some idea of the whole, we do well to begin with what Fichte himself means by 'idealism.' Like any other philosopher, we must interpret Fichte in his own terms. We must take into account the distinctions he made, the concepts he used, and the definitions he formulated. This means first and foremost that we should consider his own definition of 'idealism' and how he distinguishes it from opposing positions.

Prima facie it might seem trite to insist on an internal understanding of Fichte's idealism. "What else?" one might ask. There is a serious danger, however, that we interpret Fichte's definitions, concepts, and distinctions along Kantian lines. This is very tempting, partly because Fichte uses the same terms as Kant, and partly because he insists that his system represents the very spirit of the critical philosophy. Still, this is a temptation that we must resist. For, in significant respects, Fichte reformulated, and indeed transformed, Kant's doctrines and problems. Furthermore, his context is very different from Kant's: there is a wide difference between the philosophical concerns of the 1770s, when the critical philosophy was born, and that of the early 1790s, when Fichte first conceived his *Wissenschaftslehre*. So, even when Fichte uses the same terms as Kant, we should not take for granted that he means the same thing by them; placed in Fichte's context, they take on a completely different sense.

In the *Erste Einleitung in die Wissenschaftslehre* Fichte explains idealism in terms of his basic distinction between *criticism* and *dogmatism*.[1] He contends that these are the only possible answers to the fundamental problem of transcendental philosophy: the explanation of experience. While criticism explains experience from some *immanent* principle within consciousness, the self, ego, or I in itself (*das Ich an sich*), dogmatism accounts for it from some *transcendent* principle beyond consciousness, the thing in itself (*Ding an sich*). Criticism maintains that experience is the product of the self in itself, or that we know objects because we create them according to the laws of reason; dogmatism holds that experience is the result of the thing in itself, or that we know objects because our consciousness reflects the world that acts on it.

Fichte saw the opposition between criticism and dogmatism in terms of a dramatic choice: freedom or fatalism. While criticism preserves the possibility of freedom by seeing the subject as pure activity, the source of its entire world, dogmatism undermines freedom by viewing the subject as passive, the product of nature. For Fichte, this is a choice between Kant's critical idealism, which defends the possibility and reality of moral freedom, or Spinoza's naturalism, which stresses that everything happens of necessity according to the laws of nature.[2]

Prima facie Fichte's distinction between criticism and dogmatism is simply a reformulation of Kant's own distinction between transcendental idealism and realism, which he explained in almost the same terms as Fichte. The transcendental idealist holds that "objects conform to concepts" because the understanding is the lawgiver of nature, whereas the transcendental realist maintains that "concepts conform to objects" since they are the product of objects.[3] Moreover, Kant saw the difference between transcendental idealism and realism in terms of the choice between freedom and fatalism. Through its distinction between appearances and things-in-themselves, transcendental idealism upholds the possibility of freedom, because even though everything in the realm of appearances is determined according to the principle of sufficient reason, the world of things-in-themselves is not subject to this law. Conversely, transcendental realism, by conflating things-in-themselves with appearances, has to accept a form of determinism, an infinite series of causes, which leaves no room for the possibility of free-dom.[4] It is indeed striking that Kant himself, under the influence of the Spinoza revival of the late 1780s, saw his transcendental idealism as the only alternative to Spinozism.[5]

Although these similarities are noteworthy, they should not obscure the underlying differences between Kant's and Fichte's distinctions. While Kant's contrast between transcendental idealism and realism is essentially between those accounts of knowledge that distinguish between appearances and things-in-themselves (transcendental idealism) and those that conflate them (transcendental realism), Fichte's distinction between criticism and dogmatism takes no account of this point. Unlike Kant's transcendental idealism, Fichte's criticism does not distinguish between appearances and things-in-themselves. Rather, it explains *all* of experience as the product of the subject alone, eliminating things-in-themselves entirely. Indeed, the whole point of Fichte's criticism, at least as he explains it in the *Erste Einleitung,* is to eradicate the thing-in-itself from the body of the Kantian system.[6] Conversely, Fichte's dogmatism is a form of materialism that explains all of experience according to natural laws.[7] It does not simply regard the objects of experience as things-in-themselves—a doctrine common to materialism and dualism. Excluding the very possibility of dualism, Fichte's criticism and dogmatism are essentially *monistic:* criticism is entirely idealistic, explaining all reality in terms of the ego, while dogmatism is entirely naturalistic, explaining everything according to mechanical laws.

It is also important to see that Kant's and Fichte's distinctions arose from different formulations of the basic problem of transcendental philosophy. The purpose of Kant's transcendental idealism is to resolve the specific problem of the possibility of synthetic a priori judgments: How do we explain the truth of such judgments if they are not derived from experience and if they cannot be demonstrated according to the law of contradiction? The task of Fichte's criticism, however, is to explain how representations can correspond with objects if the mind and the world are so different from one another.[8] Hence the Fichtean problem is broader than the Kantian: it extends to *any* class of representations, even empirical or synthetic a posteriori ones, and it does not arise for synthetic a priori concepts alone. This difference between Kant's and Fichte's problems becomes especially apparent from Fichte's own interpretation of Kant's synthetic a priori. He thinks that it should be understood not simply as a unity of distinct representations but as a unity of the subject and object themselves. According to Fichte, Kant had failed to see the more general issue behind the problem of synthetic a priori judgments: How does the subject know the object if the subject and object have opposing characteristics?[9] Such a reformulation of the Kantian problem reflects the polemics against the critical philosophy in the late 1780s and early 1790s, which had stressed the difficulties of Kant's dualisms. For the entire post-Kantian generation, the basic problem of transcendental philosophy is how to surmount these dualisms.

There is another more obvious, but no less important, difference between Kant's and Fichte's distinctions. The Fichtean distinction is cast in more metaphysical terms. This metaphysical language first becomes apparent when Fichte, in the first part of the *Grundlage der gesamten Wissenschaftslehre*, states that idealism makes its first principle the *absolute* ego, which is "completely unconditioned" and not determinable by anything else outside itself (I, 97). He explains that to call something "in itself," "absolute," or "unconditioned" means that it stands above all contrast and comparison (I, 109–110, 119). Such terminology seems to derive from the metaphysical tradition, and more specifically from its modern incarnation in Spinozism. The term 'in itself' is indeed reminiscent of Spinoza's definition of substance from Book I of the *Ethica:* "that which is conceived in itself, and not in relation to something else" (I, def. 7). The similarity is indeed more than apparent, given that Fichte saw the *Wissenschaftslehre* as the antithesis and antidote to Spinoza's *Ethica.*

If we take Fichte's metaphysical language as more than a *façon de parler,* then the choice between criticism and dogmatism is not only between competing accounts of experience, but also between rival conceptions of the infinite or the unconditioned.[10] The infinite or unconditioned is either the subject in itself or the object in itself. Fichte then explains the central problem of transcendental philosophy in such metaphysical terms. To demonstrate the reality of the external world is to show how the absolute or infinite subject "goes outside itself" and becomes something limited and finite.[11] This seems to be nothing less than the ancient metaphysical puzzle about how something infinite becomes finite!

Fichte's transformation of the Kantian problematic raises some interesting and important questions. First, why the dilemma between criticism and dogmatism? Why are there only two systems of philosophy? Second, why does Fichte reject dogmatism? Why, in the end, does he think that idealism is the only possible option in philosophy? Third, why such metaphysical language? Why is the choice between criticism and dogmatism between two competing concepts of the unconditioned or infinite? And, fourth, how does Fichte square his metaphysical language with his ideal of a completely immanent transcendental philosophy?[12]

These are important questions for the later development of absolute idealism. Fichte's transformation of the Kantian problematic became decisive for Schelling and Hegel, who understood Kant's questions in essentially Fichtean terms. The main problems that Schelling and Hegel address in the 1790s are very much those first formulated by Fichte in the Jena *Wissenschaftslehre,* and their main argument in behalf of absolute idealism is that it alone resolves the questions that Fichte raised but could not answer. All the more reason, then, to examine each question in a little detail.

2. The Two Systems

Fichte's explicit explanation for why there are only two possible systems of philosophy is not very helpful. In the *Erste Einleitung in die Wissenschaftslehre* he says that anyone who disputes that there are only two systems has to prove that there are some additional components to experience besides the subject and object (I, 426). Since the subject and object are the basic entities of all experience, and since criticism and dogmatism explain experience according to either the subject or object, it seems that there cannot be any other alternative. However, this explanation would not be very convincing to the dualist, who will simply ask why there cannot be a system that explains experience according to *both* the subject and object.[13]

There is no great mystery, however, behind Fichte's exclusion of dualism. It is only necessary to consider the historical context in which Fichte's problem arose. Like Maimon and many of his contemporaries, Fichte regarded dualism not as a possible solution to his problem but as the very source of the problem itself. The central issue in explaining the possibility of knowledge is how to account for the correspondence between the mind and the world, given that the subject and object seem to be such heterogeneous things. No one in the 1780s and 1790s had forgotten Descartes' notorious problem, and it was widely held to be a *reductio ad absurdam* of the dualistic position. But the critical philosophy did not resolve Descartes' problem—it simply transformed it! Although Kant himself had rejected transcendental dualism in the *Kritik,*[14] it seemed that he had revived it in other forms with his distinctions between noumena and phenomena, things-in-themselves and appearances, and understanding and sensibility. It was the task of Fichte and the young Schelling, then, to remove those residues of dualism within the critical philosophy that left so much room for skeptical mischief. Hence they never ceased to lambast the dualism of the "dogmatic Kantians," who wanted to explain the origin of experience by the action of the thing-in-itself upon our sensibility.[15] For Fichte, any attempt to synthesize criticism and dogmatism is absurd because it presupposes *per impossible* "a continuous transition from matter to mind or vice versa."[16]

Granted that dualism is not an option, why explain criticism and dogmatism in such metaphysical language? The ultimate reason for Fichte's use of such terms as 'absolute,' 'infinite,' and 'in itself' lies less with the metaphysical tradition than with his conception of the transcendental itself. Something is absolute or infinite in the classical sense if it has no limit or end, having nothing else outside it to limit its essence or existence. This means that it cannot be determinate, because all determination involves a form of limitation; to determine a thing is to contrast and compare it with other things, so that it limits them and is limited by them. Now, Fichte reasons, the fundamental ground of experience must be absolute or infinite in just this sense. For we cannot identify this ground with any *determinate* thing—something that resembles or differs from other things—when it is the condition of all determination, the ground under which we contrast and compare things with one another. We identify a determinate thing, Fichte thinks, only by applying the principle of sufficient reason, which determines the similarities and differences between one thing and another.[17] But the ground of experience is also the basis of the principle of sufficient reason, so that we cannot apply this principle to it except on pain of circularity. Hence, in the first section of the *Grundlage*, Fichte explains that the absolute ego is indeterminable, because it is the condition under which we apply the principle of sufficient reason itself. It has no ground because it is the condition under which anything is a ground (I, 109–112).

It is now very easy to understand Fichte's identification of transcendental realism with Spinozism. If realism, like idealism, must be strictly monistic, and if its first principle too must be absolute in the sense of being beyond all contrast and comparison, then Spinoza's system seems to be the perfect candidate to fill these roles. Spinoza's substance is infinite in the sense that it is absolutely unique, inconceivable in relation to other things. It is also the source of Spinoza's monism: substance is the single reality of which mind and body are only attributes, different ways of explaining one and the same thing. Why, though, call Spinozism "realism"? It is because the first principle of Spinozism, the single infinite substance, is not within consciousness. It is therefore like the Kantian thing-in-itself in that it transcends all possible experience.

Although Fichte's language is metaphysical, it is important to recognize that he still refuses to make any metaphysical commitment with it. To say that the ego is absolute or infinite does not mean that it is the *whole* of all reality, the *totality* of all determinations. Rather, it is something purely formal and indeterminate, and so the absence of all determinations. All that can be said about it is that it *is;* as the ground of all predication, it has no predicates at all (I, 111–112, 116). For Fichte, it is a fallacy to apply determinate predicates to the absolute, because that would be to confuse the transcendental with the empirical. The very essence of dogmatism is that it hypostatizes the transcendental, placing what is a condition of our experience into experience itself (I, 120–121).

3. The Refutation of Dogmatism

If criticism and dogmatism are the only possible explanations of experience, why did Fichte choose criticism? We can answer this question, of course, only if we first know why he rejected dogmatism. The answer to this latter question proves to be rather complicated, however.

Prima facie there does not seem to be any difficulty in explaining Fichte's disapproval of dogmatism. In his review of *Aenesidemus,* he had dismissed the very idea of the thing-in-itself as an impossibility; it was nothing less than the thought of something unthinkable, a noumenon that did not exist according to any of the laws of logic. If, however, the thing-in-itself is a fiction, the main explanatory principle of dogmatism collapses. That, it seems, should be the end of the matter.

Yet Fichte did not exploit this obvious strategy. In his later 1797 *Erste Einleitung in die Wissenschaftslehre* he made some remarkable concessions to the dogmatist. To some extent he repeated his old refrain: "The thing-in-itself is a pure invention which possesses no reality whatsoever" (I, 428). Yet he no longer dismisses this fiction as a sheer impossibility. Rather, he admits that the dogmatist can give some reality to his principle after all, if he can show "the necessity of thinking of it as the basis or foundation of experience" (I, 428). He even concedes that the dogmatist can explain away the self-consciousness of freedom—the central datum of criticism—because he can point out how such an apparent "experience" is really only the result of our ignorance of the necessary laws of nature (I, 430). Such, indeed, are Fichte's concessions that he sometimes argues that there cannot be any *theoretical* basis for a choice between criticism and dogmatism, since the dispute between them concerns first principles and all demonstration and refutation presupposes a shared first principle (I, 429). Fichte then concludes that the decision between criticism and dogmatism has to be made on practical, and indeed on personal, grounds (I, 434).

Now we have come full circle. Rather than being nonsensical, dogmatism is as legitimate as criticism, and there is only a personal decision to be made between them. We shall have occasion to sort out Fichte's confusion and ambivalence about this issue in a later chapter (4.1.4). Suffice it to say for now, however, that Fichte's concessions to dogmatism were not such that he abandoned all arguments against it. If he softens his stance against dogmatism in one section of the *Erste Einleitung* (§5), he returns to attack it in the very next section (§6). He now finds dogmatism to be inadequate after all, and indeed on theoretical grounds. While he does not attempt a refutation of dogmatism in the sense of a valid deductive argument proceeding from self-evident premises, he still insists that dogmatism should be rejected because it is unable to explain experience. If the only reality the dogmatist can give to his principle is to make it the basis for the explanation of experience, and if it can be shown that this principle cannot do justice to some central features of our experience, then dogmatism will become "a helpless affirmation and assurance" (I, 438).

The starting point of Fichte's argument is his principle, first announced in the *Aenesidemus* review, that the ego or subject is essentially for itself. This means *inter alia* that self-consciousness is essential to the very nature of subjectivity, and that we hypostatize a subject if we separate it from at least the possibility of self-awareness. As Fichte now puts this point: there is an *immediate unity of being and seeing* in the case of the subject, whereas there is no such unity in the case of the object, whose existence is separable from any consciousness of it (I, 436). Now, Fichte maintains, it is just this feature of subjectivity—the necessity of self-consciousness—that dogmatism cannot explain. Rather than attempting to explain a subject from *within*, according to its self-interpretations or self-descriptions, it tries to account for it from *without*, according to some third-person point of view. It treats the subject like any other object in nature, as a mere thing conforming to mechanical laws; in other words, the dogmatist *hypostatizes* the subject. Hypostatization of the subject is indeed "the basic mistake" of all dogmatism.[18]

More specifically, Fichte's argument goes as follows (I, 435–436). If dogmatism is to explain experience, then it must account for our representations, and more specifically those accompanied by a feeling of necessity in our consciousness. To do this, it employs the principle of causality and sees the representations as effects of the thing-in-itself. But no such explanation can possibly succeed, because representations, and indeed the mind that has them, are very different from things or objects. A representation exists only for the subject who has it, and it is nothing unless the subject can be self-conscious of it. There is therefore a *double series* in the mind: the representation and the self-awareness of it, or, as Fichte puts it, "being" and the "observation of it." The essence of the mind, Fichte then stresses, consists in the *inseparability* of these two series. An object, however, differs from a representation in that it does not exist for the subject who perceives it, for by definition it is supposed to exist independent of any perception of it. Among things, therefore, there is only a *single series* of existence.

To bring out the difference between representations and things, Fichte points out that we can ask of any representation "For whom does it exist?" There *must be* some answer to this question for the representation: namely, that it exists for the subject. But there *cannot* be an answer to this question for the thing, which exists for no one because *ex hypothesi* it continues to exist even when no one perceives it. Fichte therefore concludes that we cannot explain representations, the essential units of our experience, on the basis of material things. The main problem is this: the representation and the thing "lie in two different worlds between which there is no bridge" (I, 436). It is as if the dogmatist tried to explain the origin of fire by water![19]

It is an important—and explicit—premise of this argument that dogmatism presupposes a *mechanical* model of explanation. The reason that the dogmatist cannot explain experience, Fichte contends, is that it is not possible to account for representations on the basis of mechanical causation: "all efficacious action is mechanical in character . . . and no representation can be produced in virtue of mechanical action alone" (I, 439).[20] Although Fichte is not explicit, he seems to assume that mechanical explanation operates when the cause precedes the effect in time, and when the cause imparts its force to the effect, which passively receives it. Thus he says that the cause is an event that transmits its force to another event, and so on in a series, in such a manner that it is not possible for any event to in turn *react against* the cause acting upon it (I, 436–437). Here Fichte seems to assume the law of inertia for material things; in other words, that such things cannot act unless they are acted on.[21]

So, despite his many concessions to dogmatism, Fichte finally rejects it, and indeed on theoretical grounds. The fundamental principle of dogmatism, the thing-in-itself, proves to be a fiction after all, because it cannot explain our experience. The ultimate reason for the failure of dogmatism is clear: it attempts to explain experience from some standpoint external to the mind itself, when the mind is essentially for itself, something that has to be explained internally in terms of its self-consciousness alone. The necessity of idealism is that it alone explains experience on an immanent basis according to the principles inherent in the mind itself.

4. Fichte and the Thing-in-Itself

Every student of the history of philosophy, if he knows anything about Fichte at all, knows that he rejected the thing-in-itself. That he did so is crucial to the stereotype of Fichte as the philosopher who completes and radicalizes Kant's Copernican Revolution. But, like most stereotypes in the history of philosophy, this one too is simplistic and misleading. There are at least two problems with it. First, as we have already seen, Fichte gave different, and even incompatible, reasons for rejecting the thing-in-itself. Second, Fichte did not dismiss the concept *tout court*. If he insisted on abandoning it in some senses, he demanded that it be retained in others, and indeed to such an extent that it played a pivotal role in his system.[22] This makes it necessary to raise the questions: In what senses did Fichte reject the thing-in-itself? And in what senses did he accept it?

Fichte repudiates the concept of the thing-in-itself insofar as it is the unthinkable. This is the sense he first identified and denounced in the *Aenesidemus* review, and he never retreated from this position. According to this interpretation, the thing-in-itself is something that exists not only independent of the forms of sensibility, space and time, but also independent of all the categories of the understanding. Hence it is not only something imperceptible, but also something inconceivable. For at least two reasons, Fichte finds the very idea of such a thing-in-itself absurd. First, he claims that to postulate its existence is to think the unthinkable, and so *ipso facto* destroys its very existence as the unthinkable. Second, he affirms the general idealist principle that things can exist only in the way that we must think of them. Rightly, Fichte refused to attribute such a concept of the thing-in-itself to Kant; but from this he drew the general and more problematic conclusion that Kant had no concept of the thing-in-itself at all.

Fichte also dismisses the concept of the thing-in-itself insofar as it is the transcendental cause of appearances. This concept is distinct from that of the utterly unthinkable, since the cause of appearances must at least be thinkable according to the category of causality. Still, Fichte rejected it all the same. He discovered two difficulties with the assumption that the thing-in-itself could be the cause of appearances.[23] First, it assumes that something completely unlike our representations can be the cause of our representations, so that it jumps a chasm between two worlds. Second, it involves the transcendent application of the categories of causality beyond appearances, which is flatly contrary to critical doctrine. Here, however, Fichte failed to recognize Kant's important distinction between knowing and thinking an object according to the categories.

In general, Fichte thinks that the assumption of a thing-in-itself as the cause of appearances arises from a confusion between two levels of discourse in transcendental philosophy: the standpoint of the philosopher, who reflects on and analyzes the conditions of consciousness, and the standpoint of empirical consciousness itself, which presupposes and acts according to these conditions. From the standpoint of our empirical consciousness we speak of things-in-themselves because we think that appearances exist apart from and prior to our perception of them; and we think this because we have no knowledge of the conditions that produce this object. From the standpoint of the philosopher, however, we know that these objects are only appearances that are created by transcendental synthesis (I, 482–483). Although Fichte admits that Kant sometimes does refer to the existence of things-in-themselves as the causes of appearances, he still insists that Kant then speaks only from the perspective of empirical consciousness itself. Those Kantians who postulate a thing-in-itself as the cause of the whole order of appearances fail to recognize that Kant often speaks with two voices, depending on whether he adopts the standpoint of the transcendental philosopher or that of ordinary consciousness. They not only confuse these two levels of discourse, but they also make an illegitimate use of the principle of causality, which is applicable only within the sphere of appearances themselves (I, 482). On similar grounds Fichte dismisses Jacobi's famous objection against the thing-in-itself. Jacobi confuses the empirical and transcendental levels of analysis because he thinks that Kant uses the term 'thing-in-itself' in a transcendental sense when he uses it really only in an empirical one (483n).

It is remarkable, however, that Fichte himself produces very little textual support for his reading of Kant, and that when he does so he cites passages that are more accurately read as evidence against it. In section 6 of the *Zweite Einleitung in die Wissenschaftslehre* he cites passages from Kant that he takes from, of all texts, the appendix to Jacobi's *David Hume*, the main source for Jacobi's famous attack on the thing-in-itself! There Jacobi cited a passage from the Critique of the Fourth Paralogism where Kant criticizes empirical idealism because it accepts a hidden premise from transcendental realism: that appearances are things-in-themselves, and that as such they are the cause of our representations of things outside us (A 372). In this passage Kant argued that if we assume that appearances continue to exist when we do not perceive them, then our knowledge about them will become uncertain, because we will not be in a position to know whether our representations are really caused by these things. Fichte refers to this passage as evidence for why Kant rejects things-in-themselves as the transcendental cause of our experience—as if Kant wishes to reject any kind of transcendental cause and not only the transcendental realist assumption that appearances as things-in-themselves should be that cause! But Kant is perfectly explicit in this passage, in some further sentences not cited by Fichte, that he is rejecting not things-in-themselves as the cause of our experience but only appearances understood as things-in-themselves.[24]

For all his resistance to the thing-in-itself, Fichte still endorsed the idea in important respects, assigning it a pivotal role in his own critical idealism. He does not reject the thing-in-itself provided that it is understood as a *noumenon*, the idea of something that is the product of pure thinking alone.[25] Fichte admits that Kant sometimes uses the thing-in-itself to refer to the noumenon, and that in this case it is perfectly consistent with his critical principles. The noumenon is the object that is created by the necessary laws of our reason, and that we add to appearances to give them objectivity. Such a noumenon is indeed "the cornerstone of Kant's empirical realism" (I, 483), Fichte maintains, because by it we can explain how objects appear independent of our representations and yet are not transcendent entities.

In section 5 of his *Grundlage der gesamten Wissenschaftslehre*, Fichte also reintroduces the idea of the thing-in-itself in the role of a "stimulus" or "check" *(Anstoß)* to the activity of the ego. He explains that we cannot say anything more about this entity other than it is something opposed to the ego's activity (I, 279). Although all of its known determinations are created or posited by the activity of the ego, there is still an extent to which it resists its activity and so remains forever indeterminable and unknowable. Like Kant with his thing-in-itself, Fichte feels compelled to postulate the existence of this unknowable entity to explain the finitude of the human predicament, the fact that we do not have the creative power to produce the entire world.

It is here that a serious question of consistency arises. It would seem as if this check to the ego's activity also acts on it, so that it is a cause of our representations; but this would involve, of course, a transcendent application of the category of causality. It is not possible to avoid this contradiction by claiming that the check exists only from the standpoint of empirical consciousness. For it is indeed the Fichtean philosopher who postulates the existence of this entity. Furthermore, the difficulty cannot be resolved by claiming that Fichte gives a purely regulative status to his check, for Fichte gives it an unmistakable constitutive role by stating that it acts on the subject's feelings and provokes it into activity. A merely regulative ideal is not in the position to act on anything.

Fichte himself was aware of this tension in his views, and he attempted to resolve it through a distinction between representation and feeling.[26] While representation has some objective status because it refers to some object to which we ascribe properties, feeling consists in nothing more than sensation itself. Whereas representation has a cognitive status because it issues in judgment, feeling consists in nothing more than the subjective states of the perceiver. Following this distinction, Fichte then maintains that, though we represent things only as appearances, we feel them as things-in-themselves. He explains that although we cannot know things-in-themselves directly through representation, we can know them indirectly through feeling. This removes the apparent inconsistency, he implies, because things-in-themselves are not completely unknowable after all. Their status as something felt would indeed seem to justify the application of the categories to them, so that there is no problem involved with a transcendent use of the category of causality. Thus, having initially banished the thing-in-itself as something almost nonsensical, Fichte reinstates it as the object of ineffable feeling. We shall have occasion to reexamine the role of this rehabilitated thing-in-itself in a later chapter (2.6.4).

CHAPTER 4

Freedom and Subjectivity

1. The Meaning of Freedom

Now that we have seen why Fichte repudiated dogmatism, the only question that remains is why he advocated idealism. For Fichte, the answer to this question was simple and straightforward. The great value of idealism, and its fundamental advantage over dogmatism, is that it alone can preserve freedom. This means that only idealism provides a sufficient support for the fundamental principles of morality, which are undermined by the fatalism of dogmatism. Hence Fichte saw his *Wissenschaftslehre* as "the first system of freedom."[1] Its chief purpose was to represent and defend the value of human freedom, which is the sole interest of reason itself.[2]

It is important to see, however, that freedom played an even more vital role in Fichte's thinking. It is not only the main value behind his idealism, but also its fundamental explanatory principle. Fichte saw freedom as the key to the basic problem of transcendental philosophy: how to explain the possibility of experience and the consciousness of the external world. The self-consciousness of freedom is his first principle for the deduction of experience, his basic premise to establish the awareness of an objective reality. According to Fichte, the entire sensible world has to be understood as the necessary condition for the self-consciousness of our freedom, as the means and medium by which the ego knows itself as an autonomous moral agent. "Freedom is the vehicle for our knowledge of objects; but not the converse: that our knowledge of objects is the vehicle for our knowledge of freedom."[3]

The central role of freedom in Fichte's idealism makes it imperative to raise one question: What does Fichte mean by freedom? His views on freedom are scattered throughout his Jena writings, but it is best to focus on his clearest and most mature exposition of this concept, that found in his 1798

273

System der Sittenlehre. It is also necessary to consider his 1798 *Wissen-schaftslehre novo methodo,* which in some places gives a somewhat different account.[4]

To begin, it is important to recognize that Fichte, like Kant, has two very different concepts of freedom.[5] There is the freedom of the pure will (*Wille*), which he identifies with the law of reason, the categorical imperative.[6] There is also the freedom of choice (*Willkür*), the power to do or not do something. The difference between these concepts is clear: the pure will cannot be identical with choice, which can act not only according to, but also contrary to, the law of reason. Fichte relates these two concepts by claiming that choice arises from the self-consciousness of, or reflection on, the pure will. We become aware of freedom only as choice, because we feel the moral law only as a command on our sensible nature, as an imperative that we might or might not obey.[7] Freedom in the sense of pure will cannot be an object of consciousness, Fichte explains, because it is the condition of any consciousness whatsoever.

Partly because it is so problematic, and partly because it is so important for attribution of moral responsibility, the main focus of Fichte's theory of freedom is on the concept of choice. It is this concept that is the subject of Fichte's detailed discussions of freedom in the *System der Sittenlehre* and *Wissenschaftslehre novo methodo.* To understand what he means by freedom in this sense, we do well to begin with his own thought experiment in the *Sittenlehre* (IV, 26–27, 33–34).

Imagine a steel spring that resists the motion impressed on it from outside. This spring has a principle of motion within itself, so that it is not merely passive but reacts against what acts on it. Still, we refuse to ascribe freedom to it. "Why?" Fichte asks. Our first answer is likely to be that the spring is not free because it acts of necessity. It behaves according to laws, such that if a certain pressure is applied to it, then it must react with a certain force, and it cannot do otherwise. Hence we do not regard the spring as free because we think that freedom excludes necessity, or that it involves the power to act otherwise.

Now Fichte reverses the experiment. Assume that the spring does not act of necessity, but that on one occasion it acts in one way, and that on another occasion it acts in another way, so that there is no law to predict its actions. Even in this case, Fichte insists, we would refuse to ascribe freedom to the spring. Why? Because its actions happen by chance and for no reason.

Any account of freedom, Fichte thinks, must do justice to these apparently conflicting intuitions. Freedom excludes necessity, but also chance. There must be some reason for our actions; but it cannot be a cause that compels us to act so that we cannot do otherwise. This means that any adequate theory of freedom must reject *compatibilism*, according to which a free action is consistent with natural necessity, as well as *indifferentism*, according to which the will can act without a reason so that it is indifferent whether it does one thing or another.

Fichte's own theory attempts to satisfy both these desiderata. He thinks that freedom excludes necessity because it essentially involves *independence* (IV, 24–25). Independence means that the will does *not* depend on external causes to act. Rather, the will is the cause of itself, so that we know why it acts from itself alone, and not from anything else outside itself. Hence any explanation for the acts of the will must be in terms of the will itself, of which we can only say "It is as it is, because it is so" (IV, 25).

Because he thinks freedom means independence, Fichte accepts Kant's definition of freedom as *spontaneity*, the power of the will to be a first cause, to begin a causal series without determination by some prior cause (IV, 37). For the same reason, he rejects Spinoza's definition of freedom: "That which acts by the necessity of its own nature alone."[8] Like Kant, but unlike Spinoza, Fichte thinks that freedom cannot be placed within nature, which is a realm of strict necessity. Anything that happens in nature is strictly governed by the principle of sufficient reason, according to which all events have external causes, such that, given the causes, the events cannot be otherwise (IV, 134–135).

Another reason freedom excludes necessity, Fichte argues, is because it involves choice, that is, the decision to act between opposing courses of action (IV, 81, 159). The will is free only if it has the choice to do A, B, or C, such that it is completely *indeterminate* whether it opts for A, B, or C. Those philosophers who find a contradiction in the possibility of an agent doing either X or −X on any specific occasion simply beg the question, Fichte contends, because they assume that a free agent is like something in nature. Of anything in nature we can indeed say that its essence is completely *determinate*, such that only one action is compatible with its essence. But when we assume the possibility of freedom we *ipso facto* reject the fact that a free rational agent is another thing in nature, and so we deny that it is completely determinate. Freedom, by its very nature as choice, involves *indeterminacy*, the fact that something can be either X or −X (IV, 159–161).

Although freedom involves choice, Fichte insists that it is not possible that we decide for no reason at all, as if it were completely indifferent whether we opt for X or $-X$ (IV, 35, 37, 179). Since freedom excludes chance, there must be some reason for choice. Fichte explains that we can formulate this reason in terms of a practical syllogism (IV, 179). Such a syllogism would begin with some general maxim, such as 'We must give priority to X'; it would then determine how this applies to a particular case, 'C is a case of X'; and it would then conclude with the imperative 'We ought to do C.'

But if there must be a reason for choice, how do we escape determinism? Fichte thinks that we can avoid the snares of both natural necessity and chance if we assume that the reasons for a free action lie in the realm of thought alone. The reason for a free action is not the *cause* for the action, but its *end* or *purpose* as conceived by an intelligent or rational being. Insofar as we are thinking beings, Fichte argues, we ascend to a new order of explanation outside nature itself.[9] In nature one being is the cause of another being, and so on *ad infinitum;* but in the case of a rational agent something merely thought is the reason for action. Although he does not use the same terms, Fichte anticipates the prevalent modern view that there is a distinction between reasons and causes.[10] Reasons are the purposes of an intelligent thinking being, whereas causes are events in nature that happen in space and time.

It is important to add, however, that Fichte does not think that the reasons for free actions are simply *any kind* of purpose or end. Such reasons are a *specific kind* of purpose or end: that chosen by an intelligent or rational being. Not all purposive activity is free, Fichte argues, because many organisms in nature act for ends but they do so of necessity.[11] Although Fichte does not think that the actions of living beings are explicable according to mechanical causes, he does hold that their activity is still subject to necessity and so another kind of natural law. To be free, then, an action must not only be done for some purpose; it also must be chosen by a self-conscious rational agent.[12]

Fichte summarizes his concept of freedom in the term 'self-determination' (*Selbstbestimmung*).[13] He explains that this concept means two things. First, that the self exists prior to its determinations, so that it can determine itself to be X, Y, or Z, depending on its choice; hence it must have an existence independent of any one of its determinations. In the case of a free being, then, we must make a distinction between its existence and essence. This is not the case with a thing, however. We cannot separate its existence from its essence, because its very being or existence consists in nothing more than all the properties or determinations constitutive of its nature. Thus, while the existence of a free being is *indeterminate*, that of a thing in nature is entirely *determinate;* it has all its properties of necessity, and it cannot have any others without destroying its nature. Second, self-determination means that the self acts according to its own concept of itself, that it becomes only what it conceives itself to be, so that its essence or nature conforms entirely to its own rational choice.

Like all theories of self-determination, Fichte's theory states that the agent's activity makes determinate who or what I am, and that before this activity I am only something inchoate and indeterminate. But there are two distinctive aspects to Fichte's account that distinguish it from other theories. First, it maintains that the activity of self-determination does not realize a nature that is already complete and fixed; rather, it holds that there is no such fixed nature or essence at all. Second, the activity of self-determination does not take place of necessity but conforms entirely to the acts of rational choice, which could have been otherwise. In both these respects Fichte's account of self-determination anticipates the later existentialist concept of radical freedom.[14] Thus Fichte not only implies or suggests, but explicitly states, and indeed stresses, that the self is only what it makes itself:

> Who am I really? That is, what am I as an individual? And what is the reason that I am just this one [and no other]? I answer: I am, from the moment I have come to consciousness, *that to which I make myself according to freedom, and I am this simply because I so make myself.*[15]

Fichte does not think, of course, that we are *now* free beings in the sense proposed by his concept of self-determination. Rather, he stresses that his concept lays down only an *ideal*, a *goal* for moral action; in Kantian terms, it is only a regulative, not a constitutive principle. Fichte fully recognizes that who we are depends on factors completely beyond our control, whether they are due to environment or heredity.[16] He indeed stresses that we are free only in a *formal* but not a *material* sense, that is, though we have the *power* or *capacity* to conceive purposes and to act according to them, *what* we are—our determinate properties or characteristics—still depends on nature. We can become self-determining beings, Fichte maintains, only when we make all these characteristics conform to the standards of our rational activity. What has been given to us by nature we must recreate according to reason. We approach the goal of self-determination, then, only by a struggle against nature, by striving to bring it more under our control so that it complies with the ends of reason. Only when we have complete control over nature will we be completely free, for only then will there be no external causes to make us what we are.

It is of the first importance to see that Fichte's theory of freedom—though it is conceived in the name of Kant—also involves a dramatic break with his old teacher. Fichte's ideal of complete self-determination commits him to something Kant regarded as impossible, and indeed as undesirable: *self-identity*, the unity of the noumenal and phenomenal selves.[17] According to Fichte, the more the ego gains control over nature, the more its rational character grows and the more its sensible character disappears. Although Fichte admits that the ideal of complete independence is unattainable, the mere fact that he thinks that we can approach it is significant; for this means that the Kantian dualism is no longer absolute and qualitative but only relative and quantitative. Such an assumption violates the Kantian architechtonic at its most delicate and difficult point: the relationship between the noumenal and the phenomenal, the free and the necessity. For it implies, *pace* Kant, that noumenal actions not only *harmonize* with the course of nature, as if it remains forever the same, but that they actually *change* it, forcing it to become more rational where it had once been more sensible.

2. The Theory of Subjectivity

Fichte sometimes writes that the fundamental principle of his idealism—the ultimate basis for its explanation of experience—is the 'I in itself' (*Ich an sich*). This is perfectly compatible with his other statements that his basic principle is freedom; indeed, the two formulations support one another, because Fichte thinks that the very essence of the I, self, or ego consists in freedom. Still, the two formulations are not entirely equivalent, since behind Fichte's concept of the ego lies a theory about the nature of subjectivity itself, the distinctive characteristics of a subject in contrast to an object. Some account of this theory is crucial for an understanding of Fichte's idealism; but the theory is also worth considering for its own sake, because it is one of Fichte's most original contributions to the history of philosophy.[18] It marks an important break not only with the subjectivist tradition but also with Kant himself. The theory also had a notable influence on later thinkers, most notably Hegel and Sartre.

The essence of Fichte's theory of subjectivity is captured in his odd proposition that the essence of the ego consists in "subject–object identity."[19] This proposition is best explained as an attempt to capture the *interdependence* of the two distinguishing features of the self or the rational subject: freedom and self-consciousness. Both these aspects were already formulated by Kant; but what is new and interesting about Fichte's theory is what he says about their interconnection.

The first aspect of the self is *freedom*. According to Fichte, one characteristic feature of subjectivity in contrast to objectivity, or of rational agents in contrast to things, is that subjects or rational agents are free. This point had already been stated by Kant, who held that the distinctive feature of a rational being is its autonomy, its power to create and act according to its own laws. While everything else in creation acts according to laws, Kant wrote, rational beings alone have the power to act according to the *concept* of law, that is, its universalizable form alone.[20]

The second aspect or characteristic trait of the self is *self-consciousness*. Fichte also thinks that a distinctive feature of subjectivity in contrast to objectivity is that subjects have the power of self-consciouness. We have already seen how Fichte thinks that self-consciousness is constitutive of our subjectivity, and how he maintains that we cannot separate the existence of the self from its actual or possible awareness of itself (2.2.1; 2.3.3). For Fichte, to separate the self from its self-consciousness—as if it could somehow exist even if one could not become self-conscious of itself—is to reify or hypostatize the self, to treat a subject as if it were an object. It seems strange that this point had already been foreshadowed by Kant, who, notoriously, postulated the existence of an unknowable self. But here it is important to keep in mind Kant's principle of the unity of apperception, which states that a representation is nothing at all to me unless I can be self-conscious of having it. This principle was very important for Fichte, and the starting point for his reflection on the nature of subjectivity.[21]

Corresponding to each of these characteristics, Fichte distinguishes between the subjective and objective aspects, or the ideal and the real, aspects of the self.[22] Its subjective or ideal aspect consists in its self-consciousness, its power of representing or thinking about its own activity; its objective or real aspect consists in its freedom, its power of willing and acting. While the subjective aspect is theoretical and cognitive, the objective aspect is practical and volitional. Fichte includes among the ideal or subjective side of the self its power of conceiving and deliberating about ends; the real or objective side of the self is the decision to act on one of these ends and the power to execute it. Insofar as I will some end, he explains, I make the purely subjective into something objective.[23] This is the crucial transition from the indeterminate to the determinate that is so essential for self-determination.

Fichte makes this distinction to do justice to the ordinary distinction between thinking and willing, reflecting and doing. But it is important to see that he does not intend it to correspond to any absolute distinction between cognition and volition. He is firm that this distinction holds only from the standpoint of ordinary consciousness, and not from the standpoint of the transcendental philosopher who reflects on it.[24] It is the central aim of the transcendental philosopher to show how these two aspects of the self are united.

That they are inseparable is indeed the main thrust of Fichte's theory of subjectivity. The point of his theory of the self as subject–object identity is to show that the subjective and objective, ideal and real, aspects of the self are ultimately one. This means that we cannot be self-conscious and reflective unless we are free, and that we cannot be free unless we are self-conscious and reflective. Self-consciousness and freedom involve one another, and it is especially their interconnection that is characteristic of our subjectivity.

Why does Fichte think that self-consciousness requires freedom? If we summarize his lengthy argument for this contention in the 1798 *Sittenlehre*, it boils down to the following general point.[25] Freedom consists in the activity of self-determination, which makes determinate who or what I am; before engaging in this activity, however, I am not anything specific at all but only an abstract set of possibilities. I do not have a complete and given nature that I can know prior to my acting; rather, my activity of self-determination makes me who I am. Hence it is only through freedom, the activity of self-determination, that I *know* who I am. Fichte puts the point this way in the *Wissenschaftslehre novo methodo:* to be self-conscious, the subject must know itself as an object, in other words, it must manifest, express, or objectify itself; but this activity of self-manifestation, self-expression, or self-objectification is identical with self-determination and so with freedom itself.[26]

Why does freedom require self-consciousness? Fichte has in mind partly the simple point that freedom involves choice, and that to decide between alternatives and to act on them I must know what *I* choose and how *I* attain it; in other words, I must be self-conscious.[27] But his contention goes beyond this commonplace. He remarks that we never consider our free activity to be something that goes on while we passively observe it.[28] Rather, I make the activity of the will *my* activity by making it conform to my concepts or ends;

but to make it mine, to appropriate it for myself, is to be self-conscious of it. It should be clear that self-consciousness here must be understood not simply as descriptive, but also as prescriptive; in other words, it consists in those self-conceptions or self-ideals that project the kind of person I should become. Freedom then requires self-consciousness because the activity of self-determination, of making myself who I am, involves realizing these self-conceptions.[29]

The unity of the subjective and objective sides of the self, of freedom and self-consciousness, emerges most forcefully in Fichte's idea of the *self-positing* subject, which is epitomized by the first principle of the 1794 *Grundlage der gesamten Wissenschaftslehre:* "The ego, as absolute subject, is that whose being (essence) consists only in positing itself"(I, 97). The concept of self-positing (*sich setzen*) unites both thinking and willing, conceiving and acting. This concept has two meanings. First, the I posits itself when it becomes conscious of itself, that is, when it becomes an object for itself. Second, the I posits itself when it constitutes or makes itself. Positing therefore contains an aspect of both knowing and doing, of perceiving and making. When I posit myself, I know myself; but I also make or create myself. In self-positing, self-knowing and self-making are intertwined: I know myself because I make myself; and I make myself because I know myself. Hence when the ego posits itself—when it reflects on its existence as a pure subject—it also creates or makes its existence through this very act.

Fichte's theory of the self-positing self was primarily directed against the concept of the self as a soul or substance, which had played such a prominent role in the Christian tradition and seventeenth-century rationalism.[30] Of course, this concept had come under withering criticism long before Fichte. In his *Essay* Locke had found it useless to explain self-identity; in his *Treatise* Hume had dismissed it as a fiction after failing to discover it in his stream of impressions; and in the first *Kritik* Kant had exposed the paralogisms behind the attempts to demonstrate its existence. Fichte accepted all these criticisms of the traditional concept of the self; but he believed that they had still not gone far enough. For all their criticisms of hypostasis, Locke, Hume, and Kant continued to reify the self because they persisted in thinking that it had a fixed identity apart from its free activity. To be sure, Locke had virtually identified personal identity with self-consciousness; but, despite his radical criticism of the concept of subject, he still saw self-consciousness as reflective rather than creative, as the consciousness of some thing whose real essence is unknowable.[31] Hume, for all his skepticism, had still accepted the traditional concept of the self: he assumed that if the self existed, then it had to be a substance, some kind of permanent entity behind the flow of our impressions; hence, after not finding it, he simply concluded it did not exist at all. Kant too had lapsed into the traditional error by postulating the existence of an unknowable noumenal self. Fichte's concept of the self-positing self goes beyond Locke, Hume, and Kant by conceiving of the self as nothing more than the product of its free activity.

3. Woes of the Absolute Ego

One of the most notorious problems in the interpretation of Fichte's idealism concerns the status of his subject or ego. Who is this ego? Is it my finite self? Or is it the absolute and infinite self? The questions are basic, but the texts do not speak with a clear single voice. Sometimes Fichte talks about the ego as if it must be finite; and at other times he writes about it as if it must be infinite. Not surprisingly, the result has been confusion and controversy. Let us examine the apparent inconsistencies and see if we can find a coherent interpretation.

Prima facie there seem to be some telling arguments against the Fichtean ego having a merely finite status. First of all, a finite ego cannot be the first principle or source of experience. By its very nature a finite ego has limited powers of creation, and so it confronts a given and contingent manifold; only an absolute ego has the power to produce what it perceives. It seems to be on just these grounds that Fichte writes in the *Grundlage der gesamten Wissenschaftslehre* that his first principle is the "*absolute* I" (I, 109, 112, 116). The absolute status of his ego seems further confirmed when he makes it the counterpart of Spinoza's substance, which is infinite and indeed the universe itself (I, 119–122).

Second, if the ego is the fundamental condition for the explanation of experience—as Fichte insists it is—then it would seem that it cannot be finite itself, for it is the necessary condition under which we identify or determine any finite thing. Any attempt to individuate or determine such a transcendental ego would simply presuppose it, revolving in a circle. At least Fichte himself seems to endorse this line of reasoning. Hence he argues in the *Zweite Einleitung in die Wissenschaftslehre* that the ego cannot be empirical or individual, because it is the condition under which we experience or individuate egos (I, 476, 516); he also sharply distinguishes between the concepts of selfhood (*Ichheit*) and individuality, stressing how the former is original and basic and the latter secondary and derived (502–504).

Upon closer examination, however, both of these arguments prove to be questionable, not only in themselves but also as interpretations of Fichte. The first argument presupposes the metaphysical interpretation of Fichte's idealism, which we will soon find textual reasons to reject (2.6.2–2.6.3). Furthermore, it confuses Fichte's *transcendental* account of experience with a *genetic* account of the causes of experience; in other words, it conflates the necessary conditions for objective knowledge of the world with the psychological causes of perceiving the world. The second argument commits no such basic confusion, since it considers only the *transcendental* status of Fichte's ego. Nevertheless, it is an obvious *non sequitur:* simply because the ego is the condition under which I individuate something does not mean that it cannot be individual itself; this would be to conflate the conditions under which we know something (the *ratio cognoscendi*) with the conditions under which it exists (the *ratio essendi*). Hence there is nothing about the transcendental status of Fichte's ego that necessarily commits him to its existence as an absolute ego.

Whatever the difficulties with these arguments, Fichte would be grossly inconsistent if he were to claim knowledge of the *existence* of an absolute ego. Such a claim would violate one of his fundamental principles: that all our knowledge is limited to possible experience.[32] With regard to the conditions of knowledge, which is all that is at stake here, the circularity argument indeed holds: as the basic condition of sensible experience the ego cannot be an object of sensible experience itself. Of course, Fichte seems to sidestep this argument insofar as he holds that the ego is the object of another kind of experience, an *intellectual* rather than *sensible* intuition. It is important to see, however, that Fichte stresses that an intellectual intuition gives us no metaphysical knowledge.[33] It gives us insight only into the fact *that* we are active; but it does not tell us *how* we are so. It is very far from a mystical insight into the absolute.[34]

A serious problem of consistency arises in another direction. It is one of the central teachings of the *Wissenschaftslehre,* which appears time and again in the Jena writings,[35] that existence must be determinate, or that nothing abstract exists as such. In other words, to be is to take on some determinate form and to assume some definite relations with other things. An absolute ego, however, is by definition not something determinate but the negation of all limitation. It would seem, therefore, that it could not exist, at least as such. Fichte himself drew just this conclusion, and perfectly explicitly. In the first lecture of his *Bestimmung des Gelehrten* he begins by raising the question "What would be the properly mental (*geistige*) in a person, the pure I—

absolute in itself—isolated—and apart from all relation to something outside itself . . .?" (VI, 294) He replies that, taken strictly, this question is absurd. Such a pure ego does not exist, because the ego exists only in embodied form, that is, only through its empirical determinations, and only through its relations to other selves and the world outside it (295).

There is yet another, even more powerful, consideration weighing against the existence of an absolute ego in Fichte's system. In his *Grundlage des Naturrechts* Fichte puts forward an elaborate, extended, and explicit argument about why the ego, if it is to be self-conscious as a rational and free being, must be individual, and indeed why it must be even physical, having a body that appears in space and time. The ego can become self-conscious as a rational being, he contends, only insofar as it becomes self-conscious as one individual among others in a community, or only insofar as it recognizes the equal and independent status of other egos like itself according to the principles of right (§§1–3). Furthermore, this ego can become self-conscious as a rational being only by virtue of its physical body, or only by virtue of having a spatial and temporal presence in the world (§5). The ego cannot become self-conscious simply as some rational being in general, Fichte repeatedly says, because it must assume a more determinate form as an individual (III, 8, 62). It is necessary to add that it would be a serious misunderstanding of Fichte's argument to see it only as an account of the conditions of rationality of the *finite* ego. Rather, Fichte wants to determine the conditions for the self-consciousness of rationality and freedom *as such;* and it is a result of his argument that among its conditions are individuality and material embodiment. Hence it is no accident that the argument begins with the self-positing ego of the *Wissenschaftslehre*.

4. The Two Egos

For all the problems in admitting the existence of an absolute ego in his system, the fact still remains that Fichte writes of an absolute ego. The problem is then how to interpret such language. What does such language mean? And does it commit Fichte to the *existence* of the absolute ego?

We do best to begin with Fichte's own attempt to clear up the confusion. He was very disturbed by the misunderstandings of his first principle, the absolute ego, and attempted to dispel them in the penultimate section (§11) of his *Zweite Einleitung in die Wissenschaftslehre* (515–516). Here Fichte makes a distinction between the 'I' that begins the *Wissenschaftslehre*, which is given in intellectual intuition, and the 'I' that ends it, which is only an idea (in the Kantian sense). The first 'I' is only the *form* of subjectivity, while the second also includes its *content*. The form of the 'I' is nothing more than its pure self-determining activity, prior to any of its creations and its specific determinations; the matter of the 'I' includes all its creations and determinations, both actual and possible. We have an intellectual intuition of the form of the 'I' because we can intuit *that* we are self-determining; but we have no such intuition of the matter of the 'I' because we cannot intuit *how* we are self-determining, in what specific properties or determinations its activity consists. The 'I' that is not only form but also matter is simply an *idea*, a *goal* for our infinite striving, because we are not yet everything that we posit ourselves to be; some of our characteristics are simply given to us, the product of nature rather than our own creative activity.

Fichte's distinction does correspond closely to the actual structure of the *Grundlage der gesamten Wissenschaftslehre*.[36] What Fichte means by calling the 'I' that begins the *Wissenschaftslehre* purely formal becomes clear from his first principle "I am." This principle is formal because it abstracts from all of our empirical and individual characteristics, and because it states only *that* but not *how* we exist. It expresses our existence as spontaneous, self-determining beings; but it does not make any further proposition about our nature. This hardly seems to agree with Fichte's other statements that the 'I' that begins the work is absolute; but this difficulty disappears as soon as we recognize that it is absolute in a purely formal sense. He explains that the 'I' referred to by his first principle "I am" is absolute in the sense that it is beyond all contrast and comparison. We cannot compare or contrast it to anything, since to do so already presupposes the application of the principle of sufficient reason, which, at least on Fichte's interpretation, defines a thing by determining its species and genera, its identity and difference with other things (I, 118–120). Since the 'I' that begins the *Wissenschaftslehre* is the condition of the application of this principle, it *ipso facto* does not fall under it (112). This means that the absolute I, as the condition of all determination, will have to transcend it, and so (for all we know) cannot be anything specific at all. Hence it will have to be something purely formal, stating the existence of the I and nothing more. Fichte states explicitly: "The absolute ego of the first principle is not *something* (it has no predicate, and cannot have any); it is absolutely *what* it is, and this cannot be further explained" (I, 109). He further explains that the absolute ego is the subject of a special kind of *thetic* judgment, which does nothing more than state the existence of something without ascribing any determinate property to it (I, 116). The perfect example of such a judgment is indeed "I am," because it states nothing about the 'I,' and the place of the predicate is "left empty for the possible infinite determination of the I." Thus the 'I' that begins the *Wissenschaftslehre* turns out to be purely formal because it is something completely indeterminate, its entire nature being exhausted by the form of self-identity, $A = A$.

That the ego that ends the *Wissenschaftslehre* is only an idea is also clear from the text of the *Grundlage*. In section 5 of the third and final part of that work Fichte often states that propositions of the form 'the ego posits itself as all reality,' 'the ego posits itself absolutely' have an essentially practical meaning. They do not refer to something that exists, he explains, but to something that *ought to* exist. They express the *demand* of practical reason that everything in the world conform to our rational activity (I, 260–261, 263–264, 277). The first principle of the *Wissenschaftslehre* now refers to, Fichte expressly says, "an idea of the ego, which must be presupposed by its practical infinite demand" (277).

Fichte's distinction between the two egos takes on its full meaning only when it is placed in the context of another earlier work, the first lecture of his 1794 *Über die Bestimmung des Gelehrten*. Although this is only a popular work, which abstracts from the technical details of the *Wissenschaftslehre*, it provides the original purpose and context behind Fichte's distinction. Here Fichte portrays the predicament of the ego in the world, where it is divided between its existence and essence, its rational form and sensible content (VI, 195–198). While the ego is perfectly self-determining and rational in its mere form or existence, it remains passive and sensible in its essence. It knows *that* it exists as a self-determining being, and that it has at least *the power* to act according to the demands of reason; but it also knows that *how* it exists—its essence, nature, or specific properties—depends on the sensible world outside it. Its predicament in the sensible world contradicts the fundamental law of morality: that the ego should be *completely* autonomous and independent, free not only in its mere form and existence but also in its matter and essence. The only way to resolve the contradiction between the demands of morality and the actual existence of the ego, Fichte then explains, is to read the constitutive principle 'the ego *is* self-positing' as the regulative ideal 'the ego *ought* to be self-positing' (296). This means that the ego must set itself the infinite task to make itself perfectly free and self-positing, not only in its form but also in its essence. This demands that it acquires power over nature, so that it is no longer passive and determined by it but so that

everything conforms to the requirements of its reason. Here we have, in essence, the very spirit of the Jena *Wissenschaftslehre:* self-identity, the reuni-
fication of Kant's noumenal and phenomenal selves, as the categorical imperative of morality, the goal of infinite striving.

Thus the purpose of the distinction between the ego that begins and that
which ends the *Wissenschaftslehre* is to distinguish between the ego as it exists
and the ego as it ought to be. The ego as it exists is free only in its form, having merely the capacity for self-determination. The ego as it ought to be is
free also in its content; it has complete causality over all of nature, because
that is the condition under which it ceases to be a dependent and passive being. Only the ideal ego is completely self-positing because it alone is completely independent and self-determining, not only in its existence but also
in its essence.

If we then raise the question which of these egos is absolute, we get the
surprising answer that they both are. *Prima facie* it might seem that only
the ego that ends the *Wissenschaftslehre* is the absolute ego, because it alone
has complete causality over nature, the power of an infinite being alone.
But this is not the case, for Fichte also describes the ego that begins the
Wissenschaftslehre as absolute. Hence he states in the *Grundlage* that the 'I'
of his first merely formal first principle is absolute; and he affirms in the
Bestimmung des Gelehrten that the purely formal ego has the characteristic of
"absolute being" (*absoluten Seyns*) (VI, 295–296). The crucial point to see,
however, is that this 'I' is absolute only in its mere *form* or *existence*. It is not
absolute in the sense that it is all reality, but in the sense that it is purely indeterminate and the negation of all determinate reality. Thus Fichte says in
the *Grundlage* that the 'I' of his first principle is absolute because it has no determinate properties; and in the *Bestimmung des Gelehrten* he states that the 'I'
at first consists only in the form of "pure self-identity,' "absolute unity," and
"complete uniformity with itself" because it has not realized itself fully in
the empirical world.

If we distill the main points in all these texts, we come to the following
conclusion: there are two senses in which the ego is absolute in the *Wissenschaftslehre*. It is absolute in the purely *formal* sense, in which it is self-determining only in its existence; and it is absolute in the *material* sense, in which
it is self-determining in not only its existence but also its essence. It is very
easy to confuse these two senses, so that it seems that the ego that begins the
Wissenschaftslehre in the former sense is also absolute in the latter sense. This
is indeed exactly what is done by those who give a metaphysical interpreta-

tion of Fichte's first principle, reading it as if it referrred to some *ex nihilo* creation of the world by the absolute ego.[37] But this is to conflate the very distinction Fichte wants to make between the two egos of the *Wissenschaftslehre*.

If we strictly adhere to these distinctions, we can also see that Fichte's general position is perfectly consistent. There is no real contradiction in saying that the ego is both absolute *and* individual, infinite and finite. If the ego is absolute or infinite only in the formal sense, having only the *power* of self-determination, then it is also possible for it to be individual or finite in the material sense, where all its specific determinations are still the result of nature rather than its own activity. This is indeed just the predicament in which human beings find themselves, Fichte maintains, because there is a conflict between their power of self-determination and their having a passive nature determined by external causes. The task of every human being is to resolve this conflict, so that their entire nature is the product of their self-determining activity alone.

Armed with all these caveats and distinctions, we are now in a position to resolve some of the disputes about Fichte's first principle. There has been some controversy about whether the first principle of the *Wissenschaftslehre* has a theoretical or practical meaning, whether it is a constitutive principle for the explanation of experience or a regulative principle for guiding action. It has even been argued that the *Grundlage* is an incoherent work, because Fichte shifted unintentionally and inconsistently between these two meanings of his first principle.[38] The solution to the controversy is that the first principle is *both* a theoretical and practical principle. The 'I' of intellectual intuition, the purely formal 'I,' which begins the *Wissenschaftslehre*, is indeed a theoretical principle; but the 'I' as idea, the 'I' that is the unification of form and content, is only a practical ideal, which becomes evident only in the final section of the *Wissenschaftslehre*. Although Fichte used the principle in both these senses, he did so deliberately and consistently, applying them to different aspects of the ego.

CHAPTER 5

Knowledge of Freedom

1. The Break with Kant

If there was a single decisive factor behind Fichte's break with the subjectivist tradition—one fateful move from which everything else followed—it was the pivotal role he gave to freedom in the *Wissenschaftslehre*. This forced Fichte to stress the role of volition in the constitution of experience, and so to question the contemplative tradition and way of ideas. It also compelled him to emphasize the role of free activity in the concept of the self, and thus to reject the view that the self is a special kind of substance. Most important of all, it proved vital to Fichte's attempt to break out of the circle of consciousness. As we shall soon see, both Fichte's deduction of the reality of the external world, and his proof for the existence of other minds, begin from premises about the self-knowledge of freedom.

To place such weight on the concept of freedom makes the question inevitable: How do I know that I am free? If Fichte had no proof for the reality of freedom, the entire *Wissenschaftslehre* could be in the service of an illusion, and all its demonstrations of the reality of the external world and other minds nothing but a sham. Fichte was painfully aware of this problem, which plagued him throughout the early 1790s. From 1790 to 1794 his views about this issue underwent several remarkable transformations.

Not surprisingly, Fichte's first reflections on the self-knowledge of freedom reveal a great debt to Kant. On the whole, he seemed content to reaffirm Kant's solution to this problem, the "fact of reason" of the second *Kritik*. According to this doctrine, we know we are free through the voice of conscience within us, which informs us that, despite temptation, we still have the power to act according to the dictates of duty. In his early *Versuch einer Kritik aller Offenbarung*, which he wrote in August 1791, Fichte followed this doctrine closely since he stressed that we can prove the reality of our free-dom only through some "immediate fact" (*unmittelbare Thatsache*), which turns out to be our awareness of the moral law.[1] Despite some growing doubts, Fichte adopted roughly the same position in another early work, the *Beiträge zur Berichtigung der Urtheile des Publicums über die franzöische Revolution*, whose first part was written in the spring of 1793 and then published in June 1793. Here, still true to Kant, Fichte made the moral law the *ratio cognoscendi* of freedom, the proof that there exists "an orginal form" of our-selves that is independent of all the causes of the empirical world (VI, 59, 170–171).

Fichte's first doubts about Kant's solution appeared in the second edition of the *Versuch einer Kritik aller Offenbarung*, which he wrote in the winter of 1792–1793. This edition contains a new introduction outlining a general theory of the will, which raised anew the question of the *ratio cognoscendi* of freedom. Despite reaffirming Kant's doctrine of the fact of reason in the *Beiträge*, Fichte is now much more cautious about inferring the existence of freedom from any immediate facts of consciousness. He raises the possibility that the self-consciousness of our freedom is based on nothing more than ig-norance of the underlying causes of our actions (V, 22). In this case, how-ever, the self-consciousness of freedom might be illusory, so that we would have to embrace fatalism.

To avoid such a dire and drastic conclusion, Fichte attempts to provide a demonstration that we have a moral will, a pure faculty of desire. We know that we have such a will, he argues, only if we are conscious of something that could be created only by us, something that derives from our spontane-ity alone. That we have such self-consciousness becomes clear by consider-ing the *content* of our representations of the will, that is, what it is we are aware of when we intend to act on the moral law. Unlike all other represen-tations, whose content arises from sensation and so from some source out-side ourselves, the content of this representation arises only from ourselves since it is the *pure form* of the moral law, the categorical imperative (V, 22–23). Here Fichte's argument presupposes a claim that he will often make later: that what arises from pure thinking alone, universalizability, must have its source in ourselves alone.[2]

Although Fichte had expressed some doubt about the Kantian strategy of appealing to facts of consciousness, his new demonstration of freedom did not completely dispense with them. That we are aware of some pure form, and that our will reveals itself through this form, turn out to be only facts of consciousness again (V, 23). And, indeed, that we act for the sake of duty, without any hidden empirical motive, is something we know to be true, Fichte says, only from a feeling, and more specifically the feeling of respect for the law (V, 29).

The crucial move away from Kant appeared in two reviews Fichte wrote in the autumn of 1793. The first was of Leonhard Creuzer's *Skeptische Betrachtungen über die Freiheit des Willens,* which is a critique of Kant's proof of the existence of freedom. In some respects this review simply repeats Fichte's earlier position. Regarding the possibility of freedom, Fichte again states that the unity of the realms of freedom and nature exists in some higher ground, which is incomprehensible to us (VIII, 415) Concerning the reality of freedom, however, Fichte now retreats even further from his earlier view that freedom appears in some fact. He distinguishes between the *determining* of the will as an activity and the *determination* of the will as its product or result. While the determination of the will appears as the moral law, the determining does not appear at all (413). This activity is only a postulate to explain the moral law, and it is not an object of knowledge but only a belief. We cannot even know that this act of determining is the *cause* of its determination, because that would be to apply the principle of sufficient reason to it (414).

Fichte's second review marks an even greater break with the Kantian position. This review was of F. H. Gebhard's *Über die sittliche Güte aus uninteressirtem Wohlwollen,* a work attempting to defend Kant against the criticisms of a disciple of Adam Smith's moral sentimentalism.[3] In examining Gebhard's defense of Kant, Fichte discovered what he now regarded as a fatal weakness in the strategy of appealing to facts of consciousness: that the fact of moral feeling is also explicable according to sentimentalism, which regards it as nothing more than an expression of moral sympathy (VIII, 423). The crucial question is not about the *existence* of any facts, Fichte now sees, but about competing *explanations* of them. While the Kantian derives moral feeling from practical reason, the sentimentalist deduces it from sympathy. Since he is a naturalist, the sentimentalist insists that there are natural causes for this feeling of sympathy; he does not deny that we have some feeling of moral freedom, though he insists that it is only the result of ignorance of the causes of our actions (425).

Rather than appealing to facts of consciousness, then, the critical philosopher must demonstrate the reality of freedom. He can do so, Fichte proposes, only if he shows that freedom is a necessary condition of the possibility of consciousness itself. This proof would proceed from the unity of consciousness, show that this unity is not possible without something un-conditioned in us, and then conclude that this something unconditioned is nothing less than the will or practical reason (425). Such a proof seems to envisage freedom as the necessary condition of the unity of apperception, and thus as the first principle of the possibility of experience. While Fichte did not employ exactly this strategy in the later *Wissenschaftslehre*, he did at-tempt to implement the general idea behind it: that freedom is the basis for the possibility of experience itself.[4]

2. A Philosophy of Striving

The net effect of the Creuzer and Gebhard reviews was to compel Fichte to rethink the whole problem of freedom sometime in the early winter of 1793. It was around the same time that Fichte read Schulze's *Aenesidemus*, which left him "living under the open sky," completely shaken in all his beliefs about the foundation of the critical philosophy. The turbulence of Fichte's thought during this period is captured in two notebooks, entitled *Eigene Meditationen über Elementarphilosophie* and *Practische Philosophie*. These drafts are exciting because they reveal Fichte in the very process of discov-ery: proposing, revising, and rejecting ideas, then chiding, warning, and questioning himself. Fichte thought as he wrote, and he wrote to explore the issues. As one would expect, he often contradicts himself, and he is often undecided. He does not know how to go forward; but he also realizes he cannot retreat.

Over no issue was Fichte more uncertain and troubled at this time than the question of the reality of freedom itself. The notebook entitled *Practische Philosophie* begins by expressing doubts about the very existence of freedom. Fichte is now explicit that we cannot have any proof of its reality, for a proof would belong to the realm of theoretical reason, which has no insight into the practical field. Rather than saying man is free, it is better just to say that he *strives* and *hopes* to be free. Then in plain blunt language Fichte writes: "The proposition that 'man is free' is not true" (AA, II/3, 183). But this skep-ticism is not sustained. Although Fichte bluntly denies that the will is free, he also states categorically that "all desire is absolute, independent self-ac-tivity" (185). Undecided and confused, Fichte asks himself: "The question is: which way to turn?" He eventually resolves this tension by developing the thesis that, although we are not free in the sense of having absolute independence, we still must *strive* to attain this goal.[5] It is indeed only in the striving after freedom that we prove that we are free after all. Ideal freedom requires complete independence, not only *from*, but *over* the causes of nature; it consists in having causality over everything that is not ourselves. Although we cannot achieve such complete independence, we can still strive to approach it.

This theme of striving is the leitmotiv of *Practische Philosophie*, which Fichte appropriately entitles a "*Strebungsphilosophie*." The fate of man on this earth, Fichte writes, is eternal striving and struggle, which expresses itself through a drive forever to extend the limits of our activity beyond any given point: "The condition, the sublime condition, of man is a constant striving; his joys are merely a heightening of this striving. Man always has needs; and all his satisfaction consists in the heightening of these needs; and he is the true man, for whom things are so" (189). As we shall soon see (2.6.2), striving soon became the central theme of Fichte's idealism.

Fichte developed the striving theme in his review of Schulze's *Aenesidemus*, which he wrote from November 1793 to early 1794. This theme now appears in the context of discussing Schulze's objections against Kant's doctrine of the primacy of practical reason. According to Schulze, Kant infers 'can' from 'ought,' the conditions of the fulfillment of a command from the command itself. But this begs the question, because we cannot determine whether the command is valid unless we first know that we can fulfill it. Whether something is possible can be decided only by *theoretical* principles, which determine whether something *is* or *is not* the case, so that theoretical reason has priority over practical rather than conversely.

Fichte replies that Schulze has confused the very meaning of practical reason. The condition for the validity of the 'ought' is not that some action takes place in the world of nature. Rather than commanding a physical or natural force, the moral law addresses a noumenal faculty of desire. At first it does not require any action at all, but only the constant *striving* toward one, and it does not matter if such an intention has no efficacy in the natural world (I, 22). Furthermore, reason shows that it is practical by its striving to unify the two aspects of the self: its independent intelligible or noumenal character, and its dependent empirical or phenomenal character (22). It is not practical in respect to either character alone, but only in its striving to unify them.

Prima facie it is not clear how the striving to realize complete independence, or to unify the two sides of our nature, proves the existence of our freedom. It only seems to beg the question, because even this striving could be determined by natural causes, so that it too acts by natural necessity. Indeed, in his review of Gebhard, Fichte had already admitted this very possibility. So in what sense, if any, has he advanced in his thinking? How has he come closer to establishing the reality of freedom? Though it is only implicit, it is not difficult to reconstruct the point behind Fichte's increasing emphasis on striving as a proof for freedom. Throughout his Jena writings Fichte had expressed two general principles concerning freedom and knowledge: (1) that to be free we must make ourselves free because freedom is not something given but something that we create; (2) that knowledge is the result of action rather than contemplation. It follows from these principles that there cannot be any a priori guarantee of our freedom. *If we are to know that we are free, then we must first strive to make ourselves free.* We cannot know that we are free prior to the attempt to make ourselves so, because we only become free agents through our struggle against nature and the external causes forcing us into action. We will know that we are free only when we see that we have succeeded in making nature submit to our control, and indeed only when we make the whole realm of nature disappear. So, in Fichte's view, the whole debate about the *ratio cognoscendi* of freedom rests upon a false premise: that there is some means of knowing that we are free apart from and prior to acting.

In the end, then, Fichte leaves the problem of freedom on a hypothetical and pragmatic note. We know that we are free only by striving to make ourselves free, and we know that we have become free only if we succeed in our efforts to dominate and control nature. Like all knowledge, then, the self-knowledge of freedom is the result of action, and there can be no guarantee of its reality except through the success of action. This was the essential spirit of Fichte's response to skepticism in the Jena years (see 2.2.5), which he applied to the problem of freedom itself. In this spirit, we shall soon see that Fichte came to deny the possibility of any theoretical demonstration of freedom in his later Jena years (2.5.7).

3. The Origins of Intellectual Intuition

The most formidable challenge to Fichte's attempt to establish the self-knowledge of freedom came from unexpected quarters: from the source of all his inspiration, the critical philosophy itself. In many passages of the first *Kritik* Kant wrote about the noumenal self, the source of our activity as self-determining subjects, as something unknowable, which he designated by the daunting symbol X.[6] Such a postulate is a flagrant violation, however, of the central principle that Fichte had laid down in the *Aenesidemus* review: that the the self is only for itself, or only what it conceives itself to be. Although Fichte insisted that his principle represents the very *spirit* of the critical philosophy, he had to admit that it scarcely agrees with its *letter,* which contained many unmistakable references to a mysterious unknowable self. It was therefore imperative for Fichte at least *to reinterpret* Kant, and that meant eliminating the noumenal self, the last vestige of hypostasis still lurking within the critical philosophy itself. Only such a drastic measure, Fichte was convinced, would make Kant's philosophy truly immanent and thus save it from the snares of Schulze's skepticism (see 2.2.2).

The removal of the Kantian noumenal self involved much more, however, than merely dispensing with a superfluous entity. It demanded rethinking the whole foundation of Kant's philosophy, and more specifically its central doctrine of freedom. For the inscrutable noumenal self played a fundamental role in Kant's first *Kritik:* its unknowability guaranteed the very possibility of freedom, the independence of the self from the principle of causality. It is important to see that noumenal self-knowledge and freedom are indeed *incompatible* in the first *Kritik.* Kant had maintained that self-knowledge, like all knowledge, requires the application of the categories; but among these categories is that of causality, which makes its object passive and determined by subsuming it under the principle of sufficient reason. There cannot be any self-knowledge as an active self-determining subject, then, because in becoming self-conscious I make myself passive and determined. Ironically, then, the greatest threat to freedom comes not from *outside* but *inside* myself, and more specifically from making myself the object of the categories. All heteronomy thus becomes essentially a form of *self*-enslavement. Hence, to save freedom, Kant was compelled to lay down the most severe restrictions upon self-knowledge in the first *Kritik:* he stresses that we know ourselves only as we appear to ourselves, but not as we are in ourselves as spontaneous self-determining subjects. To enforce and justify these restrictions, Kant developed some powerful arguments against self-knowledge in the Aesthetic, B Deduction, and Paralogisms.[7]

These arguments soon became a powerful challenge to Fichte. To be true to his principle that the ego is only for itself—to realize his ideal of a completely immanent transcendental philosophy—he had to develop a new theory of self-knowledge that would avoid the need to postulate an unknowable subject. Furthermore, he had to formulate a new theory of freedom, so that freedom and self-consciousness are no longer incompatible. Fichte turned to both these tasks in one of the most fascinating and frustrating doctrines of the early *Wissenschaftslehre:* intellectual intuition. The general purpose of this theory is to explain the possibility of self-knowledge, and more specifically the possibility of self-knowledge of freedom. The net result of Fichte's theory is an account of self-knowledge and freedom diametrically opposed to Kant's: freedom and self-knowledge are no longer incompatible but complementary.

The purpose of Fichte's theory of intellectual intuition has been subject to some dispute. It has been read as a critique of the dominant theory of self-knowledge in the modern tradition, the theory of 'reflection,' which creates paradoxes by distinguishing the subject of self-knowledge from acts of self-knowledge.[8] It has also been interpreted as a theory about the conditions of consciousness in general that takes special issue with Kant's unity of apperception.[9] Both of these interpretations, which are compatible, have their merits. But, if we go back to the original context of Fichte's theory, there are special reasons for thinking that Fichte was attempting to develop a purely immanent transcendental philosophy, and so was taking issue with Kant's theory of the unknowable self. This becomes clear by retracing a few steps of Fichte's intellectual development.

The first mention of intellectual intuition appears in the *Eigene Meditationen über Elementarphilosophie,* which was written in the winter of 1793–1794.[10] Fichte first developed this concept in the context of replying to Schulze's and Maimon's meta-critical skepticism. They had raised the question: How does the transcendental philosopher know that his reflections on the conditions of consciousness reflect consciousness itself? "How do his thoughts correspond with the activities of the mind, how can such a correspondence be shown?" (AA, II/3, 23–24n) To answer this question, Fichte envisages an intellectual intuition along the lines of Kant's theory of mathematical construction. Just as we prove a proposition in geometry through the construction of a figure in pure intuition, so in philosophy we should demonstrate the forms of the mind by constructing them in a pure intuition. Fichte conceives of a chain of deductions where we produce intuitions according to rules, from which we derive further rules, according to which we produce further intuitions, and so on. If we proceed in this manner, Fichte maintains, then there is no problem of a correspondence between the philosopher's reflection on consciousness and consciousness itself, because the philosopher constructs in intuition, or produces according to a rule, the very objects that he knows; it is not as if the mind were some thing-in-itself that exists apart from and prior to its reflections on itself. This is the main response to Schulze's skepticism that Fichte will develop only months later in the *Aenesidemus* review.

Prima facie Fichte's theory has little to do with self-knowledge in the specific sense of how I know myself as the *subject* of knowledge. Rather, it seems to concern the problem of how I know anything at all about myself, or more specifically how I know the general laws of my consciousness. But Fichte soon extends his theory in the direction of the transcendental subject. He asks how the transcendental philosopher knows the ego itself, which is the proposed first principle of his new *Elementarphilosophie* (AA, II/3, 26–28). In attempting to grasp it, the philosopher ensnares himself in an inescapable circle: he cannot represent the subject of all possible representations, because such a representation would simply presuppose a subject (26). This was indeed just the circle exploited by Kant to prove the impossibility of self-knowledge. Rather than drawing such a dire conclusion, though, Fichte grapples for a solution, for some means of knowing the subject of all knowledge. He resolves the difficulty by again appealing to an intellectual intuition. He explains that the first principle of the *Wissenschaftslehre* is a postulate that demands that the subject intuit itself, that it think of itself and in doing so construct itself in intuition.

This was just the salve that Fichte would later apply to the wounds Schulze had inflicted on the critical philosophy. In the *Aenesidemus* review Fichte argues against Schulze that the critical philosopher does not go beyond possible experience because he constructs the pure subject in an intellectual intuition. The transcendental ego is not a thing-in-itself, Fichte contends, but a transcendental idea, and indeed a specific kind of transcendental idea because it can be "realized in intellectual intuition" (I, 16). By appealing to intellectual intuition, then, Fichte could keep transcendental philosophy within its own self-imposed limits of possible experience.

This context shows, then, that Fichte did not develop his theory of intellectual intuition by reflecting on self-consciousness *in abstracto,* and still less from examining the conditions of consciousness in general. Rather, he formed it in reflecting on the conditions of transcendental self-knowledge, and in attempting to build a strictly immanent transcendental philosophy.

Fichte's main concern was to remove that unknowable subject that is the condition of knowledge but that cannot be an object of knowledge itself.[11] Such a subject was nothing less than the Kantian noumenal self.

4. The Meaning of Intellectual Intuition

What, more precisely, does Fichte mean by 'intellectual intuition'? The general meaning he gives to this term is self-knowledge as a spontaneous, acting subject. Fichte defines it in these terms: "Intellectual intuition is the immediate consciousness that I act, and of what I do when I act. It is because of this that it is possible for me to know something because I do it"(I, 463). When I have an intellectual intuition, I know myself as acting rather than acted on, as self-determining rather than determined. In Kant's language, an intellectual intuition is that "self-intuition which gives the determining in me (I am conscious only of the spontaneity of it) prior to the act of determination."[12] This means that in intellectual intuition the self-determining self that applies the categories knows itself as the self-determining self, and not only as the self that is determined by or subsumed under the categories. Hence Fichte often insists that an intellectual intuition consists in nothing less than the perfect identity of subject and object: the self-knowing self is the self known; there is no distinction between the subject and object of self-knowledge, such that the subject is active and self-determining and the object passive and determinable. In short, then, an intellectual intuition consists in the active self-knowing self knowing itself *as* an active self-knowing self.[13]

Why, though, does Fichte call such knowledge an 'intellectual intuition'? What does he mean by each of these terms? Fichte uses the term 'intuition' (*Anschauung*) in the Kantian sense for that form of representation that stands in an *immediate* relationship to its object. According to Kant, immediate knowledge consists in the direct intuition of a particular as a particular, so that it is a *singular* representation (*repraesentatio singularis*).[14] An intuition is *immediate* in the sense that it does not require a concept to intervene or mediate between itself and the particular. An intuition is therefore opposed to a concept (*Begriff*), which is a general representation that unifies what is common to a number of particular representations. A concept gives us a *mediate* knowledge of a particular because, as a universal, it is a representation *of* many representations of particulars. If a concept knows a particular, then, it does not know it directly as just this particular, but only indirectly or mediately through its similarities and dissimilarities with other particulars. Fichte stresses the immediacy of intellectual intuition in this Kantian sense, denying that it is a form of discursive knowledge. To say it is nondiscursive means two things: that it is *nonconceptual*—we do not use judgement to determine if it is true; and that it is *indemonstrable*—we do not prove it through reasoning. In other words, we know it to be true directly through experience.

Fichte calls an intellectual intuition *intellectual* to contrast it with a *sensible* intuition. Here again his usage is Kantian. According to Kant, the object is given for sensible intuition, while it is created or posited by intellectual intuition.[15] In a sensible intuition we are passive, since the object acts on us; but in an intellectual intuition we are active, because we produce the object we know through knowing it. Fichte emphasizes this active and creative component of intellectual intuition when he states that "It [i.e., the knowledge of intellectual intuition] *is* so, because I *make* it so"(I, 460).

If an intellectual intuition is the self-awareness of myself acting, then it must be both intuitive and intellectual in these senses. It must be intuitive for two reasons. First, I do not infer that I am acting but know this directly through experience. Second, if I know myself as an active being, then I cannot apply concepts to myself, because that would make me passive and determined, another object subsumed under the principle of sufficient reason. Self-knowledge as acting also must be intellectual because, in acting, I *create* the object that I know. Although this self-creative self-knowing appears fanciful and extravagant—as if the self somehow brings itself into being through the act of knowing itself—it is simply a requirement of knowing my own activity. The self-knowledge that I am acting creates or acts out what I know, simply because what I know is that I am acting! Self-consciousness of my activity cannot be of something *given* to me, for something that is given is not the exercise of my agency. In other words, in an intellectual intuition I know that I act because I act; it is in this sense that Fichte says that in intellectual intuition I know something is so because I make it so.

5. Fichte versus Kant on Intellectual Intuition

Prima facie the anti-Kantian motivation behind Fichte's theory of intellectual intuition appears obvious. Kant and Fichte both hold that self-knowledge of myself as an active, self-determining subject requires intellectual intuition; but Kant denies, and Fichte affirms, the possibility of intellectual intuition.

Fichte's affirmation of intellectual intuition indeed seems to violate Kant's basic teachings about the limits of knowledge. Kant was compelled to deny intellectual intuition because of two central doctrines of the first *Kritik:* that all knowledge, including self-knowledge, is *discursive,* requiring the application of concepts; and that all knowledge, including self-knowledge, is *empirical,* demanding a manifold given to sensation. The first doctrine forbids the immediacy, the second the intellectuality, of intellectual intuition. Hence, in affirming both the immediacy and intellectuality of self-knowledge, Fichte contradicts both Kantian theses about the limits of knowledge.

But if this conflict seems obvious to us, it was not so to Fichte. Such was his respect for Kant that he took pains to remove any hint of a quarrel with his former teacher. Some of the stricter Kantians saw a discrepancy between Fichte's affirmation of intellectual intuition and Kant's strictures against it. But Fichte protested that he was simply using the term 'intellectual intuition' in a different sense from Kant.[16] According to Fichte's interpretation, Kant's intellectual intuition is the divine understanding's knowledge of the archetypes, which are pure noumena transcending all experience. Fichte insisted that he too denied intellectual intuition in this sense, and he stressed that he agreed with Kant that no finite being has such powers. If he affirms an intellectual intuition, it is in a completely different sense than Kant. Namely, his intellectual intuition is not of some entity beyond our experience, but merely of an activity within it.

It is necessary to admit that Fichte does have a point. Sometimes Kant does use the term 'intellectual intuition' to refer to the divine understanding,[17] and in this sense his intellectual intuition differs from Kant's. Still, this was not Kant's only use of the term. He also uses it to refer to self-knowledge as an active, self-determining subject.[18] In this sense the conflict between Kant and Fichte is plain: both maintain that self-knowledge of my spontaneity requires intellectual intuition, a possibility that Fichte affirms and Kant denies. In any case, the whole issue does not hang on the mere use of a word. The question is whether Fichte is making claims to self-knowledge that violate Kant's critical limits; and of this there can be little doubt. In affirming that there is an intuitive and intellectual form of self-knowledge, Fichte denies Kant's claims that *all* knowledge is both conceptual and empirical.[19]

Apart from any differences in usage, the main reason Fichte is convinced that he is not in conflict with Kant comes from his interpretation of the unity of apperception. Fichte thinks that the 'I think' of this Kantian principle presupposes an intellectual intuition, a self-awareness of myself as a self-determining subject.[20] There is indeed some plausibility to this interpretation. Kant expressly says that the 'I think' expresses my spontaneity as a self-determining subject, which appears to commit him to both the immediacy and intellectuality of intellectual intuition. It is precisely in this regard, however, that the conflict between Kant and Fichte again comes to the fore. Because it would contradict his theses that all knowledge requires concepts and given intuitions, Kant refuses to call the 'I think' an intellectual intuition. The 'I think,' he insists, is not an intuition but a thought (B 157).[21] It does not give me an experience of myself because it is only a form with which any experience must comply; it merely says that any experience must be *my* experience, and to identify experiences as mine is not to identify any particular feature of them (A 346). In Kant's view, then, the claim that the 'I think' gives me an *experience* of myself simply confuses the condition of an experience with an experience itself. Here, then, is precisely where Kant and Fichte part company: while Fichte says that I have an *intuition* of myself as a self-determining subject, Kant stresses that I only have the *thought* of myself as such. To put their differences bluntly: Kant would accuse Fichte of a paralogism!

In the end, however, Fichte did come to a grudging admission that he was at odds with Kant. There are some signs in his later writings that he knew of his differences with his erstwhile teacher. Thus in his 1798 *Versuch einer neuen Darstellung der Wissenschaftslehre* Fichte makes an unmistakable allusion to Kant when he complains about how the idea of an unknowable subject infects "even the most famous lover of wisdom of our philosophical century" (I, 529–530); and in his 1798 *Wissenschaftslehre novo methodo* he mentions Kant by name and even chides him for failing to detect "the sophistry" behind the denial of self-consciousness.[22] Not surprisingly, Fichte only fully realized some of his differences with Kant after Kant's 1799 *Erklärung* denouncing the *Wissenschaftslehre*.[23]

6. Self-Knowledge and Freedom

Now that we have seen that there is indeed a conflict between Fichte and Kant, the problem is to explain how it arose in the first place. Why does Kant insist that self-knowledge as a self-determining self is impossible, and why does Fichte stress that it is necessary? What arguments did each give for his position, and why did they make them?

We have already considered why Kant denies the possibility of self-knowledge: to protect the possibility of freedom. To this end, Kant makes two arguments against self-knowledge in both editions of the first *Kritik*. The first applies to the self as subject, and appears in the Paralogism chapters; the second applies to the self as object, and derives from the Aesthetic and B Deduction.

(1) According to the first argument, the subject of all awareness, including self-awareness, is unknowable, since it is the condition of all awareness. The self-knowing self cannot know itself since its activity has to be presupposed if there is to be self-knowledge. The attempt of the self-knowing self to know itself would be circular.[24]

(2) According to the second argument, self-awareness, like all awareness, involves the application of the categories and inner sense. But the application of the categories and inner sense change their object in the act of becoming aware of it, so that it is impossible to know the object as it exists in itself, prior to their application.[25]

Fichte would reject both of these arguments because, in his view, their conclusion amounts to a virtual *reductio ad absurdum*. That there is a self that exists apart from and prior to all possible acts of self-knowledge is nothing less than hypostasis. It treats the self as if it were an object, some kind of thing, when the self is essentially for itself, something constituted by its acts of self-consciousness. The distinctive characteristic of a subject in contrast to an object, Fichte maintains, is at least the possibility of self-consciousness. Ironically, Fichte drew this conclusion from the Kantian unity of apperception itself: a self of which I could not be self-conscious would be "nothing to me, no better than a dream." Fichte, then, would simply hurl Kant's charge of paralogism back at him. In his view, the true hypostatizers of the subject are those who make it an unknowable X, beyond even the possibility of self-consciousness.

The conflict between Kant and Fichte regarding the possibility of self-knowledge is striking, because they contradict one another for the sake of the same end: freedom. We have already seen how, for Kant, freedom *excludes* self-knowledge: self-knowledge involves the application of the categories to myself, and so makes me passive and determined. Fichte maintains, however, that freedom *requires* self-knowledge. If we assume that the acting self, which is the basis of all my actions, is unknowable, then to be determined by it is to be determined by some cause external to myself. I have nothing to do with this self, which is nothing for me; and so in making me do something it acts as an alien cause. On these grounds Fichte insists that freedom *requires* self-consciousness. The self does not have an identity prior to its self-conceptions and to which they must conform. Rather, the identity of the self depends on its self-conceptions, and its freedom consists in its striving to realize them. As Fichte put the point in his *Sittenlehre:* "What it [the ego] ought to be it must make itself through its concept [of itself]; and whatever it will be, it must have been made through this concept" (IV, 29–30, 32).

Assuming that there must be self-knowledge, what are the conditions of its possibility? The main aim of Fichte's theory of intellectual intuition is to lay down two such conditions, and so by implication to reply to Kant's arguments against self-knowledge. We might call the first condition the *self-constitution* condition, the second the *self-expression* condition.[26] Each condition is necessary to reply to Kant's arguments against self-knowledge.

1. *The self-constitution condition.* The self as object does not exist apart from and prior to the self as subject. In other words, the known self is not given to the self-knowing self. Rather, the known self is only what the self-knowing self knows itself to be; in other words, the self as object is posited or constituted by the self as subject.
2. *The self-expression condition.* The self as subject expresses, manifests or embodies itself in the self as object. This means that the self-knowing self consists in nothing more than its self-expressions, self-manifestations, or self-embodiments.

These conditions are clearly distinct. If there is self-constitution, then it is still possible that there is no self-expression. Although we would know the self as object, it could still be possible that we do not know it as subject if it transcends its acts of self-objectification. These conditions are indeed the converse of one another. Self-constitution says that the self as object is constituted by the self as subject; self-expression says that the self as subject is expressed by the self as object. If we join these two conditions, then we have exactly what Fichte says is required by intellectual intuition: subject–object identity.

Each of these conditions is a necessary condition of self-consciousness. We need self-constitution for self-consciousness, because if we assume that all consciousness, including self-consciousness, acts on what it knows, and if we assume further than the object is given to it, then we cannot know the object itself. The self-constitution condition can therefore be seen as Fichte's reply to Kant's argument in the Aesthetic.

We also need self-expression, because, as Fichte argues in the *Wissenschaftslehre novo methodo,* if we assume that the self-knowing self is prior to the known self, then we cannot know it except on pain of an infinite regress.[27] To know the self-knowing self, there would be always a higher-order self-knowing self for any level of self-knowledge. Fichte's insistence on the self-expression condition can therefore be seen as his response to Kant's argument in the Paralogisms.

If these conditions are joined, then they lead to a very striking result: the self is nothing more than what it conceives itself to be. It is neither a subject nor an object existing apart from, and prior to, its actual or potential acts of self-knowledge itself. Though it is strange and radical, Fichte draws just this conclusion: "I am this [intellectual] intuition and absolutely nothing further, and this intuition itself is who I am" (I, 529).

Fichte's famous concept of the self-positing self is best interpreted as the conjunction of both these conditions. To be self-positing implies self-constitution since the self-knowing self brings itself into existence when it posits itself; there is no preexisting self who is just given prior to the self-knowing self. Self-positing also implies self-expression since to say that the self posits itself as *P,* is to say that the self simply *is P,* that it makes itself what it is through *P* or whatever it posits itself to be. In other words, *P* is not just a product of the self from which it can disassociate itself.

7. Faith in Freedom

However plausible, Fichte's theory of intellectual intuition is not without its difficulties. For one thing, the theory seems hopelessly idealistic. It seems to prescribe an ideal experience rather than to describe a real one. All that the theory does is spell out the conditions for self-knowledge of our spontaneity; but it does not show that they are actual. These conditions are indeed so demanding—complete identity of the subject and object—that one could doubt that they are ever fulfilled. For another thing, granted that these conditions could be satisfied, there is the troublesome question of how we *know* that they are so. Although Fichte insists that having an intellectual intuition is simply a question of having an experience of a certain kind—he suggests it is as simple as seeing colors and hearing sounds—one could still ask whether the experience one has is indeed an intellectual intuition.

Given such difficulties, it could well be asked how the theory of intellectual intuition could ever serve as a basis for knowledge of our freedom. The question is appropriate; but, to be fair to Fichte, it is important to realize that he never intended an intellectual intuition to provide the criterion or *ratio cognoscendi* of freedom. The purpose of the theory is only to explain the *possibility* of self-knowledge of our freedom, not to demonstrate its *reality.* We have already seen how Fichte refused to admit appeals to immediate experience as proof of the reality of freedom, and it would be remarkable if he forgot this point in developing his theory of intellectual intuition. It is indeed striking how Fichte, in section 5 of the *Zweite Einleitung in die Wissenschaftslehre,* distinguishes between the question of the possibility of an intellectual intuition and that of its reality (I, 466). Assuming that there could be an intellectual intuition, there would still be the question how we could believe that it really gave us self-knowledge of our freedom.

Fichte addresses this question in section 5 of the *Zweite Einleitung* and in various passages of the *System der Sittenlehre.*[28] Here he explains that the whole question of the reality of freedom cannot be decided on *theoretical* grounds. We cannot demonstrate or refute the reality of freedom by discovering and assessing evidence. The critical philosopher cannot demonstrate the reality of freedom through his experience, because it is always possible that there are some causes, unknown to him, of his actions. On the other hand, the dogmatist cannot refute the reality of freedom, because he cannot find sufficient evidence for the hypothetical causes of all our actions. All the dogmatist's arguments against freedom simply presuppose the fundamental point at issue: that the ego is part of nature. Since we cannot *know* that we are free, we are left with the question: Should we *believe* that we are so?

Whether we should believe we are free, Fichte argues, ultimately has to be determined on *practical* grounds. This means that we have to decide the question according to the demands of action. We have to choose between criticism or dogmatism according to which best conforms to the ends of our conduct. Seen from this perspective, Fichte thinks there can be no doubt about the outcome of the issue. We should choose to believe in the reality of freedom for the simple reason that we *ought to,* or because the moral law commands us. Morality demands that we be responsible agents, and the condition of responsibility is freedom.

Like Kant, then, Fichte attempts to decide the question of the reality of freedom by an appeal to conscience, the awareness of the moral law. We have the duty to believe that we are free because, when we do something contrary to duty, the voice of our conscience tells us that we could have always done otherwise. Fichte realizes that such an appeal is inadequate on theoretical grounds because the naturalist can always dispute the testimony of conscience, which he thinks rests on ignorance of the natural causes of our actions. But, against this objection, Fichte takes his last stand and ends the discussion. He says that he will not contest the fact of the moral law because he *ought not to*. We cannot go beyond the moral law, the experience of our own conscience, because it is a *practical* necessity. "I *cannot* go beyond this standpoint because I am not *permitted* to go beyond it" (I, 467).

In the end, then, the *Wissenschaftslehre* rests the whole question of the reality of freedom on an act of choice, the decision to be moral. Although there can be no doubt that morality commands us to adopt the belief in freedom, Fichte admits that we still have to choose the standpoint of morality. But nothing more can be expected of a philosophy devoted to freedom, Fichte insists, than resting its foundation on an act of choice.

CHAPTER 6

Critical Idealism

1. Problems of Idealism

Now that we have examined the fundamental concepts of Fichte's ideal-ism—freedom, intellectual intuition, the self-positing ego, subject–object identity—we have crossed the threshold of the *Wissenschaftslehre*. Neverthe-less, we have not entered its inner sanctum. To take that final step, we have to consider Fichte's solution to the fundamental problem of transcendental philosophy: How is it possible to demonstrate the reality of the external world? After all, this was the central problem the *Wissenschaftslehre* was meant to solve (2.1.1).

We saw in Chapter 1 how Fichte gave priority to the refutation of subjec-tivism, and in Chapter 2 how he attempted to respond to Schulze's and Maimon's doubts about the reality of experience. Still, Fichte's reply to their skepticism provided at best only one-half of his answer to the challenge of subjectivism. While it had perhaps established the possibility of knowledge, it still had not demonstrated the independent reality of the external world. In other words, it had not shown that our knowledge is of some indepen-dent reality; it is still possible that it is limited to nothing more than our own representations.

It is important to be precise about the limits of Fichte's earlier arguments. The essence of Fichte's case against Schulze's and Maimon's skepticism was essentially pragmatic: it is possible to know objects only if we act on them and make them conform to the demands of reason. The false premise behind skepticism, Fichte contended, is its contemplative model of knowledge: that we know things simply by reflecting on them and without trying to change them. Though this argument might secure the possibility of knowledge, it does not establish the reality of the external world; for it does not show that we know something *independent* of our powers. On the contrary, it demonstrates that we know an object only insofar as we create it, or only insofar as it is the product of our activity. But this seems to say that all the objects of our knowledge are only our creations, or that we cannot know any reality independent of them. This seems to confirm rather than refute the charge of subjectivism!

The weakness of Fichte's pragmatic case against skepticism is reminiscent of Kant's predicament in the Critique of the Fourth Paralogism. It will be recalled that Kant had refuted skepticism only by identifying appearances with representations; but that argument backfired because it seemed to prove the subjectivist's case that we cannot know any independent reality (1.3.1). Fichte trapped himself in the same impasse by showing how knowledge depends on our creative activity; it then seems as if all we know is what we make.

Of course, it is one thing for idealism to recognize its need to prove the reality of the external world; it is quite another thing for it to satisfy that need. It seems almost impossible to explain the external world on the principles of idealism, especially those laid down by Fichte. There are three apparently insuperable problems.

The first concerns the status of the ego or subject in itself, an issue we have already considered below (1.4.3). It would seem that this subject must be *infinite* or *absolute*, because, to avoid the problems of dualism, it must create not only the form but also the content of experience, something beyond the powers of any finite subject. The idea of the absolute ego seems much like the Kantian divine intellect or *intellectus archetypus*, which creates all of its experience in the very act of knowing it, and for whom there is no dualism between universal and particular, possibility and reality. But Kant had stressed that such an idea has no constitutive validity, and that it is only legitimate as a regulative principle for the purpose of our enquiry into nature. Hence arises the suspicion: Is Fichte not violating Kant's regulative strictures and transcending the boundaries of experience by postulating an absolute ego?

The second problem arises from the conflict between the transcendental and empirical standpoints. According to the transcendental standpoint, there is an *identity* between the subject and object, between the form and content of experience, because the self-positing ego creates its object in the very act of knowing it. According to the empirical standpoint, however, there is a *dualism* between the subject and object, between the form and content of experience, because it is a simple fact of experience that the object is given to the subject. This conflict is very ironic, however, given that the transcendental standpoint is supposed *to explain* the empirical! The subject–object identity of the transcendental standpoint must be *within* the subject–object dualism of experience if it is to account for the interaction between the subject and object. But this seems impossible, given that these standpoints contradict one another. So now we are caught in a dilemma: we must unify and separate the transcendental and empirical standpoints. It seems as if we have avoided the subject–object dualism of experience only to create an even deeper dualism between the transcendental and empirical standpoints.

The third and final problem is the infamous paradox of 'inner affection': How can the subject affect itself, and so actively make itself passive? This problem had troubled Kant in the first *Kritik;* but now it returns to haunt Fichte. If the absolute ego is infinite, active, and independent, then how does it make itself finite, passive, and dependent? Such a magical and miraculous transformation is absurd; but we seem to require nothing less to explain experience, where the subject is finite, passive, and dependent on an external world. It is no use here appealing to the idea of absolute autonomy, as if the subject limits itself because it creates the laws that restrict its activity. This only pushes the problem back another step; for the question remains: Why does the ego limit its activity by putting itself under laws?

2. The Role of Striving

Fichte was fully aware of all these problems. His solution to them is the central and characteristic theme of the Jena *Wissenschaftslehre:* the concept of striving (*Streben*). Fichte himself gave a central role to this concept in his own accounts of his philosophy. He called his early 1793–1794 *Practische Philosophie,* which anticipates the later *Wissenschaftslehre,* a *Strebungsphilosophie.* In Part III of the programmatic 1794 *Über den Begriff der Wissenschafslehre,* Fichte stated that the practical part of the *Wissenschaftslehre* was "far and away the most important part," and that the foundation of this part was played by the concept of striving.[1] In his later 1798 *Wissenschaftslehre novo methodo* Fichte continued to stress the importance he gave to striving in his earlier exposition of the *Wissenschaftslehre.* "In the first and newer version [of the *Wissenschaftslehre*]," he said, "striving . . . is regarded as the highest and first in human beings."[2]

The central text in which Fichte addresses these problems is section 5 of his 1794 *Grundlage der gesamten Wissenschaftslehre*. Fichte begins that section with his account of "a fundamental antithesis" that threatens to undermine the whole idealist program. This antithesis encapsulates all the fundamental problems of idealism in explaining the possibility of experience. The antithesis takes the following form. According to the first principle of the *Wissenschaftslehre*, the ego should be absolute and independent, because it is only what it posits itself to be. Its nature is to be completely free and self-determining, so that it must not depend on external causes (I, 248). Insofar as it is absolute and independent, the ego is infinite and unlimited, comprising all reality; everything that exists has been posited by it and is only part of its nature (255). However, this principle seems to be false by the light of our ordinary experience. Insofar as it represents something in experience, the ego depends on something else outside itself, the non-ego. It is no longer only what it posits itself to be, because it has a passive sensibility that is affected by the non-ego. Although it determines itself within the sphere of its experience, so that everything it represents depends upon its activity, the existence of that sphere itself is a limitation that does not depend on itself. The kind and manner of representation depends on the ego; but that it represents something is determined by something outside itself (248).

The absolute ego of the first principle and the ego of ordinary experience are therefore in contradiction with one another: the absolute ego is infinite and independent while the ego of ordinary experience is finite and dependent. Nevertheless, even though they oppose one another, they ought to be *one and the same* ego (249). It is only a *façon de parler*, Fichte says, that we speak of two egos, because there is really only one and the same ego seen from two aspects. Thus the fundamental antithesis is this: the absolute ego and the ego of ordinary experience ought to be one and the same, yet they have opposing characteristics.

Although it is cast in his abstract and artificial terminology, the problem Fichte poses is fundamental to the whole idealist program: How can idealism explain the reality of our experience, the fact that some representations appear to depend on causes independent of our will and imagination? This problem seems insuperable because there is an apparent contradiction between the principle of idealism, which states that everything depends on the reality of the ego, and our actual experience, which shows that our representations depend on something outside ourselves, independent of our conscious control. Fichte has also expressed the paradoxical conflict between the transcendental and empirical standpoints: that they oppose one another yet should be one and the same.

How, then, does Fichte address this question? His first proposal is to make the absolute ego the cause of the non-ego, so that when the non-ego acts on the finite ego that is its *self*-determination as an absolute ego (I, 249–250). *Prima facie* this solution seems to do justice to both the self-determination of the absolute ego and the passivity of the finite ego. Fichte explains that, for this solution to work, the absolute ego must be the cause of more than the forms of the non-ego, which have been contributed by the representing ego; it also must be the cause of the very existence of the non-ego, of the impetus (*Anstoß*) acting upon it (251).

This solution is precisely what we would expect Fichte to propose, given his idealist program. Some scholars have indeed interpreted Fichte's idealism in the light of this proposal, as if it were his final position.[3] It is striking, however, that Fichte clearly and emphatically rejects it. He argues that, according to the proposal, the ego should posit the non-ego, which means that it must limit itself; but since the ego should also posit itself absolutely, it must both posit itself as all reality and limit its reality, which is absurd (252, 257). Fichte further contends: if the absolute ego were to have complete causality over the non-ego, the non-ego would cease to be a non-ego because it would no longer be opposed to the ego. The sheer fact that the ego is opposed by the non-ego means that the absolute ego does *not* have absolute causality over the non-ego (254).

After rejecting his initial proposal, Fichte reformulates his problem. He puts the conflict between the infinite and finite ego in terms of opposing *activities:* the pure self-relating activity of the infinite ego, which posits itself as all reality, and therefore as unlimited; and the objective activity of the finite ego, which opposes itself to the non-ego, and therefore as limited (256). Fichte now admits, however, that these activities are utterly irreconcilable, and that all we can claim is that they *ought to be* equivalent. There remains nothing but the *demand* that the ego become infinite by acquiring complete causality over the non-ego (260). Although we cannot claim that the infinite ego has *causality* over the non-ego, we can state that the finite ego has a *tendency* or *striving* to determine the non-ego, to make it conform to the demands of its reason (261).

Fichte thus introduces his concept of striving (*Streben*), "a concept of the highest significance," which is his solution to the problem (I, 261–270). The main assumption behind this concept is that the activity of the ego consists in infinite striving, the ceaseless struggle against a hostile world. The finite ego never ceases to be opposed to, and limited by, the non-ego, which acts as both a stimulus and check to its activity. Although it does not have complete power over the non-ego, the finite ego must forever exert itself to acquire it, and so aspire toward the status of an infinite ego, which is now only its unattainable ideal.

This stark Faustian vision of the finite ego's struggle against an opposing world gives Fichte his middle path between the conflict of infinite and finite ego. The contradiction is resolved because the ego is now infinite and finite in different senses (258, 268–269). It is *infinite* since it never ceases to struggle against the non-ego: there is no definite point in nature that serves as an insurmountable barrier, beyond which it cannot go in its striving. It is also *finite*, however, because striving must always have an obstacle to struggle against; no matter how far it goes in its battle against nature, there will always be some point that has yet to be conquered. This infinite striving is no Sisyphean labor: the finite ego progressively *surmounts* the limits of its finitude, and it constantly *approaches* the status of infinitude. Still, it does not end in any mystical bliss: it only approaches the complete self-determination of the infinite ego. But it cannot ever attain such infinite status, for that would be to destroy its identity as a finite subject, which is doomed to struggle against obstacles forever.[4]

The concept of striving now provides Fichte with his explanation for the existence of the non-ego, which had been merely postulated in the theoretical *Wissenschaftslehre*. If we assume that the activity of the ego consists in an infinite striving, then there must be a non-ego, because only then does striving have an obstacle. Without some obstacle or resistance, it would cease to act at all and shrink to a mere infinite point, related to itself alone. This infinite striving is therefore the condition of the possibility of all objects, of experiencing a world opposed to our activity (261–262). This deduction of the object shows the priority of the practical *Wissenschaftslehre* over the theoretical: what theoretical reason simply presupposes—the existence of an external world—is now explained according to practical reason, which demands that we strive to attain complete independence.[5]

The concept of striving is also Fichte's solution to the paradox of inner affection (I, 271–276). The ego must limit itself through its free activity, he argues, because it realizes its nature as a self-conscious being only through its striving against obstacles. Here Fichte appeals to his general principle that self-consciousness is essential to the very nature of subjectivity (264, 274,

276). This means that the ego realizes its nature as a free being only insofar as it becomes *self-conscious* of its activity. It must be not only self-positing, but also for itself or self-conscious as self-positing (274). But to be self-conscious of its activity the ego must know itself as determinate, as limited or restricted, since all knowing is a form of determination, of specifying one thing in contrast to others. Activity becomes limited, however, only if it clashes against some obstacle, only if it struggles against some hindrance. Hence the ego limits itself to know itself.

After introducing the concept of striving, Fichte begins to reinterpret the concept of the absolute ego in practical and regulative terms. All that this principle should mean, he writes, is that the ego *ought to be* independent; it states only the *ideal* that everything conforms to its rational activity (260–261). The first principle of the *Wissenschaftslehre* is now reread as the *goal* of our striving, as the *ideal* of complete independence, which the finite ego attains only if it *per impossible* acquires complete control over nature (277). This ideal must remain unattainable, though, because striving is essential to our very nature as subjects; if we cease to strive, we cease to act, and activity is characteristic of subjectivity (270). Hence the complete independence and infinitude of the absolute subject belongs to God alone (253–255, 270, 275). In the end, then, Fichte is not guilty of transcendent metaphysics after all: the absolute ego has a strictly regulative status in the *Wissenschaftslehre*. It differs from the Kantian *intellectus archetypus* in that it is not only a goal for enquiry—the complete explanation of experience—but also a moral ideal—absolute independence or self-determination.

3. The Synthesis of Idealism and Realism

After expounding the concept of striving in section 5 of the *Grundlage,* Fichte develops his doctrine of 'critical idealism,' which is his preferred term for the form of idealism characteristic of the *Wissenschaftslehre.* He had already introduced this doctrine in section 4, but then only by way of anticipation. In section 5 it receives its final and formal treatment. What Fichte means by critical idealism turns out to be very surprising: it does not conform to the stereotype of a radical idealism but is much more like Kant's "formal" idealism (see 1.3.4).

Throughout section 4 of the *Grundlage* Fichte spent much effort distinguishing his critical idealism from both dogmatic idealism and dogmatic realism.[6] On the one hand, the dogmatic idealist attempts to derive the reality of the non-ego from the activity of the ego alone, asserting that the non-ego is merely an accident of the single infinite ego. Such an extreme idealism fits the interpretation of Fichte as a radical idealist who makes all reality depend on an absolute ego; it is striking, therefore, that Fichte explicitly rejects it. On the other hand, the dogmatic realist tries to derive the passivity of the ego from the non-ego alone, making the ego into a mere accident of the single infinite substance. Clearly, these positions are extreme: they make one factor of experience the cause or substance, the other the effect or accident.

Remarkably, the descriptions Fichte gives of dogmatic idealism and realism in the *Grundlage* correspond to the crude accounts he later gives of criticism and dogmatism in the *Erste Einleitung*. While in the *Grundlage* Fichte is explicit that he rejects both, in the *Einleitung* he seems to prefer criticism over dogmatism, idealism over realism.[7] Yet this does not reflect so much a change in Fichte's position as it does a difference in exposition. The account of criticism and dogmatism in the *Erste Einleitung* was intended for a broad audience, and so is deliberately simplistic. All the more reason, then, that we should not confuse it with Fichte's more detailed position.

In section 5 of the *Grundlage* Fichte repudiates both dogmatic idealism and realism precisely because they are such simplistic and extreme positions. He opposes dogmatic idealism because it fails to explain the reality of our experience by reducing it down to a mere illusion;[8] similarly, he criticizes dogmatic realism because it does no justice to the characteristic nature of our subjectivity by treating the ego as it it were no more than a thing.[9] What is characteristic of critical idealism, he maintains, is that it recognizes the equal but interdependent role of both the subject and the object, the ego and the non-ego, in the constitution of experience. Fichte insists that we cannot reduce one component down to the other, but that they are fully interdependent, such that each exists and has its characteristic properties through the other. Critical idealism is therefore a *synthesis* of both idealism and realism, and as such an idealistic realism or a realistic idealism.[10] Hence Fichte summarizes its basic idea by the slogan "No subject, no object; no object, no subject."

What, though, does such a slogan really mean? How, more precisely, do the subject and object depend on one another? How, indeed, do they differ from one another? Fichte comes closest to defining what he means by the interdependence of the subject and object when he explains that the subject is completely dependent on the *existence* of its object (I, 279–280), but that it is independent of the object in creating, if only in principle or potentially, all its *properties* or determinations. Or, as he also puts it, *how* the subject represents something in its experience depends completely on it; but *that* it represents something at all depends on the object outside it (248).

If we analyze these propositions in the context of sections 4 and 5, then the outline of Fichte's position emerges. Critical idealism has a realistic and idealistic aspect. According to its idealistic aspect, the object depends on the subject because all of the object's properties or determinations, at least insofar as they are perceived by the subject, are producible by the activity of the subject alone.[11] True to his principle that the ego is only for itself, Fichte stresses time and again in the *Grundlage* that we must explain consciousness or representation according to the ego's internal laws; he rejects the possibility of some thing-in-itself acting on our passive sensibility because such causality would have to straddle the gap between two ontologically distinct realms.[12] This means that whatever the ego perceives—all the determinations of the object of experience—must be explicable according to the inherent activity of the ego itself. According to critical idealism's realistic side, however, the subject depends on the object because the subject is finite and limited, conditioned by something outside itself, which it cannot further analyze or explain away. To account for this irreducible dimension of objectivity, Fichte postulates the existence of a check, obstacle, or impetus (*Anstoß*) to the infinite activity of the ego.[13] He stresses that this check cannot be the product of the ego's activity, for the simple reason that activity requires some obstacle, some resistance, if it is to be activity at all. We cannot distinguish between the subjective and objective sphere within consciousness, Fichte argues, unless there were something to limit and restrict the activity of the subject within a specific sphere.[14] Hence Fichte comes to the general conclusion: "According to the *Wissenschaftslehre*, the final basis for all reality for the ego is an original interchange between the ego and a something outside it, of which nothing further can be said than that it is completely opposed to the ego" (I, 279). This something beyond the ego, he further implies, is completely unknowable by us, having no other characteristic than serving as both a check and stimulus for the activity of the ego.

In Fichte's view, this commitment to the existence of a "check" or "obstacle" to the ego's activity—to something completely opposed to and beyond the realm of consciousness—is not a weakness but a strength of the *Wissenschaftslehre*. It shows that the *Wissenschaftslehre* contains an element of realism, and that it does full justice to the finitude of the human mind (I, 279–280). The distinctive feature of critical as opposed to dogmatic idealism,

Fichte explains, is that the former admits the reality of a non-ego that transcends the boundaries of consciousness, whereas the latter reduces the non-ego to a mere effect of the ego.[15] It is important to recognize, however, that this emphasis on the existence of the check or obstacle to the ego's activity marks a stronger form of realism than the mere *empirical* realism than we are led to expect from some of Fichte's more programmatic statements.[16] The realism of the *Wissenschaftslehre* is not only empirical, for it presupposes a thing-in-itself as the condition for the possibility of all consciousness. This doctrine is very close to Kant's "formal" idealism: only the forms depend on consciousness; but the existence of the object is independent of consciousness (1.3.4).

4. Reintroducing and Reinterpreting the Thing-in-Itself

Does not this concept of a check or obstacle to the ego's activity amount to a covert reintroduction of the thing-in-itself? That was Hegel's famous criticism,[17] which has been for many the final word against the *Wissenschaftslehre*. But it is, at best, an oversimplification, and, at worst, a begging of the question. The truth of the matter is that while Fichte intentionally reintroduces the thing-in-itself he also reinterprets it so that it no longer means the utterly unthinkable.

To understand Fichte's reinterpretation, we have to consider the *dynamic* element of his idealism. It is a central tenet of his critical idealism that the interrelation between subject and object is constantly moving or fluid. This means that there is not only an *interdependence* but an *interchange* between them, such that the relation between the subject and object, and indeed the subject and object themselves, is steadily changing. Hence in the early part of section 4 Fichte spends much time and effort explaining the importance of such concepts as 'change' (*Wechsel*), 'interaction' (*Wechselwirkung*), and 'interchange' (*Wechseltun*). These concepts imply some form of reciprocal alteration between subject and object where their activity and passivity are in inverse ratio to one another.[18] In section 5 Fichte explains these concepts in practical terms according to his concept of infinite striving, and it is in this context that he reinterprets the concept of the thing-in-itself.

According to the concept of striving, the more the ego strives and gains power over the non-ego, the more it makes the object, which was previously an unknowable thing-in-itself, conform to the laws of its activity so that it can become part of its consciousness; but because its activity has to be limited, there is always something more beyond its reach, which transcends the realm of consciousness (I, 280). The non-ego is therefore both a noumenon, a pure creation of reason, and an unknowable thing-in-itself, depending on the degree to which the ego strives and acquires control over nature. We are therefore caught in a circle, Fichte says, where we must both postulate something outside ourselves and yet strive to make that thing part of ourselves. But this circle is simply our fate as finite beings, who have only limited creative powers. As Fichte summarizes his position in a famous passage: "This, that the finite mind necessarily must posit something absolute outside itself (a thing-in-itself) and still recognize on the other hand that it is only there *for him* (a necessary noumenon), is that circle, which we can extend to infinity, but from which we cannot ever escape" (281).

This circle is central to the idealism of the *Wissenschaftslehre*. It expresses the heart of its teaching about the predicament of the finite subject: that it knows things only to the extent that it makes them conform to reason; and that it is always limited yet must transcend its limits. The finite knowing subject is therefore forever caught between the noumenon that it creates and the thing-in-itself that transcends it, though it can forever push forward the boundaries between them. The problem with dogmatic idealism and dogmatic realism, Fichte explains, is that they fail to recognize this circle. The dogmatic idealist refuses to see it because he denies any reality independent of consciousness; and the dogmatic realist fails to recognize it because he pushes the thing-in-itself completely beyond the bounds of human consciousness.[19]

So, in the end, despite Fichte's earlier scorn for it, the concept of the thing-in-itself does play a central role in the *Wissenschaftslehre*. It essentially serves as a limiting concept to express what remains beyond our powers in our infinite striving to control nature. But it is important to see that it is more than simply a regulative principle, that it does more than merely express the goal of infinite striving. This becomes clear when Fichte states that the check or obstacle also serves to check and limit our activity, that it is a force that can indeed be felt, even if it cannot be conceptualized (I, 279).[20] In this regard it fulfills something of its old role in the Kantian system: it acts on our sensibility, providing the source for the raw matter of experience. There still remains, however, one important respect in which Fichte's concept differs from Kant's: the Fichtean check is infinitely determinable rather than absolutely indeterminable for the powers of the understanding; in other words, its unknowability is not a matter of kind but of degree.

Fichte himself is perfectly explicit about his reintroduction of the thing-in-itself. He now states that it is "the object of a necessary idea of reason," which is presupposed by all philosophy and activities of the finite mind (283). He is anxious to lay at rest, however, two possible misinterpretations of the concept: that it is nothing more than an idea, whose reality depends on us, or that it is a mysterious entity, whose reality is completely independent of us. The truth of the matter lies somewhere in between, Fichte says, because we have to grasp it as both. The thing-in-itself is both a noumenon and an unknowable entity; which one depends on how far we progress in our infinite striving (284).

It would seem, though, that we have now relapsed into the worse kind of dogmatism. Although Fichte insists that we explain everything within consciousness according to its immanent laws, he ends by postulating the existence of something beyond it to account for its finitude. Fichte is anxious to reply to this objection. He insists that, despite its strong form of realism, the *Wissenschaftslehre* is not transcendent but simply transcendental. It explains consciousness by postulating something outside it, to be sure, but it also recognizes that in providing such an explanation it simply acts according to its own laws, so that this apparently independent thing turns out to be a mere noumenon. But this does not completely eliminate the thing-in-itself, he insists, but only points to its necessity on a higher level. The transcendental philosopher is caught in his own inevitable circle in attempting to explain consciousness. There are levels or strata of explanation, Fichte thinks. On each level the ego explains the object according to its laws, so that it becomes a mere noumenon; but such an explanation still presupposes some further conditions independent of it, and so on *ad infinitum* (280, 282–283).

It should be clear by now that Fichte does not think that the concept of the thing-in-itself is valid *only* from the standpoint of empirical consciousness, which must explain its consciousness by postulating something independent of it. This has been the prevalent interpretation of the central passages from section 5 of the *Grundlage,* and it is an understandable reading in the light of some of Fichte's statements about the thing-in-itself. Still, it does no justice to the full context of Fichte's argument. Such an interpretation assumes that the standpoint of the philosopher dispenses entirely with the thing-in-itself because the philosopher sees that the object of experience is produced rather than given. But this flies in the face of Fichte's teaching that the absolute ego is only a regulative idea; it makes nonsense of his attempt to find a middle path between the extremes of dogmatic idealism and realism; and it ignores his doctrine of the primacy of practical reason, according to which the philosopher has a right to assume only that the object *ought to be* created by the subject. In the end, then, Fichte thinks that the thing-in-itself is valid from the standpoint of the philosopher, who stresses the finitude of the human subject, its limited power to create its own world.

CHAPTER 7

The Refutation of Idealism

1. Later Arguments against Idealism

After introducing his concept of striving in the 1794 *Grundlage*, Fichte returned on several occasions to rethink his deduction of the reality of the external world. He had been very dissatisfied with the argument of the *Grundlage*, a work he had composed in great haste and that was meant only as an accompaniment to his lectures. Obviously, the whole issue was much too important for him to rest content with some sketchy first formulations. It is not surprising, therefore, that the other two major works of the Jena years—the 1796 *Grundlage des Naturrechts* and the 1798 *System der Sittenlehre*—contain several new arguments to prove the reality of the external world.[1] These are much more formal, rigorous, and precise than those of the 1794 *Grundlage*. They proceed virtually *more geometrico*, with numbered propositions, proofs, and corollaria.

Although Fichte was dissatisifed with the form of his earlier arguments, he did not alter their underlying conception. He never abandoned the theme of striving, though it would now play a more implicit role, and he retained the basic principles of the critical idealism he established in the *Grundlage*. Accordingly, the new arguments are still based on the concept of striving, and they are essentially an attempt to provide a firmer foundation for his critical idealism. These arguments attempt to establish two propositions, each of them central to and characteristic of Fichte's critical idealism. First, that the *form* of experience consists in a universal and necessary structure, so that my representations do not depend on my will and imagination but are constrained to follow one another in a definite order. Second, that the *existence* or *matter* of my experience is independent of all consciousness whatsoever. The first proposition claims only the *empirical reality* of our perceptions, their necessary conformity to the forms of the understanding; the second proposition claims the *transcendental reality* of the matter of experience, the existence of some limit to all our activity. Arguments for both theses appear in the 1796 *Grundlage* and *Sittenlehre*, though they are not precisely distinguished from one another.

Prima facie such arguments are flatly contrary to the spirit of Fichte's pragmatism. We have already seen how Fichte maintains that knowledge depends on our acting on the world and that there cannot be any theoretical refutation of skepticism. But the apparent inconsistency disappears as soon as we note the specific form of Fichte's arguments. They do not attempt to demonstrate the reality or possibility of knowledge independent of our practical activity, and still less are they meant to replace the need for practical activity. On the contrary, they attempt to show on the level of transcendental reflection the primacy of such activity in acquiring knowledge and in forming our conception of an external world. They begin from the self-awareness of our activity, and then attempt to show how such self-awareness involves awareness of an external world. In one form or another, these arguments attempt to prove that I am aware of the objective world only because it resists my attempt to change it. In other words, the world is independent of me—both in its form and content—because it is an obstacle to my will. Hence, for Fichte, the circumference of my world is equivalent to the limits of my will.

Recognizing the practical basis of these arguments is of the first importance to understanding their limits, or precisely what Fichte intends to prove. Since Fichte's arguments begin with the self-awareness of freedom, and since he does not think that there is a theoretical proof of the reality of freedom, his first premises begin only from the *demand* that we ought to believe in freedom. All that Fichte can prove from such premises, then, is that *we ought to believe in,* or that *we must assume,* the existence of the external world. The arguments therefore do not attempt to establish that such a world exists, or that we have *knowledge* of its existence. Hence Fichte's arguments work against only a limited kind of skepticism, one that states that we need not *believe in* the existence of the external world; they do not work against a more radical skepticism that holds that, whatever the necessities of our conceptual scheme, it is still possible for the world not to exist.

Fichte was aware of these limitations of his arguments, despite some carelessness of expression. Hence he sometimes formulates his arguments in a guarded manner, so that their premises only refer to what one must assume or ascribe to oneself (see section 4, premise 2). It is was indeed on these grounds that Fichte made the standpoint of moral faith superior to that of knowledge in his 1800 *Bestimmung des Menschen*. Still, it is easy to ignore or underrate these restrictions, especially because of Fichte's obscure language of positing. When he says that the ego must posit a non-ego opposed to itself, this *seems to* mean that the ego creates or makes the non-ego; and since the ego's creations are perfectly transparent to itself, it would follow that it also *knows* of the existence of the non-ego. But the language of positing really does not carry such heavy connotations. When Fichte states that the ego posits the non-ego all that he means is that it must be aware of, or assume the existence of, some non-ego opposed to itself.[2]

2. The Fichtean versus Kantian Refutation

In fundamental respects, Fichte's later arguments for the reality of the external world follow in the footsteps of Kant's Refutation of Idealism in the first *Kritik*. Like Kant, Fichte wants to show that the possibility of self-awareness requires awareness of an objective world; in other words, to be conscious of myself, I must also be conscious of some external object, which will be something in space outside me.[3]

Beyond this general similarity, however, Fichte's strategy has little in common with Kant's. The starting point of Fichte's arguments is not a form of *empirical* self-consciousness—my self-awareness in time—but a form of *transcendental* self-consciousness—my self-awareness as a rational and free being. The central thrust of Fichte's arguments is that I can be self-conscious as a free agent—I can ascribe to myself a will and rational ends—only if I am also aware of a world outside myself in which my actions take place. The existence of the external world therefore becomes a necessary condition of moral action. It is in this sense that Fichte derives the realm of objective experience not from cognition or theoretical reason but from desire or practical reason.

Fichte's arguments differ from Kant's not only in their starting point but also in their conclusion. The external world he intends to demonstrate has not only an empirical but also a transcendental reality. It is not only that which conforms to the formal conditions of experience, as in Kant's argument, but that which exists independent of any consciousness whatsoever. This is not the thing-in-itself in the Kantian sense of something completely unthinkable—obviously, to prove its existence would be absurd—but it is the check or obstacle to the ego's activity.

It is important to recognize that the general structure of Fichte's argument—quite apart from its specific premise and conclusion—is even antithetical to Kant's. We have already seen that Fichte does not think that there can be a *theoretical* demonstration of the reality of the external world, and that he denies that theoretical reason can prove or refute the existence of anything. Any demonstration of the existence of the external world, Fichte maintains, must be based entirely on *practical* principles, which tell us not what *is* the case but what *ought to be* so. Yet Kant's Refutation of Idealism operated entirely within the realm of *theoretical* reason, because it attempted to prove the existence of the world on the basis of principles that could only be regarded as constitutive (that I am aware of my existence in time). Kant had indeed maintained that it was a "scandal to philosophy" that the existence of things outside us had to be accepted on the basis of faith (B xxxix), and he stressed the need for a knock-down argument to put an end to the disgrace once and for all. But Fichte held that such an argument is problematic because of the general limits of theoretical reason. Indeed, he believed that he had good Kantian reasons for forbidding such a proof. For was it not Kant who held that philosophy is "knowledge gained by reason from concepts" (B 741), and that from concepts no reality could be inferred? Was it not Kant who insisted that the existence of objects had to be given in empirical intuition? How, then, could the transcendental philosopher exempt his reasoning from the general strictures laid down on theoretical reason? For just these Kantian reasons, Fichte insisted on a practical demonstration of the reality of the external world.

3. Problems of Exposition

The exposition of Fichte's arguments against idealism poses formidable difficulties for the historian of philosophy. Unfortunately, there are no Fichtean texts like Kant's Refutation of Idealism, which, for all its obscurity, is at least brief and to the point, laying down its argument in clearly delineated steps. The arguments of the 1796 *Grundlage* and *Sittenlehre*, though formal and painstaking, are not only obscure but diffuse, stretching over many pages of text. Even worse, they are inchoate and incomplete. There are gaps in the argument, which make it necessary to place them in a wider context to supply the missing premises. The historian of philosophy therefore faces a daunting challenge: it is necessary to *reconstruct* Fichte's argument, weaving together its premises from different texts. But this poses the danger of anachronism, selling the scholar's confabulated pastiche for real historical ware.

Though the difficulties are formidable, they are not insurmountable. Fortunately, sections 4–8 of the Second Main Section (*Zweite Hauptstück*) of the *System der Sittenlehre* present something approximating a clear step-by-step deduction of the reality of the external world. Here Fichte leaves no doubts about his intentions: to show that positing the reality of the external world is a necessary condition for the self-consciousness of my freedom. Such a proof is meant to resolve the central problem of all practical philosophy: How does a rational agent act in the sensible world? What ensures the reality of the moral law, or that it has application in experience? If we can show that our belief in the reality of the external world is based on the self-consciousness of freedom, then we will have done everything necessary to show the reality of the principle of morality itself. The fundamental concept of morality—the concept of freedom—will then prove to be the basis for our belief in all reality. This was indeed the central thesis of both the earlier versions of the *Wissenschaftslehre*, the 1794 *Grundlage des gesammten Wissenschaftslehre* and the 1798 *Wissenschaftslehre novo methodo*.

The argument in sections 4–8 consists in five propositions, which are proved in quasi-geometric form with Explanations, Proofs, and Corollaria. Never was Fichte so clear or so cogent in all his Jena writings. The *System der Sittenlehre* was indeed the most mature work of his Jena years, and it easily surpasses in clarity and concision the two versions of the Jena *Wissenschaftslehre*, whose argument is too schematic and obscure. The *Sittenlehre* was written in a period of comparative tranquility, when Fichte found more time to reflect and to spend time on his exposition. While he says that his theory of morals follows the principles of the *Wissenschaftslehre*—the work bears the subtitle *nach Principien der Wissenschaftslehre*—it would be misleading to conclude that he simply accepts a foundation he has laid down elsewhere. The argument of the first two main sections essentially rethinks the whole argument of the earlier versions of the *Wissenschaftslehre*.

The argument of the *Sittenlehre* is not, however, the solution to all exegetical problems. It is incomplete in one essential respect: it lacks a clear and indisputable first premise, which any transcendental argument against skepticism must have. Fichte had struggled to provide such a premise in other versions of the *Wissenschaftslehre*, but it does not reappear in the *Sittenlehre*. This fact alone would seem to doom the reconstruction of the argument by making it excessively speculative.

Fortunately, however, Fichte himself reveals how the argument of the *Sittenlehre* connects with the *Wissenschaftslehre*. He explains that the first premise of his argument in the *Sittenlehre*—"I find myself, as myself, only willing"—presupposes the first principle of the *Grundlage* "I am I" because to know myself as willing presupposes that I know myself (IV, 23). This suggests that the first premise of the *Grundlage* fulfills the conditional implied in the first principle of the *Sittenlehre:* "*If* I know myself, I know myself as willing.*" The premise of the argument would then be that I know myself. The same connection emerges from another angle when Fichte states that his argument in the *Sittenlehre* really begins from the same starting point as that in the *Grundlage des Naturrechts:* "If I posit myself then I must ascribe free activity to myself."[4] The first principle of the *Wissenschaftslehre* would then simply assert that the condition behind the premise is fulfilled: that I do posit myself as a rational being.

Taking this as our lead, we can reconstruct Fichte's argument for the reality of the external world so that it presents a single coherent structure. We can begin with the first principle of the *Wissenschaftslehre* and then connect it with the line of argument running through sections 4–8 of the *Sittenlehre*. To clarify that argument, I compare it in the following section with the very similar argument in the *Grundlage des Naturrechts*, and present the argument in step-by-step syllogistic form, providing a commentary on each premise. Though we shall find the argument has problems, it can claim to be at least plausible and interesting. What more can be claimed for any philosophical argument?

4. The Deduction of the External World

1. *I posit myself, or I exist only in and through the activity of thinking of myself.*

The premise of Fichte's argument is the first principle of the *Wissenschaftslehre* itself. There are various formulations of this first principle, however, which differ in the two versions of the Jena *Wissenschaftslehre*, and which also sometimes differ even in the same version. In the 1794 *Grundlage der gesamten Wissenschaftslehre* the first principle is expressed in the simple proposition "I am," or in the equally banal "I am I," but also in the more forbidding "The I posits absolutely its own being." In the 1798 *Wissenschaftslehre novo methodo* Fichte begins his philosophy with the postulate: "Think of the concept of the I, and think of oneself when one thinks of it." The differences between these versions are not as great as they first appear, however, and they all express the same fundamental point.

In both versions of the *Wissenschaftslehre,* and indeed in the *Sittenlehre* itself, Fichte prescribes the same procedure to arrive at his first principle. He demands that I abstract from all objects of consciousness and that I reflect on myself as the subject of all consciousness. Normally, the subject loses itself in consciousness of objects because it focuses its attention on them rather than on itself or its consciousness of them; only in these latter cases do we distinguish between the subject and object of consciousness. The first principle requires, however, that I become aware of myself as the subject who is conscious. In this case the subject who is conscious should be identical with the object of which it is conscious. Hence the first principle, Fichte sometimes says, should express "subject–object identity."

Fichte is also consistent throughout his Jena years that his first principle must express an act rather than a fact. He insists on this point for two reasons. First, a fact is simply the product of an activity, and so the activity that produces it is prior to it. Second, knowledge of an activity is immediate and certain, whereas knowledge of a fact or object is not. In the case of a fact or object there is a separation between the subject who knows and the object that is known because the fact or object is something given, having a source independent of me. Hence it is possible that there is no correspondence between the subject and object. In the case of an activity, however, there is no such separation because I simply create or make what it is that I know. If I want to know this object, I simply have to recreate it in myself and I do not have to search for it.[5]

If the first principle must express an act rather than a fact, then it demands that I think not only of myself but the *act* of thinking of myself. I must not think of some entity or thing that thinks—for that there is no evidence—but simply of the activity of thinking of myself. Furthermore, I must think of the act of *thinking of my existence,* and nothing more. That is, I must not think of anything more about myself than thinking that I exist. I must abstract from my individuality, from any specific characteristics of myself, and I must focus my attention simply on the I who so abstracts.[6] I must think simply that I am, and not how or what I am.

Fichte thinks that his first principle is certain or indubitable for all the classical reasons. I cannot doubt that I am thinking of myself without also thinking of myself. Of course, I can doubt that I possess certain characteristics, for example, that I am not walking when I am in fact lying in bed dreaming. But to doubt that I am thinking of myself is also to think of myself, so that to deny the proposition is to affirm it.

It is possible to view Fichte's first principle as a post-Kantian reformulation of the Cartesian *cogito*, purged of all its metaphysical intentions and implications. Like Kant, Fichte is critical of Descartes because he attempted to infer the existence of a permanent thinking substance from this principle. Such a conclusion does not follow from the principle 'I am' because it is possible that the I exists only as long as it thinks of itself; it is still possible that it goes out of existence when it is not thinking of itself. Fichte's emphasis on the activity of thinking of myself attempts to avoid this fallacy. What I know through this proposition is not the existence of a substance, Fichte is saying, but only an activity, because I know of my existence only in and through the act of thinking of it.

Though his first principle attempts to secure the existence of the 'I,' it is necessary to stress that it is still only a postulate, an imperative that prescribes an act that everyone must execute within themselves. It does not describe something that exists and that is given within the consciousness of everyone alike. That would be a fact of consciousness but not an activity, which comes into being only through an exercise of will. If someone did not care to enact his will to think of himself as acting, then he would not exist as such an activity.

2. If I posit myself, I must ascribe free activity to myself.

This is a formulation of the first principle of the *System der Sittenlehre:* "I find myself, as myself, only willing." For Fichte, to ascribe free activity to myself is to be self-conscious that I have a will; it is to be aware of myself as willing and acting. This is also the thrust of Proposition §1 of the 1796 *Grundlage:* "A finite rational being cannot posit itself without ascribing free activity to itself" (III, 17). This proposition is the starting point for Fichte's deduction of the external world and other minds in this work.

It is important to note that Fichte's propositions refer to aspects of my self-*consciousness* and not my self-*knowledge.* In other words, they claim only that I *ascribe* free activity to myself, or that I *find* myself willing. They do not state that these acts of self-ascription or self-discovery are necessarily true; in other words, they do not make the stronger claims that I am free or that I have a will. This restriction is most probably deliberate, for Fichte is firm elsewhere that we do *not* have an immediate knowledge or experience of freedom.

Why does Fichte think that, if I am self-conscious that I exist, I must also be aware of myself willing and acting? According to his account in the 1796 *Grundlage* and *Sittenlehre*, the ego cannot originally be self-conscious as thinking, because as a thinking being it is first conscious of things outside itself (III, 18; IV, 20). We first become aware of ourselves as something distinct from things when we find them to resist us, to be obstacles to us. But this means that we must be self-conscious of them resisting some *activity* within ourselves, or that we must be self-aware of them restricting some *drive* or *tendency* in ourselves toward them. In other words, we first become conscious of ourselves as acting or willing.

> 3. *If I ascribe free activity to myself, I must also assume the existence of something outside myself toward which it is directed.*

This premise is the starting point of Fichte's deduction of the objective world in the *Sittenlehre*, which takes place in the Second Main Section, appropriately entitled The Deduction of the Reality and Applicability of the Principle of Morality (IV, 64–156). The first premise of that Deduction, Proposition 1, Deduction of an Object of Our Activity in General, states: "*A rational being cannot ascribe a power [of freedom] to itself unless it also thinks of something outside itself toward which its power is directed*" (§4; IV, 76–83).

In the *Sittenlehre* Fichte provides two arguments for this premise. Both arguments consist in an analysis of what is involved in ascribing free activity to myself. Both presuppose a similar analysis of freedom: that to ascribe freedom to myself is to conceive of several specific actions as possible through me; in other words, it is to attribute a power of choice to myself, such that I can choose between opposing courses of action (IV, 7).

According to the first argument, to choose one course of action means that I act in the world, or that I produce some effect outside myself (80). But the mere fact that my purposive activity involves the production of something, Fichte argues, involves a distinction between myself and the external world. To aim to realize my ends means that I intend to bring something into existence, something that will continue to exist independent of me (81–82, 24). I contrast my own subjective status as someone who conceives an end with the objective status of what I intend to achieve.

According to the second argument, I ascribe freedom to myself only if I also assume the permanent *existence* of the world outside me. To attribute a power of choice to myself, Fichte contends, I must also conceive of some object that exists independent of whatever choice I make. I must assume the existence of some object A that continues to exist independent of my will, although it is either X or $-X$ depending on my choice. In other words, this thing A must be conceived of as permanent or enduring, as one and the same thing, whether I choose X or $-X$. Hence, Fichte concludes, I must assume that there exists some matter or stuff (*Stoff*) outside me, something that is infinitely modifiable according to my choice. Although I can alter its *form*, it must continue to remain the same at least in its *content* or *matter* (82–83). This argument works only on the assumption that I cannot create the entire world; it is just this assumption, however, that a skeptic will question.

The argument Fichte offers for this premise in the 1796 *Grundlage* is more plausible and straightforward. It is essentially a variant of his contention in section 5 of the 1794 *Grundlage* that all striving requires an obstacle to resist it. Fichte now reasons that I know myself as acting or willing only if there is something that resists my activity; what resists my activity is not something within me but something distinct from me, and indeed something opposed to me (III, 18–19). Hence I am self-conscious as an active being only if I am also conscious of something opposed to myself. As Fichte formulated this point in the two versions of the *Wissenschaftslehre:* consciousness of an 'I' involves of necessity consciousness of a 'not I.'[7]

Fichte explains in the *Rechtslehre* that the world outside me originally has the character of being something opposed to my activity, something that resists my efforts or striving to control it. An object is an object, he says, only insofar as it should not exist according to my free activity, which aims to destroy it (III, 19). Thus the original character of the world—the first form in which I am conscious of it—is that it is an obstacle to my activity.

We can now see how Fichte's practical proof of the external world works against the skeptic. The proof of the reality of things is that it resists my will, frustrates my desires, or restricts my activity. If the world were only the product of my will and imagination, as the skeptic suggests, then I should perceive no such resistance or restriction; the object should immediately conform to my wishes. If the skeptic insists that he could be dreaming that there is an object in front of him now, the reply to him is that, if this is so, he should be able to remove it right away, since dreams remain under the control of our will and imagination. How, indeed, can a mere object of imagination be an obstacle to his acting? The discrepancy between the skeptic's doubts and his deeds had always been a favorite counter against Pyrrhonism; Fichte's argument can be seen as a variation of this venerable strategy.

4. *If I ascribe free activity to myself, I also must assume that I have the power to act on and change things in the sensible world.*

This premise takes the conclusion of the third premise a step further by stating that the object outside myself must consist in the sensible world, that is, it must be an empirical manifold. The argument for this premise is explicit in sections 5–6 of *Sittenlehre* (IV, 83–91). The premise itself also appears explicitly as the conclusion of Fichte's argument for Proposition §1 of the 1796 *Grundlage*. This conclusion (§2 *Folgesatz*) states: "*Through its positing of its capacity for free activity the rational being posits and determines a sensible world outside itself*" (III, 23–24).

In *Sittenlehre* §§5–6 Fichte justifies this premise by a closer analysis of what is involved in ascribing freedom to myself. If I assume I am a free agent, he argues, I must be able to choose a specific action. In other words, I must will something determinate, this or that end, and not simply something in general; and I must do something determinate, this or that action, and not just act in general. My end or action is determinate, however, only by virtue of its limitation, by virtue of its opposition to other possible actions. Thus I will a determinate action X only by virtue of X not being Y or Z.

If my actions must be determinate, the proof continues, then they must take place in the sensible world. For I know what limits my activity, what gives it its determinate character, only through experience or through feeling. To know the determinate character of anything I must consult experience; I must know what it is not, or that to which it is opposed, and I know this only through perception of things outside me. Although I know *that* I act through an a priori intellectual intuition, I know *how* I act only by virtue of my opposition and relation to an external world.

The Proof concludes by introducing the idea of a temporal manifold. If I know my specific actions only through experience, then my awareness of them involves the sensible intuition of a temporal magnitude, a definite degree or quantity (*ein Quantum*). This quantum is a manifold because it is, at least in principle, divisible into smaller units *ad infinitum*. This means that I know my activity through sensible intuition when it passes through a succession of distinct moments. But to act throughout time, Fichte concludes, is what it means to act in the external sensible world (90–91).

5. If I have the power to act and change things in the sensible world, then I must perceive this power in a manifold having a definite and irreversible order, that is, my experience must have a necessary and universal form.

Fichte arrives at this conclusion by a further analysis of the conditions of my acting in the sensible world. He argues that we attain the final end of our action only by passing through a series of intermediate ends. Thus we achieve our final end *X* only if we also realize *a;* and we realize *a* only if we also realize *b;* and so on. Our ends are such that we cannot realize them all at once, but we are bound to a definite order of means (IV, 94–95). Fichte then suggests that this is the paradigm for all objective order in our experience. We experience events as having an objective order, independent of our will and imagination, because we encounter resistance to our actions and have to realize them in a definite circumscribed order.

Fichte's proof of this premise consists in two propositions. (1) *My causality is perceived in succession or as a manifold in a continuous series.* This is because the perception of my causality falls within time, and occupies a quantum of time. This quantum involves a manifold because time is in principle infinitely divisible. The instants of this manifold follow a determinate, irreversible order and cannot be otherwise. In other words, what I perceive in this series does not depend on me, but on the order of the series itself. It does not depend on me because each moment of time in which I perceive my activity consists in the perception of some resistance to my activity (97). (2) *The successive order of the manifold is determined independent of me, and it is only as such a limitation of my activity.* It is independent of me not only in that my thinking does not determine the specific order of the manifold, but it is also independent of my practical activity. This is again because the successive order is an order of resistance to my activity, and as such resists all forms of my activity, whether theoretical or practical (98).

The result we have reached here is significant: that I cannot be aware of my activity as a free agent unless I am also aware of an objective time order of events, an order that is independent of my representation and my will. Such an objective order constitutes empirical reality, the independence of experience from the subjective order of my own representations. This objectivity follows from (a) the series of events having an irreversible order, independent of my will and imagination, and (b) such an order not depending on me but on the world outside me, which provides resistance to my activity. I arrive at an objective view of the world, Fichte concludes, because my activity encounters resistance, so that it can be realized only through follow-ing a definite order of means to ends.

Fichte suggests that all properties of the material world—apart from its formal characteristics—are explicable in terms of their relation to my activ-ity. For example, that this object is such and such a distance from me means that I must perceive so many other things between it and me, and that I must encounter so much resistance in such and such a time when I ap-proach the object.[8] That an object is hard means that I feel such and such a degree of resistance when I touch it, and so on (99).

> 6. *If I have the power to act in the sensible world, then that world must also have a power to act on me, that is, it must follow its own objective laws.*

This premise is the general conclusion of Proposition 5, the final proposi-tion of Section II of the *Sittenlehre*.[9] This Proposition states: "*A rational being cannot ascribe any power to act to itself without also presupposing a certain power to act of its objects.*"

Fichte attempts to prove this premise by introducing the concept of a drive (*Trieb*). The ego first knows itself as an active being, he contends, through its drives, for example, hunger, thirst, sex, and so on. Its first actions are at-tempts to satisfy these drives. It perceives its drives, their satisfaction or dissatisfaction, through feeling (*Gefühl*) (105–106). Fichte insists, however, that insofar as I feel, I am constrained. Both what I feel, and that I feel, does not depend on my self-positing activity; in feeling I am not positing but pos-ited (107). As a free being I do have some control over my drives: I can choose to satisfy or not satisfy them; but that I have these drives, and that they are satisfiable only in certain ways, does not depend on me. Insofar as I am a thinking and willing being I am free; but insofar as I have drives and feelings I am part of nature (109–110).

Appealing to some of his early propositions, Fichte now contends that it is not only that through these drives I posit myself as nature; I also posit a *na-ture* outside my own. This is because (1) there must be some matter outside me for my activity to shape and form (Prop. 1), and (2) this matter must have a definite form because it is necessary for me to realize my ends in a de-terminate order (Prop. 4). My nature and the nature outside me are similar to one another (as nature) but also opposed to one another (mine versus what is not mine). Since they therefore reciprocally condition one another, there must be a whole of which both are only parts. This is to say that my nature should be explained according to the whole system of nature (109–

110). Fichte thus concludes his argument by placing the subject within the whole of nature. The subject is not the whole of nature but only one of its parts.

Such is, in rough outline, Fichte's argument for the existence of an objective world. Although I have tried to do justice to the details of Fichte's argument, the richness and obscurity of the texts permit other readings. But it is the general strategy and main point behind Fichte's argument that is of greatest importance and interest here. This consists in his practical refutation of subjectivism, his attempt to prove the reality of the external world by appealing to the limits of our activity as agents having a will. For Fichte, the only effective proof of the reality of the external world is that I cannot make that world conform immediately, entirely, and automatically to my desires. Hence the limits of the objective world consists in that which resists or opposes my activity. Again, the problem with skepticism is that it has a much too *contemplative* or *theoretical* attitude toward the world; it is only once I try to change the world, to make it submit to the demands of my activity, that I see that the world cannot be only the product of my will and imagination.

CHAPTER 8

The Structure of Intersubjectivity

1. Kant versus Fichte on the Problem of Other Minds

Fichte's concern with the refutation of subjectivism is scarcely exhausted by his attempt to demonstrate the reality of the external world. There was another respect in which he was greatly preoccupied by the challenge of subjectivism: the question of the reality of other minds. Fichte's attempt to resolve this problem—his general argument for intersubjectivity—is one of the most original and interesting aspects of the Jena *Wissenschaftslehre*.[1] It was only by solving it, Fichte was firmly convinced, that he could finally slay the monster of nihilism.

Fichte first devoted himself to the problem of other minds sometime in the summer of 1795. With some justice, he complained that this issue had not received the attention it deserved: "It is a weighty question in philosophy, which, to my knowledge, has never been resolved: Why do we attribute the concept of rationality to some objects in the sensible world and not to others? What is the characteristic difference between these classes?"[2] His interest in this question originated with his attempt to find a foundation for the principles of right and morality, and more specifically with his fear that skeptical doubts about other minds could undermine these principles. For with what right do I apply these principles to others if I do not know that they are rational beings like myself? After all, if they are only very complicated machines, why should I treat them as ends in themselves?

In Fichte's view, this question had been neglected even by Kant, who had been all too willing to follow common sense and general opinion. But this was simply not good enough from a philosophical standpoint, and especially from a moral one. "I ride a horse without asking its permission . . . Why do I have more qualms when it comes to the man who lends me the horse?"[3]

334

Fichte pointed out that it does not work simply to appeal to general opinion, which also accepts that the Russian nobleman sells and beats his serfs. We need some general criterion to know when to apply the principles of morality, some means of determining which beings have rights and duties. It does not help much to say morality makes demands on us insofar as we are *rational* beings. For the questions remain: In what does rationality consist, and in whom does it really exist?

Fichte had some reason to chide Kant, who had not fully appreciated the problem of other minds. He came closest to considering the issue only in the third *Kritik*, Fichte says, where he lay down the criteria for ascribing purposive activity to things in my experience.[4] But even here the main subject of his attention was living beings, not rational ones. When his doctrine was extended to rational beings it had troubling implications, for Kant had stressed that all judgments about ends have only a regulative validity, so that although we can *think* of living beings acting for ends it does not follow that they *really* do so.

In the first edition of the Paralogisms in the first *Kritik* Kant raised the issue of other minds *en passant*, but only to dismiss it (A 346–347). He noted that it is strange that the condition under which I think should be valid for everyone alike. We have an apparently empirical proposition 'I think,' and from this single case we attempt to base a universal proposition, namely, that whatever thinks must, in all cases, be constituted as it is for my own self-consciousness. The reason for this strange assumption, Kant explained, is that "we must assign to things necessarily and a priori all the properties that constitute the conditions under which alone we think them." Since I can conceive of other thinking beings only by analogy with my own self-consciousness, I am justified in concluding that they have a consciousness like my own. Kant then came to the conclusion: "Objects of this kind [i.e., other thinking beings] are, therefore, nothing more than the transference of this consciousness of mine to other things, which in this way alone can be represented as thinking beings" (A 347).

Kant's dismissive treatment of the problem only raised more questions than it answered. He left it unclear what justified the analogical inference to other minds like my own. It simply begged the question against the solipsist to claim that *we had to assume* that beings who acted and spoke like ourselves had minds like ourselves; for he would insist that we could equally well assume that they are mere robots. This was indeed the very possibility that Descartes had raised in the First Meditation. But even if we had to assume that they were like ourselves—even if we had no other way of representing them to ourselves—this still left the question what justified such a rule or habit of thought in the first place. And here Kant was very short on answers. He seemed to be willing to regard other minds as little more than "the transference (*Übertragung*) of this consciousness of mine to other things" (A 347). But to say that the attribution of consciousness to others was simply a projection from my own consciousness was virtually to abandon the case to the solipsist.

Kant's suggested argument for other minds also raised serious questions of consistency. It began from the assumption that I can at least prove my own existence, and then transfer the conditions under which I think my existence to others. But, as the context makes clear, the basis of this assumption is the 'I think,' the principle of the unity of apperception, which is only an *apparently* empirical proposition. This principle is in truth a transcendental proposition about the formal conditions of experience, which states only that it must be possible for me to be self-conscious of my own representations.[5] In the Paralogisms, however, Kant argued repeatedly against any attempt to derive existential propositions from transcendental ones. More specifically, he contended that I have no right to infer my existence as a permanent, self-identical substance from the principle of the unity of apperception, which is a merely formal condition of the possibility of experience. In the second edition of the Deduction he does state that the 'I think' expresses my spontaneity as a thinking subject, so that it shows at least *that* I exist if not *how* I exist (B 157–158n). But even in this case it at best shows that I exist *at the moment* I utter it, and nothing more. What I cannot demonstrate in my own case, however, I *a fortiori* cannot do in the case of others. If I cannot know from my own case that I am a thinking thing, I am deprived of the basis for any analogical inference that others are such things.

Kant's neglect of the issue of other minds had serious consequences for the critical philosophy as a whole, because it brought into question the intersubjective status of the formal conditions of experience. There was now room for a skeptical challenge to the thesis of the Transcendental Deduction itself. Assuming that the formal structure of experience—the twelve categories and the forms of space and time—is valid for all human beings, the problem remains how I know that there are other human beings. How do I know that I am *not* the only human being? There are other beings who act and talk like myself, to be sure, but for all that I know they might not have a human sensibility and understanding. They might simply be robots, or they might be creatures having a body similar to my own but a sensibility so different that they perceive four-dimensional objects and time in two directions. Kant often posed the question 'What if *our* experience were completely chaotic?,' where it is assumed that there are many *human beings* that could suffer such an experience; but we must also raise the question: 'What if the experiences of creatures *apparently like myself* were radically different from my own?' This additional question raises doubts about the claim to intersubjective validity of the categories and forms of sensibility; for it seems as if they could be valid, as far as I know, *only in my own case.* We could still accept the argument that they are valid for all human beings, for all beings with a sensibility and understanding like my own; but we still would need to know that there are other human beings having a sensibility and understanding like mine; otherwise, I would not know whether they are valid for anyone else except myself.

We can formulate the general issue as follows. If intersubjectivity means *everyone* sharing the same structure for experiencing and explaining the world, then it involves at least two elements. First, that every self-conscious or human being has a conceptual structure like my own, which, at least on the Kantian analysis, consists of the twelve categories and the forms of intuition, space and time. Second, that the other creatures who inhabit my world are really self-conscious or human beings like myself. The weakness of the Transcendental Deduction is that it has established at best the first but not the second element of intersubjectivity. We can see Fichte's efforts to demonstrate the reality of other minds as an attempt to fill in this gap in Kant's argument.[6]

2. First Reflections

Fichte's concern with the problem of other minds goes back to his 1794 lecture series *Die Bestimmung des Gelehrten.*[7] There he posed the problem in the context of discussing the foundation of natural right. Such a foundation, he explained, had to answer two questions, which had been rightly raised by the skeptic, but which had been too often ignored by philosophers. First, with what right does someone call a specific portion of the physical world *his* body? It seems odd that we do this because the mind and body have opposing characteristics. Second, with what right does someone assume the existence of other rational beings outside himself? We ascribe rights and duties to others on the assumption that they are rational beings like ourselves. But how do we justify this assumption, given that we have no evidence from our own self-consciousness or outer experience that such beings exist? Both these questions demand an answer, Fichte insisted, if natural right is to be based on a solid foundation.

In this popular work, which was intended for a general audience, Fichte did not develop a systematic answer to either of these questions. Here his main concern was not with the foundation of natural law so much as with the consequences of some of its principles. Nevertheless, though he provided little argument for them, he did sketch some of his main ideas on the topic of other minds. These are important because they lay much of the foundation for his later position.

Most significant, Fichte is emphatic and explicit in his opposition to empiricism. We cannot prove the existence of other minds through experience, he argues, because a skeptic will claim that all the evidence of our senses provides us only with a *representation* of other beings like ourselves, and that does not prove that the representation corresponds with some mind outside it (VI, 303).[8] Furthermore, what is essential to our subjectivity is our freedom, our spontaneous activity, which cannot ever be an object of experience (305). This rejection of empiricism has broader implications, because Fichte, no less than Kant, held that the limits of theoretical reason are also those of experience. This means that there cannot be a *theoretical* solution to the problem of other minds; in other words, we cannot prove the existence of other minds, or know of it on the basis of sufficient evidence. Fichte himself drew just this conclusion when he indicated that the solution to the problem had to be based on *practical* principles (304). Although he does not explain what these principles are, nor indeed how they are practical rather than theoretical, his general philosophical position demands that we interpret them along Kantian lines. In that case, these principles should have a *regulative* rather than *constitutive* validity, that is, although they cannot provide us with knowledge that other minds exist, they lay down moral imperatives that we ought to act *as if* they exist.

It is also of significance that Fichte attempts to develop a criterion for the knowledge of other minds. The essential distinguishing feature of subjectivity, Fichte holds, is rationality. So if some other mind exists, it will have to be a rational being like myself. The question is then how to determine whether another being is rational. It is not sufficient to show that such a being acts according to concepts or purposes, he argues, because some forms of purposive activity are not necessarily rational. Some organisms act according to purposes, though they are not necessarily rational beings (304–305). The distinguishing feature of rationality is not only action according to ends, Fichte claims, but action according to ends determined by freedom. Such free actions will not be explicable according to natural laws alone.

The problem has now been pushed back another step. To determine whether another mind exists we need to demonstrate that its action occurs according to freedom rather than mere necessity (305). But how can we know this? This is a difficult question, Fichte admits, because I cannot have the immediate awareness of freedom outside myself, nor indeed even inside myself; as the final basis for the explanation of consciousness, freedom does not appear within consciousness itself. However, I can be aware of my freedom in a negative sense, Fichte thinks, when I am not aware of any other cause for my acting than my will. Now if I know that the law governing my free actions is the only way to explain the actions of some other being like myself in the sensible world, then I will also have reason to believe that this being is free, and so a rational agent like myself (305). Unfortunately, Fichte does not further explain here what these laws are, and indeed how we show that they would apply to someone else as the unique way of explaining their actions. We shall soon see that these laws are nothing other than the principles of natural right.

In the *Vorlesungen* Fichte also states the central conception of human nature that underlies his later argument for intersubjectivity. He is perfectly explicit that man is a social being who exists only among others, and that he contradicts his nature if he lives apart from them. "The human being is determined to live in society; he ought to live in society; he is not a complete human being and contradicts himself if he lives in isolation" (306). We only realize our nature as rational beings, Fichte argues, when we live in reciprocal interaction with others according to freedom, granting others the same rights as we would have them bestow on us. This was not a Hobbesian conception of humanity, nor even a Kantian one. Rather, Fichte drew his inspiration from Rousseau, whom he also did not hesitate to correct. Rousseau said that *some* who regard themselves as masters are really slaves themselves; but he should have really gone further and said that *all* who want to dominate others are really slaves (309). Only he is free, Fichte stated categorically, who wants to make everyone free around him. It was this Rousseauian intuition, appropriately generalized, that Fichte would now apply to the problem of other minds. Its ultimate implications were clear: that I could be a free and rational being only if I was willing to recognize a similar stature on the part of others.

3. The Argument for Intersubjectivity

Fichte's systematic and mature position on the problem of other minds is developed in the first main section of his later 1796 work *Grundlage des Naturrechts*.[9] For its clarity of exposition, rigor of argument, and boldness of conception, this text remains one of Fichte's best. Though it has been little studied outside the context of political philosophy, it is indeed one of the central works of German idealism. Nowhere else in the modern tradition is the problem of other minds made so central, and nowhere else is the case for an intersubjective normative order made so well. The text is of considerable historical significance because it marks a clear break with the privacy of the subjectivist tradition. On point after point Fichte's argument anticipates Hegel's later position in the famous 'Herrschaft und Knechtschaft' section of the *Phänomenologie des Geistes*.

In the introduction to his work Fichte returns to the original context of his discussion of the problem of other minds: the need to provide a foundation for natural right. To give a deduction of the concept of natural right, he argues, we must show it to be a necessary condition of self-consciousness. More specifically, we must demonstrate that it is a necessary condition of a rational being's self-consciousness as an individual, as one among other rational beings; in other words, we must show that its self-awareness as an individual depends on it recognizing the equal and independent reality of others outside itself (8). We know ourselves as rational individuals, and we ascribe an equal and independent reality to other rational individuals, Fichte further explains, only by virtue of the principles of natural right. These principles demand that I treat others as free agents like myself; if they respect my freedom by not interfering with my actions, then I have an obligation to respect their freedom by not interfering with their actions. But to recognize the freedom of another being is to accept its status as another rational being, as another mind equal to and independent of my own.

Fichte is eager not only to explain the conditions for knowledge of other minds, but also to demonstrate that these conditions hold. In other words, he intends to show that we are indeed justified in applying the principles of natural right to other beings. Accordingly, he then develops a detailed argument in sections 1–3 of the first section of the *Rechtslehre* to show that a finite rational being knows itself as a free agent only if it ascribes a similar rationality to other free agents outside itself. The argument culminates in Proposition §3: "The finite rational being cannot ascribe to itself a power of free action in the sensible world unless it also ascribes it to others, and consequently assumes the existence of other finite rational beings outside itself."

Fichte intends his argument to be first and foremost a refutation of 'egoism,' the doctrine that I am the only mind in existence. But he also casts it in an even stronger role by making it his refutation of empirical idealism, the view that everything exists only in my own mind. The argument has indeed such implications: if I have to ascribe equal and independent reality to the minds of others, then I can no longer assume that everything exists only in my own mind. Fichte generalizes his argument when he states that it proves "the reality of the world . . . is the condition of self-consciousness" because "we cannot posit ourselves without positing something outside ourselves to which we ascribe the same reality as ourselves" (III, 40). That which we posit outside ourselves turns out to be, in the course of his argument, some other rational agent (33–36).[10]

If we abstract from Fichte's technical jargon and the details of his dialectic, then the essence of his argument in sections 1–3 consists in these premises:

1. *For a rational being to posit itself as a rational being it must ascribe free activity to itself* (§1).

It is essential to the nature of a rational being, Fichte says, that it consists in self-reflective and self-determining activity (17). His rationale for this premise, though not fully stated here, is his argument in the *Vorlesungen* that freedom is the distinctive characteristic of a rational being (see 2.4.2).

2. *To posit my free activity, I must oppose it to my activity in the perception of the external world* (§1, II, III).

Fichte reasons that to be conscious of my *free* activity, I must abstract from my activity in the perception of an external world, for in the perception of that world my activity is bound and constrained. This is because the content of my perception—what I perceive—does not depend on my will and imagination. He then concludes that there must be a sharp distinction between subject and object, self and world. Because my free activity is constrained and limited by the perception of objects outside me, I *oppose* it to these objects. "The objects are objects simply insofar as they should not exist according to the free activity of the ego, and [insofar] as it must be constrained and limited insofar as they should exist" (19).

3. What limits and opposes my activity must be the source of a demand (Aufforderung) that I act freely.

This is the most surprising, and also the pivotal step in the argument. The object outside me and opposed to me turns out to be not *any* kind of object but *one* very specific kind: it is something that makes a demand or request on me that I act in a certain way. Of course, we cannot say at this stage of the argument that what makes such a demand or request is a rational or even living being; that is what is to be proved. But we do know that it is something that communicates with me in such a way as to make a demand on me. It is still left open whether this is a robot or not.

Why, though, must the object outside me make a demand on me? Fichte's brief explanation for this point is that what opposes or restricts my activity must have an effect or influence on it, and that this influence must be limited to a demand on me, because this alone leaves me free to act or not act; it is up to me, a free decision of my will, whether I act on the demand. If, however, the influence of the object were a form of physical causality, then it would compel me to act in one way rather than another, and so destroy the very freedom I am to know (34–35).

Fichte also arrives at this conclusion, however, by a more intricate and formal argument, which considers an apparent contradiction in the conditions for self-consciousness of our freedom.[11] He argues that if I am to be self-conscious of my freedom, then my freedom must be an object for me, since all consciousness requires an object; but it is absurd for my freedom to be an object for me, something I find outside myself and simply given to me, for my freedom is something that I create. Furthermore, if my freedom became an object for me, then it would be something conditioned and limited, like all objects, which destroys the nature of its spontaneous activity (32–33). On either count, it would seem impossible for me to be self-conscious of my freedom.

This contradiction arises, Fichte contends, if we assume that the object would be something definite and limited in my sense experience. But it disappears as soon as we assume that the object is not some determinate thing in my experience but a representation of my own free activity. This representation of my free activity must come to me in the form of a prescription rather than a description, an imperative instead of a concept, because to describe or conceive freedom is to destroy it, making it a definite and limited object in my experience (32–33). This imperative can be nothing other than the demand that I engage in free activity.

It is only later in his argument, after coming to his central conclusion, that Fichte identifies more concretely what the demand involves. It becomes clear that this demand is the claim someone has against me to respect their rights as they have respected mine (43). But it is also more generally any attempt to control and direct the actions of others: "The demand to free activity is that which one calls education" (39).

4. *What makes the demand on me must have a concept of me as something rational and free; otherwise, its demand that I act freely would be pointless* (36).

This step is troublesome. The demand that I do or refrain from certain actions would not be pointless if I were a robot that could be conditioned by the appropriate training. The step is unproblematic only if we read the demand more narrowly as a demand *for free activity,* which already involves the idea of a self-conscious rational agent.

5. *What assumes that the object of its activity is rational and free must be rational and free itself* (36).

Fichte argues that this is indeed the criterion to determine rational agency. We know that an action has a rational agent for its cause if we know that its reason or purpose is to bring about some *knowledge* on the object of the action (38). What attempts to bring about knowledge in others—in this case, the knowledge that I am free—must also be an intelligent agent itself.

From these premises, Fichte comes to his main conclusion: that to posit myself as a free and rational being I must posit the existence of another free and rational being; I must ascribe to someone else the same free activity that I ascribe to myself (39).

4. The Normative Structure of Intersubjectivity

Although his formal argument suffers from serious weaknesses, Fichte's later account of the intuition and general idea underlying it is more plausible and interesting. In sections 4–7 Fichte gives some account of this intuition and idea when he explains the specific conditions under which we assume the existence of other rational beings outside ourselves. He makes it clear that we do so because we are part of a general normative order established by natural right. This requires that I ascribe the same rights to others as I would have them ascribe to me; alternatively, it demands that I freely decide to limit my external freedom in a manner consistent with the external freedom of others.

Now it is because of this system of mutual rights and duties, Fichte explains, that we assume the existence of other minds outside ourselves. According to this system, the being outside me has limited its own freedom in respecting my rights, and it has made a similar claim against me to limit my freedom with regard to it. I assume that there is another rational being outside me, then, because it has the power to limit its actions by respecting my rights to free action, and because it makes a similar claim against me to respect its rights. I suppose that others have the same *inner* freedom—the power to make decisions—to respect my outer freedom as I have to respect theirs.

Fichte goes on to explain that even our concept of ourselves, our sense of self-identity, depends on the normative order of which we are part. We define ourselves in terms of the rights and duties we have with respect to others, and that others have with respect to us. Each individual has a certain sphere of action where he has a right to act without the interference of others. He determines this sphere by opposing it to a similar sphere of others. He then forms a concept of himself as a determinate individual through his possible actions within this sphere. As Fichte explains: "That which exclusively chooses within this sphere is *his* self (*Ich*); it is the individual, that determinate rational being formed through opposition to other rational beings; and his self is characterized through a determinate expression of freedom that exclusively belongs to him"(42).[12]

For all its interest and plausibility, Fichte's argument remains problematic. It is not clear that it escapes an obvious vicious circle: I must assume the existence of other minds only because of the principles of natural right; but I am justified to apply the principle of natural right only because I must assume the existence of other minds. Although Fichte is aware of this circle, he is still caught in it. He attempts to prove the existence of other minds before applying the principles of right; but his proof makes use of some of the fundamental concepts of these principles, which are already implicit in the concept of a "demand." He assumes that the other has a right to make this demand against me, and that I should recognize such a right; only its having such a right gives it the status of rationality and prevents it from being a robot. But, of course, that the other has such a right already presupposes that the principles of right apply.

This means that Fichte's argument has not met the challenge of the skeptic after all. The skeptic would happily admit that *if* I assume the concept of natural right, then I am indeed obliged to assume the existence of other beings outside myself; but he would then point out that I am not under any obligation to make such an assumption in the first place, because I still do not know whether the concept of natural right applies. I know that it should apply, he will argue, only if I also know that the beings within my experience are rational agents like myself; if they are only robots then I have no reason to treat them according to the principles of natural right.

The argument also suffers from serious ambiguity. Sometimes Fichte seems to aim for the strong conclusion that I really *know* that there is someone outside me who is a rational being like myself; but at other times he appears content with the weaker conclusion that I ought *to assume* that there is such a being. Fichte's insistence on the limits of theoretical reason limits him to the weaker conclusion; but his need to show that the principles of natural right apply to experience compels him to argue for the stronger one.

Fichte could establish his stronger conclusion only if he could somehow satisfy his criterion for rational action. But his criterion is too strict, setting impossible standards of proof. It states that a rational action is that which is explicable only under the assumption that the agent intends to bring forth some kind of knowledge (38). Apart from the question whether this is a sufficient test for rationality—it could be argued that even a robot could have such intentions—it is very difficult to establish with certainty that there is such an intention on the part of the agent, or that his action is explicable only by such an assumption. According to Fichte's own arguments, we cannot demonstrate the existence of such intentions from experience; and if all the empirical data are explicable according to the assumption that the action was produced by a robot, then we seem to have no reason at all to postulate an intention.

For all its problems, Fichte's attempt to solve the problem of other minds remains of interest and importance. Though the technical argument proves weak, it is also suggestive. That the intersubjective order is a normative one, that the radical privacy of the subjectivist tradition is incompatible with the self-consciousness of moral agency, that I become self-conscious only through having a sphere of rights and duties for my freedom—these were ideas at least worth later exploration. It was no wonder that Hegel soon followed in Fichte's footsteps.

PART III

Absolute Idealism

CHAPTER 1

Absolute Idealism:
General Introduction

1. The *Dramatis Personae*

From 1795 to 1801, a completely new form of idealism evolved in Germany, one unlike the critical idealism of Kant and Fichte, and even more unlike the "skeptical idealism" of Descartes and Hume or the "dogmatic idealism" of Leibniz and Berkeley. This idealism was deeply influenced by Kant and Fichte; but it also grew up in reaction against them. We do best to call this new form of idealism by the name occasionally used by some of its protagonists: 'absolute idealism.'[1] There were other cognate terms, such as 'objective idealism,' 'syncriticism,' 'transcendental idealism,' or, more often and simply, 'idealism.' Since, however, the term 'absolute idealism' is more customary, I will use it here.

There were three main groups of thinkers who advocated absolute idealism. One group consisted in leading figures from the "romantic circle" in Jena and Berlin: Friedrich Schlegel (1772–1829), Friedrich Wilhelm Joseph Schelling (1775–1854), and Friedrich von Hardenberg (1772–1801), who is best known by his pen name Novalis.[2] Another was the so-called *Bund der Geister* in Frankfurt and Homburg, a circle of friends comprising Friedrich Hölderlin (1774–1843), Georg Wilhelm Friedrich Hegel (1770–1831), Isaak von Sinclair (1775–1815), and Jakob Zwilling (1776–1809).[3] Yet a third group was the *Bund der freien Männer* in Jena, a fraternity modeled on Fichtean principles, whose members included August Ludwig Hülsen (1765–1810), Johann Erich von Berger (1772–1833), Johann Smidt (1773–1857), Johann Georg Rist (1775–1847), Johann Casimir Böhlendorff (1776–1825), and Johann Friedrich Herbart (1776–1841).[4] All these groups could be regarded as offshoots of early romanticism or *Frühromantik*,[5] and

349

for this reason I will sometimes refer to the absolute idealists as romantics, though this is to use the term 'romantic' in a broad sense.

These circles sometimes overlapped with one another. Schelling was a close friend of Hölderlin and Hegel, who were his classmates at the *Tübinger Stift;* Sinclair cavorted with the *freie Männer,* though they did not admit him into their ranks; Böhlendorff and Hölderlin were friends; and Hülsen was an associate of the romantic circle in Berlin. But these circles do not coincide, not only because their meetings, membership, and location differ, but also because their interests, ideals, and beliefs sometimes do. What all these groups have in common, however, is a shared intellectual heritage and *Weltanschauung.* Their origins can be traced back to the University of Jena around the time of Fichte's tenure there (1794–1799).[6] All of them reacted against Fichte's idealism for very similar reasons; and all of them shared a sympathy for Spinozism. Their *Weltanschauung* was a synthesis of Spinozism, Platonism, and vitalism.

With some justice, Schelling and Hegel are the best known among the absolute idealists. They gave absolute idealism its most elaborate and systematic formulation; and they edited a common journal to defend it, the *Kritisches Journal der Philosophie.* It is important to recognize, however, that they were not the progenitors but only the propagators of the doctrine. The essential ideas behind absolute idealism had already been formulated years earlier by Hölderlin, Novalis, Schlegel, Zwilling, and Hülsen. While Hegel has gone down in history as the grand representative of absolute idealism, his main achievement was to systematize ideas already formulated by his contemporaries. To be sure, Hegel broke with the romantic movement around 1804; but that break has little to do with the content of absolute idealism and much to do with how to justify or defend it.

It is extremely difficult to determine who, if anyone in particular, was the founder of absolute idealism. This title has often been claimed for Hölderlin.[7] It is possible to determine with reasonable accuracy that he developed the foundations of his position in the early spring of 1795.[8] But there is also evidence that his criticisms of Fichte's philosophy were a commonplace in Jena, and that Hülsen developed the rudiments of his views by 1794.[9] In any case, Zwilling, Novalis, and Schlegel formulated their positions very shortly after Hölderlin, and independently of him. It is necessary to stress that the essential ideas of absolute idealism were "in the air" in Jena after 1794. They were the subject of discussion among a whole generation of students, many of whose views are now lost to us. The general atmosphere was such that many could have developed similar views around the same time. Under these circumstances, then, it becomes difficult, indeed impossible, to sustain any claim to originality.[10]

2. The Meaning of Absolute Idealism

What did these thinkers mean by 'absolute idealism' or its cognates? We will address this question in detail in the following chapters; but it is important now to have at least some schematic idea, so that we know what is to be explained, and so that we can see the forest as well as the trees. Since there is no generally accepted meaning to the term, which is often associated with the most different, even opposing, doctrines, it is all the more imperative to provide some preliminary account of its meaning.

Unfortunately, none of the advocates of absolute idealism gave a precise definition or explicit explanation of the term, or indeed any of its cognates. This reflects partly their mistrust of definitions, partly their view that the meaning of a term rests on its precise place in a system, and partly their reliance on an historical context of meaning that is now lost to us. In the absence of a formal and final definition, the historian has no recourse but to reconstruct the meaning of the doctrine from various sources.

To recover the meaning of 'absolute idealism,' it is necessary to begin with its qualifying adjective, the term 'absolute.' True to name, absolute idealism was first and foremost a doctrine about the absolute, or, to use some synonyms, the unconditioned, the infinite, or the 'in-itself.' Like the term 'absolute idealism,' however, 'absolute' is rarely explicitly defined or explained. One of the very few definitions appears in a later work of Schelling, his 1804 *System der gesammten Philosophie.*[11] There Schelling says that the absolute is, according to its general idea, something which is "from itself and through itself" (*von sich selbst und durch sich selbst*).[12] In the same vein Schelling and Hegel sometimes refer to the absolute as "the in-itself" (*das An-sich*). These short phrases offer the best key to the meaning of the term. For they are obvious allusions to Spinoza's definition of substance in the *Ethica:* "By substance, I mean that which is in itself, and is conceived through itself: in other words, that of which a conception can be formed independently of any other conception."[13] Spinoza understood substance to be that which has an *independent* or *self-sufficient* existence and essence, or that whose being and nature does not depend on anything else. It was on the basis of this definition that he argued that substance must be infinite, equivalent to the universe as a whole, because anything less than the whole of all things must depend on something else outside itself. While the absolute idealists often disagreed with Spinoza's specific conception of the absolute, they understood the concept of the absolute in the same general sense as Spinoza. Their absolute was like Spinoza's substance because it was that which has a self-sufficient essence or existence. For the same reasons as Spinoza, they insisted that the absolute has to be nothing less than the universe as a whole.

It is this Spinozist context, then, that defines the general meaning of the term 'absolute' among the romantics. Though it has religious and mystical associations, the term usually meant nothing more than the universe as a whole. Hence its cognates were sometimes 'the universe' (*das Universum*), 'the one and all' (*Hen kai pan*) or, more simply, 'being' (*Seyn*).

Of course, the romantics had a much more specific conception of the absolute than simply the universe *simpliciter*. Their conception could be summarised in three theses. The first thesis is straightforward *monism:* that the universe consists in not a plurality of substances but a single substance; in other words, the only independent and self-sufficient thing is the universe itself. The second thesis is a version of *vitalism:* that the single universal substance is an organism, which is in a constant process of growth and development.[14] The third thesis is a form of *rationalism:* that this process of development has a purpose, or conforms to some form, archetype, or idea. Putting these theses together, absolute idealism is the doctrine that everything is a part of the single universal organism, or that everything conforms to, or is an appearance of, its purpose, design, or idea.

Clearly, these are distinct theses. It is possible to be a monist and not a vitalist: one might hold, with Spinoza, that the universe is static and eternal. Conversely, it is also possible to be a vitalist and not a monist: one might maintain, with Leibniz, that there are a plurality of substances that consist in living force. It is even possible to be a vitalist and monist but not a rationalist: one might claim, with Schopenhauer, that the universe consists in a single irrational will struggling for power. What is distinctive of absolute idealism is its *synthesis* of monism, vitalism, and rationalism: it is a monistic vitalism or a vitalistic monism; or it is a monistic rationalism or a rationalistic monism.

According to this interpretation, one distinctive trait of absolute idealism—what makes it a species of idealism in general—is its monism, its thesis that there is one and only one being that has an independent existence and essence. It is important to add that this monism opposes not only *pluralism,* the doctrine that there are many beings having an independent existence and essence, but also, more specifically, *dualism*, the doctrine that there are *two* kinds of substance, the mental and the physical, the ideal and the real. It is this latter point that Schelling, Novalis, Hegel, and Schlegel emphasize as central to their idealism. They explain that absolute idealism consists in the doctrine that the opposition between the real and the ideal, the mental and the physical, disappears in the absolute, which is a single reality.[15]

What, though, makes absolute idealism *idealism?* What is the genus of which monism and vitalism are only the species? The idealist dimension of absolute idealism comes from its rationalism. It should be obvious that this makes it idealism in a very different sense from the critical idealism of Kant and Fichte, or even the empirical idealism of Descartes and Berkeley. The ideal does not refer to the mental, subjective, or conscious, but to the rational, archetypical, or intelligible. To claim that everything is ideal in this sense does not mean that it is an appearance existing for some consciousness, but that it is a manifestation or embodiment of the rational, archetypical, or intelligible. In this latter sense the ideal can have manifestations in either the subjective or objective, in mind or matter, and it would be a mistake to limit it to either the mental or the physical. In absolute idealism a distinction is finally made between two senses of the ideal that had been constantly confused before Kant and by Kant: the distinction between the noumenal and archtypical on the one hand and the mental and spiritual on the other hand.

It is important to note two completely distinct reasons why some absolute idealists, especially Schelling and Hegel, call their doctrine "idealism." First, insofar as it holds that everything is a part of the absolute, which is identified with the idea or reason, absolute idealism maintains that everything is a manifestation or appearance of the idea or reason. Idealism in this sense is the doctrine that everything is ideal because it is a part, aspect, or appearance of the absolute idea. Hence Schelling sometimes identifies absolute idealism with "the doctrine of ideas" (*Ideenlehre*), and Hegel with the thesis that finite things do not exist in themselves but only in the "universal divine idea."[16] Second, it is sometimes held that all oppositions between finite things, and especially that between the ideal and the real or the subjective and objective, have not a *real* but only an *ideal* existence. To say that they have only an ideal existence in this sense does not mean that they are an appearance of the absolute idea, but that their appearance of an independent reality *outside* the absolute exists only for reflection, or only for the intellect as an artificial and arbitrary abstraction.[17] This sense of ideal is virtually opposed to the first because it attributes ideal status to that which is *outside* the absolute, whereas the first sense attributes ideal status to that which is *inside* it.[18]

Regarding the various uses of the term 'idealism' in this period, two caveats are necessary. First, sometimes the term is used to refer to one aspect or form of the absolute, whereas at other times it refers to the entire or whole standpoint of the absolute, of which this idealism is only a part. Second, sometimes Schlegel, Schelling, and Novalis use the term 'critical idealism' to describe their own doctrine of absolute idealism. This does not imply, however, any endorsement of the critical idealism of Kant and Fichte, though it does express their common goal with that idealism of providing a synthesis of idealism and realism.

Another word of caution should be added. While all the absolute idealists follow, more or less, the general theses ascribed to them here, this should not be taken to imply that they always agreed with one another, as if they formed a solid phalanx against their opponents. These general theses provide only the *genera,* not the *differentia specifica.* Each of these thinkers developed their own specific form of absolute idealism, so that, not surprisingly, there were sometimes quarrels between them. Schelling and Schlegel, Hölderlin and Schelling, Schelling and Hegel, Schlegel and Hegel—all differed with one another about one point or another. Still, while these differences are not to be overlooked, they should not obscure the fundamental points of agreement.

This very general account of the meaning of absolute idealism should be relatively uncontroversial. Many would agree that absolute idealism is a form of monism, rationalism, and vitalism. However, even if the definition is uncontroversial, its application is not. It is controversial to claim that such a definition applies to the early romantics, more specifically to Hölderlin, Novalis, and Schlegel. It might well be admitted that it fits easily enough the doctrine developed by Schelling and Hegel around 1801; but it will be protested that we should not read all early romantic philosophy in such terms. One reason for distinguishing between absolute idealism and early romanticism, it has been argued, is precisely that the early metaphysical doctrines of Novalis, Hölderlin, and Schlegel are not a form of rationalism.[19] Their epistemology has been characterized as a form of radical skepticism, and their metaphysics has been identified with the view that the absolute is pure being, a ground of consciousness transcending all consciousness.[20]

But such an interpretation of early romantic metaphysics is much too narrow, and it derives from focusing all one's attention on a few early manuscripts to the extent of their philosophy as a whole.[21] Most significantly, it completely underrates the Platonic heritage of Hölderlin, Novalis, and Schlegel, which becomes more explicit in their later years, though it was always present from the very beginning. This Platonic heritage means that—in one form or another—the absolute is identified with the *logos* or *telos*, the archetype, idea, or form that governs all things. The absolute is not transcendent being, which is somehow presupposed by reflection and consciousness, and so can never be its object. To be sure, Hölderlin, Novalis, and Schlegel were critical of the powers of a *discursive* reason; but, true to the Platonic tradition, they clung all the more firmly to the powers of an *intuitive* reason. Hence they all developed—in one form or another—a doctrine of intellectual intuition, which they identified with aesthetic feeling or perception.[22] Their mysticism or faith in an immediate form of knowledge should be placed within the Platonic tradition, which had always claimed that an insight into the forms transcends discursive elaboration.[23] It should not be seen in terms of the religious mysticism characteristic of the Protestant tradition. In the following chapters we will have occasion to consider the Platonic legacy of Hölderlin, Novalis, and Schlegel in more detail, which should leave no doubt about its importance for their metaphysical views.

3. Absolute versus Critical Idealism

It should be obvious by now that absolute idealism is in fundamental respects antithetical to the critical idealism of Kant and Fichte. There are two major differences between these species of idealism. The first is that absolute idealism involves a much greater degree of *naturalism* than critical idealism. It is not simply a form of *empirical* naturalism, which explains everything in the phenomenal world according to natural laws, but which leaves the noumenal realm untouched. Rather, it maintains that we can explain not only empirical consciousness, but transcendental self-consciousness according to its place within nature.[24] Even the Kantian 'I think' and the Fichtean 'I am' will now be understood as expressions of the absolute. Hence there is no self-sufficient noumenal realm that somehow transcends the phenomenal world of nature. Reason in its subjective form is simply the highest degree of organization and development of all the powers of nature, the manifestation of absolute reason.

The second major difference is that absolute idealism involves a much greater degree of *realism* than critical idealism. Its stronger realism derives from the very idea of the absolute, which is nothing less than the whole of nature. The single universal substance cannot be reduced down to the realm of subjectivity, not when all individual subjects are simply its modes, parts, or aspects. This is not merely because the whole is greater than *all* its parts, but also because all finite subjects amount to only *some* among the infinitude of its parts. Its parts include not only individual minds, but also material things, and indeed everything from the great chain of being, whether animal, vegetable, or mineral. Clearly, this is not merely the *empirical* realism of Kant and Fiche, which defines the independent existence of an object in terms of its conformity to universal and necessary forms of consciousness. However, it is important to see that it is also not *transcendental* realism in the Kantian sense. Absolute idealism does not hold that the absolute exists *fully* and *entirely* apart from and prior to all subjectivity, as if consciousness were simply irrelevant to its essence and existence.[25] For the absolute idealists insist that subjectivity is a *necessary* manifestation of the absolute, and indeed its *highest* manifestation, apart from which it cannot *fully* exist or *completely* realize its nature. Of course, it could exist in some *inchoate, indeterminate,* and *undeveloped* form apart from its subjective embodiment; but it exists in its *organized, determinate,* and *developed* form only in and through them.

To understand the relation of the absolute to subjectivity, it is important to keep in mind that the romantics regard the absolute first and foremost as an *organic* whole. Like any organism, the whole determines the identity of each of its parts, and each part also determines the identity of the whole. This means not only that each subject becomes determinate only from its place within the whole, but also that the identity of the whole becomes determinate only in and through each subject. Hence the absolute will realize its nature—it will become completely organized, determinate, and developed— only in and through finite consciousness. This holds for all parts of the absolute, of course, but it holds especially for finite minds, which occupy a privileged place within the hierarchy of nature. They are the *highest* degree of organization and development of all the living powers of nature, so that the absolute will come to its final realization and manifestation only through them.

It was because of this organic conception of the absolute that Novalis, Schelling, and Hegel rejected the whole dilemma that placed the absolute either inside or outside consciousness.[26] They argued that since the absolute is an organic whole it is both inside and outside consciousness: inside it, because the identity of the whole depends on each of its parts; and outside it, because the very identity of the part depends on the whole, which is not reducible to one of its parts alone. The usual way of viewing nature as something outside consciousness is simply a legacy of Cartesian dualism, which saw nature as a *res extensa* outside the *res cogitans*. Once we accept the organic paradigm of nature, however, this entire dualism proves to be illegitimate.[27]

Prima facie it might seem that the differences between critical and absolute idealism cannot be so great because the absolute is simply the Kantian–Fichtean transcendental ego stripped of its individual and empirical limitations. According to this interpretation, the absolute is simply the transcendental ego insofar as it is *universal,* not individuated one per person, and insofar as it is *pure* or *infinite,* unlimited by objects in the empirical world. Hence this interpretation sees the absolute of absolute idealism as essentially subjective, as one super-subject or gigantic ego.[28]

That this still-popular interpretation of absolute idealism cannot be sustained becomes evident as soon as we take into account the early romantic critique of Fichte. The young romantics argued against Fichte that it is impossible for the absolute to be anything subjective at all—even a cosmic or infinite ego—because something is subjective or objective only *within* the context of experience where one thing is opposed to another. The absolute, however, is not within experience because it is that which makes all experience possible. Insofar as we talk about an ego or subject at all—whether it is empirical or transcendental—we are still within the realm of experience, and so have not ascended to the first ground of being, which is neither subjective nor objective, neither ideal nor real.

The discrepancy between the romantics' absolute idealism and this radicalized version of Kant's and Fichte's subjective idealism becomes all the more apparent when we consider the early romantic stance on the role of self-consciousness in philosophy. The young romantics broke with Kant and Fichte, and indeed the whole subjectivist tradition, because they no longer regarded self-consciousness as the self-evident starting point of philosophy. The Kantian 'I think' and the Fichtean 'I am' were to be first principles because they made the 'I' the condition of all thinking, which had no higher thought as its condition. Hölderlin and Novalis, and then Sinclair and Schelling after them, dispute just this point, however, for they contend that the very possibility of self-consciousness requires a higher ground that transcends it.[29] Their arguments proceed by way of an immanent critique of Fichte. Like Fichte, they point out that self-consciousness requires the pure identity of subject and object; but they then argue that this identity cannot, on pain of circularity, be given within self-consciousness itself. Furthermore, they maintain, again on impeccable Fichtean grounds, that all consciousness, even self-consciousness, requires some distinction between the subject and object; but if this is so, then subject–object identity will transcend the sphere of consciousness entirely. Because subject–object identity transcends self-consciousness, it cannot be regarded as something subjective; hence the romantics identify it with being, substance, or the absolute. This was in effect to reverse the entire subjectivist tradition: the starting point of philosophy, its highest first principle, is no longer the subject but the universe itself. The romantics follow their mentor Spinoza, who held that philosophy must follow the order of the universe itself, beginning from "that idea that represents the origin and source of the whole of nature."[30]

The romantic break with the Kantian–Fichtean starting point becomes even clearer when we consider their conception of the self's place within nature. Because the identity of the self depends on its place within nature, it ceases to be self-sufficient and perfectly transparent to itself. The identity of the self depends on the whole of nature, which it can know but imperfectly. Deep within myself there lie the mysterious energies and powers of nature itself, which I cannot entirely know or control. Hence the self cannot know itself by abstracting from everything outside itself and then by reflecting on itself, as Fichte advises, because it then separates itself from the very whole on which its identity depends. Of course, this does not imply that the self cannot know many things about itself with certainty, for example, that it is suffering pain right now; but it does imply, *pace* Kant and Fichte, that the self cannot be the spontaneous or original ground of all its own activity. The romantic conception of the self's place within nature deprived the Kantian–Fichtean subject of its alleged autonomy, spontaneity, and self-sufficiency. It was no longer the 'I' that was the source of all its thinking but the universe itself that thought through the 'I.' The thinking and acting of the subject now becomes—unbeknownst to the subject itself—the medium and instrument of the absolute itself. The subject's consciousness is not therefore simply *its* consciousness but also the absolute's consciousness through it. Perfectly explicitly, Schelling drew just this conclusion: "That I say: I know or I am the knowing is already the *proton pseudos*. I know nothing, or my knowledge, insofar as it is really mine, is no true knowledge. It is not that I know but that the universe knows through me" (VI, 140).

The distance of absolute idealism from a radicalized form of subjective idealism is most obvious when the romantics state that their fundamental goal is to provide a *synthesis* of Fichte and Spinoza.[31] This ideal is explicitly expressed by Hölderlin, Novalis, and Schlegel, and it is later endorsed by Schelling and Hegel. All admit that Fichte's idealism is an important part of the truth; yet it is only a part. They insist that the other side of the truth appears in Spinoza, who was of course Fichte's great antipode. The challenge was how to square the circle: how to unite Fichte's idealism with Spinoza's naturalism and realism. That synthesis would usually take the form of seeing the Kantian–Fichtean subject as the culminating point, the purpose of all of nature; yet its starting point, and its ontological foundation, was nothing less than nature itself.

4. The Break with Critical Idealism

Why, more precisely, did the young romantics break with Kant's and Fichte's critical idealism? Here again the specter of nihilism played its fateful role. The very problem that pushed Kant beyond the empirical idealism of Berkeley and Leibniz—and that forced Fichte beyond the critical idealism of Kant—moved the romantics beyond the ethical idealism of Fichte. They reacted against Fichte's idealism chiefly because, contrary to its express purpose, it had not explained the reality of the external world. Rather than giving independent reality to nature, Fichte had made it either a product of our activity or an unknowable thing-in-itself.

This reaction to Fichte's subjectivism appears in several forms in the writings of the young romantics. Its most obvious and visible form emerges in Schelling's and Hegel's criticisms of Fichte's circle of consciousness. For the young Schelling and Hegel, nothing better revealed the limitations of Fichte's idealism than the circle that ends the 1794 *Wissenschaftslehre*.[32] There, it will be recalled, Fichte had condemned the ego to an infinite striving against a forever resistant non-ego (see 2.6.4). To the degree that the ego had dominated the non-ego, it had made the non-ego a mere noumenon; but to the degree that the non-ego resisted its activity, the non-ego remained an unknowable thing-in-itself. There was no middle path, however, where the ego could know a nature independent of itself.

Another form of the reaction against Fichtean subjectivism emerges in Hölderlin's, Schelling's, and Hegel's criticism of Fichte's interpretation of the principle of subject–object identity. They attack Fichte's interpretation not least because they think that it has solipsistic consequences. Fichte confines this principle to the realm of subjectivity because he construes subject–

object identity in terms of the ego's self-consciousness or intellectual intuition. But if subject–object identity is also the first principle or paradigm of *all* knowledge, as Fichte also insists, it then follows that the subject knows nothing but itself. All its knowledge will be of nothing more than its own activity and its products. The principle of subject–object identity will then be useless in explaining how we have knowledge of an *external* object in ordinary experience. Rather than explaining such knowledge, the principle of subject–object identity *contradicts* the opposition between subject and object in everyday consciousness. The only escape from this solipsistic impasse, Schelling and Hegel argue, is to *objectify* the principle of subject–object identity, so that it refers to the single universal substance that appears equally within the subject and object of ordinary experience.

Yet another form of the reaction against Fichte's subjectivism appears in Hölderlin's and Hegel's complaint that Fichte has reduced the realm of nature down to a mere instrument and medium of moral action.[33] Rather than treating nature as an end in itself, as something worthy of religious and aesthetic contemplation, Fichte subordinates it to the striving of the ego, so that all its value derives from the ends *imposed* on it. Nature is to be dominated, manipulated, and controlled in the interest of morality, whose purposes are alien to nature itself. "My world is the object and sphere of my moral duties and absolutely nothing else" (II, 261). For the romantics, that statement from Fichte's *Bestimmung des Menschen* epitomizes the crude utilitarian view of nature; their aesthetic and religious view of nature is its direct antithesis. The romantics insist that nature is not a mere means to our moral ends; rather, it should be appreciated as an end in itself, an object of aesthetic contemplation. Since the identity of the self depends on its place within the universe, nature is not the enemy of the self but its complement.

Prima facie such opposing attitudes toward nature do not seem to have any connection with the ontological question of its independent reality: after all, nature might exist independent of me even though I want to conquer it. Yet there was a deeper metaphysical view underlying this critique of Fichte. The romantics' insistence that we should treat nature as an end in itself derived from their claim that purposiveness, rationality, and value are intrinsic to nature itself and not simply the product of what our activity imposes on it.

The romantics' disapproval of Fichte's attitude toward nature also reveals their underlying disagreement with his fundamental principle for the deduction of the reality of the external world: the primacy of practical reason. They believed that this principle is entirely inadequate to support the belief in the reality of the external world. They rejected this principle not only because of its moral consequences—the subjugation and destruction of nature—but also because of its underlying logic. The essence of Fichte's deduction, it will be recalled (see 2.6.3–2.6.4), is that the external world must exist because all moral activity requires some obstacle to stimulate and restrain it. But this is to reason from our moral needs to the existence of the conditions for their fulfillment. For the romantics, such an inference is patently invalid: just because something ought to be the case does not mean that it is the case; just because we have a legitimate demand does not mean that we can fulfill it. As the young Schelling put the point: "A need, however pressing it may be, cannot make the impossible possible."[34] The romantics had indeed rejected all acts of faith—whether that was Jacobi's *salto mortale*, Kant's moral faith, or Fichte's belief in freedom—on the grounds that the mere need to believe in something, no matter how moral, cannot justify its truth.[35] To the young romantics, such a doctrine is vulnerable to skepticism, and it violates the fundamental demand of reason itself: that we give sufficient evidence for all our beliefs. They believed it was necessary, then, to provide some *theoretical* justification for our belief in reality. Yet such a justification had to be careful not to lapse back into the old syllogisms and abstract reasoning of the Leibnizian–Wolffian school, whose arguments had been so mercilessly devastated by Kant. We shall soon see how they rose to this challenge (3.1.6–3.1.7).

5. Intellectual Sources

To have a more concrete idea of absolute idealism it is necessary to consider its main sources, the chief influences on it. There were three such sources: Spinozism, Platonism, and vital materialism. All these doctrines enjoyed a remarkable renaissance in late-eighteenth-century Germany, the gestation period of absolute idealism. What is characteristic of absolute idealism is its synthesis of all these strands of thought.

Spinozism

One of the strongest influences on absolute idealism—an influence to vie with that of Kant and Fichte—was the remarkable rise of Spinozism in the late 1780s. The revival of Spinoza began in 1786 with the publication of F. H. Jacobi's *Briefe über die Lehre von Spinoza*, which grew out of Jacobi's dispute with Mendelssohn about Lessing's alleged Spinozism. To a stunned world, Jacobi revealed the content of his private conversations with Lessing in the summer of 1780. According to Jacobi, Lessing had told him that the orthodox concepts of the divinity were no longer of any value, and that he could believe in only the God of Spinoza. "Εν χχαι Παν! [one and all] I know nothing else," Lessing said.[36] In making this revelation, Jacobi's motives were much more than biographical; he was making a very provocative philosophical point. Since he held that Spinozism is the only tenable system of philosophy, and that it is tantamount to atheism and fatalism, he was in effect warning his contemporaries of the dangerous consequences of *all* philosophy or enlightened rationalism. Lessing was the perfect figure to make this point since he had a reputation for being the most daring and radical, the most honest and scrupulous, thinker of the *Aufklärung*. If Lessing were honest enough to admit his Spinozism, Jacobi insinuated, then every other *Aufklärer* should have the integrity to do the same. Jacobi then threw down a gauntlet to the German public: they had to choose between a rational atheism and fatalism or take a leap of faith in freedom and a personal God.

Jacobi's *Briefe* was a sensation. It shocked the orthodox, and it provoked the *Aufklärer*. But, worst of all, it backfired. It was avidly read by the young, who were inspired by it. Rather than heeding Jacobi's warnings about Lessing's secret religion, the new generation was drawn to it. Here was a tempting *credo*, all the more alluring just because it was forbidden and unorthodox. The young romantics lined up in solidarity with Lessing, whose *En kai pan* soon became their slogan.[37] Although they were not doctrinaire Spinozists themselves, they were very sympathetic to some of the main strands of Spinoza's thought.

Why were the young so sympathetic to Spinoza? There were several reasons, all of them complex, which we can only roughly summarize here.

First, Spinoza's vision of the universe was both religious *and* scientific, combining an account of the infinite with a complete naturalism. This seemed to provide a solution to that persistent and notorious conflict between science and religion, reason and faith, that Jacobi had so dramatized in his *Briefe*. There was no need to make Jacobi's *salto mortale*—his leap of faith in a personal God—to save oneself from Spinoza, for he was a man who saw God in all things. He was indeed "*ein Gott betrunkener Mensch,*" as Novalis called him. His creed was pantheism rather than atheism. To brand him an atheist was simply to confuse the *natura naturans*, the immanent and infinite creative force of nature, with the *natura naturata*, the sum total of all finite things. For a generation who held that the old orthodox concepts of the divine were nothing but mythology, but who also shuddered at a purely mechanical materialism, Spinoza seemed to provide the answers. Spinozism seemed to be nothing less than the religion of science, the science of religion.

Second, Spinoza's critique of the Bible, his defense of democracy, and his separation of church and state seemed to provide the realization of such classical Protestant ideals as the priesthood of all believers and the liberty of the Christian. Spinoza seemed to liberate the Protestant spirit from its two self-imposed shackles: adherence to the letter of the Bible and allegiance to the state. This was the reason for Spinoza's appeal to those sympathetic to the Radical Reformation, thinkers such as Gottfried Arnold (1666–1714), Johann Christian Edelmann (1698–1767), Johann Gottfried Herder (1774–1801), and, of course, Lessing himself. But Spinoza continued to have the same attraction to the younger generation, who wanted to throw off the yoke of Protestant orthodoxy without abandoning its classical ideals.

Third, Spinoza's monism seemed to provide a solution to the dualisms that had plagued philosophy since Descartes, and continued to do so after Kant, who, it seemed, had overcome Descartes' mental–physical dualism only to reestablish some dualisms all his own. The sharp distinctions between noumena and phenomena, understanding and sensibility, were just as bad as that between Descartes' mind and body. Spinoza's doctrine that the mental and the physical are simply two different attributes of one and the same thing seemed to provide a path out of the dualistic impasse. It applies *mutatis mutandi* to the Kantian dualisms, so that the noumenal and phenomenal, or the intellectual and the empirical, can also be attributes of a single thing. Hence Spinoza's doctrine was the chief source of the monism of absolute idealism.

For all their sympathy with Spinozism, his young admirers were anything but strict followers of his doctrine. Without fully admitting or recognizing it, they departed from Spinoza in two basic respects. First, they did not accept Spinoza's rationalism, his strict geometrical method that begins with axioms and definitions and derives every proposition as a theorem.[38] This method smacked too much of the old scholasticism of Wolff, which had been discredited by Kant. What they did find in Spinoza, however, was just the opposite of rationalism: his mystical love of God, the *amor intellectus dei*, with which he ends the *Ethica*. Second, they were not advocates of Spinoza's strictly mechanistic conception of the laws of nature, which they saw as simply the product of his allegiance to the sciences of his day. Contrary to Spinoza's banishment of final causes, they would attempt to introduce a form of telology into the natural order.

Platonism

A second source of the worldview of absolute idealism was Platonism. Such was the growth of Platonism in the late 1790s and early 1800s in Germany that it is fair to speak of a Platonic renaissance. It is in any case difficult to exaggerate the influence of Plato's writings on the generation of the 1790s. Hölderlin, Hegel, Novalis, Sinclair, Schelling, and Schlegel all began their philosophical education by reading Plato, especially the *Phaedo* and *Symposium*, in the original Greek. Hölderlin, Schlegel, and Novalis were inspired in particular by the writings of the Dutch Platonist Franz Hemsterhuis, whose writings first appeared in Germany in the 1780s.[39] Many Platonic themes in Hemsterhuis—desire as longing to return to the eternal, the unity of truth and beauty, the role of poetry as a medium of knowledge, the fundamental role of love as a power of the soul—reappear in the writings of the young romantics in the late 1790s.[40]

Platonism plays a central role in the worldview of absolute idealism.[41] Its rationalism derives as much from Plato as its monism from Spinoza. The *En kai pan* was often described in Platonic terms, whether as an "hypostasis," "archetype," or "the form of all forms." The unity of universal and particular in the Platonic form provided the perfect model for the unity of the one and many in the absolute itself. The doctrine of intellectual intuition, which became so important for Schelling, Novalis, Schlegel, and Hölderlin, also has Platonic sources, whether they lie in the ectasy of the poet in *Phaedo* or the intellectual perception of the guardian in the *Republic*. The point is important if only because the mysticism of the early romantic idealists has so often been described as "antirationalist."[42] This is to assume, however, that their mysticism arises from the Protestant tradition, which limited the realm of reason to the earthly sphere; but the mysticism of the idealists does not go *beyond* the realm of reason but *into* it, aspiring toward insight into the archetypical world.[43]

The Platonic renaissance of the 1790s was the climax of decades of interest in the classical texts; but it was in sharp contrast to the earlier eighteenth century.[44] At the dawn of the century Plato was almost as good as forgotten, having been eclipsed by the Aristotelian scholasticism in German universities. Because of theological controversies, Germany had turned further away from the Platonic currents of the Renaissance than either France or England. In France Descartes and Malebranche kept the spirit of Plato alive, while in England there were the Platonists of the Cambridge school. Germany had no equivalent. It had its great Platonist in Leibniz; but his Platonism was one of the more esoteric aspects of his teaching, and so it remained largely without influence. The neglect of Plato in the early eighteenth century is evident from the fact that the last major edition of Plato's writings had appeared in 1602.

Interest in Plato began to appear only in midcentury, largely due to the growth of classical philology, a formidable weapon in theological controversy. In the 1750s the classicists J. A. Ernesti and David Ruhnken did much to revive classical philology by insisting on reading Greek sources in the original. Admirers of Plato, both Ernsti and Ruhnken delivered influential academic orations on his philosophy. It was also in 1757 that Winckelmann read Plato, who became one of the central influences on his aesthetics. By the 1760s interest in Plato had grown enormously. The writings of Rousseau and Shaftesbury, which were filled with Platonic themes, began to have their impact. It was also in the 1760s that Hamann, Herder, Winckelmann, Wieland, and Mendelssohn all wrote about Plato or Platonic themes. By the 1770s Plato had become a popular author. New editions and translations of his writings frequently appeared. By the 1780s the Plato renaissance had truly begun. In Halle, F. A. Wolf began a more rigorous philological study of Plato, publishing several editions of some of his writings. From 1781–1787 the Zweibrücker edition of Plato's writings appeared, making Plato more accessible than ever before.

Vital Materialism

Another crucial source of the worldview of absolute idealism was the rise of vital materialism around the close of the eighteenth century. Among the chief exponents of this doctrine in France were the *philosophes* Diderot, La Mettrie, and Maupertuis; and among its main spokesmen in England were the freethinkers John Toland, Matthew Tindal, and Anthony Collins. According to vital materialism, the essence of matter does not consist in extension, as in Cartesian physics, but in motion. The modern grandfather of this doctrine was no less than Leibniz, who had developed a dynamic view of matter against the mechanism of Cartesian physics. According to Leibniz, the essence of matter consists in living force (*vis viva*), which is not only a tendency toward motion but also the development or realization of the essence of a thing. Self-consciously going back to the Aristotelian tradition, Leibniz designated this concept with the old scholastic term *entelechy*, which refers to the form inherent in matter, or what has its purpose within itself.[45]

This concept of matter never disappeared, despite the increasing mechanization of science in the late seventeenth and eighteenth centuries. It was not only defended by members of the Leibnizian–Wolffian school in Germany, but it was also adopted by radical republican and masonic circles, who were eager to undermine the alliance of throne and alter.[46] They were attracted by this view because if matter has the power to move and organize itself, there is no need for a supernatural creator and designer of the physical cosmos, so that revealed religion, the main pillar of that alliance, crumbles. The spread of masonic ideas in Germany in the late eighteenth century would only have made this view more popular. Its radical political implications made it attractive to some of the younger generation, who were no less intent on undermining the alliance of throne and alter.

The vitalist conception of matter only gained in prestige with the new developments in natural science in the late eighteenth century. The new experiments with electricity, magnetism, and chemistry seemed to give evidence for a more dynamic view of matter, according to which matter consists in attractive and repulsive forces. Because they seem to involve action at a distance, these forces had always been difficult to explain according to mechanism, which accounts for motion by the impact of one body on another. Mechanism could explain attraction and repulsion only by postulating ethers or subtle matters through which the forces worked; but ether theory had been subject to constant experimental criticism in the late eighteenth century.[47] While the physical sciences were becoming less mechanistic, the life sciences were becoming more materialistic. Lavoisier's chemistry suggested that the very stuff of life was oxygen, while Galvani's experiments with "animal electricity" seemed to show that vital forces operated according to the same laws as matter. These complementary developments appeared to demonstrate that there was no clear dividing line between the mental and physical because the same kinds of forces were active in both the organic and inorganic worlds.

The vitalist conception of matter had some powerful spokesman in late-eighteenth-century Germany. One of its earliest protagonists was C. F. Kielmeyer (1765–1844), who, in a celebrated speech given in 1793,[48] put forward a view of nature as a single organic whole, a hierarchical continuum from the inorganic to the organic. Another important figure behind the new dynamic view of matter was Kant himself, whose *Metaphysische Anfangsgründe der Naturwissenschaften* analyzed matter in terms of its constitutive forces. Although Kant stoutly resisted the move toward vitalism, drawing a sharp line between merely active and living forces, his work helped to bury mechanism and inspired many vital materialists. The most powerful and influential voice behind the new vitalism in Germany was Herder. His 1778 *Vom Erkennen und Empfinden der menschlichen Seele* argued that the the mental and physical are simply different degrees of organization and development of organic force; and his *Gott, Einige Gespräche* (1786) took his vitalism one giant leap forward by applying it to Spinoza's substance, which was no longer a static thing but a living power, "the force of all forces."

Herder's synthesis of vitalism and monism in *Gott* set an important precedent for the romantic generation. Such a synthesis is a defining characteristic of absolute idealism, which is indeed a vitalistic monism or monistic vitalism. Whether self-consciously or not, the younger generation followed Herder in *vitalizing* Spinoza's concept of substance, which now becomes nothing less than the single cosmic living force. To be sure, Spinoza himself said that the essence of substance consists in power; but his conception of power was by no means organic, for his substance underwent no development and it excluded all final causes.[49] With the young romantics, however, Spinoza's *natura naturans* ceases to be dead and static but becomes alive and dynamic. Like all organic things, it undergoes a distinctive pattern of development: it begins from a stage of inchoate unity; it then differentiates itself; and it then reintegrates itself, so that its development consists in the stages of unity, difference, and unity-in-difference. Although Hegel is the thinker best known for this idea of "dialectical development," the idea was formulated by Hölderlin, Novalis, Schlegel, and Schelling long before him.

This vitalist concept of nature had profound epistemological implications, which the absolute idealists did not hesitate to explore and exploit. One important implication is that it provided a completely new paradigm for understanding the relationship between the mental and the physical. They are no longer distinct kinds of substances, which stand in some mysterious causal connection with one another; rather, they are only different degrees of organization and development of a single living force. The mental is only the highest degree of organization and development of the living forces of the body, whereas the body is simply the lower degree of organization and development of the living forces of the mind. As Schelling metaphorically summarized this view in his first work on *Naturphilosophie:* "Nature should be visible spirit, spirit should be invisible nature."[50] The young idealists then reinterpreted Spinoza's dual-attribute doctrine in such vitalist terms. Unlike Spinoza, the mental and the physical are no longer simply different perspectives, or different forms of explanation, of a single substance, which themselves cannot interact with one another. Rather, the mental and the physical refer to only different appearances, manifestations, or embodiments of a single living force. Another important implication of vitalism is that the mental and the physical are no longer in a purely *causal* relation with one another, where the cause retains its identity after acting; instead, they are in an *expressive* relation where one becomes what it is, or develops its determinate character only through the other. The mental is not simply the effect of the physical, then, but its realization or development; conversely, the physical is not merely the effect of the mental, but its embodiment or organization.

6. The Rehabilitation of Metaphysics

Spinoza's monism, Herder's vitalism, and Plato's ideas are the basic components of absolute idealism. But it does not seem possible to imagine a more heady metaphysical mixture. Absolute idealism appears to be "metaphysical" in the very sense condemned by Kant and Fichte: it involves speculation about the unconditioned, about entities that cannot be given in any possible experience, whether that is Plato's ideas, Spinoza's substance, or Herder's vital forces. So absolute idealism appears to be "transcendent," going beyond the limits of possible experience, the borderline separating knowledge from fantasy and mysticism. It was indeed on just these grounds that Kant rejected Herder's vitalism as "metaphysics," that Erhard, Schmid, and Niethammer criticized Fichte's "Transcendentism," and that Fichte dismissed Schlegel's talk of the absolute as "mysticism." All this raises some difficult questions: How did the absolute idealists defend their worldview against Kant's critique of metaphysics? How did they attempt to justify the greater realism and naturalism involved in their absolute idealism?

The absolute idealists were well aware of Kant's challenge, and they were eager to meet it on his terms. No new metaphysics could come forward as a science alone until it had withstood the tribunal of critique. Their first response to Kant's challenge is a paradox: only absolute idealism realizes the true *spirit* of the Kantian philosophy.[51] Ironically, the young idealists revive metaphysics in the name of Kant, the very thinker who banished it.

Behind this paradox lies their belief that only absolute idealism can remain true to the basic principle of Kant's philosophy—the principle of subject–object identity—*and* solve its fundamental problem—the explanation of the possibility of objective knowledge. Although absolute idealism is indeed metaphysics, and in the very sense prohibited by Kant and Fichte, its metaphysics is necessary to solve the outstanding problem of Kant's philosophy according to its own guiding principle. The central dilemma of the critical philosophy is that it can resolve its fundamental problem only if it answers metaphysical questions, and so goes beyond its own limits on knowledge.[52]

To explain this paradox, it is necessary to consider one influential line of criticism of Kant's philosophy in the early 1790s, a set of objections put forward by Platner, Hamann, Maimon, and Jacobi.[53] They argued that Kant had failed to provide a convincing answer to the central question behind the transcendental deduction: 'How do a priori concepts apply to the given empirical manifold of sensibility?' Their diagnosis of this failure put the blame on Kant's unbridgeable dualism between understanding and sensibility. Kant insists that knowledge requires the most intimate interchange between the concepts of the understanding and the intuitions of sensibility—"concepts without intuitions are empty, intuitions without concepts are blind"—yet his dualism is so drastic that it forbids any interaction at all. For the understanding is an active, intellectual faculty, whose operations do not appear in space and time; and sensibility is a passive, empirical faculty, whose workings are in space and time. How, then, could these faculties interact with one another?

Of course, Kant himself realized the problematic status of his dualisms, and in the *Kritik der Urteilskraft* went some way toward addressing the problem. He attempted to bridge the gap between his dualisms by postulating the idea of an organism, "a technic of nature," as a principle of reflective judgment. According to this principle, the understanding should proceed in its investigation of nature as if nature is the product of an intelligent design, since this alone explains how the manifold of empirical laws form a systematic unity. Such an idea seems to bridge the gap between the understanding and sensibility, and indeed noumena and phenomena, by conceiving all of nature as an organic whole. The intellectual or noumenal world is now the *design* or *purpose* behind the sensible or phenomenal world. But Kant no sooner proposed a solution to his problem than he seemed to retract it, for he insisted that his principle of reflective judgment is only *regulative:* that we have no right to assume that there *is* such a design, but only to proceed *as if* there were one. It was just this restriction, however, that disappointed his successors, who insisted that it was insufficient to solve the problem of the deduction. For to explain the *actual* interaction between understanding and sensibility, noumena and phenomena, nothing less was needed than a *constitutive* principle. Whatever mediated or synthesized these opposites would have to be as real as themselves and their interaction. To make the organic principle only regulative was to admit that it might not be true, and so to leave the mystery still standing.

Kant's problematic dualisms continued to be a central topic among young philosophers in the later 1790s. It seemed as if Fichte's idealism did not remove Kant's dualisms but only reinstated them in a new form. Of course, it was Fichte's grand aim to bridge the outstanding dualisms of Kant's philosophy with his principle of subject–object identity. According to that principle, the subject is one and the same as its object because the subject knows a priori only what it creates, what it produces according to a plan of its own. However, there seemed to be a fatal gap between Fichte's principle and system, his promise and the execution. While his principle demands nothing less than subject–object identity, his system sanctions all kinds of dualisms, which appear on at least two fronts. First, there is the dualism between the striving ego and the "obstacle" or "check" (*Anstoß*), which seems to be nothing better than the Kantian thing-in-itself. Second, there is also the dualism between our rational activity and the given material of experience. While that activity is purely spontaneous, formal, and noumenal, the manifold of sense is inert, material, and phenomenal. How, then, can there be any interaction between them? The problem is not only that infinite striving cannot end, but that it cannot even begin.

The net result of Kant's and Fichte's dualisms was a complete *aporia* regarding the explanation of the possibility of knowledge. All the options seemed to have been exhausted. Contrary to its own principles, subjective idealism left an insurmountable dualism between subject and object. Materialism could not explain the *sui generis* characteristics of the mental, and so it too ended in another kind of dualism in the form of epiphenomenalism. Transcendental realism not only presupposed a mysterious preestablished harmony between subject and object, but it also could not answer obvious skeptical challenges about how we know representations correspond to things that exist external to them. But if subjective idealism, materialism, and realism are not options, what is left?

The only answer, of course, is absolute idealism, which solves the problem of the deduction by its *reinterpretation* of the Kantian–Fichtean principle of

subject–object identity. All the absolute idealists agree with the basic assumption behind this principle: that we can explain the possibility of knowledge only if there is some point of identity between the subject and object.
The starting point of absolute idealism is a rejection of all forms of dualism,
because these make it impossible to explain the correspondence between
the subject and object involved in knowledge. It is imperative to reinterpret
the principle of subject–obect identity, however, because if it is understood
only subjectively, in terms of the self-consciousness of the transcendental
subject, dualism still remains. There is still a gulf between the transcendental
self-consciousness of the transcendental ego and the empirical manifold.
This principle must be reformulated in two respects. First, it is necessary to
universalize or *objectify* it, so that all its restrictions to the subject are removed;
in other words, subject–object identity does not refer simply to the self-consciousness of the subject but to the single infinite substance of which the
subjective and objective are only appearances or attributes. Second, it is necessary to *vitalize* it, so that it refers to a single living *force*, of which the subjective and objective are only its different degrees of organization and development.

Applied to the problem of knowledge, this interpretation of the principle
of subject–object identity finally removes the troublesome dualisms that
prohibited the solution to the transcendental deduction. As aspects of a single absolute, the subject and object of knowledge are no longer divided into
distinct ontological worlds but are different degrees of organization and development of living force. The vitalist metaphysics, which seemed so speculative and transcendent, now plays a crucial role in solving the problem of
the transcendental deduction. For it establishes the requirements for an intimate interchange between understanding and sensibility, the intellectual
and the empirical. If the intellectual and empirical are both manifestations
of living force, they not only interact with one another in causal fashion, but
each is the expression, realization, or development of the other. This means
that the subject's consciousness of the object is nothing less than the self-
realization of the nature of the object itself.

Seen from another angle, the absolute idealist interpretation of the principle of subject–object identity means that the act of knowledge must be
placed within the context of nature as a whole. Both the subject and object
are now parts of a single universal force. Since this substance is an organic
whole, where the identity of each part depends on every other, the subject
and object are not completely self-sufficient and independent of one an-

other but interdependent aspects of a single living force. This means that each has its specific nature through the other, so that the subject becomes determinate through the object and the object determinate through the subject. This implies that the subject's knowledge of the object is not extrinsic to the object but the realization and development of its nature. The subject's knowledge of the object is then nothing less than the object knowing itself through the subject.

We are now in a position to explain—if only in a very abstract way—the paradox with which we began. The absolute idealists believe that they are true to the spirit of the critical philosophy because they develop its principle of subject–object identity to resolve the outstanding problem of the transcendental deduction. Although their reinterpretation of this principle involves absolutizing it, and so transcending the Kantian–Fichtean limits on knowledge, they insist that it is by this means alone that we resolve the metaphysical problem that the deduction poses but cannot answer. Hence the ideas of the absolute and vital force prove themselves to be necessary conditions of the possibility of experience itself. Thus they receive their own transcendental deduction, their own Kantian justification.[54]

7. The Aesthetics of Absolute Idealism

Granted that the metaphysics of absolute idealism resolves the problem of the transcendental deduction, this still does not give us the right to assume its truth. For we are still left with the skeptical *quid juris?:* How do we *know* that there is an absolute? How do we know that anything exists beyond our own representations? Until we have an answer to this question, we cannot claim to solve the problem of nihilism, still less to remove the suspicion of dogmatism.

The young romantics were, of course, perfectly aware of the challenge of skepticism. They had themselves developed a form of radical skepticism that questions all first principles and all acts of faith. They also accept much of Jacobi's and Kant's critique of reason, especially its central thesis that the unconditioned or absolute cannot be known by discursive or conceptual means. Following Kant and Jacobi, they make two arguments against such knowledge. First, all conceptualization is determination, involving some form of negation where one predicate is contrasted against another; but the absolute is the indivisible whole of all that exists, and so it cannot be determinate or contrasted against anything else. Second, all explanation is conditional in form, assuming that something happens only *if* some other condition is fulfilled; but the absolute is the unconditioned, acting from the necessity of its own nature alone. All discursivity therefore transforms the absolute into something it is not, whether that is a finite determination or something conditional. As Novalis summed up the predicament: "We seek the unconditioned (*das Unbedingte*) and always find only things."[55]

Yet the romantics' skepticism and critique of reason was only the negative side of a much more positive and imaginative program: their attempt to establish the sovereignty of the aesthetic, the primacy of art over the realms of reason and action. One of the characteristic tenets of absolute idealism around the late 1790s and early 1800s is its faith in the powers of art, its attempt to displace the primacy of practical reason in critical idealism with the supremacy of the aesthetic. The romantics' belief in the powers of art fully emerges when they make aesthetic experience the organon or *ratio cognoscendi* of absolute knowledge. While they insist that we cannot know the existence of the absolute through reason, they also stress that we can know it, if only vaguely and obscurely, through immediate aesthetic intuition. We know that there is an infinite universe outside us, that there is something much greater than us on which we depend, through aesthetic experience. The feeling of the sublime, the longing to reunite ourselves with all things, and the experience of love, in which I see myself in others as others see themselves in me, show us that we know an other that transcends our own circle of consciousness.

The absolute idealists recognize that the skeptic doubts the veracity of such experiences, and they admit that they cannot *demonstrate* anything from them. Nevertheless, they also insist with equal justice that the skeptic also cannot *refute* such experiences. The province of the skeptic is the realm of discursivity because he can criticize only a proposition, something we can put in words; but these experiences are not expressible in words. Whether we accept the veracity of such experience simply depends on whether we have sufficient sensitivity. This is not an escape from criticism, the idealists believe, because the same is the case with our normal sense perception. We cannot verbalize, conceptualize, or prove our experience of colors, sounds, and tastes. Either we have the experience or we do not. All that we can do is provide some figurative or allegorical expression of them, which is, of course, the province of poetry, painting, and music.

This faith in the sovereignty of art went hand-in-hand with the absolute idealists' organic concept of the universe: to regard nature as an organism and as a work of art are one and the same. The universe is nothing less than a *natural* work of art, and a work of art is nothing less an *artifical* organism. Hence the realms of truth and beauty, the natural and the aesthetic, coincide. As Schlegel explained the general standpoint of idealism: "Idealism considers nature as a work of art, as a poem."[56]

Here we seem to be very far from Kant, who had famously criticized the claims of genius and mysticism. But the irony is that, more than anyone else, Kant had prepared the ground for the aesthetics of absolute idealism. In the *Kritik der Urteilskraft* he made the idea of organic unity the keystone of the critical philosophy. This idea not only unified the realms of freedom and nature, of noumena and phenomena, but it also systematized the multiplicity of empirical laws, thus closing the remaining gap between the categories of the understanding and the manifold of sensibility. In giving such a fundamental role to the idea of organic unity, Kant in effect gave priority to the aesthetic itself. For, more or less explicitly, he had stressed the fundamental analogy between the concepts of the organic and the aesthetic. Both concepts came together in the idea of purposiveness (*Zweckmäsigkeit*): both the living organism and the work of art were created according to a rational plan where the idea of the whole precedes the possibility of its parts.

These facets of the *Kritik der Urteilskraft* were to prove very suggestive to the absolute idealists, who argued in true Kantian fashion that all the sciences presuppose the idea of organic unity, which they conceive as an aesthetic whole.[57] Yet the romantic view of Kant's aesthetics remained ambivalent. While they smiled on the speculative potential of the third *Kritik*, they frowned on its regulative constraints. Although the implicit structure of the third *Kritik* supported the sovereignty of the aesthetic, Kant also denied aesthetic experience any metaphysical stature. In his view, aesthetic judgements are not cognitive, but only express a universalizable pleasure, which is not an objective property of appearances. Aesthetic experience is thus demoted to a status worse than in Plato's cave: it tells us only about our *feelings* about appearances, and so nothing even about appearances, let alone things-in-themselves. Hence Kant's aesthetics would prove to be as much a challenge as an inspiration to the romantic generation. We shall soon see how Hölderlin, Novalis, and Schlegel rose to the occasion.

CHAPTER 2

Hölderlin and Absolute Idealism

1. Philosophy versus Poetry

For absolute idealism to be born, it had to go four steps beyond Fichte's critical idealism. First, it had to deny that subject–object identity consists in the self-consciousness of the ego alone, and it had to affirm instead that it exists only in the single universal substance, of which the subjective and objective are only appearances. Second, it had to dispute the purely regulative status of the absolute and to stress its constitutive role; in other words, it had to contend that the absolute is not only an ethical ideal but an existing reality. Third, it had to transcend the Kantian–Fichtean limits on knowledge and to claim cognition of the absolute. Fourth, it had to hold that nature is not a projection of consciousness, still less an obstacle to the will, but an autonomous organism having independent reality and inherent rationality.

Among the very first, if not the first, to take all these steps was Friedrich Hölderlin, the close friend and roommate of Schelling and Hegel from their days at the *Tübinger Stift*. While Schelling, Schlegel, and Novalis were still under Fichte's magical spell, and while Hegel was busy applying Kantian ideas to religion, Hölderlin was already a critic of the *Wissenschaftslehre*, striving to move beyond its confines. As early as the spring of 1795, Hölderlin had argued against the subjective status of the principle of subject–object identity; he had postulated an aesthetic intuition of the absolute; he had criticized Fichte's concept of nature; and he had given nature a standing independent of the ego. There is indeed good reason to think that it was Hölderlin who first impressed such views on Schelling and Hegel. For all these reasons, Hölderlin has been considered the father of absolute idealism.[1]

Hölderlin's significance for the development of absolute idealism is not least apparent from his pivotal role in the formation of the Schelling–Hegel alliance. It was probably Hölderlin who forged the intellectual bond between Schelling and Hegel that eventually led to their collaboration from 1801 to 1804. For, otherwise, it is a very remarkable fact that Schelling and Hegel joined forces at all in 1801, given that they had not seen one another for several years, and given that they had developed in different directions after leaving the *Tübinger Stift*. From October 1793 to Autumn 1796, Hegel was preoccupied with a modern *Volksreligion* and the source of religious positivity, while Schelling had become involved in Fichte's philosophy and the study of natural science. What eventually brought them together in 1801 to forge a united front against Fichte's subjective idealism was probably Hölderlin's common influence. Although Schelling and Hegel saw little of one another before their Jena period,[2] Hölderlin saw them both. He had visited Schelling twice in Tübingen in 1795, and Schelling had come to see him in Frankfurt in 1796. Though we know little about these encounters, we do know that they were the occasion for philosophical dispute.[3] After getting Hegel a position as a *Hauslehrer* next to him in Frankfurt, Hölderlin was in constant contact with Hegel from January 1797 until September 1798, when they very often had philosophical discussions.[4]

Whatever the precise content of these discussions, many of the anti-Fichtean themes of Schelling's and Hegel's Jena writings reveal the influence of Hölderlin. The critique of a subjective principle of subject–object identity, the concept of the absolute as the one dividing itself, the belief in the independent reality of nature, the rejection of all forms of dualism, and the role of art in the comprehension of the universe—all these ideas are found in Hölderlin before they emerge in Schelling's and Hegel's Jena writings. Although some of these themes were already implicit in Schelling's development apart from Hölderlin, it was still his older friend who first criticized Fichte, and who urged Schelling to go in his own direction. When Schelling complained about how far behind he was in philosophy, Hölderlin consoled him: "Do not worry; you are just as far ahead as Fichte; I have just heard him."[5]

Whether Schelling and Hegel intended Hölderlin to collaborate with them in the production of their *Kritisches Journal* we can only speculate.[6] But it was clear that such a triumvirate was never to be. In July 1802 Hölderlin returned from a stay in France in a desperate and disturbed state of mind. Shortly after leaving Jena in 1803, Schelling wrote Hegel about the sorry sight of their old friend, who was already showing signs of "derangment" (*Verrückung*).[7]

However formative was Hölderlin's role in the development of absolute idealism, it is necessary to admit that this can be said only with the benefit of hindsight and a touch of anachronism. For Hölderlin never saw himself in such a light. He did not attempt to systematize his ideas, and never self-consciously formulated a doctrine he called "absolute idealism." These tasks would later fall to his fellow *Stiftler,* Schelling and Hegel. The reason for Hölderlin's failure to execute them lie not so much in the accidents of his tragic fate—though he constantly complained about the lack of peace and freedom to do his own work—as in his own ambitions. All his life Hölderlin regarded himself as primarily a poet rather than as a philosopher. Although he had an education in, and indeed a passion for philosophy, he believed that his real calling and talent lay with poetry.[8] True to his profession, the main preoccupations of his creative years in Jena, Frankfurt, and Homburg were his novel *Hyperion* and his tragedy *Empedokles.*

There cannot be any doubt, however, about the importance of philosophy in Hölderlin's intellectual development. Since his early days in the *Tübinger Stift,* philosophy had been one of his chief concerns, and indeed something of a consuming passion. He once advised his stepbrother: "You must study philosophy even when you have no more money than to buy a lamp and oil, and even when you have no other time than from midnight to the crack of dawn."[9] In the early 1790s he had exerted himself to master the writings of Kant, Plato, Spinoza, Schiller, and Fichte, and his remarks on them clearly show his abilities. Such indeed was Hölderlin's philosophical training and acumen that, in the early 1790s, Schelling and Hegel looked to him for advice and inspiration, and he even considered plans for a professorship in Jena.[10] Although Hölderlin would sometimes complain about philosophy as "a tyrant," he also regarded it as a tonic because, with its insistence on clarity, precision, and objectivity, it had the power to cure the excess and isolation of poetic subjectivity. Hence he once wrote his friend C. L. Neuffer: "There is a hospital where every unhappy poet like me can take refuge with honor—philosophy."[11]

There is no better proof of the importance of philosophy for Hölderlin, however, than the role it plays in his own literary work. The early hymns are essentially didactic poems expounding Platonic and Schillerian themes; *Hyperion* is quintessentially the "philosophical novel"; and *Empedokles* is a philosophical drama.

Hölderlin's twin devotion to poetry and philosophy was the crux and crucible of his intellectual development, creating both its agenda and problems. His loyalty to poetry made it necessary for him to justify the realm of art; and his involvement with both disciplines made it imperative that he provide some account of the proper relationship between them. Hence his main goals, throughout his creative life from his Tübingen to his Homburg years, were to defend poetry and to explain its connection with philosophy.

Hölderlin's struggle with these issues eventually led to a controversial conclusion, which became the guiding theme of his intellectual career: the sovereignty of poetry over philosophy, the supremacy of aesthetic sense over reason. Unlike many *Aufklärer*, Hölderlin insisted that poetry is not simply a popular medium for philosophical truths; it is not as if philosophy and poetry have the same content but simply represent them in different forms, one appealing to feeling and imagination and the other to reason. Rather, poetry is the source of insights and ideas that philosophy presupposes but cannot express in its discursive language. The only appropriate medium for these insights and ideas lies in the metaphorical and concrete language of poetry. To establish the primacy of poetry, Hölderlin adopted a bold strategy: he would show how the discursive procedures of philosophy ultimately presuppose an intuitive awareness of the whole, which is accessible only to aesthetic sense. Only such awareness saves philosophy from skepticism and the illusions of pure reason.

This philosophical program is crucial for understanding Hölderlin's move toward absolute idealism. For the main reason Hölderlin reacted against Fichte's subjective idealism is that it gave so little place to aesthetic values. The primacy of practical reason in the *Wissenschaftslehre* threatened to dominate and destroy nature, turning it into something of value only for our moral ends. Fichte's circle of consciousness reduced nature, insofar as we know it at all, into nothing more than a mere representation, having no reality beyond our own activity. This meant that nature would lose its magic, its mystery, and its harmony—in a word, its beauty. Nowhere did Fichte's idealism permit anything like the feeling of the sublime, the awareness of something infinitely transcending our meager human powers. Aesthetic sense demands a contemplative rather than active relation to nature: we must treat nature as if it were an end in itself, as if it had a value and existence in its own right apart from our moral purposes. As Kant saw and Schiller stressed, aesthetic perception demands the autonomy of its object, its freedom from moral ends, the recognition of its inherent value.

For the same reason, however, Hölderlin could not bear the regulative constraints of Schiller's and Kant's aesthetics. While Hölderlin accepted Kant's and Schiller's belief in the autonomy of aesthetic values, he held that they had not gone far enough, stopping short of recognizing the *metaphysical* or *ontological* status of beauty. For Hölderlin, beauty is not simply pleasure in appearances, and still less merely a symbol of the good; rather, it is nothing less than the harmonic structure of reality itself. It was Hölderlin's great step beyond Kant and Schiller to remove their *as if* clause behind aesthetic contemplation, making the aesthetic not merely a regulative principle or a way of looking at things but a constitutive principle about reality itself.

In *Hyperion* and *Empedokles* Hölderlin drove home his theme of the sovereignty of poetry over philosophy by showing how some of the central issues of philosophy are best treated by the novel or drama. He took the central philosophical issue of the 1790s—the conflict between Fichte's idealism and Spinoza's naturalism—and showed how it arose from his characters' personal experience, and how it could be resolved only through their spiritual development. The strengths and weaknesses of a philosophy, Hölderlin believed, could only be lived through and experienced, and not determined through pure reason. Since personal character and spiritual development are the proper subject of drama and the novel, they prove to be the only proper medium to explore and resolve philosophical problems.

2. Sources of Absolute Idealism

Because of their historical importance, it is worthwhile to consider Hölderlin's intellectual origins, the influences on him that eventually led to his absolute idealism, making a negative reaction to Fichte's idealism virtually inevitable. These influences, all of which go back to Hölderlin's early years in the *Tübinger Stift*, came from four main sources: Spinoza, Schiller, Jacobi, and Plato.

It is well known that in the early 1790s the *Bund der Geister* in Tübingen—a reading circle of young students including Schelling, Hegel, and Hölderlin—closely followed the pantheism controversy between Mendelssohn and Jacobi. Some of the evidence for Hölderlin's involvement in this controversy comes from one of the few remaining manuscripts of his Tübingen years, his notes on Jacobi's *Briefe über die Lehre von Spinoza*, which he probably wrote sometime in late 1790 or early 1791.[12] These notes are essentially a summary of Jacobi's arguments, revealing little of Hölderlin's own thinking. They are important, however, because some passages lay the ground for his later response to Fichte. Hölderlin notes Jacobi's argument that Spinoza's immanent *ensoph* cannot have either will or understanding, because these require some objects outside themselves, while the *ensoph* is infinite, having nothing outside itself (IV/1, 207).[13] This was the very argument Hölderlin would later make against Fichte's claim that the absolute is the ego. Just as Spinoza's absolute cannot have personality, Hölderlin would reason, so Fichte's absolute cannot be subjective. From a later perspective it is also striking that Hölderlin carefully notes an anti-idealist remark of Lessing's: "It belongs to our human prejudices that we consider thinking the first and best and want to derive everything from it."[14] This was the same prejudice that Hölderlin, Schelling, and Hegel later saw behind Fichte's idealism.

In his February 14, 1791 letter to his mother, Hölderlin revealed the dramatic effect "writings about and by Spinoza" had on his religious beliefs. He explained that he had been enquiring into the basis of religious faith, and that he had come to the conclusion that reason cannot support any of the fundamental dogmas of natural religion, such as the beliefs in God and immortality. He stated in his latest sermon he had preached that, without faith in Christ, there cannot be any belief in God or immortality, and indeed no religion at all. If one takes a "cold and heartless" reason to its ultimate limits, then one has to accept Spinozism; the only rescue from such a labyrinth, the only hope for the heart, came with faith in Christ (VI/1, 63–64). This letter shows that the young Hölderlin had accepted Jacobi's dilemma and taken his *salto mortale:* to escape the abyss of Spinozism, he had made a leap of faith in the historical Christ.

It was not for long, however, that Hölderlin would follow Jacobi. Though he first heeded Jacobi's warnings, he soon became tempted by Lessing's *credo*. By 1795, at the latest, Hölderlin adopted Lessing's *En kai pan* as his own formula for the universe.[15] But he had been moving in this direction for years. Thus the early Tübingen hymns 'Lied der Liebe' and 'An die Göttin der Harmonie,' which were published in late 1791, are filled with pantheistic sentiments.[16] Whenever the move occurred, Hölderlin had reversed his early attitude toward Spinoza. For some reason, Spinozism now seemed to satisfy the demands of his heart as well as his head.

What had happened? Why did Hölderlin endorse Lessing's *credo* after initially rejecting it? There is no concrete and compelling historical evidence to give a decisive answer to this question. All that we can do is consider some of the general forces pushing Hölderlin away from Jacobi and toward Spinoza. One probable factor was the growing influence of Kant. Although Hölderlin had apparently read Kant as early as February 1791,[17] his influence seems to have been weak and filtered through other sources. But he later renewed his study of the Königsberg sage,[18] becoming especially impressed by his demand for a thorough criticism of all beliefs. "I am accustomed from the Kantian philosophy to examine something before I accept it," he once wrote his brother.[19] A leap of faith in a personal God like Jacobi's is always vulnerable to rational criticism, and very likely to prove to be what Jacobi admitted it was: a *salto mortale*. It is improbable, then, that Hölderlin's faith in a personal and historical Christ survived his later study of Kant.

Another significant factor behind Hölderlin's growing sympathy for Spinozism was his poetic ambition.[20] What Hölderlin saw in Lessing's *En kai pan* was a basis for his inspiration, a rationale for his artistic vocation, and more specifically a confirmation for his aesthetic attitude toward nature. Since his earliest poems, he had seen nature as a source of both consolation and inspiration. Nature was not a threat to our autonomy, as in Kant and Fichte, but the complement to our identity, or that which makes us whole once again. Nature was also sublime, infinite, and divine. In this respect Spinoza's nature must have suited Hölderlin. For what could be more sublime than Spinoza's single infinite substance?

It is important to recognize, however, that the *En kai pan* never had a strict Spinozist meaning for Hölderlin. The concept of nature that emerges from the early poems is clearly vitalist. Thus the Tübinger hymns celebrate the force of love behind all of creation, which animates all of nature, and which realizes itself in the love between human beings. But such an animated world does not square well with Spinoza's banishment of final causes, and still less with his endorsement of Cartesian mechanism. It is indeed difficult to understand how Spinoza's universe, which is cold, indifferent and mathematical, can excite much *sympathy* for nature. If Spinoza's universe is sublime, it is not friendly or alive. It is a cosmos designed more for stoical self-control than poetic sentiment. So, clearly, Hölderlin had to reinterpret Spinoza. The crucial question then concerns the sources of his reinterpretation.

One obvious candidate is Herder's *Gott, Einige Gespräche*, which was first published in 1787 in response to Jacobi's *Briefe*. All the elements of a vitalistic Spinozism are clearly present here. Herder argues against Jacobi that Spinzoism is not atheism and fatalism, and he reinterprets Spinoza's substance as the single living force behind all of nature, the *Urkraft aller Kräfte*. Still, while Herder's works had become widely read in the 1780s, there is no direct evidence that Hölderlin was influenced by, or even read, this tract.[21] Another plausible source of Hölderlin's vitalism came from Spinoza's great adversary, Leibniz. Hölderlin himself stated that Leibniz's monadology inspired much of his early cosmological poem 'Hymne an die Göttin der Harmonie.'[22] It could well have been Leibniz, then, who taught Hölderlin that everything in nature is alive, consisting in an entelechy or conatus. Still, it could not have been Leibniz, the adament pluralist, who taught Hölderlin his monism.

The most likely source of Hölderlin's vitalism *and* monism was Schiller's early *Philosophische Briefe,* which was published in *Thalia* in 1786. Schiller had been Hölderlin's hero from his earliest days, and he read all his work avidly. The *Briefe* sketched a vitalistic monism especially important for Hölderlin. It anticipates all the fundamental themes of the Tübinger hymns: that love is the creative force behind the universe; that the structure of the cosmos is revealed in beauty; that everything in nature has a soul; and that the creation consists in a hieroglyph, a secret language. Schiller's early cosmos was indeed just as pantheistic as Spinoza's:

> God and nature are two quantities that are perfectly equal. The whole sum
> of harmonic activity, which exist *together* in the divine substance, is in na-
> ture, the image of this substance, individuated in innumerable degrees,
> measures and stages. Nature is the infinitely divided God.[23]

Another important influence that pushed Hölderlin away from Kant's and Fichte's idealism came from Platonism. Since the early 1790s, Hölderlin had been an avid reader of Plato, and was especially fond of the *Symposium, Phaedrus,* and *Timeus.* In 1793 and 1794 he stated that his main reading had been "Kant and the Greeks,"[24] a point stressed by his leaving testimony from the *Tübinger Stift:* "Philologiae, imprimos graecae, et philosophiae, imprimus Kantianae . . . assiduous cultor" (VII/1, 479). There can be little doubt that, among "the Greeks," he meant Plato.[25] His early enthusiasm for the ancient philosopher is especially evident from his July 1793 letter to Neuffer, where he fantasizes that he is "lying down among the students of Plato" watching the flight of Plato's spirit across the heavens and into the abyss (VI, 86). What he would give to be present at a symposium where, "drunk from the Socratic goblet," he could listen to "the divine Socrates himself" teaching about love! His heart's desire is to impart some of this Platonic inspiration to his own work, especially the novel he was now planning on writing, which he calls "Hyperion." True to his ambition, the Tübinger hymns and *Hyperion* are replete with allusions to Platonic themes, such as the world soul, eros, reminiscence, and friendship.

What did Hölderlin get from his reading of Plato? If we go beyond the Tübingen poems and consider his later work as well, the Platonic influence proves to be as persistent as it was pervasive. One dominant and recurrent theme is *eros*. Like Diotima in the *Symposium*, Hölderlin saw love as the basic creative force of the soul, the source behind every desire for the good. Applying this idea to the philosophical issues of the 1790s, he made love the solution to the apparently intractable Kantian–Fichtean dualisms, the single source of Kant's understanding and sensibility, and the unifying force behind Fichte's infinite and finite activities. Another central theme is the myth of the fall in the *Phaedrus*. That our souls were once in contact with reality itself, that they have fallen, and that they now strive to return to their origins is a motif that appears time and again in Hölderlin's thought. Of course, there were other sources of this myth, not least Kant and Schiller; but Hölderlin never ceased to see the history of the soul in Platonic terms. Still another Platonic theme is Socrates' account of madness in the *Phaedrus*. This was crucial for Hölderlin's own defense of poetry, and specifically for his belief in the powers of inspiration. Needless to say, Hölderlin's Plato was not the one who banished the poets in the *Republic*, but the one who celebrated the poetic muse in the *Phaedrus*.

The influence of Plato must be stressed in considering Hölderlin's anticipation of absolute idealism. For one of his decisive moves toward this idealism—granting constitutive status to aesthetic ideas—was ultimately inspired by Plato. This becomes clear if we consider Hölderlin's October 10, 1794 letter to Neuffer, where he first reveals his intention of writing an essay on the aesthetic ideas. This essay, he explains, will show the necessity of going beyond the limits that Kant and Schiller assign to aesthetic judgment (VI/1, 137). To go beyond their restrictions could mean only one thing: refusing to see aesthetic ideas merely as regulative principles that we should read into appearances, and granting them instead a constitutive status to refer to the structure of reality itself. The Platonic inspiration for this move becomes apparent when Hölderlin explains that his essay will take the form of a commentary on a specific passage from Plato's *Phaedrus*. Unfortunately, Hölderlin does not reveal the specific passage. It has been conjectured that Hölderlin had in mind 249b–c, where Socrates explains that the power of reason to unify a multiplicity of particulars presupposes recollection, and more specifically the memory of our previous perception of reality itself.[26] That this is probably at least one passage Hölderlin had in mind finds support from another text, the preface to the penultimate draft to *Hyperion*. For in this passage Hölderlin makes an argument much like Socrates: that beauty must be real because to strive for it, and even to think about it, we must already have had some experience of it. The Platonic provenance of the argument is made more than plain when, after expounding it, Hölderlin exclaims: "I believe we will in the end all say: holy Plato, forgive us, for how much have we sinned against you!" (III, 236–237).

Hence Hölderlin's attempt to go beyond Kant and Schiller was an attempt to restore the integrity of the Platonic ideas, to give them back their status as creative principles that they had lost in the critical philosophy. It does not work to see them simply as regulative principles, Hölderlin holds, because we can unify a manifold only if we already presuppose the form inherent in it. His argument here ultimately goes back to Socrates in the *Meno:* that we can search for unity, a pattern in particulars, only if we have already had some experience of that unity or pattern itself. We shall soon see that Hölderlin proposed other arguments of a less Platonic kind for the constitutive validity of the aesthetic ideas; but it seems that his original argument drew its inspiration from Plato.

Along with Spinoza, Schiller, and Plato, the other crucial figure in pushing Hölderlin away from Fichte was Jacobi.[27] *Prima facie* this might seem surprising, given that Hölderlin had rejected Jacobi's *salto mortale* in the early 1790s; yet there were other aspects of his thinking that had a more lasting and positive effect. Hölderlin's break with Fichte's idealism came in April 1795 when he began to contest Fichte's analysis of the absolute as the ego and to replace it with his own concept of the absolute as pure being. Contrary to Fichte, Hölderlin insisted on the primacy of being over consciousness, the priority of existence over subjectivity, as an analysis of ultimate reality. It was in just this regard that Jacobi had such an important influence on Hölderlin. There were several strands of Jacobi's thinking that aided him in making this break with Fichte.

The first strand was Jacobi's insistence that the concept of existence is something simple, immediate, and fundamental. According to Jacobi, existence is *simple* because we cannot reduce it down to, or infer it from, a collection of properties; it is not a special kind of property itself, because all the properties of a thing remain the same whether the thing exists or not. Existence is also *immediate* because we cannot demonstrate or refute it through reasoning; whether something exists depends on whether it is given to us in our experience. Finally, existence is *fundamental* because it is the basis of all our identity and thoughts: while who we are and what we think depends on existence, existence does not depend on us. The centrality of the concept of existence in Jacobi's philosophy emerges unmistakably from a famous passage of his *Briefe über Spinoza:*

> In my judgment, the greatest merit of the investigator is to disclose existence, to reveal it . . . Explanation is only a means, a path toward the goal— never the final end. His final goal is that which cannot be explained: the irresolvable, immediate and simple. (IV/1, 72)

No single statement of Jacobi had a greater impact on the romantic generation, and especially on Hölderlin.

A second strand was Jacobi's realism, his belief that we have an immediate knowledge of the existence of things outside ourselves. In his *David Hume* and *Briefe über Spinoza* Jacobi had already developed a realist epistemology that he pitted against Kant's idealism. According to his realism, we cannot demonstrate or refute our belief in the reality of external things, which we hold on the basis of immediate perception alone. The existence of these things, and their determinate qualities, is simply given to us, and not something that we create by means of our cognitive powers. Although Jacobi did not deny that our cognitive faculties are active in determining the constitution of experience, he still insisted that existence, and the particular content of our perception, is passively received from sources outside ourselves. Contrary to Kant's idealism, Jacobi believed that it is a serious mistake to think that we make ourselves and the world in which we live; rather than the lawgiver of nature, we are dependent on the world, both in what we are and in what we know. The fundamental concept should be the concept of existence rather than thought; the *sum* should precede the *cogito*, and prior to even the *sum* is the impersonal *est*, of which the *sum* is only a variant.[28]

The third and final strand was Jacobi's interpretation of Spinoza. In the second edition of his *Briefe über Spinoza* Jacobi had interpreted Spinoza's immanent *ensoph* in terms of the concept of being (*Seyn*). Spinoza's single universal 'substance' is nothing less than being itself, which is "the pure principle of actuality in everything actual, of being in all existence."[29] It is not difficult to see what led Jacobi to such an interpretation. Spinoza's term 'substance' is somewhat misleading because it makes it seem as if it is only a thing, or one kind of thing, when it is really the whole of all things, and as such present within the mental as well as physical, the subjective as much as objective. We cannot use any property to characterize substance, however, because a property involves some negation whereas substance is pure positive reality. What terms are there to characterize such reality, then, other than the term 'being itself'?

When Hölderlin later made his criticism of Fichte he brought together all these strands of Jacobi's thinking—though in a manner that would have horrified their creator. Hölderlin accepted Jacobi's arguments that the concept of being is simple and fundamental, that we know existence only through some immediate experience, and that we must interpret Spinoza's substance in terms of being. However, he used these points to reinterpret Fichte's concept of the absolute. While Jacobi had rejected the whole concept of the absolute as a moral and religious abomination, Fichte had revived the concept by making it the fundamental condition of the possibility of experience. Hölderlin then combined Fichte's transcendental concept of the absolute with Jacobi's interpretation of Spinoza to produce a surprising result: that the fundamental transcendental basis of all consciousness is not the ego but being itself.

3. The Critique of Fichte

Soon after arriving in Jena in the autumn of 1794, Hölderlin met Fichte and attended his lectures. He was deeply impressed. "Fichte is the soul of Jena," he wrote his friend Neuffer in mid-November 1794 (VI, 139). He deeply admired Fichte's acumen, energy, and idealism. Never had he met anyone who could speak so passionately, and reason so subtly, about the first principles of knowledge and morality. So taken was Hölderlin by Fichte that he quickly became immersed in the study of his philosophy, not bothering to attend any other lectures.[30]

Hölderlin's admiration for Fichte was not uncritical. The competing influence of Spinoza, Plato, and Jacobi would never have allowed complete acceptance, only careful asessment. Furthermore, there were other factors in his immediate intellectual environment that would have only encouraged criticism. For, as early as the autumn of 1794, Fichte's philosophy had been coming under heavy criticism in Jena from those students of Reinhold who had become disillusioned with foundationalism.[31] Niethammer, Erhard, Schmid, Weißhuhn, and Herbert saw Fichte's philosophy as a desperate attempt to rehabilitate a lost cause. There can be no doubt that Hölderlin was familiar with some of these criticisms, for he was an intimate friend of Niethammer, who had invited him to contribute articles to the *Philoso-*

phisches Journal.[32] Some of his literary plans in the mid-1790s clearly reveal the influence of Niethammer's skepticism about first principles, especially his thesis that a first principle is not a given reality but an infinite task.[33]

Stimulated by this atmosphere, Hölderlin began to write down his first doubts about Fichte's philosophy shortly after his arrival in Jena. The early fragment 'Hermokrates an Cephalus,' which was probably written in early 1795, criticized Fichte for thinking that philosophy can create a complete system of knowledge such as the *Wissenschaftslehre.* The task of infinite striving applies as much to transcendental as empirical knowledge, Hölderlin argues, so that a complete system of transcendental philosophy is also only a regulative ideal. The belief that we can finish such a system amounts to a "scientific quietism," because it either completely denies the limits of knowledge or remains content with some specific limit (IV, 213). The theme of Hölderlin's article shows that it was probably intended as a contribution for Niethammer's *Philosophisches Journal,* which made the possibility of foundationalism its chief agenda. The draft is interesting not least because it reveals how Hölderlin—like Schlegel, Schelling, and Novalis after him—developed his romantic philosophy through a critique of classical foundationalism. The critique of Fichte's foundationalism was indeed the first step in his program to establish the sovereignty of poetry over philosophy, for he would soon argue that only poetry avoids the infinite striving involved in philosophy.

It was also in early 1795 that Hölderlin took his most important step beyond the idealism of the *Wissenschaftslehre.* Anticipating Schelling and Hegel, who will make the same point only years later, he objects against the purely subjective status of the principle of subject–object identity. He insists that this principle cannot be equated with self-consciousness but must be identified with pure being (*reines Seyn*) itself. The paradigm of subject–object identity is not self-consciousness, he implies, but the single universal substance of which thought and extension, the subjective and objective, are only manifestations or appearances.

There are two crucial pieces of evidence for Hölderlin's early move beyond the subjective idealism of Fichte. The first is his January 26, 1795 letter to Hegel, and the second his short fragment 'Urtheil und Seyn,' probably written in early 1795.[34] In both texts Hölderlin takes issue with Fichte's claim in the 1794 *Grundlage* that the absolute is subjective, consisting in the ego or self-consciousness.

In his letter to Hegel, Hölderlin does not develop his own positive account of the absolute identity but simply points out an inconsistency in the *Wissen-schaftslehre*.[35] The essence of Hölderlin's argument is that Fichte's absolute cannot be subjective because there is a tension between it and one necessary condition of subjectivity—namely, the possibility of consciousness. Hölderlin reasons as follows: if the absolute ego contains all reality, like Spinoza's substance, then it should be everything, having nothing outside itself; this means that the absolute ego canot have an object, because this would be to postulate something outside it; since, however, there cannot be conscious-ness without an object, the absolute ego cannot be conscious; but what can-not be conscious cannot be an ego; and hence Fichte's absolute cannot be subjective.

Such a condensed argument needs further explanation. Why cannot the ego have an object if it is all reality? It would seem that the ego could still have *itself* for an object and still be all reality. The suppressed premise of Hölderlin's argument comes from Fichte himself, and more specifically from his 'law of reflection': that to know anything determinate, to be conscious of it as this rather than that, I must oppose it to something; hence to know even myself as an ego, I must oppose myself to a non-ego. This was exactly Fichte's reasoning in the *Wissenschaftslehre*,[36] which Hölderlin now turns against him. From the law of reflection Hölderlin draws the conclusion that the ego cannot be absolute. Since to know itself the ego must oppose itself to the non-ego, it follows that the ego cannot be all reality because it must have something outside itself. Hence, on Fichte's own reckoning, the ego must be *finite*, and it becomes nonsense to speak of an *absolute* or *infinite* ego.

In his letter to Hegel, Hölderlin writes *as if* he were a Kantian himself, chiding Fichte for transcending the limits of experience. Thus he says that he suspects Fichte of a dogmatism just like that of the older metaphysicians, be-cause his absolute cannot be within consciousness. It would be wrong to conclude from this, however, that Hölderlin *was* a Kantian at this time, as if he wished to uphold the critical limits against all forms of dogmatism.[37] For, long before 1795, Hölderlin was champing at the bit, eager to move beyond the Kantian limits himself. This becomes clear from his January 16, 1794 let-ter to Neuffer, where he says that Schiller should have gone further beyond the Kantian limits in his *Anmut und Würde,* implying that he would do just that if he were to write his own an essay on the aesthetic ideas (VI, 137). So, rather than towing the Kantian line himself, Hölderlin simply accuses Fichte of an inconsistency for not doing so.

While the letter to Hegel merely points out an inconsistency in Fichte's position, the fragment 'Urtheil und Seyn' states Hölderlin's own positive account of the absolute. He identifies the absolute, the unity of subject and object, with *being (Seyn)*. Hölderlin implicitly equates being with Spinoza's single universal substance. This substance can be described as the identity of subject and object because both the subjective and objective, the ideal and the real, are aspects of it. That Hölderlin called subject–object identity "being" was probably due to the influence of Jacobi, who had already identified Spinoza's immanent *ensoph* with being pure and simple.[38]

Hölderlin's claim that the absolute is not the ego but being seems to pit a realistic concept against an idealistic one. Rather than holding that thought precedes being, Hölderlin now appears to maintain that being precedes thought. It is as if he were endorsing Jacobi's interpretation of Spinoza: "Thinking is not the source of substance, but substance is the source of thinking."[39] But it is important to see that Hölderlin does not mean this. When he claims that the absolute is being he means that it is neither idealistic nor realistic, neither subjective nor objective alone, but that it is both of them yet still neither of them because it is nothing more nor less than their pure unity. The whole point of Hölderlin's principle is indeed to overcome *all* forms of dualism, whether they completely separate the subject or object or emphasize one at the expense of the other. The term 'being' was perfectly appropriate to express such pure identity, because both the subjective and objective are aspects of being and share in it equally; being is not determinate in any respect, neither more subjective nor more objective. Hence if Hölderlin sides with Spinoza, it is not because he thinks that Spinoza's naturalism and realism are more true than Fichte's idealism, but because he thinks that Spinoza's substance overcomes the oppositions between idealism and realism. Hölderlin does not want to side with dogmatism against criticism—the false dilemma Fichte presented him—but to develop a single standpoint that encompasses them both.[40] It is in this sense that he anticipates Schelling, who will later call this single standpoint "criticism" or "the indifference point."

Whatever his positive views, Hölderlin's main aim in 'Urteil und Sein' is still essentially negative and anti-Fichtean. Still taking issue with Fichte, Hölderlin now makes a new argument for why the absolute identity cannot be the ego. The thrust of his argument is that the distinctive feature of the ego is self-consciousness, but that self-consciousness necessarily involves some *distinction* between the subject and object, and so is incompatible with the *pure* subject–object identity of the absolute. Of course, Hölderlin concedes, self-consciousness also involves some element of *identity* because the knowing subject is the object known; but he also insists that self-consciousness also implies a *distinction* between the subject and object. Self-consciousness is only possible, Hölderlin explains, insofar as I distinguish myself from myself but still regard myself as one and the same throughout this distinction (IV, 217). But then the question arises: To what extent am I the same? I can, and indeed must, ask this question, Hölderlin implies, because to another extent I can distinguish myself from myself simply because I can ask the question whether I the knowing subject am the same as the known object. But insofar as I can ask to what extent or degree they are the same, Hölderlin maintains, there cannot be a *complete* or *absolute* subject–object identity.

The most difficult aspect of Hölderlin's argument is his claim that *self*-consciousness involves some distinction between subject and object. It seems as if Hölderlin already made this point in his letter to Hegel; but it is important to see that he is no longer simply repeating the Fichtean point that self-consciousness requires consciousness of an external world. He is now making the more radical claim that there must be a distinction between subject and object within *self*-consciousness itself. This is a point that Fichte would resist to the last, because it implies that complete self-consciousness is impossible.[41] If there is a distinction between the subject and object within self-consciousness, the subject will know itself only on pain of an infinite regress.

What is Hölderlin's basis for this stronger claim? There are at least three reasons for it, all of them implied by, or at least consistent with, the text of 'Urtheil und Seyn.'

The first is that it is possible to *formulate* or *express* self-knowledge only by making some distinction between the subject and object. This is because any attempt to formulate or express self-knowledge requires judgment, which involves some distinction between subject and predicate. Hence, playing on the presumed etymology of the term 'judgment' in German (*Urteil*), Hölderlin explains that judgment is the act of original separation (*Ur-teilung*) because it is divided into a subject and predicate (IV, 216). He argues that this distinction holds even for the judgment '*Ich bin Ich*,' the first principle of the *Wissenschaftslehre*, which is supposed to state the self-consciousness of the self-positing subject. Although the *content* of the judgment '*Ich bin Ich*' affirms the identity of the subject and object, its *form* implies a separation between them because it is expressed as a distinction between subject and predicate.

The second reason consists in the application of Fichte's law of reflection to self-consciousness itself: that to identify one term as the subject and another as an object, even in cases of self-knowledge, requires making a distinction between subject and object; it is possible to distinguish between the self who knows itself and the self who is known because they oppose one another as subject and object. Hölderlin seems to suggest this line of argument in 'Urteil und Seyn' when he writes that I must oppose myself to myself in self-consciousness.

The third reason is skeptical: we can always ask how the subject knows itself, or how it knows that it is the same as its object. If this question is legitimate or meaningful—and it would be simply dogmatic to dismiss it—then that alone seems to warrant the possibility of at least a *logical* distinction between the subject and object. Hölderlin appears to gesture in this skeptical direction when he says that he can at least raise the question to what extent the subject and object are identical.

Whatever the precise form of his argument, Hölderlin's general intent in 'Urtheil und Seyn' is to provide something on par with a *transcendental deduction* of Spinoza's concept of substance, and so to avoid any charge that he is simply relapsing into metaphysical dogmatism. The whole point of the critique of Fichte is to show that the fundamental condition of all knowledge cannot lie within the realm of subjectivity alone. Hölderlin agrees with Fichte that subject–object identity is the necessary condition of all knowledge; but he disagrees with him that this identity is subjective, given that subjectivity implies the possibility of self-consciousness, which involves some distinction between subject and object. In Hölderlin's view, only Spinoza's substance, pure being, expresses the pure subject–object identity that is a necessary condition of the possibility of experience itself.

With his argument for the primacy of being in 'Urtheil und Seyn,' Hölderlin had taken another crucial step in his program to establish the primacy of the aesthetic. Since in *Hyperion* Hölderlin identifies the one and all with beauty (III, 81), and since being is the element of identity or unity of the one and all, it follows that being is an essential element in beauty itself. The priority of being over the ego—its more basic role as the fundamental condition of experience—is then tantamount to the primacy of the aesthetic itself.

4. Aesthetic Sense

Hölderlin anticipated absolute idealism not only by postulating the existence of the absolute, and not only by denying its merely subjective status, but also by affirming the possibility of actual knowledge of the absolute. If, for

Hölderlin, the absolute is not only an ideal for action, as in Fichte, neither is it merely an object of faith, as in Kant. Rather, the absolute is the object of a special kind of experience, the intuition or feeling that arises from aesthetic sense. Following Fichte's terminology, though not his meaning, Hölderlin called such an experience "intellectual intuition" (*intellektuelle Anschauung*).

Of course, even to affirm such a possibilty is to contradict Kant's and Fichte's teachings about the limits of knowledge. Hölderlin was clearly intent, however, on taking just such a bold and controversial step. The first sign of his intentions appear as early as the Tübinger hymns, especially the 'Hymne an die Schönheit' and the 'Hymne an die Göttin der Harmonie,' which were composed in 1791. It is striking that the first poem begins with a quote from Kant's *Kritik der Urteilskraft:* "Nature in its beautiful forms speaks figuratively to us, and the gift of explaining its ciphers is bestowed upon moral feeling."[42] The citation is from §42 where Kant explains why we find a taste for natural beauty morally superior to that for fine art: that reason takes an interest in the *objective reality* of its ideas, which appear to be realized in the beauty of nature. Nowhere does Kant come closer to admitting the constitutive status of the ideas than in these passages of the third *Kritik.* The young Hölderlin readily endorses Kant's train of thought; but he then goes an important step further when he insists that we *perceive,* if only through a glass darkly, the objective reality of the ideas through their appearance in nature. Thus Urania, the goddess of truth and harmony, addresses the poet:

> Herrlicher mein Bild in dir zu finden
> Haucht' ich Kräfte dir und Kühnheit ein,
> Meines Reichs Geseze zu ergründen,
> Schöpfer meiner Schöpfungen zu sein.
> Nur im Schatten wirst du mich erspähen,
> Aber liebe, liebe mich, O Sohn!
> Drüben wirst du meine Klarheit sehen.
> Drüben kosten deiner Liebe Lohn. (I, 132)[43]

> To find my image more
> splendid within you
> I breathed power and boldness within
> To fathom the laws of my world,
> [I made you] the creator of my creations.
> Only in shadows will you sense me,

but love me, love me, my son!
Above you will see my clarity
Above you will taste the reward of your love.

What Hölderlin first declared in poetry he eventually planned to defend in philosophy. In early 1795 he had sketched plans for a new epistemology of aesthetic ideas, which would show not only the limits of reason but also the necessity of an aesthetic awareness of the absolute. While Hölderlin never completed this project, it is possible to reconstruct his ideas from a few remaining fragments, some letters, and the final published version of his novel *Hyperion*.[44] The fundamental thesis of Hölderlin's epistemology—that understanding and reason require an aesthetic awareness of the absolute—reemerged years later in Schelling's *System des transcendentalen Idealismus* and Schlegel's *Vorlesungen über Transcendentalphilosophie*.

That Hölderlin should postulate some form of consciousness or awareness of the absolute might at first sight seem odd, given that the apparent consequence of his argument against Fichte is that the ground of consciousness must transcend consciousness itself. For just this reason it is sometimes said that Hölderlin saw this ground as something unknowable, as indeed something unthinkable presupposed by all thinking.[45] It is important to see, however, that Hölderlin never drew such a strong conclusion. He certainly did not regard the one and the all as something unknowable or transcendent. While he indeed argued that this ground is the condition of all *sensible* intuition or *discursive* thinking, and so cannot be the object of such intuition or thinking, he also held that it is the object of an *intellectual* intuition. This intellectual intuition, he maintains, can be found only in aesthetic experience.

That Hölderlin had assumed the possibility of some form of knowledge or experience of the absolute becomes clear from two letters he wrote in late 1795 and early 1796. On September 4, 1795 he wrote to Schiller about his idea of infinite progress in philosophy, according to which the complete analysis of the absolute can be approached but never attained through endless striving (VI, 181). This was roughly the thesis of his earlier fragment 'Hermokrates an Cephalus.'[46] But Hölderlin now made one telling and striking addition to it: that, though the unity of subject and object is not attainable *theoretically*, it is so *aesthetically* in intellectual intuition. Hölderlin took a further step in this direction when he wrote Niethammer on February 24, 1796 that he wanted to find *theoretically* in intellectual intuition the principle that would dissolve the opposition between subject and object (VI, 203).

While in his earlier letter he had opposed the realm of theory and intellectual intuition, in this later letter he had virtually identified them. The shift is
significant, for it now makes clear that intellectual intuition is indeed a form
of knowledge. Hölderlin is now reclaiming some of the rights of knowledge
that had been so restricted by the primacy of practical reason in the *Wissenschaftslehre*.

That there is some kind of intuition or experience of the absolute is also a
leitmotiv of *Hyperion*. When Hyperion describes the consolation he finds in
the arms of nature, he often describes his experience as a direct awareness of
the one and all itself. He writes, for example, that "Just as Jupiter's eagle
heard the song of the muses, so I listen to the wonderful infinite tone within
me" (III, 48). Hyperion admits that he cannot demonstrate or analyze this
experience, and that words fail him in trying to express it; still, he insists that
it exists all the same. Thus he assures his less mystical friend Bellarmin: "I
cannot speak of it [the inner peace found in the beauty of nature] but there
are indeed hours where the best and most beautiful appears as if in clouds,
and the heaven of perfection opens itself to love; there Bellarmin! There
think of your being, there bend your knee with me and think of my serenity! But do not forget that I had what you felt, that I saw with eyes what appeared to you only in the clouds" (III, 51). As if to banish further doubt,
Hyperion then declares that he not only believes in or thinks of the beauty
characteristic of the one and all, but that he has "seen and gotten to know
it" (*ich hab es gesehn, ich hab es kennen gelernt*) (52).

Hölderlin wanted to call his new tract on the epistemology of aesthetic
ideas *Neue Briefe über die Ästhetische Erziehung des Menschen*. The polemical reference to Schiller's *Ästhetische Briefe*, which had only recently appeared, is
unmistakable. These *Neue Briefe* would take that extra step beyond Kant that
Schiller had failed to take in *Anmut und Würde*. Although Hölderlin never explains how he plans to go beyond Schiller, his intentions become clear by
comparing his ideas with Schiller's in the early 1790s. Although Schiller had
put forward some grand claims in behalf of beauty in his 1786 *Philosophische
Briefe*, his study of Kant in the early 1790s had greatly sobered him, making
him much more critical about the metaphysical significance of the aesthetic.
He no longer sees beauty as the perfection of nature or as the harmony of
the cosmos, but simply as a property of appearances. This critical turn is apparent not so much from the *Aesthetische Briefe* itself but from his first major
writing on aesthetics in the 1790s, the incomplete and unpublished *Kallias
Briefe*. Here Schiller defines beauty as *freedom in appearance*, insisting that the

ascription of freedom to objects in nature is a purely *regulative* judgment made on the basis of an *analogy* to our free activity.[47]

Given Hölderlin's abiding Platonic sympathies, it is easy to imagine his reaction to Schiller's Kantian doctrine. First, he would be disturbed by the limitation of beauty to the realm of appearances; second, he would reject the purely regulative validity of aesthetic judgment; and, third, he would be repelled by Schiller's definition of beauty because it subordinates the aesthetic to the moral through the concept of freedom. Hölderlin wanted to go beyond all these limits by making aesthetic contemplation the medium for knowledge of being itself. The irony is that no one inspired him more to transcend these limits than the young Schiller himself!

While Hölderlin knew that his doctrine of aesthetic intuition transcended the Kantian–Fichtean limits on knowledge, he was also intent on avoiding any relapse into precritical dogmatism.[48] He was still enough of a Kantian to realize that he would have to provide some justification, some rationale for his claims to knowledge of the unconditioned. On no account did he want to lapse into the complacency of the old metaphysics of the Leibnizian–Wolffian school, whose failure to examine its own methodology had resulted in all the 'paralogisms,' 'antinomies,' and 'amphibolies' so ruthlessly exposed by Kant. Hölderlin indeed accepted some of the main arguments behind Kant's critique of reason, especially the doctrine that the unconditioned is inaccessible to the concepts of the understanding or the demonstrations of reason. Where he disagreed with Kant was the conclusion that there could be no knowledge whatsoever of the unconditioned. Hölderlin saw this as a *non sequitur,* resting on the hidden premise that knowledge of the absolute must be discursive. It was just this premise, however, that his new epistemology of aesthetic ideas would contest.

How did Hölderlin attempt to justify his bold step beyond Kant? How did he attempt to establish the necessity of some intuitive knowledge of the absolute? His letters to Schiller and Niethammer, and some passages from the final version of *Hyperion,* show that he had developed a definite strategy, even though he never put it into practice. What Hölderlin wanted to provide is something like a transcendental deduction of the aesthetic ideas by showing how they are a necessary condition for the proper functioning of reason and the understanding. It is only the aesthetic ideas, he suggested, that set the proper limits to these faculties, preventing them from self-destruction and protecting them against skepticism. Reason will not produce anything rational, and the understanding will not create anything understandable, he writes in *Hyperion*, unless each of these faculties are directed by aesthetic sense (III, 83). This is because reason and the understanding *presuppose* but can never *experience* the idea of the whole. Both of these faculties are essentially discursive or analytical, proceeding from the parts to the whole. They operate effectively, however, only if there is some prior knowledge of the whole, some intuitive or synthetic power that proceeds from the whole to its parts. It is just this synthetic capacity that is provided by aesthetic sense.

Aesthetic sense is necessary in philosophy, Hölderlin believes, chiefly because it is the only means of rescuing reason from skepticism.[49] This view emerges clearly from *Hyperion* where he suggests that aesthetic sense is immune from doubt because the skeptic himself presupposes it (III, 81). The source of all the skeptic's doubts and objections against reason, he explains, is that he has vague sense or feeling for the whole. It is this feeling that allows the skeptic to see that our discursive faculties cannot know the whole, and that they contradict themselves whenever they attempt to do so; but this feeling comes from the skeptic's own latent aesthetic intuition. A similar view about skepticism appears in Hölderlin's September 4, 1795 letter to Schiller, where he explained that one of the aims of his new aesthetics is to show the extent to which the skeptics are right and wrong (VI, 181). Though he never went into any details, it is not difficult to reconstruct his meaning: the skeptics are right to think our discursive powers, which are analytical, cannot grasp the whole; but they are wrong to conclude that there cannot be *any* knowledge of the whole, given that even their own doubt presupposes some awareness of it.

The problem still remains, however, how it is possible to justify an aesthetic intuition. How do we explain or verify its content, what it purports to know? Here Hölderlin, like any artist, confronts a grave dilemma. To explain the meaning of an aesthetic intuition, and to establish the truth of its content, it is necessary to give it a determinate sense or to put it in more concrete terms; for, on its own, it amounts to only a vague sense or feeling for the whole. But to give the intuition a determinate sense means that it must be possible to verbalize or conceptualize it; but all verbalization and conceptualization kills because it dismembers the unity of the whole, transforming the living and individual into the artificial and the abstract.

Hölderlin himself was all too aware of this dilemma, which plagued him all his life. Obviously, the problem is endemic to all poetic creation, which involves formulating intuition and feeling into words. From time to time Hölderlin stressed both horns of the dilemma: that to explain or demonstrate aesthetic intuition is to destroy it; and that all intuition proves its truth only if it is expressed in determinate terms.[50] It is only in a later fragment, 'Über Religion' that Hölderlin provides something like a solution to the problem. Here he is clear that the intuition and feeling for the universe characteristic of religion cannot be expressed in concepts or demonstrated in syllogisms, because they would make the purely immediate and concrete into something mediate and abstract (IV, 276–277). Nevertheless, he also stresses that we have a natural tendency to express religious feelings and intuitions in thoughts and words (IV, 275–276). The only solution to the dilemma is for expression of the religious to be mythical. The great value of mythical language is that it avoids the abstract and analytical language of reason yet it puts our intuitions and feelings into some more concrete form. Mythical language is a synthesis of the intellectual and the historical: it has all the determinacy of the intellectual but also all the immediacy, unity, and wholeness of the historical (IV, 281). Hölderlin's solution favors the poetic over the philosophical, and it is indeed part of his general program to establish the priority of the aesthetic. Hölderlin does not hesitate to express his general thesis: "Hence all religion is in its essence poetic" (IV, 281). This is indeed Hölderlin's main difference with the later Hegel, who will later attempt to express the intuitions and feelings of religion into systematic form.

5. The Concept of Nature

Criticizing the subjective status of the absolute, postulating its existence, and then affirming knowledge of it were three fundamental steps toward absolute idealism. They do not exhaust, however, the extent to which Hölderlin anticipated absolute idealism. It is also necessary to consider Hölderlin's role in formulating the romantic concept of nature. Before Hegel and around the same time as Schelling, Hölderlin developed the vitalist conception of nature that later became so crucial for the philosophy of identity.[51] To be sure, Hölderlin was not the founder of this conception; and he did not develop the implications, nor remove the inconsistencies, in his own view until the late 1790s. Nevertheless, it is not the case that Hölderlin's vitalism was mere poetic enthusiasm, a vague and imaginative idea he left for Schelling and Hegel to systematize and rationalize. For Hölderlin played an important *philosophical* role in the development of vitalism: he was the first to defend it against Fichte's concept of nature. Schelling and Hegel will later resume his struggle only in the late 1790s.

There are already intimations of vitalism in some of Hölderlin's early Tübingen hymns, especially the 'Hymne an die Göttin der Harmonie' and the 'Liede der Liebe.' These poems celebrate the force of love behind creation, a force that unites, harmonizes, and animates all things. This was not mere poetic fancy, since Hölderlin wanted to expound a view of nature that he had discovered in Plato, Schiller, and Leibniz. Still, it was only after his encounter with Fichte in 1794 that he began to explain and justify his intuitions and feelings. It then proved necessary for him to defend them against the more negative concept of nature in the *Wissenschaftslehre*.

Hölderlin's defense of his own view of nature begins in 'Urtheil und Seyn' and the various versions of his novel *Hyperion*, which were written around 1795. While these fragments contain some perceptive criticisms of Fichte, they also show that Hölderlin was still far from a consistent view of his own. There was indeed a deep tension in his own positive account of the absolute. In the preface to the penultimate version of *Hyperion* he identifies the absolute, or the one and all, with "serene unity, being in the strict sense of the word" (III, 236). This agrees with his account of the absolute in 'Urtheil und Seyn.' However, in the ultimate published version of *Hyperion*, Hölderlin equates the absolute not with being but beauty, which consists in "the one distinguishing itself" (*das Eine in sich selber unterschiedene*) of Heraclitus (III, 53, 81). This raises a serious question of consistency: How can the one and all be both mere unity and the one distinguishing itself? If it is being alone, then it would be mere unity, subject–object identity. If, however, it is oneness distinguishing itself, then it cannot be just unity, but it must also be unity within difference, the identity of identity and nonidentity. With the first view, Hölderlin seems to have in mind Parmenides; but with the second, he refers us explicitly to Heraclitus.

This tension in Hölderlin's thinking derives from the conflicting sources in his intellectual development. It was the influence of Spinoza that led him to identify the one and all with pure being. If we follow Spinoza, then the absolute is pure unity, the single universal substance, so that any difference between subject and object will be only a difference in attribute or perspective, alternative forms of explanation of one and the same thing. It was the legacy of Plato, Schiller, and Leibniz, however, that pushed Hölderlin toward a view of the absolute as oneness differentiating itself. For these thinkers gave Hölderlin a vision of an animate universe, of a cosmos that changes and evolves as a living being. If the universe is animate, if it is one vast organism, then it should be more than mere oneness; it should be instead oneness separating itself, for organic development involves differentiation, a process by which an inchoate, indeterminate unity becomes an organized and determinate multiplicity.

Hölderlin eventually resolved this tension in favor of the more vitalist concept of nature. When he did so exactly is not clear. But in his 1799 fragment *Grund zum Empedokles* he identifies the unity of the subjective and objective with "pure life" (*reines Leben*) rather than with "pure being" (*reines Seyn*) (IV, 152). He also makes it clear that pure life is more than unity alone, because life involves the process of growth, organization, or differentiation, the development from the unified, inchoate, and indeterminate into the manifold, organized, and determinate. Indeed, far from the serenity of pure being, Hölderlin now insists that life consists in struggle, a conflict between extremes where each realizes itself only by becoming its opposite, so that the moment of greatest conflict is also that of greatest reconciliation (153). In the slightly earlier fragment *Das Werden im Vergehen* Hölderlin also develops an explicitly dynamic concept of the absolute. The "world of all worlds," "the everything in everything" (*Alles in Allen*) presents itself "genetically" in the beginning and end of time (282). The life that manifests itself in time does not consist in being but in a process of becoming that is "between being and non-being" (*Seyn und Nichtseyn*) (283). The same dynamic concept of nature also emerges in the late essay *Über die Verfahrungsweise des poetischen Geistes*, where Hölderlin maintains that the poetic spirit must grasp the "infinite unity" involved in the interchange between oneness and multiplicity (251). Here Hölderlin is especially clear that the absolute must be viewed not only as a unity in opposition to difference, but as the whole process by which unity involves opposition and conversely (251, 255–257).

The point behind Hölderlin's vitalism was to surmount that dualism between the subjective and objective, the ideal and the real, which had continued to plague Kant and Fichte. Unlike Kant and Fichte, Hölderlin refuses to see the subjective and objective, the ideal and the real, as belonging to distinct realms of being, such as the noumenal and the phenomenal. By 1799 he also came to reject one Spinozist solution to this difficult problem. Spinoza had made the mental and the physical different attributes of substance, defining an attribute as "what the intellect perceives as constituting the essence of substance."[52] This ensured the perfect unity of the universe; but, at least on one reading of attribute, it also made the differences between the subjective and objective only a matter of perspective or kind of explanation. To be sure, Hölderlin sees the subjective and objective as different *ap-*

pearances or *manifestations* of the same thing; but he does not think that these differences have an only *ideal* or *intellectual* status. Rather, they are perfectly real, existing within nature itself. This does not destroy the unity of nature, however, because they are different degrees of organization and development of a single living force. This view of the relation between the subjective and objective becomes perfectly explicit in the *Grund zum Empedokles,* where Hölderlin states that the objective is the indeterminate, inchoate, and universal form of life, whereas the subjective is its determinate, organized, and particular form (IV, 152–153).

It becomes clear from the *Grund zum Empedokles* that Hölderlin postulates a special kind of organic connection between the subjective and objective. Their relationship is not purely causal or mechanical. It is not that they are reciprocally cause and effect of one another. Since cause and effect are distinct terms, this is much too dualistic. It is also not accurate to think of them as force and manifestation of one another, if that means that each has an inherent force and complete identity apart from the other and only shows itself upon the stimulus of the other. This too would be much too dualistic. Rather, Hölderlin stresses how both the subjective and objective become what they are only through the other, or how each realizes its nature only through the other. The objective realizes itself as the subjective because nature reaches its perfection in art and human consciousness, which is its highest degree of organization and development. Conversely, the subjective realizes itself as the objective because art attains its perfection in becoming nature, and because human activity realizes its final end only in becoming one again with all of nature (IV, 153–154).

It is a distinctive feature of Hölderlin's organic vision of the universe that it consists in a *cyclical* process of continual formation *and* dissolution. The universe does not develop only progressively by infinite growth, as if were constantly becoming more differentiated and organized, but it also develops regressively through decay and death, where the organized and determinate returns to its primal mass and unity. "We have long ago agreed," he wrote his brother June 4, 1799, "that all the erring streams of human activity return to the ocean of nature as they have gone forth from it" (VI, 329). Hölderlin especially emphasized both aspects. The movement from difference back to unity, from the organized back to the inchoate, was no less important for him than that from unity to difference, from the inchaote to the organized. Hölderlin stressed the first aspect as much as the second as a corrective to an anthropomorphic or idealistic concept of nature, which saw humanity as the sole end of creation. That had been indeed a salient feature of Fichte's idealism, which saw human morality as the very purpose of things. Hölderlin did not deny—as Schelling will later stress—that human self-consciousness can be seen as the culmination of nature, the highest organization of its powers. But for him it was also important to see that human self-consciousness is only one part of the universe, which greatly transcends it, and that it is to the great ocean of the one and all that everyone eventually returns. Thus death was an essential part of the cosmos.

This is a central theme behind Hölderlin's incomplete tragedy *Der Tod des Empedokles*. Hölderlin's hero, Empedocles, the ancient Greek philosopher, thinks that he is the very height of creation, because he has magical powers over nature. Since nature does whatever he commands, he imagines that he himself is a god. But, of course, such hubris is the cause of his fall. Empedocles eventually realizes that rather than being a god himself, he is really only the mouthpiece of the gods, whose powers infinitely surpass his own. He finally sees that his self is not the end of creation, but only one part and moment of an infinite cosmos. To achieve unity with nature means not only having power over it but surrendering oneself to it; it means losing one's individuality and returning to the universal whole. Hence Empedocles sees no more deserving fate for himself than leaping into the crater of Mount Etna.

6. Philosophy in Literature

Hölderlin's study of Fichte in the winter of 1794–1795 plunged him into a deep intellectual crisis. Fichte's concept of infinite striving in the 1794 *Wissenschaftslehre* presented a completely different picture of nature from anything he expressed in his poems. Rather than seeing nature as something inherently alive and rational, as a system of ends existing apart from human activity, Fichte viewed it as a mere obstacle to the striving of the will, as a mechanism whose rationality had to be forcefully imposed on it by the ego. Nature was no longer a friend, a source of consolation and companionship, but an enemy, a hindrance to every desire and action. Ultimately, both Fichte and Hölderlin shared the same goal: subject–object identity, the unity of the self with nature. But they had diametrically opposed means of achieving it: for Fichte, it demanded the will's titanic struggle to subdue nature; for Hölderlin, it required an intuitive sympathy with nature, a feeling of oneness with it.

Fichte's concept of striving had raised a general question for Hölderlin: How should the self relate to nature? Should the self become everything and nature nothing? Or should nature become everything and the self nothing? That is how Hölderlin himself phrased the issue in the preface to the incomplete penultimate version of *Hyperion* (III, 236), which he wrote between August and December 1795. With this question Hölderlin had raised the most topical philosophical issue of the early 1790s, for he was in effect posing the choice between Fichte and Spinoza.[53] Fichte wanted the ego to be everything, because the aim of infinite striving is for nature to disappear; but Spinoza demanded that nature be everything, because he saw the self as a mode of the single infinite substance.

Hölderlin wrestled with this problem throughout the 1790s, beginning with his Jena episode (November 1794–July 1795) and continuing in his Homburg period (September 1798–April 1800). His first response to it appears in the various versions of *Hyperion*. The drafts of the metrical version, the penultimate version, and *Hyperions Jugend* begin with a discussion of a view of nature that is unmistakeably Fichtean. It was indeed no accident that Hölderlin started his intensive study of Fichte around the autumn of 1794, the very time he wrote these early versions of the novel.[54] Though the final published verion of the novel omits any reference to a Fichtean concept of nature, it continues to consider the broader issues raised by it.

What is so striking about Hölderlin's solution to this problem is that he rejects *both* Fichte and Spinoza. He thinks that they represent two extreme attitudes, and that to find the truth it is necessay to find some middle path between them.[55] The proper attitude toward nature, Hölderlin suggests, must be a synthesis of Fichte and Spinoza that preserves their truths and cancels their errors. The argument of *Hyperion* is an essential part of Hölderlin's aesthetic program, for what he attempts to show throughout the novel is that each attitude toward nature evolves from and depends on a person's life and stage of development. Since both attitudes are united only through the complete story of a person's life, their synthesis is the proper subject of literature rather than philosophy.

For all the problems it posed for him, Hölderlin did not simply reject Fichte's ethical vision of the world.[56] If he was repelled by Fichte's view of nature, he was also attracted to his concept of freedom, and especially to his stirring picture of the ego's heroic struggle against nature. He could not help but admire the humanism behind Fichte's vision: like Prometheus, the Fichtean ego went to do battle against fate, and in doing so it rescued the powers of reason and freedom. Following Schiller's example, Hölderlin had celebrated titanic striving in some of his early poems.[57] The great strength of Fichte's concept of striving is that it recognizes how we have to struggle against nature to develop our powers of reason and freedom. We cannot forever live in a state of harmony with nature, and we cannot simply reconcile ourselves to the necessity of nature, as Spinoza would like, because that would not foster the growth of the powers most characteristic of our humanity. Hence the wise old man of *Hyperions Jugend* advises the younger and more cynical narrator: "You carry the germ of infinity within you! Hold it upright throughout all the barrenness of life! Your free spirit invincibly exercises its rights against the resistance of nature" (III, 204).

Hölderlin had no trouble incorporating Fichte's concept of striving into his worldview, for he simply Platonized it, interpreting striving in terms of *eros*, the longing of the soul to return to the eternal. This Platonic theme appears in *Hyperions Jugend*, where Hölderlin wrestles with the same problem that led Fichte to his concept of striving: how to conceive of the infinite within the finite, pure activity in a finite world (III, 202). Hölderlin's solution is also the concept of striving, but he reinterprets it in the light of the Platonic concept of love. Striving is not sheer will power, the obedience to an ethical command, as in Fichte, but the soul's spontaneous longing for the eternal. Love unites the infinite and the finite, pure activity and limitation, because it involves not only a striving for the eternal that transcends any specific limit, but also a feeling that requires some obstacle or resistance. The concept of love explains the origin of limitation and finitude, Hölderlin maintains, because love involves feeling, and feeling is possible only because it is lacking something and something restricts it. "There is something within us that happily carries our chains," the old man says in *Hyperions Jugend*, "for if the spirit were not limited by some resistance we would not feel ourselves or others. But not to feel is the same as death" (III, 202). After all, as Diotima once put it, love consists in striving and longing because it is the offspring of both plenty and scarcity, of both wealth and poverty.[58]

For all its merits, there were problems with Fichte's concept. The striving ego threatened to destroy nature, turning it into a wasteland bereft of beauty, mystery, and magic.[59] There was simply no place left for aesthetic values. Fichte treated nature as if it had a mere use value: nature is the field for the exercise of moral duty. Fichte's concept of striving also ran counter to the doctrine of aesthetic education that Hölderlin inherited from Schiller, which maintains that natural desires and feelings are not to be annhilated or dominated but cultivated and developed into a beautiful whole. Fichte did battle against the passions and instincts, attempting to extirpate them to prepare the ground for the total triumph of reason.[60]

The greatest danger for Hölderlin posed by Fichte's concept of striving is nihilism. Since the self sees the purpose of life as its struggle against nature, it lapses into despair as soon as it recognizes—as it eventually must—that its foe is ultimately insurmountable. The striving self then sees the futility of its efforts and so peers into the abyss. After realizing that all his labors to restore the glory of Greece have been in vain, Hyperion grows despondent and gives vent to the darkest brooding: "we are born for nothing, we love nothing, believe in nothing, work for nothing, and gradually convince ourselves of nothing" (III, 45–46).

It is just at this point, Hölderlin thinks, that the opposing Spinozist view of our relation to nature has its value. For the only cure for such nihilism is to turn to nature. If we cannot achieve unity with nature through our own efforts, we must attain it by surrendering ourselves to the whole of nature. This is how Hyperion saves himself when all his hopes and plans have come to naught. Whenever his struggle fails, he surrenders himself to the arms of nature:

> To be one with everything that lives! With these words virtue lays down its angry armor and the spirit of man its scepter; all thoughts die away before the image of the eternally one world, like the rules of the struggling artist before his Urania; and iron fate renounces its rule. Death fades from the bond of all beings, and inseparability and eternal youth blesses and beautifies the world. (III, 9)

Granted that both Fichte's and Spinoza's views have their merits, how is it possible to synthesize them? Hölderlin is most explicit about his solution in the preface to the penultimate version of *Hyperion*. Here he places each attitude toward nature in a broader *historical* framework: the innocence—fall—redemption scenario of the Christian tradition, which had been secularized by Kant and Schiller.[61] Following the Genesis myth, Kant and Schiller had seen history as the story of mankind's struggle to regain paradise, which consists in its original unity with nature. That which had once been given by nature to ancient man would have to be recreated by modern man through his own efforts, through the use of his freedom and reason. While Kant and Schiller realize that their ideal of unity is unattainable, a utopia we can only approach through constant effort, they also stress that the struggle to regain paradise has had one good result: it has led to the development of reason and freedom.

This theory of history reappears in Hölderlin, who applied it to the development of the individual as well as mankind. Clearly referring to this view of history in the preface to the penultimate version of *Hyperion*, he wrote:

"Blessed unity, being (*das Seyn*) in the only sense of the word, is lost for us, and we must lose it, if we should strive to achieve it. We tear ourselves away from the peaceful one and all of the world, so that we can produce it through ourselves" (III, 236). In the final version of the novel the theory often recurs, now formulated in the mantra "*Ideal wird, was Natur war*" (III, 63). Placing both Fichte and Spinoza in the context of this theory, Hölderlin saw a clear justification for each attitude toward nature: while Spinoza's unity with nature represents the lost ideal, Fichte's concept of striving expresses the struggle to regain paradise.

The historical schema appears biased in favor of Fichte, given that his infinite striving belongs to the future, whereas Spinoza's unity with nature belongs to the past, the state of original oneness lost forever. But Hölderlin's synthesis gives a remarkable twist to the historical schema that grants equal validity to both standpoints. Rather than placing one standpoint in the past and the other in the future, Hölderlin thinks that both belong to extreme but recurring phases of individual development, neither of which is more mature and wise than the other. These stages are not progressive, as if one supersedes the other, but they are circular, moving between opposite extremes. Our life consists in an "eccentric orbit," Hölderlin writes in his *Fragment von Hyperion*, where we move back and forth between opposing extremes or peripheries but where the essential direction seems to be forever the same (III, 163).[62] Both of these extremes are found in Hyperion's life, which constantly oscillates between them. His life is a striking example of the eccentric orbit because the novel ends as it began—with his finding his sense of unity and harmony with nature after failing to recreate the republic of ancient Athens.

Hence the standpoints of Fichte and Spinoza have equal legitimacy because they represent the two poles of the orbit. "Often it seems to us as if the world were everything and we are nothing; but also it often seems as if we were everything and the world nothing," Hölderlin writes in the preface to the penultimate version of *Hyperion* (III, 236). Which standpoint is valid, Hölderlin implies, simply depends on the phase of personal development. "If the life of the world consists in the change from expansion and enclosure, in the flight and return into oneself, why should this not also be the case for the heart of man?" (III, 38) Ultimately, Hölderlin makes the validity of the philosophy depend on the individual's own choice. "In which sense they should be valid for everyone, a free will must decide," he writes in the *Fragment* (163).

Making the validity of a philosophy depend on personal choice and experience was Hölderlin's final trump card in his program to establish the primacy of the aesthetic, the priority of literature over philosophy. If the truth of a philosophy depends on choice, stage of development, or experience, then the conditions of its validity are ultimately better represented in literature than in philosophy, given that it is only in literature that it is possible to portray such personal factors. Hölderlin reached this radical conclusion by taking some of Jacobi's teachings about the limits of reason and exploiting them in the interests of art rather than religion. Since the first principles of a philosophy are indemonstrable, as Jacobi taught, it follows that the choice of a philosophy cannot depend on reason, and so falls outside the realm of philosophy itself.

Such a radical doctrine seems to make philosophy entirely subjective, as if its validity were a matter of choice alone. This hardly squares with Hölderlin's own attempt to break outside the limits of Fichte's subjective idealism, and his insistence on the metaphysical role of the aesthetic. It is important to see, however, that Hölderlin thinks that the eccentric orbit is not only personal but also natural, reflecting not only the spirit of the individual but also the movements of the universe itself. Here, as so often among the romantics, it is crucial to recall that the microcosm is a mirror of the macrocosm, because every individual is inseparable from the organic unity of the universe as a whole. Thus Hölderlin maintains that nature itself has its own dialectical rhythms corresponding to the idealist and realist phases of our personal development. If the idealist phase mirrors nature's movement from the universal and inchoate to the individual and organized, where all the energies of the universe seem to concentrate themselves in self-consciousness, their highest organization and development, the realist phase corresponds to nature's movement from the individual and organized back to the universal and inchoate, where the individual disappears and is swallowed up again in the infinite. It is the task of the poet, Hölderlin insists, to represent both these movements as a unity (IV, 251, 259). To achieve this task would be to show how one's personal development mirrors the movement of the universe itself. That is a demand of a tall order, of course, but Hölderlin's faith in the sovereignty of the aesthetic requires nothing less.

CHAPTER 3

Novalis' Magical Idealism

1. Novalis and the Idealist Tradition

Sometime in the autumn of 1795, not long after Hölderlin wrote 'Urteil und Seyn,' another young thinker sat down to write his critical reflections on Fichte's philosophy. For one long year he entered his reflections into notebooks, which gradually swelled in size. These jottings laid down the basis for much of his later philosophy, and they were to prove no less fecund for the development of absolute idealism than the fragments of Hölderlin. This youth was none other than Friedrich von Hardenberg, or, to use his more commonly known pseudonym, 'Novalis.'

Like Hölderlin, Novalis has gone down in history as one of the foremost lyric poets of early romanticism. But he too was a philosopher, and not only in an incidental way. "Philosophy," he wrote his friend Friedrich Schlegel in the summer of 1796, is "my *Lieblingsstudium*," "the soul of my life and the key to my innermost self."[1] Novalis' philosophical background was very much like Hölderlin's. He too was trained in Jena, where some of the foremost Kantians—K. L. Reinhold and K. C. Schmid—were his tutors. He too was an ardent admirer of Schiller, whose work and conversation proved crucial for his intellectual development. Again like Hölderlin, Novalis was part of the Niethammer circle, and counted Niethammer, Erhard, and Herbert among his intimate friends. He was indeed a member of that circle from 1790 to January 1792, its most formative and fecund years when its critique of foundationalism was first formulated. It was in the house of Niethammer in May 1795 that Novalis first met Fichte, and crossed paths—for the first and last time—with Hölderlin.[2]

No less than Hölderlin, Novalis deserves a prominent place in the history of German idealism. Around the same time as Hölderlin,[3] and long before

Schelling and Hegel, he formulated some of the basic themes of absolute idealism. That the absolute is the divine *logos*, the identity of the subjective and objective; that the ideal and the real are only parts of a single living whole; that thinking lapses into falsehood and contradiction in abstracting parts from the whole; that unity is not possible without difference; and, finally, that only art has the power to perceive the absolute—these themes are found in Novalis' notebooks as early as 1796. Along with Hölderlin and Schlegel, Novalis was also a leader in the reaction against Fichte's subjective idealism. While Schelling was still a Fichtean and Hegel still a Kantian, Novalis insisted that Fichte's principles are too abstract and one-sided: they could not explain the organic structure of nature, still less establish the systematic unity of the empirical sciences. Like Hölderlin, Novalis doubted whether self-consciousness could provide philosophy with a self-evident starting point, and he too questioned the very possibility of first principles. In all these respects, Novalis' critique of Fichte anticipates—and indeed goes beyond—Hegel's later *Differenzschrift*.

Recognition of Novalis significance in the history of German idealism has been late in coming.[4] The traditional picture of Novalis has been that of a mystical poet who had neither training nor discipline to think through a philosophical problem. While his philosophical interests were sometimes acknowledged, they were regarded as at best amateurish, and in their content dependent on Fichte.[5] To be sure, Novalis was recognized as the creator of a form of idealism—his so-called magical idealism—but this was considered extravagant and occult, a poetic version of Fichte's *Wissenschaftslehre*. It was only in 1954 that Novalis' philosophical stature was finally and fully recognized by Theodor Haering in his magisterial *Novalis als Philosoph*.[6] While it must be said that Haering viewed Novalis through Hegelian spectacles, he at least did justice to the full depth and range of his philosophical interests. In the 1960s the traditional picture of the mystical poet was completely exploded with the publication of the critical edition of Novalis' works. Sheer size alone shows the intensity and extent of Novalis' philosophical and scientific concerns: while the literary works make up a single volume, the philosophical notebooks encompass more than two larger volumes. Now that these notebooks have been carefully edited and published, the study of Novalis' philosophy has begun in earnest.[7]

While Novalis' philosophical importance is now widely recognized, his place in the history of German idealism has become the subject of controversy. In the past some scholars placed Novalis in this tradition, either because he was influenced by Fichte or because he anticipated Schelling and Hegel.[8] More recently, however, other scholars have argued that Novalis falls outside this tradition. They have put forward two arguments for their view. First, Novalis' general position is more akin to realism than any form of idealism because it makes being rather than the ego the first principle of consciousness.[9] Second, in the name of art Novalis developed a radical criticism of all philosophy, so that he places himself outside any philosophical tradition, not least idealism.[10]

There is some truth to these contentions. Regarding the first, it is true that Novalis was *not* an idealist in the Kantian–Fichtean sense. It does not follow, however, that he is not in the tradition of *absolute idealism*.[11] While Novalis, no less than Hölderlin, gives a central role to the concept of being, this is not a form of realism, as if his absolute transcends all subjectivity. For Novalis insists that the absolute has both a subjective and objective aspect, that it unites idealism and realism. In this respect Novalis belongs in the same tradition as Hölderlin, Schlegel, Schelling, and Hegel.

Regarding the second point, it is true that, unlike Hegel, Novalis held that true philosophy should end in ignorance because the absolute transcends the grasp of discursive reason.[12] It is also the case that, with Hölderlin, he believed in the sovereignty of art over philosophy, holding that only poetic imagination could fathom the absolute. Still, for all his criticism of philosophy, Novalis never turned away from it.[13] His critique of foundationalism should *not* be taken as a rejection of philosophy *tout court*. For Novalis insisted that, even though it cannot provide knowledge of the absolute, and even though it cannot establish an infallible first principle of all knowledge, philosophy is still the source of regulative ideas that are crucial for guiding human action.[14] No less than Kant and Fichte, Novalis prized the critical role of philosophy, taking to task those who had failed to scrutinize their own methods and goals. The goal of philosophy, as he formulated it in his 1798 *Allgemeine Brouillon*, was "to make everything loose," that is, to show how all standpoints on the absolute are only relative (no. 622; III, 378). By 1798, however, Novalis began to assign philosophy a much more positive role: it provided the key for the construction of his encyclopedia, the template for the system of the sciences. It was philosophy that founded the principles of scientific method, and that systematized all special sciences (nos. 622–624; III, 378). Though Novalis gave poetry sovereignty over philosophy, he still stressed the two disciplines were interdependent, so that good poets are good philosophers and conversely (nos. 29, 31; II, 531, 533) Philosophy indeed became for him the guardian and helpmate of poetry, the basis for "the theory of poetry" that would show the importance and necessity of art (nos. 31, 280; II, 590–591).

Both arguments for placing Novalis outside the idealist tradition draw invalid generalizations from his early notebooks, failing to consider his later philosophical development. While Novalis was critical of almost all philosophical pretensions in his early notebooks, he continued to nurture systematic ambitions, which eventually grew into his project for the encyclopdia of all the sciences. No less than Schelling and Hegel, Novalis was a systematic philosopher, whose goal was to show how all the sciences form a unity. Furthermore, the transcendent absolute of the early notebooks disappears in the later writings, which emphasize a neo-Platonic conception of God. Rather than a *deus obsconditus*, Novalis' God becomes the divine *logos* of Plotinus, who reveals himself in all creation. Indeed, Novalis wanted to make the idea of God into the organizing principle of his encyclopedia, so that the definition of God became the basis of all definitions; he also made God into the object of a rational perception or intellectual intuition along neo-Platonic lines (nos. 896,934; III, 440, 448). The stumbling block of nonrationalist interpretations of Novalis is his allegiance to the Platonic tradition, which goes back to his earliest years, but which became even more pronounced in his later ones.[15]

2. Fichte Studies

In the autumn of 1795 Novalis began a career as an administrator of the Saxon government, becoming secretary to a local official in Tennstedt. His job left him three free hours a day, when he would devote himself to "urgent introductory studies, [filling] basic gaps in my knowledge, and the exercise of my thinking powers."[16] It was during his Tennstedt days that Novalis began to write notes on Fichte, a task that preoccupied him from autumn 1795 until late summer 1796. His notebooks consist in six different groups of manuscripts, which were written at varying intervals, and which differ in content and style. They have been given the title *Fichte-Studien*, though the name is somewhat misleading since they do not consist in studies of, or commentaries on, any of Fichte's writings. Rather, they represent Novalis' effort to formulate his own position by thinking his way through what he called the "dreadful thread of abstractions" of Fichte's system.

After long neglect, the importance of the *Fichte-Studien* for Novalis' philosophical development has been fully recognized, and they have even been called "the most significant philosophical contribution of early German romanticism."[17] The notebooks anticipate, and lay the foundation for, many of Novalis' later views, especially those concerning the limits of philosophy and the role of art. Novalis sketches the rudiments of a philosophy of language, develops a dialectical methodology, and proposes an absolute idealism that is a synthesis of Fichte and Spinoza. But perhaps the most striking feature of the notebooks is Novalis' radical criticism of philosophy itself. He questions the very possibility of foundationalism, doubting the feasibility of any transcendental philosophy that would determine the first principles and conditions of human knowledge.

For all their importance, the notebooks are also an early and immature work, riddled with doubt, hesitation, ambivalence, and inconsistency. While some of their themes proved fecund, others fell sterile. After all, the notebooks are just that: notebooks, collections of jottings written on various occasions and never intended for publication. Their main purpose was exploratory and pedagogic, and their results were provisional and tentative. Often Novalis asks himself what he means, chides himself for vagueness, and even admits that he engages in sophistry. While it is wrong to dismiss the notebooks as an incoherent miscellany of fragments, it is also naive to see in them the preliminary exposition of a system.[18] Novalis did not have a principle, program, or system *before* writing the notebooks, but at best some vague ideas *after* writing them. But the main reason for caution in dealing with the notebooks comes from Novalis himself, who became dissatisfied and bored with them, complaining that they were superficial and lacked any organizing principle.[19] This does not mean that the notebooks are of marginal value for the study of Novalis—the very opposite is the case—but it does mean that there is a danger of anachronism where one treats the notebooks only as an anticipation of later ideas. Any complete and accurate account should treat them as a whole, considering them in all their ambivalence, incongruity, and tentativeness.

Nothing better reveals the provisional and immature character of *Fichte-Studien* than a profound tension running throughout it. While Novalis criticizes the very possibility of a system of philosophy, he also searches for one of his own. Hence he states that he is looking for a theory that will reveal the fundamental laws behind our mental life (no. 465; II, 250); he also often writes of "my system" (nos. 11, 108; II, 108, 153); and he even proposes his own first principle of philosophy.[20] Nevertheless, Novalis' investigation into the possibility of philosophy comes to a negative conclusion, casting doubt on the feasibility of both a system and a first principle. This tension eventually became fully apparent to Novalis himself when he wrote in one of the closing entries: "The proper philosophical system must bring freedom and infinity, or, to put it more paradoxically, systemlessness into a system"(no. 648; II, 289).

Whatever his views about systematicity, Novalis' central concern in the notebooks is to investigate the very possibility of systematic transcendental philosophy. This interest is never explicitly stated, but it emerges clearly enough from several of the early fragments. Thus Novalis makes his subject of enquiry "philosophy in general—the possibility of a system" (no. 11; II, 108), raising the question of "grounding the possibility of reflection or systematic thinking" (no. 12; II, 111). In effect, Novalis' enquiry is *meta*-critical or *meta*-epistemological: to determine whether a transcendental epistemology like that of Kant or Fichte is possible.

Throughout the notebooks Novalis finds a systematic transcendental philosophy problematic for several reasons. The first concerns the circularities and infinite regresses of self-knowledge.[21] These difficulties arise because the transcendental philosopher attempts to determine within the self the ultimate conditions of all thinking, which cannot themselves be an object of thinking. Novalis raises these thorny issues almost immediately by asking whether philosophy can consist in self-reflection (*Selbstbetrachtung*) (no. 15; II, 113). He answers in the negative for the following reason. To reflect on itself, the self would have to be an object to itself; in other words, it would have to perceive itself and determine its specific characteristics; but the self cannot be such an object to itself when it is the ultimate condition of all thinking, the basis under which anything is an object of thought.

Although Novalis doubts that the self can know itself through reflection, he does not deny the possibility of *all* self-consciousness or self-knowledge. His argument excludes the possibility of *discursive* self-knowledge, but leaves open the possibility of *immediate* or *intuitive* self-consciousness. Novalis raises just this prospect when he states that the self is "perhaps" aware of itself through feeling (*Gefühl*) (no. 115; II, 113; no. ll; II, 25–26). If philosophy cannot be self-reflection, he says, it is still possible for it to be self-feeling (*Selbstgefühl*). He then affirms this possibility by stating that philosophy is originally feeling, and that there must be at least some feeling of the activities behind consciousness.

While Novalis concedes the possibility of self-consciousness in the form of feeling, he also insists that feeling determines the ultimate limits of all transcendental enquiry. "The limits of feeling are the limits of philosophy. Feeling cannot feel itself" (no. 15; II, 114). Feeling is essential to self-consciousness, and so all consciousness; but it resists all discursive analysis, which presupposes its presence. Fichte would have agreed with Novalis that feeling marks the limits of all philosophy, for he too insisted in the *Wissenschaftslehre* that the realm of feeling is undeducible. This indeed helps to explain Novalis' own use of the term 'feeling.' But Novalis turns Fichte's point against him, maintaining that undeducible feeling exists in not only the empirical manifold but self-consciousness itself. It is impossible for transcendental philosophy to articulate and systematize feeling, Novalis argues, for here the same vicious circle reappears. We cannot think about this feeling without presupposing it. If we reflect on the feeling in consciousness, that is possible only if we lay down some prior mediating intuition (*Mittelanschauung*); but this intuition is in turn possible only through some prior feeling and reflection, and so on *ad infinitum* (no. 17; II, 114–115).

Of course, Fichte himself was aware of all the difficulties involved in self-knowledge, and he postulated intellectual intuition precisely to avoid them. Novalis does not deny the possibility of intellectual intuition; and he indeed affirms its necessity, insisting that it lies at the basis of all consciousness (no. 22; 119). While he sometimes seems to think it is composed of, and based upon, feeling and reflection (nos. 16–17; II, 114–115), he also insists that its analysis into these components holds only for reflection itself and that originally it lies at the basis of even that reflection (no. 22; II, 119; no. ll; II, 18–22). Nevertheless, Novalis holds that simply appealing to intellectual intuition does not resolve the difficulties posed by self-knowledge. The same problems reappear all over again, for the issue now is how the purely immediate intellectual intuition is to be made into the subject of a transcendental system. How do we make something purely intuitive and immediate into an object of thought without destroying its very immediacy and intuitiveness? Hence Novalis reasons as follows: "Intellectual intuition alone gives *mere reality*—but this is in reflection as good as nothing. It should be for reflection and it is not—i.e., it cannot be opposed.—Hence it is for reflection nothing" (no. 22; II, 120).

Novalis' doubts about the possibility of transcendental philosophy are based on not only the problems of self-consciousness but also the difficulties of establishing any first principle. His skepticism about foundationalism begins from impeccable Kantian premises: that reason is limited to experience, to the knowledge of given objects (no. 15; II, 113), and that it should not step beyond experience in the attempt to know the absolute or the unconditioned. But Novalis turns this doctrine against Kant and Fichte, using it to criticize the ambitions of transcendental philosophy itself. The incapacity of reason to know the absolute means that it cannot discover the first principles of knowledge, or develop a system about the conditions of experience itself. For these principles or conditions are themselves not within experience, and they too are unconditioned or absolute as the ultimate and final conditions of all thinking or experience. We should treat first principles or a complete system, Novalis thinks, only as regulative ideas, as ways of bringing unity into our thinking about the conditions of experience. We should be aware, however, of assuming that there is some first principle or complete system already there within ourselves, for that would amount to nothing less than hypostasis, the very fallacy Kant and Fichte so often warn against. Hence Novalis likens the search for such first principles or such a system to the quest for "the philosopher's stone" (no. 566; II, 270). Applying Fichte's doctrine of striving to transcendental philosophy itself, Novalis states that the only absolute given to the transcendental philosopher is the *striving* or *search* for first principles, which can be approached but never attained.

Novalis' reflections on the possibility of transcendental philosophy eventually lead him to the harsh conclusion that it is nothing but a form of what he calls the "sophistry of the ego" (nos. 44, 49; II, 136, 138). He arrives at this conclusion on the basis of a general critique of reflection, or abstract and systematic thinking, which reveals the influence more of Jacobi than Kant. The problem with transcendental philosophy is that it explains the first conditions of knowledge by postulating something absolute, which it then attempts to know through reflection, though the absolute cannot be grasped through reflection. Throughout his notebooks Novalis gives several reasons why reflection cannot know the absolute. First, the absolute is the unconditioned, the cause of itself; but reflection explains all events by the external causes acting on them. Second, the absolute is an indivisible unity; but all reflection divides. Third, the absolute is infinite, not limited by anything outside itself; but reflection is determination, defining a thing through negation, by how it contrasts with other things. Hence Novalis likens reflection to one-half of a sphere whose properties are the opposite of the other it represents (no. 17; II, 115). Reflection falsifies whatever it reflects on, so that whatever image or picture of reality it produces is the very opposite of the truth (no. 64; II, 142). It creates an inverted world, an *ordo inversus*, whose statements have to be denied to find the truth.[22]

Novalis' criticism of transcendental philosophy eventually expands into an attack on discursive thinking in general, culminating in his striking claim that "all thinking is the art of illusion" (no. 234; II, 181). He indeed goes so far as to insist that illusion (*Schein*) is constitutive of experience itself, and nothing less than "the original form of all truth." His choice of terms here is significant: *contra* Kant, Novalis deliberately conflates appearance (*Erscheinung*) with illusion (*Schein*), because he thinks that experience is constituted by judgments, all of which are false. Novalis comes to this shocking conclusion from two perfectly pedestrian and plausible premises. The first is the Kantian claim that all knowledge, and indeed perception, involves the use of concepts, and so an (implicit and subconscious) act of judgment. The second is a conventional analysis of the logical form of judgment, which Novalis could have found in any textbook.[23] According to this analysis, the subject term of a judgment stands for a bare particular, which is formless, while the predicate represents a universal or form, which is contentless (nos. 227–230; II, 172). If we put these premises together, then the conclusion is inevitable: all thinking and experience will have to consist in illusion. For when we apply a predicate to a subject, we attribute the determinate to the indeterminate, a form to something formless. All thinking or judging involves an act of determination, carving a whole into distinct parts, which destroys the unity of the particular it attempts to know. All illusion arises, Novalis explains, when we elevate the part to a whole or degrade a whole to its part (no. 234; II, 180). But this is precisely what we do in judgment when we attempt to understand an indivisible and unique bare particular through a determination or property, which divides it and compares it to other things.

It has been argued that the intention behind Novalis' critique of philosophy in the *Fichte-Studien* was to establish the sovereignty of art.[24] Supposedly, Novalis wanted to show how the absolute cannot be known through reason but only through art. This reading is plausible, not least because it shows how Novalis fits into a common romantic project. Unfortunately, however, there is little textual evidence to support it. While Novalis later argues for the sovereignty of poetry over philosophy, no such claim appears in the notebooks.[25] He does suggest that beauty should be the criterion for truth in philosophy, and he even states the basis of representation and intuition consists in the "principle of beauty" (no. 234; II, 177). But these remarks are left unexplored. Novalis' distance from his later position becomes especially clear when we find him baldly reaffirming Fichte's doctrine of the sovereignty of practical reason: "The highest philosophy is ethics" (no. 536; II, 267).

Whatever Novalis' motives in criticizing philosophy, they did not prevent him from trying to develop his own system. Already in the first group of manuscripts he thinks that he has provided something of a "deduction of philosophy," the possibility of reflection to formulate intellectual intuition (no. 19; II, 116–118). Although reflection cannot conceive pure form or pure content, it can grasp *determinate* form—some unity of form and content—and it is just this that is provided by intellectual intuition. The method to construct a system, Novalis explains, is to see how each level of unity of form and content is opposed by another unity, and then to ascend to that unity that cannot be opposed by anything else (no. 20; II, 118). This method will be both analytic and synthetic, moving from the whole to its parts and then back to the whole from the parts (no. 271; II, 192). Novalis not only expresses systematic ideals but also attempts to practice them, proposing different ways of organizing and deducing the Kantian categories from a single idea or principle. This was the staple fare of transcendental philosophy in the 1790s; not even Novalis could resist the pastime of *Architektonikspiel*.

The tension between Novalis' critique of philosophy and his own philosophical ambitions runs even deeper, however. Although he doubts the possibility of a first principle, he attempts to discover one himself; and although he casts doubt on all knowledge of the absolute, he does not hesitate to speculate about its nature. There are some remarkable passages in the first group of manuscripts where Novalis attempts to synthesize and go beyond Spinoza and Fichte. While Spinoza's first principle is nature, and Fichte's is the ego or the person, his is nothing less than God (no. 151; II, 157). Novalis sees God as the highest thesis, the sphere of all analysis and synthesis (nos. 151–152; II, 157). God is what remains when we abstract from everything in the spheres of nature and person (no. 156; II, 158). Nature and person are only aspects of God, which come together in him like two pyramids with a common apex (no. 153; II, 157). In seeing the ego or the person as only one aspect or attribute of God, Novalis deliberately demotes the status of the *Wissenschaftslehre*. Rather than dealing with the first principle of philosophy, the *Wissenschaftslehre* is now nothing more than "*Subjektslehre*," treating the subjective rather than the objective side of the absolute (nos. 157, 186; II, 158, 163). Like Hölderlin, Novalis finds it difficult to understand why Fichte calls his absolute an ego when it is not something subjective opposed to the objective but the unity or indifference of the subjective and objective (nos. 5–7; II, 107).[26]

Yet does not Novalis' own critique of philosophy also apply to his own first principle? If all first principles are only regulative, and if the belief in some reality corresponding to them is only an illusion, then the same would seem to hold for the idea of God himself. There are passages in the notebooks where Novalis appears to endorse this very conclusion. The idea of God is only an hypostatization of the idea of an absolute whole, he suggests, because it is only a *personification* of this idea, which is itself only a fiction (no. 462; II, 249). Whether God exists, he also implies, depends on whether we believe in him: "Where man lays down his reality, what he *fixes* upon, that is his god, his world, his everything" (no. 396; II, 233). Novalis comes closest to undermining the reality of the idea of the absolute when he later insists that the whole idea of pure being is nothing more than a fiction: "What does it mean, *pure* and *empirical*[?] What are these for concepts? Pure—what is not related, not relatable. The forms of the relatable are the empirical forms a priori. The concept *"pure"* is therefore an empty concept—i.e., a concept corresponding to no intuition—a concept that is neither possible, nor actual, nor necessary—everything pure is an illusion of imagination—a *necessary* fiction" (no. 234; II, 179). Novalis later expands this argument by stating that pure being does not designate anything, that one knows nothing about a thing if one knows only that it exists, and that a thing is for us nothing more than the totality of its properties (nos. 454–455; II, 247).

It seems possible to remove this tension simply by claiming that Novalis ascribes a strictly regulative validity to his own concept of God or absolute being. But the texts do not permit such an easy reconciliation. The tension persists because Novalis also makes the absolute into an object of feeling and faith (nos. 3, 15; II, 106–107, 113–114), which implies that it exists. If we claim that the absolute is only a regulative idea, that it is indeed only a *"fiction,"* then it cannot also be made into an object of feeling and faith.[27] For this is to imply that there is nothing for us to feel or believe in; to assume that there is something in existence corresponding to the idea is just the fallacy of hypostasis all over again.

The source of the tension probably lies in Novalis' own religious feelings, which he had nurtured from childhood, but which clashed with the critical legacy of Kant's philosophy. Friedrich Schlegel had complained about Novalis' indulgence in pietist mysticism, which did not cease while writing his notebooks. On July 8, 1796 Novalis wrote Friedrich Schlegel that he now felt part of an infinite whole, and that he missed Zinzendorf's and Spinoza's idea of infinite love in Fichte's philosophy (IV, 188). These feelings only grew during the illness of Novalis fiancée in November 1795, and they emerge with perfect frankness and clarity after her death when Novalis said that he would now have to live in "belief in God and immortality."[28] It was probably these kinds of feeling that inspired Novalis to make God into his absolute rather than merely nature or the ego. Whatever their source, Novalis' growing religious views were difficult to reconcile with the radical critical philosophy of Fichte and the Niethammer circle, which ascribed a purely regulative and moral status to the traditional objects of religious belief.

3. Fichte in Novalis' Idealism

Since the publication of Haym's magisterial *Die romantische Schule* in 1870, the prevalent interpretation of Novalis' idealism in histories of literature and philosophy has been that it is "poetically exaggerated Fichte," an imaginative, mystical, or occult form of the *Wissenschaftslehre*.[29] According to this interpretation, the starting point of Novalis' idealism is the Fichtean principle that the world is the creation of the absolute ego, the objectification of productive imagination. Supposedly, Novalis simply extended and radicalized this principle, making it the basis for his natural philosophy and poetry. Hence Novalis made self-knowledge the key for the study of nature, and productive imagination the source of poetry.

There is some truth to this interpretation. Novalis was indeed inspired by Fichte's idealism, which did play a central role in his aesthetics and natural philosophy. But there are also serious problems with this reading, which has to be heavily qualified to yield an accurate account of Novalis' idealism. Though it has come under increasing criticism, Haym's interpretation is still far too entrenched to ignore.[30]

The first difficulty with his interpretation is that it ascribes a very crude reading of Fichte to Novalis, whose understanding of Fichte—it must be said—was much more subtle and sophisticated than some of his expositors. It is clear from the *Fichte-Studien* that Novalis grasped perfectly well the limits of Fichte's critical idealism, its restriction of knowledge to experience and the regulative status of its basic principle. Novalis does not think that the Fichtean ego is some kind of universal creative principle or activity that creates the entire finite world. Rather, he maintains that it is only a regulative ideal, a goal for our action, which we can approach but never attain (nos. 479, 502; II, 256, 258). It is a crude fallacy, he further explains, to assume that this merely regulative idea has the power to create anything (no. 476; II, 255). While Novalis makes much of the powers of the creative imagination, just as his commentators stress, he does not think that these have the capacity to create the entire world. He indeed insists that the realm of feeling is given to us, and that no philosophy is in a position to deduce or to explain it (nos. 15–17, 515; II, 113–114, 261). The Fichtean ego is not "an encyclopedia" that contains the whole content of the empirical world within itself, but only "a universal principle" that assimilates content *after* it is given to it (no. 168; II, 273). Later, in his *Allgemeine Brouillon*, Novalis is explicit about the purely fictional status of the Fichtean ego, which he insists is only an ideal, something that we should construct, so that it belongs in the realm of art rather than nature (nos. 76, 717; III, 253, 405). The fact that the Fichtean ego belongs in the realm of art means that we, the multitude of finite agents, create it through our striving to become purely rational beings. It is our collective work of art, our creation, no less than society and the state.

Another grave problem with this interpretation is that it neglects a powerful anti-Fichtean influence upon Novalis' thinking: Spinoza. Like Schelling, Hölderlin, and Hegel, Novalis had read Jacobi's *Briefe*,[31] and he too was attracted by Lessing's *credo*. Spinoza became for him "*der Gott betrunkene Mensch*" (no. 562; III, 651), who rightly saw the divine presence in all things. Novalis was especially inspired by Spinoza's idea of the infinite, and by his intellectual love of God, which demands reconciliation with the world through a rational identification with it. Such ideas, he realized, could not be easily accommodated in Fichte's system. Because Fichte stressed that we must change the world, forcing it to conform to reason, he had failed to recognize that we must also change ourselves, learning how to adapt to, and become one with, the world. Novalis' sympathy for Spinozism, and his growing reservations about Fichte, are perfectly apparent from this passage in his July 14, 1796 letter to Friedrich Schlegel:

> I feel more in everything that I am the sublime member of an infinite whole, into which I have grown and which should be the shell of my ego. Must I not happily suffer everything, now that I love and love more than the eight spans of space, and love longer than all the vascillations of the chords of life? Spinoza and Zinzendorf have investigated it, the infinite idea

of love, and they had an intuition of its method, of how they could develop it for themselves, and themselves for it, on this speck of dust. It is a pity that I see nothing of this view in Fichte, that I feel nothing of this creative breath. But he is close to it. He must step into its magic circle—unless his earlier life wiped the dust off his wings. (IV, 188)

The Fichtean interpretation of Novalis' idealism is only a half-truth, then, because Novalis' goal is to *synthesize* Fichte and Spinoza. Like many of his generation, Novalis wanted to find the *common principle* of Fichte's idealism and Spinoza's naturalism, the point of identity of which the subjective and objective, the ego and nature, are only appearances. This synthesis of idealism and realism would not simply subordinate realism to idealism, as in the transcendental idealism of the *Wissenschaftslehre*, but it would give both an equal and coordinate role. Novalis' search for this single principle appears repeatedly in some of his later notebooks, especially the *Allgemeine Brouillon*.[32] But we have already seen him stumbling toward such a principle in the *Fichte-Studien*, where he made the ego and nature two different appearances of a single reality, which he identified with God.

A final problem with the Fichtean interpretation of Novalis' idealism is that it does not consider the profound extent to which Novalis *reinterpreted* and *transformed* Fichte's basic concepts according to neo-Platonist principles. In the autumn of 1798 Novalis made a momentous discovery: Plotinus! Plato and Hemsterhuis had been his favorite authors since he began his study of philosophy,[33] but he became acquainted with the ideas of the great neo-Platonist only much later by reading Tiedemann's *Geschichte der Philosophie*. Novalis found that Plotinus' ideas were exactly what he had been looking for in his attempt to fuse idealism and realism, and that no other philosopher suited him so well. So pleased was Novalis with his find that he later told Caroline Schlegel that Plotinus was the first philosopher to enter the sacred temple, and that no one after him had penetrated so far inside it (IV, 276). This is how he explains his discovery to Friedrich Schlegel on December 10, 1798:

> I do not know if I already wrote you about my dear Plotinus. I learned about this philosopher, who was born for me, from Tiedemann—I was almost astonished by the similarity with Fichte and Kant—and his *idealistic* affinity with them. He is more to my heart than the two of them . . . In Plotinus there is still much unused—and he is well worth making better known. (IV, 269)

After his discovery of Plotinus, Novalis began to give many of the concepts of Fichte's philosophy a neo-Platonic interpretation. In his *Allgemeine Brouillon* Novalis praised Plotinus for anticipating many of the fundamental results of modern philosophy, such as the need for a synthesis of idealism and realism (no. 924; III, 443). But rather than making Fichte the standard to judge Plotinus, he made Plotinus the standard to judge Fichte. The concept of intellectual intuition now became the inner light or ectasy (no. 896; III, 440), and Fichte's ego was the forerunner of reason or the divine *logos* (nos. 908, 1098; III, 443, 469). Where Fichte went astray, Novalis complained, is in not having any idea of the *hypostases* (no. 1067; III, 465); because of this, he had grasped only half of what is meant by the creative mind. This was Novalis' way of saying—what Schelling and Hegel would insist on two years later—that Fichte had only a subjective idealism; in other words, Fichte had failed to see that reason is something objective in reality itself and not only a form of self-consciousness.

Novalis' discovery of Plotinus, his lifelong sympathy with Plato, and his enthusiasm for Hemsterhuis casts doubt on another aspect of the Fichtean reading of his idealism: the claim that Novalis poeticized Fichte's system by replacing reason with the imagination.[34] For all his criticisms of philosophy in the *Fichte-Studien*, Novalis never lapsed into irrationalism, denigrating the value and necessity of reason itself. While reason did not have the creative power of imagination, he still saw it as the characteristic trait of humanity (no. 476; II, 255), and indeed as the basis to unify all our mental powers (no. 86; II, 543). Reason was nothing less than "the sole salvation of humanity," "the only genuine and true *logos* coming from God and returning to him."[35] While Novalis had prized mystical insights that lie beyond our discursive powers, these had more to do with the hyperrational intuition of Plato and Plotinus than the arational perception of Luther and the Protestant tradition.

4. The Elements of Magical Idealism

In several fragments Novalis devised the name 'magical idealism' for his own philosophy, and it is under this title that his views have become known to history. The name appears repeatedly in his 1798 *Allgemeine Brouillon*, though the essential ideas behind it emerge in some fragments from the *Vorarbeiten*, the 'Logologische Fragmente,' which were written in late 1797.[36] Novalis wrote of "*Mein magischer Idealismus*," and he sketched a progression of philosophical positions culminating in his doctrine.[37] There is more than sufficient justification, then, for regarding magical idealism as his personal philosophy.

However, the exact meaning of this doctrine is obscure and ambiguous, and it has been the subject of some dispute. Some maintain that Novalis abandoned it in his final years,[38] while others hold that it is not truly representative of his complete philosophy.[39] There is indeed an apparent difficulty in reconciling magical idealism with other aspects of his philosophy: it postulates the possibility of a complete control over our bodies and all of nature, so that it appears to clash with Novalis' sympathy for Spinozism.[40] Before we examine these thorny issues, it is best to consider the basic meaning of the doctrine.

The germ of magic idealism lies in an analogy that appears in a few fragments from the *Vorarbeiten*.[41] In one fragment Novalis imagines that someday we will have the power to control our external senses just as we now have the power to direct our internal ones (no. 111; II, 546–547). This analogy appears in the context of the common eighteenth-century distinction between inner and outer sense. Novalis locates external sense in the body, internal sense in the soul. Through the body we perceive stimuli in the external world, whereas through the soul we perceive stimuli within ourselves. Thanks to our powers of attention and abstraction, Novalis writes, we have great control over our internal senses. We have the power to determine what we perceive within ourselves by abstracting from, or directing our attention to, some things rather than others (no. 235; II, 577–578). Is it also not possible, Novalis asks, for us to have the same degree of control over our external senses, if we only educate this latent power?

In another adjacent fragment Novalis somewhat alters the terms of the analogy, now focusing on the relationship between mind and body in general rather than that between internal and external sense. He imagines that one day we will be able to control the inner organs of our body just as we are now able to control our thoughts, actions, and speech (no. 247; II, 583). That the soul has much greater power over the body than we normally think is apparent, Novalis says, from psychosomatic phenomena, and from those individuals who have some power over usually involuntary functions. We can make the whole body dependent on our will, Novalis thinks, if we can only learn how to direct the will itself. The more control we have over our bodies, the more we will have over our senses, and so we will influence the world we perceive, so that we will ultimately be able to live in a world of our own making (nos. 247–248; II, 583–584). The body is the tool for the education and modification of our world, so that the more we modify it, the more we create our world (no. 256; II, 587).

Though their formulations differ, the underlying analogy in both fragments is roughly the same. The essential idea is that we should have the power to control our external senses or body just as we now have the power to control the internal senses or the mind. In either case, the power of the will is to be extended further over our nature—"everything involuntary is transformed into something voluntary" (no. 273; II, 589)—so that the world we perceive is made to approximate the world in which we want to live. Novalis sometimes took his utopian thinking to extremes, postulating the ideal of a complete control over nature, so that we human beings finally attain the status of God (nos. 78, 320; III, 253, 297). Though this seems fantastic and even perverse, it is important to stress that Novalis, like Fichte, saw it only as a regulative ideal that we could approach but never attain. The utopian dimension of Novalis' thinking here is already clearly stated by Fichte in his *Vorlesungen über die Bestimmung des Gelehrten*,[42] and it should not be taken as evidence for the excesses of romanticism.[43]

Such is, if only very crudely, one essential idea behind magical idealism. Novalis gave his doctrine this name because magic is for him the art of making nature conform to our will (no. 109; II, 546), and because idealism is the doctrine that what we perceive depends on our own creative activity. It should be obvious that much of the provenance of this doctrine is Kantian–Fichtean. Novalis began from the general principle behind Kant's new method of thought: that we know or perceive what we create or produce. He gave this principle an especially clear formulation in a fragment from the *Vorarbeit:* "We know something only insofar as we *express* it—i.e., can *make* it. The more completely and diversely we can *produce, execute* something, the better we *know* it. We know a thing perfectly when we can communicate it everywhere and in every manner" (no. 267; II, 589). But Novalis then added to this principle a basic Fichtean doctrine: that our cognitive faculties stand under the direction of the will. Fichte taught Novalis that we can do whatever we will to do, and that the limits of our powers are determined only by those of our will.[44] He then took this voluntaristic element of Fichte's thinking to its final conclusion when he wrote that the will is nothing less than "the basis of all creation" (no. 512; II, 354). Now if we add Kant's principle that knowing is making with Fichte's doctrine that making depends on willing, we arrive at the view that the world we know and live in depends on the will itself. What Novalis adds to these Kantian and Fichtean elements is an aesthetic dimension: that the will should create the world according to the standards of beauty, so that it becomes a work of art. According to Novalis' own definition, magical idealism is the *romantic* doctrine because romanticism is making the world into a work of art, so that it regains its magic, mystery, and beauty.[45]

These Kantian and Fichtean elements of magical idealism have been one of the chief reasons for the Fichtean interpretation of Novalis' philosophy. It is important to see, however, that they do not exhaust the meaning of magical idealism, but express only one of its aspects, more specifically its subjective or idealistic side. For, true to Novalis' attempt to find a system that would unify Fichte and Spinoza, there is also an objective or realistic side to magical idealism. The purpose of magical idealism is to give us power over ourselves and nature, to be sure, but that power does not consist simply in being active, in creating nature and making it conform to our will. Rather, it also consists in being passive, in learning how to integrate ourselves with nature and to receive her stimuli. Unlike Fichte and more like Schiller, Novalis' goal is not the annhilation of the realm of sensibility, but the unity of our powers, an aesthetic whole where activity and sensibility, inner and outer sense, are harmonized with one another.[46] The ideal constitution, Novalis states, is that where the highest degree of sensitivity is united with the highest degree of energy (no. 235; II, 577). Control over our body and senses means making them not only instruments to change the world, but also more sensitive organs to perceive it. Novalis further explains that his ideal is where our inner and outer sense enjoy an *interplay* with one another, so that they work in perfect harmony (no. 111; II, 546–547). This harmony means that they must each retain their specific characteristics when united with one another. The elements of harmony are not only the will but also chance; the goal is to unite them so that the voluntary appears like chance and the chance voluntary (no. 112; II, 547–548). This is precisely what would be involved in making our lives more like a work of art or novel.

That Novalis had in mind Schiller's aesthetic unity more than Fichte's titanic will becomes apparent from his allegiance to the physiology of John Brown. No less than Kant's and Fichte's epistemology, Brown's physiology was an essential basis for Novalis' magical idealism.[47] According to Brown's doctrine, the state of health of an organism depends on it finding a balance between overstimulation and understimulation, activity and passivity. There are diseases that result from overstimulating the organism, and those that result from understimulating it. True to Brown's theory, Novalis recognizes that too much activity of the will, and too little receptivity to the outside world, would result in danger to the organism. Thus he warns that too great activity of our inner powers results in delusions (II, 376, 451). The point behind magic idealism was to give longer life to the organism by counteracting the overwhelming stimuli of the external world with a stronger source of stimulation from within (no. 399; III, 315).

One of the major stumbling blocks to Novalis' philosophical rehabilitation has been the very term 'magical idealism,' which has connotations of the occult. There can be no doubt that Novalis had some sympathy with the hermetic and cabalistic traditions, and that some of its ideas play a crucial role in his magical idealism (nos. 137–143; III, 266–268). But rather than denying or wishing away these elements of Novalis' thinking, it is necessary to ask what lay behind them. All too often in Novalis the mystical and magical is simply a poetic or religious formulation for philosophical or scientific doctrines. Nowhere is this more apparent than in Novalis' fascination with one of the central ideas of the cabalistic tradition: the sympathy of the sign with the signified, the doctrine of the *signatura rerum*, according to which everything in nature is a secret language. This idea was central to Novalis' whole conception of magic. He became so excited by it because it seemed to rest on a profound scientific truth: that the external appearances of nature reveal an underlying chemical structure. Novalis' insistence on this doctrine was crucial to his program of unifying the sciences, and it was one of the main points of his disagreement with the physicist A. G. Werner, who denied that the external empirical features of a phenomenon provide any clue to its underlying structure.[48] Novalis' hope was that we could achieve greater control over nature, and as a result acquire better health, by learning how to read these signs of nature. The magical idealist would become versed in the art of interpreting the signs of nature, learning how to read the inner structure of things from their external and empirical characteristics.

The connotations of the occult disappear when we realize that Novalis never believed that the control over nature could be achieved by supernatural means, by reciting formulas, waving wands, or casting spells. No less than Bacon, who also influenced him,[49] Novalis wanted to achieve the grand ambitions of traditional magic—control over nature—through method, rule, and reason. Hence Novalis insists that magic is an art, which means for him that it must conform to definite rules (nos. 111, 252; II, 546–547, 585). There are indeed two arts that the magical idealist must cultivate:

medicine and poetry. It is through medicine that the magical idealist learns how to increase our inner stimuli, and to achieve a balance between over- and understimulation; and it is through poetry that he learns how to achieve a magical transformation of the sensible world.

The distance from the occult grows even further when we realize that Novalis distinguishes between good and bad forms of magic.[50] The appeal to the supernatural, the hope to achieve something simply by willing it or by influencing a spirit, was simply a bad form of magic. There were both magical idealists and realists, as Novalis put it, and both of them could become forms of illness if they sought complete control and perfection, failing to grasp the limits of their activity (no. 638; III, 384–385). The sick magical idealist failed to recognize the limits on his activity imposed by the physical world. Any one who tried to achieve certain goals has to take into account the properties of the means and instruments he uses, which impose definite limits on what he can achieve. The hindrances and obstacles of the real world have indeed their point in our overall mental economy since they prevent us from delusions of power and grandeur (no. 80; II, 451).

5. Syncriticism

Although Novalis' had sketched a synthesis of idealism and realism in the *Fichte-Studien*, his ideas did not move beyond the very rudimentary. He had postulated a single absolute, God, of which the ideal and real are only appearances; but he did not explain this in any detail, let alone give any hint about how he could resolve the apparent contradiction between idealism and realism. Novalis tackled some of these issues in his later notebooks, especially the 1797–1798 *Entwürfe* and the 1798–1799 *Allgemeine Brouillon*. Never did he form his scattered reflections into a system, though, so only programmatic and suggestive fragments remain. Still, if we collect all these fragments, the outlines of an interesting and original system emerge.

There should be no doubt that Novalis' synthesis of idealism and realism would go beyond the boundaries of the *Wissenschaftslehre* by making realism not subordinate but coordinate to idealism. Around the same time as his friend Friedrich Schlegel, Novalis insists that idealism and realism should each provide a basis to prove the other, and that both are opposing perspectives on a single truth. This emerges especially clearly from a fragment in the *Allgemeine Brouillon*:

Philosophy. The perfect coincidence of idealism and realism—the most perfect independence gives each the most perfect proof of the correct procedure. One should be converted into the other . . . Idealization of realism—and the realization of idealism leads to truth. One works for the other—and so indirectly for itself. The idealist must, in order to work directly for idealism, attempt to prove realism—and so conversely. The proof of realism is idealism—and conversely. (no. 634; III, 382–384)

Unfortunately, Novalis does not explain in any detail how idealism and realism would demonstrate one another. He does give some further indication, however, about the nature of the synthesis he has in mind. The synthesis of idealism and realism means that we can treat nature as if it were visible spirit, and spirit as if it were invisible nature (no. 69; III, 252). It also means that it is one and the same whether we put the universe within ourselves, like Fichte, or whether we put ourselves in the universe, like Spinoza (no. 633; III, 382). Whether things conform to concepts, or concepts conform to things, is ultimately one and the same, Novalis writes, alluding to Kant's own formulation of the distinction between transcendental idealism and realism (no. 268; II, 589).[51]

Novalis calls the system that will be a synthesis of idealism and realism 'syncriticism.' This term, used to refer to the mystical and eclectic tendencies of neo-Platonism, once had derogatory connotations. Undaunted and defiant, Novalis attempted to co-opt it in a positive sense.[52] For him, syncriticism is that form of criticism that synthesizes idealism and realism; standing above both standpoints, it assigns each of them their necessary part in a whole (no. 457; III, 333). One central thesis of syncriticism is that we understand nature on analogy with ourselves, as if all nature were one great mind (no. 820; III, 429). But another basic thesis is just the converse: that we understand ourselves on analogy with nature, as if the self is only a microcosm that reflects the order of nature as a whole (nos. 69, 338; III, 252, 301). Rather than being a mature view that supersedes magical idealism, syncriticism seems to be another formulation of it, for Novalis explains magical idealism in similar terms. The magical idealist, he writes, should have the power to make not only his thoughts into things but also his things into thoughts (no. 338; III, 301). He shows how the soul externalizes itself in the things of nature as well as how the things in nature internalize themselves in the mind (no. 69; III, 252).

Although Novalis is never so explicit, the basis for his synthesis of idealism and realism lies, in part, in his general organic concept of nature. Like many of his contemporaries in the 1790s, Novalis reacted against the mechanical physics of Descartes, and developed a more dynamic concept of nature, which analyzes matter into living force. Like Schelling, Novalis revived the concept of the world soul, seeing all of nature as a single organism. Each individual living thing is comprehensible only by how it depends on all other living things; and the organic system of all individual living things forms another single individual living thing, which is the world soul (nos. 460, 477; III, 334, 341). Life, which consists in power (no. 598; III, 660), is indeed the *universale menstruum* of all things, what gives them their form, shape, and being (no. 235; III, 281). Novalis ascribes to something like the "great chain of being," a hierarchy of powers in nature where each higher power organizes and develops lower ones. The hierarchy begins with pure *stuff* (*Stoff*), or first matter, whose material form is due to power; it is followed by the *soul,* which is the power of all powers in matter; the soul is succeeded by *spirit* (*Geist*), which is the soul of all souls; and finally spirit reaches its culmination in God, who is the spirit of all spirits (no. 24; II, 529). While each higher stage might be *temporally* consequent to the lower one, it is *logically* prior to it, for it determines the purpose and rationale of all lower forms of activity. Clearly, such a doctrine was the very opposite of materialism.

On the basis of this organic concept of nature, Novalis could overcome the dualism between the mental and the physical, which had dominated the dispute between idealism and realism in the eighteenth century. Both idealism and realism had attempted to overcome this dualism, of course, but they could do so only by reducing one entity down to the other, by explaining matter in terms of the mind or mind in terms of matter. Novalis avoids this dilemma by denying the common premise behind it: that matter consists in inert extension. By analyzing all nature into living force, he has a unified means of understanding both the mental and the physical, which are simply different degrees of organization and development of living power or force. Matter is inchoate and nascent force, whereas mind is organized and developed force. Depending on one's perspective, matter could be seen as a primitive form of mind, or mind as a developed form of matter.

As explained so far, Novalis' ideas for a synthesis of idealism and realism seem very much like those of Schelling. The resemblance is by no means coincidental, for Novalis had been studying Schellings's writings since early 1797. The two philosophers eventually met in December 1797, a meeting that pleased Novalis, who said he had become Schelling's friend after spending "several precious hours symphilosophizing with him."[53] A correspondence was planned, though nothing of it survives, if it ever took place. There are indeed surprising parallels between Novalis and Schelling regarding their attempts to develop a system of idealism and realism. Both wrote of the absolute as a point of identity that is neither ideal nor real; and both described a critical standpoint that stood above both idealism and realism. Nevertheless, it cannot be said that Novalis developed his ideas under Schelling's influence. Although Novalis had read Schelling's *Briefe über Dogmatismus und Kritizismus*, he did so only in the summer of 1797, a year after expounding the basic ideas of a philosophy of identity in the *Fichte-Studien*.[54] Indeed, while Schelling still remained loyal to Fichte in 1797 and would only break from him in 1801, Novalis was already struggling to break the spell of Fichte's "magic circle" in 1797.[55]

Novalis soon became increasingly critical of Schelling, defining his own philosophy against that of his new friend. The most notable point of friction concerns the status of nature itself. While Schelling, in 1797, still believed that the foundation of *Naturphilosophie* ultimately lay with transcendental philosophy, he also held that, within *Naturphilosophie* itself, nature should be treated as a self-sufficient realm. The world soul, the highest hypothesis of *Naturphilosophie*, did not depend on any supernatural realm outside itself but stood for the self-dependent organism of all nature. For Novalis, however, nature is not a self-sufficient whole, but only an emanation of the divine, while the world soul too is only the earthly embodiment of God (no. 453; II, 643). In reaction against Schelling's naturalism and Spinozism, Novalis increasingly stressed the distance between the natural and divine while also the dependence of nature on a higher moral order.[56] This difference emerges clearly in Novalis' July 20, 1797 letter to Friedrich Schlegel, where he writes that he has made "the interesting discovery of the religion of the visible cosmos," an allusion to his concept of the moral world order, which he insists transcends nature. He then explains that with this discovery he will be able to treat all of physics symbolically, and thus "far to surpass Schelling" (IV, 255).

Schelling, for his part, was not blind to these growing differences. When Novalis read his 'Christenheit oder Europa' to the romantic circle in Jena, he was so repelled by its pious tone that he wrote a satiric poem to mock it, his 'Glaubensbekenntnis des Heinz Widerporsteins,' the most irreligious of all his writings.[57]

What is distinctive of Novalis' synthesis of idealism and realism, as he implies in his letter to Schlegel, is the idea of a "symbolic physics." This idea is indeed absent in Schelling's thinking in the late 1790s and early 1800s, though it did play an important role in his later thought. What did Novalis mean by a symbolic physics? The inspiration for his idea seems to have come from the neo-Platonist Hemsterhuis and the Paracelsian tradition,[58] which taught that everything in visible nature symbolizes something invisible, or that everything sensible represents something intelligible.[59] Novalis was especially attracted to the ancient mystical idea of the *signatur rerum*, the idea that nature is the secret language of God, his esoteric way of communicating with his creatures: "Everything that we experience is a *communication*. In fact, so is the world too a *communication*—the revelation of spirit. The time is gone when the spirit of God was comprehensible to us. The meaning of the world has been lost to us. We have only seen its letters. We have lost that which is appearing behind the appearance" (no. 316; II, 594).[60] Novalis fused this idea with the neo-Platonic *Emanationslehre*, according to which everything in nature represents or symbolizes everything else.[61]

That this symbolic physics played a central role in Novalis' synthesis of idealism and realism becomes clear as soon as we see how he applied it to the problem of mental–physical interaction. Novalis used the idea of representation to explain the mutual dependence between the subjective and objective. Both can be understood as signs or symbols of the other. If the meaning of the subjective lies in its externalization in nature, so the meaning of the objective lies in its internalization in the mind; the mental and the physical therefore represent or signify one another. This is how Novalis applies the idea of representation to this problem in a passage from the *Allgemeine Brouillon:*

> Something becomes clear to us only through representation. One understands an idea most easily when one sees it represented. Hence one understands the ego only insofar as it is represented by the non-ego. The non-ego is the symbol of the ego and only serves the self-understanding of the ego. So, conversely, one understands the non-ego, only insofar as it is represented by the ego, and this is its symbol. (no. 49; III, 246)

Thus Novalis' syncriticism had two models for explaining the connection between the subjective and objective, the ideal and the real. One of these is vitalist, according to which the subjective and objective are simply aspects of living force; and the other is neo-Platonic, according to which the subjective and objective are each the representation or symbol of the other. If the former model is a common idea in the late eighteenth century, the latter is more characteristic of Novalis' own syncriticism, his unique synthesis of idealism and realism.

We can now see more clearly the connection of Novalis syncriticism with his magical idealism. For, as we saw, magic idealism too is based on the idea of *signatura rerum*. Novalis made this connection very clear in several fragments of the *Allgemeine Brouillon* where he defined magic in terms of the "sympathy of the sign with the signified," and connected the art of medicine with that of magic (nos. 137–143; III, 266–268). These fragments show that the magician gains his power over nature not only by moral striving or the use of technology—as Fichte had imagined it—but by learning how to read and interpret the signs of nature. If we only know how to interpret these signs, Novalis thinks, then we will know how to find that balance between ourselves and the world on which our health depends.

6. Models of Knowledge

The reason many commentators stress the Fichtean dimension of Novalis' idealism, and overlook his attempt to synthesize Fichte and Spinoza, is his clear adoption of the Kantian–Fichtean model of knowledge. There can be no doubt that he accepts Kant's and Fichte's account of knowledge as a form of creation or making. "We *know* only insofar as we *make*," as he puts it in his *Hemsterhuis-Studien* (II, 378). True to Kant and Fichte, Novalis explains how all knowledge depends on *appropriation*, that is, making an object conform to the laws of my own activity so that it is no longer alien to me (no. 468; II, 646).[62]

Novalis allegiance to this model of knowledge seems to place him so firmly in the Kantian-Fichtean camp that it appears impossible for him also to be a realist of any kind. If we know the world only insofar as we create it, making it conform to the laws of our activity, then how do we know it in itself, apart from and prior to the application of our knowing instrument? We seem trapped here inside the circle of consciousness, which it is the very purpose of absolute idealism to escape.

Novalis knew this impasse all too well, and he struggled to avoid it. In some interesting passages from the *Vorarbeiten* and *Allgemeine Brouillon* he attempted to supplement and synthesize his idealist model of knowledge with another more realistic one. Here Novalis stresses how knowledge of an object involves not only an act of *appropriation*, but also one of *alienation*; in other words, the subject must not only make the object its own, but it must also make itself into the object. This means that all knowledge also involves an act of identification with the object, which requires that I put myself in its place. Hence Novalis writes in the *Allgemeine Brouillon* that we understand what is alien to us only through *self-alienation* (*Selbstfremdmachung*) (no. 820; III, 429).

Novalis provides a further account of the realistic dimension of knowledge, and its connection with the idealistic dimension, in *Vorarbeiten* no. 118. Here Novalis states that to know an object completely I must *enliven* (*beleben*) it. To enliven it means that I give the object its "soul," that unity of elements characteristic of its individuality alone (II, 551). The act of enlivening the object involves not only my appropriating it, making it an element of my own living whole, but also my identifying and becoming one with it. I create and extend the nature of the object by making it conform to me; and I create and extend myself by making it conform to the object. What I know is a product of both acts, the point of indifference between them. This means that I see the object of my perception as both mine and as alien to me. It is mine insofar as I appropriate it according to my forms of perception; and it is alien to me insofar as I am made to perceive it in a determinate manner (II, 551–552).

The crucial question remains how my appropriating the object develops *its* individuality, revealing rather than concealing its nature. Why are we not left with an unknowable thing-in-itself? Novalis addresses this very issue in another fragment of the *Vorarbeiten* (no. 125; II, 554). My mental activity does not involve a "decomposition" or "recreation" of the world, he says, because it consists in only its "variation operation" (*Variations Operation*).[63] That is, it gives the world one of its many possible specific forms. This is because the world in itself is not entirely determinate but it becomes so, at least partly, through me. Apart from the subject who knows it, the object in itself is something relatively inchoate and indeterminate, at least in some respects, and especially with respect to the knower; it then becomes organized and determinate, and so what it is, only through my act of knowing it. Novalis implies, then, that it is wrong to make a distinction between the nature of the object and the knowledge of it because the object realizes *its* determinate nature only through me and in my act of knowing it. The converse holds for the knowing subject: it becomes what it is only through the object.

Novalis comes to this conclusion because he places the act of knowing within his general organic view of nature. Like Schelling, he refuses to place the knowing subject in some transcendental sphere where it remains sealed against the influences of nature. Thus, in the *Vorarbeiten*, he stresses how my senses and body, the instruments of my knowledge, are determined to act as they do because all of nature, the "world soul," acts through them. They are inseparable from the world, and indeed only a variation of it (no. 118; II, 551). And in the *Allgemeine Brouillon* he states that the subject and object of knowledge are both members of the organic whole of nature, where each has its identity only through the other and the whole (no. 820; III, 429). Since the identity of each thing in nature depends on every other, it would be false to separate the subject and object of knowledge; both become determinate only through the other, so that the subject's knowing activity makes the object more determinate just as the object's activity makes the subject more determinate by acting upon it.

In Novalis' view, then, the problem of knowledge appears insolvable only because one forgets the general natural context in which the act of knowing takes place. We conceive the subject and the object as self-sufficient entities and then ask how they correspond with one another; we then attempt to explain their correspondence by the interaction between them. Since each is conceived as self-sufficient, the only relation between them is conceived to be one of external causality. Either the subject is the cause of the object (idealism) or the object is the cause of the subject (realism). But since these entities are so self-sufficient and heterogeneous, even such a causal interaction becomes impossible. To get beyond this *aporia*, it is necessary to conceive the relation between subject and object in more organic terms, such that each becomes what it is only through the other.

Novalis' attempt to fuse realism and idealism also leads him to reassess the account of self-knowledge in the Kantian–Fichtean tradition, which he thinks is very one-sided. According to Fichte's account of self-knowledge, the self attains its self-awareness only through abstraction and reflection, that is, by abstracting from everything that is an object of knowledge and by reflecting on itself as a subject of knowledge. In some revealing fragments from the *Vermischte Bemerkungen* Novalis evaluates this very model of self-knowledge (nos. 26, 43; II, 422, 430). He agrees with Fichte that abstraction and reflection are indeed essential to the development of self-consciousness; but they are not sufficient, he thinks, because the reverse activity is also necessary. If the self is to know itself, then it should not only go inside but also outside itself, becoming part of the world of which it is a part; it must *negate* the very act by which it abstracts from the world and makes its activity visible in the world. The self knows itself, Novalis suggests, only by embodying or manifesting its activity in things, by identifying and becoming part of something outside itself. "Self-alienation is the source of all self-abasement, but also just the opposite: the basis of all self-elevation" (no. 26; II, 422). So important is this theme of self-alienation to Novalis that in the *Fichte-Studien* he regarded it as "the highest philosophical truth" (no. 98; II, 56).

Such, if only very crudely, is the general drift of Novalis' fragments on the criterion of knowledge, his last will and testament on how to fuse idealism and realism. Though his views are sketchy, they are also suggestive and interesting. It is obvious that, in their own inchoate way, they anticipate the more elaborate and systematic ideas of Schelling and Hegel. Novalis could indeed claim to have lived up to his namesake: he had indeed broken new ground.[64]

CHAPTER 4

Friedrich Schlegel's
Absolute Idealism

1. Philosophy, History, and Poetry

Along with Hölderlin and Novalis, Friedrich Schlegel is a central figure in the development of absolute idealism. Schlegel is best known as the leading aesthetician of the romantic school. He was a founder of its journal *Athenäum*, and the father of its famous concepts of 'romantic poesy' and 'irony.' Yet Schlegel was even more a philosopher than Hölderlin and Novalis. His interests spanned every field of philosophy, but his main concerns were in metaphysics and epistemology. With some justification, he has been regarded as *the* philosopher of the romantic movement.[1] "Metaphysics," he wrote Jacobi in November 7, 1812, "has been for a long time, indeed from my youth (since 1790), the chief preoccupation of my life."[2] This inclination to metaphysics derived from the same source as Hölderlin and Novalis: Plato. "It is now thirty-nine years ago," he said in the preface to his 1827 *Philosophie des Lebens*, "that I read through the complete works of Plato in Greek with indescribable curiosity; and since then . . . this philosophical enquiry has always been my proper main concern" (X, 170–180).[3]

But Schlegel's philosophical stature is somewhat controversial. Because his best known works are in literary history, and because he rarely succeeded in systematizing and refining his profusion of ideas, he has been dismissed as a "philosophical dilettante."[4] Such a judgment is understandable. There can be no doubt that Schlegel lacked rigor, precision, and organization, and that he failed to direct his energies sufficiently to produce a solid, lasting result. Most of Schlegel's philosophical remains are lectures, which are informal and loosely organized, or notebooks, which are fragmentary and chaotic. Nevertheless, such a judgment is also unfair. It ignores not only Schlegel's considerable philosophical output, but also his own statements about the importance of his philosophical interests. Worst of all, it begs philosophical questions. For perfectly plausible reasons, Schlegel was very skeptical of much of the scholastic apparatus of definition, analysis, and proof that is part of the conventional picture of the philosopher. He saw this as a useful measure of intellectual technique, not as a secure method to attain truth. Hence the proper medium for philosophy was not the treatise but the fragment, or even a novel.

There is another reason why it is a serious mistake to underrate Schlegel's philosophical work. Some of his most important and influential aesthetic ideas, especially romantic poesy, irony, and the new mythology, have their source and foundation in his epistemological and metaphysical reflections in the 1790s. The origin and meaning of these ideas cannot be recaptured simply by considering their literary dimension, by examining how they continue with or depart from the historical use of such terms as 'romantic' and 'irony.' Schlegel's later romantic aesthetic took the form it did chiefly because of the antifoundationalist epistemology and absolute idealist metaphysics that he developed from 1796 to 1798.[5]

Nowhere are Schlegel's philosophical interests more in evidence than in his attempt to formulate an absolute idealism around 1796–1797. The same constellation of ideas that are found in Hölderlin, Schelling, and Novalis emerge in Schlegel: the synthesis of Fichte and Spinoza, the indifference point of the ideal and the real, the Platonic concept of the ideal, and the sovereignty of art as the means and criterion of absolute knowledge. Although Schlegel never went as far as Schelling in systematizing his absolute idealism, he did go further than Novalis and Hölderlin in giving explicit lectures on the subject. He was indeed the first to present the fundamental ideas of absolute idealism to a public audience.[6]

Like Novalis and Hölderlin, Schlegel came to his absolute idealism by critical reflection on Fichte's 1794 *Wissenschaftslehre*. His reflections on Fichte were made only a little later than Hölderlin's and Novalis', in the winter of 1796–1797, but they seem to have been developed independently of them. Though Schlegel knew little of Hölderlin,[7] he was the close friend of Hülsen, Novalis, and Schleiermacher; and until 1799, he was on at least good terms with Schelling.[8] Although Schlegel had debts to his friends, he in turn was an important influence on them.[9] Novalis gave eloquent witness to Schlegel's importance for him when he wrote him in June 1797:

> You have been elected to protect the striving young thinker against Fichte's magic. I know from experience how bitter this understanding can be—I am

thankful to you for many hints, for many indications, in how to find one's way through this horrible labyrinth of abstractions, and for the idea of a free, critical spirit. (XXIII, 372)

What is distinctive of Schlegel's absolute idealism—if we compare it to that of Schelling, Novalis, and Hölderlin—is its *historicism*, that is, the central role it assigns to history.[10] Usually, Hegel is given credit for creating an historicist absolute idealism, but Schlegel developed such a doctrine well before him. Like Hegel after him, Schlegel stressed that the absolute realizes itself only through human activity, and more specifically its actions in history. No less than Hegel, he emphasized that historical development is dialectical, a synthesis of externalizing and internalizing activities. It is indeed with Schlegel that we begin to see the first clear outlines of what Dilthey was later to call "the historical critique of reason."[11]

2. The Break with Fichte

Fichte was a major philosophical influence on Schlegel, just as he had been for Novalis and Hölderlin. Schlegel's first opinions about Fichte were deeply flattering, revealing all the hyperbole and enthusiasm of youth. He wrote his brother August Wilhelm from Dresden in August 1795 that Fichte was "the greatest metaphysical thinker now living," and that he was the kind of intellectual Hamlet had sought in vain because "every trait of his public life seemed to cry out: here is a man" (XVIII, 242). Such, indeed, was the young Schlegel's admiration for Fichte that he placed him as a thinker above Kant and Spinoza, and as a popular writer above Rousseau.[12] It is noteworthy that Schlegel had formed these opinions of Fichte before he met him, and apparently independently of his friend Novalis, who had already encountered Fichte in the spring of 1795.[13]

The reasons for Schlegel's admiration for Fichte were complex. They were in part philosophical. Like many in the 1790s, Schlegel saw Fichte as the first thinker to complete Kant's Copernican Revolution. It was Fichte who had finally discovered the foundation of the critical philosophy, and who had created a complete and consistent system of idealism.[14] While Schlegel would soon voice his doubts about Fichte's idealism, he never ceased to regard it as an achievement of the greatest cultural significance. He wrote in a famous aphorism that Fichte's *Wissenschaftslehre*—along with the French Revolution and Goethe's *Wilhelm Meister*—was one of the greatest tendencies of the age.[15] Fichte's idealism had become "the central point and foundation of the new German literature," he wrote in 1802, because it expressed the spirit of freedom characteristic of the modern age, the spirit that was the heart and soul of the new romantic literature.[16]

There were not only philosophical but also political motives behind Schlegel's admiration for Fichte. Since 1793 Schlegel had supported the cause of the Revolution in France, and his political interests became so strong that they eventually began to overshadow and displace his classical studies.[17] In 1796 he published an essay, 'Über den Begriff des Republikanismus,' which defends a left-wing interpretation of republican principles, and which criticizes Kant for both restricting the franchise and denying the right of revolution.[18] It is not surprising, then, that Schlegel came to admire Fichte, who was notorious as one of the most outspoken champions of the Revolution. It is indeed telling that when Schlegel praises Fichte so highly in his August 1795 letter he refers to *Beiträge zur Berichtigung der Urtheile des Publikums über die französische Revolution,* Fichte's radical defense of the course of the Revolution. No doubt, Schlegel came to regard Fichte as his ally in the philosophical and political struggle against the *ancien régime.*

If Schlegel were ever a disciple of Fichte, it was only for a short period, probably only a year, from the summer of 1795 to the summer of 1796. During this period some of Schlegel's writings show that he accepted Fichte's foundationalist program of beginning philosophy with self-evident first principles.[19] In his *Über das Studium der Griechischen Poesie,* which he had completed by December 1795, he had praised Fichte for discovering the foundation of the critical philosophy, which would now provide the basis for an objective aesthetics (I, 357). Then, in his early 1796 essay 'Von der Schönheit der Dichtkunst' he reaffirmed his faith in an objective aesthetics, which would be based on the fundamental principles of practical philosophy, whose foundation had been established by Fichte (XVI, 5, 17–18, 22). Finally, Schlegel endorsed not only Fichte's foundationalist program but even its first principle, for, in his 'Über den Begriff des Republikanismus,' he attempts to derive republican ideals from the Fichtean principle 'The ego ought to be' (VII, 15–16).

It was most probably in the summer of 1796 that Schlegel began to have his first doubts about Fichte's philosophy. In late July he visited his friend Novalis, who might well have imparted to him some of his own reservations about Fichte's idealism; and in early August he went to Jena where he associated with the Niethammer circle, whose antifoundationalism seemed to rub off on him.[20] Some of the notebooks entries from the autumn of 1786 indicate a growing skepticism and disillusionment with foundationalism. Thus Schlegel now wrote of skepticism: "There is still no consistent σκ [skepticism]; it is surely worthwhile to establish one. σκ [skepticism] = permanent insurrection" (no. 94; XVIII, 12).[21] And he complained about Reinhold's foundationalist program: "Reinhold, the first among the Kantian sophists, has organized Kantianism and created misunderstanding.—He is a seeker after foundations (*Grundsucher*)." (no. 5; XVIII, 19). Schlegel also began to distance himself from the Kantians who swore by the spirit of his philosophy (no. 191; XVIII, 36); he referred to "the regressive tendency of the hypercritics" (no. 4; XVIII 19), which could be an allusion to Fichte and Schelling.[22]

Whatever the source of Schlegel's doubts, his enthusiasm for Fichte's philosophy was certainly short lived. He first met Fichte in August 1796, and saw him often after that. His first impressions were very positive, since he found Fichte even better in conversation than on paper and lectern. A friendship grew, which only strengthened over the years. Still, friendship is one thing, philosophy another. Sure enough, Schlegel's doubts about Fichte's philosophy only intensified soon after meeting him. Thus he complained to C. G. Körner in September 1796 about his disappointment with his last conversation with Fichte.[23] It is remarkable, he confided to Körner, that Fichte has so little idea of things that do not directly concern him, and that he is especially weak in every science that has an object. Schlegel was puzzled that physics and history simply did not interest Fichte. He then went on to make an astonishing revelation: Fichte told him he would rather count peas than study history! These misgivings proved to be decisive, for one of the main reasons for Schlegel's later break with Fichte came down to the lack of realism and history in his system. Schelling would later break with Fichte for almost the same reasons.

Schlegel began an intensive study of Fichte's philosophy sometime in the winter of 1796. He began to write down some of his criticisms, which he hoped to publish in the form of an essay provisionally entitled 'The Spirit of the *Wissenschaftslehre*.'[24] The result of his investigations, he told Körner January 30, 1797, is that he had not only become clear about some fundamental points, but that he had also "decisively separated himself from the *Wissenschaftslehre*" (XVIII, 343). Though the essay was never written, the notes for it remain, revealing many of Schlegel's early reservations about Fichte's philosophy.

Many of his doubts concern the form and method of the *Wissenschaftslehre*.

Schlegel is especially critical of Fichte's foundationalism, casting scorn on Fichte's claims to have a complete system and irrefutable first principles. It is easy simply to deny some of his fundamental first principles (no. 126; XVIII, 31), which themselves stand in need of proof. Why not say, for example, that the *non*-ego posits itself absolutely? (no. 51; XVIII, 510) It is futile to think, however, that these principles could be proven because there is never an end to deduction, given that any proposition can be proven in myriads of ways (no. 129; XVIII, 30; nos. 9, 12; XVIII, 518). Furthermore, Fichte's system is far too mathematical and abstract, leaving out the positive reality of experience; all his deductions can at best only derive abstractions, not individual facts of experience (no. 141; XVIII, 152). Given such doubts about Fichte's foundationalism, it is not surprising to find Schlegel treating the *Wissenschaftslehre* as a work of literature rather than philosophy. The *Wissenschaftslehre* is Fichte's *Werther* (no. 220; XVIII, 38), and as rhetorical as Fichte himself, "a Fichtean exposition of the Fichtean spirit in Fichtean letters" (no. 144; XVIII, 33). All Fichte's bluster and seriousness makes him a comic figure: he is like the drunk who tirelessly climbs up on his horse and, "transcending it," falls off again (no. 138; XVIII, 32).

Schlegel's other doubts about Fichte's philosophy concern more the content than the form of the *Wissenschaftslehre*. Significantly, they are especially focused on its idealism. Schlegel saw the Fichtean obstacle or check as very problematic—"*An seinem Anstoß bin ich immer angestossen*" (no. 140; XVIII, 32)—because it is not only a relapse into the Kantian thing-in-itself (no. 83; XVIII, 25), but also the source of an insurmountable dualism in a philosophy that should be completely idealist. Schlegel's main objection to Fichte's idealism is that Fichte is "not enough of an absolute idealist" and "not realist enough in every sense and respect" (no. 134; XVIII, 31). What Schlegel means by this becomes clearer from a later fragment when he complains that Fichte has established only "the ideality of the real" but not "the reality of the ideal" (no. 209; XVIII, 38). Fichte does not grant sufficient reality to the ideal because he limits it to the sphere of appearances and the finite subject.[25]

Besides his notes for the 'Geist der Wissenschaftslehre', Schlegel had several other collections of fragments in his notebooks that also focused on Fichte.[26] These too show how much Schlegel had completely broken with Fichte's philosophy. One central theme of these collections is that Fichte is a mystic, and that like all mystics he begins his philosophy by postulating something absolute (no. 2; XVIII, 3). This makes everything too easy, however, because once we postulate the absolute we can explain everything; but the real question is what gives us the right to postulate it in the first place (no. 71; XVIII, 512). Schlegel thinks that in relying on a mystical experience—he has in mind intellectual intuition—Fichte has forfeited the demands of criticism, which do not allow us to appeal to some infallible experience (nos. 52, 93; XVIII, 8–9, 12). Another basic theme of these notes is that Fichte has ignored the whole realm of history, which is vital to show the necessity of his own system. To justify the *Wissenschaftslehre* we should see how it arose, why it was necessary to solve the problems of its historical context; but that means we cannot separate the *Wissenschaftslehre* from the history of philosophy itself (no. 20; XVIII, 520). Although it is indeed necessary to distinguish between the transcendental and empirical ego (no. 135; XVIII, 31), Fichte's philosophy is still guilty of a kind of "empirical egoism," Schlegel argues, because it limits the experience of the subject down to the eternal present, ignoring the historical dimension of self-consciousness that links us to the past and the future (no. 31; XVIII, 508).

If we were to summarize the positive recommendations deriving from Schlegel's critique, then it would be that philosophy must become completely regulative and nonfoundationalist. The only dimension of Fichte's philosophy that Schlegel wants to maintain are the doctrines that the ego consists in activity, and more specifically the activity of infinite striving. It is with striving, he insists, that philosophy should begin and end (nos. 18, 101; XVIII, 5, 13). Although Schlegel is skeptical of mysticism, he insists that it should be permitted, though again only on a regulative basis where the mystic's intuitions become an ideal for practice or enquiry (no. 23; XVIII, 507). In the same manner, he reads Fichte's first principle 'The ego posits itself absolutely' as an imperative: 'The ego *ought* to be absolute' (no. 187; XVIII, 36). But there was another less critical and more speculative result of Schlegel's critique, which emerges in some later collections of fragments. This is Schlegel's insistence that "absolute idealism" must also be an "absolute realism" (no. 606; XVIII, 80). The growing realism in Schlegel's thinking becomes especially apparent from the remarks in his notebooks about Spinoza, who now virtually displaces Fichte as his philosophical mentor. There is in Spinoza's writings, he comments, "the fragrance of infinity," "an infinite persuasiveness," "a majesty of thought" (no. 567; XVIII, 75). Since Spinoza, philosophy has only gone backward in its attempt to find the basis of all knowledge (no. 234; XVIII, 40–41), because his philosophy provides the model for the synthesis of the ideal and the real (no. 252; XVIII, 43).

Spinoza alone has formed a coherent system of the universe (nos. 724, 727; XVIII, 90), and no other moral philosophy is more in tune with the dignity of reason (no. 775; XVIII, 94). The growing importance of Spinoza for Schlegel is most probably due to the influence of Schleiermacher, whom he had met in the summer of 1797.[27]

It should be clear that Schlegel's absolute realism is not only an *empirical* realism in the Kantian sense, because it does much more than postulate the independent reality of the external world *within* a transcendental framework. Rather, it is a form of *transcendental* realism because it maintains that the realm of nature exists apart from and prior to any subject, whether that subject is empirical or transcendental. It is important to add, however, that this transcendental realism will not affirm the existence of the thing-in-itself in the Kantian sense, which exists apart from all subjectivity. Rather, it postulates the existence of a single reality within nature, which is both subjective and objective, ideal and real, because it manifests itself equally in both.

Why had Schlegel become so dissatisfied with the lack of realism in Fichte's *Wissenschaftslehre*? What made him break with Fichte's subjective idealism? It is tempting to see it as the result of external influences, whether they came from Hülsen, Schleiermacher, Schelling, or Novalis. The temptation grows when we consider that these thinkers had been moving in a more realistic direction before Schlegel, and that he knew all of them intimately. He had been a close friend of Hardenberg since January 1792, and he greatly admired Schelling, whom he placed alongside Fichte on his Parnassus.[28] He had read virtually all of Schelling's early writings, and he especially liked his *Briefe über Dogmatismus und Kritizismus,* which sketches the rudiments of an absolute idealist position. The evidence indeed suggests that he read the *Briefe* around the winter of 1796–1797, just when he was settling his accounts with Fichte.[29]

Still, it is not possible to explain Schlegel's growing realism from external influences alone. Whatever impetus Schlegel received from Novalis in the summer of 1796, he had been out of touch with Novalis for over a year when he wrote his notes on Fichte. Furthermore, the influence also went in the other direction, because Schlegel sent his notes to Novalis, who later thanked him for freeing him from Fichte's influence.[30] While Schlegel might well have derived some impetus from Schelling's *Briefe,* it is clear that this could have taken him only so far, given that Schelling was still a loyal Fichtean and had been very tentative in suggesting absolute idealism.[31]

Though Schleiermacher had probably reinforced his implicit realism, it would be wrong to trace the source of Schlegel's realism to Schleiermacher alone, for the critique of Fichte's subjective idealism is already clear before his first meeting with Schleiermacher.[32] Schlegel's friendship with Hülsen most probably began in the winter of 1797, and he had already read his most important writings, which show a realistic tendency; yet Schlegel's notebooks show him to be confused or critical about the direction of Hülsen's thought.[33] All in all, then, the evidence seems to suggest that Schlegel came to his conclusions about Fichte largely, though not entirely, on his own initiative.

But, even if Schlegel had been influenced by Schelling, Novalis, Schleiermacher, or Hülsen, the question remains: What *predisposed* him to be so? What strands of realism were already inherent in his thinking prior to his encounter with the *Wissenschaftslehre?* Here it is important to recognize that Schlegel had been subject from his earliest years to some of the same influences as Novalis, Schelling, Schleiermacher, and Hölderlin: Plato, Hemsterhuis, and Spinoza. Plato's eternal forms, Hemsterhuis' longing for the infinite, and Spinoza's one and all had already imparted a deep and ineradicable realism to his thinking. Schlegel himself recognized this tendency within himself when he wrote of his "longing for the infinite," "his fondness for the absolute," or his "loyalty to the universe."[34] So deep was this passion for the one and all that he admitted to being "absurdly in love, and indeed infatuated" with it. This metaphysical strand of his early thought is especially apparent from his August 28, 1793 letter to his brother where he defends the Platonic conception of the ideal against August Wilhelm's anti-rationalism:

> The source of the ideal is the hot thirst for eternity, the longing for God, and so it is the most noble of our nature . . . Enthusiasm is the mother of the idea and the concept its father.—What is then our dignity other than the power and the decision to be like God, to have infinity constantly before our eyes?—The restless striving after activity, the highest criterion of judgment, does not exclude all the virtues of receptivity but can only exist with them. (XXIII, 130)[35]

Given such such predispositions, it was difficult, if not impossible, for Schlegel to accept Fichte's idealism, which threatened to reduce the entire objective world down to the level of appearances. Was it any accident, then, that he regarded Fichte's *proton pseudos* to be his attempt to derive the reality of the objective world from the self?[36] Yet, as we shall soon see (3.3.6), the Platonic influence upon Schlegel would soon lead him to develop his own form of objective or absolute idealism. The infinite would soon be identified with the archetypical and ideal.

3. An Antifoundationalist Epistemology

In the course of his reflections on Fichte's philosophy in the winter of 1796, Schlegel developed the outlines of an antifoundationalist epistemology, which appears in his notebooks and the later *Kritische* and *Athenäums Fragmente*. Like Novalis and Hölderlin, Schlegel seems to have imbibed some of the skepticism about the foundationalist methodology of Reinhold's *Elementarphilosophie* and Fichte's *Wissenschaftslehre* that was prevalent in the Niethammer circle; but he developed this skepticism in much greater detail than his contemporaries. This skepticism is crucial for an understanding of Schlegel's absolute idealism and his romantic aesthetic, especially his ideas of irony and romantic poesy.

There are several respects in which Schlegel breaks with foundationalism.

First Principles

Schlegel criticized the classical foundationalist doctrine, reaffirmed by Reinhold and Fichte, that philosophy must begin with a self-evident first principle and then derive all other beliefs in a chain of deduction from it. Schlegel made two objections against this doctrine. First, that any proposition, even the apparently self-evident, can be doubted; it too must be demonstrated, so that there is an infinite regress of justification. Second, that there is an infinite number of ways of proving any proposition, such that we can continue to perfect our proofs *ad infinitum*.[37] For these reasons, Schlegel concluded: "There are no first principles that are universally efficient companions and guides to truth" (no. 13; XVIII, 518).

Schlegel's skepticism about first principles is also apparent in his attitude toward the geometric method, which had for so long been the model for foundationalist epistemology. In his *Athenäumsfragment* no. 82 he laughed at its pretensions, claiming that defining and demonstrating a proposition is pointless. There are an infinite number of real definitions for any individual, and any proposition can be demonstrated in all kinds of ways. The main point is to have something interesting to say and then just to say it, following the "thetical method" where we set down "the pure facts of reflection without concealment, adulteration, or artifical distortion" (II, 178).

Critique

Schlegel accepts the fundamental demand of the critical philosophy: that *all* beliefs submit to criticism. However, he insists on applying this demand to the critical philosophy itself, so that it becomes *meta-critical*. This demand for a meta-critical philosophy appears throughout the notebooks where Schlegel calls for a "philosophy of philosophy." The same theme emerges in the *Athenäums Fragmente:* "Now that philosophy criticizes everything that comes before it, a critique of philosophy would be nothing better than a justified reprisal" (no. 56; II, 173). The radicalization of criticism into meta-criticism involves skepticism, of course, but Schlegel does not shirk from this conclusion, insisting upon the value of a real skepticism that "begins and ends with an infinite number of contradictions" (no. 400; II, 240–241).

Schlegel rejects the premise behind the critical philosophy that it is necessary to criticize all claims to knowledge prior to making any such claims. We cannot bracket all claims to knowledge, and then evaluate them before we make them; for not only does the application of a standard of knowledge imply a claim to knowledge, but also we know the powers and limits of our cognitive powers only by using them. This means that we should be critical of our cognitive powers not *before* but *while* using them. Criticism must be integrated with the process of enquiry and cannot stand apart from it.[38]

The Myth of the Given

Schlegel is as critical of empiricism as rationalism regarding the possibility of providing a secure foundation of knowledge. He believes the given hard data of sense no more than infallible first principles. This is the message that emerges from *Athenäumsfragment* no. 226 where Schlegel maintains that we can do history only with the guidance of hypotheses (II, 202). We cannot state *that* something is, he argues, unless we can say *what* it is; but to determine what it is we must use concepts. Hence facts are such only through the concepts we use to identify them. This does not imply that anything can be a fact, and that we can use any concept, Schlegel insists, given that among the large number of possible concepts only some are necessary. Still, it is the task of the critical philosopher to be aware of which concepts he uses; otherwise, he will simply accept them according to chance or caprice. The main mistake to guard against, Schlegel warns, is that one has "pure solid empirical facts [*Empirie*] entirely a posteriori," for this is only to sanction "an extremely one-sided, highly dogmatic, and transcendent a priori view."

System

Schlegel's antifoundationalism makes him ambivalent about the ideal of a system.[39] He both affirms and denies it. He denies it in the classical Kantian sense of a body of knowledge derived from, and organized around, a single self-evident first principle. There is no perfect system, in his view, because there are so many ways of organizing knowledge, and no single one can claim to be the sole truth. But Schlegel also affirms the ideal of a system because the only criterion of truth now left to him is internal coherence. Following the Kantian tradition, Schlegel abandons the standard of truth as correspondence and replaces it with coherence. Rather than correspondence with some unknowable realm of being, and rather than deduction from some indubitable first principle, the only standard of truth is now the mutual support of propositions in a whole (*Wechselerweis*). The proper form of a system is not *linear*, where we derive all propositions from a single principle in a unique deductive chain (no. 16, 22; 518, 521), but *circular*, where we can begin from any proposition and return to it because all propositions are interconnected.[40]

Schlegel's ambivalent attitude toward the possibility of a system is perfectly summarized by a fragment from the *Athenäum:* "It is equally false for the spirit to have a system, and not to have one. It therefore must decide to unite them both" (no. 52; II, 173). Both horns of the dilemma are inescapable. On the one hand, it is dangerous to have a system, because it sets arbitrary limits to enquiry, and because it imposes an artificial order on the facts. On the other hand, it is necessary to have a system, because unity and coherence are essential to all knowledge, and it is only in the context of a system that a proposition is justifiable.

If we must have and also cannot have a system, all that remains is the persistent *striving* for one. For Schlegel, the ideal of a system takes on purely regulative status, a goal we approach but never attain. Of course, there is no perfect system; but that does not mean that all systems are on the same footing. There are better and worse ways of organizing our knowledge. The ideal system is that which combines the greatest unity with the greatest multiplicity, or which organizes the most data according to the fewest principles.

4. Romanticism and Absolute Idealism

Schlegel's critique of Fichte's idealism and foundationalism had the most important effect on his aesthetic doctrines, which were very much in evolution in 1797. In his earlier works on classical poetry, especially his 1795 *Über das Studium der griechischen Poesie,* Schlegel had defended a very rigid, almost fanatical neoclassical aesthetic, according to which all works of art should be judged according to a rigorous "objective" standard of beauty.[41] This neoclassical aesthetic began to fall apart, however, because it could not match his own demands for relentless self-criticism. Schlegel's critique of first principles meant that there are no universal and necessary standards of criticism, and hence that there is no single canon to judge all works of art. When Schlegel disavowed his earlier classicism in the *Kritische Fragmente,* he duly drew attention to the connection between it and his erstwhile naive foundationalism: "The revolutionary rage for objectivity in my earlier philosophical musicals had something of that fundamental rage that was so so virulent around the time of Reinhold's consulate in philosophy" (no. 66; II, 155). Understanding this comment in its proper context is important, for it means that Schlegel's romanticism is not as Fichtean as is often thought. It was not Schlegel's discovery and appropriation of Fichte that led him to reject classicism but almost the very reverse: his *critique* of Fichte's idealism and foundationalism.[42]

Now that Schlegel rejected that "rage for objectivity," the problem was to find a new aesthetic adequate to his antifoundationalism. The result was nothing less than his romanticism, more especially his famous concepts of 'irony' and 'romantic poesy,' which he expounded in the *Kritische* and *Athenäums Fragmente.*

The connection of Schlegel's aesthetics with his antifoundationalism is especially clear in the case of the concept of irony. This was Schlegel's reponse to the apparent *aporia* of his antifoundationalist epistemology. Although there are no first principles, no perfect demonstrations, no criteria of criticism, and no complete systems, Schlegel does not despair. He consoles himself with the idea that we are still left with the eternal *striving* toward the truth, the constant *approximation* to our ideals. This is where irony plays a crucial epistemological role: it consists in the recognition that, even though we cannot attain the truth, we still must strive toward it. This was the attitude of Socrates, that great master of irony, who now became Schlegel's model.[43] Socrates was a perpetual gadfly, of course, but he was also the wisest man precisely because he knew that he knew nothing.

Schlegel gives his best characterization of what he means by irony in the 1797 *Kritische Fragmente*. There he explains irony as a response to two kinds of predicament encountered in the attempt to know the truth. The first kind consists in "the feeling of the irresolvable conflict between the unconditioned and conditioned" (no. 108; II, 160). The ironist feels a conflict between the unconditioned and conditioned because any attempt to know the unconditioned would falsify it and make it conditioned. The whole truth is the unconditioned, because it completes the entire series of conditions; but any form of conceptualizing and explaining the unconditioned makes it conditioned, either because it applies the principle of sufficient reason, which determines conditions, or because it applies some determinate concept, which has its meaning only by negation.[44] The second kind of predicament consists in "the impossibility and necessity of a complete communication." The ironist feels that complete communication is *impossible* because any perspective is partial, any concept is limited, and any statement perfectible; the truth is intrinsically inexhaustible, defying any single perspective, concept, or statement of it. But he also sees that complete communication is *necessary* because it is only by postulating the ideal of the whole, which guides and organizes our otherwise blind and scattered efforts, that we approach the truth. We must never cease to strive after completion because we can always achieve a deeper perspective, a richer concept, and clearer statement of the truth, which is more adequate to the wholeness, richness, and depth of experience.

The ironist's response to these predicaments consists in "the constant change from self-creation to self-destruction"(no. 37; II, 151).[45] In other words, the ironist creates forever anew because he always puts forward a new perspective, a richer concept, a clearer formulation; but he also destroys himself because he is forever critical of his own efforts. It is only through this interchange between self-creation and self-destruction that he moves forward in the eternal search for the truth. Schlegel's *via media* between this self-creation and self-destruction is *self-restraint:* limiting our creative powers, and adopting a critical distance toward them, so that we do not completely exhaust them in the heat of inspiration.

In fundamental respects, Schlegel's concept of romantic poesy is also the result of his antifoundationalist epistemology. Romantic poesy, as stated by Schlegel in the famous *Athenäumsfragment* no. 116 (II, 182–183), is essentially the aesthetic version of the philosopher's eternal striving for truth. The romantic poet cultivates the same ironic attitude as the philosopher. Both the poet and philosopher are engaged in endless enquiry, an eternal striving, to provide the best description of their object. Hence Schlegel states in no. 116 that the "characteristic essence" of romantic poesy is that it forever becomes and is never complete. Furthermore, both poet and philosopher vascillate between self-creation and self-destruction because, though critical of all their efforts to describe their object, they always create anew. Thus Schlegel also says in no. 116 that the romantic poet "hovers in the middle on the wings of poetic reflection between the object depicted and the act of depicting it." Still further, both poet and philosopher realize that there is no end to self-criticism, and that there are no objective rules of criticism that somehow stand above criticism itself. Hence Schlegel writes again in no. 116 that the romantic poet multiplies reflection *ad infinitum*, as if in an endless series of mirrors. Finally, both poet and philosopher refuse to acknowledge any final rules in their search for the truth, because these serve as artificial and arbitrary limits on the creative process. Thus Schlegel declares in no. 116 that the romantic poet will not be bound by any definite rules of genre, and that he recognizes no laws on his own free will.

There can be no doubt that Schlegel's concepts of irony and romantic poesy have a great debt to Fichte. What Schlegel had done is transfer Fichte's ethical concept of infinite striving into the aesthetic sphere. The infinite striving of the Fichtean ego to attain its absolute independence became the infinite striving of the artist to attain perfection and to express absolute truth. This analogy has often been made, and rightly so. However, it is of the first importance to see that Schlegel appropriated this theme without endorsing Fichte's idealism. The artist's infinite striving did not imply any form of idealism, according to which all of reality is a construction of my will or imagination, and still less did it endorse the circle of consciousness at the close of the *Wissenschaftslehre*.[46] Schlegel's romanticism is decidedly *not* the aesthetics of Fichte's idealism.

That this Fichtean interpretation is very problematic should already be clear from Schlegel's critique of Fichte's idealism in his notebooks, which was formulated only shortly before his romantic aesthetic. But there is another factor telling against this interpretation: that Schlegel's romantic aesthetics depends on the realism of Spinozism. This is apparent in the *Athenäums Fragmente*, where Schlegel not only defends Spinoza,[47] but also stresses that the mystical feeling for the one and all is essential to aesthetics. Schlegel had already said in his earlier *Kritische Fragmente* that the concept of irony presupposes the philosopher has some intuition or feeling for the infinite, "the mood that surveys everything and rises infinitely above all limitations" (no. 42; II, 152); it is indeed just this mood that makes him doubt that any of his particular statements or formulations will be adequate to the truth. But this mystical dimension is even more explicit in the *Athenäums Fragmente* where he insists that the ideas of irony presuppose mysticism, the perspective from which "the spirit regards everything as mystery and miracle" (no. 121; II, 184).

What the new Spinozistic realism meant for Schlegel's aesthetics becomes clear from his *Gespräch über die Poesie*, which he wrote in late 1799. Schlegel now states unequivocally that only an absolute idealism that is in the same measure an absolute realism provides the foundation for the new mythology or poetry (II, 314–318). He explains that the new poetry must come from the inner depths of the spirit, from the spirit's eternal striving to find its creative center, and that idealism aids poetry by discovering the inner depths and creative center. But the idealism Schlegel has in mind here is not a Fichtean *subjective* idealism; rather, it is his new *absolute* idealism, of which Fichte's idealism is now only one aspect or moment. Hence he insists that idealism must have within itself "an equally unlimited realism" if it is to do full justice to the creative process. This creative process is a dialectical development where the spirit not only goes outside itself, externalizing its activity in things, but also returns into itself, recognizing its limits and internalizing the world outside itself (II, 314). Such a process expresses not only the ideality of the real—the dependence of nature on spirit—but also the reality of the ideal—the dependence of spirit on nature. While the first aspect represents idealism, the second signifies the "equally unlimited realism." Now this second aspect has to be fully recognized, Schlegel insists, to establish the possibility of the new poetry. For this poetry should not only stem from the inner spirit, but it should also reveal the infinite in the finite, the divine within every individual thing. Because Spinoza has shown how all finite things exist within the infinite, his philosophy becomes the basis for poetry. "In fact I hardly understand how one can be a poet," the character Ludovoko says, "unless one honors, loves, and appropriates Spinoza" (II, 317).

These passages make it clear that Schlegel's romanticism was the aesthetic not of the *Wissenschaftslehre* but of *absolute* idealism itself. An essential element of the romantic aesthetic—whether in Schlegel, Novalis, or Hölderlin—is its mystical and realistic dimension, the idea that we must see everything finite as part of the infinite, as an appearance of the absolute. It is this dimension that cannot be explained if we construe romanticism as a derivative of Fichte's subjective idealism.

5. The Mystical

While Schlegel's absolute idealism is wedded with his romantic aesthetic, it appears to conflict with his antifoundationalism. The source of the tension lies in Schlegel's irrevocable demand for criticism, a demand so uncompromising that it approaches a complete skepticism. Schlegel had indeed called irony, the capstone of his new epistemology, "the highest, purest skepticism"(no. 1023; XVIII, 406). But such skepticism poses a serious challenge for absolute idealism: How do we know the existence of the absolute? Absolute idealism postulates the existence of the absolute, the reality of the one and all, which exists independent of finite consciousness. Yet it would seem skepticism permits at best only an agnosticism about its existence, granting at most only *regulative* status to this idea.

Schlegel had already faced this problem in his earlier years when his Platonic tendencies, his "longing for the infinite," came crashing against the Kantian limitations of knowledge. Thus in his October 16, 1793 letter to his brother, where he first explains his concept of the Platonic ideal, he also expresses his disagreement with Kant, mentioning explicitly his doctrine of "the regulative use of ideas" (XXIII, 141). While Schlegel's early Platonism contains no explicit postulate of the existence of the absolute—he explains that the longing for the infinite is rooted in human nature, thus giving it only a practical rather than theoretical legitimacy—he also plays around with mystical ideas that suggest we have some feeling or sense of the infinite (XXIII, 130). In any case, it is clear that Schlegel had as yet no clear position on this all important question. To his brother he expressed his willingness to reread Kant's first *Kritik*, "the first [philosophical work] of which I understood something, and the only one from which I still hope to learn much."

Once Schlegel committed himself to absolute idealism, the problem of knowing the absolute became especially acute. But his skeptical epistemology seemed to undermine any solution. He had agreed with Jacobi and Kant that we cannot know the absolute by *discursive* means. He accepted the thrust of one of their main arguments against such knowledge: that reason operates according to the principle of sufficient reason, which demands that there is always another cause or condition for any event, so that reason cannot grasp first causes or the unconditioned (no. 64; XVIII, 511). But if there cannot be any discursive knowledge of the absolute, then it would seem that the only possibility is some form of mystical knowledge, a purely immediate intellectual intuition. This was indeed the solution of Hölderlin and Novalis, and Schelling too spoke of intellectual intuition as the ultimate ground of

Spinoza's philosophy. But here again Schlegel's skepticism stood in the way. If there cannot be pure empirical data, neither can there be pure mystical insights. Whatever we know or see will be mediated by concepts, by a web of belief, and so subject to interpretation.

Initially, Schlegel himself drew just this conclusion. Unlike Novalis and Hölderlin, he forcefully repudiated mysticism, at least in his published work around 1796–1797. His new hero around this time was Lessing, who represented for him the ideal of free enquiry, the willingness to examine all beliefs regardless of social convention and religious orthodoxy.[48] But Schlegel's insistence on constantly pushing forward the boundaries of enquiry, and subjecting all beliefs to criticism, made it difficult for him to accept mysticism, which implies the existence of some ultimate and unquestionable experience. This becomes especially apparent in his early 1796 reviews of Jacobi's *Woldemar* and of J. G. Schlosser's *Der Deutsche Orpheus*.[49] Schlegel criticized both for appealing to some mystical experience that transcends all criticism, and for forcing rational enquiry to follow the guidelines of their own faith. "Whoever demands of philosophy that it creates a Julia for him, will have to come sooner or later to the sublime maxim of Shakespeare's Romeo: *Hang up Philosophy! Unless philosophy can make a Juliet!*" (II, 70). Schlegel censures mystics as enthusiasts, as dreamers who prefer to reach truth immediately by fantasy rather than by the painful effort of enquiry (VIII, 10). His criticism of indubitable first principles made him especially skeptical of Jacobi's appeal to some immediate intuition as the basis of knowledge. He argues that Jacobi's claim that every proof ultimately presupposes something unproven, some self-evident insight or experience, works only if we assume that all knowledge is based on a single fundamental principle; but it is not necessary to appeal to such an experience if the justification for a proposition is based on the mutual support of other propositions in a coherent system (II, 71–72).

Schlegel's published reviews are only half of the story, however. His more private reflections reveal that he had a much more complicated and ambivalent view of mysticism. In December 1796 he sent Novalis a packet containing his latest philosophical musings, which revolve around the theme of mysticism.[50] Rather than simply condemning mysticism as a betrayal of the ideal of free enquiry, Schlegel now has a much more positive view of it. He states that the mystics are those from whom we should learn philosophy (no. 11; XVIII, 5), that they are the masters of the original science of the absolute (no. 39; XVIII, 15), that they are more moral and consistent than empiricists, skeptics, and eclectics (nos. 9, 20; XVIII, 4–5), and that mysticism is the beginning of progressive history, whose central goal is a mystical idea (no. 23; XVIII, 6). Not all mystics, Schlegel admits, are like Jacobi, who is a *false* mystic because he mixes empirical motives with purer mystical ideals (nos. 3, 26, 60; XVIII, 3, 6, 9).

There can be no doubt that Schlegel's interest in mysticism in these notebooks stems from his concern with the problem of how to know the absolute. He restates this problem explicitly: "*What* can I know is only one-half of the problem; the other half is: *how* can I know?" (no. 33; XVIII, 7). Mysticism is one of the most serious attempts to answer these questions because "Its *essence* and its *beginning* consists in the free positing of the absolute" (no. 7; XVIII, 4). Mysticism consists in the aspiration toward absolute unity (no. 39; XVIII, 7), and in the positing of the existence of the absolute, from which it is possible to explain everything (no. 2; XVIII, 3). So seriously does Schlegel now take mysticism that he thinks that both Fichte and Spinoza are mystics, because they both postulate the absolute and appeal to some form of intellectual intuition (nos. 2, 12; XVIII, 3, 5).

Although his attitude toward mysticism is more positive than his published reviews suggest, Schlegel still rejects it. His new appreciation of mysticism goes along with a new criticism of it. Schlegel thinks that skepticism, eclecticism, and mysticism are three "degenerate forms" (*Abarten*) of philosophy, three kinds of "logical sickness." Although mysticism is the most instructive and consistent of these forms, it is still deviant, a form of "unphilosophical philosophy" (no. 101; XVIII, 13). All these aberrant forms not only destroy one another, but also themselves (no. 6; XVIII, 4). Mysticism ends in "dull inner brooding." The main problem with mysticism is still the same as that which Schlegel had insisted on in his reviews: it is uncritical (nos. 52, 93; XVIII, 8–9, 12). Schlegel reaffirms his commitment to the endless creative activity of free enquiry, which he now sees as the basis of philosophy itself. The essence of philosophy is "the striving for unity in our knowledge" (no. 101; XVIII, 13), and the only given from which it begins is the principle "I strive after unity of knowledge" (no. 18; XVIII, 5). Hence the only cure for mysticism is *Bildung*, going gradually through all the stages of one's education and realizing that one cannot attain insight except after a long process of enquiry (no. 13; XVIII, 518).

It was only after his first meeting with Schleiermacher, which took place in July 1797, that Schlegel embraced the mystical as the basis of his philosophy. A fragment from that year shows its growing importance: "With the *mystical* everything begins and ends. Only from the mystical must be derived physics, logic, poetry, ethics" (no. 656; XVIII, 84). There is now a major, though subtle, shift in Schlegel's views about the nature of philosophy: it does not begin and end with the infinite striving of reason, but with some intuition or feeling for the universe. Hence he writes that philosophy in the strict sense should provide a *characteristic* of the universe (no. 494; XVIII, 70), that this is to be had only in poetry (no. 231; XVIII, 141), and that it requires something like an intellectual intuition (no. 1005; XVIII, 103). This new understanding of philosophy emerges fully in his essay *Über die Philosophie*, which he wrote in August 1798 and then published in the *Athenäum* in 1799. Here Schlegel is explicit that "The thought of the universe and its harmony is my one and all" (VIII, 49), and he makes religion the heart and soul of all *Bildung*. Hence, rather than being the antidote to enthusiasm, *Bildung* now derives from it. Schlegel further explains that "the *universe* remains my slogan" because there must be in all human feeling, thinking, and acting an interaction between individuality and universality, the single person and the universe as a whole (48–49). The more we love a person, the more harmony we find in the world; and the more harmony we find in the world, the more we will see the depth and richness of every individual. If we truly love someone, we also love the world in our beloved; and to do this we already must have at least a sense for the world. This was the mysticism of Diotima in the *Symposium* and of Schiller in the *Theosophie des jungen Julius*. It was indeed the mysticism involved in the Platonic longing for the ideal, which had been implicit in Schlegel's thinking ever since 1793.

We are still left with the questions, however, how Schlegel could square his new mysticism with his radical criticism, and how it could provide a sufficient support for his absolute idealism. These were issues that Schlegel only fully faced in his lectures on transcendental idealism in 1801, to which we must now turn.

6. Lectures on Transcendental Idealism

Since July 1797 Schlegel had been living in Berlin, leading an insecure bohemian existence while trying to earn his living as a writer. But he never abandoned hopes for an academic career, and considered returning to Jena someday as a university lecturer. That opportunity finally came in the summer of 1800. Fichte and Schelling, the most popular champions of the new transcendental philosophy and the main rivals for prospective students, had left Jena. It now seemed as if Schlegel could establish himself, unchallenged, as the chief spokesman for transcendental philosophy, and at the very university that had become the center of philosophy in Germany. So Schlegel duly returned to Jena and announced two lecture series for the winter semester, a public one entitled *Philosophiam transcendentalem* and a private series called *de officio philosophi*, an intended successor to Fichte's very popular lectures on the vocation of the intellectual. He began the first set of lectures on October 27, and concluded them on March 24, 1801; the second seems never to have been given.

Schlegel's lectures on transcendental philosophy were his most serious and sustained attempt to explain his new absolute idealism. Rather than simply suggesting his ideas in a few witty fragments, as he had done in the *Athenäum*, Schlegel now had to explain himself before a student audience. Furthermore, he also had to organize his ideas, casting them into something approaching systematic form. Unfortunately, however, the lectures have been lost. Schlegel's manuscript has disappeared, and all that remains are some fragmentary and incomplete notes by an unknown hand.[51] Still, these notes are invaluable, providing the only insight into the details of Schlegel's thinking about absolute idealism around 1800.

One of the conditions of becoming a faculty member at the University of Jena was holding a public disputation, in which the candidate had to defend theses against opponents. Holding his dispute March 14, Schlegel chose to defend eight theses from his lectures.[52] Some of them are very revealing about the nature of his absolute idealism. That his philosophy had a Platonic inspiration, and that it understood the ideal in Platonic terms, is clear from his first thesis: "I. *Platonis philosophia genuinus est Idealismus.*"[53] That his absolute idealism involved a preponderant element of realism is evident from his second proposition: "II. *Realismi majores sunt partes in Idealismo producendo quam Dualismi.*" And that he would conceive his idealism in aesthetic terms, by giving art a fundamental role as its organon and criterion, is clear from his fourth proposition: "IV. *Enthusiasmus est principium artis et scientia.*"

Schlegel's Jena lectures are important first and foremost because they are his only attempt to provide a systematic account of his absolute idealism. Unlike Novalis and Hölderlin, Schlegel half succeeded in organizing some of his ideas systematically, even though it was only in his lectures and in no published form. *Prima facie* this seems to contradict his earlier antifoundationalist views, especially those about the impossibility of creating an ideal system. The inconsistency appears all the greater when Schlegel begins his exposition in foundationalist fashion, employing the geometric method with all the apparatus of definitions, axioms, and theorems. The inconsistency is only apparent, however, once we realize that Schlegel makes no claims whatsoever for the finality of his system.[54] Rather, he continues to stress that there is no ideal system, and that there are many different ways of organizing our views, none of which can make a claim to absolute truth. His old antifoundationalist scruples are still very much in evidence. Hence he insists that philosophy is only an experiment, whose success cannot be known a priori (XII, 3); he denies that philosophy can begin with formal definitions, which presuppose the knowledge it should attain (4); and he recognizes that there are an infinite number of proofs about the infinite (23). The lectures indeed end with Schlegel strongly reaffirming his antifoundationalism: that philosophy cannot start from a presuppositionless beginning, that all truth is relative, and that absolute truth can never be given (93–94). Given such antifoundationalism, we might wonder why Schlegel attempts to formulate a system at all. The reason is that he still thinks the philosopher has an obligation to strive after the systematic ideal: the maximum amount of unity for the greatest diversity of ideas (10, 28).[55]

The introduction to the lectures sketches the foundation of Schlegel's absolute idealism. He begins with a short characteristic of philosophy itself, stating that "The tendency of philosophy is toward the absolute" (4). The absolute consists in a positive and negative factor: the positive factor is the unconditioned, the negative is the conditioned or the infinite series of individual finite things. Now what philosophy seeks in its attempt to know the absolute is some account of the unity of the unconditioned and conditioned, the unity of unity and multiplicity. The main problem of philosophy, as Schlegel puts it, is to find the central point of all *principles* and *ideas*. A 'principle' is that which gives us knowledge of the original or primary, the unity of all things, while an 'idea' is that which gives us knowledge of the whole, the totality of all finite things (4). The central point of all principles and ideas would then be the unity of the conditioned and unconditioned, of unity and multiplicity (7).

How do we find this central point? We first must abstract from everything that is not absolute, Schlegel urges, until we come to some point from which we cannot abstract any further. We then must "constitute" the absolute, that is, we must posit it absolutely as all reality (5). We do this through the "annihilation of every imagination of the finite."[56] In other words, we must affirm the absolute not only negatively, as that which is opposed to the finite, but also positively, as that which has infinite reality. This demands

completely negating the reality of the finite as something opposed to the absolute, because such a reality would limit it. How such negation is to take
place the notes do not explain.

Still, the crucial question remains: What gives us the right to postulate the
infinite? Schlegel replies that the consciousness of the infinite is given to
the individual through the *feeling of the sublime.* Here indeed is the core of
Schlegel's aesthetic idealism: the feeling of the sublime is the guarantee for
the reality of the infinite, the criterion for knowledge of the absolute.[57]
Schlegel states that this feeling consists in *enthusiasm,* which is the positive
factor of philosophy just as skepticism is its negative factor (4, 6). In choos-
ing this term, Schlegel was attempting to give a positive meaning to what
had derogatory connotations ever since the Reformation. The *reductio ad
absurdam* of any philosophy was once said to be that it "opens the gates of
enthusiasm." Schlegel insisted, however, that it is one of the *strengths* of his
philosophy that it does just this (42). But the main source of Schlegel's enthusiasm was Platonic rather than Protestant: it was nothing less than the
third kind of madness of Plato's *Phaedrus,* that which comes from the muses
and consist in poetic inspiration (245a).

Schlegel insists that the feeling of the sublime cannot be explained or
defined. The absolute thesis of all philosophy—the postulation of the existence of the absolute—cannot be demonstrated because it contains its proof
within itself (24). It is not, however, simply a form of faith (*Glaube*), because
this feeling is a form of knowledge. All faith contains something uncertain,
whose opposite is also possible, which is not the case with the first principle
of philosophy (24). Although this feeling cannot be explained or demonstrated, it can still be interpreted, Schlegel insists, and the media of its interpretation is poetry.[58]

But is it not possible that the feeling of the sublime is mistaken? Is
the feeling the poet has for the infinite perhaps only a delusion? Schlegel's
reply to this objection is suprising: he admits that this feeling is a fiction
(*Erdichtung*), but he insists that it is still a necessary fiction because it is inherent in the most fundamental tendency of human nature. This tendency
consists in the longing for the infinite, the striving to reunite ourselves with
the universe (9). In calling it a fiction, Schlegel does not mean that it is false,
but simply that it is an ideal that we cannot verify or falsify by discursive
means. In other words, he admits that there is no proof for the infinite, and
that we must simply *experience* its reality, which can no more be proved than
the existence of colors to a blind man.

Whatever the problems of knowing the infinite, Schlegel devotes most of his attention in the introduction to exploring the *implications* of postulating its existence. No sooner does he posit the infinite than he comes to an important conclusion about the two basic elements or concepts of his idealism. If we abstract from the finite, and if we posit absolutely the infinite, we are still left with something outside the infinite from which we cannot abstract, namely the acts of positing and abstracting themselves. Since these acts belong to the *consciousness* of the infinite, it follows that the consciousness of the infinite remains something outside the infinite itself. Hence Schlegel concludes that *consciousness* and the *infinite* are the two basic elements of all philosophy, the two fundamental poles around which it forever revolves (5). With this argument, Schlegel had made his basic concession to Fichte, who had always maintained that the subjective is irreducible because the ego forever remains after abstraction from every object of consciousness.

Now that he has found his two irreducible poles, Schlegel states that the task of philosophy is to synthesize Fichte and Spinoza (6, 29–30). The pole of the infinite represents the philosophy of Spinoza, while that of consciousness stands for the philosophy of Fichte. His philosophy is to be a synthesis of Fichte and Spinoza because it insists on the necessity of each pole and the complementarity of both. They are interdependent, Schlegel says, because the only object of consciousness is the infinite, and the only predicate of the infinite is consciousness (6). The infinite and consciousness relate to one another as matter and form, he later explains, where matter gives substance and reality to form and form determination to matter (39).

Schlegel states that the basic formula of his philosophy, his synthesis of Fichte and Spinoza, is that "*the minimum of the ego is equal to the maximum of nature, and the minimum of nature is equal to the maximum of the ego;* in other words, the smallest sphere of consciousness is equal to the greatest of nature, and conversely" (6). This formula implies that the ego and nature, the subjective and objective, or ideal and real, are not *absolute* opposites, which are qualitatively opposed to one another, but *polar* opposites, which are quantitatively opposed to one another. The subjective and objective, the ideal and the real, therefore stand in a continuum where they are in inverse ratio to one another. The more we proceed in one direction, the further removed we are from the other. The middle point, where the two poles are perfectly balanced with one another, Schlegel calls by the neutral term "reality" (6). Following Schelling, he sometimes calls this center "the indifference point."

What allows Schlegel to reconceive the subjective and objective in these quantitative terms is his organic worldview, which he shares with Novalis, Hölderlin, and Schelling. The subjective and objective, the ideal and the real, differ only *quantitatively* because they are simply different degrees of organization and development of a single life force. In the first part of the lectures Schlegel makes the fundamental concept of his theory of nature the concept of 'life' or 'energy' (*Energie*). He then divides nature into two fundamental elements, form and matter. What unites these two elements, he explains, is the concept of an organism. It is the essential characteristic of an organism that it is matter making itself form and form making itself matter. The concept of energy designates the living inner power, the principle of organization, behind every organism (35). The concept of energy means that all things have only as much power (*Kraft*) as they have sense (*Sinn*), and that all things in nature are alive (33). Schlegel then applies this concept of an organism on a grand macrocosmic scale: "The universe is a work of art—an animal—a plant" (40).[59]

Schlegel calls his synthesis of Fichte and Spinoza "idealism." It is idealism not in the sense that it holds all reality depends on the ego, but in the sense that it maintains all reality depends on an "absolute intelligence" within the universe itself (96). This absolute intelligence is not something subjective, having personality and consciousness, but it is that rational principle or archetype active in all things, the idea of all ideas. As Schlegel formulates idealism in an entry from the notebooks: "Idealism means nothing more than all reason is universal. It is the organ of man for the universe" (no. 701; XVIII, 252). Such idealism, Schlegel maintains, consists in two basic elements, 'dualism' and 'realism' (14). While dualism corresponds to the element of consciousness, because all consciousness involves some distinction between subject and object, realism corresponds to the element of the infinite. Schlegel is emphatic and explicit that this realism is not an *empirical* realism, because it goes beyond ordinary experience and concerns the infinite (14n).

The higher realism involved in Schlegel's absolute idealism is most apparent from some of the notebook entries written around the same time as the lectures. Sometimes Schlegel simply identifies idealism with "absolute realism" (no. 1174; XVIII, 418); and sometimes he insists that, though the ideal disappears in the real as the real in the ideal, it is always realism that dominates (no. 1236; XVIII, 298). So close is the connection of idealism with realism that he holds Spinoza is "the highest idealist" (no. 975; XVIII, 401–402). Schlegel's usage is not entirely consistent, however, because he also sometimes continues *to contrast* idealism with realism, saying that idealism becomes realism when the absolute appears as nature (no. 451; XVIII, 358). On the whole, however, Schlegel stresses the predominance of realism in his absolute idealism, fearing that his doctrine could be confused with the more subjective idealism of Kant and Fichte. It is this realist dimension of idealism, he claims, that undermines Jacobi's objections against its purely subjective status (no. 459; XVIII, 358). The realist dimension of Schlegel's idealism ultimately derives from his postulate of the infinite, the one and all, which transcends all finite consciousness. This is not, however, Spinozism pure and simple, given Schlegel's vitalism. This injection of life into Spinoza's static universe restores the subjective component on a cosmic scale.

Schlegel maintains that, properly conceived, idealism is opposed to not realism but dogmatism.[60] The distinguishing characteristic of dogmatism is that it seeks reality in merely formal principles (12). It begins from the merely phenomenal and assumes that the categories (for example, causality, quality, and quantity) are true of reality itself (14). What Schlegel means by 'dogmatism' here is not the fallacy exposed by Kant: ascribing to things-in-themselves what is true only for the understanding. Rather, it is the sin later descried by Schelling and Hegel: assuming that the categories valid for the finite world are also applicable to the infinite. In opposing idealism to dogmatism in this sense, Schlegel apparently means that idealism is committed to the doctrine that there is something infinite that transcends expression in the finite or conceptual terms.

It is striking that Schlegel, like Schelling around the same time, virtually identifies the standpoint of idealism with *Naturphilosophie*. Physics is the first of all the sciences, he says, because all science is ultimately the science of nature (16). He is almost ready to conclude that the standpoint of idealism completely coincides with physics, but then stops himself by asking what is the distinction between them. It is as if Schlegel now intends to work out his differences with Schelling. The distinction between philosophy and physics, he answers, is that the philosopher has to deal with the maximum and minimum of reality themselves, the two poles of the absolute, whereas the physicist has to deal with only the finite members that lie between these poles (17). In finally assigning the physicist such a subsidiary task, Schlegel had put a distance between himself and Schelling's *Naturphilosophie*. This distance indeed grew with the years, as Schlegel increasingly allied himself with Novalis' efforts to go beyond Schelling.[61]

Schlegel reformulates the basic problem behind his lectures—how to think the unity of unity and multiplicity—by raising the question why the infinite goes outside itself and makes itself finite. In other words, why are there individual things? His answer to this question again reveals the pivotal role of the aesthetic in his idealism. He explains that there are two fundamental opposing concepts that must be reconciled: the infinite, which is indivisible and eternal, and the finite or the individual, which is divisible and transitory. The mediating concept between these two is that of the image (*Bild*), presentation (*Darstellung*), or allegory (*Allegorie*). The individual is the image of the single infinite substance, its presentation of the essence of substance. The allegorical form of this explanation is that "God creates the world in order to portray himself" (39). This means that the infinite is a kind of divine artist, creating the entire world for its self-knowledge. The infinite is therefore to be conceived as a kind of intelligence, what Schlegel, anticipating Hegel, calls "spirit" (*Geist*) (39).

Schlegel's postulate of the infinite, his fondness for Spinoza, and his identification of reality itself with the divine, makes his absolute idealism appear essentially pantheistic.[62] This is indeed the case; but it is important to stress that it is a pantheism with a difference. True to his organic vision, Schlegel sees the divine as in a process of becoming, as undergoing a process of organic development whereby it moves from unity, to difference, to unity-in-difference.[63] Schlegel further insists that this process of divine development is something in which all human beings participate. The universe itself is imperfect and in development, gradually realizing itself through our finite actions.[64] Hence history becomes a constitutive part of the absolute. This historical dimension of Schlegel's metaphysics becomes especially apparent when Schlegel states that God is really only a task for us, and that we create him through our own actions.[65]

All these aspects of Schlegel's lectures—the Platonic inspiration, the emphasis on the unity of Fichte and Spinoza, the aesthetic vision of the universe, the organic conception of reality—make them an *almost* perfect epitome of absolute idealism. All that they lack is rigor and detail, which is not surprising for a student transcript. It is all the more a pity, therefore, that the original manuscripts are missing. Yet, given Schlegel's restless creative spirit, we might well doubt if he would have ever sat long enough to perfect them.

PART IV

Schelling and Absolute Idealism

Introduction: The Troublesome Schellingian Legacy

Schelling is no longer a prominent name in the history of philosophy, at least not in the Anglo-Saxon world. There are few books devoted to him,[1] no entry on him in the latest reference book on metaphysics.[2] For all too long he has been treated as a predecessor to others, "an intermediate figure" between Kant and Hegel. Marxists have praised the dialectical elements of his *Naturphilosophie;* Hegelians have acknowledged the importance of his absolute idealism; and existentialists have recognized the significance of his later critique of essentialism. But all these parties value Schelling essentially as a stepping stone for later developments. Schelling is rarely taken as a figure in his own right, deserving close examination for his own sake. Despite some notable exceptions,[3] scholars have failed to take into account the advice of Karl Rosenkranz, who, more than a century ago, declared: "*Schelling ist einmal Schelling und man muß ihm nehmen, wie er ist.*"[4]

The tendency to treat Schelling as a foot stool has been especially misleading with regard to his role in the development of German idealism. Persistently, Schelling has been valued only as the predecessor of Hegel. That, at any rate, is how Hegel portrayed his erstwhile friend and colleague in his *Geschichte der Philosophie,*[5] which relegated Schelling to a few subparagraphs in a vast system. But such a fate is unfair, a caricature of Schelling's real contribution. It was Schelling who fathered the basic principles and who forged the central themes of the absolute idealism that Hegel loyally defended and systematized from 1801 to 1804. Even if we admit that Hegel eventually saw farther than Schelling—a very generous concession—it is also necessary to add that he did so only because he stood on Schelling's shoulders. While Hegel broke with Schelling around 1804, he did so chiefly because Schelling had failed to justify and develop *his own* principles. If Hegel was not simply "the spear carrier" for Schelling, neither was Schelling merely the footrest for Hegel.

465

The reason for Schelling's decline in contemporary philosophy has much to do with the ill repute of metaphysics. No one nowadays wants to be near metaphysics, the bogeyman of postivists, pragmatists, neo-Kantians, and postmodernists alike. But Schelling has had the reputation for being a full-blown metaphysician, and so has suffered accordingly. Such notoriety is somewhat ironic, given that, after 1809, Schelling himself turned against the metaphysical tradition, developing an interesting critique of conceptual thought in his later *Positivephilosophie*. It is indeed for just this reason that most contemporary efforts to revive him lay stress upon his *Positive-philosophie*.[6] Still, the *Positivephilosophie* was only one phase in Schelling's development, one period in a very protean intellectual career. In the earlier phases of his thought from 1796 to 1800, Schelling was indisputably a metaphysician, and indeed in a perfectly straightforward sense. His *Natur-philosophie* attempted to know the fundamental forces of nature, the infinite productive powers of Spinoza's *natura naturans;* and his *Identitätssystem* put foward a system of knowledge of the absolute. What Kant claimed reason could not know—the absolute or unconditioned—Schelling wrote volumes about. Should we not shun, then, Schelling's earlier metaphysics?

To do so fails to appreciate the context behind that metaphysics; even worse, it just begs the question. For in his early years Schelling saw something that many of his contemporaries, and many still today, fail to appreciate. He recognized that the solution to the fundamental problems of epistemology requires nothing less than metaphysics. The basic question of epistemology—'How do we know that our concepts correspond to the world?'—is resolvable, Schelling argued, only if we can also explain the interaction between the mental and physical, the subjective and objective, the ideal and real. If these terms refer to complete opposites—if they denote entities in separate worlds—then the correspondence between representation and object in knowledge becomes impossible, at best a complete mystery. Rightly, Schelling saw that the problem of dualism would be surmountable only if philosophers rethought the nature of matter itself. If matter is only bare extension, and if mechanism is the paradigm of explanation, then the only options are dualism and materialism. But neither is satisfactory. If the former makes mental–physical interaction mysterious, the latter fails to recognize the *sui generis* status of mental life. Hence the task of Schelling's *Naturphilosophie*—the goal behind all his speculations about the nature of matter—was to find some middle path between dualism and materialism, some way of explaining the mind naturalistically without reducing it down to a mechanistic straitjacket. Although his *Naturphilosophie* was indeed metaphysics, it was a metaphysics designed to get beyond the *aporia* of classical epistemology. It is simply question begging, then, when we appeal to epistemology to criticize his metaphysics.

Behind Schelling's engagement with metaphysics lay his recognition of the ambivalent and problematic relationship between metaphysics and natural science. He saw all too well that philosophy could not solve its basic problems without natural science; but he also knew that philosophy should not uncritically accept science, lapsing into a scientism that sees technology and mechanism as the only solutions to metaphysical questions. Such an attitude is a marked improvement on those philosophers who either ignore or worship natural science, who make philosophy either completely independent of, or totally dependent on, it. There are few philosophers today who could combine Schelling's critical outlook on the metaphysical pretensions of science with such a profound knowledge of its latest results.

Whatever Schelling's abiding relevance, there can be no doubt that he deserves a prominent place in any history of German idealism. He was the most inventive, brilliant, and productive of all the absolute idealists, and indeed the most fertile. His thinking had a deep impact on Schlegel and Novalis as well as Hegel, even if they often quarreled with him. Schelling's role in the development of absolute idealism comprises only one phase of his protean intellectual career: the period from 1799 to 1804, that of the so-called *Identitätssystem*. During these years Schelling wrote some of the most subtle, sophisticated, and systematic works of absolute idealism: the 1801 *Darstellung meines Systems der Philosophie* and its important sequel *Fernere Darstellung des Systems der Philosophie,* the 1802 *Philosophie der Kunst,* and the unpublished but climactic 1804 *System der gesammten Philosophie.*[7] What was merely fragmentary, inchoate, and suggestive in Hölderlin, Novalis, and Schlegel became systematic, organized, and explicit in Schelling.

Schelling's significance for the history of absolute idealism lies primarily in his *Naturphilosophie,* which laid the foundation for the new organic concept of nature so central to the romantic *Weltanschauung.* Absolute idealism is inconceivable apart from *Naturphilosophie* because the solution to its fundamental problem—'How does the subject know the object when they appear to be in opposite worlds?'—depends on the organic concept of nature. No one deserves more credit for developing this concept than Schelling. Only implicit and embryonic in Novalis, Schlegel, and Hölderlin, this concept becomes fully explicit and systematic only in Schelling. To be sure, Schelling was not the creator of *Naturphilosophie;* the discipline has a long history, and he was only one of many in his generation to revive it. Nevertheless, Schelling could still claim to be its foremost spokesman in the 1790s and early 1800s. He deserves this title not only because of the many works he wrote in the field, but also because of his influential role as the editor of the *Zeitschrift für spekulative Physik.*

Given Schelling's abiding relevance, and given his pivotal role in the development of German idealism, the following chapters are devoted to a detailed examination of his early thought, more specifically, his early Fichtean phase and the later period of the *Identitätssystem.* We shall investigate the growth of Schelling's *Naturphilosophie,* his break with Fichte, and finally the method and meaning of his absolute idealism.

CHAPTER 1

The Path toward Absolute Idealism

1. The Fichte–Schelling Alliance

The development of Schelling's absolute idealism is a long and complex story. Like all his contemporaries, Schelling served his intellectual apprenticeship under Fichte, and he formed his absolute idealism in reaction against the "subjective idealism" of his erstwhile mentor. But Schelling's struggle to liberate himself from Fichte was much more protracted, tortured, and violent than any contemporary. What took months for Hölderlin, Novalis, and Schlegel took years for Schelling. This is not because he had formed a more intimate friendship with Fichte—Schlegel could claim to be on closer terms—but because he had so publicly linked himself with Fichte's cause. To break with Fichte therefore involved creating a whole new literary persona for himself.

Schelling's first contact with Fichte came when he was still very young. In September 1794, when he was only nineteen and still a student at the *Tübinger Stift*, Schelling wrote Fichte a flattering letter, expressing deep admiration for his work. Along with his letter he sent Fichte a copy of his first philosophical publication, *Über die Möglichkeit einer Form der Philosophie überhaupt*.[1] Schelling told Fichte that he had been thinking about the foundation of Kant's philosophy, and that he found his ideas the most promising to secure it against skeptical objections.[2] Accordingly, his tract is a defense of the Fichtean thesis that the first principle of philosophy is the self-positing ego. In the most polite and humble terms, Schelling requested Fichte's response to his work. Though his reply has been lost, Fichte encouraged his young admirer, sending him a copy of the first part of his *Grundlage der gesamten Wissenschaftslehre*.[3]

Thus began Schelling's alliance with Fichte, a sometimes fruitful but always fraught collaboration that would last another six years. Though twelve years younger than Fichte, Schelling was never simply his disciple or student. From the very beginning, he was an independent thinker, and even in his earliest days his philosophical development took him down paths never traveled by his older colleague. Still, there can be no doubt that Schelling also saw himself as a defender of at least the *spirit* of Fichte's philosophy. His 1795 *Über das Ich als Princip der Philosophie* argues that the only tenable system of philosophy makes the ego its first principle; and his 1797 *Abhandlungen zur Erläuterung des Idealismus der Wissenschaftslehre* is a partisan exposition of Fichte's early system. Though Schelling had been in Tübingen and Leipzig during the heady days in Jena, he was not ignorant of the *Grundsatzkritik* of the Niethammer circle, and he was well aware of the criticisms of Fichte's subjectivism.[4] Nevertheless, he did not abandon his faith in Fichte's foundationalism; and he would begin to criticize Fichte's subjectivism only many years after his contemporaries in Jena.

It was only by late 1799 that it had become clear to Schelling, and only by late 1800 that it had become plain to Fichte, that there were fundamental differences between them, and that these were irresolvable. The story of how they became aware of these differences, and how they attempted and ultimately failed to to settle them, unfolds in their correspondence from 1800 to 1802. These letters tell a sad tale about a collaboration gone astray. While they begin with expressions of the warmest regard and respect, they end in mutual contempt and recrimination. After 1802 Fichte and Schelling will regard one another as archenemies.[5]

Schelling's break with Fichte is a crucial episode in the development of absolute idealism.[6] Its main effect was to make public and explicit all the differences between subjective and objective idealism. In their correspondence around 1800–1801 Fichte and Schelling finally became clear about all the fundamental points dividing their idealisms. They now realized that they had opposing concepts of nature, conflicting interpretations of subject–object identity, competing conceptions of realism and naturalism, and rival accounts of rationality. Never had these issues been explored in such depth and detail before. All these differences then became public when, in May 1801, Schelling published his *Darstellung meines Systems,* the first systematic exposition of absolute idealism. The differences became even more explicit when, in October 1801, Hegel published his defense of Schelling, his *Differenz des Fichteschen und Schellingschen Systems der Philosophie.*

Seen from a broader historical perspective, Schelling's dispute with Fichte marks a radical break with the Cartesian heritage, and more specifically with the tradition of epistemology as *philosophia prima*. While Schelling, unlike Hölderlin, Novalis, and Schlegel, did not reject Fichte's foundationalism, he did form a completely different conception of the foundation of philosophy. In the course of the development of his *Naturphilosophie*, he began to question the whole Cartesian tradition of beginning philosophy with the knowing subject, a tradition that had been continued by Kant, Reinhold, and Fichte. Schelling became convinced that rather than providing a presuppositionless starting point, epistemology had some dubious presuppositions all its own. The epistemological tradition assumes, for example, that the self-conscious subject is a self-sufficient noumenon or *res cogitans*, though this is only a false abstraction from its place in nature. If philosophy were ever to escape from the impasse of Cartesian solipsism and dualism, Schelling firmly believed, then it had to follow the path of nature itself—reconstructing the natural history of consciousness, the laws by which nature gradually produces self-consciousness itself.

It is noteworthy that Fichte and Schelling saw their quarrel in just these terms. While Fichte claimed the title of *philosophia prima* for his *Wissenschaftslehre*, Schelling attempted to usurp that honor for his *Naturphilosophie*. Throughout his correspondence with Schelling, Fichte firmly and self-consciously remained loyal to the Cartesian heritage by insisting that philosophy begin with self-consciousness. He stressed time and again that we must explain nature by reference to our consciousness of it, and that we cannot account for our consciousness in terms of nature. By 1801, however, Schelling had given his *Naturphilosophie* not only independence from, but priority to the *Wissenschaftslehre*. The true starting point of philosophy, he argued, should be nature itself, the universe as a whole. Rather than beginning with self-consciousness, the philosopher should start with the *natura naturans* and derive self-consciousness from it. The self-awareness of the transcendental subject now became simply the highest potency of the organic powers of nature. In making this move, Schelling deliberately turned the Cartesian tradition on its head.

2. Early Fault Lines

Schelling's first major work, published in April 1795, was his *Vom Ich als Princip der Philosophie*. With good reason, this work usually has been placed in his early Fichtean period. In many respects it closely follows Fichte's

Grundlage, whose first part had appeared only months before. Schelling not only applies Fichte's methodology and vocabulary, but he also endorses many of his central theses. Like Fichte, he sees philosophy essentially as a dispute between criticism and dogmatism, and he leaves no doubt that he is on the side of criticism. Nevertheless, Schelling betrays a great sympathy with Spinozism. In his preface he insists that Spinozism is "infinitely more worthy of respect" than all the eclectic systems of the present (I, 151),[7] and he even wrote Hegel in February 1795: "I have become a Spinozist."[8] Still, this was mere flirtation. For in his preface Schelling is explicit that his intention is to write "a counterpart to Spinoza's *Ethica*" (159), and so "to destroy the foundation" of Spinoza's system (151). The basis of Schelling's early allegiance to Fichte was fully sincere and deep: it rested on his Fichtean belief in the primacy of freedom, which he regarded as "the alpha and omega of philosophy."[9] For all the attractions of Spinozism, Fichte's system was preferable to it because it gave a foundation for the belief in freedom. Spinoza had undermined this belief by hypostasis, by placing the unconditioned outside rather than inside ourselves. Freedom was precious for Schelling for political as well as moral reasons. Ultimately, it was his radical republicanism that attracted him to the *Wissenschaftslehre*.[10]

Despite his Fichtean convictions, Schelling's early tract departs from his mentor in important respects. In subtle and unconscious ways the ground is already laid for the later break with Fichte. One basic difference with Fichte concerns the status of the absolute itself. It is Schelling's central thesis that the absolute is Fichte's ego and not Spinoza's substance, or that the absolute is within myself rather than outside myself in the universe. Yet he also qualifies and hedges this contention so that it is unclear what sustains it and why he says it at all.[11] Thus he writes that the unconditioned cannot be found in the subject anymore than the object, for both the subject and object are conditioned and determinable only in contrast to one another (§2; I, 165); and he contends that any system that begins with the subject contradicts itself no less than dogmatism (§5; I, 172). We are then left wondering why Schelling calls his absolute subjective at all. Why is it not instead being or the indifference point?

Our doubts about the subjective status of Schelling's ego only increase when we find that he holds that the absolute ego can never be an object to itself, and that it excludes the possibility of self-consciousness (§8; I, 180). If the absolute 'I' were to be an object to itself, he argues, then it would lose its identity as the absolute; for whatever becomes an object is something conditioned. Furthermore, as the condition of all consciousness, the absolute cannot on pain of circularity become an object of consciousness. Although Schelling insists that the ego is given to itself through an act of intellectual intuition (§8; I, 181), this act does not seem to be the same as self-consciousness itself, which would destroy the absolute by making it conditioned. The closer one examines the Schellingian ego, the more it appears to be little more than sheer existence, something like Hölderlin's 'pure being.' Sure enough Schelling writes: "*I am.* My ego contains a being that precedes all thinking and representing" (§3; I, 167). If we ask why this being preceding all thinking and representing is *myself,* we cannot receive any answer, for that would be to determine it as something when it is that which precedes all determination.

Schelling's tract departs from Fichte in another crucial respect: it gives the idea of the absolute not a regulative but a constitutive status. Contrary to Fichte's teaching that the absolute ego is not the object of belief but only an ideal for action, Schelling maintains that the absolute ego is an existing reality that we know through intellectual intuition. Most probably, this departure from Fichte was unintentional, for Schelling wrote his tract before reading the third part of Fichte's *Grundlage* where the primacy of practical reason, and the regulative status of the absolute ego, is most explicit.[12] The model for Schelling's interpretation of Fichte came from the early programmatic *Über den Begriff der Wissenschaftslehre* and the first part of the *Grundlage,* where these doctrines are not in evidence.

That Schelling gives the absolute ego a constitutive status in *Vom Ich als Princip* becomes perfectly clear from several passages. He states that the ego is *not* only an idea (§15; I, 205, 208), and that it *exists* absolutely, containing all being or reality within itself (§10; I, 187). He ascribes to the absolute ego all the characteristics of Spinoza's substance: it is *causi sui,* infinite, the immanent cause of all things, and it has absolute power and infinite attributes. Just as Spinoza held that his substance exists necessarily, so Schelling holds the same for his ego. For Schelling, the fallacy of Spinoza lay not in thinking that such an infinite being exists—in mistaking a regulative for a constitutive principle—but in projecting such a being outside us when it really should be placed inside us.

Why did Schelling give constitutive status to his absolute ego? It appears as if he is guilty of one vast Kantian paralogism, of reifying the transcendental subject. Aware of this very issue, Schelling replies that he is entirely innocent. Rather than being transcendent, the affirmation of the existence of the absolute 'I' is "the most immanent of all affirmations," and indeed "the condition of all immanent philosophy" (§15; I, 205). This affirmation is anything but a paralogism, Schelling contends, since it is the very means to avoid them. The central argument of *Vom Ich als Princip* is indeed that we should not conceive the absolute 'I,' which is the condition of all experience of things, as a thing itself. Playing on the etymology of the German word for the unconditioned, "*das Unbedingte*," Schelling argues that to say that the 'I' is unconditioned means precisely that it is not some thing (*ein Ding*), which is by nature conditioned (*bedingt*) (§3; I, 166–167). We commit a paralogism and make a transcendent claim, he explains in Kantian fashion, only when we attempt to objectify this condition of the experience of objects.

This argument still does not explain, however, how Schelling knows that the absolute ego exists. Granted that we cannot conceive the ego as some *specific* or *finite* thing, we still need to know why it exists as the absolute or infinite. There is indeed something very misleading in Schelling's appeal to the Kantian paralogisms. While he is on firm Kantian ground in stressing that we must not reify the conditions of experience, he also goes beyond Kant in maintaining that the 'I' is more than the merely formal unity of our representations. He admits Kant's doctrine that the 'I' of the unity of apperception is merely the formal condition of the possibility of our experience; but he stresses that this 'I' is possible only through the 'I' of the absolute ego, which is neither merely an idea nor just a formal or logical condition of experience (§15; I, 207).

Schelling flatly rejects any demand to prove the existence of the absolute ego. He stresses that we cannot prove the existence of the absolute, since all demonstration is valid only in the sphere of the conditioned (§3; I, 167). We cannot even conceive or describe the 'I,' he argues, because it is the condition under which we apply all concepts (§8; I, 180). All that we can say about the 'I,' he admits, is that it exists (§15; I, 210).

Yet the question remains: How do we know even this much? Schelling answers: we *know* that the I exists because it is the referent of the self-confirming proposition 'I am.' This proposition is self-validating since we cannot deny it without also affirming it; to deny that I exist is to assume that I do (§3; I, 168). He further claims that this ego cannot be empirical or individual, because, as the condition of all experience, even that of myself as an individual subject, it cannot be individuated (§2; I, 165). Like Fichte, Schelling characterizes the act of intuition by which I know my existence through the 'I am' as an intellectual intuition (*intellektuelle Anschauung*) (§8; I, 181).

It is obvious, however, that the 'I am' still does not give *conclusive* evidence for the existence of the *absolute* I. Even if the 'I' does not refer to an empirical or individual subject, it is still possible that it designates a completely *formal* and *indeterminate* one. This is indeed just the point stressed by Kant, and then reemphasized by Fichte. But, like Spinoza's substance, and unlike Fichte's ego, Schelling's ego is not simply indeterminate, the negation of any specific determination; rather, it is the whole of all reality, the unity of all specific determinations (§10; I, 186–187).

It seems, then, as if Schelling's argument is a *non sequitur,* its weakness symptomatic of his hasty metaphysical ambitions. Because of the claims he advances for his absolute 'I,' he has been duly criticized for having *dogmatized* Fichte's philosophy, for having turned his purely immanent project into a full-blown metaphysics.[13] These Fichtean critics point out how Schelling, ignorant of the third part of the *Grundlage,* interpreted Fichte's absolute ego in a constitutive rather than regulative sense. If Schelling had only known the critical caution of his wiser mentor, these critics argue, then he would have known better and reined in his metaphysical ambitions.

Yet these criticisms miss the point. While Schelling's explicit arguments are indeed weak, they do not reveal his underlying reasoning. The ultimate basis for his belief in the existence of the absolute 'I' goes back to his reading of the idealism of the *Wissenschaftslehre,* which he interprets strictly according to Fichte's original principles. According to Schelling's *Abhandlungen über das Idealismus der Wissenschaftslehre,* the idealism of the *Wissenschaftslehre* is entirely antidualistic: it denies the existence of the thing-in-itself, affirming the ego alone as the source of all experience; and it repudiates any distinction between the form and the matter of cognition (I, 357, 360–361, 427). These principles were indeed avowed by Fichte; but then qualified by him in the third part of the *Grundlage.* It is striking, however, that Schelling reads Fichte's idealism *according to its original conception,* and does not take account of the more critical doctrine expounded in the third part of the *Grundlage.*

Now if we insist on reading the idealism of the *Wissenschaftslehre* according to its original conception, then it is clear that the 'I' must have an absolute status, because only as such does it have the power to create the matter as well as the form of experience. It is only for an absolute subject, not for the merely formal transcendental subject of Kant and Fichte, that the thing-in-itself, and the dualism between the form and matter of experience, disappears. Rather than a dogmatic and arbitrary postulate, then, Schelling's belief in the existence of the absolute ego has to be seen as a conclusion of his many arguments against dualism, which are advanced in the *Abhandlungen* and *Vom Ich als Princip*. Hence Schelling would no doubt reply to his critics that he was only carrying through Fichte's original antidualistic program, and that it is only by giving such constitutive status to the absolute ego that it is possible to surmount the disasterous Kantian dualisms. So, ironically, Schelling's tract was more Fichtean than Fichte himself!

Yet, for all its genuine Fichteanism, Schelling's *Vom Ich als Princip* looked forward to his absolute idealism in two fundamental respects. First, it suggested that the absolute could be neither subjective nor objective; and, second, it gave the absolute a constitutive status. These theses will assume a greater importance for Schelling in the years ahead, helping to prepare the ground for his eventual break with Fichte.

3. An Independent Standpoint

No sooner had Schelling finished *Vom Ich als Princip* than he started writing his next work, his *Philosophische Briefe über Dogmatismus und Kriticismus*, which appeared in two installments in the *Philosophisches Journal* in late 1795 and early 1796.[14] While *Vom Ich als Princip* is essentially a Fichtean work—despite its implicit views about the nonsubjective and constitutive status of the absolute—the same cannot be said for the *Briefe*. Though still under Fichte's influence, Schelling is much more free and explicit in putting forward his own position. Probably due to Hölderlin's prodding, Schelling now questions openly whether the absolute can be described as subjective alone, and he maintains that the standpoints of criticism and dogmatism have equal theoretical and practical validity. Ultimately, however, his loyalty to Fichte does not falter: he still chooses criticism over dogmatism and defends Fichte against some of Hölderlin's objections.

The *Briefe* foreshadow Schelling's later system of absolute idealism to a remarkable degree. More than five years before the *Darstellung meines Systems*, Schelling states one of its central and characteristic doctrines: that idealism and realism, or criticism and dogmatism, are both equivalent from the standpoint of the absolute. These systems are essentially identical, Schelling explains, since both attempt to describe the pure subject–object identity of the absolute. While criticism makes the subject absolute and demands that the object disappear, dogmatism makes the object absolute and demands that the subject vanish (315, 334–335). Both standpoints become identical in the absolute, Schelling says, because the subject of idealism and the object of realism each have their distinctive character only in opposition to one another, yet all opposition dissolves in the absolute (330–332). Here Schelling finally seems to admit Hölderlin's point that the absolute cannot be subjective since subjectivity involves finitude, the contrast with something objective.

Flatly at variance with Fichte's teaching, Schelling maintains that criticism and dogmatism, idealism and realism, are equal to, and coordinate with, one another. Perhaps disingenuously, he says that he cannot see anything wrong in principle with dogmatism: "As far as I am concerned, I believe that there is a system of dogmatism as well as a system of criticism" (306). He thinks that the standpoint of the critique of pure reason, which he also identifies with the *Wissenschaftslehre*, should provide *the canon* for both systems. While not being identifiable with any single system, the critique should be the basis for both (301–302). Its task is to show why both systems are necessary, and to examine their powers and limits (306). The role of the critique of pure reason in the *Briefe* will later be played by the standpoint of the absolute in the *Identitätssystem*.

Prima facie Schelling's interpretation of the standpoint of the critique of pure reason seems to be blatantly contrary to Kant's teaching, since Kant never permitted dogmatism in this sense, which he would have described as "transcendental realism." Aware of this very objection, Schelling replies that when Kant forbids dogmatism he is really excluding only *the dogmatic use of reason*, its tendency to speculate about the unconditioned without an antecedent investigation of its powers. However, Kant does not mean to prohibit dogmatism in the sense of transcendental realism, Schelling assures us, given that he retains the concept of a thing-in-itself. This must be at least the spirit of Kant's teaching, Schelling contends, because if we interpret the critique simply as a system of idealism, we cannot escape all the inconsistencies that arise regarding the thing-in-itself (303). Rather than excluding dogmatism or transcendental realism, then, the critique endorses it, if only implicitly, so that it plays a role just as important as idealism itself.

Why does Schelling stress the *equal* status of criticism and dogmatism? He explains that criticism cannot refute dogmatism, and that both theories are indemonstrable because they are about the unconditioned or the absolute, which transcends the limits of knowledge. Because they cannot be refuted or demonstrated, Schelling concludes that dogmatism and criticism are on a par from the viewpoint of *theoretical* reason. Furthermore, he insists—flatly contrary to the very spirit of Fichte's teaching—that they are also on an equal footing from the standpoint of *practical* reason. They are on the same footing morally speaking, Schelling claims, because both provide equally viable solutions to the problem of how to act in the world. Criticism demands that the subject assert itself, that it become completely active, so that it makes the world conform to its reason, while dogmatism insists that the subject deny itself, that it become totally passive, so that it learns how to conform to the world (315, 334–335). Which system one chooses, Schelling maintains, depends on an act of free choice (308). That, of course, was just the doctrine that Hölderlin had been expounding in his *Hyperion*.

Schelling's move away from Fichte in the *Briefe*—his concept of an absolute identity that is neither subjective nor objective, and his insistence that idealism and realism are on the same footing, both theoretically and practically—strongly suggests the influence of his friend Hölderlin. The evidence for Hölderlin's influence on Schelling is circumstantial but striking. Schelling probably wrote the *Briefe* between April and July 1795, immediately after or right around the time Hölderlin was developing his criticisms of Fichte in Jena. While Hölderlin visited Schelling in Tübingen between July and August 1795, too late to have any effect upon the *Briefe*, it is likely that Schelling was already aware of his anti-Fichtean standpoint, which Hölderlin had communicated to Hegel as early as January. During his visit to Tübingen, Hölderlin did his best to persuade Schelling of the limitations of Fichte's standpoint, and Schelling gave way, at least to some extent. Hence, referring to the Fichteanism of *Vom Ich als Princip*, Hölderlin noted with some satisfaction in his December 22, 1795 letter to Niethammer: "Schelling has become a little disloyal to his first convictions" (GSA, VI/1, 191).[15]

But Hölderlin was not entirely successful. Schelling did not completely abandon the Fichteanism of his earlier work, and to some extent he even attempted to defend it. Many passages of the *Briefe* read like a criticism of Hölderlin, elements of whose views reappear in Schelling's fictional correspondent.[16] Schelling's loyalty to Fichte is most apparent when he continues to defend criticism against dogmatism. Although he insists that criticism and dogmatism have an equal theoretical and practical validity, he cannot resist criticizing dogmatism on both theoretical and practical grounds. He makes several theoretical criticisms: that it hypostatizes intellectual intuition (319–320), that it cannot explain our moral striving to change the world (284), and that its demand we lose ourselves in the absolute is self-contradictory because we cannot deny our own existence (315–316, 320). But his main reason for preferring criticism over dogmatism is moral and practical. Although Schelling has some sympathy for the aesthetic side of dogmatism—

the sublimity involved in surrendering ourselves to nature—he still rejects dogmatism because it demands the forfeiture of the most important moral quality: freedom. The last hope for humanity, Schelling writes in the final letter, is for it to recover its autonomy, to recognize that the powers we have projected onto the world have really arose from within (339). Indeed, throughout the *Briefe*, Schelling continues to affirm the unconditional value of freedom, which remains for him "the alpha and omega of all philosophy." Ultimately, it was this belief in freedom that kept Schelling so firmly attached to Fichte, and still so clearly divided from Hölderlin, whose pantheism seemed to provide no clear place for it.

4. The First Quarrel

Fichte's reaction to Schelling's *Vom Ich als Princip* was favorable. He wrote Reinhold that he was very pleased with its publication because it gave a clear exposition of his system.[17] Fichte said nothing, however, about Schelling's absolute ego, ignoring how its constitutive status had violated his critical strictures, his severe warnings against leaving the limits of finite consciousness. Most probably, this was because he read Schelling's tract very cursorily. Hence he told Reinhold that, "as far as he could read of it," Schelling's work was only a commentary on his own.

But Fichte was not so sanguine about the *Briefe*. Regarding that work he was indeed troubled, because he could already see growing differences between himself and Schelling. This put him in an awkward position: he had to set the record straight to prevent the conflation of his position with Schelling's; but he also did not want to alienate his young disciple with public criticism. The only solution was to take silent issue with Schelling, never mentioning him by name. This Fichte did as early as 1797 in his *Einleitungen in die Wissenschaftslehre*.[18] Although Fichte never cites the *Briefe*, and indeed avoids any allusion to Schelling, there can be no doubt that he was taking issue with him; for in his later years, when his split with Schelling seemed inevitable, Fichte himself finally confessed as much.[19] In fundamental respects Fichte's early reaction to the *Briefe* anticipates his later quarrel with Schelling, raising the main issues that eventually led to their parting of ways in 1801.

Given his general principles, it is not difficult to imagine Fichte's reaction to the *Briefe*. Sure enough, his main complaint concerned the *coordinate* status of criticism and dogmatism. Fichte saw this as a grave misunderstanding of the idealism of the *Wissenschaftslehre*, which gives only a *subordinate* place to realism. If we put realism on a par with idealism, Fichte warned, we quit the boundaries of possible experience by postulating the existence of things-in-themselves. To Fichte's alarm, then, Schelling's sympathy with dogmatism failed to observe the completely immanent constraints of the *Wissenschaftslehre*. Hence, in the *Zweite Einleitung*, Fichte went to pains to stress the strictly *subordinate* role of realism within the *Wissenschaftslehre*. He insists that while the *Wissenschaftslehre* permits *empirical* realism—the doctrine that objects exist independent of empirical consciousness—it forbids *transcendental* realism—the doctrine that the thing-in-itself exists with all its properties independent of any consciousness whatsoever.[20] Responding to Schelling's standpoint of absolute identity, Fichte insists that criticism and dogmatism, transcendental idealism and transcendental realism, are two completely opposed systems, which cannot be united in any higher canon, whether that of the critique of pure reason or the *Wissenschaftslehre*.

Although Fichte is intent on refuting dogmatism or realism in anymore than a subordinate sense, he equivocates regarding Schelling's claim that idealism and realism are theoretically and practically equivalent. This point caused him great consternation, which he never completely resolved. He is compelled both to admit and to deny Schelling's point. On the one hand, he has to concede it because he recognizes that any refutation of realism goes beyond the limits he and Kant have assigned to reason; but, on the other hand, he also has to repudiate it because it gives coordinate status to realism, which robs him of any rational basis to choose idealism over realism. Fichte wavers between these positions in the *Erste Einleitung* to such an extent that he flatly contradicts himself. While in section 5 he argues that dogmatism and criticism are both irrefutable, he argues in section 6 that dogmatism cannot explain experience after all, and that idealism is the only possible philosophy. Though he insists in section 5 that dogmatism and criticism have equal moral validity, he then turns around and contends in section 6 that dogmatism arises from a life of decadent sensuality and that it leads to fatalism and the forfeiture of all moral responsibility.

This ambivalence in Fichte's position did not appear only in 1798, after his reaction to Schelling's *Briefe*. It was more deeply rooted, having already emerged in the 1794 *Grundlage*. There Fichte had virtually anticipated the whole argument of the *Briefe:* that there cannot be any proof of idealism or criticism, and that idealism and realism are equally justified on theoretical grounds (I, 156). Still, this did not prevent Fichte, anymore than Schelling after him, from criticizing dogmatism on theoretical grounds. Thus Fichte argued that dogmatism hypostatizes the subject which is the ground of experience (I, 120), that it fails to arrive at the first ground of experience because of insufficient abstraction (I, 121, 155), and that it ends in skepticism (I, 120–121). So, in stressing the equal validity of dogmatism and criticism while also arguing against dogmatism, Schelling was simply repeating Fichte's own ambivalence.

However much Fichte disliked giving equal validity to criticism and dogmatism, his teaching about the limits of theoretical reason compelled him to do so. In the *Erste Einleitung* and *Grundlage* he gave several powerful reasons why there could not be any theoretical refutation of dogmatism.[21] First, the dispute between criticism and dogmatism concerns first principles, so that any refutation would have to presuppose them (I, 429). Second, both idealism and realism concern the infinite or the absolute, and to claim demonstrative conclusions about it amounts to a transcendent use of reason, as Kant had already argued in the first *Kritik*. Third, Fichte accepted Jacobi's argument, which Schelling had also cited in the *Briefe* (308–309), that all demonstration is valid only in the sphere of the conditioned, because it attempts to determine how one thing depends on another *ad infinitum* according to the principle of sufficient reason. This too means that there cannot be any valid demonstrations about the nature of the unconditioned (I, 433). Fourth, although criticism has the advantage over dogmatism that it can find its first principle within consciousness, the dogmatist can reply that this is not really a first principle after all, since everything in consciousness is the product of the thing-in-itself, even the apparent consciousness of freedom (I, 430). Because there is no theoretical refutation of criticism or dogmatism, Fichte concludes that the decision between them must be based on practical grounds, which must be strictly personal, depending on one's individual interests and preferences. Hence he writes in some famous lines: "Which philosophy one chooses depends on what kind of person one is; for a philosophical system is not a dead household utensil that one can lay down or pick up as one wishes, but it animates the very soul of the person who adopts it" (I, 434).

Yet Fichte no sooner made this concession than he wanted to retract it. It had the most disturbing consequences for his philosophy as a whole. For, if the decision is ultimately only personal, then there cannot be any rational grounds for being an idealist rather than a realist. Furthermore, this would also be to lend weight to Schelling's conclusion that the *Wissenschaftslehre* is not the highest standpoint after all. For if criticism and dogmatism are on a level, should there not be a more comprehensive standpoint that includes both of them?

Unwilling to accept this conclusion, Fichte reverses course and begins to criticize dogmatism on both theoretical and practical grounds. In section 6 of the *Erste Einleitung* he contends that dogmatism cannot explain experience, and more specifically the self-consciousness that is characteristic of the self. Ultimately, this means that dogmatism is theoretically inadequate, and should be rejected on speculative grounds alone. The argument in section 6 then culminates in a resounding verdict against dogmatism: "Seen from the standpoint of speculation, dogmatism is not even a philosophy, but only a feeble declaration and assurance. As the only possible philosophy there remains only idealism" (I, 438).

So intense was Fichte's zeal against dogmatism that he went on to provide a *practical* refutation of it. If in section 5 he was generous enough to admit that one's choice of philosophy depends on the kind of person one is, in section 6 it becomes clear that some people are better than others precisely because of their choice of philosophy. Those who opt for criticism over dogmatism stand on a higher level of moral development, because they have recognized that they are free. The problem with dogmatism is that it alienates our freedom, abandoning our power to make our own laws by surrendering to some imaginary universe outside us (I, 433–434). It becomes clear from Fichte's bitter railing against dogmatism that he never valued what Schelling and Hölderlin saw in it: the tranquility that comes from resignation and submission to the eternal laws of nature, or, as Schelling described it, "the silent surrender to the immeasurable, peace in the arms of the world" (284). This went against the very fiber of Fichte's temperament, and indeed against the nerve and spirit of his philosophy: namely, its activism, its mission to reform the social and political world.

The ultimate reason for Fichte's rejection of dogmatism is his belief that he has a moral duty to do so. It was a fundamental requirement of acting according to the moral law, he held, that we recognize our autonomy, or that the ultimate source of our actions is our will. To fail to do this is tantamount to forfeiting responsibility for our actions. The basic problem with dogmatism, Fichte contended, is that it leads to just such a consequence. All dogmatism, if it is only consistent, ends not only in determinism but fatalism, that is, in resignation and passivity to fate.[22] Hence in the *Zweite Einleitung* Fichte said that he opted for transcendental idealism because it alone is in accord with our moral duty. We should not further question its foundation because we *ought not to;* we *cannot* go beyond it because we *may* not (I, 467).

CHAPTER 2

The Development of
Naturphilosophie

1. The Claims of *Naturphilosophie*

Schelling's break with Fichte is largely a tale about the development of his *Naturphilosophie*. This project was Schelling's own brainchild, and the extent of his growing independence from Fichte can be readily measured by the degree to which he gave it autonomous status apart from the *Wissenschaftslehre*. *Naturphilosophie*, in its mature and complete form, involved two assumptions completely at odds with Fichte's *Wissenschaftslehre:* first, transcendental realism, the thesis that nature exists independent of all consciousness, even that of the transcendental subject; second, transcendental naturalism, the doctrine that everything is explicable according to the laws of nature, *including* the rationality of the transcendental subject. The more Schelling developed his *Naturphilosphie*, making it independent from the *Wissenschaftslehre*, the more he articulated and defended these two assumptions. Since it was just these assumptions that Fichte had so stoutly resisted in the *Einleitungen*, the growth of the *Naturphilosophie* made a break with him all but inevitable.

The genesis of *Naturphilosophie* is not only a story about its struggle for *independence* from the *Wissenschaftslehre*, but also a tale about its battle for *domination* over the *Wissenschaftslehre*. For *Naturphilosophie* eventually acquired not only equality to, but priority over the *Wissenschaftslehre*. Rather than making both kinds of philosophy equal partners in one system, Schelling made the *Wissenschaftslehre* part of *Naturphilosphie* itself. Hence there was a complete reversal: *Naturphilosophie* began as the servant to the *Wissenschaftslehre* but ended as its master.

How did such a remarkable reversal come about? Why did Schelling change his position so dramatically? We can begin to answer these questions

483

only by carefully retracing Schelling's steps, the stages of development of his *Naturphilosophie* from 1797 to 1799.

2. The Early Fichtean Phase

The starting point of the story is Schelling's early 1797 *Abhandlungen zur Erläuterung des Idealismus der Wissenschaftslehre,* the most Fichtean of all his early writings and the furthest removed from his later position. In this work Schelling virtually forbade the possibility of *Naturphilosophie* as he later understood it. He does not regard *Naturphilosophie* as a complementrary science to the *Wissenschaftslehre,* as he will do in 1799 and 1800, and still less does he consider it the foundation of the *Wissenschaftslehre,* as he will do in 1801. Rather, he denies the very possibility of a *Naturphilosophie* that begins with the reality of nature and then derives the self-consciousness of the 'I' according to necessary laws. Thus, in the *Abhandlungen,* Schelling argues that we have only two options in philosophy: either we explain matter from spirit or spirit from matter. Since we cannot understand matter in itself, and since we originally understand only ourselves, we have no choice but to explain matter from spirit (I, 373). Schelling even denies one of the central premises of his later *Naturphilosophie:* that there is some inner dimension to matter. To be sure, matter is not merely passive and inert; but it still does not have the capacity to reflect on itself, which is characteristic of subjectivity. In other words, the power of matter works outward, reacting to stimuli; but it does not return into itself, and so it has no self-consciousness, the necessary characteristic of having some inner life (379).

The distance of the *Abhandlungen* from the later *Naturphilosophie* becomes all the more apparent when Schelling attempts an idealist deduction of the concept of an organism. Rather than the mediating concept between subject and object, as in the later *Naturphilosophie,* the concept of an organism is now derived from the subjective realm alone. Hence Schelling explains the self-causing activity characteristic of an organism from the subject's tendency toward self-consciousness. Insofar as the subject knows that it is the cause of its own representations, it knows that it is the cause and effect of itself, and so that it has a *self-organizing* nature (386). Schelling then generalizes the argument, deriving the whole organic concept of nature from the subject's striving toward self-consciousness: "Since there is in our mind an infinite striving to organize itself, a universal tendency toward organization must also reveal itself. Hence it is really the case. The system of the cosmos is a kind of organization that has formed itself from a common center" (386).

Schelling's first writings on *Naturphilosophie*—his 1797 *Ideen zu einer Philosophie der Natur* and his 1798 *Von der Weltseele*—make clear its dependence on the *Wissenschaftslehre*. In the preface to the *Ideen* Schelling explains that *Naturphilosophie* is simply the *application* of pure theoretical philosophy, whose task is to investigate the reality of all of our knowledge. Rather than developing new concepts and arguments, *Naturphilosophie* simply illustrates the principles of the *Wissenschaftslehre* as they relate to nature itself (II, 3–4). In both of these works Schelling stresses that the two basic concepts of *Naturphilosophie*—attractive and repulsive force—are in need of a "transcendental explication."[1] These forces have to be presupposed in *Naturphilosophie*, because their foundation lies in transcendental philosophy, which derives them from the main activities of the mind. Starting from Fichte's analysis in the 1794 *Grundlage*, Schelling maintains that imagination, the fundamental faculty of the mind, consists in two basic activities: one directed outward and extending to infinity, another directed inward and tending toward a single point.[2] These activities have their analogues or embodiments in nature: the first activity corresponds to repulsive, the second to attractive force. Just as the object of intuition is a synthesis of these activities, so the object in nature is a product of the equilibirum of these forces. Thus the object of nature simply objectifies and manifests these basic activities of the mind, so that matter turns out to be "nothing other than the mind intuited in the equilibrium of its activities."[3]

The subordinate role of *Naturphilosophie* to *Wissenschaftslehre* was inevitable, of course, as long as Schelling continued to avow the fundamental principles of Fichte's idealism. One of these principles is that the absolute is subjective, the ego rather than nature. If the absolute is the ego, then nature must be only its mode or manifestation. Since the ego is the subject matter of the *Wissenschaftslehre* and nature the object of *Naturphilosophie*, it follows that the *Wissenschaftslehre* must have precedence over *Naturphilosophie*. The priority of *Wissenschaftslehre* over *Naturphilosophie* in this regard becomes plain when Schelling says that the former deals with the infinite and unconditioned while *Naturphilosophie* treats only the finite and conditioned. Though, as we have seen, Schelling had his doubts about the subjectivity of the absolute (4.1.3), he still continued to affirm its subjective status. While the *Briefe* proposed that the absolute is both subjective and objective, Schelling did not persist with this suggestion but relapsed into the more Fichtean standpoint. Indeed, as we have also seen, even in the *Briefe* he continued to defend idealism over realism.

On the basis of this principle, Schelling continued to admit the subordinate role of *Naturphilosophie* as late as 1799. In his *Entwurf eines Systems der Naturphilosophie* he states that every science has the right to regard its subject matter as unconditioned and self-sufficient, and he stresses that even *Naturphilosophie* is entitled to view nature as an independent realm (II, 17). Nevertheless, Schelling does not abandon but reaffirms his idealism. He states that the autonomy of nature is only a *regulative* or *methodological* principle of *Naturphilosophie*, which means that it should proceed only *as if* nature were the unconditioned. Still in keeping with his idealistic arguments in *Vom Ich als Prinzip*, Schelling concedes that only transcendental philosophy has the *real* unconditioned or absolute for its object (II, 11).

Schelling was further held back from developing his *Naturphilosophie* because of his adherence to another central principle of Fichte's idealism: that the ego is only for itself. Fichte invoked this principle against Schelling in the *Erste Einleitung* in his attempt to show the limitations of naturalism. But the irony is that Schelling himself reaffirmed it around the same time as Fichte. In the 1797 *Abhandlungen* Schelling appealed to this principle to defend idealism against materialism (I, 373); and in his 1797 *Einleitung zu den Ideen einer Philosophie der Natur,* he employed it against Spinoza's naturalism. The naturalist cannot explain the possibility of self-consciousness, Schelling argued, because he treats the ego as if it were only an optical glass reflecting the rays of the world impinging on it (II, 21, 32–33). Like Fichte, Schelling maintained that the problem with naturalism is that it cannot bridge the gap between consciousness of the world and the world itself, so that in the end it too cannot avoid dualism. Only idealism, Schelling concluded, provides a remedy for the patent inadequacies of naturalism and dualism (II, 32–33).

Schelling's arguments against dogmatism hardly seem to square with his more charitable view, already espoused in *Briefe über Dogmatismus und Kritizismus*, that dogmatism and criticism have an equal validity. To liberate *Naturphilosophie* from the confines of the *Wissenschaftslehre*, it would seem, Schelling only had to stress the equal status of dogmatism. Still, this was a step that Schelling was not ready to take in 1795, or even for several more years. We have just seen how Schelling—a more loyal student than Fichte imagined—reinvoked and reiterated his idealist principles against Spinoza's naturalism. But even in the *Briefe*, which is his work most sympathetic to

Spinoza, Schelling did not refrain from expressing his reservations about dogmatism. And, in any case, his defense of dogmatism in the *Briefe* is very limited. If Schelling maintained that dogmatism cannot be refuted, he also insisted that it cannot be demonstrated; and he gave it only a strictly *practical* legitimacy alongside criticism. Schelling will take the crucial step toward *Naturphilosophie* only when he declares that dogmatism has an equal *theoretical* legitimacy to criticism.

3. The First Decisive Step

That step was taken sometime in 1799 in the *Einleitung* to the *Entwurf eines Systems der Naturphilosophie*, which Schelling probably wrote shortly after the *Entwurf* itself. Schelling now states explicitly that transcendental philosophy and natural philosophy are equal to and independent from one another, both providing necessary perspectives on a single reality: the activity of reason or intelligence. This activity has two appearances: a necessary or subconscious form in nature, and a free or conscious form in the ego. Since these are simply different aspects of a single reality, Schelling argues, we should be able to explain each in terms of the other. Transcendental philosophy begins from the free and conscious activity of the ego and derives its necessary and subconscious appearance in nature; natural philosophy begins from the necessary and subconscious activity of nature and derives its free and conscious appearance in the ego (II, 271).

The methods and aims of *Naturphilosophie*, Schelling further explains, are completely independent of those of transcendental philosophy. *Naturphilosophie* banishes all idealistic explanations, such as the theory that nature is nothing but an organ for self-consciousness. These kinds of explanation are as bad as the old teleology, Schelling claims, because they treat nature as if it were made for our ends. The first maxim of *Naturphilosophie* is that of all natural science: to explain everything on the basis of natural powers alone (273). This principle means treating nature as a self-sufficient and autonomous realm, whose investigation should be free from the guidelines of the transcendental philosopher.

It is striking that in the *Einleitung zu dem Entwurf*, in contrast to the *Entwurf* itself, Schelling no longer insists that the autonomy of nature is a mere fiction. Now that idealism and realism have equal status as explanations of the absolute, the *Naturphilosoph* has as much right as the *Wissenschaftlehrer* to consider his object as the absolute. *Naturphilosophie* is no longer beholden to the *Wissenschaftslehre* to determine the real nature of the unconditioned, as if *Naturphilosophie* were relegated to deal with an artificial abstraction. Hence Schelling now calls *Naturphilosophie* the "Spinozism of physics" because it posits nature as the absolute and unconditioned (III, 273).

The equal and independent status of *Naturphilosophie* seems to entail accepting the very naturalism Schelling had once rejected in the *Ideen*. If we can begin from the powers of nature and derive all the free and self-conscious activities of the ego, then these activities will be nothing more than the highest organization and development of the powers of nature. But now Schelling embraces just this conclusion. Remarkably, he insists on extending the principles of naturalism to the highest forms of intelligence, so that reason itself proves to be nothing more than "a play of higher and necessarily unknown natural powers" (*ein Spiel höherer und notwendig unbekannter Naturkräfte*) (273–274). This means, as Schelling later put it, that the subject's awareness of nature amounts to nothing more than nature coming to its *self*-awareness through him. This was indeed a decisive move, for it involved abandoning Fichte's principle that the ego is for itself, explicable in terms of its self-consciousness alone.

It is important to recognize, however, that Schelling is ready to extend the principles of naturalism only because he denies one central premise behind Fichte's argument against naturalism: the assumption that naturalistic explanation is mechanistic. Schelling's willingness to extend naturalism to the Fichtean ego goes hand-in-hand with his growing conviction that the idea of an organism has to be given a constitutive status to resolve the outstanding Kantian dualisms.

4. The Priority of *Naturphilosophie*

In the *Einleitung zu dem Entwurf* Schelling made the vital move in giving equality and independence to his *Naturphilosophie*. But this was far from the final step in the evolution of the *Identitätssystem*. For Schelling had still not conceived of the *single* absolute standpoint that would unite both transcendental philosophy and philosophy of nature. In the preface to his 1800 *System des transcendentalen Idealismus* he reasserted the equality of transcendental philosophy and philosophy of nature; but he insisted that, just because of their complementarity, they would never be able to form a unity (III, 331). To be sure, he had envisaged something like a single standpoint in his *Briefe*, when he conceived of the critique of pure reason as the canon of both realism and idealism. But Schelling was now searching for something more than what that standpoint had ever promised or provided: namely, a *theoretical* foundation for both realism and idealism. As we have just seen, the standpoint of critique in the *Briefe* could ensure at best only a *practical* foundation for idealism and realism.

Shortly after writing the *System*, which he had completed in March 1800, Schelling took another decisive—and dramatic—step toward the development of the *Identitätssystem*. In his 1800 *Allgemeine Deduktion des dynamischen Prozesses* Schelling is no longer content simply to demand equality and independence for his *Naturphilosophie*. Rather, he insists on its *priority* over transcendental philosophy.

This move is at first puzzling and surprising—a complete *volte face* for the former idealist—but it follows inevitably from the development of *Naturphilosophie*. Schelling now recognizes that there is something abstract and artificial in the standpoint of idealism: it reverses the order of nature itself, treating the *ratio cognoscendi* as if it were the *ratio essendi*, or what is first in the order of knowledge (the subjective) as if it were the first in order of being. The net result of such a confusion is that it removes the self-consciousness from its place in nature, treating it as if it were eternal and given, when it is in fact the product of the development of the powers of nature. The self-consciousness of the transcendental ego is not something self-sufficient, but it is really nature coming to consciousness through him. What the transcendental philosopher therefore presupposes—an intellectual intuition of his own activity—has to be reconstructed by the philosopher of nature, who provides "a physical explanation of idealism" (§63; IV, 76). Schelling says that the philosopher can proceed in either of two directions: from nature to us, or from us to nature; but he then makes his own preferences all too clear: the true direction for he who prizes knowledge above everything is the path of nature itself, which is that followed by the *Naturphilosoph* (IV, 78).

In his next writing on *Naturphilosophie*, his essay 'Über den wahren Begriff der Naturphilosophie und die richtige Art ihre Probleme aufzulösen,' which he wrote shortly after *Allgemeine Deduktion*, Schelling took stock of the fateful step he had now taken. That he had now overthrown the hegemony of the *Wissenschaftslehre* was clear; but he still had to explain its place in the new philosophy that was coming into being. The main interest and subject matter of the *Wissenschaftslehre*, Schelling now said, is the philosophy of philosophy. Of course, to know the nature of philosophy it is necessary to begin with the knowing subject, and to abstract from everything objective, in the

Fichtean manner. But, for just this reason, Schelling insists, the *Wissenschafts-lehre* is not philosophy proper, which consists in knowledge of nature itself. Thus Schelling identified *Naturphilosophie* with philosophy itself. He thinks there will still be room for the transcendental ego in his new system of philosophy; but it will no longer be the starting point but the result. The self-consciousness of the transcendental ego will be nothing less—though also nothing more—than the highest potency of nature, the final stage of organization and development of all its powers.

As we shall soon see, to understand the *Identitätssystem* it is of the first importance to keep in mind the *priority* of *Naturphilosophie* over *Wissenschafts-lehre*. The *Identitätssystem* is really a *Naturphilosophie* whose highest level, stage, or "potency" is the *Wissenschaftslehre*. Although Schelling sometimes continues to write of the parity between the two sciences even after 1800, the *Identitätssystem* is ultimately based on *Naturphilosophie*. Nowhere is this so clear as in 'Über den Begriff,' for here Schelling argues that the principle of subject–object identity exists properly, purely, and completely only within the realm of nature itself. He explains that the identity of the subjective and objective means, only in the *popular* sense, that the ego and nature have parity with one another; but, in the *philosophical* sense, it signifies that nature is *pure* and the ego is a *derived* or *subjective* subject–object identity (IV, 86–87).

'Über den wahren Begriff' appeared only months before the *Darstellung meines Systems*, the first exposition of the *Identitätssystem*. Schelling's concept of *Naturphilosophie* had come full circle: once the maidservant of the *Wissen-schaftslehre*, it had now become its master. The *Wissenschaftslehre* is no longer the foundation of *Naturphilosophie*, but *Naturphilosophie* is the foundation for the *Wissenschaftslehre*. The break with the subjectivist tradition could not have been more total.

CHAPTER 3

Schelling's Break with Fichte

1. Background

What was Fichte's reaction to Schelling's *volte face*, to the dramatic development of his *Naturphilosophie?* Strangely, for many months, he had none at all. Fichte had never studied Schelling's writings on *Naturphilosophie*, admitting that they fell outside his field of competence.[1] But even the surprising reversal in Schelling's thinking—his ascription of priority to *Naturphilosophie* over *Wissenschaftslehre*—had escaped his notice. Such blissful ignorance was largely due to circumstances. From late 1799 to early 1800, the crucial period for the formation of Schelling's later views, Fichte was caught in the vortex of the atheism controversy, and so he had little opportunity to study Schelling's latest writings. He also had few occasions to speak with Schelling. From July to December 1799 Fichte had been in Berlin, where he had sought his new home after his dismissal from Jena; though he returned to Jena for a short while, from December 1799 to early 1800, he rarely saw Schelling, who was never at home. During these months Schelling himself had something more on his mind than philosophy: he was immersed in a scandulous love affair with Karoline Schlegel.[2]

Yet *eros* had not completely vanquished *minerva*. For all his new preoccupations, Schelling was eager to know how Fichte would react to the latest direction of his thought. Even though he had self-consciously gone beyond the *Wissenschaftslehre*, he did not intend to break with Fichte. He saw the development of his *Naturphilosophie* more as an extension of Fichte's principles than a supersession of them, more as a new demonstration of their common *credo* than a refutation of Fichte's own.[3] For all their differences, Fichte and Schelling were still wedded together as heirs of the Kantian philosophy, as champions of the principle of subject–object identity. Schelling knew all too

491

well that the naturalism and realism of his *Naturphilosophie* broke with the limits of Kant's and Fichte's critical idealism; but he still saw such naturalism and realism as the inevitable development of their common principle. Once Fichte understood this, he hoped, they could continue to work together on a new project. Hence Schelling had planned to co-edit with Fichte a common journal, a *Revision der Fortschritte der Philosophie,* whose purpose was to defend the Kantian legacy against its growing detractors and desertors.

So despite his growing differences with Fichte, Schelling still saw Fichte and himself as representatives of a common viewpoint. They were the last true heirs of the Kantian tradition, the last defenders of the spirit, if not the letter, of the critical philosophy: its principle of subject–object identity. The mounting reaction against this tradition from so many quarters—whether it it came from the older *Aufklärer* (Nicolai and Biester), from aging *Sturmer und Dränger* (Jacobi and Herder), from the more orthodox Kantians (C. G. Schütz and K. C. Schmid), from the new skeptics (Schulze and Maimon), or from the latest logicians (Reinhold and his latest apostle C. G. Bardili)—gave him a sense of solidarity with Fichte that their growing differences otherwise would have long since have dissipated.

But did Fichte see things in the same way? How did he view Schelling's new *Naturphilosophie* with its transcendental realism and naturalism? Would he be able to regard this as nothing more than an elaboration of their basic common principle? Schelling was still in the dark. Accordingly, he wrote Fichte May 14, 1800 soliciting his reaction to all his latest writings, and sending him copies of his *System des transcendentalen Idealismus, Einleitung zu dem Entwurf,* and Heft 2 of the *Zeitschrift für spekulativen Physik,* which contained the most controversial sections of the *Allgemeine Deduktion.*[4] Schelling added that he was especially anxious to hear Fichte's views about the first work.

But this request seemed to fall on deaf ears. Schelling had to wait. As late as September 1800 he had yet to learn Fichte's reaction. Though they had corresponded with one another on several occasions about their new journal, Fichte still said nothing about Schelling's writings. In the meantime he heard some disturbing gossip from Friedrich Schlegel: that Fichte had reservations about Schelling's new philosophy.[5] The nature of these misgivings was unclear. Perhaps it was some skeptical remarks about the *Naturphilosophie,* perhaps it was Fichte's disappointment, which he admitted expressing to Schlegel, that no one had mastered his synthetic method. Because Schelling's letters are lost, it is difficult to know.

But, whatever the nature of the rumors, and whatever the truth behind them, Schlegel had reasons for engaging in intrigue. He disliked Schelling, whose affair with Karoline Schlegel was humiliating his brother, August Wilhelm, who happened to be her husband. More professional motives might have played a role: it is possible that Schlegel and his brother wished to pry Schelling away from Fichte, so that Schelling would collaborate with them on their own journal.[6] But there was an even more powerful motive at work: Schlegel wanted to inherit Fichte's mantle as the spokesman for transcendental philosophy in Jena.[7] Alienating Schelling from Fichte would help him secure this prestigious title against his most threatening competitor.

After hearing Schlegel's gossip, Schelling decided that he could wait no longer. His whole friendship with Fichte stood in the balance. Probably around September 1800 he wrote Fichte to solicit again his reaction to his writings. In bitter terms he also reprimanded Fichte for his lack of candor—for telling Schlegel rather than himself about his reservations. Clearly, that was no basis for any kind of collaboration.[8]

Naturally, Schelling's letter distressed Fichte. He was deeply hurt by Schelling's accusations, of course, but he also feared for their friendship. His next letters to Schelling, written October 3 and 21, are desperate attempts to reestablish trust and to restore relations.[9] He assured Schelling that he had every confidence in his abilities, and that he never expressed reservations about his work to anyone, least of all to Friedrich Schlegel, whose machinations he now suspected. Although he did tell Friedrich Schlegel that he regretted no one had mastered his synthetic method, he could not understand how that should offend Schelling.

Since Schelling's reply to the October 3 letter has been lost, it is difficult to know how he received Fichte's reassurances. But his October 31 letter to Fichte shows that their friendship had been restored.[10] Schelling again asked Fichte to join him in co-editing a journal. Inadvertantly, he revealed another reason for renewing his bonds with Fichte. Schelling told Fichte that Friedrich Schlegel had announced his lectures on transcendental philosophy, and he was so troubled by this that he planned to stay in Jena to compete with his new rival. It was now obvious to Schelling that Schlegel was not to be trusted, and that he needed Fichte's friendship more than ever.

2. The Dispute Begins

Though their friendship had been restored, Fichte could no longer postpone his response to Schelling's writings. Sooner rather than later, he would have to consider all the troublesome issues raised by his *Naturphilosophie*. On November 15, 1800, Fichte finally wrote Schelling to give his reaction to his *System des transcendentalen Idealismus*.[11] This letter proved to be fateful. Now, for the first time, Fichte states openly to Schelling his reservations about his philosophy. The first irreparable cracks in their alliance appear.

Of course, Fichte praised Schelling's work—"it is everything that could be expected from your brilliant style of exposition"—but he also did not hesitate to state his main objections to it. "I still cannot agree with your opposition between transcendental and natural philosophy," he wrote, adding that "it seems to rest upon a confusion between ideal and real activity." Fichte did not explain this obscure remark, but it was essentially his way of saying that the opposition between the subjective and the objective, the real and the ideal, should fall *inside* the *Wissenschaftslehre* and should not lead to a new science outside it. If ideal activity is that by which the ego acts on its world, and if real activity is that by which the world acts on the ego, then the *Wissenschaftslehre* explains real activity by ideal activity, as the result of the *self*-limitation of the ego's spontaneity, so that there is no need to postulate an independent source of real activity outside of the ego.

Whatever the precise meaning of this remark, Fichte clearly contradicted the autonomy or independent status of nature, the main presupposition behind *Naturphilosophie*. The reality of nature is only something given, found, and complete in transcendental philosophy, he stressed, and it is not something that acts according to its own laws but only those of self-conscious intelligence. Fichte went on to complain about Schelling's description of the methods of transcendental and natural philosophy. It is absurd to write as if we can begin with the subjective or the objective and then derive its counterpart, he argued, because this implies that they are separable from one another, as if one can be added to another, when they are really completely united with one another in pure subject–object identity.

The philosophical issues behind Fichte's reaction to Schelling's *Naturphilosophie* are much more explicit in some of his unpublished manuscripts, which he wrote in late 1800. In some jottings written down during the reading of the *System des transcendentalen Idealismus*,[12] Fichte made it clear that he was locked in a struggle with Schelling for the coveted title of *philosophia prima*: just as he wants to bring *Naturphilosophie* inside the circle of the *Wissenschaftslehre*, so Schelling wants to bring the *Wissenschaftslehre* inside the *Naturphilosophie*. Fichte flatly denies that nature can be given the priority Schelling ascribes to it. While Schelling wants to regard knowledge as only a "manner of being," he fails to see that "being is possible only in relation to some knowledge." Fichte then bluntly states his own idealist principles: "I say: that nature, as object, is still something you only think of; it is something for you only insofar as you think it." Fichte realizes, however, that he cannot refute Schelling simply by restating his own principles. How, then, can he defeat Schelling? The only escape from this apparent *aporia*, Fichte thinks, is to show that Schelling's principles cannot achieve what he demands of them. It is necessary to demonstrate that we cannot explain self-consciousness according to the laws of nature, that it cannot be only "the reflexion of nature upon itself." Schelling thinks of nature as an activity; but the ego is more than this: it is a *self-comprehending* activity. Thus Fichte was adamant that his 'I' would remain irreducible, resistant in principle to all forms of naturalistic explanation.

In another short manuscript, 'Sätze zur Erläuterung des Wesens der Thiere,'[13] also written in late 1800, Fichte develops his own concept of nature in reaction to Schelling. He flatly rejects Schelling's thesis that intelligence is only a higher potency of nature if this means—as it did indeed in Schelling—that reason is only a higher manifestation of nature. Such a proposition has been refuted by transcendental philosophy, Fichte states confidently. If we demonstrate in transcendental philosophy that nature is a product of intelligence, then it is circular to turn around and derive intelligence from nature. Like Schelling, however, Fichte sketches an hierarchical account of nature, whereby minerals, plants, and animals are ordered according to their degrees of organization and development of attractive and repulsive force. It is striking that Fichte does not have a strictly mechanical conception of nature, but attributes a drive or striving to act, and be acted on, to everything in nature. Yet Fichte stops short of Schelling. While he ascribes a drive or striving to act to natural things, he denies that it amounts to a form of consciousness, and he even implies that the predication of drives to nature is analogical, having only a regulative validity. For Fichte, the rationality of nature is something that we *read into* nature; it is not something that nature has within itself because of its purposive structure.[14]

Fichte's reaction to Schelling's philosophy is also implicit in one of his published writings, the final sections of his *Sonnenklarer Bericht*, a popular exposition of his philosophy, whose last half was composed in the autumn of 1800. Nowhere does Fichte mention Schelling by name, but now and then his language and context show that Schelling is his target. In the fourth 'Lehrstunde' Fichte makes a passing negative reference to a system based on a different kind of intellectual intuition than his own.[15] In the fifth he puts forward an interesting objection against the natural history of consciousness that Schelling proposes in the *Allgemeine Deduktion*.[16] It is a logical error, he argues, to assume that philosophical reconstruction of consciousness from its simple elements corresponds to some kind of natural history, as if the *logical* priority of the elements were also some kind of *temporal* priority. Although we do have a right to treat consciousness *as if* it develops from its simple elements, we have no right to assume *that* it actually does so. Schelling's natural history of consciousness, Fichte implies, is a kind of category mistake, offering us "the history of man before his birth." Fichte then insists that it is a mistake to assume the independent reality of nature apart from consciousness: this would be to relapse into the old dogmatism. The *Sonnenklarer Bericht* concludes with a rollicking diatribe against Fichte's reviewers, many of whom are advised to devote themselves to more useful vocations, such as law, forestry, medicine, and animal husbandry.[17] Among these vocations Fichte includes lens grinding, an unmistakable reference to Spinoza. This allusion was probably made only in passing, but Schelling later read it as a rebuke for his admiration of Spinoza.[18]

3. Schelling States His Case

Though convalescing from a severe illness, Schelling responded to Fichte's letter on November 19, 1800, probably immediately after receiving it.[19] Schelling stressed that the issues between himself and Fichte were of the first importance to idealism, but that they still stood in need of clarification. Like Fichte, he saw the main source of disagreement in the opposition between transcendental and natural philosophy. He advised Fichte not to put too much weight on his description of the methods of transcendental and natural philosophy. What he wrote about beginning from the object and deriving the subject, and conversely, was only from a popular standpoint, and he too did not believe that the subject and object were somehow separate from and then added to one another. From a philosophical standpoint, they still agreed on the main principle: that both ideal and real activity are one and the same and indissolubly united in the ego. He pointed out, however, that the basis for this opposition did not lie in any distinction between ideal and real activity, but in something higher still: namely, in the fact that, in its objective aspect, the productive ego is nothing less than nature itself. This means that nature is not only something found and given, something produced according to the laws of intelligence, but that it consists in productive and intelligent activity itself. For Schelling, the objective side of subject–object identity permitted, and indeed required, that the philosopher postulate rationality inherent within nature itself, independent of the finite minds in which it realized itself. *Pace* Fichte, nature is not a mere phenomenon, an appearance for consciousness. We do not impose our reason on it, but it has reason inherent within itself.

Such a conclusion was, of course, unpalatable to Fichte. But there was even worse to come, for Schelling's letter contained much more indigestible material. Although it states that the *Wissenschaftslehre* is a perfect and complete science in itself, it also makes clear that it is so only within very circumscribed limits. The *Wissenschaftslehre,* Fichte is told in so many words, is not *philosophia prima* after all. This is because it is not really philosophy at all, but only the philosophy of philosophy. While it is the task of the *Wissenschaftslehre* to analyze the logic of our knowledge, and so to provide a *formal* proof of idealism, the business of philosophy proper is to know the nature of reality itself, and so to supply a *material* proof of idealism. Schelling then made it clear that the *Wissenschaftslehre* is really derivative, its foundation resting on the material proof of idealism of *Naturphilosophie.* This material proof abstracts from the principle of subject–object identity of the *Wissenschaftslehre,* from subjectivity or the act of self-consciousness constitutive of the ego, and it begins from the principle of *pure* subject–object identity of nature itself, which is now the fundamental principle of the *theoretical* part of philosophy. The ego of the *Wissenschaftslehre* is then derived from this fundamental principle, and it is therefore only its final potency, the highest degree of organization and development of the productive powers of nature.

Attempting to distinguish his system from the older materialism, which denied all reason to nature, Schelling stressed that his principle of pure subject–object identity is not something simply real, the merely objective in abstraction from the subjective. Rather, it postulates the identity of *both* real and ideal, objective and subjective, because it affirms the existence of some intelligence or reason within nature itself. Schelling denied that this intelligence or reason exists completely independently of the ego, because he now saw the ego as the goal and culmination of its activity; but he also affirmed that this ego exists independent of the philosophizing subject, who simply observes its activity.

4. A Botched Reconciliation

Schelling's November 19 letter had laid down all his cards. It lacked nothing in frankness, bluntly setting forth all his differences with Fichte. That the ego is only the highest potency of the powers of nature, that nature is the source of intelligent productive activity, that philosophy has theoretical powers of demonstration, that we can abstract from the subjectivity of the ego to reach the pure subject–object, and that the *Wissenschaftslehre* is not *philosophia prima* but only the philosophy of philosophy—all these were points flatly contradicting some of Fichte's fundamental principles. It would seem, then, that the Fichte–Schelling alliance now lay in ruins. In expressing such irreconcilable differences in such plain terms Schelling appeared to be only provoking the inevitable parting of the ways.

It must be said, however, that Schelling did not see things this way. Although he deliberately exploded the limits of the *Wissenschaftslehre*, he still nurtured hopes that Fichte would agree with him and follow him down his new path. After all, the material proof of idealism was only a new demonstration of the same general doctrine, of their common principle of subject–object identity, the very principle that Fichte had made into the cornerstone of his *Wissenschaftslehre*. "If I seem to distance myself from you," Schelling assured Fichte, "then it is only to come closer to you." He stressed that he still agreed with Fichte on all the fundamental points, and that, though they were traveling down different paths, they still had the same goal. In any case, all their differences were not reason to prevent them from collaborating on their new journal.

Probably because of these conciliatory remarks, Fichte's December 27 reply to Schelling seemed very promising.[20] He wrote that he too did not regard the differences in their views as an obstacle to future collaboration. It was indeed the case that some of Schelling's propositions were contrary to transcendental philosophy, and that they could be established only by going beyond the limits of the *Wissenschaftslehre*. But, remarkably, Fichte did not exclude this possibility, and he even hinted that he was already moving in just this direction in the final section of his *Bestimmung des Menschen*. What was required to remove their differences, and indeed all the misunderstandings of the *Wissenschaftslehre*, he now said, was a "transcendental system of the intelligible world." Such a system would postulate the existence of an intelligible or noumenal world whose fundamental laws govern all finite rational beings. Schelling's statement that the individual (*das Individuum*) is only a higher potency of nature could be explained according to this system, Fichte wrote, if nature were conceived not only as a phenomenon but also as intelligible within itself.[21]

The December 27 letter gave Schelling some reason to believe, then, that

Fichte was going beyond the narrow limits of his old doctrines.[22] The draft of his December 27 letter, and the final section of the *Bestimmung des Menschen*, show that this was indeed the case. In the draft he explains that if he could only show "the right to go beyond the ego," then he could explain the original limitation of the ego in its sense experience, and so transcend the *Wissenschaftslehre* or transcendental idealism, understood as the system that remains within the limits of the sense experience of the finite intelligence. If we assume the existence of a noumenal world, Fichte explains, then we can derive conscience and feeling as manifestations of the intelligible in the sensible. In the final section of the *Bestimmung des Menschen* Fichte had indeed already taken this very step. He postulated the existence of a single infinite reason, which manifests itself in the conscience and reason of every finite individual.[23] This infinite reason is now the transcendental condition of each finite reason: whatever it thinks, perceives, or wills is what the infinite reason thinks, perceives, or wills through it. Such a doctrine is not far from the doctrine of absolute reason that Schelling was to develop only months later.

The promise of the December 27 letter soon disappeared, however. While Fichte was struggling to find common ground with Schelling he committed a *faux pas* that undermined all his best efforts. On January 24, 1801, he made a public announcement in the *Allgemeine Literatur Zeitung* about the forthcoming publication of the new exposition of his *Wissenschaftslehre*, in which he complained about the poor reception of his philosophy.[24] This was the occasion to recognize Schelling's efforts in behalf of transcendental idealism. Fichte duly mentioned them, but he did so in such a clumsy and ambiguous manner that it could only trouble a very sensitive younger colleague. Fichte simply said that he would not now comment on whether his "talented co-worker" (*geistvollen Mitarbeiter*), Professor Schelling, had greater success in disseminating the transcendental viewpoint with his writings on natural philosophy and *System des transcendentalen Idealismus*.

Such a lack of commitment on Fichte's part was enough to raise eyebrows and to encourage speculation.[25] Worst of all, Fichte had given comfort to some of his most bitter enemies. In the *Allgemeine deutsche Bibliothek* Friedrich Nicolai, notable Berlin *Aufklärer* and enemy of transcendental philosophy, noted Fichte's announcement with *Schadenfreude* and wondered what Schelling's reaction would be. He read Fichte's annoucement as a public rebuke to Schelling for not having understood the *Wissenschaftslehre*. For Nicolai, of course, this was clear proof that no one, not even Fichte's most talented disciple, could comprehend his hopelessly obscure writings.

Sure enough, Schelling was annoyed by the ambiguities and innuendos of Fichte's announcement.[26] While Fichte had gone out of his way to mention him, he did not endorse his efforts, and it even seemed as if he wanted to withhold judgment. What especially annoyed Schelling was the insinuation that he was a only disciple of Fichte, whose main goal was to propagate the principles of the *Wissenschaftslehre*. Fichte implied that this was the case even for Schelling's writings on *Naturphilosophie*—just at the time when he admitted that these writings were going beyond the limits of the old *Wissenschaftslehre*. So, in sum, it seemed as if Schelling were nothing more than a well-intentioned, but not necessarily successful expositor of Fichte's philosophy! That was too much for Schelling to bear. After reading the announcement Karoline Schlegel wondered how Schelling could even consider further collaboration with Fichte. She advised him to follow his own path.[27]

That Schelling did. After Fichte's fateful announcement there passed five months of silence while Schelling was busy writing his own system of philosophy. He entitled this work *Darstellung meines Systems* to give notice to the world that he was not simply Fichte's follower.

5. Persistent Hopes

When Schelling finally wrote Fichte on May 15, 1801,[28] he duly reprimanded him for saying that the aim of his writings on *Naturphilosophie* had been only to introduce the public to the principles of the *Wissenschaftslehre*. But, given Fichte's gaffe, Schelling's letter is remarkably conciliatory. Fichte's remarks in the December 27 letter that he had been understood, and that he was planning an extension of the principles of his idealism, made Schelling hopeful that they could still agree with one another. He expressed his "ardent wish" that Fichte could now devote himself to developing his system of the intelligible world, which he too felt would resolve all their differences.

Schelling wrote again on May 24, now much more sanguine about the prospects of future collaboration with Fichte.[29] He had just read Fichte's *Antwortschreiben*, a polemic against Reinhold, which had completely "captivated" and, in places, even "moved" him. He was now more confident than ever that Fichte and he were at one, and that he could say "what I want is the same as what Fichte thinks, and my expositions are only variations on his themes." Schelling explained that it had become clear to him from *Antwortschreiben*, and that it would becomes obvious to Fichte from *Darstellung meines Systems*, that both ascribed to one and the same standpoint of absolute knowledge. Though they might express this standpoint in different ways, they were still agreed about its existence and importance.

To reassure Fichte and to minimize their differences even further, Schelling told Fichte that he now planned to write another part to *Darstellung meines Systems*, where the 'I' of the *Wissenschaftslehre* would play the central role. He would now show how the 'I' is the center of "existing absolute identity" and how nature is the same absolute identity "insofar as it contains the ground of its own existence." From this central point "idealism" would emerge as the "all inclusive, all comprehending, and all penetrating sun." It would then be possible to understand the higher sense in which everything is the 'I' and exists only in the 'I.' These passages make it clear that Schelling still saw his *Naturphilosophie* as a proof of idealism. If the ego of the *Wissenschaftslehre* was no longer the starting point of philosophy, it was at least its center point and culmination. The ego lost its self-sufficient essence and existence, to be sure, but it had now become the highest manifestation and development of all the organic powers of nature.

Even a cursory reading of the *Antwortschreiben* shows that Schelling's enthusiasm was not completely unfounded. In this work Fichte had protested against Reinhold's purely subjectivistic and psychologistic interpretation of the *Wissenschaftslehre*, according to which the 'I' denotes nothing more than the individual consciousness. If this were the only referent of the 'I,' then the *Wissenschaftslehre* would be indeed guilty of solipsism, just as Jacobi, Reinhold, and Bardili had complained. But, Fichte protested, he never meant anything like this. The 'I' of the *Wissenschaftslehre* did not denote the the individual, but a single universal reason that is equally present in all individuals. The 'I' expressed an act of intellectual intuition that is neither subjective nor objective but the identity of them both. We grasp the true root of reason, Fichte argued, only if we conceive of it as the absolute identity of the subjective and objective.[30] Schelling had used similar expressions to describe the standpoint of absolute reason in *Darstellung meines Systems*. It is not surprising, then, that in his May 25 letter to Goethe, Schelling says that all Fichte had to say for them to be perfectly agreed is that all positing is that of the infinite.[31]

Schelling's May 24 letter marks the high point of his hopes for an alliance with Fichte. Despite his growing differences with Fichte, despite Schlegel's gossip, and despite Fichte's announcement, Schelling was more keen than ever to collaborate with Fichte. All the obstacles had been overcome, and he now looked forward to producing their journal.

Or, at least this is what Schelling told Fichte. Privately, he seems to have had his doubts about a reconciliation. Around this time Karoline Schlegel wrote about Schelling's "valiant disposition" and his readiness for a forthcoming public debate with Fichte.[32]

6. The Irresolvable Differences

Fichte was indeed ready to attack. He had just read Schelling's *Darstellung meines Systems,* which completely repelled him. This had finally convinced him that now was the time to draw his line in the sand. He began to write Schelling only a week later, on May 31; due to circumstances, however, Fichte did not complete his letter until August 7, when he finally sent it to Schelling via A. W. Schlegel. In the interim, rumors were rife. Schlegel knew something about the contents of the letter, which he passed on to Karoline, who speculated about what would happen when Schelling received "*der große Brief.*" That a dispute was brewing was clear to the Schlegels and Schleiermacher by the end of June.[33] It was in this tense atmosphere that Schelling began to steel himself for a battle.[34]

Finally received on August 7, Fichte's May 25 letter proved to be a bombshell, but even more than anyone expected. Never was Fichte so savagely critical, never so brutally frank. Though he told Schelling his last letter gave him more hopes for science, he made it clear that science would have to be on his own terms. All that he could see in Schelling's *Naturphilosophie* was "the old errors once again," which he had tried to point out several times in the past. The *Darstellung meines Systems* demonstrated to Fichte that he had not been understood, and that Schelling's position was completely untenable. Fichte conceded that they might agree about the subject matter and differ in their manner of exposition, but he added, somewhat ominously, that the exposition was essential to the subject matter. Rather than developing or reformulating his principles, as Schelling once expected, Fichte only dug in his heels. There was no need for a realism alongside his idealism, Fichte insisted, because there is only one science, of which all others are only parts, and that science is the *Wissenschaftslehre*. Fichte then reaffirmed the priority of the *Wissenschaftslehre* over *Naturphilosophie*. Instead of beginning from being, philosophy had to start from a seeing, and it was obviously circular to infer seeing from being and then being from seeing, as Schelling did. Furthermore, Schelling had gone completely astray, Fichte implied, when he ascribed autonomy and independence to nature. The realm of nature amounted to nothing more than the world apparent to our senses, which consisted in appearances of "the immanent light." Although it was possible for a *Naturphilosophie* to begin from the concept of a complete and fixed nature, as Schelling explained in his *System,* Fichte stressed that this concept was only an artificial abstraction from the system of knowledge.

It was clear from Fichte's May 25 letter that his differences with Schelling were irresolvable. They had been much too optimistic, and indeed much too superficial, in their belief that they were converging toward a new doctrine, an extension and revision of the principles of the *Wissenschaftslehre.* There were indeed some points of convergence: they both affirmed the existence of an absolute reason, and they both maintained that it consists in subject–object identity. But beyond such general formulae there were only discrepancies, deeper dissonances, which reflected a fundamental conflict in principle. These differences were most apparent in their contrasting attitudes toward the first principle of philosophy. While Schelling insisted that the infinite is an object of knowledge and the starting point of philosophy, Fichte continued to write of it as an object of faith that is only the end or ideal of philosophy. Also, Schelling was simply much too hasty in conflating Fichte's intellectual intuition or ego with the infinite. Although the ego of the *Wissenschaftslehre* is not the individual, it is also not the infinite or the single universal substance either. Rather, it is only the structure common to every rational being, which arises from abstracting from all our individual and empirical features.[35] To be sure, Fichte had written in his December 27 letter of going beyond the limits of the *Wissenschaftslehre* and of establishing a new system of the intelligible world; but this did not involve the radical reversal Schelling had hoped. Fichte went beyond his older principles in postulating *the existence* of the infinite; he persisted, however, in maintaining that it is only an object of *faith,* and that all *knowledge* must remain confined to the realms of experience.[36] This was not the extension in the powers of theoretical reason involved in Schelling's *Naturphilosophie.*

There were also profound discrepancies between Fichte's and Schelling's concepts of nature. *Prima facie* their differences were not so great because both affirmed a dynamic concept of matter, and both attributed drives to nature itself. It is indeed true that Fichte did not have the mechanistic concept of nature that has been so often attributed to him, and that he believed we should have apply organic concepts as well as mechanical ones.[37] But there was still an unbridgeable difference: Fichte insisted that the organic concepts had a strictly regulative validity, which we simply read into nature, whereas Schelling stressed their constitutive worth. So even though Fichte does not regard nature as a mechanism, it is only a mechanical model of explanation that has constitutive validity for him.

Fichte also remained a resolute opponent of Schelling's naturalism, or more specifically his explanation of the ego as the highest potency of nature, because this failed to explain the characteristic feature of subjectivity—namely, self-consciousness. More significantly, it undermined the concept of freedom, which it was the central purpose of the *Wissenschaftslehre* to support. It was useless, therefore, for Schelling to try to diminish his differences with Fichte by insisting that the 'I' of the *Wissenschaftslehre* was still the center point of his system, the highest potency of nature and the culmination of all its powers, for this was still to presuppose the naturalism Fichte so deeply despised.

All these unbridgeable differences eventually came to the light of day when Schelling finally replied to Fichte on October 3, 1801.[38] Now that Fichte had laid down his ultimate principles, Schelling decided to do the same. He first made it clear that he could not accept Fichte's views about the starting point of philosophy. He insisted that philosophy must begin not from a seeing, from subjectivity or the 'I,' but from pure being itself, which is not just reality or the objective but the indifference point of the ideal and the real, the subjective and objective. While Fichte had indeed postulated a principle of infinite reason, he had made it the result, the final synthesis, of his system, when it should have been the beginning. The starting point of philosophy must be the universe as a whole, the one and all, of which the ego is only the highest potency, and it is a perversion of the order of nature to make this potency the first principle itself.

Schelling then went on to criticize Fichte for his concept of nature. Rather than seeing nature as an end in itself, as having its own inherent purposes, Fichte demoted it to a mere means for the exercise of moral purposes. His aim was indeed "to annihilate" the reality of nature, to shrink it down into nothing more than "a little region of consciousness." For all these criticisms of the *Wissenschaftslehre*, Schelling still concedes its value, but only as one part of his system. It is indeed true that we can regard all of the universe as ideal, he explains, but that is only one of its attributes, for we can also consider the whole universe as real or objective. Spinoza was not a mere dogmatist or realist, as Fichte assumed, because he saw that there is a single reality that can be regarded as either subjective or objective, subsumed under the attribute of thought or extension. It rankled Schelling that Fichte recommended lens grinding for failed philosophers, and he reminded Fichte that Spinoza was a much greater thinker than he ever imagined.

Naturally, Fichte's May 25 letter and Schelling's October 3 reply shattered all hope for future collaboration. While Fichte accused Schelling of having never understood him, Schelling retorted that Fichte had scarcely read his work. "I am not your enemy," Schelling told Fichte, "though you are in all probability mine." The only question now was not whether to end their collaboration but how. In no uncertain terms Schelling told Fichte to cease calling him his collaborater, and warned him that their differences could no longer be concealed before the public. He would no longer idly stand by for Fichte to end the relationship on terms to his advantage, and he would not allow himself to be referred to a second time as a failed disciple. No, the die had already been cast. For Schelling had some very unpleasant news for his erstwhile colleague:

> Peaceful over the end and sure of my cause, I gladly leave everyone to find out for himself the truth of the affair. But I also cannot deprive someone of their own healthy sight and seek in any manner to hide something. Today a book appeared by a very superior head, which has as its title *Difference between the Fichtean and Schellingian Systems of Philosophy;* I had no part in it, but I also could not prevent it.

With these lines the Fichte–Schelling alliance came to its formal and final close.[39] A new one had been born. This "superior head" was, of course, Hegel, who had now, at least for the time being, thrown in his lot with Schelling.

CHAPTER 4

Problems, Methods, and
Concepts of *Naturphilosophie*

1. Absolute Idealism and *Naturphilosophie*

Above the portals of the academy of absolute idealism there is written the inscription *'Let no one enter who has not studied Naturphilosophie.'* Without an understanding of at least the central doctrines, basic arguments, and fundamental problems of *Naturphilosophie* the absolute idealism of Schelling and Hegel is all but incomprehensible. This should be clear enough simply by a cursory look at almost any of Schelling's and Hegel's texts, where so much *Naturphilosophie* appears. But no one should be tempted to dismiss this material for the sake of some deeper philosophical substance that exists underneath it. For the philosophical substance of Schelling and Hegel is absolute idealism, which is inseparable from *Naturphilosophie*.

The close connection between absolute idealism and *Naturphilosophie* is clear in two respects. First, as we have already seen (4.2.4; 4.3.6), Schelling's absolute idealism arose from his *Naturphilosophie*, and more specifically from its struggle for independence from, and then hegemony over, the *Wissenschaftslehre*. We should recall that, by late 1799, Schelling maintained that the principle of subject–object identity, the fundamental principle of absolute idealism, is the prerogative of *Naturphilosophie* alone. The *Wissenschaftslehre* and *Naturphilosophie* are not just equal to one another, he argued, but the former is based on the latter, since the self-consciousness of the transcendental ego is derived from the laws of nature in "the physical proof of idealism." It is only in a *popular* sense that the principle of subject–object identity means that ego and nature are equal to one another; in the proper *philosophical* sense it signifies that the ego is derived and nature is fundamental. In other words, subject–identity is originally found not in the self-consciousness of the ego but in the single universal substance. That there is a single universal substance, of which the subjective and objective are only manifestations, is the fundamental proposition of *Naturphilosophie;* but it is also the sum and substance of Schelling's absolute idealism around 1800.

Second, the intimate bond between absolute idealism and *Naturphilosophie* is also apparent from Schelling's own use of the term 'absolute idealism' (*absoluter Idealismus*).[1] In the early 1800s, Schelling used the term specifically to refer to the standpoint of *Naturphilosophie*. Absolute idealism is not a synthesis of the idealism of the *Wissenschaftslehre* with the realism of *Naturphilosophie*, a combination of both standpoints where each has equal legitimacy. Rather, it is nothing less than the inversion of the *Wissenschaftslehre*, the derivation of transcendental idealism from the realism and naturalism of *Naturphilosophie*. In other words, it is Fichte standing on his head.

Despite its importance for absolute idealism, *Naturphilosophie* has been ignored or spurned for decades, by historians of philosophy and science alike. Its reputation suffered greatly under the shadow of neo-Kantianism and positivism, which had dismissed it as a form of pseudoscience. *Naturphilosophie* had its heyday in Germany from 1800 to 1830. After the rapid growth of the empirical sciences in the 1840s, however, it came under increasing criticism. It was attacked for its a priori methodology, unverifiable speculations, and disregard for experiment. Allegedly, rather than carefully limiting their conclusions to definite experimental results, Schelling and the *Naturphilosophen* sketched grand theories, resorted to farfetched analogies, and forced preconceptions on a few scanty facts. For many philosophers and scientists, *Naturphilosophie* became the very model of how *not* to do science. It indeed became "the pestilence and black death of the century."[2]

Fortunately, there is no longer much need to justify the study of *Naturphilosophie*. After the blossoming of the history of science in the 1970s, there has been a virtual renaissance in the subject.[3] There have been books, conferences, and journals devoted to *Naturphilosophie*,[4] and there are now special editions of Schelling's and Hegel's writings in the field.[5] While there are few who would defend *Naturphilosophie* as a method for doing science today,[6] it has been recognized by many as a phenomenon of fundamental historical importance for the growth of modern science and philosophy.

Unfortunately, however, the legacy of positivism remains, and the old image of *Naturphilosophie* persists to this day. Some scholars would like to distinguish between the development of modern biological science and *Naturphilososophie* on the grounds that the early biologists and physiologists eschewed the metaphysical principles and transcendental methodology of *Naturphilosophie*.[7] According to this distinction, the pioneers of modern biology, such as Albrecht von Haller, J. F. Blumenbach and K. F. Kielmeyer, Alexander von Humboldt, and C. F. Wolff, observed Kant's regulative constraints and strictly followed an empirical methodology, while the *Naturphilosophen* flew in the face of these constraints and recklessly indulged in an priori procedure. Yet this distinction is more a positivistic construction than an historical reality. It suffers from several difficulties. First, Kant's regulative doctrine was *not* the foundation of empirical science in the late eighteenth and early nineteenth century; rather it was completely at odds with it. It is striking that virtually all the notable German physiologists and biologists of the late eighteenth and early nineteenth centuries conceived of their vital powers as causal agents rather than regulative principles.[8] Second, the fundamental program of *Naturphilosophie*—to explain life and the mind on a naturalistic yet nonmechanistic foundation—was shared by all the physiologists and biologists. Third, it is wrong to equate *Naturphilosophie* with a priori reasoning, system building, and speculation, as if it had no concern with experiment and observation.[9] Not only does this rest on a misunderstanding of the method of *Naturphilosophie*, which stressed the role of observation and experiment (see 4.4.6), but it also ignores how many *Naturphilosophen* were critical of excessive speculation and a priori theorizing.[10] The history of science needs to cast off the legacy of positivism—especially that lurking under Kantian guise—and to realize that *Naturphilosophie* was nothing less than the normal science of its day, not some freakish philosophical or metaphysical alternative to it.

Nowhere is the legacy of positivism more persistent, however, than in scholarship on German idealism. This seems paradoxical, given the conceptual distance between positivism and German idealism. But, since the Hegel renaissance of the 1970s, this scholarship has been under pressure to make its subject appear more respectable to contemporary analytic philosophy, where positivism still casts a dark shadow. Much recent Hegel scholarship, for example, has attempted to separate Hegel's "rational core" from his "mystical shell."[11] While the rational core consists in his system of categories, his adherence to the Kantian transcendental project, and whatever "arguments" can be reconstructed from his texts, the mystical shell comprises his Spinozistic metaphysics, his dialectical logic, and, worst of all, his lingering involvement with *Naturphilosophie*. Because so much contemporary Hegel scholarship still consists in the anachronistic attempt to reinterpret Hegel according to current intellectual orthodoxies, it has had more interest to conceal rather than reveal his considerable debt to Schelling's *Naturphi-*

losophie. As a result, it has failed to understand the origins and meaning of Hegel's own absolute idealism.

The purpose of the next two chapters is to examine the purpose, problem, and method of Schelling's *Naturphilosophie*. I shall argue that *Naturphilosophie* belongs to the rational core rather than the mystical shell of Schelling's and Hegel's absolute idealism. We shall find that we cannot so easily separate the epistemological concerns of absolute idealism from its metaphysics, for *Naturphilosophie* arose from the attempt the solve the problem of knowledge, and more specifically the outstanding problem of the transcendental deduction. To dismiss the metaphysics of absolute idealism and *Naturphilosophie* is simply to beg the question against Schelling and Hegel, who believed that they had no choice but to go beyond the Kantian limits to resolve its fundamental problems. Rather than attempting to interpret away Schelling's and Hegel's violation of the Kantian critical limits, it is much more important to reconstruct their reasons for doing so.

2. The Problematic of *Naturphilosophie*

Schelling's *Naturphilosophie* has often been placed outside the Kantian–Fichtean tradition of philosophy.[12] The usual justification for this historical location is that Schelling, in attempting to derive the transcendental ego from the laws of nature, self-consciously broke with some of the main principles of Kant's and Fichte's idealism. Some scholars, particularly those of Marxist loyalties, have regarded this development in a positive light, as a crucial step toward a scientific and materialist conception of nature.[13] But others, especially neo-Kantians, have seen Schelling's *Naturphilosophie* in a more negative light as a relapse into the metaphysical dogmatism of the past.[14] They complain that Schelling simply presupposed knowledge of the independent reality of nature as a whole, and so begged all the critical questions about how such knowledge is attained. But, whether by Marxists or neo-Kantians, Schelling's *Naturphilosophie* has been placed *outside* the tradition of Kantian–Fichtean idealism as a new competing development.

There is some truth to this account of Schelling's *Naturphilosophie*. Schelling did indeed self-consciously break with some of the central principles of Kant's and Fichte's idealism, and so cannot belong to the Kantian–Fichtean tradition in all respects. But this view of *Naturphilosophie*—if pushed to extremes—is also problematic. If we place *Naturphilosophie* completely outside the Kantian-Fichtean tradition—as if it ignores its main problems and disregards its central values—it becomes impossible to explain the development of absolute idealism itself. It is important to recognize that Hegel's argument on behalf of absolute idealism in the *Differenzschrift* is based on his defense of *Naturphilosophie*, and consists in the thesis that *Naturphilosophie* is necessary to resolve the outstanding problems of the Kantian–Fichtean tradition. Hegel's argument makes perfect sense if we place Schelling's *Naturphilosophie* within the Kantian–Fichtean tradition; but it makes none at all if we place it outside it.

More problematically, this historical location of Schelling's *Naturphilosophie* does scant justice to its origins and context. The more closely we examine its genesis, the more it becomes apparent that its original motivation and problematic came from the Kantian–Fichtean tradition, and indeed ultimately from the Transcendental Deduction itself. Schelling's central concern in developing his *Naturphilosophie* was to devise a new strategy for solving the very problem that had so troubled Kant and Fichte: 'How do we explain that correspondence between representation and object on which all knowledge depends?' His belief in the importance of *Naturphilosophie* for epistemology came from his recognition that the answer to the question behind the Transcendental Deduction—'How do synthetic a priori concepts apply to the manifold of a posteriori intuitions given in sensibility?'—requires a broader metaphysical theory about the relationship between the subjective and objective, the noumenal and phenomenal, or the mental and the physical.

Schelling's early concern with the problematic of transcendental philosophy becomes evident from his first publication on *Naturphilosophie*, his 1797 *Ideen zu einer Philosophie der Natur*. In the long introduction explicitly devoted to the problems of *Naturphilosophie*, Schelling stated that it begins with the same fundamental problem as all philosophy: "How a world outside us, how nature, and with it experience, is possible?" (II, 12) Often Schelling emphasized that the problem of *Naturphilosophie* was to accout for not the origins of nature itself but our *consciousness* of it (II, 12, 15, 30). The goal of *Naturphilosophie*, he further explained, is to develop a general theory of nature that unifies the mental and physical according to a single idea (II, 56). Although *Naturphilosophie* underwent important changes since its original conception in 1797, Schelling always held that its main goal is identical to that of transcendental philosophy: to provide a demonstration of the principle of subject–object identity, which is the fundamental presupposition of all knowledge.[15]

The strategy behind Schelling's *Naturphilosophie* was to approach the classical problem of mental–physical interaction from the opposite direction of transcendental philosophy itself. Rather than beginning from the subject and investigating the realm of consciousness, Schelling would begin from the object and study the nature of matter itself. He recognized that the whole problem of mental–physical interaction involves the question 'What is matter?' as much as the question 'What is mind?' Schelling contended that we should not view the nature of matter as a given, as if the only mystery were the mind and its relation to matter. Rather, we have to recognize that the very nature of matter is mysterious—it is indeed "the most obscure of all things, and indeed to some obscurity itself" (II, 359).

It should be clear, then, that if we place Schelling's *Naturphilosophie* completely outside the Kantian–Fichtean tradition, we fail to see its philosophical relevance, how it became an important part of the conversation of the post-Kantian tradition regarding the solution of the problem of knowledge. If we were to summarize the relevance of *Naturphilosophie* in a single phrase, we might call it a *naturalistic epistemology*, that is, one which attempts to explain the origin and possibility of knowledge by placing the subject and object of knowledge within nature as a whole.[16] According to this epistemology, the subject's awareness of nature does not take place in some *sui generis* transcendental realm, which transcends the natural world as the condition of its possibility. Rather, such awareness is simply another expression or appearance of the powers of nature itself, so that both the mental and physical, the subjective and objective, become parts or aspects of the natural world as a whole. While Schelling at first only vaguely conceived this project,[17] he soon developed it much more explicitly, so that in his 1799 *Einleitung zu dem Entwurf eines Systems der Naturphilosophie* he writes of deriving the whole transcendental realm from nature (III, 273–274). The epistemological relevance of *Naturphilosophie* therefore consists in its attempt to resolve the classical problem of knowledge in a purely naturalistic manner.

3. Rethinking Matter

Schelling's main strategy for dealing with the mind–body problem—reconsidering the nature of matter itself—faced one serious challenge: the Cartesian account of matter as *res extensa*. This concept of matter was the foundation of Descartes' mechanical physics, and the basis for his disasterous mental–physical dualism. It was the central aim of Schelling's *Natur-*

philosophie to replace it with a new concept of matter that did not have dualistic consequences.

According to Descartes' cosmology, the nature of matter consists in extension, that is, in having a certain length, breadth, or depth.[18] Since it does nothing more than occupy space, matter is essentially inert or static, so that it changes its state only if it is moved or acted on by something else.[19] All change of motion therefore happens through impact, by one body directly exerting pressure on another, when the degree of impact is measured in terms of quantity of motion, that is, by how much the body changes place in a definite time. The causes of all events in the natural world are explained in terms of this concept of matter, in other words, by the shape, size, position, and motion of particles, and by their impact on one another; hence there is no need to refer to final causes or inner powers.[20]

The main point behind such a concept of matter was to justify the mathematical treatment of the natural world.[21] Since extension has a definite size, shape, and weight, it is perfectly measurable and calculable. The price to be paid for such a concept, however, is an insurmountable mental–physical dualism. The problem is that consciousness does not appear to occupy space, because ideas—whether as acts or objects of thought—do not have a definite size, shape, and weight. Furthermore, it becomes impossible to explain how the external world acts on the mind; for if nothing in the mind changes place, it is impossible to measure, or even think of, impact.

Though it was coming under increasing criticism in the late seventeenth century, the Cartesian legacy was still very much alive in the late eighteenth. There was no dearth of natural philosophers who attempted to explain the new phenomena of magnetism, electricity, and chemistry according to mechanical principles.[22] According to one of its leading expositors, Friedrich Albert Gren, the central principles of this mechanical physics were the following: (1) that matter fills space through its mere existence, (2) that it is absolutely impenetrable, (3) that it is not infinitely divisible, but consists in indivisible and extended particles called atoms, (4) that there are empty spaces between atoms, (5) that the parts of elastic fluids (air, heat, light) do not touch, and (6) that the hollowness or density of body depends on the number of interstices between its particles.[23] The most prominent and radical of the mechanical physicists was George-Louis Le Sage (1724–1803), who applied such principles to gravity, chemical affinity, and magnetism. He explained chemical affinity by the compatibility between the size and shape of atoms, gravity by the motions of atoms in a fluid, and magnetism by the special affinity of two kinds of atoms in a subtle medium. Because of his prestige and uncompromising mechanism, Le Sage later became the main target of Schelling's critique of materialism.[24]

Schelling was not the first in late-eighteenth-century Germany to criticize the Cartesian legacy. The most important and influential step away from the mechanical physics came from Kant himself. In his 1786 *Metaphysische Anfangsgründe der Naturwissenschaften* Kant sketched a dynamical theory of matter to replace the traditional Cartesian concept. According to Kant, the essence of matter does not consist in extension but in moving force (*bewegende Kraft*). Extension is not the fundamental characteristic of matter, Kant contended, because the occupation of space needs to be explained in terms of something even more basic: the moving force to repel any other motion impinging on a space. Hence impenetrability is not an *absolute* quality, as if matter filled space by its very nature, but only a *relative* one, the result of the specific force by which it resists any body penetrating its space.[25]

The heart of Kant's theory of matter in the *Anfangsgründe* is his analysis of a physical body into two fundamental but opposing forces: the force of *repulsion*, by which one body causes another to go away from it, and the force of *attraction*, by which one body causes another to come close to it. These are the only two possible forces, Kant argued, because all forces express themselves in motion, and motion is representable as a line between two points, which can only approach or go apart from one another.[26] Though they conflict with one another, moving in opposite directions, both forces are necessary to matter. If matter consisted only in repulsive force, which strives constantly *to expand* its space, then it would scatter to infinity.[27] If, on the other hand, it were composed only of attractive force, which strives constantly *to diminish* its space, then it would shrink to a mere point.[28] What makes a body possible, therefore, is *a balance* between its attractive and repulsive force.

This theory of matter had a profound influence on Schelling. More than any other work, Kant's *Anfangsgründe* provided him with the conceptual basis for his own break with the Cartesian legacy. Although Schelling later became extremely critical of Kant's dynamics, it still provided most of the inspiration and impetus for his own theory of inorganic nature. In his *Ideen zu einer Philosophie der Natur* Schelling paid tribute to Kant's work by praising its analysis of matter. It is an account so perfect, he said, that it is only necessary to add some supplementary comments (II, 231).

Schelling was not, however, the first among his contemporaries to develop Kant's dynamic concept of matter. That direction of thought had already been firmly established by several of his contemporaries before he began to write his *Naturphilosophie* in 1797. A. C. A. Eschenmayer, C. F. Kielmeyer, H. F. Link, and A. N. Scherer had all taken Kant a step further by applying his ideas to the growing field of chemistry, and by trying to develop a comprehensive dynamical theory to explain all the phenomena of electricity and magnetism.[29] Schelling's *Naturphilosophie* has to be placed within a broader tradition, then, situated among all those late-eighteenth-century thinkers who attempted to construct a more speculative philosophy on the basis of Kant's concept of matter. There can be no doubt that Schelling was strongly influenced by the work of Eschenmayer and Kielmeyer.[30]

Schelling's own settling of accounts with the Cartesian legacy began with his 1797 *Ideen zu einer Philosophie der Natur.* It is striking how Schelling turns the critical tools of Kant's epistemology into a weapon against mechanistic materialism. True to the regulative strictures of transcendental philosophy, he accuses the mechanists of having hypostatized the concept of matter. They reify matter when they assume that it is something in which forces inhere (*materiae vis insita*), when it really consists in nothing but these forces themselves (II, 192, 194–195). By assuming that forces of attraction and repulsion must work by immediate impact, they also confuse the transcendental conditions of experience (these very forces) with events in experience itself (II, 192, 213). Following a line of argument sketched by Kant in the *Anfangsgründe,* Schelling then attacked the atomistic tenet of the absolute indivisibility and impenetrability of matter, accusing it of setting artificial restrictions to empirical investigation. There is no limit to indivisiblity or impenetrability, he argued, since for any degree of division or compression there can always be some greater (II, 196, 201).

After criticizing mechanistic materialism on these grounds, Schelling then broadened his offensive by attacking the physics of Le Sage. The main stumbling block of this physics, he argued, is that it presupposes what it should really explain: the possibility of matter and motion. It simply assumes the existence of fundamental particles in motion, and then explains the variety of kinds of matter from the quantity and motion of their parts; but the fundamental problem is the very existence of matter, the occupation of space, in the first place (II, 208, 212). Furthermore, the mechanical physics explains the motion of a body from the impact of another acting on it, but it cannot explain the source of this impact itself, that is, why one body moves and acts on another (II, 40, 205).

But the *Ideen* is much more than simply a critique of the Cartesian legacy, a mere polemic against Le Sage's mechanical physics. The heart of the work is its attempt to provide a deeper transcendental foundation for Kant's dynamics. Schelling explained that there are two possible procedures regarding the transcendental explication of the concept of matter: an *analytic* one that begins from the concept of matter and derives its necessary conditions, and a *synthetic* one that begins from more fundamental principles and then derives the concept of matter from it (II, 214). While Schelling praises Kant for his analytic account of matter, he also thinks it is necessary to go further and determine the conditions of the possibility of matter itself.[31] What Fichte had done for the Kantian categories and forms of intuition that Schelling would now try to do for the Kantian principles of dynamics: they too were to be derived from even more fundamental principles.

The basis of Schelling's deduction is Fichte's analysis of the fundamental activities of the mind in the *Wissenschaftslehre*. According to Fichte, there are two basic activities that are completely opposed to one another: an indeterminate activity extending outward to infinity, and a determinate activity reflecting inward to a single point. These activities are necessary conditions of the possibility of having an intuition of any determinate body in space. While the first activity gives content to our intuition, the second provides it with form. Schelling now applies this analysis of the conditions of experience to Kant's fundamental forces. Attractive and repulsive force, Schelling argues, represent or objectify these two activities in our outer experience. The fundamental conditions of the possibility of matter—attraction and repulsion—then turn out to be the fundamental conditions of the possibility of any object of intuition. What we are aware of in our experience, the object in space and time, is the synthesis of these two fundamental powers (II, 214, 220, 231–234).

It is doubtful, however, whether such a deduction would have met with Kant's blessing. Kant stressed that the forces of attraction and repulsion were fundamental, and *ipso facto* could not be explained themselves.[32] Here again we can see how Fichte and Schelling pushed the search for foundations beyond the Kantian limits.

4. Nature as Organism

Since the main subject matter of the *Ideen* is material nature, Schelling did not deal directly with organic nature, and still less with the mind–body problem. In the preface to the first edition he announced a continuation of the work that would treat aspects of organic nature, especially teleology and physiology. But this promise he never kept.

Only in the retrospective and later introduction to the work did Schelling begin to discuss organic nature and the mind–body problem. His treatment of these issues is tentative and schematic, yet central to his later *Naturphilosophie*. In the course of a rambling polemic against mechanistic materialism, Schelling suggests that the paradigm for the unity of the mental and physical, ideal and real, should be the concept of an *organism* or *self-organizing matter* (II, 44, 47). Since the idea of organization involves that of a unity of form and content, concept and object (II, 40–41, 44), and since such a unity is possible only if there is some directing intelligence or governing mind (II, 42, 47), self-organizing matter must be understood as a unity of mind and body, ideal and real. The purpose or concept of an organism must be *inherent* in the object itself, and not something imposed on it from outside, Schelling argues, because it is necessary not only for its structure or form but its very existence. Hence it is necessary to assume that there is some intelligence or reason within matter.

Very boldly but also very tentatively, Schelling generalizes this paradigm, applying it to all of nature. The unity of mental and physical in organic nature now becomes the paradigm for the unity of organic and inorganic in nature as a whole. Schelling suggests that one idea for uniting the realms of the organic and inorganic, the purposive and mechanical, is the purposiveness of nature as a whole (II, 54). This idea means that there is a hierarchy of life in the universe, and that any form of organized matter is a form of life, even if a very limited kind (II, 46).

What was a mere proposal in the *Ideen* soon became a full-blown program in Schelling's next work on *Naturphilosophie*, his 1798 *Von der Weltseele*. We can overcome the opposition between the organic and inorganic, the mechanical and purposive, Schelling argues in the preface to this work, only if we conceive all of nature as an organism. Since all attempts to explain the organic in mechanical terms have failed, there remains only the possibility of explaining the mechanical in terms of the organic. Mechanism is then simply the *negative* side of life, its lowest stage of organization and development. In a daring move, Schelling neatly reversed the usual order of explanation in seventeenth- and eighteenth-century philosophy. Rather than taking mechanism as his model of explanation and reducing the organic and mental to its terms, he makes the organic his model, seeing the mechanical relation of cause and effect only as a manifestation of a universal organic development. In a few short sentences Schelling makes this dramatic reversal perfectly explicit:

> What then is that mechanism with which you frighten yourselves, as if with a ghost? Is mechanism really something existing for itself? Is it not rather only the negative side of the organism? Must not the organism be prior to the mechanism, the positive be prior to the negative? If in general the negative presupposes the positive, and not conversely, our philosophy cannot begin from mechanism (as the negative) but from organism (as the positive); organism is so little to be explained from the mechanism that mechanism is to be explained from organism. (II, 349)

The concept of an organism provides the root metaphor, the guiding principle, behind Schelling's *Naturphilosophie*. Schelling extends this metaphor to the universe as a whole, so that all nature is one vast organism, one living whole, which is undergoing constant growth and development. According to his organic vision, there is a single living force acting throughout all nature, and all the different species of minerals, plants, and animals, and even all the different forms of matter itself, are simply so many different degrees of its organization and development. All nature forms one vast hierarchy, which consists in the various stages of organization and development of living force. This hierarchy begins from the most simple forms of matter, passes through the more complex minerals, plants, and animals, and finally ends with the most complex forms of life, such as the self-consciousness of the transcendental philosopher and the creativity of the artistic genius.

What, more precisely, did Schelling mean by 'organism'? To understand his usage, it is necessary to go back to Kant's classic account of this concept in sections 64–65 of the *Kritik der Urteilskraft*, which Schelling closely follows.[33] Kant maintained that the distinctive feature of an organism, when it is considered as an end of nature (*Naturzweck*) rather than of art, is that it is the cause and effect of itself. Rather than being produced by causes external to itself, an organism produces itself according to ends, so that the effect of its activity can also be understood as its cause. Kant further defined this self-causing activity through two more specific characteristics. First, the idea of the whole contains and precedes all its parts, so that every part has its identity only in the whole. Second, the parts produce the whole because they are reciprocally cause and effect of one another. Kant emphasized the second feature as especially characteristic of products of nature as opposed to products of art. Both works of art and nature could be seen as organic wholes, because, in art as in nature, the idea of the whole precedes the parts. Unlike a work of art, however, a product of nature is *self*-generating and *self*-organizing. Rather than the idea of the whole being imposed on it by some external agency, a natural organism produces itself through the reciprocal interaction of all its parts.

Like Kant, Schelling distinguished an organism, which is *self*-causing and *self*-generating, from a mechanism, which is something produced according to external causes alone. He maintained that the concept of an organism is *sui generis,* irreducible to the laws that apply only to a machine, because mechanical explanation cannot account for the self-causing and self-generating activity of an organism. Mechanism presupposes that the series of causes and effects is *unidirectional* because no effect can react on its cause but can only be the cause of some other effect. In an organism, however, the series of causes is *bidirectional* because the effect can also react on the cause, so that cause and effect interact with one another reciprocally (II, 40–41). Although Schelling denies that an organism is reducible to a mechanism, he does not make any sharp or absolute distinction between these concepts. He does not intend to banish mechanism from the sphere of nature, and he indeed insists that it plays a necessary role in the explanation of all phenomena.[34] It's only that mechanical explanation must now be placed in the broader context of the purposiveness of nature as a whole: it is the means and medium by which organic activity realizes itself.

This organic concept of nature was Schelling's solution to the dilemma that had troubled physiology ever since the early seventeenth century: dualism versus mechanistic materialism. These extremes seemed to be the only possibilities if one adopted the Cartesian concept of matter and its paradigm of mechanical explanation. If all naturalistic explanation is in terms of motion on extended bodies, then either we place life and the mind outside nature—and so become dualists—or we reduce it down to matter in motion—and so become mechanists. But both alternatives are unsatisfactory. While the mechanist upholds the principles of naturalism, he seems to ignore the characteristic qualities of life and the mind; and whereas the dualist recognizes such qualities, he transports them into a mysterious *sui generis* realm where they cannot be explained according to the methods and principles of the new sciences.

It was the purpose of Schelling's organic theory to provide some middle path between the horns of this dilemma. Schelling agreed with the dualist that mechanism could not explain the *sui generis* characteristics of life and the mind; but he also sympathized with the efforts of the materialist to explain life and the mind according to natural laws. The organic concept of nature alone, he believed, could avoid the problems of both dualism and materialism and provide a *naturalistic yet nonreductivistic* account of life and the mind. Since an organism is not reducible to a mechanism, it does not reduce life and the mind down to a machine; but since it also acts according to natural laws, there is no violation of the principles of naturalism. The organic concept thus calls into question the false common premise behind both dualism and materialism: that all natural explanation is mechanical. Rather than accounting for natural events by external causes acting upon them, it explains them by their necessary place in a systematic whole. The paradigm of explanation is now holistic rather than analytical or atomistic.

Schelling's *Naturphilosophie* attempts to bring life and the mind into the naturalistic world view by regarding them as aspects or appearances of living force. He refuses to regard them as *sui generis* forces or substances, as if they were somehow inexplicable according to the laws governing physical nature. Rather, he insists that they are simply the higher degrees of organization and development of the same living forces that are inherent in matter. According to his organic view, then, there is no distinction of *kind*, but only one of *degree*, between the mind and body. They are different levels of organization and development of the single living force throughout all of nature. The mental is the highest degree of organization and development of the living forces active in matter; and matter is the lowest degree of organization and development of the living forces present in the mind. We can therefore regard mind as highly organized and developed matter, and matter as less organized and developed mind. Nature is visible mind, and mind is invisible nature, by virtue of their being different stages in the development of living force.

5. Regulative or Constitutive?

Whatever its explanatory value, it is obvious that Schelling's organic theory has problems of its own. The main difficulty concerns the epistemic status of the original metaphor. Is it possible to give the idea of life a *constitutive* worth, so that we can assume that nature *is* an organism? Or is it necessary to assign it a merely *regulative* status, so that we can investigate nature only *as if* it were an organism?

Prima facie Kant's position on this question was clear and firm. It is one of the central teachings of the *Kritik der Urteilskraft* that we cannot attribute objective validity to teleological judgments that ascribe purposes to things in nature.[35] We assume that organisms act for ends only by analogy with our actions, and we have no evidence that such an assumption is warranted because nothing in our experience could possibly confirm it. We do not derive the concept of purposiveness from nature but read that concept into it.[36] This concept therefore has only a heuristic value in helping us to systematize the multiplicity of empirical laws. We should proceed in our investigation of nature *as if* it were created according to a divine intelligence since this will help us to find such systematic unity as exists; but we have no right to conclude that there really is such an intelligence or complete unity.

Although Kant himself had sketched a dynamic theory of nature in his *Metaphysische Anfangsgründe*, he was always careful to distinguish his position from any form of hylozoism or vital materialism, according to which matter has some living principle within it. In the third part of the *Anfangsgründe*, Kant had provided a demonstration of the law of inertia, which, he insisted, proves that matter is lifeless.[37] According to this law, every change in matter must have an *external* cause, such that a body persists in motion, in the same direction, and with the same speed unless there is some external cause to make it change its direction and speed. This means that there cannot be any internal or living principle in matter, something that would make it self-moving and self-organizing. We have a right to ascribe such an internal principle to a body, Kant further argued, only if we can show that it has some faculty of desire, some intention or purpose of changing its state; but experience provides no possible evidence for such a claim. As if he intended to crush all speculative impulses in the bud, Kant then proclaimed his damning indictment against hylozoism: "*der Tod aller Naturphilosophie.*"

What was Schelling's response to this Kantian challenge? Initially, it was to avoid any confrontation at all, and even to concede the Kantian limits. In several passages of the *Ideen*, for example, Schelling stressed that the idea of an organism has only a heuristic value. Although it is a necessary principle of reflective judgement, it gives us no right to assume that nature itself is organized according to some design (II, 54–55). Schelling also conceded Kant's point that the idea of purposiveness involves that of a creative understanding, which cannot be demonstrated by theoretical reason (II, 42). Even in *Von der Weltseele*, where Schelling had first generalized the organic metaphor, he sometimes insists that we have no right to assume the existence of ultimate powers, and that they are only useful as limiting concepts in pushing back the boundaries of explanation (II, 384, 386).

It is striking, however, that the general direction of Schelling's thought is on a collision course with Kant. Even when he insists on the Kantian strictures, he also commits himself to transcending them. This becomes apparent from his protracted polemic against both dualism and materialism in the introduction to the *Ideen*, where the upshot of his argument is that the idea of a purpose must have more than a merely subjective validity. Schelling criticizes materialists and dualists alike for their incapacity to explain the unity of form and content in an organism. We cannot separate form from content, as if form were imposed on content from the outside, whether by God or some material cause, because the form is *inherent* in the object, the conditions not only for its structure but for its very existence (II, 41, 44–45, 47). Now, Schelling reasons, if the form, the idea of a purpose, is necessary for the very existence of an object, as Kant himself concedes, then in what sense do we only read it into the object? The claim that we only project our ends into the object is implausible, Schelling suggests, because it does not explain why we do so for some objects rather than others. Surely, there must be something in the object itself that distinguishes it from the inorganic and that makes us think that it is purposive (II, 43–44). While the Kantians are right to insist that the idea of a purpose involves that of some guiding intelligence, they also must admit that, in the case of an organism, this intelligence is *within* the object itself.

Despite his methodological caution in some passages, the thrust of Schelling's organic metaphor in *Von der Weltseele* was to give constitutive status to the idea of life. In seeing matter as only the negative side of life, as its lowest degree of organization and development, Schelling had virtually embraced the very hylozoism Kant had condemned. And when he claimed that we must understand mechanism as part of a wider organic whole, he had clearly gone beyond Kant's limits by making the organic a necessary condition of causality, and so of the theoretical knowledge of experience itself. While the implications of Schelling's theory are clear, they were not drawn by him until much later. They became more explicit only after 1799 when he developed a specific methodology for his *Naturphilosophie*, and when he established a foundation for his *Naturphilosophie* independent of the *Wissenschaftslehre*.

Although Schelling himself did not provide an explicit account of his reasons for going beyond Kant's regulative constraints even after 1799, it is easy to reconstruct why he did so. The main point is simple: the problem of knowledge could be resolved only by granting constitutive validity to teleology. Schelling's problem was to explain the correspondence between representation and object, subjective and objective, ideal and real, involved in all knowledge. Any satisfactory explanation of this correspondence required giving some account of how such apparently heterogeneous factors could interact with one another. To explain this interaction, Schelling postulated the idea of an organism, which makes the subjective and objective simply different degrees of vital activity. Clearly, however, to account for the *actual* interaction it is necessary to assume that the living powers are *in* the phenomena. To say that we have a right only to proceed *as if* they are in them is only to leave the mystery that is to be explained; we would then still not know why there is any interaction at all. Of course, Kant himself insisted that we leave the interaction a mystery, denying that we can have any insight into the single source of our faculties. But there is a clear retort to this line of argument: that leaving things a mystery does not explain the possibility of knowledge itself, which it is the purpose of transcendental philosophy to explain.

It is indeed noteworthy that Kant himself was never very clear and firm about the distinction between the regulative and constitutive himself, and that in places he came very close to the position of Schelling and Hegel.[38] Nowhere are his vascillations more apparent than in the Appendix to the Transcendental Dialectic of the first *Kritik*. Here Kant sometimes staunchly maintains that we must assume there is some systematic order in nature itself, for otherwise we would have little rationale or motivation to look for it. Proceeding simply according to an "*as if* assumption," he insists, will not be sufficient to justify or motivate enquiry.[39] Kant then blurs his distinction between the regulative and the constitutive, reason and understanding, when he states that the assumption of systematicity is necessary for the application of the catgories themselves. Without the idea of systematic unity, he says, there would not be "coherent employment of the understanding," not even a "sufficient criterion of empirical truth."[40] The same equivocation extends into the *Kritik der Urteilskraft* itself, where Kant sometimes states that we cannot have a coherent experience without the application of the maxims of reflective judgment itself.[41] In insisting that we assume the existence of intelligent design, and in making such an assumption a necessary condition of experience, of the application of the catgories themselves, Kant himself had completely violated his own distinction between the transcendental and the transcendent. The metaphysical idea of the organic had virtually become a necessary condition of experience itself.

6. The Methodology of *Naturphilosophie*

Once we raise the question of the epistemic warrant for Schelling's main principles we immediately broach the topic of method. How did Schelling attempt to justify his principles? By what means did he claim to know them? These questions are all the more pressing when we consider that the brunt of the positivisitic campaign against Schelling was that he did not have a scientific methodology. This makes it necessary to examine Schelling's own methodology and how he attempted to defend it. Rather than condemning Schelling out of hand by positivisitic standards, which he would only have rejected, it is necessary to examine him in the light of his own philosophy of science.

After 1799, in response to growing criticisms, Schelling began to reflect on the proper procedure for *Naturphilosophie,* and he went to some pains to explain it in various passages of his works, especially in his *Einleitung zu dem Entwurf eines Systems der Naturphilosophie* and some articles in his *Zeitschrift für spekulative Physik*.[42] In reading these texts one is struck by Schelling's methodological sophistication and caution, which is all the more remarkable given his reputation for naivité and carelessness. As if by foresight, he anticipates the caricatures later attributed to him, warning the reader that is not him. He deplores the vices of speculation, especially 'formalism,' the tendency to impose simplistic ideas on the variety and complexity of facts.[43] While he does use analogies, and indeed sometimes indulges in them, he also stresses that they have only a preliminary and heuristic value, and that they should later be more precisely formulated by quantification.[44] In his earlier works Schelling insists that basic forces and ultimate units are only regulative ideas, useful fictions for guiding enquiry, which should on no account be hypostatized.[45] Indeed, he warns against postulating elemental substances, such as caloric, on the grounds that they cannot be justified by experience.[46] Finally, rather than rashly developing some general hypotheses, Schelling often advises waiting for more empirical data.

One reason for the notoriety of Schelling's *Naturphilosophie* has been its common association with vitalism, with speculation about some *Lebenskraft* or *élan vital* behind all the phenomena of nature. It is important to recognize, however, that Schelling was a sharp critic of vitalism, and took pains to distinguish his position from it.[47] Indeed, he rejected vitalism on the same grounds as many a positivist: that it postulates an occult force inexplicable by natural laws. In general, Schelling abjured all hypotheses about supernatural powers, insisting that we cannot postulate any force beyond nature because every force is finite, having its efficacy and magnitude only within a system of forces.[48] The interpretation of Schelling as a vitalist is simply too crude, failing to distinguish his theory from the many theories of life at the close of the eighteenth century.

Rather than a proponent of the occult and the supernatural, Schelling was a stout champion of naturalism, the doctrine that everything that happens acts of necessity according to the laws of nature. *Naturphilosophie* was "the Spinozism of physics," and as such its naturalism was just as uncompromising as that in the *Ethica*. Although Schelling does reject the *mechanistic* paradigm of naturalistic explanation advocated by Descartes and Spinoza, this does not mean he abandons naturalism in general. Rather, the very opposite is the case: he expressly affirms its necessity. The first maxim of true natural science, he writes in his *Einleitung,* is to explain all events on the basis of natural powers alone (III, 273). Nature is a completely self-sufficient and autonomous realm, he states explicitly in the *Entwurf,* so that everything that happens within it must be explained according to its laws alone (III, 17). In insisting on such naturalism, Schelling means to exclude several kinds of theories: (1) all references to the supernatural, such as miracles; (2) all explanations in terms of occult powers; (3) the old physico-theology, which explained all things by their place in providence; and finally (4), by 1799, any idealist explanation of nature that makes it only an instrument of self-consciousness.[49] Indeed, naturalism was so important to Schelling that it became one of the main reasons for his abandonment of the *Wissenschaftslehre.*

Another major reason for the notoriety of Schelling's *Naturphilosophie* is its method of a priori speculation. It has been severely criticized for its lack of careful induction, and for its neglect of experimentation. There is some rationale for this interpretation, since Schelling himself stressed the need for starting from a priori principles and criticized the procedure of empirical physics. But, before we pass judgement on such a method, it is necessary to understand the epistemology behind it. Why did Schelling think that the method of *Naturphilosophie* should be a priori? Why, too, did he criticize empirical physics?

In the *Einleitung zu dem Entwurf* Schelling cast some light on the first question by making some general distinctions between *Naturphilosophie* and empirical physics (III, 282–283). He first distinguished between their *subject matters:* while *Naturphilosophie* treats the first causes of nature, its deeper sources, and its inner activity, empirical physics deals only with its secondary causes, its external appearances, and the results or products of its activity (III, 274–275). He then distinguished between their *methodology: Naturphilosophie* begins from a priori principles and constructs all propositions from them, whereas empirical physics begins with experience and derives its principles from them. The difference in subject matter determines that in methodology: the fundamental principles of *Naturphilosophie* have to be a priori simply because the first causes of nature cannot be given in experience itself. The central task of *Naturphilosophie* is explicitly and self-consciously *transcendental* or *metaphysical,* because its principles precede any possible experience and so cannot be derived from it.

Schelling's critique of empirical physics has to be placed within its specific historical context and understood as the critique of one specific kind of methodology: that practiced by the mechanical physics of his day. The central target of Schelling's critique, and indeed his paradigm of empiricist methodology, was the mechanical physics of George-Louis Le Sage.[50] According to Schelling, Le Sage attempted to derive his principles from experience, but he did so by constantly modifying his theory to accomodate any new data that came along; he would invent *ad hoc* all kinds of particles, shapes, and subtle media so that his theory would correspond to any kind of fact.[51] Schelling saw two difficulties with this kind of theorizing: first, it is circular, because one derives causes from effects and then effects from causes; and, second, it is constantly subject to revision whenever new data arises. The problem with empiricism, then, is not that it resorts to facts, but that it begins from them and constructs its theories *ad hoc* only in the light of them.

The ultimate basis for Schelling's a priori methodology, and his critique of empiricism, lay with his Kantian paradigm of knowledge. True to the idealist tradition, Schelling stresses the role of mental activity in cognition. We know only what we create, he says, so that all knowledge in the strictest sense is a priori (III, 276). To know an object is to determine the principles of its possibility, and to determine these is to be able to construct it, to reproduce its activity in thought (275). Schelling is confident that such a priori constructions will conform to nature itself, because he thinks that the philosopher and nature share one and the same productive reason. The principles by which nature creates its objects in reality are the same as those by which the philosopher constructs his objects in thought. As Schelling puts it, nature too works a priori, because it brings forth all its products according to a rational plan (III, 279; IV, 530).

This paradigm of knowledge is also the foundation for Schelling's ideal of science. Like Kant, Schelling thinks that the ideal of science is a system, a complete body of propositions organized around and derived from a single principle. This ideal of a system follows directly from his concept of knowledge as construction. If to know an object is to construct it, and if to construct it is to show its place in a whole, or to demonstrate how it follows of necessity from a single idea, then the proper form of knowledge will be a system.[52] The ideal of *Naturphilosophie* will then be to express the vast multitude of phenomena in nature according to a single universal principle (III, 276).

On the basis of his paradigm of knowledge, Schelling then developed some striking views about the role of experiment in natural science. Since knowing is acting, we gain knowledge of nature not when we passively record its operations but when we actively interfere with them. Such intervention is an experiment, which is an attempt to compel nature to answer questions (III, 276). Accordingly, Schelling stresses the role of theory in the framing of experiments. We ask nature the questions we do, he argues, only because we are led by a theory. If we are without theory, we will be like those tourists who do not ask questions because they know nothing about what they see. Indeed, Schelling sometimes goes so far as to contend that facts in themselves are nothing, having their meaning and validity only in the context of a specific theory: "whoever does not have the correct theory also cannot have a correct experience, and conversely" (IV, 532).[53]

It is clear that Schelling's paradigm of knowledge and science have their origins in Kant's philosophy of nature, especially as it is expounded by Kant in his *Metaphysische Anfangsgründe der Naturwissenschaften.* That the laws of science have a transcendental or metaphysical foundation, that a discipline is a science only insofar as it is systematic, that the method of science is a priori construction, that the basic parts of natural science should be organized according to the architechtonic of reason itself, and that we make experiments according to the demands of theory—all these themes of Schelling's methodology are inspired by Kant, most of them deriving directly from the *Anfangsgründe.* Schelling differs from Kant not regarding any issue of methodology, but rather in how far he takes his methodology. Schelling attempts to take the method a step further by providing a foundation for the laws that Kant himself regarded incapable of further deduction.[54] Clearly, showing the

Kantian provenance of Schelling's methodology does not legitimate it; but the extent of Schelling's debt to Kant is remarkable considering that Kant's name is so often invoked as a talisman against the excesses of metaphysical speculation after Kant. The irony is that, more than anyone else, Kant was the father of these metaphysical tendencies.

Though it is more prominent, the a priori aspect of Schelling's methodology is only one of its aspects. For all his criticism of empiricism, and for all his insistence on a priori principles, Schelling also stresses the indispensable role of experience in *Naturphilosophie*. In reply to the criticism that *Naturphilosophie* neglects experience Schelling counters with the lines: "We know not only this or that, but we originally know nothing at all except through experience and by means of experience" (III, 278). To be sure, the *Naturforscher* comes to the facts with his ideas and questions; but that does not mean that they are only what he reads into them. While his first principles cannot be discovered by experience, they can still be falsified by it. Schelling is clear and firm that the scientist's first principles have at first only the status of an hypothesis, and that their value rests on their ability to explain the facts. The test of his principles is whether he can derive all the facts from it. If there is just a single phenomenon that cannot be derived from his principles, Schelling stresses, then it is necessary for this reason alone to reject them (277).

In the *Einleitung zu dem Entwurf* Schelling complains that it is a complete misrepresentation of *Naturphilosophie* to think that it ignores experience. Although every proposition in a system should be derived a priori, this does not mean that the *Naturphilosoph* does not consult experience to discover it in the first place. Schelling locates the source of this misunderstanding in a common confusion about the nature of the a priori (III, 278). We tend to think that the distinction between a priori and a posteriori knowledge corresponds to distinct kinds of propositions, so that it seems as if one and the same proposition cannot be confirmed by reason and discovered by experience. But the a priori or a posteriori status of a proposition attaches not to the propositions themselves but simply to our mode of knowledge of them. Hence a proposition that we first know a posteriori through experience can later become a priori by its role within the system itself (III, 278).

For several reasons, this point is of general importance for understanding Schelling's methodology. First, it shows how he thinks reason and experience are both necessary to understand phenomena. We need experience to learn about the existence and specific properties of phenomena, and reason to determine their necessary place in a system. Second, it also demonstrates how his polemic against empiricism combines with his insistence on the role of experience in forming knowledge. The problem with empiricism is not that it appeals to facts, but that it does not give a proper a priori foundation for them, which requires showing how they relate to one another in a system. Third, it makes clear, contrary to a popular stereotype, that Schelling is not trying to deduce specific empirical laws from a priori principles without the aid of experience. The role of a priori deduction is only to determine the proper systematic order or structure of the materials gathered from experience.

If, however, the materials of a system have to be derived from experience, is that system not subject to falsification and constant revision? Schelling was always ready to concede this regarding the details of the system. He sometimes stressed that the system of *Naturphilosophie* is more an ideal than a reality, a goal for investigation that will be complete only when all the facts are fully known. But what about the fundamental principles themselves? Schelling wavered on this crucial question. Sometimes he emphasized that even the fundamental principles were subject to falsification if they did not derive all the data of experience (III, 277); at other times, however, he insisted that there could be no conflict between reason and experience, and any appearance of one only went to show that some apriori principles are not really principles of reason after all (IV, 530).[55] Aware of the distance between a priori principles and specific empirical data, Schelling held that the goal of empirical research should be not random induction for its own sake, but the discovery of those *mediating terms* (*Zwischenglieder*) between a priori principles and the multitude of empirical data (III, 280; IV, 532). Only these would be able to determine the true application and legitimacy of the principles themselves.

Such, in brief, were Schelling's methodological views. It should be clear by now that there is indeed some rationale for them, and that it is simply question begging to dismiss them by empiricist standards. Yet a question remains. While it is necessary to admit that Schelling had a clear and consistent method, did he actually practice it? Some of Schelling's fairer critics were ready to admit his methodological sophistication, and even the value of his ideals; where he went astray, they argued, is not following them. Whether this is so is best left to a close reader of Schelling's texts to judge.

CHAPTER 5

Theory of Life and Matter

1. The Spinozism of Physics

So far we have only scratched the surface of Schelling's *Naturphilosophie*. We have considered its general concept of nature, its method, and its fundamental problems. But we have still not examined its doctrines in any detail. Given Schelling's identification of absolute idealism with *Naturphilosophie*, such an examination is crucial for a more concrete idea of absolute idealism itself. Schelling's absolute idealism involved first and foremost his organic concept of nature. But until we see how Schelling developed that concept, it is bound to appear to be nothing more than a metaphor. If Schelling's view of nature was poetic in inspiration, it was also meant to be scientific in execution. We must not forget that Schelling, unlike Hölderlin, saw himself mainly as a philosopher whose special business was to rationalize and systematize poetic intuition.

To consider the detail of Schelling's doctrines, it is necessary to consider their evolution, for Schelling's views were constantly changing as he developed new approaches to the same problem. Our task now is to consider the development of Schelling's views on matter and life during the crucial period from 1798 to 1800.

Such was the rapid development of Schelling's *Naturphilosophie* that by 1799 he began to rethink its foundation. In his first two writings on *Naturphilosophie*—his 1797 *Ideen zu einer Philosophie der Natur* and his 1798 *Von der Weltseele*—Schelling had given a Fichtean foundation to both his dynamics and theory of life. But in his third major writing in this field, his 1799 *Entwurf eines Systems der Naturphilosophie*, he virtually abandoned these Fichtean foundations. Rather than attempting to ground the fundamental forces of nature in the basic activities of the transcendental ego, Schelling now insisted on placing their foundation in nature itself. He explained that every science has the right to assume that its subject matter is self-sufficient and independent, and this holds for *Naturphilosophie* as much as transcendental philosophy. If transcendental philosophy could postulate the absolute reality of the ego, *Naturphilosophie* could do the same for nature itself. The fundamental presupposition of *Naturphilosophie* is therefore the autonomy of nature, which means that the basic forces of nature must be sought within it. True to this new, more naturalistic standpoint, Schelling now called his *Naturphilosophie* "the Spinozism of physics."

The central principle of Schelling's new dynamics is that nature in itself consists in infinite productivity, absolute activity. Schelling warns against considering nature in itself as a 'substance,' or even as the 'totality of things,' for these terms imply a static view of nature. He also advises against supposing that activity somehow inheres in some substance or thing. A substance or thing is never as basic as activity because it is only the result or product of it. Strictly speaking, then, nature is not even an organism, since that would be again only the product of its activity (*natura naturata*). Instead, nature is nothing less than living activity or productivity itself (*natura naturans*) (III, 284). What Fichte once said about the ego—that its nature is only activity— Schelling now declares to be true of nature itself. In one move Schelling had both objectified the subjective and subjectified the objective: the ego became nature as nature became the ego.

Prima facie this dynamic outlook seems to be the antithesis of Spinoza, who saw all of nature as the single infinite substance. But we must not forget that Spinoza also conceived of substance in dynamic terms: "God's power is identical with his essence."[1] Where Schelling differs from Spinoza is in his reintroduction of final causes into nature, in seeing substance as living and evolving. For Spinoza, God's power is not purposive but simply acts according to the necessity of its own nature. In this regard Schelling, like Hölderlin, Novalis, and Schlegel, is less a strict Spinozist than a follower of Herder's vitalist reinterpretation of Spinoza.

Like Spinoza, Schelling maintains that nature in itself, considered as absolute productivity, is completely positive and infinite, so that it is not possible to distinguish anything within it. But he also holds that this productivity results in definite products, in specific things, which are distinguishable from one another. This raises the difficult question: How do we explain the limitation of the absolute productivity of nature? How is it that something absolutely productive limits itself to create a definite product? This is, of course, the classic problem of the origin of finitude, of how the infinite limits itself, the very problem that plagued Spinoza. It is also Fichte's problem of how to explain the reality of the external world from the absolute ego. Now Schelling brings this very issue into *Naturphilosophie*. He claims that to resolve this problem is nothing less than "the highest task of all *Naturphilosophie*" (III, 18, 102, 220).

In his writings on *Naturphilosophie* Schelling's approach to this problem is to postulate two fundamental opposing forces in all of nature. The restriction of the absolute productivity of nature is conceivable, he argues, only if we postulate a fundamental dualism or opposition of force. The limitation of the activity of nature to some definite product is possible, Schelling argues, only if there are two primal tendencies in conflict with one another (III, 17). One of these tendencies is centrifugal, expanding to infinity; the other is centripetal, contracting to a single point. These powers mutually restrict or limit one another: the first would expand to all reality if it were not limited by something tending to a single point; the second would shrink to a single point and evaporate into nothing if it were not opposed by something expanding to infinity. For different reasons, each power is necessary to understand the creation of something determinate, a definite product. Without the infinitely expanding tendency, there will be nothing at all, and so nothing to restrict, because it is the condition of any existence; and without the infinitely contractive tendency, there will be nothing *determinate*, because negation is the condition of all determination. The product of nature must be seen, then, as the result of both these forces. It comes into existence through their mediation, the point at which their opposed directions cancel one another and equals zero (III, 288).

Clearly, these basic tendencies are modeled on Kant's account of attractive and repulsive force in the *Anfangsgründe*. Schelling does not deny the analogy, but he insists that the Kantian forces are really only the empirical analogues of a more basic metaphysical distinction (III, 17n2). Where Schelling once only praised Kant's dynamics, he now criticizes it for not being sufficiently dynamical.[2] He maintains that Kant has not gone far enough, beginning from a point that should be really derived. Rather than determining the origin of his forces, Kant begins with something extended, some definite product of nature's activity, and only then analyzes it into its basic forces. A genuine dynamical philosophy, however, begins from the fundamental activities of nature in itself and then derives its definite products, something extended in space. In other words, matter should be the result and not the starting point of its method. Accordingly, in the *Entwurf,* Schelling derives Kant's repulsive and attractive forces from a Spinozistic foundation, so that they are only the empirical manifestations of the fundamental process by which the *natura naturans* becomes *natura naturata.*

Schelling's postulate of an original opposition in nature is the basis for one of the central and characteristic principles of his *Naturphilosophie:* polarity. This principle was already implicit in the *Ideen,* and it now becomes much more explicit in the *Entwurf.* Polarity comprises several interrelated claims: (1) that every force in nature is limited by an opposing force; (2) that the degree of one force increases or decreases in *inverse* ratio to the other; and (3) that opposing forces are complementary, such that one cannot be conceived without the other. We cannot conceive of one force without the other, Schelling contends, anymore than we can conceive of something positive without something negative, and conversely. It is a fundamental maxim of *Naturphilosophie* that there cannot be any single absolute force in nature, for any force must have a definite magnitude or quantity, and to have such it must be restricted or limited by a countervailing force (II, 49–50, 386). As proof of the omnipresence of polarity throughout nature, Schelling cites such phenomena as magnetism, electricity, and gravity. He insists that all these phenomena are manifestations of the deeper opposition between the basic tendencies of nature.

True to his dynamic principles, Schelling insists that the opposition between forces is not static but active. If nature is absolute productivity, then its opposed forces must be in a constant struggle with one another, where one constantly tries to increase at the expense of the other. If they were to come into a stable or lasting equilibrium, then the activity of nature itself would cease, and everything would freeze into a static product. Absolute productivity therefore must appear as *eternal* conflict, as an infinite series of ceaseless struggles between antagonistic forces (III, 14–15). This means that there cannot be anything really permanent or lasting in nature. The equilibrium of forces that yields a definite product of nature lasts but for an instant, and it then immediately passes over into disequilibrium again. The products of nature are only apparently permanent and enduring, because the ceaseless struggle between their constituent forces means that they are constantly destroyed and recreated (III, 289).

If nature consists in a perpetual conflict between opposing forces, then why is it that its forces stabilize at all, if only for an instant? Why is there ever a balance between them? We cannot explain this momentary stability through the opposition of forces, because it is unceasing; nor can we account for it through some third thing or factor, for originally there is only opposition. The only possible explanation, Schelling then concludes in true Fichtean fashion, is that there is in nature a *striving* to return to its original identity (III, 309). The momentary balance of forces is the result of nature's tendency to achieve its primal state of pure self-identity. According to this theory, then, we must conceive of the activity of nature as a progression from identity, to opposition, and to a new higher identity, which incorporates its opposition. Since, however, the conflict of forces in nature is eternal, this higher identity, which Schelling calls the "indifference point," is only an unattainable goal (III, 312).

Although it cannot resolve its fundamental opposition, the activity of nature approaches, if it does not attain, the ultimate synthesis by unifying opposites *within* this more fundamental opposition. Schelling asks us to imagine an infinite line of two opposing end points, within which there are infinitely many opposing terms (III, 310). The more these opposed terms are synthesized, the more nature approaches its ultimate synthesis. Each of these more specific syntheses, however, is also incomplete, because it becomes opposed on a higher level by another opposing synthesis. This opposition too must be synthesized on yet another higher level, and so on. This progression leads to the creation of a hierarchy (*Stufenfolge*) of stages or levels of development, where each stage is more inclusive than the previous ones. Schelling calls these stages "potencies" (*Potenzen*), because each of them marks a stage of development of living force. Each potency is a synthesis of the products of a lower level, and so it is a product of products.

Granted that we can explain the determinate products of nature only from an opposition between basic forces, granted too that there cannot be any such thing as a single basic force, and granted finally that the opposition between forces is unceasing, the question still remains: Why there are *two* forces in the first place? In short, what justifies Schelling's original postulate of a duality in nature? Here Schelling admits that he has come to the absolute limits of his *Naturphilosophie*, which must presuppose this duality and cannot explain it (III, 18, 102). Although he postulates a common cause of the duality, he does not dare to name it (III, 220). The sheer imponderability of this issue would soon lead Schelling to the most drastic of conclusions: that the problem is irresolvable because it is absurd (4.6.1).

2. The Dynamic Construction of Matter

The dynamic vision of nature sketched in the *Entwurf* and the *Einleitung zu dem Entwurf* remained, at best, general and programmatic. While Schelling postulated the basic forces of nature and their hierarchic organization, he gave only the roughest of outlines about how the basic phenomena of nature were interrelated.[3] He was still far from his central objective: a definitive and detailed account of how all the basic forces of nature—magnetism, electricity, chemistry, light, and life—create matter and form a systematic unity. Schelling moved much closer to this goal in his next major work on *Naturphilosophie*, his 1800 *Allgemeine Deduktion des dynamischen Prozesses*.

The central task of this work was to develop what Schelling called a *dynamic construction* of matter. To construct something dynamically is to show how it arises of necessity from the interrelationship of its basic forces. It is not an *analytic* procedure that begins from the concept of matter and then regresses to its basic forces—Kant's procedure in the *Anfangsgründe*—but a *synthetic* or *genetic* account that starts from basic forces and then shows how matter arises from their interrelation. These moments are not temporal but logical, Schelling explains, because they determine the necessary conditions under which it is possible for anything to occupy space (§30; IV, 25). Thus dynamic construction is to physics as transcendental deduction is to philosophy: it shows the necessity of a phenomenon from the original conditions of matter in general (§63; IV, 75–76).

Schelling's *Allgemeine Deduktion* addresses two central problems in dynamics. The first problem concerns the interrelationship between three basic kinds of phenomena: magnetism, electricity, and chemistry. In the late eighteenth century these phenomena were still being intensively investigated; and though there was a wealth of experimental results, there was still little understanding of the connection between them. The second problem concerns how the dynamic forces fill space, that is, why they fill it to a definite degree, and why they constitute a *three-dimensional* space. It is not sufficient, Schelling argues, to construct matter, the filling of space, from the opposition of forces; it is also necessary to know *how* a space is filled through these forces, and more specifically why they fill space to a determinate extent and in three dimensions.[4]

Schelling attempts to resolve both of these problems with one bold stroke: he argues that each kind of phenomenon (magnetism, electricity, and chemical process) expresses a definite relation of the basic powers of matter to space. More specifically, he tries to demonstrate how each kind of phenomenon corresponds to a definite dimension of space, and how each dimension arises from the interplay of its forces (§4; IV, 4–5). Thus magnetism corresponds to the line (length), electricity to the plane (breadth), and chemistry to the cube (depth). If this deduction can be achieved, then it will show that magnetism, electricity, and chemistry are essential to matter as such; each will be as necessary to a body as its having a length, breadth, and depth in space. Furthermore, it will show the systematic unity or interconnection of these phenomena. Since there is ultimately one dynamic process that creates the line, plane, and cube—these moments are distinguishable only for reflection—there will also be one and the same cause behind magnetism, electricity, and chemistry (§45; IV, 48–49).

The starting point of Schelling's construction is his analysis of the basic forces of nature given in the *Entwurf* and *Einleitung*. He assumes that nature was originally a unity that became divided into two opposing forces (§6; IV, 5–6). One of these is expansive, and directed outward to infinity; the other is retarding, and directed inward to a single point (§§5–6; IV, 5–6). Although opposed to one another, these forces strive to return to the primal identity of nature. This striving expresses itself as a synthesis, an equilibrium, that leads to a common product (§7; IV, 6–7). The schema of primal identity, division, and then identity-in-division provides the general structure of his deduction.

The first stage in the construction of matter shows that the opposition requires synthesis. The forces of attraction and repulsion cannot oppose one another, Schelling contends, unless there is some common point of unity between them (§§8–9; IV, 7–8). If the positive force works from point A to B, and if the negative force moves from B to A, there must be some central point C in which the two forces mutually limit and balance one another. Each force can only limit the other if there is some sphere where each is limited, and also some sphere where one prevails over the other. Hence from A to C the positive predominates, from B to C the negative, while in C their powers equal and annul one another. Both forces thus acting in opposing directions and uniting in a single point give the line A—C—B, and thus the dimension of length (§§8–11; IV, 7–9).

The physical appearance corresponding to length, the first stage of the construction of matter, is magnetism. The three points on the line correspond to the positive and negative poles of the magnet and its neutral central point (§12; IV, 9–10). As empirical proof for this construction, Schelling cites several experiments that show how magnetic forces work lineally or in a straight line (§21; IV, 15–17). That magnetism arises from the dimension of length alone demonstrates, Schelling says, that it is a universal force of nature, and not the result of any special kind of medium (§§14–15; IV, 10–12).

The second stage of the construction of matter is the converse of the first. While the first shows that there must be unity if there is opposition, the second shows that there must be opposition if there is unity. Just as we must conceive of the two forces as united in some common point C, so we must also conceive them as opposed to one another, and so fleeing C. Since the two powers infinitely oppose one another and so flee one another *ad infinitum*, there comes a moment in which they separate from one another. The common point C in the line A—C—B disappears, and so there are two separate forces represented by the two distinct lines AC, CB (§16; IV, 12). Since their shared point C is dissolved, each force returns to its tendency to act in all directions. But this means that for any given direction in which the force acts from A, there will be an infinite number of other possible directions it could act, which form angles to A. From these angles arises the dimension of breadth (§18; IV, 14).

The physical appearance corresponding to the second stage of the construction of matter is electricity. This is because electricity works between distinct bodies and throughout a plane. This is evident empirically, Schelling argues, because bodies become electrified through their entire surface (§22; IV, 19). That electricity corresponds to the dimension of breadth shows that it is as much a universal function of matter as magnetism, and that the physicist should not postulate any special kind of ether or matter to explain it. Just as in their first dimension, as a line, all bodies are magnetic, so in their second dimension, as a plane, they must be electric (§23; IV, 19–20).

The third stage in the construction of matter attempts to show how there can be *both* unity and opposition between the forces. If the first moment shows how the two forces are united, and if the second moment demonstrates how they are separate, the third establishes that there is a synthesis of the two opposing moments, an identity-in-difference. Since each power on its own represents a plane, their synthesis will have to be a common product of both planes, which would be a cube (§34; IV, 31). The cube is the product of the line of the first moment and the plane of the second moment, and so gives the third dimension of space, depth.

After constructing the three dimensions of space, Schelling warns us that this still has not yielded the idea of matter. Matter involves the further idea of a *filled* or *occupied* space; so far, however, we have only a *geometrical,* not a *physical* space. Schelling therefore takes his construction a step further to show how the unity and opposition of forces must give a filled space. The space in which the two powers act should be represented as a continuum of points, where the positive power is limited to a definite degree by the negative power acting on it. The limitation of the positive expansive force to a determinate magnitude is the source of impenetrability, the resistance to any other body occupying a space and the defining characteristic of matter (§35; IV, 32).

Schelling argues that the construction of matter requires not only two forces—the attractive and repulsive—but three. This third force will be a synthesis, a compound of the other two, that unifies *and* separates them. It is necessary to postulate such a force because impenetrability requires that, in every point of space, the two forces are united without destroying one another. This third force is nothing less than gravity.

Against Newton and Kant, Schelling insists that it is a mistake to equate gravity with attractive force alone, since gravity is that which gives a definite magnitude to attractive force, namely, the power of working in proportion to mass (§39; IV, 38). The magnitude of attractive force of a body can be determined not by its counteracting repulsive force, which has to be limited by the attractive force in the first place, but only by the general system of bodies—the mutual relations of attraction and repulsion—of which the body is a part (§§32–39; IV, 28–41). This general system of attraction and repulsion, however, corresponds to gravity.

The physical appearance resulting from gravity is the chemical process. The action of gravity makes it possible for opposing powers to interpenetrate, and so to occupy a common space. The reciprocal interpenetration of bodies in a common space is nothing less than the chemical process itself (§41; IV, 43–44). The chemical process is the moment of unity amid opposition, unifying both magnetism and electricity. Since it unites distinct bodies in the same space, it contains both the unity of magnetism and the difference of electricity (§41; IV, 43–44).

With the deduction of the chemical process Schelling had completed the first two orders or potencies of the dynamic process. The first potency consists in the various relations between attractive and repulsive force, in all those elements necessary for something to be matter at all, that is, to fill a three-dimensional space to a definite degree. This order of nature does not appear to the senses, Schelling maintains, because it determines the necessary conditions under which anything can do so. The second potency consists in magnetism, electricity, and the chemical process, which are the *appearances* of the relationships between the forces on the first level. There is, however, yet a third potency, which is a function of the second, and therefore an appearance of magnetism, electricity, and chemical process. Like any potency, this third order or level must manifest, unify, and reproduce the forces of its lower level. What could this potency be?

Schelling has a short and simple answer: light. Light is the central phenomena of the third potency because it is an appearance of all the phenomena of the second: it is no accident that magnetism, electricity, and the chemical process all manifest themselves as light. What makes light especially suitable for the third potency, however, is that it makes visible or apparent the three-dimensional space of the first and second potencies. It is through light that we recognize that an object has a length, width, and breadth (§43; IV, 45).

With the third potency nature transcends the more material stages of the first and second potencies. Although light makes matter apparent, it is not a form of matter itself because it reveals space without filling it. Light reveals the productive activity of nature, but it does so in such a pure way that it reveals it as an activity, so that it is, as it were, a second-order construction of constructive activity. Light is the final potency before the organic, which is only a higher potency of all the lower ones preceding it. Schelling then goes on to suggest that thinking itself is only a more intellectual and spiritual form of light itself, "the last outbreak (*Ausbruch*) of that which light made the beginning" (§43; IV, 46–47). However fanciful the analogy, it shows the close connection that Schelling wished to forge between the intellectual and the sensible, the mental and the physical. Light is the highest stage of the physical world—or the lowest stage of the mental world—before the appearance of rationality itself. The deduction of light was thus a crucial step in Schelling's "physical explanation of idealism."

3. The Theory of Life

What, more precisely, is Schelling's theory of the relationship between the mind and body? We have seen that, according to his dynamic and organic concept of nature, they are only different degrees of organization and development of living force. We still need a more precise account, however, of how these degrees differ from and relate to one another. For the question arises whether Schelling, in attempting to avoid all forms of dualism, lapsed into a new kind of dualism all his own. If the concept of the organic is so sharply formulated that it differs in kind from the inorganic, then the struggle against dualism has been lost on another front. But there is also another danger Schelling has to avoid: reductivism. He must not escape dualism at the cost of reducing the organic to the inorganic, or conversely. In short, we must examine whether Schelling avoided the Scylla of mechanistic materialism and the Charybdis of dualism after all.

The problem of finding an explanation of life that is neither dualistic nor mechanistic is central to Schelling's *Naturphilosophie*, and he devoted most of *Von der Weltseele* and *Entwurf eines Systems der Naturphilosophie* to it. It is important to recognize, however, that Schelling was not alone in his quest for a middle path between the extremes of dualism and materialism. Such a search was one of the main preoccupations of many natural philosophers in the eighteenth century.[5] For decades thinkers like Lamarck, Buffon, and Maupertuis in France, and Blumenbach, Kielmeyer and Humboldt in Germany, had been looking for a "third approach" to avoid the problems of mechanism and vitalism. Schelling's *Naturphilosophie* was thus only one of many theories in the late eighteenth century that attempted to unify the organic and the inorganic without reducing one to the other.

Schelling's first attempt to develop such a theory appears in the long section entitled 'Über den Ursprung des allgemeinen Organismus' in *Von der Weltseele*. The theory of life Schelling developed here, though crude, vague, and still encumbered with Fichtean assumptions, laid the foundation for much of his later work. It is therefore necessary to consider it in a little detail.

Schelling begins by setting forth three theories about the basis of life: (1) that it lies solely in the animal matter itself, that is, in the chemical composition of the body; (2) that it rests completely outside the animal matter in some vital spirit or force; and (3) that it is contained in opposed principles, one of which is outside the individual and the other inside it. The first view is that of materialism; the second that of vitalism; and the third, a synthesis of the others, is Schelling's own.

Schelling flatly rejects the first or materialist option as the height of *Unphilosophie* because it understands chemical laws purely mechanically as specific instances of the laws of impact and gravity (II, 496–497). Such a theory cannot account for matter itself, let alone life, given that we must explain chemical laws themselves dynamically, according to the laws of attraction and repulsion. But what if we explain chemical laws purely dynamically? In that case Schelling has no objection against biochemistry (498). He does not reluctantly admit, but readily endorses the possibility of an organic chemistry, which explains such phenomena as assimilation and reproduction according to chemical laws (499). Nevertheless, he insists that a complete biochemistry, even when it is understood dynamically, is only a *necessary*, not a sufficient basis for the explanation of life. Rather than viewing life as the product of organic chemistry, Schelling insists we view organic chemistry as the product of life (500).

Whence this reversal in the order of explanation? Why does Schelling reject organic chemistry as a sufficient explanation of life? He gives several reasons, all in the form of questions for the materialist (500–502). First, since all chemical processes come to an end when their forces balance themselves, why is the balance constantly *disturbed* in a living organism? What prevents it from attaining the more stable equilibrium of chemical interaction? Second, if the chemical parts of the body are undergoing constant change, why do the same *kind of changes* (for example, the constriction of the heart muscles) constantly recur in the body? Third, why do the chemical processes of the body remain within the limits of the organism? Why do they not continue to spread their effects in all directions to their surroundings? Why, in short, do the chemical processes of life always reproduce the same matter and form? Fourth, what is the cause of the organic process itself? What brings together just this material to produce just this organization? Here Schelling has in mind a point he makes elsewhere: all chemical explanation assumes the existence of certain basic components, and from them explains the general structure of living matter; but it cannot give the reason for the existence of these components themselves.[6]

Schelling also makes short work of the second or vitalist option, dismissing it because it violates one of the general principles of his dynamism: that of polarity (502). The problem with placing the source of life completely outside the body, he explains, is that it makes the body entirely passive, as if it simply receives vitality like a lump of clay. However, there is nothing in nature that is totally passive, that does not *react* when it is acted on. For every positive principle in the world there is another negative principle opposed to it. Hence the positive principle outside the organic body presupposes a negative principle inside it, so that the body must be at least as important. What the vitalist fails to see, Schelling further explains, is that life does not consist in a specific kind of substance or thing, and still less in a specific kind of force, which somehow miraculously and magically animates the body when added to it; rather, it consists in only a *state* of being, or, more precisely, in a *play of forces (Spiel der Kräfte)* (566).

Schelling's own theory of life attempts to combine the strengths and to avoid the weaknesses of both theories. He maintains that the basis of life is contained in two principles: a *positive* principle that is outside the organic body, and a *negative* principle that is inside it. While the vitalists have rightly stressed the value of the positive principle, the materialists have correctly emphasized the negative one. The vitalists have gone astray in placing the source of life completely *outside* the processes of organic chemistry, while the materialists have been mistaken in placing theirs totally *inside* it (505, 526–527).

What are these positive and negative principles? The positive principle is nothing less than the universal *ether*, the world spirit itself, which is a universal medium spread throughout creation, penetrating every individual thing, both organic and inorganic (505, 567, 569). The negative principle consists in the structure and chemical composition of each organic body, which is distinctive or characteristic of that body. While this positive principle is diffused throughout nature, it only animates those bodies that are capable of fully assimilating or appropriating it. There must be something about the chemical constitution of organic bodies, Schelling says, that makes them more apt to assimilate this vital principle than inorganic bodies (567–568). He likens the action of the positive principle on living things to the action of magnetism or electricity. Just as magnetism and electricity are spread throughout nature, but only act on specific bodies capable of reacting to them, so life is extended throughout all of nature and only is assimilated by bodies that react to it.

Clearly, Schelling's positive and negative principles are based on his general theory of polarity. But it is important to see that they are not specific instances of the positive and negative forces of nature but these universal forces themselves. The positive principle is that indeterminate, centrifugal force that strives to fill infinity, while the negative principle is that determinate, centripetal force that tends toward a single point. While the positive principle is universal, unifying all things, the negative principle is that which makes all things different, distinguishing them from one another. In this still Fichtean phase of his thought, Schelling stresses that this dualism has its origins in transcendental philosophy itself, and that it cannot be demonstrated a posteriori (396).

Schelling sees the positive principle as the proper *cause* and *source* of life, and the negative principle simply as its *condition* (505). The positive principle constantly stimulates and maintains the living processes characteristic of the organic body; yet it is not part of these processes itself (505, 567). The specific role of the positive principle is to *upset* or *disturb* the equilibrium of forces characteristic of the organic body, so that there must be a constant attempt to restore equilibrium (507, 513, 568). What is characteristic of life, in contrast to the merely material, Schelling says, is that life consists in the constant *activity* of unifying and separating forces, of *struggling* toward equilibirium. Purely material things, by contrast, are much more stable, quickly achieving a more lasting equilibrium of elements.

In making such a distinction between the organic and inorganic, Schelling seems to lapse into a new kind of dualism all his own: namely, the organic is that which strives, and the inorganic that which does not strive, toward higher stages of equilibrium. It is possible to read this distinction, however, in a manner consistent with Schelling's general theory while avoiding any sharp dualism between organic and inorganic. More closely considered, the distinction between organic and inorganic *must be* only one of degree rather than kind. It must be a matter merely of the *greater or lesser* degree of equilibrium, or more accurately *duration* of equilibrium, between opposing forces, because Schelling denies the possibility of a complete or lasting balance of forces anywhere in nature.[7] Such an equilibrium is only an ideal, which all things approach but never attain. The difference between the organic and inorganic is then only between *the degree of duration* of their equilibrium of forces: there is more stability in the equilibrium of forces in the inorganic than organic. It is possible to conceive a *continuum* of degrees of stability from the lowest levels of the inorganic to the higher levels of the organic.

The theory of life contained in *Von der Weltseele* raises other serious questions, however, which are less easily solved. The main problem concerns the status of his positive principle, which is somehow transcendental, lying behind and beyond all its physical manifestations. This raises two questions. First, is not the positive principle simply an obscure quality, no better than the *vis animae* of the vitalist? If so, then Schelling seems to violate the principles of his naturalism. Second, does not another kind of dualism arise between the transcendental positive principle and the physical negative principle? In that case, Schelling also infracts the law of continuity, which he invokes to banish all forms of dualism.

Schelling's response to the first question is to stress that the concept of an ultimate power, such as that of the world soul, is a purely limiting concept.

He denies that it it serves as an *explanation* of anything that happens in nature, and even admits that it becomes a stumbling block to enquiry, an obscure quality, if it is given a constitutive status (II, 386, 527). Rather than limiting natural investigation, though, such a concept extends and stimulates it, because it states that anything given inside experience and within the chemical process will not be the *ultimate* ground. It demands that we continue our search for the final cause *ad infinitum*.

It is doubtful, however, that this reply completely solves the difficulty. While Schelling stresses its purely regulative status in some places, he also gives it a constitutive status in others. This becomes fully apparent when he argues that it acts as *a cause* on the organic body, disrupting the equilibrium of forces that would otherwise turn the organic process into something inorganic. If the principle acts as a cause, then it surely must exist.

It is in just its role as a cause of the organic process, however, that Schelling's positive principle flagrantly violates the principles of his own naturalism. If Schelling sometimes insists that his positive principle is *outside* the organic body—serving as a transcendental principle to explain anything within it—he also has to admit that it is in some respects *inside* it, because its activity extends into the realm of phenomena by disturbing the balance of forces. This raises the question of *the mechanism* by which such disruption occurs—a question that Schelling himself sees as a necessary part of all natural explanation.[8] It would seem, however, that the more we discover and determine the nature of this mechanism, the more it will be simply part of the organic process itself. Schelling resists this conclusion, however, because of its materialist consequences.

Schelling does little better in answering the second question. If the positive principle is indeed transcendental, such that no amount of experience ever fully exemplifies it, then the nasty old question arises how a transcendental cause can have an empirical effect. Schelling has no direct response to this problem, and seems unaware of the difficulty. He stresses that his principle does not come from the outside, impressing itself on each individual thing, but that each thing somehow appropriates and forms it in its unique fashion (567). But this does not remove the difficulty that there must be some *interaction* between the positive principle and the body—according to the general principle of polarity—and that interaction between such heterogeneous things, one transcendental and the other empirical, does not seem possible.

In the end, then, the theory of life in *Von der Weltseele* was vulnerable to objections of obscurantism and dualism—the very problems the theory was designed to avoid. Yet such difficulties did not daunt Schelling. The theory of life in *Von der Weltseele* was only his first approach to the issues, and he continued to think about them in succeeding years.

4. Irritability, Sensibility, and World Soul

Schelling returned to the problem of the nature of life in his next major work, his *Erster Entwurf eines Systems der Naturphilosophie,* which appeared around Easter 1799. Here again he attempted to steer a middle path between materialism and vitalism, and again he tried to formulate a naturalistic yet nonreductivistic account of life. Nevertheless, Schelling's new theory differs in important respects from that of *Von der Weltseele.* Schelling now refined and reformulated his earlier position, utilizing the concepts of irritability and sensibility of eighteenth-century physiology.[9] But, while the theory gains in clarity and precision, some fundamental problems remain.

Schelling explains materialism and vitalism in different terms than those in the earlier work. He now says that there are two opposing systems about the nature of life, which he calls *physiological materialism* and *physiological immaterialism.* According to the physiological materialist, the activity of an organism is determined entirely by its passivity, by the effect of external causes acting on it. The influence of these external causes happens solely according to the laws that govern matter, that is, according to the interchange between attractive and repulsive forces. All the different phenomena of life are functions of the different chemical elements and the different ratios between their attractive and repulsive forces (III, 74–78). This biochemical explanation of life is not merely mechanical but also dynamical, Schelling says, because chemical interactions take place according to the ratios between their forces (74n1).

According to the physiological immaterialist, however, the passivity of an organism is determined completely by its activity, by the vital force assimilating and transforming material and stimuli from outside (78–81). The immaterialist stresses the extent to which the organism *reacts* to the stimuli acting on it. He denies that there is any such thing as a pure effect of matter on an organism, since both the kind and degree of action on an organism depends on the kind and degree of its reaction. The immaterialist contends that, in assimilating and transforming inorganic matter in its unique manner, the organism disrupts and changes the laws of chemistry that apply to inanimate matter. This is possible only in virtue of a *sui generis* principle in the organism, which is an immaterial vital force (*Lebenskraft*).

Seeking the *via media* between these extremes, Schelling argues that both materialism and immaterialism have expressed but one aspect of the truth. The materialist is correct in attempting to explain life according to natural causes; but he goes astray in reducing it down to *chemical* causes alone. While he is right in stressing the importance of external causes, he is blind to the internal activity of the organism itself, which reacts on these causes and makes them conform to its own nature. Conversely, the immaterialist is correct in resisting reduction to chemical causes, and in seeing some higher cause that organizes and controls chemistry itself; but he makes the mistake of thinking that his vital force is supernatural and somehow changes the laws of nature. Though the immaterialist is right to stress the importance of the organism's activity, he fails to see that chemical causes are central to life itself.

Schelling attempts to synthesize both systems by stressing the *interdependence* of receptivity and passivity. Both materialist and immaterialist fail to see that activity and passivity are interdependent, and that an organism can be active only to the extent that it is passive, and conversely. Schelling stresses the interdependence of passivity and activity chiefly because it follows from his general principle of polarity. He explains that we should conceive of the action of the external world on the organism, and the reaction of the organism on the external world, as *complementary forces* that depend on one another. Just as we cannot have a negative force without a positive, so we cannot have passivity without negativity. Life consists in the *synthesis* of both forces, in the constant *struggle* to find some mean between them (85–86).

Schelling thinks that the fundamental concept to understand the interdependence of passivity and activity in an organism is excitability or irritability (*Erregbarkeit*). A central theme of eighteenth-century physiology, irritability usually designated the capacity of certain parts of the body (for example, the muscles) to contract when stimulated. Schelling latched onto this concept because it seemed to express how an organism consists in both activity and passivity, in a capacity both to receive and react to external stimuli. Irritability seemed to be the perfect concept for his middle path between physiological materialism and immaterialism.

Schelling gives credit to the Scottish physiologist John Brown (1735–1788) for first recognizing the full importance of the phenomenon of irritability.[10] It was Brown, he says, who made irritability the distinguishing characteristic of life, who saw that activity and passivity are complementary, and who held that, though irritability is not reducible to chemistry, it should still be explicable in natural terms (90–91n, 153). Schelling recognizes that, to a certain extent, Brown anticipated his own position, because he too attempted to avoid the extremes of both materialism and vitalism. Nevertheless, Schelling thinks that Brown did not go far enough, for he could not explain the causes of irritability itself.[11] If he sketched the possibility of a third position between vitalism and materialism, Brown did not provide it with a proper foundation. This is indeed Schelling's central task in the *Entwurf*, where he attempts to provide an a priori deduction of the concept of irritability itself.

The starting point for Schelling's deduction of irritability is his analysis of the organism into two aspects or functions (146–148). There is the higher function, the organism as subject, which *reacts* to external stimuli, and is only *mediately* affected by them; and there is the lower function, the organism as object, which *receives* the external stimuli, and is *immediately* affected by them. We can explain the lower function simply from the influence of chemical causes; but this still does not account for the higher function, which *controls* and *directs* these chemical causes. Such a cause, reacting on and controlling all the chemistry of the body, cannot be a chemical cause itself (149–150). All that chemistry explains is the specific cases or instances of irritation, Schelling argues, but it cannot explain the existence of the power of irritability itself.

What, then, is the cause of this power? Schelling locates the source of an organism's activity in its *sensibility* (*Sensibilität*), which he defines in terms of its characteristic way of organizing and responding to stimuli (169). It is sensibility that constantly disturbs and restores the balance of forces in an organism, preventing it from ending in that more stable characteristic of matter alone (162).[12]

No less than irritability, sensibility was a central concept of eighteenth-century physiology. It was usually understood to be a higher function than irritability, involving not only the physical reaction to a stimulus, but also sensation—feeling or, at the highest level, conscious notice of a stimulus. The great physiologist Albrecht von Haller (1708–1777) distinguished between irritability and sensibility: while irritability was regarded as a function of the muscles, sensibility was seen as a function of the nervous system. But Haller's distinction was contested by Théophile de Bordeu (1722–1776) and other physiologists of the Montpellier school, who had argued that all living matter is sensible and that irritability is only a special function of sensibility.[13] In making sensibility into the source of irritability, Schelling was now following—consciously or not—Bordeu and the Montpellier school.[14]

It would seem that we can push our enquiry further by asking: What is it about sensibility that makes it function this way? But here, Schelling says, we come to the limits of all empirical investigation. We cannot determine anything about the nature of sensibility as such from experience, he argues, because, as the condition of all organic activity, it does not appear in experience itself (159, 169, 190–191). There should be no doubt that we can investigate sensibility according to natural laws because we can analyze its *products* or *effects* into their chemical elements; but we cannot determine anything about the source of the activity—what creates the products—according to these laws, since it is the origin of all activity in nature.

It is at this point that Schelling's theory about the first cause of life becomes very metaphysical. Where the path of empirical investigation ends, speculation begins. Following the central theme of *Von der Weltseele* Schelling maintains that the source of sensibility is one and the same as that of all nature (160). The origin of sensibility is nothing less than the single productive force active throughout nature: the world soul itself. The sensibility of individual plants and animals, and even of inorganic things, is only a modification of the sensibility of the universal organism (160n2, 190–191). What creates and maintains life in every individual thing is simply its participation in the soul of nature, the *natura naturans*. All particular things are simply modes or functions of the growth and development of this original productive activity, corresponding to the various stages in its differentiation and growth.

In the *Entwurf*, unlike *Von der Weltseele*, the postulate of a world soul assumed a much more straightforward constitutive status. There was no longer any pretense of regulative constraint: as the animating source of life in every individual, the world soul, the *natura naturans*, simply had to exist. This raised anew, however, the difficult question of how the universal animating force, which transcends experience, acts on or within specific organisms in experience itself. Schelling again faced the difficult question of how the transcendental and empirical, the infinite and finite, interact with one another. The classical dualism between the mental and physical, it seemed, had now been replaced by a new more metaphysical dualism between the transcendental and empirical, the infinite and finite.

5. The Mental and Physical as Potencies

In both *Von der Weltseele* and the *Entwurf* Schelling was struggling to find a theory to encompass organic and inorganic nature, a common expression for both worlds, which would unlock the secret to the relationship between the mental and physical, the subjective and objective. Schelling's goal was to avoid the extremes of both dualism and materialism, to find a common concept of the mental and physical, the subjective and objective, that would not reduce one term to the other. The positions Schelling took in these works was very tentative, and he did not cease to think about the underlying problem in later works.

In both the *Entwurf* and *Von der Weltseele* Schelling failed to achieve his goal. The problem was that, to avoid materialism, he regarded the cause of life as something transcendental; but he thus placed the cause of life outside the sphere of experience itself, and so introduced another dualism between the transcendental and the empirical. All the problems Kant once had about accounting for the interaction between these domains returned to haunt him.

After writing the *Entwurf*, however, Schelling began to eliminate every vestige of the transcendental from his *Naturphilosophie*. "The physical explanation of idealism" envisaged at the close of the *Allgemeine Deduktion* would derive the highest forms of self-consciousness from the order of nature itself (§63; IV, 76). Now the transcendental dimension began to disappear, and the vestigial dualism haunting the theory of life in *Von der Weltseele* and *Entwurf* was finally removed.

It is not surprising, then, that in the *Einleitung zu dem Entwurf* and in the *Allgemeine Deduktion* itself Schelling approached the whole problem of the relationship between the organic and inorganic from a new more promising direction. The best way of explaining this relationship, he now believed, was by the concept of a potency (*Potenz*) (III, 317–326). This concept had already appeared in his earlier works, but now Schelling developed it in more detail, applying it to the problem of life itself.

The essence of Schelling's new theory is that the organic is only the higher potency of the inorganic.[15] In other words, the organic is the higher degree of organization and development of the inorganic. What is implicit, inchoate, and disparate on a lower level or potency becomes explicit, organized, and unified on the higher one. Since a higher potency unifies the factors of a lower potency, it reproduces them and so is not completely distinct from them.

The question of the relationship between the organic and the inorganic now becomes a question of how a higher potency relates to a lower. The difference between the organic and inorganic is now only one of degree rather than kind since both differ only in terms of their degree of organization and development, and not in terms of their being distinct kinds of substance. Both are one and the same substance—living force—that has developed and organized itself in different degrees, first as the inorganic phenomena of matter and then as the organic phenomena of life.

With the concept of a potency Schelling finally arrived at his middle path between dualism and materialism. There is no dualism since the higher potency includes and presupposes the lower; but there is also no materialism because, as a greater degree of organization and development, the higher potency cannot be reduced down to the lower. The middle path is based on the potencies differing only in form but not in content or substance: they are only different kinds of manifestation of one and the same thing, namely, living force.

Schelling sometimes put this point—the identity in substance but the difference in form—in terms of a distinction between nature as subject and as object (III, 325–326). Nature as subject is the single activity that is controlling, directing, and organizing itself throughout all of its potencies; but nature as object consists in these different potencies themselves, which are indeed distinct from one another. The distinction between nature as subject and as object is therefore one between nature as productivity and nature as product, or, as Spinoza put it, between *natura naturans* and *natura naturata*. Now the organic and the inorganic are one and the same insofar we consider nature as subject, but they are different from one another insofar as we view nature as object.

The fact that the higher potency differs from the lower only in form, but not in substance, makes Schelling's theory appear like a form of epiphenomenalism. There are many materialists who would grant the mental a *sui generis* status apart from the material; but such status is derivative and caused by the material. But Schelling's theory of potencies is the very opposite of epiphenomenalism, and more accurately described as form of holism. Rather than giving priority to the material parts of an organism and seeing the whole only as their product, it regards the whole as prior to its parts, and indeed as the source of their activity. Here it is important to recall Schelling's view that mechanism is the result of teleology, and not conversely.

Seen from a broad historical perspective, Schelling's theory of the relationship between the mental and the physical is a synthesis of the vitalism of Leibniz with the monism of Spinoza. From Leibniz, Schelling took the idea that the essence of matter consists in living force; from Spinoza, he borrowed the concept of nature as a *natura naturans,* a single power and productive force. Hence his *Naturphilosophie* was the monism of Spinoza spelled in vitalistic terms, the vitalism of Leibniz stretched to the universe as a whole. In this manner Schelling resurrected the two great dogmatic philosophers, whose ideas now seemed more relevant than ever as the only means of resolving the outstanding problematic of the Kantian philosophy.[16] The rebirth of metaphysics was thus, for Schelling, not a relapse into dogmatism but part of the immanent development of the critical philosophy itself.

CHAPTER 6

Schelling's Absolute Idealism

1. The Blinding Light of 1801

All the growing forces in Schelling's intellectual development in 1799 and 1800—his sympathy for Spinozism, his belief in the autonomy and omnipresence of nature, and his argument for the priority of the *Naturphilosophie* over the *Wissenschaftslehre*—came to their culmination in his *Darstellung meines Systems*, which was published in May 1801.[1] Schelling now naturalizes the absolute, or he absolutizes nature, so that the absolute is identical with the universe itself. This was the final triumph of *Naturphilosophie*, which had now become identical to the standpoint of reason itself, representing the *entire* principle of subject–object identity. *Naturphilosophie* was no longer just the equal partner to transcendental philosophy, still less the handmaiden to the *Wissenschaftslehre*. Rather, it had usurped the title of *philosophia prima*, of which the *Wissenschaftslehre* is only the result.

With the *Darstellung meines Systems* Schelling finally comes into his own. True to its title, this work represents *his* philosophy in contrast to Fichte's. While Schelling did not exclude the possibility of Fichte's still agreeing with him,[2] he also made it plain that he was no longer toeing a master's line. If the possessive adjective in the title was not a formal act of repudiation, it was still a declaration of independence.[3]

Schelling himself regarded the *Darstellung meines Systems* as the fulfillment of all his previous work. He later wrote that it was the beginning of his true and proper system, and that it was the result of a great illumination.[4] In the preface to the work he gives us some hint about the nature of this inspiration. For several years now, he explains, he had expounded one and the same philosophy from two sides, from the angles of both transcendental and natural philosophy (IV, 107). He now puts forward the single system that these different expositions have presupposed but not articulated. Transcendental and natural philosophy are merely opposed poles of the single true system; and with his present exposition he now finds himself in "the indifference point," which each has constructed from opposing directions (108).

Judging from the preface, Schelling's "great light" seems to have consisted in the insight that the absolute is neutral, the indifference point of the subjective and objective. After that illumination, all his earlier work seemed like complementary expositions of this absolute standpoint. The absolute could no longer be merely the ego, as Fichte once thought, because as the pure identity of subject and object, it is the center of both transcendental and natural philosophy, and so no more subject than object, no more ego than nature. This interpretation is not only suggested by the preface to the *Darstellung*; some forty years later, Schelling explained the development of the *Identitätssystem* in similar terms.[5]

But, in one respect, this explanation is surprising and misleading. The problem is that Schelling again seems to demote *Naturphilosophie* to the status of a subordinate standpoint within his system, and he says—quite falsely—that he has always seen it as one of the opposed poles of philosophy. What Schelling's explanation omits, of course, is the remarkable development of his doctrines in 1799 and early 1800 when *Naturphilosophie* gained *priority* over transcendental philosophy. The very dialectic of that development meant that the standpoint of *Naturphilosophie* became that of the indifference point itself and not merely one subordinate standpoint within it. I will attempt to unravel this apparent inconsistency in the next section.

Schelling's account of his intellectual development is misleading for another reason. He wrote that his present system did not represent any change in his views, but that he had it "always before his eyes" (IV, 107–108). It was as if his entire intellectual growth had been continuous and consistent, a constant and sure progress toward the development of his current doctrines. This was another oversimplification, a shortsighted attempt to see purpose and order in a career notable for its protean changes. It was indeed legitimate to see some pattern in his past, to see some anticipation of the principle of subject–object identity. Thus the *Briefe über Dogmatismus und Kritizismus* foresaw a critique of pure reason above both dogmatism and idealism; and the *Einleitung zu dem Entwurf* conceived transcendental and natural philosophy as opposing poles of the principle of subject–object identity. But, in considering only these points, Schelling took an anachronistic and selective view of his own past; he was abstracting from many other phases of his development that did not fit such a tidy pattern. He was willfully ignoring, for example, his earlier view of *Naturphilosophie* as an applied part of transcendental philosophy, his preference for idealism over dogmatism in *Vom Ich als Princip* and in the *Abhandlungen*, and his statement in the preface to the *System des transcendental Idealismus* that, because of their complementarity, transcendental and natural philosophy would *not* be able to form a unity. The path toward the *Darstellung meines Systems* was not always the smooth transition, the organic development, that Schelling wanted it to be. Rather, it demanded some change from his former views, not only in the weaker sense of *reformulating* them but also in the stronger sense of *renouncing* them.

2. Objective Idealism

The *Darstellung meines Systems* has an important place in the history of German idealism. It is the first *systematic exposition* of 'objective' or 'absolute' idealism, the first *technical exposition* of the '*En kai pan*,' that pantheistic *credo* that had become so popular in Germany in the 1790s. What Hölderlin, Schlegel, Novalis, and Hülsen had left in fragments—what they regarded as a mystical insight transcending conceptual articulation—Schelling would now try to rationalize and systematize.[6] Like Hegel after him, Schelling complained about the lack of rigor and form among his contemporaries. It is not enough to leave the insight into the one and all on the level of intuition and feeling, he argued, because it is also necessary to objectify and embody it, to give it a strict scientific form.[7] Some kind of intuition is necessary to *begin* philosophy, of course, but it is not its resting point and should never replace the business of conceptual elaboration. Hence the method of the *Darstellung meines Systems* would be the most rigorous possible: it would proceed *more geometrico* like Spinoza, starting from self-evident propositions and definitions and then proving every proposition from preceding ones. The result was a disciplined parade of numbered paragraphs, an exposition as dry and routine as anything from Christian Wolff.

True to its pantheistic *credo*, Schelling's treatise is essentially a defense of a *monistic rationalism* or a *rationalistic monism*. The whole work is a demonstration of three fundamental propositions: that there is a single, indivisible substance, which is identical with the universe itself; that this substance does not transcend reason but is identical with the fundamental law of reason, which is the principle of identity, $A = A$; and that the principle of identity expresses the complete unity of the subjective and objective, the ideal and real, the mental and physical. The first part of the work (§§1–50) consists in an argument for these three propositions, while the second part (§§51–159) attempts to develop the details of *Naturphilosophie* from them.

The obvious historical ancestor for Schelling's rationalistic and monistic vision of the world was, of course, Spinoza. Sure enough, in his preface Schelling pays explicit homage to him. He explains that it is not only the method but the doctrines of Spinoza that are closest to his own. Schelling had now come full circle. Although in his Fichtean days he once told Hegel "*Ich bin Spinozist geworden!*," that was more an expression of his sympathy for Spinoza than a statement of doctrinal affiliation; then Schelling's goal was to write the *antithesis* of Spinoza's *Ethica*, the main work of dogmatism. Now, however, Schelling considers Spinoza the apostle of the principle of subject–object identity itself, the first spokesmen for that broader view of the universe that encompasses the *unity* of the subjective and objective, the truth of *both* dogmatism and criticism.[8]

Although the *Darstellung meines Systems* is the first system of absolute idealism, it is striking that Schelling refuses to discuss the whole issue of idealism versus realism. The reason for his resistance to enter into this quagmire is sensible enough: "for what is idealism and realism, and what is also a possible third system of both, is just that which is unclear and needs to be investigated" (109). He insists that the terms 'idealism' and 'realism' have only the meaning that he assigns to them in the context of his system, and that their proper sense will emerge only at the end of his exposition. It is somewhat disappointing, therefore, that the work does not contain any concluding definitions or final summary. The reader simply has *to infer* Schelling's meaning from the various contexts in which he uses his terms.

Despite his refusal to give an introductory account, Schelling does not hesitate to suggest how his idealism differs from Fichte's. These are only *possible* differences, he insists, because he does not want to beg any questions in advance. Accordingly, his explanation is very schematic: while Fichte uses the term 'idealism' in a *subjective* sense, he uses it in an *objective* one. In its subjective meaning idealism is the statement that the ego is everything (*das Ich sey Alles*); in its objective meaning it signifies just the converse: that everything is the ego (*Alles sey = Ich*) and there is nothing but the ego (IV, 109). Schelling says that these views are clearly opposed, but that both can be described as 'idealism.'

These remarks are cryptic and confusing, but their general sense is plain enough if we place them in the context of Schelling's polemic against Fichte.[9] Both statements equate the ego with everything, which is what makes them both forms of idealism. What makes them opposed to one another is the position of subject and predicate. In the subjective meaning the ego is the subject and the universe is its predicate; in the objective meaning the universe is the subject and the ego the predicate. The logical form is crucial because, in eighteenth-century logic, the subject stands as the *reason* or *ground* for its predicate. The conflict between idealism and realism then concerns which term is more fundamental: the universe or the ego? In making the universe the subject rather than predicate in his formula for objective idealism, Schelling was reversing the order of logical priority from subjective idealism. The universe was now the ground or explanans of the ego, and not conversely, as in the *Wissenschaftslehre*.

Another formulation for the difference between subjective and objective idealism appears in an earlier work of Schelling's, his *Einleitung zu dem Entwurf eines Systems der Naturphilosophie*, which he wrote shortly before the *Darstellung meines Systems* (III, 272). Here Schelling does not explicitly use the terms 'subjective' and 'objective' idealism, and his main concern is only to explain the difference between transcendental and natural philosophy. Still, he makes a contrast very similar to that which appears in the preface to the *Darstellung*, though he now replaces the term 'I' with 'reason' (*Vernunft*). He explains that both these disciplines attempt to explain the *rationality* of nature, that is, its conformity to law or systematic order. But there is a fundamental difference between them: whereas transcendental philosophy sees rationality as the product of the activity of the ego alone, natural philosophy regards it as the result of the activity of nature itself. *Naturphilosophie* ascribes rationality to nature because it holds that nature acts for ends, that it is not purely mechanical but also organic, having a systematic structure developed from its own intelligent activity. According to the view of natural philosophy, then, rationality is inherent in nature itself, implicit within its purposive activity, and not simply imposed on it by the understanding.

If we read Schelling's doctrine of objective idealism in this context, then it essentially consists in the central thesis of *Naturphilosophie*. Objective idealism is then the view that reason is *within* nature itself, that its rationality is not created by the transcendental ego alone but is inherent in the purposive activity of nature itself. The difference between subjective and objective idealism then reflects two opposing theories about the *ontological status* of reason itself, or about the sources and conditions of its existence. The main question at stake between these forms of idealism is whether rationality is something that we create and impose on the world, or whether it is something that exists within the world itself and is reflected in our own activity. Is human reason the lawgiver of nature, as Kant maintains, or is nature its own lawgiver, so that it is autonomous, as Schelling claims? That, in short, is the issue between subjective and objective idealism.

These formulations of objective idealism reflect Schelling's intellectual development around 1800 when he gave *Naturphilosophie* priority over the *Wissenschaftslehre*. They both equate objective idealism with the standpoint of *Naturphilosophie*, which begins with the independent reality of nature and derives the ego from it (rather than conversely). The first formulation makes the universe the fundamental term and the ego derived, corresponding to Schelling's "physical proof of idealism," which attempts to derive the self-consciousness of the ego from the laws of nature. The second formulation places reason within nature itself rather than the ego, corresponding to Schelling's claim that the principle of subject–object identity exists properly and primarily within nature itself and only secondarily in the self-consciousness of the ego.

How, though, do these formulations square with Schelling's frequent statements that the system of identity gives *equal standing* to both transcendental and natural philosophy? If we take these statements seriously—as we must—then the meaning of objective idealism should comprise *both* the idealism of the *Wissenschaftslehre* and the realism of *Naturphilosophie*. This reading of objective idealism as a *synthesis* of idealism and realism seems to be confirmed by Schelling's statement in the preface to the *Darstellung* that he has now arrived at the indifference point of transcendental and natural philosophy. It acquires even more plausibility when we consider how, in his later works, Schelling continues to describe idealism and realism as subordinate perspectives within the standpoint of absolute identity.[10]

The source of the confusion rests with the very terms Schelling warns us against, namely 'realism' and 'idealism.' These terms are ambiguous because they can describe the standpoint of absolute identity itself or the subordinate perspectives contained within it. The standpoint of absolute identity can be described as *realism* because it maintains that the absolute is the universe as a whole, the one and all, of which consciousness is only one mode; it can also be regarded as *idealism* because it sees the absolute as reason, as the idea of all ideas, and holds that everything is a manifestation of it. There is also, however, a realism and idealism *within* or *subordinate* to this standpoint because there are complementary manifestations or appearances of the absolute, and realism and idealism each describe one of them. Realism considers its appearances from the infinite to the finite, from unity to difference; and idealism treats its appearance from the finite back to the infinite, from totality back into unity.[11] Schelling himself would later draw attention to these ambiguities by distinguishing between an absolute and relative idealism, and a general and more specialized *Naturphilosophie*.[12]

If we consider these ambiguities, then Schelling's position is perfectly consistent. When he says that *Naturphilosophie* represents the absolute standpoint itself he is *not* denying that there is another kind of subordinate standpoint within it that can be described as idealism. He is simply making two claims, both of them perfectly compatible: that the absolute is the universe as a whole, nature in itself, and that it appears in two forms, one of which can be described from an idealistic standpoint and another from a realistic one.

The main point at issue between subjective and objective idealism is where we place the principle of subject–object identity: whether in nature or in the ego itself? In either case we can speak about two aspects or manifestations of the principle. If subject–object identity is in nature, then the subjective and objective, the mental and physical, are different attributes or appearances of a single universal substance. If, however, subject-object identity is in the ego, then the subjective and objective, the mental and physical, are different attributes or appearances of a single subject.

The crucial point to keep in mind, however, is that the realism and naturalism of *Naturphilosophie* does describe the absolute standpoint itself, for the absolute is now the universe as a whole, nature in itself, the *natura naturans*, which subsists apart from consciousness and explains its very possibility according to necessary laws. Relative to this realism and naturalism the idealism of the *Wissenschaftslehre* assumes a merely subordinate status as the *relative* idealism within the absolute standpoint.

All this brings us to a significant conclusion: objective idealism is not a *synthesis* of the *Wissenschaftslehre* and *Naturphilosophie* after all. Rather, it is nothing less than the standpoint of the *Naturphilosophie* itself, an absolute or transcendental realism and naturalism.[13] Schelling calls his position *objective* idealism precisely because of this realism and naturalism, and precisely because it places reason outside the subject as the structure of the universe as a whole or nature in itself. It is indeed no accident that he later virtually identifies the standpoint of *Naturphilosophie* with absolute idealism itself.[14]

3. The Kantian–Fichtean Interpretation

It should be obvious by now that Schelling's absolute idealism—and Hegel's in the years of his collaboration with Schelling—cannot be the same as the transcendental or critical idealism of Kant and Fichte. In their early Jena years, Schelling and Hegel were indeed very anxious to distinguish their doctrine from Kant's and Fichte's, and they were tireless in their attempts to spell out their differences with them. These amount to two fundamental distinctions. First, they contrast their *objective* idealism with the *subjective* idealism of Kant and Fichte. Kant's and Fichte's idealism is *subjective* because it regards reason as the product of the transcendental subject, or because it limits subject–object identity to transcendental self-consciousness. Schelling and Hegel maintain that their idealism is objective, however, because it sees reason as the intelligible structure of reality itself, and subject–object identity as the archetypical structure of the absolute itself. In short, objective idealism holds that reason is not created by or imposed on reality by the transcendental subject but is inherent in nature itself; it sees the rational or the intelligible not as the form of consciousness but as the form of being itself. Second, they distinguish their *absolute* idealism from the *relative* idealism of Kant and Fichte. Relative idealism attempts to derive the objective from the subjective, the real from the ideal, as if one appearance or aspect of the absolute has priority over the other; but absolute idealism maintains that the subjective and objective, the ideal and the real, are only different appearances or aspects of the absolute, and that both have an equal and independent standing. For this reason, Schelling and Hegel sometimes claim that Kant's and Fichte's idealism is still caught in the realm of appearances.[15]

If we consider the full implications of both these points, it becomes clear that Schelling's and Hegel's absolute idealism, at least in its initial formulation from 1801 to 1803, is not even a *radicalized* version of Kant's and Fichte's idealism. According to this neo-Kantian interpretation, absolute idealism is transcendental idealism *without* the thing-in-itself and the given manifold, and *with* the unity of apperception universalized, so that it refers to the single transcendental subject within all individual and empirical subjects.[16] In Schelling's and Hegel's terms, however, this would still be a form of subjective or relative idealism, because it sees the subject as the source of reason, and because it attempts to derive or reduce the objective down to the subjective, one of the mere aspects or appearances of the absolute. It makes no difference here if this subject is conceived as universal and transcendental rather than individual and empirical, or indeed if it is considered absolute or infinite instead of finite; the result is still the same because this would be to make the absolute subjective or ideal when Schelling insists that it is neither subjective nor objective, neither ideal nor real, but the *indifference point* of both.

The main stumbling block of the neo-Kantian interpretation is that absolute idealism involves a form of *transcendental* realism and naturalism completely at odds with the Kantian–Fichtean tradition. This is not an *empirical* realism and naturalism, which is valid only from *within* the absolute standpoint and limited to only one of its partial perspectives, namely, its real or natural pole where the infinite appears as the finite. Rather, absolute idealism includes a *higher* realism and naturalism, because it equates the absolute with the universe as a whole, and because it begins with the independent reality of nature to derive *transcendental* self-consciousness.

This higher realism and naturalism is especially evident from Schelling's identification of the absolute standpoint with *Naturphilosophie*. This identification was not a passing moment in Schelling's development, a mere stage on the way toward the system of identity, because it reappears frequently in his writings from 1801 to 1804. Its persistence is apparent in several respects. First, Schelling continues to identify the absolute with nature in itself or the *natura naturans*. This is his formula for the absolute in itself, the indifference pole of the subjective and objective, and not only one pole or appearance of the absolute.[17] Second, Schelling continues to identify the doctrine of absolute idealism with the standpoint of *Naturphilosophie*, which, he says, expresses not one side but the whole principle of subject–object identity.[18] Third, Schelling does not abandon but develops in detail his program for the *"physical explanation of idealism,"* which will derive the self-consciousness of the Kantian–Fichtean 'I' from the powers of nature as a whole.[19] It is especially in this regard, in this attempt to develop a naturalistic account of the Kantian–Fichtean 'I,' that Schelling breaks most sharply from the Kantian–Fichtean tradition. His aim is to reintegrate the transcendental 'I' into nature, to take it outside its self-sufficient noumenal realm and to show how its reason is the expression and manifestation of the rationality inherent in nature itself.

All this does not mean, of course, that the absolute is somehow objective, completely transcending the realm of consciousness, and existing apart from and prior to it. This would be a serious mistake because Schelling and Hegel made it one of their chief aims to combat the illusion that the absolute is somehow beyond us, existing on its own in some supernatural and heavenly realm. This was one form, and indeed the worst, of that dualism between the subjective and objective which it was the central purpose of the philosophy of identity to overcome. They were explicit that, as the whole of all reality, the absolute had to include the realm of consciousness within itself, and that this realm is indeed one of its necessary manifestations. They even give pride of place to the Kantian–Fichtean 'I' by making it the highest potency, the greatest organization and development of all the powers of nature. The 'I' was indeed that point where the absolute became self-conscious in the finite world, "the magical formula with which the world reveals itself."[20] But for all its importance—even though it is the highest manifestation of the absolute—the 'I' is still only *one* of its manifestation. It is indeed the *terminus ad quem* and culmination of the *Identitätsystem*, but not its *terminus a quo* or foundation.

4. The Interpretation of Subject–Object Identity

Some of Schelling's accounts of absolute idealism virtually equate it with the doctrine of subject–object identity, the principle that the absolute is neither subjective nor objective but the complete indifference of both. What did Schelling mean by this principle? And what role did it perform in his *Identitätssystem?*

We have already seen that the purpose of this doctrine is to surmount that dualism between the noumenal and the phenomenal, the intellectual and empirical, the subjective and objective, which had been such a problem in the Kantian tradition. But to say this much is not to say very much. It is not enough to say that the theory surmounts dualism, as if it were sufficient simply to postulate the identity of the subjective and objective; we need to know *how* this principle overcomes this dualism, and indeed what right someone has to postulate such an identity in the first place. In short, our task is to be more precise about how Schelling thinks that his principle explains the unity of the ideal and real, the mental and physical. What model of explanation does this principle apply to the relationship between the mental and physical?

This question goes to the very heart of the *Identitätssystem*. Unfortunately, there is no simple answer to it. It is in just this respect that Schelling's doctrine becomes very vague and complex. There are three possible interpretations of Schelling's principle, corresponding to three different models of the unity of the subjective and objective. Each of these interpretations finds some support in the texts, but there is also some evidence that counts against them. What is worse, these interpretations are in some respects incompatible.

The Dual-Aspect Doctrine

According to this interpretation, to say that the absolute consists in subject–object identity means that the subjective and objective, the ideal and real, or the mental and physical are simply different *attributes, perspectives, or explanations* of one and the same thing. This means that there is no *real* opposition between these terms in the sense that it does not describe different properties of reality itself, let alone distinct substances. Rather, there is only an *ideal* opposition in the sense that it exists only for reflection, for our way of explaining things. The principle of subject–object identity is then something like a cosmic dual-aspect doctrine, according to which idealism and naturalism, the mental and physical, are incommensurable but equally valid ways of explaining the world. This kind of dual-aspect doctrine differs from that prevalent in the philosophy of mind only in its subject matter: the whole universe rather than just a single person.

This interpretation seems to follow immediately from several characteristic Schellingian doctrines: that the absolute is pure identity, that all opposition is purely ideal, and that the whole absolute can be described according to the principles of idealism or realism.

The historical antecedent of this doctrine is Spinoza's theory that the mental and the physical are different attributes of a single universal substance (at least on a subjectivist reading of Spinoza's concept of an attribute). It is striking evidence in behalf of this interpretation, then, that Schelling explicitly endorses Spinoza's doctrine, and sometimes uses his language of attributes.[21] When one considers that Spinoza's distinction between thought and extension belongs only to the *natura naturata*, and that he regarded extended and thinking substance as one and the same thing viewed under different attributes, Schelling argues, then one must recognize that Spinoza did hold that the absolute is the unity of ideal and real.

There are, however, difficulties with this reading, which does not apply easily to all of Schelling's texts. First, Spinoza's dual-aspect doctrine forbids any interaction between the mental and the physical, which are regarded as completely independent forms of explanation of one and the same thing.

This is a residual form of dualism in Spinoza's doctrine that Schelling does not want to share. The whole point of his *Naturphilosophie* is to explain the *interaction* between the mental and physical by regarding each as an *expression* or *embodiment* of the other. Second, Schelling sometimes writes as if idealism and realism both describe real aspects, appearances, or "uniformations" (*Ein-bildungen*)[22] of the absolute itself, so that they are not only different forms of explanation of one and the same thing (as they are on at least one reading of Spinoza's attributes). Third, by 1804 Schelling became critical of Spinoza's dual-aspect doctrine on the classical grounds that it cannot explain the origin or necessity of its modes.[23]

The Hylozistic Interpretation

According to this reading, the principle of subject–object identity of the *Identitätssystem* must be understood in the context of Schelling' general theory of life in his *Naturphilosophie*. The principle of subject–object identity then simply states that the subjective and objective, or the mental and physical, are essentially one and the same in themselves because they are only different manifestations, expressions, and embodiments of a single reality— namely, living force. The absolute of the *Identitätssystem* is essentially the single living force of the *Naturphilosophie*, but it is that force as it is in itself, prior to its manifestations in the potencies of nature. The purpose of the principle of subject–object identity in the *Identitätssystem* is indeed the same as that of the theory of life in the *Naturphilosophie:* to explain the possibility of knowledge by surmounting all forms of dualism.

This interpretation implies that there is a *real* difference between the subjective and objective, the mental and physical, although it is only a difference in degree rather than kind. There is a difference in degree in that the mental is the *highest* degree of organization and development of the living powers of the body, while the body is the *lowest* degree of organization and development of the living powers of the mind. This seems to be indeed the essence of Schelling's concept of quantitative differences, which played a central role in the *Identitätssystem* (see below, 4.7.3).

There is an important difference between this interpretation of the principle of subject–object identity and the Spinozist dual–aspect interpretation: Schelling's hylozistic account of nature demands teleology, the attribution of purposes to nature, which is expressly forbidden by Spinoza. Although Spinoza does conceive of substance in terms of power,[24] he does not think of power as acting for ends, and still less does he consider its attributes as expressing different degrees of the development of this power.

There are some obvious advantages to this interpretation: it ensures continuity in Schelling's philosophical development; it accounts for how the ideal and real, the subjective and objective, are *real* aspects, appearances, or manifestations of the absolute; and it explains why Schelling analyzes the absolute in terms of quantitative differences.

The disadvantage of this interpretation is that it stresses the continuities of Schelling's development at the expense of its changes. It does not account for a major shift in his views from the *Naturphilosophie* to the *Identitätssystem*, because Schelling no longer writes of the absolute in terms of living force, and indeed he ceases to regard it as an activity. The absolute is not the force of all forces, the potency of all potencies; rather it is that in which all potencies are extinguished, the point of indifference that is potencyless.[25] Similarly, the dynamic, organic worldview of the *Naturphilosophie* begins to disappear in the static indifference point of the *Identitätssystem*. Rather than being the paradigm of the union of the mental and physical, the organic is now demoted to one form of the absolute, the real pole of the absolute as the highest potency of the natural world.[26]

The Platonic Interpretation

According to this reading, the principle of subject–object identity means that the absolute consists in reason, the archetype, or the idea, and this is neither mental nor physical, neither subjective nor objective, because an intelligible form is neither kind of entity or property. It is neither of them exclusively, but it is also both of them equally because it manifests or embodies itself in them. The mental and the physical are united on this model not because they are really one and the same thing, as in the dual-aspect theory, or because they are different degrees of organization and development of a single living force, as in the hylozistic model, but because they both instantiate or embody a single kind of law or rational structure.

The advantage of this interpretation is that it reflects the Platonic strands in the *Identitätsystem*, which later become explicit in *Bruno*. There are indeed clear passages in his later works where Schelling formulates the principle of subject–object identity expressly and entirely in Platonic terms.[27] He illustrates the union of the subjective and the objective, the ideal and the real, by the unity of universal and particular in geometric construction. While these

Platonic themes are not evident in the *Darstellung meines Systems*, the case could be made that they were already implicit from the very beginning.[28]

Which of these interpretions applies best to the *Identitätsystem?* Appropriately enough for a philosophy that wants to overcome all oppositions, all and none of them. The texts are so rich that they support each of them and do not give any single one the exclusive title to the truth. The *Identitätssystem* was essentially eclectic, a medley of various doctrines—Spinozist, Leibnizian, and Platonic—reflecting the different influences on Schelling.

It is difficult to see, however, the synthesis, the unity behind the manifold. To some extent these doctrines support one another; but to another extent they appear irreconcilable. Spinozism does not completely jibe with vitalism: for how does an eternal substance go outside itself, undergoing development like an organism? Nor does Spinozism go well with Platonism: for how does this single indivisible substance split itself into the plurality of forms? Finally, vitalism does not square with Platonism: for how does the active energy of life become the static eternity of the form? It is a sign of both the richness and poverty of Schelling's texts that they raise all these questions but provide no straightforward answer to them.

CHAPTER 7

The Dark Night of the Absolute

1. The Dark Parmenidian Vision

In the *Darstellung meines Systems* Schelling develops a vision of the absolute that is strictly monistic and severely Parmenidian. The absolute is pure one-ness, complete unity, utter self-sameness, and there is no difference, distinction, or multiplicity in that dark night. Hence Schelling repeatedly, emphatically, and explicitly defines the standpoint of absolute reason as that of pure self-identity, the complete indifference of subject and object. The highest law, and indeed the sole law, to express the absolute is therefore the law of identity, $A = A$ (§§7, 15; 117, 120).[1] The absolute is not an identity of identity *and* nonidentity, but purely and simply an identity of identity (§16Z; 121). The absolute standpoint therefore *excludes* all opposition between things or any differences between subject and object (§23; 123). From the absolute standpoint, the finite simply does not exist, because nothing considered in itself is finite (§14; 119).

This was the view of the absolute that Hegel famously parodied as "the night when all cows are black." But what led Schelling to such a dark vision in the first place? Why is his absolute so black? Schelling offers only the sketchiest of explanations in the *Darstellung*. He reasons that if the absolute were not purely one, there would have to be some other reason for its existence beside itself, and so it would no longer be absolute (§3; 116). If we keep in mind Spinoza's concept of substance, which is the basis for Schelling's concept of the absolute (see 3.1.2), it is not difficult to see his point. According to Spinoza's concept, substance is that which has an independent essence and existence, or that which does not depend on anything else in order to be. Hence substance must be one, unique, and indivisible. For if we were to divide it, then there would be two things, each of which is conceivable only through the other; hence neither would have an independent essence.

This reasoning led Schelling to a significant general conclusion, which is characteristic of this phase of his philosophical development. He stresses that it is "the basic error of all philosophy" to assume that the absolute has "gone outside itself," that is, that it has ceased to be pure self-identity and has differentiated itself in the finite world (§§14, 30; 119–120, 128). This is an error, Schelling argues, because it implies that the absolute destroys itself: from being purely one it becomes many, and so ceases to be. The absolute cannot be both one and many, both pure unity and difference, because that would be a contradiction. Those who assume that the absolute goes outside itself entangle themselves in this contradiction, because they must assume that the differences are somehow within it. It is a fundamental maxim of reason, however, that *ex nihilo nihil fit*, so that the differences cannot emerge from its opposite, unity. True philosophy therefore consists in the proof that the absolute is pure self-identity, and that it cannot destroy itself by going outside itself. Schelling says that the only philosopher who fully understood this point, though even he did not make a complete proof of it, was Spinoza.

Such a drastic conclusion marks a new phase in Schelling's philosophical development. As recently as the *Entwurf eines Systems der Naturphilosophie*, which was published in 1799, Schelling had contended that it is "the highest task of philosophy" to explain how absolute identity becomes duplicity (III, 220). It was indeed the central problem of his early thought—as it was later of Hegel's—to think of the unity of unity and multiplicity, the identity of identity and nonidentity. The fundamental task of philosophy, Schelling said in the *Briefe*, is to explain the possibility of the synthetic a priori, which means understanding how the absolute could go outside itself to posit the multitude of things in the empirical world (I, 294). Schelling had now convinced himself, however, that this was a *pseudoproblem*, that it involved the false presupposition that the absolute could *per absurdam* destroy itself.

Still, there was some precedent for this doctrine in Schelling's earlier writings, and indeed the whole basis of his later reasoning was already implicit within them. In his *Briefe über Dogmatismus und Kritizismus* Schelling had argued that theoretical reason cannot postulate any transition from the infinite to the finite (I, 313), for that violates the maxim *ex nihilo nihil fit*, according to which nothing determinate can be derived from something indeterminate. Schelling agreed with Jacobi that this maxim was the spirit of Spinozism, and that Spinoza was therefore right to deny any transition from the infinite to the finite. He was even willing to concede—despite all his sympathy for Fichte—that Spinoza's solution to this problem was the only one possible (I, 314). The later philosophy of identity simply carried through this earlier insight to its final conclusion. Now that Schelling cast himself in the role of a modern Spinoza, he would have to endorse a doctrine so essential to his spirit.

2. The Dilemma of Absolute Knowledge

Whatever the reasons for Schelling's Parmenidian vision, the results were still problematic, and indeed for all the classical reasons. There could be no denying the fact that there are differences between things, that there are individual things, or that there is a finite realm where things are limited by one another. Even if we downgrade this realm to the status of a mere *Ens imaginarius,* there is still the problem of explaining the origin of so prevalent and natural a illusion. So, like it or not, it seems as if Hegel had a point after all: there must be some white cows in that dark night. The problem is then to explain how they got there.

While we now seem to be deep in metaphysical territory, far removed from the epistemological concerns of the Kantian–Fichtean tradition, it is important to keep in mind that the main problem here is still that central to all German idealism: How do we explain the reality of the external world? This problem has now been formulated in metaphysical terms, but it remains all the same. It became just as much a problem for Schelling's and Hegel's absolute idealism as it was for Kant's and Fichte's critical idealism.

In attempting to explain empirical reality, Schelling and Hegel confront a dilemma very similar to that which troubled Fichte in his 1794 *Grundlage.* Fichte had to unite the transcendental standpoint of subject–object identity with the empirical standpoint where there is a subject–object dualism. Now the same problem returns for Schelling and Hegel, though the formulation is more metaphysical. On the one hand, it is necessary *to exclude* the realm of the finite from the absolute, because the finite and absolute contradict one another; more specifically, the absolute is independent and indivisible while the finite is dependent and divisible. On the other hand, however, it is also necessary *to include* the realm of the finite in the absolute, because, as the whole of all reality, the absolute cannot be limited by something outside itself; as the being in itself, having an independent essence and existence, the absolute cannot be conceived in contrast to something it is not. An absolute that excludes the finite becomes, by just that token, a finite absolute, and so not really an absolute at all.

Of course, Schelling was acutely aware of this problem, and his solution to it in the *Darstellung meines Systems* is his theory of *quantitative* differences (§20, 23; 123, 127n). According to this theory, there cannot be any *qualitative* differences between things in the absolute, that is, differences where one thing opposes another or can be posited without the other. There can be, however, *quantitative* differences, that is, differences where two things are posited together and are inseparable from one another, but where one is given more reality than the other. This concept therefore implies that there can be differences in degree but not in kind. The source of this doctrine is the principle of polarity in the *Naturphilosophie*, which stresses that opposites are complementary and differ only in degree. Schelling now integrated this principle into his vision of the absolute because it seemed to resolve the serious dilemma facing him. While differences in degree appear to explain the realm of the finite, they still do not posit oppositions within the absolute.

However strategic, the doctrine of quantitative difference still does not fully resolve the dilemma. There is first of all the problem that the doctrine of purely quantitative difference does not seem to account for all the *qualitative* differences seen in the finite world—a point that Schelling himself had made in his critique of Kant's dynamism. Even worse, however, Schelling has to admit that, as the *pure* identity of subject and object, as the *complete* indifference between them, the absolute cannot include even *quantitative* differences. Sure enough, he is forced to place these differences too outside the absolute standpoint (§25, 26Z; 125). Like qualitative differences, these differences too are created by reflection, by the intellect's capacity for carving out firm distinctions between things originally one. In this regard, then, quantitative differences are no better than qualitative ones: both fall outside the absolute standpoint, and both therefore serve as limits on the absolute.

Another related problem with Schelling's Parmenidian vision is that it forbids the possibility of all intellectual discourse about the absolute. The proper conclusion to draw from it is that we cannot say anything at all about the absolute, because to do so would be to ascribe some property to it, which is to posit some difference within it. To attribute some property to the absolute is to divide it, because any property has its determinate meaning only in contrast to its negation. *Omnis determinitio est negatio*, Spinoza said, and Schelling agreed. But if this so, then the sum and substance of absolute wisdom should be nothing more than $A = A$. After uttering this empty tautology the philosopher should, like all better mystics, observe a strict silence.

But Schelling never had the makings of a Trappist. True to his prodigal and prolific nature, he provides a rather elaborate account—stretching more than fifty pages—of the various potencies of the absolute, that is, of its various levels of organization and appearance in the natural world. How could Schelling justify such a theory in the face of his vision of the absolute as pure oneness, utterly undifferentiated unity?

His response to the difficulty is to distinguish between the *essence* and the *form* of absolute identity. While the essence of the absolute is its nature considered in itself, its form is its manner of being. Such a distinction, Schelling argues, is already implicit within the single valid principle of the absolute, the law $A = A$. On the one hand, this principle asserts the complete identity of the subject and predicate; it does not posit the A of the subject or the A of the predicate but simply the identity of them both (§6; 117) On the other hand, it is possible to distinguish within this principle between a subject and predicate. It is this distinction that constitutes the form of the absolute, that is, the specific manner of its existence (§15, 120). Now all knowledge of the absolute, and so all discourse about it, belongs to its form rather than its essence (§18, 122). Anything that we know about the absolute—apart from the simple statement that it is what it is—will belong to its form or manner of being.

With this tenuous and artificial distinction, Schelling believed he had justified the possibility of knowledge of the absolute. Since knowledge of the absolute does not belong to its essence, it does not introduce any distinction into its pure self-identity; but since it does belong to its form, the manner in which it exists, it also does not stand completely outside it, at least not in the manner of pure reflection, which knows only the appearances of the finite world.

But this distinction clearly could not provide what Schelling wanted. The difficulty is that whatever belonged to the form of absolute identity still could not grasp it in itself, in its intrinsic nature (§15, Z2; 122). Any form whatsoever—even the very sparse form limited to the distinction between the subject and predicate of $A = A$—involved some distinction and so could not grasp, but only falsify, absolute identity itself. The main problem is that the absolute, as pure undifferentiated unity, cannot have any form at all, any specific manner of being, given that all determination involves negation.

This means, however, that all discourse about the absolute must stand outside it, so that it has a purely imaginary status, consisting in nothing more than arbitrary and artificial abstractions of the understanding. Schelling had criticized Kant and Fichte for limiting knowledge to the circle of our own finite consciousness; but, ironically, his own Parmenidian doctrine of the absolute leads to a similar impasse.

Schelling's distinction between the essence and the form of the absolute was a self-conscious attempt to revive Spinoza's doctrine of the attribute.[2] But it also suffers from all the problems of that notoriously ambiguous doctrine. For it is unclear from Spinoza's definition of the attribute—"that which the intellect perceives as constituting the essence of substance"— whether the attribute is purely subjective, belonging only to the intellect's perception of it, or whether it is also objective, constituting its essence. While Spinoza said that substance has infinitely many attributes, the question remains how it has any attribute at all, given that it is pure indivisible unity. Rather than resolving Spinoza's difficulty, Schelling's distinction between the essence and form of the absolute merely restated it.

3. Rethinking the Absolute

In the years immediately following the publication of his *Darstellung meines Systems* Schelling did not cease to reflect on the problem of absolute knowledge. He recognized the difficulties in the position he had so baldly and boldly declared in the *Darstellung,* and he attempted to resolve them in two subsequent works, *Bruno* and the *Fernere Darstellungen aus dem System der Philosophie,* both of which were published in 1802. In these works Schelling reaffirms some of the cardinal doctrines expressed in the earlier work: that the absolute is pure self-identity, that it cannot go outside itself, and that its appearances consist in only quantitative differences. Yet, in grappling with the problems posed by these doctrines, he reformulated and revised them to a significant degree.

There is a remarkable passage in *Bruno* where the character Bruno, Schelling's spokesman, bluntly states the main difficulty confronting the Parmenidian view of the absolute: if the infinite excludes the finite, or if unity opposes opposition, then the infinite and unity cannot be absolute, because then they become limited by the finite or opposition (IV, 235–236, 247). The absolute cannot be the infinite in contrast to the finite, unity in opposition to opposition, Bruno therefore concludes, but it must be the unity of the infinite *and* finite, the identity of identity *and* opposition. Bruno then defines the true idea of the absolute as that "wherein all opposites are not so much unified as one, and not so much negated as rather not separated at all" (IV, 235); and he describes the unity of the absolute as that in which "unity and opposition, the self-identical and the nonidentical are one" (236).

This passage is noteworthy, not least because it shows that Schelling did not always hold the naive Parmenidian view that the absolute is a pure unity that excludes difference. While criticisms of that view apply against Schelling's position in the earlier *Darstellung meines Systems,* they do not work against his later standpoint in *Bruno* and the *Fernere Darstellungen.*

Schelling's new definition of the absolute seems to be an abrupt reversal of his position in the *Darstellung meines Systems,* where his formula for the absolute was the identity of identity (§16Z2; IV, 121). Yet the change in Schelling's views is not that drastic, and amounts more to a reformulation than an abandonment of his earlier doctrine. This becomes clear when Bruno argues that the finite as such—particular things in all their variety and differences from one another—belongs outside the absolute and in the realm of appearance (IV, 259, 261, 298). Although all finite things are indeed within the absolute, Bruno explains, they are so only insofar as they are identical with one another; insofar as they are distinct from one another, they belong only to the realm of appearance.[3]

This means that the absolute is still pure unity and identity after all. It is an infinite that includes the finite insofar as all finite things are identical with one another; but it is still an infinite that excludes the finite insofar as all finite things are distinct from one another. In this respect, then, Schelling's position in *Bruno* does not diverge from his earlier Parmenidian views. It was no doubt on these grounds that he felt himself justified, in the *Fernere Darstellungen,* in reaffirming the pure self-identity of the absolute (IV, 374).

Schelling's new thinking about the absolute around 1802 becomes especially clear in some passages from the *Fernere Darstellungen* where he lays out three possible views of the absolute (IV, 375). Schelling explains that his own position is a middle path between two problematic extremes. According to one extreme, the absolute is an abstract unity that excludes all difference, or it is the infinite in contrast to the finite. Schelling rejects this view because such an absolute becomes limited by the finite. According to the other extreme, the absolute is the unity of the infinite and the finite, but a unity that contains all the differences of the finite world within itself. He discards this view because such an absolute would lose its unity, becoming divided by all the differences within itself. The challenge is then to find a concept of the absolute that explains how it can include the finite without losing its unity. Again, Schelling's solution is that the finite is within the infinite, but not as such or as a determinate thing. In other words, all individual things are within the absolute, but only insofar as they are identical with one another, and not insofar as they are distinct from one another. The mineral, plant, and animal are all within the absolute whole, not as this particular mineral, plant, or animal, but only insofar as they all share the same essential nature in themselves (IV, 394). If we are to see the finite in the infinite, if we are to see it as part of the universal whole, Schelling explains, then we have *to negate* its differences from all other things and see how it merges with everything else (IV, 393, 408).

For all Schelling's efforts to reformulate his theory, it still faced some obvious difficulties. Although he had now placed the finite within the infinite, he still did so only in a halfhearted and nominal way by insisting that all finite things within the absolute had to be identical with one another. This still left the realm of difference, the multitude of finite things outside the absolute. The question then remained: Why did they not limit the absolute? If they were outside it, then it could not be conceived only in relation to itself, and so it could not be really absolute.

Schelling deals with this problem in several passages of *Bruno* and the *Fernere Darstellungen,* but he does not develop a completely consistent stance toward it. Sometimes he grants the world of difference some status by saying that it is somehow contained *potentially* within the absolute (IV, 258, 359); but he does not develop this view, leaving unanswered the troubling question how this potentiality becomes an actuality. His usual attitude toward the realm of difference is much more damning: he consigns it to the realm of mere illusion. He begrudges it only the most negligible status by insisting that the finite as such does not have a *real* existence, that it belongs to the realm of appearance, and that it is ultimately nothing at all (IV, 298, 385). All the different finite things in the universe are only the creations of reflection, the work of the abstracting and dividing intellect (IV, 259, 261, 387). Since it is really nothing at all, a mere world of appearance, it cannot limit the absolute.[4] It is probably for this reason that Schelling continued to deny the legitimacy of the question of how the absolute creates the world of appearance, and that he reaffirmed his original uncompromising doctrine that even quantitative differences belong outside the absolute (IV, 413).

If we place Schelling's thinking about the absolute around 1802 in a general perspective, it is clear that it does not deserve all the criticisms later made against it, especially by Hegel after his break with Schelling. Schelling's concept of the absolute was not always "the abstract absolute" or "bad infinite," the infinite opposed to the finite, which Hegel made it appear to be in the preface to the *Phänomenologie*. While this criticism does apply to Schelling's position in the *Darstellung meines Systems,* it does not work against his later standpoint in *Bruno* and the *Fernere Darstellungen.* Like Hegel, Schelling had then argued that the absolute had to be the unity of the infinite and finite, the identity of identity and nonidentity.[5]

Nevertheless, Schelling's development of this concept proved to be insufficient and halfhearted because he continued to exclude from the absolute the finite as such, the multiplicity of finite things. Of course, this was not enough for Hegel, who wanted to place that multiplicity within the absolute. It is important, however, to formulate Hegel's criticism correctly. In Hegel's view, the problem with Schelling was not that he had the wrong formula for the absolute—that he did not conceive of the finite within the infinite—but that he did not take this formula to its proper conclusion. It was not that Schelling excluded finite things from the absolute, but that he included them only insofar as they are identical with one another. In other words, the night when all cows are black did include cows within it; it was only that they were all black. Hegel wanted more: that there should be white cows in that dark night, or that the absolute should include the finite insofar as things are also different from one another. This difference with Schelling was already apparent during the Jena years, and it would be one of the more important factors in Hegel's split from Schelling.[6]

4. The Fall

After leaving Jena in 1803 Schelling continued to think about the problem of the absolute. His critics gave him no choice. Relentlessly, they pressed him on the question of the origin of the finite. If the absolute were the source of the finite, Carl Eschenmeyer wrote,[7] then it had difference within itself; but if it were not the cause, then there was a dualism between the infinite and finite.

This kind of objection drove Schelling to his most sustained and subtle reflections on the problem of the relationship between the infinite and finite, his 1804 tract *Philosophie und Religion.* This work is Janus-faced. While it explicitly defends the position developed in the earlier works, it also implicitly abandons it. Rightly, it has been regarded as a transitional work, the beginning of Schelling's later "philosophy of freedom."

Schelling's first line of reply to Eschenmeyer is to stand his ground and to deny the very problem facing him. There is no problem of explaining the origin of the finite world, he argues, for the simple reason that this world does not exist. Philosophy should have a completely negative relationship to the world of appearances, so that it should not attempt to derive the reality of the finite world; rather, it should try to prove that such a world does *not* exist (VI, 38). In any case, Schelling insists, it is impossible to explain the origin of the finite from the absolute (VI, 42). There cannot be any transition from the infinite to the finite, either in a logical or a causal sense, because this would entail that the absolute has real differences within itself. Whether we conceive of the origin of the finite through the *self-differentiation* of the absolute or through its gradual *emanation,* we end out dividing its reality by assuming that the finite is somehow inside it (VI, 35–38). Hence Schelling reaffirms his original position, first announced in the *Darstellung meines Systems,* that the absolute, as pure self-identity, cannot go outside itself. The whole problem of the reality of the finite world is dispatched as irresolvable, and indeed as a pseudoproblem.

Schelling implicitly admitted, however, that the problem could not be so easily dismissed. He betrays his own denial of the existence of the world of appearances by continuing to speculate about its origin. After all, what does not exist, what is pure nothingness, cannot have a cause. If it has some reality, even of a marginal kind, the question remains of its origin.

Without acknowledging the legitimacy of the question, Schelling struggled to answer it through the most abstruse neo-Platonic speculations. Here he fell back on a strategy he hit on in *Bruno*. In his attempt to explain how the infinite and the finite are one in the absolute, Schelling introduced the Platonic theory of ideas (IV, 229, 242–243). This theory seemed to provide a foundation for his view of the absolute as the unity of the infinite and finite. The unity of universal and particular in the Platonic idea or archetype became the model for the unity of the infinite and finite in the absolute. While the infinite is the universal because it applies to an indefinite number of particular things, the finite is the particular because, like any particular, each finite thing is limited by others and definable only in contrast to them. Now just as the universal and particular are one in the archetype, so the infinite and the finite should be one in the absolute.

In *Philosophie und Religion,* however, Schelling took this theory a step further, introducing an explanation for the source of the ideas themselves. The starting point for his explanation is the *self-knowledge* of the absolute. In its self-knowledge the absolute subject objectifies itself, and its image or reflection consists in its idea, which is the primal idea (*die Uridee*). Because this idea is an image or reflection of the absolute, whose nature consists in its independence, it takes on an independent status of its own. This independent status of the primal idea gives it freedom from the absolute, some reality in itself. This freedom is the source of the finite world, Schelling says, because the idea too knows itself, and the objects of its reflection, the ectypes of the finite world, also acquire an independent nature (VI, 39–40).

There is, then, some relationship between the absolute and finite after all. To be sure, it is not a *direct* transition; but there is at least some *indirect* connection between them through the world of ideas. The absolute knows itself through the ideas, which are its image; and the ideas know themselves through finite things, which are their images. The world of ideas has a twofold existence, then, one in the absolute and another in itself, by which it relates to the finite (VI, 41).

Although they are indirectly joined, Schelling still denies that the absolute is *the cause* of the finite world. The immediate source of the finite world is the idea, whose self-reflection is objectified in the finite. But this does not mean, Schelling thinks, that the absolute is even the *mediate* cause of the finite world. This is not the case for two reasons. First, the idea asserts its independence from the absolute in giving rise to its reflections. Second, even the ideas are not the proper causes of the finite world. They provide only the principles of its *possibility*, he explains, but not of its *reality* (VI, 40). So the question still remains: Whence the *reality* of the finite world?

Schelling's answer is simple but surprising: the reality of the finite world arose from a "breaking off," "a leap," "a distancing" and "a defection" from the absolute by the finite itself (VI, 38). This was, of course, nothing less than the ancient myth of the fall, not what we expect from a Spinozian naturalist. Still, Schelling self-consciously embraced this venerable myth, seeing it as the perfect solution to his problem insofar as it seemed to explain the origin of the finite world without invoking any cause within the absolute itself. If philosophy only appropriated this myth, Schelling explained, then it could make the required division between the realms of reality and nothingness. Paradoxically, though, Schelling then went on to insist that, once separated from the realm of being, the realm of nothingness could shine forth in its true glory. He then bade philosophers to read Dante: "Whoever pretends to know the principle of the good without evil commits the greatest of all errors; for in philosophy, like in Dante's poem, the path to heaven is only through the abyss" (VI, 43).

But Schelling's explanation of the origin of the finite, and his wholehearted affirmation of the realm of sin, still left him with the problem of dualism. If the cause of the reality of the finite world lay within itself, then it had to have some reality outside the absolute. But if it is real and exists outside the absolute, it then limits the absolute, which must be conceived in contrast to it. Like it or not, then, Schelling was flirting with a Manichean view of the world.

Schelling's explanation of the origin of the finite did not help him resolve the problem of dualism, but only reinvoked it from another angle. The threat of dualism now arose from within the absolute itself. Schelling had given such an independent status to the image of the absolute, to its self-objectification, that he had even called it "the other absolute" (*das andere Absolute*) (VI, 39). He could deny the damage from this concession, of course, by insisting that the self-objectification is indeed ultimately identical with the absolute because of the principle of subject–object identity. But he then faced a dilemma: if the self-objectification is identical with the absolute, there is no basis to explain the finite; and if it is not identical, there is a dualism.

For all his speculations, then, Schelling never escaped Eschenmeyer's dilemma. If he made the absolute the cause of the finite, he divided it; and if he made the finite its own cause, he gave it a reality that limited the absolute. The whole of philosophy of identity was fracturing under the stress of this dilemma. The original Spinozian inspiration was giving way, slowly but surely, to a Christian theism. It was this factor more than any other that eventually drove Schelling away from the philosophy of identity and toward his new philosophy of freedom.

In the meantime, Hegel drew his own conclusions from Schelling's difficulty. Seeing the dualism implicit in Schelling's account of the fall, he was convinced that it is necessary to make negativity an essential element of the absolute itself.[8] Here indeed lay the crossroads for Schelling and Hegel in Jena, the source of their eventual parting of the ways.

CHAPTER 8

Absolute Knowledge

1. In Defense of Speculation

The philosophy of identity was no sooner born than it had to struggle to survive. There could be no doubt that the position sketched by Schelling in the *Darstellung meines Systems* was metaphysics in the grand style, and indeed in the very sense condemned by Kant: knowledge by reason of the absolute or unconditioned. This plain fact raised a question much too obvious to be ignored: How is it possible to justify the possibility of such knowledge? How, indeed, is metaphysics possible?

According to one common view, Schelling simply refused the demand for justification. Since he held that absolute knowledge is indemonstrable and esoteric, he had to reject any attempt to prove or explain it. The philosophy of identity therefore represents a relapse into dogmatism, because it claims to possess a knowledge of the absolute that stands above all criticism.

But this objection is unfair. Although Schelling did hold that absolute knowledge is indemonstrable and esoteric, he still believed that he had to justify its possibility. To prove its *reality* was one thing; but to establish its *possibility* another. This conviction stemmed from Schelling's own adherence to some of the fundamental values of the Kantian critique, especially its demand to examine the possibility of knowledge. 'Dogmatism' was a *Schimpfwort* for Schelling no less than Kant. Rather than rejecting the critique, Schelling insisted on its necessity, making it into the introduction to his system.

Nowhere is Schelling's distance from dogmatism, and his loyalty to the values of criticism, more apparent than with his *Kritische Journal der Philosophie*, which he founded and co-edited with Hegel. The main purpose of the *Journal* was to criticize the prevailing forms of nonphilosophy (*Unphiloso-*

phie), and especially all forms of 'dogmatism,' which consists in the transcendent application of finite concepts or forms of knowledge to the absolute. The chief aim of criticism, Schelling and Hegel explained in their
leading essay, is *negative:* to reveal the limitations of the prevailing kinds of
philosophy, and more specifically the problems of dogmatism.[1] But they also
added that criticism has a more *positive* task: to show the possibility of absolute knowledge itself.

This was not mere lip service. During their Jena years Schelling and Hegel
took pains to explain the possibility of their new metaphysics, and they
went to some lengths to justify it before the tribunal of critique. Schelling
engaged in these tasks in his essay 'Über die Konstruktion in der Philosophie,' and in parts of his *Fernere Darstellungen* and *Vorlesungen über die
Methode des akademischen Studiums,* while Hegel turned to them in his *Differenzschrift* and essay 'Verhältniß des Skeptizismus zur Philosophie.'[2]

For Schelling and Hegel, the defense of metaphysics involved surmounting another even more basic challenge than the Kantian–Fichtean critique
of metaphysics: the Kantian–Fichtean circle of consciousness. Their attempt
to demonstrate absolute knowledge became inseparable from their attempt
to establish a more general realism, a knowledge of reality in itself. The
source of the connection is plain: since the absolute is the universe—the
whole of reality, which is not reducible to the dimensions of my subjectivity—there can be knowledge of it only if there can also be knowledge of
something independent of my own representations. Hence to defend the
possibility of absolute knowledge, Schelling and Hegel somehow had to
show that not all our knowledge is determined by, and therefore limited to
the results of, subjective activity; they had to demonstrate, in other words,
that we have knowledge of things-in-themselves and not only appearances.
We shall soon see how their defense of speculation became linked to their
criticism of subjective idealism and their attempt to break outside the
Kantian–Fichtean circle of consciousness. The task of the present chapter is
to examine Schelling's and Hegel's early attempt to justify both the metaphysics and realism of absolute idealism.

2. The Strategy for the Defense

To defend their project, Schelling and Hegel first had to come to terms
with the Kantian critique of metaphysics, pinpointing its weaknesses and
strengths. It is indeed striking how much they value Kant's ruthless and re-

lentless attack on the metaphysical tradition.[3] They praise Kant for having exposed the bankruptcy of the methods of Leibnizian–Wolffian rationalism, and more specifically for having shown that the concepts of the understanding cannot be applied to the unconditioned. They maintain that Kant was perfectly correct in arguing that these concepts cannot be extended beyond experience, and that in their transcendent employment they end in paralogisms, antinomies, and amphibolies.[4]

But for Schelling and Hegel, the value of the Kantian critique was essentially *negative:* it had rightly destroyed the bankrupt Leibnizian–Wolffian *Verstandesmetaphysik;* but in doing so it had only cleared away the rubbish lying in the path of a true metaphysics. Where Kant went astray was in concluding that *all* metaphysics is impossible, and in inferring that there cannot be *any* knowledge through reason of the unconditioned. Kant drew this unwarrented conclusion, Schelling and Hegel insisted, only because he had unwittingly accepted one of the main premises of the older rationalism: that *all* knowledge through reason has to be through the principle of sufficient reason. Kant had indeed a much too limited concept of reason: he reduced it down to logic, and saw it as nothing more than an extension of the concepts of the understanding.[5]

Here, then, lay Schelling's and Hegel's strategy for the resurrection of metaphysics. It was only necessary to question, they contended, Kant's underlying premise, his limited paradigm of reason and his tacit acceptance of the methods of the older rationalism. Schelling and Hegel would therefore attempt to show that there is a form of rational knowledge of the unconditioned that is not limited by the principle of sufficient reason, and hence that there is a kind of knowledge of the absolute that is not subject to Kant's strictures about the limitations of the understanding. If they could only establish this, they would have truly outflanked the Kantian critique, being able to endorse its devastating criticisms without having to accept its fatal conclusions.

It is important to stress—if only because of the frequent charges of irrationalism and mysticism hurled against them[6]—that Schelling's and Hegel's strategy was to revive a *rational* knowledge of the absolute. While they wanted to escape the mistakes of the older rationalism and its narrow reliance on the principle of sufficient reason, they also wanted to avoid the excesses of mysticism, of any appeal to intuition that transcended conceptual elaboration and methodological guidance. They demanded that knowledge of the absolute must be *systematic* and *methodological,* and they were critical of those romantic visionaries who could not develop their inspirations into systematic form.[7] It is indeed striking that Schelling's standard of knowledge during the Jena years is provided by mathematics, and that his method of exposition is *more geometrico*.

3. Intellectual Intuition

Schelling and Hegel saw the solution to the problem of metaphysics in "a wonderful and secret faculty": *intellectual intuition*. They made great claims for this faculty, and rested all their hopes for metaphysics on it. Intellectual intuition was hailed as the new organ for speculative thought. "Without intellectual intuition no philosophy!" Schelling proclaimed in his *Vorlesungen*. "Without intellectual intuition one cannot philosophize!" Hegel trumpeted in his *Differenz*. Such enthusiasm in appealing to a marvelous and mysterious faculty makes it seem as if Schelling and Hegel are indulging in the very mysticism they deplored. But that this is not the case becomes clear from a closer look at the meaning they give this term.

Schelling defines intellectual intuition in general terms as "the capacity to see the universal in the particular, the infinite in the finite, and indeed to unite both in a living unity."[8] An intellectual intuition, he explains, consists in my grasping an individual as a member of a whole, in seeing how its essential nature or inner identity depends on the totality of which it is only a part. When I have an intellectual intuition of an object, Schelling says, I do not *explain* it, and I do not *deduce* it, but I *contemplate* it. To explain an object is to show how other objects act on it and cause it to act as it does; to deduce an object is to derive it from higher principles, showing how it is only a single instance of a general universal. But to contemplate an object is to consider it in itself, apart from its relations with other objects. When I contemplate an object, Schelling maintains, I also see how it is part of a wider whole, how it represents the entire universe from its own point of view, because in themselves all objects are one and the same.[9]

Schelling calls this kind of knowledge intellectual intuition to distinguish it from both *sensible* intuition and *conception*. To grasp the universal in the particular in this way cannot be *sensible* intuition because the senses grasp each object singly and individually, and they therefore do not recognize the wider whole of which it is a part. To see the object in itself, apart from its relations to other things, also cannot be an act of *conception*, because to conceive an object is to subsume it under some universal, and so to compare or contrast it in some respect to other things. When I grasp the universal in the particular through an intellectual intuition I do not simply *subsume* the particular under some general concept or universal; for then there is no real identity between particular and universal. When a particular is subsumed under a universal there are other universals true of it, and there are other particulars that instantiate this universal. In an intellectual intuition, however, what I intuit is the *identity* of the universal and the particular; I see how the particular is inseparable from the whole of which it is a part, and how the whole cannot be without that particular. Because I do not use a concept, and because I grasp the object directly or immediately, apart from its relations to other things, I have an *intuition* of it. Here, of course, Schelling follows Kant's definition of an intuition as purely immediate representation.

Now it is in terms of this concept of intellectual intuition that Schelling and Hegel define reason itself. Theirs is not an arbitrary or stipulative definition, but it is based on a common general sense of the term, according to which knowing the reason for a thing involves seeing its place in a whole. Schelling's and Hegel's concept of reason is therefore essentially holistic. According to their definition, the task of reason is to comprehend something by showing how its identity depends on its place within a whole. This is how they explained reason in the *Fernere Darstellungen:*

> Only for reason is there one universe, and to conceive something according to reason means: to conceive it as an organic member of an absolute whole, in a necessary connection with the whole, and by this means as a reflection of absolute unity. (IV, 390)

Schelling's and Hegel's definition of reason marks an important change from that prevalent in the eighteenth century. The earlier concept of reason was essentially based on a mechanical model of explanation, according to which events have to be understood by the causes acting on them. According to this mechanical concept, reason is governed by the principle of sufficient reason, which (at least on this interpretation) states that there must be a sufficient reason or cause for every event, such that given the cause the event occurs of necessity. It is then the task of reason to seek the reasons or causes for events, to find the conditions for everything conditioned in the universe. This was the concept of reason that Kant and Jacobi had made into the target of their critique of rationalism, and whose limitations they had so ruthlessly exposed.

Schelling and Hegel defined their own organic or holistic concept of reason in contrast to this mechanical concept. They now called the power of explaining events according to the principle of sufficient reason the "understanding" (*Verstand*), which they sharply distinguished from reason (*Vernunft*). Like Kant and Jacobi, they believed that reason in the sense of the understanding could not grasp the absolute or the unconditioned. Schelling and Hegel too do not stint in their criticisms of this kind of rationalism, making several criticisms of this principle: that it never considers an object in itself but only in its relations to other objects; that it leads to an infinite regress and so never to the unconditioned; that it subordinates one thing to another, seeing one as cause and the other as effect, when all things are equal in the absolute.

It is now easy to understand why Schelling and Hegel believed that they had outmanuevered Kant. They could endorse all of Kant's criticisms of metaphysics as valid for the *understanding,* but they did not regard them as true for *reason* itself. That is because Kant had simply presupposed a mechanistic paradigm of reason, a view of reason that reduced it to the understanding. He never really considered the concept of reason in its proper sense as the power of intellectual intuition, the capacity to grasp things as parts of the whole. Hence the path lay open for the new metaphysics based on intellectual intuition.

It should now also be clear why intellectual intuition is not a mystical faculty. The power to see the universal in the particular is essentially that which is involved in the construction of a system. Schelling and Hegel indeed insist that intellectual intuition has to be executed and realized through systematic construction, which serves as its demonstration. It is the system that proves the truth of the intuition, through its internal coherence and adequacy to experience, and not the intuition that proves the truth of the system. In other words, the intuition does not carry its warrant in itself. Notoriously, any appeal to intuition is weak because it leaves open the possibility for someone else to claim an opposing intuition. Aware of this very point, Schelling and Hegel insist on the need for conceptual elaboration or systematic development to test the truth of the original intuition.

4. Fichte versus Schelling on Intellectual Intuition

Of course, "intellectual intuition!" was an old refrain. Fichte had already made intellectual intuition into the organ of the *Wissenschaftslehre,* and there could be no doubt that his discovery was a precedent for Schelling and

Hegel. They indeed use the term in the same general sense as Fichte. For Schelling and Hegel too, an intellectual intuition is a form of self-knowledge, and its structure consists in subject–object identity. It is also an immediate intellectual insight into its object, which cannot be demonstrated or explained by concepts. But here the similarities end.[10] Rather than simply following Fichte, Schelling and Hegel develop their concept of intellectual intuition in reaction against him. In their view, Fichte was right to point to the existence of this faculty; but he misdescribed it, and failed to realize its full potential.

There are at least two important differences between Fichte's concept of intellectual intuition and that of Schelling and Hegel. First, while Fichte, Schelling, and Hegel all see intellectual intuition as self-knowledge, they have different conceptions of the self and its place in nature, and so opposing conceptions of the self-knowledge of intellectual intuition. For Fichte, intellectual intuition gives me knowledge of my noumenal self, which transcends the phenomenal realm of nature. Through it I recognize my autonomy, that I am the sole source of my own actions. For Schelling and Hegel, however, intellectual intuition consists in the knowledge of my identity with the universe as a whole. Through intellectual intuition I do not see myself acting but all of nature acting through me. Second, Fichte expressly denies that intellectual intuition can be the source of metaphysical knowledge, as if it gives insight into the archetypes or eternal forms. Schelling and Hegel affirm this very possibility, however, defining intellectual intuition as archetypical knowledge. It is by intellectual intuition that I grasp the unity of universal and particular, the ideal and the real, that is characteristic of the Platonic forms.

The provenance of Schelling's concept of intellectual intuition lay less with Fichte than his antipode and nemesis: Spinoza. This concept was Schelling's formulation for Spinoza's "intellectual love of God," that self-knowledge of one's identity with the universe that he made into the capstone of his *Ethica*. According to Spinoza, the more the self understands of God, the more it understands of its mind and body, since all things exist in God and are only modes of his attributes; furthermore, the self attains an adequate idea of itself only when it knows how its nature follows of necessity from the divine essence.[11] My self-knowledge grows with my knowledge of God, because I am only a mode of the single infinite substance, so that whatever I think and do is ultimately only God thinking and acting through me. Schelling appropriated this concept, and duly made it the epitome of his own system.[12] From his earliest years he had been attracted by Spinoza's sublime theme of "the silent surrender of myself in the arms of the absolute," and he had even contrasted Fichte's and Spinoza's concepts of intellectual intuition: while Fichte made it the self-knowledge that I am the absolute, Spinoza made it the self-knowledge that I am part of the absolute.[13] Schelling first rejected Spinoza's concept—despite his fascination for it—as part of his defense of Fichte. But his growing distance from Fichte, and his increasing affinity for Spinozism, made it only natural for him to appropriate Spinoza's concept and to reinterpret intellectual intuition according to it.

5. Art versus Philosophy

How does one attain an intellectual intuition? And how does one know that it even exists? Obviously, these are crucial questions. Because it is so easy to doubt the possibility and reality of such a rare experience, the burden of proof falls on Schelling and Hegel. These questions troubled them throughout their Jena years, and they gave different, not completely consistent, answers to them.

Schelling's first response to them develops the doctrine of the sovereignty of art so characteristic of the romantic circle in Jena. Like Hölderlin, Novalis, and Schlegel before him, Schelling makes art into the organon and criterion of intellectual intuition. In his 1800 *System des transcendentalen Idealismus* he maintains that aesthetic experience is the medium and proof for our awareness of the absolute (III, 612–629). Schelling's deduction of the primacy of aesthetic experience attempts to demonstrate how it alone can synthesize the two fundamental aspects of the absolute, its subjective and objective pole. Since the subjective pole of the absolute manifests itself in free and conscious activity, and since its objective pole appears as necessary and subconscious activity, the perfect synthesis of these activities is nothing less than the creative activity of the artist. This is because only the artist creates with choice and conscious intention (according to the subjective pole), but also follows subconscious forces beyond his control (according to the objective pole). Although the artist begins his work with a conscious design in mind, nature subconsciously works through him, producing much in his work that he cannot intend or predict. The work of genius consists precisely in the expression of the subconscious forces of nature. All great artists testify, Schelling insists, that in creating their work they feel that they are directed by higher powers beyond themselves (617–618). Their works too show that they are not entirely the product of intention and design, because the artist himself cannot explain entirely how they arose and how they are to be interpreted. They present the infinite in a finite form because they are capable of an infinity of interpretations (620). Intellectual intuition comes with that self-consciousness after the moment of creation when the artist recognizes that he alone does not produce the work of art according to his conscious design but nature also acts to produce it through him. He then sees that his work of art is nothing less than the highest development and organization of all the powers of nature. What the genius creates is what nature creates through him, so that in contemplating works of art and their production one perceives the absolute itself, the highest synthesis of its subjective and objective poles.

With good reason, Schelling's apotheosis of the artist in the *System des transcendental Idealismus* has often been seen as the culmination of the aestheticism of the romantic school.[14] Schelling seems to dissolve the problems of philosophy into those of art. Philosophy now becomes the virtual handmaiden of art because "art is the model of science, and wherever art is science should follow" (623).

But Schelling's hymn to the poetic muse was not sung for long. For in his next publications on the philosophy of art—the 1802 lectures on the *Philosophie der Kunst* and his 1803 *Vorlesungen über die Methode des akademischen Studiums*—Schelling restored philosophy to sovereignty over art. Philosophy stood on a higher level of reflection than art, because it could understand the forces behind artistic creation better than the artist himself (V, 348). Although Schelling still gave a privileged position to art, because it grasped the appearance of the absolute in its eternal forms, he still did not give it the status of philosophy, which perceived absolute identity itself (§§14–15; V, 380–381). Philosophy is indeed more comprehensive than art: while the realm of art is that of beauty, philosophy comprises the unity of truth, goodness, and beauty (§16 Anm; V, 382–383).

6. The Method of Construction

Schelling's demotion of the role of art reveals the more rationalist direction of his thought, that penchant for systematic or discursive thinking that separates him from some of his romantic contemporaries, especially Hölderlin, Schlegel, and Novalis. Following this tendency, Schelling began to develop his own philosophical methodology in his later Jena years: the method of construction. The aim of this method is not only to establish the reality of an intellectual intuition, but also to provide a procedure for its systematic elaboration.[15]

The inspiration for Schelling's method is that old mainstay of all foundationalism: mathematics. That our reason has the power of intellectual intuition—that it has the capacity to perceive archetypes—is clear from the example of mathematics, Schelling maintains. Every mathematical demonstration shows the identity of the universal and the particular, the ideal and the real, which is characteristic of the archetype. The geometer knows that his demonstration holds for all figures as such, and he does not have to see whether it corresponds with any particular ones in his experience. When he makes his proof by constructing a figure in intuition, he abstracts from all the particular features of the figure so that it represents all figures of its kind. After this abstraction, he then perceives the universal in the particular, the properties of all figures of a certain kind in this particular one. Now when the geometer grasps this unity of universal and particular by constructing a figure in space, Schelling explains, he does so through an intuition or act of perception. Of course, this act of intuition alone does not function as a proof; but the proof will only articulate and embody the original intuition.

Schelling thinks that these features of a mathematical proof—the pure intuition of the universal in the particular—show the possibility of intellectual intuition in philosophy itself. Philosophy and mathematics are alike, he argues, because both presuppose the absolute unity of the universal and particular, and both employ intuition. The mathematician's construction of a proof according to the forms of space and time is the *primitive sensory form* of the philosopher's intellectual intuition. Just as the geometer abstracts from the accidental properties of his particular figure and considers its essential properties as pure instances of space in general, so the philosopher abstracts from all the contingent features of a particular and sees it as a pure case of the absolute whole. Both mathematician and philosopher aspire to a unity of thought and intuition, an identity of universal and particular. The only difference between them is this: the geometer deals with a universal that is the a priori form of *sensible* intuition (space and time), whereas the philosopher deals with a universal that is the a priori form of *intellectual* intuition. Mathematics and philosophy have indeed a different *content* or *subject matter:* mathematics deals with space and time, whereas philosophy examines the universe as a whole; but they still have the same *form* or *structure:* the demonstration of the unity of the universal and particular through intuition.

Following this analogy, Schelling then lays down his philosophical method. The proper method of philosophy, the means by which to attain and confirm an intellectual intuition, is through *construction*. Just as the mathematician constructs a figure in space, so the philosopher constructs a particular in his system. In each case we show the universal in the particular through an act of intuition. The task of philosophical construction, Schelling explains, is to grasp the identity of the particular with the universal, to see the ideal in the real and conversely (IV, 393–395). To establish such an identity, the philosopher has to abstract from each particular's determinate characteristics, to negate those distinctive features of the thing by which it differs from everything else. He then has to focus on the thing itself, apart from all its relations with other things, and to contemplate it for its own sake, regardless of its moral value or physical utility. If he does this, he will then see its identity with all things, grasping the entire universe within it. This is because all things are in themselves identical with one another, differing from one another only through their properties, which are abstracted away through intellectual intuition.

The acknowledged source of Schelling's method of construction was Kant's theory of mathematics. According to Kant, proof in mathematics proceeds according to the construction of a concept a priori in intuition; "to construct a concept," he explains, "is to exhibit a priori the intuition which corresponds to the concept" (KrV, B 741). Construction treats the particular as a pure case of the universal, Kant says, because it abstracts from all its accidental features. It is furthermore strictly a priori, because in drawing a figure the geometer does not have to borrow anything from his experience. Schelling closely follows this theory. Like Kant, he sees mathematics as a form of intuition, and he regards geometry as the intuition of space and arithmetic as the intuition of time. He indeed praises Kant for having grasped the idea of construction.[16]

There is, however, a sticking point between Kant and Schelling that goes to the heart of the issue about intellectual intuition. Namely, Kant saw construction as the method of mathematics *alone*, and denied that it could be the method of philosophy. Unlike the mathematician, the philosopher has no a priori intuition by which he can construct his concepts, and he must content himself with an analysis of concepts through discursive reason alone. Because of this lack of a priori intuition, Kant saw no hope for philosophy becoming a science like mathematics. Kant was therefore depriving Schelling of the very analogy by which he tried to establish intellectual intuition as the organ of philosophy.

Of course, Schelling was aware of the irony of appealing to Kant's method of construction as a model for philosophy. In his essay 'Über die Construktion in der Philosophie' he turned to the issues raised by Kant's distinction between mathematics and philosophy.[17] While he praised Kant for having accurately explained the true nature of mathematical construction, he criticized him sharply for limiting this method to mathematics. Kant distinguished between mathematics and philosophy by saying that mathematics considers the universal in the particular, while philosophy treats the particular in the universal. But this is an artificial and arbitrary distinction, Schelling argues, because this very distinction falls within mathematics itself: arithmetic treats the particular in the universal and geometry the universal in the particular. In both mathematics and philosophy there is a unity of universal and particular, of ideal and real. Although the subject matter of mathematics is the form of sensible intuition, mathematical intuition is not entirely sensible but also partly intellectual. Both mathematics and philosophy employ intellectual intuition, Schelling insists, and the only difference between them is that mathematics has an intellectual intuition reflected in sensibility whereas philosophy has a pure intellectual intuition reflected into itself.

7. Head over Heels into the Absolute?

In some famous lines in the preface to his *Phänomenologie*, several years after the dissolution of their philosophical alliance, Hegel criticized Schelling for beginning his system directly with absolute knowledge, as if it could be somehow "shot from a pistol." These lines seem to be directed against the very first proposition of the *Darstellung meines Systems*, where Schelling virtually catapults the reader into the realm of absolute knowledge. This proposition consists in a definition of absolute reason: the total indifference of the subjective and objective (§1; IV, 114–115). To think of reason as absolute, Schelling explains, it is necessary to abstract from everything subjective, the activity of thinking itself. But to do this is also to abstract from the objective, because the subjective and objective have meaning only in contrast to one another. Through this feat of abstraction, then, reason is grasped as neither subjective nor objective, but as something indifferent between them. In this manner, Schelling assures us, we grasp reason as the true being in itself.

In so quickly launching the reader into the realm of absolute knowledge, Schelling again seems to be transcending the limits of experience and to be engaging in a dogmatic metaphysics. Is this not to beg the question against

Kant and Fichte, who both deny that it is possible for the subject to abstract from his own activity as a thinker? According to Kant, the 'I' of the 'I think' accompanies every act of consciousness, so that to abstract from the 'I' would be to have no representation at all. According to Fichte, we cannot abstract from the 'I' because even the attempt to abstract from it presupposes it. Schelling explained that all he wanted is an abstraction from the intuiting subject of an intellectual intuition.[18] But it was just this, of course, that neither Kant nor Fichte was willing to grant him.

Schelling knew that he was, in Kant's and Fichte's terms, demanding the impossible. Yet he still attempted to meet them on their own ground by staying within the realm of transcendental philosophy itself. He argues that Kant and Fichte have drawn the limits of knowledge much too tightly, for by restricting knowledge to the subject they unwittingly undermine the possibility of knowledge in general. The nub of Schelling's strategy is therefore nothing less than a transcendental argument: that if there cannot be abstraction from the purely subjective dimension of knowledge, there cannot be any such thing as knowledge at all. All knowledge presupposes the pure identity of subject and object, Schelling argues, and such pure identity demands that we abstract from the subject as much as the object of knowledge. Hence Schelling denies that postulating absolute knowledge involves transcending the limits of knowledge. It goes beyond the narrow limits postulated by Kant and Fichte, to be sure, but it does not go beyond these limits in general, for it simply articulates a necessary presupposition of all knowledge.

Schelling put forward this transcendental argument in several texts, each time expounding it from a different angle.[19] His argument consists in two stages: (1) that subject–object identity is the necessary condition of all knowledge; and (2) that subject–object identity has to be conceived not as pure self-consciousness, or as the self-consciousness of the transcendental 'I,' but as the self-knowledge of the absolute itself.

Schelling put forward the first step of his argument in most detail in the opening section of his *System der gesammten Philosophie* (§1; VI, 137–140). Here he maintains explicitly that the central and characteristic principle of the philosophy of identity—that the absolute is the identity of subject and object—is the first presupposition of all knowledge. If the subject and object are not entirely and utterly identical, if the the knower and the known are not one and the same, there cannot be knowledge in the proper sense at all. Schelling attempts to provide an indirect proof of this principle by showing how *any* distinction between the subject and object makes knowledge impossible. If we assume that the subject and object are *completely* distinct from one another, then there cannot be any correspondence between them, and so no knowledge will be possible. This is because there cannot be any connection, interaction, or correspondence between utterly heterogeneous entities. It is necessary to assume, therefore, that the subject and object are only *partially* distinct, so that they have some kind of connection with one another. This connection must be such that either the object determines the subject or the subject determines the object. In either case, Schelling contends, we conceive of knowledge as arising through some form of causality; but then knowledge in the true and proper sense, knowledge of reality in itself, becomes impossible. If the object determines the subject, there will be no knowledge of the object in itself, because then the subject will know the object only insofar as the object affects it; it will see the effects of the object's activity but not the object in itself. If, conversely, the subject determines the object, then the subject will know the object only insofar as it affects the object, or only insofar as it makes the object conform to the conditions of its knowing; but insofar as the subject does not affect the object, it remains an unknowable thing-in-itself. For these reasons, Schelling concludes that if there is *any* dualism between the subject and object—if they are at all distinct from one another—then true knowledge is impossible. The necessary precondition of all knowledge is therefore complete and total subject–object identity.

Of course, Kant and Fichte were themselves ready to admit that subject–object identity is the principle of all knowledge. They had made the principle that we know only what we create into the paradigm of all knowledge. In this respect Schelling only continues with the Kantian–Fichtean tradition, which was in spirit, if not in letter, completely antidualistic. Where he goes beyond them is in his *interpretation* of this principle: he insists that subject–object identity cannot be construed simply as the self-consciousness of the pure or transcendental subject that is presupposed by all empirical consciousness. Rather, he insists that it must be read as nothing less than the self-knowledge of the absolute itself, which is present within all individual selves but also transcends them.

The second step of Schelling's argument consists in a *reductio ad absurdum* of the Kantian and Fichtean position. If we adopt the Kantian–Fichtean reading of the principle of subject–object identity, Schelling argues, then we are trapped inside the circle of our own consciousness, incapable of knowing anything more than our own passing representations. Kant and Fichte assume that this subject is nothing more than the 'I' that accompanies all my representations, or that it is nothing more than my pure self-consciousness abstracted from all its empirical elements. This is not the infinite 'absolute I,' of course, but still a 'finite I,' because all experience is still given and contingent for it. Since, however, this 'I' knows only what it creates, only what it subordinates to its own activity, it knows nothing more than the products of its own activity, and so it cannot know the object in itself, the object as it exists apart from and prior to its creative activity. It is then caught in a dilemma: either it knows itself or it knows nothing. There is no middle path, however, where it is possible for the subject to know reality itself, something that exists apart from and prior to it.

This was indeed, Schelling pointed out, the very dilemma with which Fichte had closed the *Wissenschaftslehre*. When Fichte admits that his subject is caught inside an inescapable circle in which the object is either a noumenon or a thing-in-itself, he virtually condemns the knowing subject inside the circle of his own consciousness. For Schelling, as for so many of his generation, this dilemma is nothing less than the *reductio ad absurdum* of the *Wissenschaftslehre*, the final proof of its nihilism.

The only way to avoid the nihilism of subjective idealism or the skepticism of dualism, Schelling held, is *to reinterpret* the principle of subject–object identity. This principle has to be reconstrued so that it no longer refers to the self-knowledge of the finite subject but to the self-knowledge of the absolute within him. While the subjective reading of this principle traps each subject inside the circle of its own representations, the objective reading lifts it outside this circle by making true self-knowledge equivalent to the self-knowledge of the absolute itself.

Schelling and Hegel believed that only their objective interpretation of the principle of subject–object identity ensures the possibility of knowledge because it alone means that knowledge is not simply *my* knowledge—something I know to be true from my own case or my own consciousness—but the knowledge of the object itself. The Kantian–Fichtean interpretation left a residual dualism between subject and object, because the finite subject could not create the entire manifold and knew it only insofar as it acted on it. If, however, we make subject–object identity into *absolute* self-knowledge, there is no such dualism, no remaining given and contingent manifold, and so there is the required complete identity between knower and known.

It is clear, however, that this interpretation of the principle of subject–object identity saves the objectivity of knowledge only on the further assumption that my knowledge as a finite subject is part or a mode of absolute knowledge. In other words, I as a finite subject know the object itself, as opposed to merely its appearance for my consciousness, if my knowledge of the object is the absolute knowing itself through me. It presupposes, in short, the ancient Platonic theme that all knowledge participates in divine self-knowledge, or that when I know something God knows it through me. Schelling did not shirk from putting forward just this doctrine: "Not I know, but the all knows in me, if the knowledge that I call mine is an actual and true knowledge" (§1; VI, 140). The 'I am' and the 'I think' have been the basic mistake of all philosophy, he wrote, because thought is not *my* thought and being is not *my* being but they are *the* thought and being of the absolute or the universe itself.[20]

This was, of course, high metaphysics. Explicitly and emphatically, Schelling had postulated the existence of something that transcends the limits of finite consciousness, and he had refused to degrade it to the status of a mere regulative ideal. But his final line of defense against the charge of engaging in transcendent speculation is that only this postulate explains the possibility of knowledge itself. Although this postulate cannot be confirmed in finite experience, it is still a necessary condition of its possibility. For Schelling, then, the final paradox is that it is not possible to explain the possibility of our knowledge as finite subjects unless we transcend the limits of finitude itself.

But if this is not bad metaphysics, is it what it claimed to be—namely, a good explanation of the possibility of knowledge? Here, indeed, serious doubts could be raised, doubts so grave that Schelling's explanation seemed to be little more than wishful speculation after all. Such an explanation of the possibility of knowledge seems to create more problems than it solves, because it does not answer the skeptical challenge of how I *know* that my knowledge participates in divine self-knowledge. Simply to maintain that this is the only means to explain the possibility of knowledge begs the question by assuming that there is knowledge in the first place. Schelling's theory also had problems of internal consistency. It seems as if there is a new kind of dualism between the finite subject and absolute, because the finite subject cannot be one and the same as the absolute; and if there is such a dualism, then the finite subject cannot fully enjoy or participate in the subject–object identity required for knowledge. Even worse, as we have already seen, Schelling places the discursive knowledge of the finite subject *outside* the absolute and even condemns it to the realm of illusion. In what sense, then, can he be said to guarantee the objectivity of *its* knowledge? This was a question for which Schelling had no ready answer.

8. The Paradox of Absolute Knowledge

In spite of all Schelling's and Hegel's attempts to explain the possibility of absolute knowledge there lay a deep paradox behind the philosophy of identity. It was one of Schelling's and Hegel's cardinal doctrines that there cannot be any distinction between knowledge of the absolute and the absolute itself.[21] We cannot claim that the knowledge of the absolute is distinct from the absolute itself, they argue, for the simple reason that the absolute is all reality and has nothing outside itself. If there is any knowledge of the absolute it therefore must consist in nothing more nor less than the *self*-knowledge of the absolute.

The same result arises from their paradigm of knowledge. Since they contend that subject–object identity is the necessary condition of *all* knowledge, the subject who knows the absolute must be identical with the absolute itself. There cannot be any distinction between absolute knowledge and the absolute itself, because that would create a dualism between subject and object, violating the fundamental condition of all knowledge.

This result is paradoxical, however, because it denies legitimacy to the very problem Schelling and Hegel are trying to solve. The question how *we* know the absolute becomes a pseudoproblem because it is not we, you, or I who can know the absolute, but it is only the absolute that can know itself. Schelling not merely concedes but stresses this point: "Not we, not you, not I, know of God. For reason, insofar as it affirms God, can affirm *nothing else*, and it destroys itself as a particularity, as something *outside God*."[22]

It is a complete mistake, Schelling further explains, to seek the capacity to know the absolute within ourselves. We do not have a power of reason by which we know the absolute, as if it were something existing outside us. Rather, the only reason that knows the absolute is that of the absolute itself. It is not *we* who know the absolute through our reason, then, but the absolute that knows itself through its reason.[23] According to Schelling, the whole question of how *I* can know the absolute commits the fundamental error of all modern philosophy: that I, not God, am the subject of knowledge.

The net result of such teaching, however, is that it is virtually impossible for the finite subject to know the absolute. If the subject knows the absolute, then *ipso facto* it ceases to be finite and becomes the same as the absolute itself! There is an insurmountable chasm, then, between our knowledge as finite subjects and the infinite self-knowledge of the absolute itself. The subject–object identity of the absolute is thus bought only at the price of another dualism between the finite subject and the absolute itself. Hence Schelling had *not* escaped the very objection he once hurled against Fichte: that if *we* know something, then it becomes limited to our finite nature, so that we are caught between our finite self-knowledge and the self-knowledge of the absolute outside us.

Schelling sometimes attempts to ameliorate the paradox by explaining that there is a *partial* identity between our knowledge of the absolute and the absolute itself.[24] Complete self-knowledge exists only in its perfection in the absolute; but we more or less participate in it. When the absolute knows itself it does so through us, so that we are the organs of its self-knowledge.[25] Our knowledge is an ectype of the divine archetypes, so that we do see the absolute after all, if only through a glass darkly.

Schelling never fully developed this doctrine, however. He never explained in any detail how finite subjects share in the self-knowledge of God. The reasons for this silence were probably the obvious problems with the doctrine itself: if knowledge requires *complete* subject–object identity, there cannot be any sense in which we share *more or less* in the divine self-knowledge, for that would be to admit some kind of a dualism between the subject and object, which destroys all knowledge. For the same reason, there cannot be any ascent to the knowledge of the absolute, some procedure by which the subject strips off its finitude and comes to know God by becoming like him.[26] For becoming *like* God is not enough to fulfill the strict standards of subject–object identity; the subject must *be* God to know God.

In the end, then, Schelling's uncompromising insistence on subject–object identity as his standard of knowledge placed him in an impossible position: to know the absolute we have to be the absolute, which is to say that we, as finite subjects, cannot know it at all. For all Schelling's insistence on explaining the possibility of absolute knowledge, for all his attempts to avoid the charge of dogmatism, and for all his efforts to develop a scientific method of knowledge, his ideals of knowledge were in the end simply impossible to fulfill. So the Kantians were right after all: Schelling was guilty of dogmatism, though not in the first-degree, as charged, but only in the second-degree. For he was a dogmatist not by intention but only by implication, and indeed in spite of himself.

Schelling's abject failure to solve the problem of absolute knowledge left a difficult legacy for Hegel, whose own attempt to resolve this problem finally led him to his *Phänomenologie des Geistes* in 1807. Just how Hegel resolved Schelling's problem—how he tried to show that finite knowledge involves the knowledge of the infinite—is a complex and difficult question that we cannot pursue here. My purpose has only been to sketch the origins of Schelling's absolute idealism; Hegel's later reformulation of that doctrine is another story.

Notes

Abbreviations

AA   *J.G. Fichte: Gesamtausgabe der Bayerischen Akademie der Wissenschaften,* ed. R. Lauth, H. Jacob, and H. Gliwitsky. Stuttgart–Bad Cannstatt: Friedrich Fromann, 1964–.

AT   *Oeuvres de Descartes,* ed. C. Adam and P. Tannery. Paris: Vrin, 1964–1976.

GSA Hölderlin, Friedrich. *Sämtliche Werke: Grosse Stuttgarter Ausgabe,* ed. F. Beißner and A. Beck. Stuttgart: Cottanachfolger, 1943–1985.

KA   *Friedrich Schlegel Kritische Ausgabe,* ed. E. Behler, Jean-Jacques Anstett, and H. Eichner. Paderborn: Ferdinand Schöningh, 1958–.

KrV Kant, Immanuel. *Kritik der reinen Vernunft.* All references to this work are to the pagination of the first (1781) and second (1787) editions, designated "A" and "B" respectively. All references to Kant's other works are to the Academy edition, *Kants gesammelte Schriften,* ed. W. Dilthey et al. Berlin: de Gruyter, 1902–.

L   Leibniz, Gottfried Wilhelm. *Philosophical Papers and Letters,* ed. L. Loemker. 2nd ed. Dordrecht: Reidel, 1969.

NA   *Schillers Werke. Nationalausgabe,* eds. J. Peterson, L. Blumenthal, and B. von Wiese. 42 vols. Weimar: Böhlau, 1943–.

NS   *Novalis Schriften,* ed. R. Samuel, H. Joachim Mähl, and G. Schulz. Stuttgart: Kohlhammer, 1960–1988.

Introduction

1. Some recent popular expositions of this interpretation can be found in Robert Solomon's *Continental Philosophy since 1750: The Rise and Fall of the Self* (Oxford: Oxford University Press, 1988), pp. 1–7, 53–55; and in Frederick Copleston, *A History of Philosophy* (New York: Doubleday, 1994), pp. 1–31. This interpretation has been defended even by more careful scholars. See, most recently, Karl Ameriks, *Kant and the Fate of Autonomy* (Cambridge: Cambridge University Press, 2000), pp. 227, 308.

2. On the influence of the Scottish commonsense school in Germany, see Manfred

Kuehn, *Scottish Common Sense in Germany, 1768–1800* (Kingston: McGill–Queen's University Press, 1986) (McGill–Queen's Studies in the History of Ideas, No. 11).

3. On the early reactions to idealism in Germany, see Manfred Kuehn, 'Kant and the Refutations of Idealism in the Eighteenth Century,' in *Man, God, and Nature in the Enlightenment,* ed. Donald Mell, Theodore Braum, and Lucia Palmer (East Lansing: Colleagues Press, 1988), 25–35.

4. Of course, "naturalism" is a very vague term. Here there are two relevant senses, one weak and another strong. In the weak sense, "naturalism" means that not only everything objective, physical, or material, but also everything subjective, mental, or conscious is explicable according to laws of nature (however we define these laws). In the stronger sense, "naturalism" involves the added claim that not only everything subjective, mental, or conscious, but also everything ideal, normative, and formal is explicable according to laws of nature. The growing naturalism within German idealism was in the weaker sense. The stronger sense involves a form of empiricism that would be rejected by all German idealists. What separates the idealist from the pragmatist tradition is precisely the idealist rejection of any derivation of the logical, formal, or transcendental from experience itself.

5. Most notably, this was the interpretation of Josiah Royce's popular and influential *The Spirit of Modern Philosophy* (Cambridge: Houghton Mifflin, 1892), pp. 143–145, 162, 484, 487. Royce developed this interpretation in more technical detail in his "Baltimore lectures," published posthumously as *Lectures on Modern Idealism* (New Haven: Yale University Press, 1919), pp. 44, 49, 51, 73–74, 90. Royce's role in the reception, understanding, and criticism of German idealism has not been fully appreciated. It was his interpretation of German idealism that was taken over by the American pragmatists, especially William James and John Dewey. See James, *Pragmatism* (New York: Longmans, 1907), pp. 145, 165; and Dewey, *Reconstruction in Philosophy* (Boston: Beacon, 1948), pp. 49, 50–51. Royce's influence is still apparent in Richard Rorty's criticism of the idealist tradition, which follows largely in James's and Dewey's footsteps. See his *Philosophy and the Mirror of Nature* (Oxford: Blackwell, 1980), pp. 147–148, 353. My criticisms of Royce are not meant to deprecate him; he was, and still remains, the deepest American scholar of the German idealist tradition.

6. See Royce, *The Spirit of Modern Philosophy,* pp. 144–145.

7. The meaning of this concept will be explained in more detail below, 3.1.2.

8. Royce believed that there was a tension in post-Kantian idealism between its concept of an impersonal absolute and its emphasis upon the self. See *Lectures on Modern Idealism,* pp. 70, 74–75. "The crucial issue of the time," he wrote, was that the self was "the center of the universe, while the Absolue was nevertheless impersonal" (70). Unfortunately, Royce did not explore the issue.

9. On the importance of the Platonic legacy for Marburg neo-Kantianism, see Ernst Cassirer, 'Paul Natorp,' *Kant-Studien* 30 (1925), 273–298, esp. 291–296; and 'Hermann Cohen, 1842–1918,' *Social Research* 10 (1943), 219–232.

10. The foundationalist interpretation appears in Royce, *Lectures on Modern Idealism,*

pp. 44, 49, 51, 73–74, 90; Copleston, *A History*, vol. 8, p. 9; Dewey, *Reconstruction*, pp. 19, 20–21. It has been reaffirmed most recently by Karl Ameriks in his *Kant and the Fate of Autonomy*, pp. 81–84.

11. See Karl Ameriks 'Kant's Transcendental Deduction as a Regressive Argument,' *Kant-Studien* 69 (1978), 273–287; Henry Allison, 'Reflections on the B-Deduction,' *Southern Journal of Philosophy* 25, Supplement (1986), 1–15; and Stephen Engstrom, 'The Transcendental Deduction and Skepticism,' *Journal of the History of Philosophy* 32 (1994), 359–380.

12. Reinhold's influence has been overestimated by Ameriks, *Kant and the Fate of Autonomy*, pp. 81–160.

13. Hegel's interesting and complex response to the problems of foundationalism has been the subject of a number of recent studies. See, for example, Tom Rockmore, *Hegel's Circular Epistemology* (Bloomington: Indiana University Press, 1986); Kenneth Westphal, *Hegel's Epistemological Realism* (Dordrecht: Kluwer, 1989); Michael Forster, *Hegel and Skepticism* (Cambridge: Harvard University Press, 1989); and David Lamb, *Hegel: From Foundation to System* (The Hague: Martinus Nijhoff, 1980).

14. See especially Dieter Henrich, *Konstellationen: Probleme und Debatten am Ursprung der idealistischen Philosophie (1789–1795)* (Stuttgart: Klett-Cotta, 1991); and Manfred Frank, *Unendliche Annäherung: Die Anfaänge der philosophischen Frühromantik* (Frankfurt: Suhrkamp, 1997).

15. Among the Hegelian histories of German idealism are Karl Rosenkranz, *Geschichte der kantische Philosophie* (Leipzig: Voss, 1840); Richard Kroner, *Von Kant bis Hegel* (Tübingen: Mohrn, 1921); and Nicolai Hartmann, *Die Philosophie des deutschen Idealismus* (Berlin: de Gruyter, 1954). Though neither Kroner nor Hartmann were strict Hegelians like Rosenkranz, their sympathy with Hegel was enough for them to see his system as the culmination of German idealism. Royce's *Spirit of Modern Philosophy* and *Lectures on Modern Idealism* were also written from an essentially Hegelian standpoint.

16. See, for example, Jean Hyppolite, 'The Concept of Life and Consciousness of Life in Hegel's Jena Philosophy,' in *Studies on Marx and Hegel* (London: Heinemann, 1969), pp. 3–21.

17. While I agree with Hegel about the need to distinguish between subjective and objective idealism, my formulation of the distinction is not Hegelian. The distinction will be further explained and defended below, 3.3.2–3.

18. This point will be explored in more detail below, 3.3.3.

Part I. Introduction

1. The subjectivist interpretation first arose in the 1780s; see the historical sources cited in 1.2.1, note 1. The foremost modern exponents of the subjectivist interpretation have been in the Anglo-Saxon tradition. See especially H. A. Prichard, *Kant's Theory of Knowledge* (Oxford: Clarendon Press, 1909), pp. 1–26, 115–139; P. F. Strawson, *The Bounds of Sense* (London: Metheun, 1966), pp. 21–22, 35, 56–

57, 197; and Jonathan Bennet, *Kant's Analytic* (Cambridge: Cambridge University Press, 1966), pp. 22–23. Also in this tradition are those scholars who have stressed Kant's affinity with Berkeley; on them, see the sources in 1.5.2, note 16.

2. The first exponents of the objectivist interpretation were some of the early romantics, especially Hölderlin, Novalis, and Friedrich Schlegel. Their interpretation of Kant will be discussed in Part 3. The main modern exponents of the objectivist interpretation have been the members of the Marburg school, especially Hermann Cohen, Paul Natorp, and Ernst Cassirer. For a good example of their interpretation, see Cohen, *Kants Theorie der Erfahrung*, 2nd ed. (Berlin: Ferdinand Dümmler, 1885), pp. 575–616. There have been few representatives of this interpretation in Anglo-Saxon literature; but two prominent scholars, Edward Caird and Norman Kemp Smith, have endorsed aspects of the objectivist interpretation. See Caird, *The Critical Philosophy of Immanuel Kant* (Glasgow: James Maclehose, 1889), I, 442–443, and II, 560–561, 645–646; and Smith, *A Commentary to Kant's Critique of Pure Reason* (London: Macmillan, 1923), pp. 274–275. More recently, there has been a new form of the objectivist interpretation that attempts to explain the Kantian subject in terms of the concepts of cognitive science. See the sources listed in 1.8.1.

3. On the objectivist interpretation of the transcendental subject, see Cohen, Kants *Theorie der Erfahrung*, pp. 319, 325, 589–592; and Ernst Cassirer, *Substanzbegriff und Funktionsbegriff: Untersuchungen über die Grundfragen der Erkenntniskritik* (Berlin: Cassirer, 1910), pp. 410–411.

4. The neo-Kantians of the Marburg school were much closer to the absolute idealism than they would often allow. Although they often stressed the merely regulative role of the forms of experience, they also conceived them as constitutive of nature itself. See, for example, Cohen, *Kants Theorie der Erfahrung*, pp. 590–592, who conceives the a priori conditions of experience as "die Grundlagen der Dinge." On Natorp's affinity with absolute idealism, see Ernst Cassirer, 'Paul Natorp,' *Kant-Studien* 30 (1925), 273–298, esp. 291–296.

5. An example of the former position is Strawson; the latter position is taken by Karl Ameriks. See his 'Kant's Transcendental Deduction as a Regressive Argument,' *Kant-Studien* 69 (1978), 273–287; 'Recent Work on Kant's Theoretical Philosophy,' *American Philosophical Quarterly* 19 (1982), 1–24; and *Kant and the Fate of Autonomy*, pp. 37–80.

6. For views similar to my own in this regard, see Ralph Walker, *Kant* (London: Routledge, 1978), pp. 122–135; and Sebastian Gardner, *Kant and the Critique of Pure Reason* (London: Routledge, 1999), pp. 87–114, 271–306.

7. I have in mind, of course, Barry Stroud's famous criticism of transcendental arguments. See his 'Transcendental Arguments,' *The Journal of Philosophy* 65 (1968), 241–256. While I think that Stroud makes some compelling criticisms of Strawson's interpretation of Kant, I do not accept them as criticisms of Kant himself. As we shall see in Chapter 6, Kant's arguments do not attempt to prove the reality of the external world in the strong transcendental sense.

8. In addition to the work of Karl Ameriks (see note 5), see Henry Allison, 'Reflections on the B-Deduction,' *Southern Journal of Philosophy* 25, Supplement (1986), 1–15; and Stephen Engstrom, 'The Transcendental Deduction and Skepticism,' *Journal of the History of Philosophy* 32 (1994), 359–380.

9. The advocates of the antisubjectivist interpretation have been Graham Bird, *Kant's Theory of Knowledge* (New York: Humanities Press, 1962), pp. 1–52; Gerold Prauss, *Kant und das Problem der Dinge an sich* (Bonn: Bouvier, 1974), pp. 13–42; and Henry Allison, *Kant's Transcendental Idealism* (New Haven: Yale University Press, 1983), pp. 3–34. Also see Allison's important defense of his interpretation, 'Transcendental Idealism: The Two Aspect View,' in *New Essays on Kant,* ed. Bernard den Ouden and Marcia Moen (New York: Lang, 1987), pp. 155–78. More recently, the antisubjectivist interpretation has been defended vigorously, if onesidedly, by Arthur Collins, *Possible Experience* (Berkeley: University of California Press, 1999).

10. This is striking from a broader historical perspective. In the early twentieth century, philosophers tended to see Kant as the precurser of Hegel. See, for example, James' *A Pluralistic Universe* (New York: Longman, 1909), pp. 238–241, and Dewey's early essay 'Experience and Objective Idealism,' in *The Influence of Darwin on Philosophy* (New York: Holt, 1910), pp. 198–226.

11. Hence in 'Two Aspect View,' pp. 156–157, Allison writes of epistemic conditions as "subjective" because "they reflect the structure and operations of the human mind" and because they involve "a reference to mind." In this regard Allison is much closer to the subjectivist tradition than any objectivist.

12. The *locus classicus* of the patchwork theory is Hans Vaihinger, 'Die transcendentale Deduktion der Kategorien in der Erste Ausgabe der Kritik der reinen Vernunft,' in *Philosophische Abhandlungen* (Halle: Niemeyer, 1902), pp. 24–98; reprinted and translated in *Kant: Disputed Questions,* ed. Moltke Gram (Chicago: Quadrangle Books, 1967), pp. 23–61. Throughout his *Commentary* Kemp Smith closely follows, and indeed widely extends, Vaihinger's theory.

1. Idealism in the Precritical Years

1. See, for example, Brigitte Sassen, 'Critical Idealism in the Eyes of Kant's Contemporaries,' *Journal of the History of Philosophy* 35 (1997), 421–455, esp. 428. See also Heinz Heimsoeth, *Transzendentale Dialektik* (Berlin: de Gruyter, 1966), p. 129.

2. On early reactions to idealism, see the general introduction, note 3.

3. On the reception of Berkeley's idealism in Germany, see Eugen Stäbler, *Berkeley's Auffassung und Wirkung in der deutsche Philosophie* (Tübingen: Sporn, 1935), pp. 5–38; Henry Bracken, *The Early Reception of Berkeley's Immaterialism: 1710–1733* (The Hague: Nijhoff, 1959), pp. 1–39, esp. 16–24, 83–84; Désirée Park, 'Kant and Berkeley's Idealism,' *Studi Internazionali die Filosofia* 2 (1969–1970), 3–10; and Dietmar Heidemann, *Kant und das Problem des metaphysischen Idealismus* (Berlin: de Gruyter, 1998) (*Kant-Studien Ergänzungsheft* 131), pp. 15–46. On the recep-

tion of Hume, see G. Gawlick and L. Kreimendahl, *Hume in der deutschen Aufklärung: Umrisse einer Rezeptionsgeschichte* (Stuttgart–Bad Cannstatt: Fromann-Holzboog, 1987) (Forschungen und Materialen zur deutschen Aufklärung, Part 2, vol. 4).

4. On the influence of the Scottish commonsense school in Germany, see the general introduction, note 2.

5. It is striking that Kant identifies dogmatic egoism with Spinozism. See Metaphysik L1, XXVIII, 207. This is apparently because both the egoist and the Spinozist think that there is only one subtance. *Reflexion* 3803 states: "All Spinozists are egoists. Query: whether all egoists are necessarily Spinozists." XVII, 297.

6. See Metaphysik Herder, XXVIII, 42; and Metaphysik L1, XXVIII, 206–207.

7. Metaphysik Herder, XXVIII, 43. See also Metaphysik K2, XXVIII, 770.

8. This is noted by Kemp Smith, who, in his *Commentary*, p. 300, maintains that "By idealism Kant means any and every system which maintains that the sensible world does not exist in the form in which it presents itself to us. The position is typified in Kant's mind by the Eleatics, by Plato, and by Descartes, all of whom are rationalists." While essentially valid, Kemp Smith's statement needs correction in two respects. First, Platonic idealism was not the only form of idealism for Kant, not at any stage of his development. Second, the paradigm of Platonic idealism for Kant was Leibniz and not Descartes, who was a problematic idealist.

9. This is Kant's formulation in the *Monadologia physica*, Prop. VII, I, 481. The same distinction is already implicit in the *Nova dilucidatio*, I, 413–416.

10. On the dispute surrounding this problem, see Benno Erdmann, *Martin Knutzen und seine Zeit* (Leipzig: Voss, 1876), pp. 55–83; L. W. Beck, *Early German Philosophy* (Cambridge: Harvard University Press, 1969), pp. 187–188, 225–226; and Eric Watkins, 'From Pre-established Harmony to Physical Influx: Leibniz's Reception in Eighteenth Century Germany,' *Perspectives on Science* 6 (1998), 136–203, and 'The Development of Physical Influx in Early Eighteenth-Century Germany: Gottsched, Knutzen, and Crusius,' *Review of Metaphyiscs* 49 (1995), 295–339.

11. For a more detailed account of Kant's early theory of interaction and its role in his philosophical development, see Eric Watkins, 'Kant's Theory of Physical Influx,' *Archiv für Geschichte der Philosophie* 77 (1995), 285–324.

12. On the details and various versions of physical influx theory, see Watkins, 'The Development of Physical Influx'; and Eileen O'Neill, "Influxus Physicus," in *Causation in Early Modern Philosophy: Cartesianism, Occasionalism, and Pre-Established Harmony*, ed. Steven Nadler (University Park: Penn State University Press, 1993), pp. 27–55.

13. This is the objection of Moltke Gram, 'What Kant Really Did to Idealism,' in *Essays on Kant's Critique of Pure Reason*, ed. J. N. Mohanty and Robert Shahan (Norman: Oklahoma University Press, 1982), pp. 127–155, esp. 129–130. It could be, however, that Kant really intended the argument to work against only egoism. A Reflexion from the late 1760s puts forward essentially the same argument specifically against the egoist rather than idealist. See R 4094, XVII, 413.

14. This is a leitmotif of Kant's early philosophy. See *Gedanken von der wahren Schätzung der lebendigen Kräfte* §9, I, 23; *Nova dilucidatio*, Prop. XIII, Usus. 1, 5; I, 414, 415; and *Monadologia physica*, Prop. V, Scholion; I, 480.

15. For a discussion of the materialism inherent in Kant's doctrine, see Alison Laywine, *Kant's Early Metaphysics and the Origins of the Critical Philosophy* (Atascadero: Ridgeview, 1993) (North American Kant Society Studies in Philosophy, vol. 3), pp. 25–54.

16. These objections were made by *inter alios* J. P. Reusch, J. C. Gottsched, and C. A. Crusius, whose works were widely influential. On these developments, see Watkins, 'From Pre-established Harmony to Physical Influx,' pp. 182, 191–192, 196, and 'The Development of Physical Influx,' p. 306.

17. As Leibniz formulates his doctrine in the *Discourse on Metaphysics*, "even if everything were destroyed, except God and myself, I would still have all the perceptions I now have" (§14). See too 'A New System of the Nature and Communication of Substances': "[T]he perceptions or expressions of external things reach the soul at the proper time by virtue of its own laws, as in a world apart, and as if there existed nothing but God and itself" (§14). Leibniz would later regret these statements, which were famously attacked by Pierre Bayle in the first and second editions of his *Dictionaire historique et critique* (1697, 1702). Leibniz admitted that the statements were extreme and insisted that they were hypothetical, because he did not mean to deny that our perceptions correspond to external objects. See his replies to Bayle, in *Schriften*, IV, 517–524, 554–571.

18. See Metaphysik Mrongovius, XXIX, 867. See too R 4785, XVII, 727, from the mid-1770s, where Kant refers to the the world of the egoist as "ein monadisches Daseyn." In his later 1790 *Streitschrift* against Eberhard, Kant is explicit that Leibniz's preestablished harmony leads to idealism (VIII, 249).

19. On Swedenborg's Leibnizian metaphysics and their role in his mysticism, see Laywine, *Kant's Early Metaphysics*, pp. 55–71.

20. See, for example, Kant's *Prolegomena*, where, in language reminiscent of the *Träume*, he complains about Berkeley's "mystical and visionary idealism" and "dreaming idealism" (IV, 293). See too R 6050, 'Von der philosophischen Schwarmerey,' XVIII, 434–37; and the late 1796 essay 'Von einem neuerdings erhobenen vornehmen Ton in der Philosophie,' VIII, 398–399.

21. Laywine, *Kant's Early Metaphysics*, p. 70.

22. In Metaphyik L Kant characterizes dogmatic idealism as Platonic idealism, and says that Leibniz was "attached to Platonic idealism," XXVIII, 207. Metaphysik Mrongovius also portrays Leibniz as a Platonist, XXIX, 761, 763.

23. On these grounds Paul Guyer has referred to the "ontological realism" of the Inaugural Dissertation and stressed that Kant's doctrine of the ideality of space and time did not imply the ideal status of objects themselves. See *Kant and the Claims of Knowledge* (Cambridge: Cambridge University Press, 1987), pp. 20–24. This term is ambiguous, however. Kant's realism did not involve *transcendental realism*, the doctrine that appearances are properties of things-in-themselves; rather, it committed him to only a belief in the reality of things-in-themselves, whose intrinsic properties are unknown to us. Already in the late 1760s Kant had repu-

diated direct realism and affirmed the subjectivist principle that the objects of awareness are representations. See, for example, R 3929, XVII, 351.

24. *Pace* Gram, 'What Kant Really Did to Idealism,' p. 152n7.

25. Leibniz would counter this argument, of course, by claiming that all mathematical propositions are based on the law of identity: "The great foundation of mathematics is the *principle of contradiction or identity*, that is, that a proposition cannot be true and false at the same time and that therefore A is A and cannot be non-A" (Leibniz's Second Letter to Clarke, L, p. 677). Clearly, Kant's argument presupposes his theory that mathematical propositions are synthetic a priori. Though Kant had not yet developed his general classification of judgments, and more specifically his theory of the synthetic a priori, the Inaugural Dissertation lays down the basis for his later doctrine by arguing that mathematical propositions require some form of intuition (§15B; II, 403). On the development of Kant's theory of the synthetic a priori character of geometry, see Ted Humphrey, 'The Historical and Conceptual Relations between Kant's Metaphysics of Space and Philosophy of Geometry,' *Journal of the History of Philosophy* 11 (1973), 483–512, esp. 490–500.

26. See Lambert to Kant, October 13, 1770, *Schriften*, X, 103–111; and Mendelssohn to Kant, December 25, 1770, *Schriften*, X, 113–116.

27. See also R 4718, XVII, 685–686.

28. See *Träume eines Geistersehers*, II, 323, 368. Kant had already anticipated this conclusion in his 1763 Prize Essay when he argued that the objects of philosophy, unlike those of mathematics, must be given in experience.

29. Kant first came to this conclusion in the general remark to his essay on negative quantities, II, 201–204. He reiterates the point at the close of the *Träume*, II, 307.

30. The point has been stressed by Karl Ameriks, *Kant's Theory of Mind* (Oxford: Oxford University Press, 1982), p. 110. I will attempt to defend this interpretation in more detail in Chapter 7.

31. For example, Strawson, *The Bounds of Sense*, p. 257, and T. E. Wilkerson, *Kant's Critique of Pure Reason* (Oxford: Oxford University Press, 1976), p. 82.

32. See R 4285 (XVII, 496), R 4536 (XVIII, 586), R 5400 (XVIII, 172), R 5461 (XVIII, 189), R 5563 (XVIII, 234), R 5636 (XVIII, 268), R 5642 (XVIII, 280).

33. See Kemp Smith, *Commentary*, p. 300, who finds Kant's failure to describe Hume as a skeptical idealist very puzzling.

34. *Meditations on First Philosophy*, AT, VII, 38–40.

35. See also the argument in the *Prolegomena*, IV, 313.

36. *Treatise of human Nature*, Book I, Part ii, section 6, and Part iv, sections 2 and 3.

37. See Benno Erdmann, 'Kant und Hume um 1762,' *Archiv für Geschichte der Philosophie* 1 (1888), 62–77, 216–230, esp. 65–68.

38. On Kant's knowledge of English, see Erdmann, as above, p. 64. In his article 'Hat Kant Hume's Treatise gelesen?' *Kant-Studien* 5 (1901), 177–181, Karl Groos suggested that though Kant was indeed not fluent in English he could still read it with the help of a dictionary. He points out that Kant owned and cited the *Gentleman's Magazine*. But it is one thing to read an article in a popular magazine

and quite another to master the delicate phrasing and dialectical nuances of the *Treatise*.

39. See James Beattie, *Versuch über die Natur und Unveränderlichkeit der Wahrheit; im Gegensatze der Klügeley und der Zweifelssucht* (Leipzig, 1772). On this work as the source of Kant's knowledge of the *Treatise*, see Kemp Smith, *Commentary*, pp. xxviii–xxix; Robert Paul Wolff, 'Kant's Debt to Hume via Beattie,' *Journal of the History of Ideas* 21 (1960), 117–123; and L. W. Beck, 'A Prussian Hume and a Scottish Kant,' in *Essays on Hume and Kant* (New Haven: Yale University Press, 1978), pp. 117–120. On the continental reception of the *Treatise*, see Ernest Mossner, 'The Continental Reception of Hume's *Treatise*, 1739–41,' *Mind* 56 (1947), 31–43. That this translation might have been the source of Kant's awakening by Hume is doubtful, however. Since it appeared only around Easter 1772, it would have been too late for the events usually regarded as decisive: 1769, when Kant discovered the antinomies, and February 1772, when Kant wrote Beck about the problem of the objective validity of the concepts of reason.

40. Not too much stress should be placed on these informal contacts. Hamann confessed he had not closely studied the *Treatise* (see note 44); and Kant's friendship with Kraus began only in 1773, much too late for the discovery of the antinomies and the formulation of the critical problem as stated in the 1772 letter to Herz.

41. See *Prolegomena*, IV, 272; and *Kritik der praktischen Vernunft*, V, 52.

42. See *Treatise*, I, iii, 1, and I, iv, 1.

43. This is the argument of Manfred Kuehn, 'Kant's Conception of Hume's Problem,' *Journal of the History of Philosophy* 21 (1983), 176–193; and Gawlick and Kreimendahl, *Hume in der deutschen Aufklärung*, pp. 189–198. Kreimendahl has elaborated his argument in *Kant—der Durchbruch von 1769* (Cologne: Dinter, 1990). For an incisive review of this work, see Lorne Falkenstein, 'The Great Light of 1769—A Humean Awakening?' in *Archiv für Geschichte der Philosophie* 77 (1995), 63–79. See also Wolfgang Carl's review of *Hume in der deutschen Aufklärung*, *Philosophische Rundschau* 35 (1988), 207–214.

44. The article is in Hamann's *Sämtliche Werke*, ed. J. Nadler (Vienna: Herder, 1949–1957), IV, 364–370. For a long time it was assumed that the article was Hamann's own work; it appears in the Nadler edition without any note that it was a translation. Apparently, the first to see that it was a translation was Rudolf Unger, *Hamann und die Aufklärung*, 2nd ed. (Halle: Niemeyer, 1925), II, 932.

45. Kuehn maintains that Kant knew of the translation through its publication, while Kreimendahl claims that he must have known of it in the late 1760s. Only if we assume Kant knew it much earlier, Kreimendahl argues, could it have been an influence on his discovery of the antinomies, which Kant made in 1769. Kreimendahl brings forth all kinds of hypothetical and circumstantial evidence that Kant would have known of the article earlier than its publication in 1771. See *Durchbruch*, pp. 83–101. The evidence is far too weak, however, to support the enormous weight Kreimendahl places on it.

46. There are two statements by Kant about the source of his critical philosophy.

One is his statement in the *Prolegomena* that Hume awoke him from his dogmatic slumber (IV, 260); the other is his statement in his September 21, 1798 letter to Christian Garve that the discovery of the antinomies first roused him from his dogmatic slumber (XII, 257). On these statements, see Kreimendahl, *Durchbruch*, pp. 9–13.

47. Kreimendahl cites as evidence to clinch his case Hamann's May 7, 1781 letter to Hartknoch, where Hamann states with reference to the first *Kritik* that "Hume's treatise on human nature is Kant's Pegasus." See Gawlick and Kreimendahl, *Hume*, p. 198; and Kreimendahl, *Durchbruch*, pp. 98–101. But this is only Hamann's opinion, not a hard fact. Furthermore, Hamann did not necessarily mean that Kant was literally studying the *Treatise*, but only that Humean views were important to Kant. This was part of his general assessment of Kant as a "Prussian Hume." In any case, as Erdmann points out, 'Kant und Hume,' p. 65, Hamann himself confessed in 1781 that he had not studied the *Treatise*. Kuehn, 'Kant's Conception,' p. 185n42, rightly corrects Erdmann for holding that Hamann did not know the work at all; but Erdmann was indeed right to question the depth of Hamann's knowledge.

48. See *Treatise*, I, iv, 7. The contradiction to which Hume refers is not evident from this text, and it must be read in the light of *Treatise*, I, iv, 4, and I, iii, 14.

49. This is the interpretive premise of many scholars, most notably Smith, *Commentary*, pp. xxv–xxx, 61–64; Strawson, *The Bounds of Sense*, pp. 85–112; Robert Paul Wolff, *Kant's Theory of Mental Activity* (Gloucester, Mass: Peter Smith, 1973), pp. 78–183; and Patricia Kitcher, *Kant's Transcendental Psychology* (Oxford: Oxford University Press, 1990), pp. 65–116.

50. See the literature cited in the introduction, notes 5 and 8.

51. This conclusion is confirmed by Wolfgang Carl's study of the development of the Deduction, *Der schweigende Kant: Die Entwürfe zu einer Deduktion der Kategorien vor 1781* (Göttingen: Vandenhoeck and Ruprecht, 1989), pp. 7, 11–12, 146–158. Though we proceed from very different starting points, we agree about the limited significance of Hume's skepticism for Kant's development.

2. Transcendental Idealism and Empirical Realism

1. Among the empiricists see the Garve-Feder review of the first *Kritik, Zugaben zu den Göttinger gelehrte Anzeigen*, January 19, 1782, 3. Stück, 40–48; Feder, *Raum und Causalität* (Frankfurt: Dietrich, 1788), pp. 48–51, 56–57, 107–108; Adam Weishaupt, *Gründe und Gewissheit des menschlichen Erkennens: Zur Prüfung der kantischen Critik der reinen Vernunft* (Nürnberg: Gratenau, 1788), pp. 20–21, 62–63, 119–120, 125–126; Pistorius, review of the *Prolegomena* in *Allgemeine deutsche Bibliothek* 59 (1784), 322–356, review of second edition of *Kritik, Allgemeine deutsche Bibliothek* 81 (1788), 195–238, and his review of Schultz's *Erläuterung, Allgemeine deutsche Bibliothek* 66 (1793), 191–200. Among the rationalists, see Eberhard, *Philosophisches Magazin* I/1 (1788), 17, 28, and I/3 (1789), 264–265; and Mendelssohn, *Morgenstunden, Schriften (Jubiläumsausgabe)*, III/2, 56–57, 59. Among the *Glaubensphilosophen*, see Jacobi, the Beylage to *David Hume, Werke*, II,

291.ff; and Hamann, 'Metakritik zur Purismum der reinen Vernunft,' *Sämtliche Werke*, III, 283–289. Though Hamann does not directly accuse Kant of subjectivism, he does place him, here and elsewhere, in the tradition of Locke, Berkeley and Hume. See Hamann to Herder, May 10 and December 9, 1781, *Briefwechsel*, IV, 293–294, 355.

2. See, for example, B 59, 66, 164, 235, 236, 518, 519, 527, 534, 535, 553, 554, 591: A 104, 339, 373, 375, 384, 385, 386, 391.

3. See A 38, 42, 251–252, 358, 537; B xxvi, xxvii, 69, 566.

4. This has been the the interpretation of many scholars, most notably Gerold Prauss, *Kant und das Problem der Dinge an sich*, pp. 13–42; Henry Allison, *Kant's Transcendental Idealism*, pp. 8–9, 237–242; Erich Adickes, *Kant und das Ding an sich* (Berlin: Pan, 1922), pp. 20–27; Martin Heidegger, *Kant und das Problem der Metaphysik* (Frankfurt: Klostermann, 1952), pp. 36–39; H. J. Paton, *Kant's Metaphysic of Experience* (London: George Allen and Unwin, 1970), I, 61–62; George Schrader, 'The Thing in Itself in Kantian Philosophy,' *Review of Metaphysics* 2 (1949), 30–44; and, more recently, Rae Langton, *Kantian Humility* (Oxford: L. W. Beck, *A Commentary on Kant's Critique of Practical Reason* (Chicago: University of Chicago Press, 1960) pp. 29–41; Oxford University Press, 1998), pp. 12–13. There are important differences between these scholars, more specifically regarding whether the distinction is between different properties of things (Langton, Adickes), different explanations (Beck), or different perspectives or standpoints (Allison, Prauss). However, all affirm that there is one thing that has two aspects, whether properties, explanations, or perspectives.

There is an important ambiguity in dual aspect theories depending upon the reading of the term "appearance" (*Erscheinung*). This term might refer to the *relation* between subject and object, the *act* or *manner* in which objects are perceived; or it might also refer to the *object*, what is perceived. Some dual aspect theorists maintain that appearances are only the former, so that the sole object of perception is the thing-in-itself; others maintain that appearances are the latter, so that the object of perception is an appearance. Advocates of the dual aspect reading sometimes make both these claims, vacillating from one sense of appearance to another. To avoid this ambiguity in what follows, I distinguish between *weaker* and *stronger* dual aspect doctrines, where the weaker uses appearance in strictly the former sense and the stronger uses it in strictly the latter sense.

5. This is the interpretation of Kuno Fischer, *Immanuel Kant und seine Lehre* (Heidelberg: Winter, 1898), I, 603–620; Benno Erdmann, *Kants Kriticismus in der ersten und zweiten Auflage der Kritik der reinen Vernunft* (Leipzig: Voss, 1878), pp. 91–94, 202–203; Ernst Vahinger, 'Zu Kants Widerlegung des Idealismus,' *Strassberger Abhandlungen zur Philosophie* (Freiburg: Mohr, 1884), pp. 87–88, 121–124; Bird, *Kant's Theory of Knowledge*, pp. 308–321; and Smith, *Commentary*, pp. 157, 298–321. More recently, a version of this interpretation has been put forward by Alfons Kalter, *Kants vierter Paralogismus* (Meisenheim am Glan: Verlag Anton Hain, 1975), pp. 265–267.

6. The footnote states: "I have also, elsewhere, sometimes entitled it *formal* ideal-

ism, to distinguish it from *material* idealism, that is, from the usual type of idealism which doubts or denies the existence of outer things themselves" (B 519).
This seems to moderate or qualify the extreme subjectivism of the earlier definition, because Kant now appears to commit himself to "the existence of outer
things." The meaning of the term 'formal idealism' will be explained below,
1.3.4.

7. The meaning of this definition has been the source of some controversy. Allison
has claimed that, contrary to appearances, it is evidence for his own two aspect
interpretation, and he has taken it as an example for how apparently subjectivist
passages can be read in a two aspect light. According to his reading, the characterization of appearances as "mere representations" must be understood to refer
to "the manner in which they are represented." See *Kant's Transcendental Idealism*, p. 27. Allison has been taken to task for such a counterintuitive reading by
Hoke Robinson, 'Two Perspectives on Kant's Appearances and Things in Themselves,' *Journal of the History of Philosophy* 32 (1994) 411–441, esp. 419–420. Robinson contends that the identification of appearances with representations has
to be taken at its face value and maintains that the passage "insofar as they are
represented" *(so wie sie vorgestellt werden)* qualifies the two forms of appearances
as representations. In a later defense of his reading, Allison explains that the relative pronoun "which" *(die)* refers back to "the objects of any possible experience" *(Gegenstände einer uns möglichen Erfahrung)*. See his 'Transcendental Idealism: A Retrospective,' in *Idealism and Freedom* (Cambridge: Cambridge University
Press, 1996), p. 13. Allison is indeed correct to read the passage in this manner,
because, as he correctly argues, if the pronoun refers to "appearances, that is,
mere representations," we attribute unrepresented representations or appearances to Kant. However, this syntactical point does not provide any evidence for
his two aspect reading. Even if the pronoun qualifies "objects," it is still consistent with the text for the appearances to be mere representations. This is indeed
exactly what the text states, and it is only if this passage is ignored that there is
any evidence for Allison's reading. In any case, Allison's reading hardly agrees
with Kant's later identification of appearances with representations at A 492.

8. Allison, *Kant's Transcendental Idealism*, p. 8. Allison's account of the distinction
between the transcendental and empirical is completely false for the first edition
definitions.

9. For more general criticisms of the dual aspect interpretation, see Richard Aquila,
'Things in Themselves and Appearances: Intentionality and Reality in Kant,'
Archiv für Geschichte der Philosophie 61 (1979), 293–307; Karl Ameriks, 'Recent
Work on Kant's Theoretical Philosophy,' *American Philosophical Quarterly* 19
(1982), 1–19, esp. 5–11; and Gardner, *Kant and the Critique of Pure Reason*,
pp. 289–298. See Allison's response to some of these criticisms in his 'Two Aspect View,' in *New Essays on Kant*, pp. 157–178, and his 'A Retrospective' in *Idealism and Freedom*, pp. 3–26. The weakest point of Allison's defense remains his in-
ability to explain the many passages where Kant identifies appearances and
representations. See his 'A Retrospective,' p. 13, where he virtually admits that
he cannot explain these passages.

10. See below, 1.4.1.

11. See also R 5400, XVIII, 172.

12. It is striking that in his initial explanation of the empirical reality of space in the Aesthetic, Kant states that to say there is something outside me means that it appears in a different region of space than my own body (A 28). He does not say that the empirical reality of space is evident from objects existing apart from one another, where my body is only one such object. For some reason, Kant seems to think that my body is privileged in providing me with the concept of an external reality. Why? Although the reasons for Kant's emphasis upon the body are not explicit in the very dense exposition of the Aesthetic, they become clearer from his early 1768 essay 'Von dem ersten Gründe des Unterschieds der Gegenden im Raume.' Here Kant argues in some detail that the ultimate basis for knowing that things are outside us in space lies in their relationship to our body (II, 378–379). This relationship is crucial, he explains, in determining the three dimensions of space. The three-dimensionality of space can be represented as three planes intersecting at right angles to one another. The body is central in determining these three dimensions because it lies along the axis of intersection of these three planes. One of the planes is horizontal, giving rise to the distinction between *above* and *below.* The other two planes are vertical, one of which divides the body into *right* and *left,* and the other of which separates it into *front* and *behind.* Now Kant maintains that our knowledge of direction in space derives essentially from these primitive variables. For even if we know the positions of objects relative to one another, we still do not know how to locate the whole system of such objects, which could be to my right or left, in front of me or behind me. The system remains the same, even though its orientation in space is very different.

13. Some scholars have pointed out that Kant's phrase "outside me" is ambiguous and means not only in another space from me but also different from or other than me. See Langton, *Kantian Humility,* pp. 36–37, and Guyer, *Kant and the Claims of Knowledge,* p. 311. This is indeed correct. In the Fourth Paralogism and the Aesthetic, however, Kant's stress is on the spatial meaning, which is primary for him because he thinks that objects are distinct from me in virtue of the fact that I assign them a different position in space. In the empirical sense nothing more should be read into the distinctness or otherness of the object than its appearance in another place than myself. Kant's criterion for the empirical identity of objects is chiefly spatial.

14. Kant formulates the distinction between appearance and illusion more explicitly in the second edition, B 69–70. It was already in place, however, in the 1770s. See R 5395, XVIII, 171.

15. Kant's rejection of problematic idealism should be treated, therefore, as a repudiation of phenomenalism. The *locus classicus* for the phenomenalist interpretation of Kant is Bennett, *Kant's Analytic,* pp. 22–23. For some telling criticisms of this interpretation, see Bird, *Kant's Theory of Knowledge,* pp. 1–17, 54–60; Richard Alquila, 'Kant's Phenomenalism,' *Idealistic Studies* 5 (1975), 108–126; and Gardner, *Kant and the Critique of Pure Reason,* pp. 156, 271, 273–277. For an inter-

esting attempt to pour new wine into the old bottle of phenomenalism, see James Van Cleve, *Problems from Kant* (Oxford: Oxford University Press, 1999), pp. 6–12.

16. See G. E. Moore, 'Kant's Idealism,' *Proceedings of the Aristotelian Society* 4 (1904), 128–140, esp. 135–136; Prichard, *Kant's Theory of Knowledge*, pp. 71–76; and Strawson, *Bounds of Sense*, pp. 38–39.

17. This point has been made in greater detail by Bird, *Kant's Theory of Knowledge*, pp. 1–17; and Allison, *Kant's Transcendental Idealism*, pp. 5–9.

18. See KrV, B 62–63, 314, 333–334; *Prolegomena*, IV, 289–290; and *Preisschrift über die Fortschritte der Metaphysik*, XX, 269.

19. See Descartes, *Meditations*, AT, VII, 37, 38, 39, 75.

20. The most important addition is Section III of §8, where Kant clarifies the distinction between appearances and illusion (B 69–71). Kant drew this distinction in the first edition, but in the Dialetic rather than Aesthetic (A 293–294).

21. Compare A 27–28 and Dissertation §15D, II, 404–405.

22. Compare A 28, 34, and Dissertation §11, II, 397.

23. This is the reading of Erich Adickes, *Kants Lehre von der doppelten Affektion unseres Ich als Schlüssel zu seiner Erkenntnistheorie* (Tübingen: Mohr, 1929), p. 38; Henry Allison, 'Kant's Critique of Berkeley,' *Journal of the History of Philosophy* 11 (1973), 43–63; and Margaret Wilson, 'The Phenomenalisms of Kant and Berkeley,' in *Self and Nature in Kant's Philosophy*, ed. Allen Wood (Ithaca: Cornell University Press, 1984), pp. 167–168.

24. See Adickes, *Kants Lehre*, pp. 32, 37, 38–39; Vaihinger, 'Zu Kants Widerlegung,' pp. 145–147, and *Commentar zu Kants Kritik der reinen Vernunft*. (Stuttgart: Deutsche Verlags Anstalt, 1922), II, 53–56; and Kemp Smith, *Commentary*, pp. 615–616.

25. My task here is only to assess the interpretation of empirical realism in the theory of double affection. For a more general critique of the theory, see Prauss, *Kant und das Problem der Dinge an sich*, pp. 192–227; Bird, *Kant's Theory of Knowledge*, pp. 18–35; and Moltke Gram, *The Transcendental Turn* (Gainsville: University of Florida Press, 1984), pp. 11–57.

26. This point was admitted by Vaihinger himself. See his *Commentar*, II, 51–53.

27. See note 18 above.

3. The First Edition Refutation of Skeptical Idealism

1. See too A 367 where Kant defines idealism as the doctrine that "the existence of all objects of outer sense is doubtful."

2. As we shall see below, 1.4.1 and 1.5.2.

3. See Kant's comments in the preface to the second edition of the *Kritik* regarding the failure of philosophy to refute skepticism, B xxxixn; his critique of the Scottish philosophy of common sense in the preface to the *Prolegomena*, IV, 257–260; and his criticism of Mendelssohn in 'Was heißt: Sich im Denken orientiren?' VIII, 140. I take issue here with the view of Karl Ameriks that Kant's starting point was "the common standpoint" that consists in "what all normal people re-

ally do believe." See his *Kant and the Claims of Autonomy*, pp. 2, 39, 57. Ameriks maintains that rather than attempting to answer skeptical doubts about our ordinary beliefs, Kant held that "philosophers should simply accept . . . common knowledge . . . and move on from there" (57). Such an interpretation has difficulty in explaining not only Kant's rejection of common sense but also his high opinion of skeptical idealism.

4. See R 6050, "Von der philosophischen Schwärmerey,' XVIII, 434–437; and the late 1796 essay 'Von einem neuerdings erhobenen vornehmen Ton in der Philosophie,' VIII, 398–399.

5. See second preface, B xxxvii–xxxviii.

6. See especially the Sixth Meditation, AT, VII, 75, 77.

7. This is to simplify matters. Kant's detailed account of the structure of the paralogisms at A 402–403 applies only with difficulty to the fourth paralogism. For example, Kant maintains that the major premise of a paralogism applies a *category* in a transcendental sense while the minor applies it in an empirical sense. But this does not apply to the fourth paralogism as expounded at A 366–367. Here the basic confusion concerns not the empirical and transcendental use of a category but the empirical and transcendental use of the concept of external objects or appearances. Still, apart from these technical details, Kant's general point that the paralogisms conflate the transcendental and empirical senses of a concept (taken in a wide sense) applies to the fourth paralogism.

8. This is how Kant presents the argument of the Aesthetic in the Critique of the Fourth Paralogism (A 370). In fact, Kant was simplifying his own position. There are indeed some places in the Aesthetic where Kant states that "outer objects are nothing other than mere representations of our sensibility" (A 30). Yet Kant's position was more complicated because he also states in the Aesthetic that appearances are not just representations but how objects appear to us (A 26–27). Whatever the proper reading of appearance in the Aesthetic, Kant's tactic against the Cartesian skeptic demanded the stronger identification of objects with representations. To argue against the Cartesian, Kant had to identify appearances with representations alone, given that the skeptic would deny that the representations of space are appearances of anything external to them.

9. Compare A 372–373 with B 278–279.

10. See also Kant's *Logik*, IX, 49–50; and R 5642, XVIII, 281.

11. This argument becomes much more explicit in the *Prolegomena*, §49, IV, 336–337. But it is already in place in the first edition version of the Transcendental Aesthetic. See Kant's attempts to explain the empirical reality of objects in space, A 27–29, 36, 39, 45. Kant had already developed the coherence strategy against skepticism in the *Reflexionen* of the 1770s. See R 4285 (XVII, 496), R 4536 (XVIII, 586), R 5400 (XVIII, 172), R 5461 (XVIII, 189), R 5563 (XVIII, 234), R 5636 (XVIII, 268), and R 5642 (XVIII, 280).

12. This kind of Cartesian objection has been made by Margaret Wilson, 'Kant and the Refutation of Subjectivism,' *Proceedings of the Third International Kant Congress*, ed. L. W. Beck (Dordrecht: Reidel, 1970), pp. 597–605.

13. See A 58, 104; and *Logik*, IX, 49–50.

14. There are, of course, precedents for reading Kant's distinction in this light. See W. H. Walsh, *Kant's Criticism of Metaphysics* (Edinburgh: Edinburgh University Press, 1975), pp. 28–33, 39–44, and his 'Kant's Transcendental Idealism' in *Kant on Causality, Freedom and Objectivity,* ed. William Harper and Ralf Meerbote (Minneapolis: University of Minnesota Press, 1984), pp. 83–96. See also Bird, *Kant's Theory of Knowledge,* pp. 36–51, and his 'Kant's Transcendental Idealism,' in *Idealism Past and Present,* ed. Godfrey Vesey (Cambridge: Cambridge University Press, 1982) (Royal Institute of Philosophy Lecture Series: 13), pp. 71–92.

15. This is the contention of Kemp Smith, *Commentary,* pp. 140–141. The same point was made by Prichard, *Kant's Theory of Knowledge,* pp. 75–76.

16. This is the solution of Bird, *Kant's Theory of Knowledge,* p. 51; and Allison, *Kant's Transcendental Idealism,* pp. 8–9.

17. See also the following passages: A 358, 391, 494.

18. Although this is more explicit in the second edition, there can be no doubt that it is fully present in the first. See, for example, A 38, 251–252, 385, and the passages in the preceding note.

19. This shift in Kant's doctrine was first noted and explained by Erdmann, *Kant's Kriticismus,* pp. 91–94.

20. Kant gives this definition in R 6316, XVIII, 621–622; in his December 4, 1792 letter to J. S. Beck, XI, 395; in the footnote to the Antinomies, B 519; in the marginal note E xxvi, XXIII, 23; and in the Appendix to the *Prolegomena,* IV, 376–377. Later on, to distinguish his transcendental idealism from empirical or material idealism, Kant sometimes calls his position *formal* or *critical* idealism. See *Prolegomena,* IV, 293, 337, 374. He grew to prefer the term 'critical' over 'transcendental' idealism because the word 'transcendental' seemed to imply a special knowledge of things, whereas the critical philosophy is limited to an examination of the faculty of knowledge.

21. See especially §§22–23, B 146–148. See also the materials cited in 1.5.4, note 26.

22. We shall soon see that this is one of the fundamental points dividing Kant from Berkeley, 1.5.3.

23. I take issue here with the article by Stephen Barker, 'Appearing and Appearances in Kant,' *Monist* 51 (1967), 426–441.

4. The First Edition Refutation of Dogmatic Idealism

1. See Kemp Smith, *Commentary,* p. 301; and Colin Turbayne, 'Kant's Refutation of Dogmatic Idealism,' *Philosophical Quarterly* 5 (1955), 243.

2. That the unnamed dogmatic idealist of the first edition was Leibniz was first argued by George Miller, 'Kant's First Edition Refutation of Dogmatic Idealism,' *Kant-Studien* 62 (1973), 315–335. Though Miller saw the importance of Leibniz's idealism for Kant, he placed Kant's critique of Leibniz in the Second Antinomy alone. He also did not consider Kant's criticisms of Leibniz's idealism in his earlier lectures and writings.

3. Kant describes Leibniz as an idealist in Metaphysik L1, XXVIII, 207, and Metaphysik Mongrovius, XXIX, 761, 763.

4. Kant places Leibniz in this tradition also in the *Metaphysische Anfangsgründe der Naturwissenschaften*, IV, 507; and in the *Streitschrift* against Eberhard, VIII, 248. One source of Kant's Platonic interpretation of Leibniz is the letter to him from David Ruhnken dated March 10, 1771, *Schriften*, X, 118–119. Kant is correct in placing Leibniz in this tradition. See, for example, Leibniz's 'On the True Theologica Mystica,' L, pp. 367–369; *Discourse on Metaphysics* §§26–27; and his 1702 letter to Sophia Charlotte, L, p. 549. On Leibniz's Platonism, see Paul Schrecker, 'Leibniz and the *Timaeus*,' *Review of Metaphysics* 4 (1951), 495–505.

5. See 'The Metaphysical Foundations of Mathematics,' L, p. 666; Third Paper to Clarke, §4, and Fourth Paper, §41; March 24/April 3, 1699 to de Volder, L, p. 516; June 30, 1704 to de Volder, L, p. 536.

6. Kant is probably summarizing Leibniz's view of space in the Aesthetic when he states the view that "Are they [space and time] only determinations or relations of things, yet ones that would pertain to them even if they were not intuited" (A 23).

7. Even detailed studies of Kant's relationship to Leibniz fail to see it as a critique of his idealism. See, for example, H. J. Paton, 'Kant on the Errors of Leibniz,' in *Kant Studies Today*, ed. L. W. Beck (La Salle: Open Court, 1969), 72–87; and Charles Sherover, 'Kant's Evaluation of his Relationship to Leibniz,' in *The Philosophy of Immanuel Kant*, ed. Richard Kennington (Washington: Catholic University Press, 1985) (Studies in Philosophy and the History of Philosophy, No. 12), pp. 201–228. Allison treats Leibniz only as a transcendenal realist. See his *Kant's Transcendental Idealism*, pp. 18, 19–21. Although Heimsoeth conjectures that Kant is criticizing Leibniz's idealism (*Transzendentale Dialektik*, pp. 130–131n), he falsely places this critique in the Fourth Paralogism, where Kant's avowed target is Descartes' problematic idealism.

8. Compare KrV, A 854 and *Prolegomena*, IV, 274.

9. See, for example, the *Specimen Dynamicum*, L, p. 445; the Fifth Letter to Clarke, §§33, 47.

10. See, for example, the *Discourse on Metaphysics*, §12; October 9, 1687 to Arnauld, L, p. 343; 'First Truths,' L, p. 270; to de Volder, June 20, 1703, L, p. 530, and June 30, 1704, L, p. 536.

11. See 'On the Method of Distinguishing Real from Imaginary Phenomena,' L, pp. 363–365.

12. For a further analysis of the distinction between their doctrines, somewhat different from but compatible with that given here, see Margaret Wilson, 'The Phenomenalisms of Leibniz and Berkeley,' in *Ideas and Mechanism* (Princeton: Princeton University Press, 1999), pp. 306–321.

13. See the *New Essays*, pp. 131–133, 403–404.

14. In her interesting article 'Confused Perceptions, Darkened Concepts: Some Features of Kant's Leibniz Critique,' in *Kant and His Influence*, ed. G. M. Ross and T. McWalter (Bristol: Thoemmes, 1990), pp. 73–103, Catherine Wilson raises the

important question of whether Kant's attribution of a single faculty theory to Leibniz is accurate. Rightly, she maintains that the historical significance of Kant's criticism depends on the accuracy of the attribution (p. 73). Wilson finds some evidence that it is not accurate (pp. 82–88), and then argues that Kant probably attributed the single faculty theory to Leibniz under the influence of his successors, Christian Wolff, A. G. Baumgarten, and C. F. Meier (pp. 88–94). While she is probably correct in thinking that Kant's interpretation of Leibniz was influenced by Wolff, Kant also could have learned of the confusion doctrine directly from Leibniz himself, especially from the *Nouveaux Essais*, which had been published in 1765. On the influence of this text on Kant, see Ernst Cassirer, *Kants Leben und Lehre* (Berlin: Cassirer, 1921), pp. 102–104. For a defense of Kant's interpretation of Leibniz and Wolff, see Gottfried Martin, 'Kant's Auseinandersetzung mit der Bestimmung der Phänomene durch Leibniz und Wolff als verworrene Vorstellungen,' in *Kritik und Metaphysik*, ed. F. Kaulbach and J. Ritter (Berlin: de Gruyter, 1966), pp. 99–105.

15. See Leibniz, *New Essays*, pp. 403–404.
16. See Leibniz's analysis of sense qualities in ibid., pp. 131–133; and his letter to Sophia Charlotte, 1702, L, p. 547.
17. See Leibniz's taxonomy of ideas, 'Meditations on Knowledge, Truth, and Ideas,' L, pp. 291–292.
18. Kant rightly emphasizes this point in the first *Kritik*, A 43, 270–271, 275–276.
19. Needless to say, Kant's arguments cannot be reconstructed in all their depth and detail here. For a fuller account, see Vaihinger, *Commentar*, II, 202–290; Paton, *Kant's Metaphysic of Experience*, I, 107–186; and Lorne Falkenstein, *Kant's Intuitionism* (Toronto: University of Toronto Press, 1995), pp. 217–252.
20. See KrV, B 93; and *Logik*, IX, 91.
21. See KrV, A 24–25; and Dissertation, II, 402.
22. See A 438; and Dissertation, §15, Corollarium (II, 405). In 3789, XVII, 293, Kant formulates the distinction as one between a *totum analyticum* and a *totum syntheticum*. In R 6178, XVIII, 481, he formulates it as a distinction between intuitive and discursive universality. See also §76 of the *Kritik der Urteilskraft*, V, 401–404.
23. The Fifth Letter to Clarke, §47, L, pp. 703–4.
24. Kant employed the argument from incongruous counterparts on several occasions, and sometimes drew very different conclusions from it. In the Dissertation and Amphiboly it is used to support the intuitive structure of space or the distinctive characteristics of phenomena. It first appeared in the early essay 'Von dem ersten Gründe des Unterschieds der Gegenden im Raume,' II, 380–383, where it was employed to prove the absolute status of space. In the *Prolegomena* (§13, IV, 285–286) and in the *Metaphysische Anfangsgründe* (IV, 483–484) it is cited to establish the subjectivity of space. For some contrasting views on its various uses, see Kemp Smith, *Commentary*, pp. 161–166; and Allison, *Transcendental Idealism*, pp. 99–102. For an interesting attempt to reconcile these uses, see Jill Vance Buroker, *Space and Incongruence* (Dordrecht: Reidel, 1981), pp. 50–68.

25. See Leibniz to de Volder, June 20, 1793, L, p. 529; and *Monadology,* §9.

26. This was Kant's argument in *Träume eines Geistersehers,* II, 321–324. See above, 1.1.5.

27. See above, 1.2.1, note 4 for the distinction between weaker and stronger dual aspect doctrines. According to the weaker version, appearances consist entirely in the manner or act of perception, and their sole object is the thing-in-itself.

28. Here I take issue with the reading of Sadik Al-Azm, *The Origins of Kant's Arguments in the Antinomies* (Oxford: Clarendon Press, 1972), pp. 46–85, who maintains that the Thesis represents Newtonian atomism and the Antithesis Leibniz's criticism of it. Al-Azm fails to explain, however, all the points noted here. While he recognizes that Kant describes the Theses as Platonic (p. 4), he does not seem to realize that Kant describes Leibniz's idealism in such terms.

29. Only one passage seems to provide evidence against this reading. In the Remark on the Antithesis Kant portrays the monadist as holding that *matter* is not infinitely divisible (A 439). This does not imply, however, that matter is the simple, but only that it is the appearance of the simple. Admittedly, Kant's description of the monadist as holding that matter is not infinitely divisible is very odd, given that Leibniz argued the opposite on many occasions. The oddity disappears, however, when we consider that the Leibnizians had two views of matter: as mere extension, which is infinitely divisible, and as an appearance of substance or *phenomenon bene fundata.* It is decidedly the second view that is at stake in the Thesis, as Kant makes clear (A 440).

30. Compare A 439 and 441. Kant vascillates between saying that the proof *might* be valid, and that it *is* so. See *Schriften,* III, 305, lines 29–30, and 307, lines 10–12. Only the more cautious formulation is true to his critical agnosticism; the bolder one is a throwback to the rationalism of the Inaugural Dissertation.

5. Kant and Berkeley

1. See the *Zugabe zu den Göttinger gelehrte Anzeige,* January 19, 1782, 40–48. Garve later published his own review in the *Allgemeine deutsche Bibliothek,* Anhang zu 37–52 (1783), 838–862. Some question remains whether Garve's later published version was the same as the version he sent to Feder. According to Erdmann, *Kants Kriticismus,* p. 99, he rewrote some of the sections. Yet Garve claims that he did not alter it. See Garve to Kant, July 13, 1783, in Kant, *Schriften,* X, 330–331. In any case, Garve said that he lost the much longer original draft.

   The edited Garve-Feder version has been reprinted in Karl Vorländer's edition of Kant's *Prolegomena* (Hamburg: Meiner, 1969), pp. 167–174. There is a translation of both the original Garve review and the Feder version by James Morrison in Johann Schultz, *Exposition of Kant's Critique of Pure Reason* (Ottawa: University of Ottawa Press, 1995), pp. 171–199.

2. On the authorship of the review, and the differences between its original and edited versions, see *The Fate of Reason,* pp. 175–177.

3. See Garve to Kant, July 13, 1783, *Schriften*, X, 331.

4. According to Emil Arnoldt, who made an exhaustive comparison of the texts, only one-third of the review came from Feder's hand. See his *Kritische Exkurse im Gebiete der Kant Forschung*, in *Gesammelte Schriften* (Berlin: Cassirer, 1908), IV, 9–11.

5. Feder was responsible for equating Kant's idealism with Berkeley's. Garve's original review has no such equation, contending instead that Kant's position is more akin to Descartes' rather than Berkeley's idealism. Feder himself later admitted that he added the offending passages about Berkeley. See his *J. G Feders Leben, Natur und Grundsätze* (Leipzig: Schwickert, 1825), p. 119. On Feder's critique of Kant, see Kuehn, *Scottish Common Sense in Germany*, pp. 214–221; and Reinhardt Brandt, 'Feder und Kant,' *Kant-Studien* 80 (1989), 249–264.

6. See Garve to Kant, July 15, 1783, *Schriften*, X, 328–333.

7. It is questionable, however, whether Garve really disowned the opinions expressed in the review. Beck wrote Kant that Eberhard told him that Garve still could not see any difference between Kant's and Berkeley's idealism. See Beck to Kant November 10, 1792, *Schriften*, XI, 384.

8. See Kant to Herz, November 24, 1776, *Schriften*, X, 198.

9. On the reception of Berkeley's idealism in Germany, see above, 1.1.1, note 3.

10. The pertinent sections of the *Prolegomena* are §13, Anmerkung II and III (IV, 288–294), and §49 (IV, 336–337). According to Benno Erdmann, many other sections of the *Prolegomena* were written in response to the Göttingen Review; the most important of these were the Anhang to §39 (IV, 322–326), the Anmerkung I to §13 (IV, 287–288), and the final section 'Auflösung der allgemeinen Frage der Prolegomenen' (IV, 365–371). More controversially, Erdmann argued that Kant's indignation over the Göttingen Review made him change his plans to publish a popular summary of the *Kritik* and to write instead a much more polemical work, the *Prolegomena* as we know it. The *Prolegomena* thus became a compound work, both a popular summary and a polemic. See his rare but still valuable 'Einleitung' to *Immanuel Kant's Prolegomena* (Leipzig: Voss, 1878), pp. i–xvii. Erdmann's theory was criticized by Emil Arnoldt, *Kants Prolegomena nicht doppelt redigiert: Widerlegung der Benno Erdmannschen Hypothese* (Berlin: Leipmannsohn, 1879). Hans Vaihinger attempted to resolve the dispute in 'Die Erdmann-Arnoldt'sche Controverse über Kants Prolegomena,' *Philosophische Monatshefte* 16 (1880), 44–71. Erdmann returned to the fray in his *Historische Untersuchungen über Kants Prolegomena* (Halle: Niemeyer, 1904). The whole dispute is ably summarized by Vorländer, *Prolegomena*, pp. xvi–ix.

11. See especially §8 (B 69–72) of the Transcendental Aesthetic. However, the 'General Note on the System of Principles,' B 288–294, and the 'Refutation of Idealism,' B 274–279, are primarily directed against Descartes' problematic idealism.

12. Here I take issue with Kemp Smith, *Commentary*, p. 306.

13. See Kant's comment on Berkeley in his anthropology lectures for 1781–1782, XXV/2, 880.

14. According to Erdmann, another possible influence was Hamann's contention

that Kant was a Prussian Hume. He maintains that Kant probably knew of Hamann's remark and wrote several sections of the *Prolegomena* in response to it. See his 'Einleitung,' pp. xvii–x. Erdmann assumes, however, that Kant understood Hume as a skeptical idealist, which we have found reason to question (see above, 1.1.6).

15. See H. W. B. Joseph, 'A Comparison of Kant's Idealism with That of Berkeley,' *Proceedings of the British Academy* (1929), 213–234; and Colin Turbayne, 'Kant's Refutation of Dogmatic Idealism, *Philosophical Quarterly* 5 (1955), 225–244. The most notable modern advocate of Kant's affinity with Berkeley is Strawson, *The Bounds of Sense*, pp. 21–22, 35, 56–57, 197. But the tradition continues. See, for example, T. E. Wilkerson, *Kant's Critique of Pure Reason* (Oxford: Oxford University Press, 1976), p. 27.

16. See George Adams, 'Berkeley and Kant,' in *George Berkeley*, ed. S. Pepper, K. Aschenbrenner, and B. Mates (California: University of California Publications in Philosophy, 1957), pp. 189–206; Margaret Wilson, 'Kant and "The Dogmatic Idealism of Berkeley,"' *Journal of the History of Philosophy* 9 (1971), pp. 459–475; Henry Allison, 'Kant's Critique of Berkeley,' *Journal of the History of Philosophy* 11 (1973), 43–63; Gale Justin, 'On Kant's Analysis of Berkeley,' *Kant-Studien* 65 (1974), 21–32, and 'Re-Relating Kant and Berkeley,' *Kant-Studien* 68 (1977), 77–89; Ralph Walker, 'Idealism: Kant and Berkeley,' in *Essays on Berkeley*, ed. John Foster and Howard Robinson (Oxford: Oxford University Press, 1985), pp. 109–129; and William Harper, 'Kant on Space, Empirical Realism and the Foundations of Geometry,' *Topoi* 3 (1984), 143–161. Many of these articles are a reaction against Turbayne, cited above in note 15.

17. This is the position of Erdmann, *Kants Kriticismus*, pp. 202–203; and Kemp Smith, *Commentary*, pp. 157, 304–306, who follows Vaihinger, 'Zu Kants Widerlegung des Idealismus,' pp. 131–134.

18. This is the argument of Turbayne, 'Kant's Refutation,' pp. 229–236.

19. Compare KrV, A 360 with Berkeley, *Principles of Human Knowledge* §§87–88.

20. See Kemp Smith, *Commentary*, pp. 157, 304–306.

21. Thus Turbayne, 'Kant's Refutation,' pp. 240–244. We will consider the question of Berkeley's possible influence on Kant below, 1.5.5.

22. See KrV, B 25: "I call *transcendental* all knowledge which is occupied not so much with objects as with the mode of our knowledge of objects insofar as this mode of knowledge is to be possible a priori." Compare Kant's explanation of the term in R 5642, XVIII, 279, where he lays emphasis upon the critical role of his idealism, and especially the exposure of fallacies.

23. In his December 4, 1792 letter to Beck, *Schriften*, XI, 395, Kant dismisses the conflation of his idealism with Berkeley's on the grounds that he speaks of the ideality of space and time with regard to the *form* of representation, while Berkeley thinks of it with regard to its *matter.* See above, 1.3.5, note 20.

24. Both Erdmann and Vaihinger see this as the fundamental distinguishing feature between Kant's and Berkeley's idealism. See Erdmann, *Kant's Kriticismus*, p. 88, and Vaihinger, *Kommentar*, II, 494–505. They do not discuss, however, whether

Kant is inconsistent in holding this point, and whether, as a result, his idealism is identical with Berkeley's after all.

25. Some have indeed interpreted Kant's critique of transcendental realism in the Fourth Paralogism as an attack upon transcendental affection, as if Kant wants to deny the possibility of things-in-themselves acting upon a passive sensibility. See, for example, Bird, *Kant's Theory of Knowledge*, pp. 21–27; and Gerd Buchdahl, *Kant and the Dynamics of Reason* (Oxford: Blackwell, 1992), pp. 137, 143. In these passages Kant does criticize inferences from our perceptions to things-in-themselves as their causes. The main target of his criticism, however, is the equation of outer appearances with things-in-themselves, and more specifically the assumption that *empirical* objects, thus understood, are the causes of our representations. The possibility that some *transcendental* object is their cause remains open; and if the inference to its reality and causality is not necessary, it is also not absurd or impossible. Indeed, Kant himself makes just this distinction (A 372).

26. In R 6319, which was written around 1790, Kant identifies this, along with the problem of knowing oneself solely as appearance, as one of the two basic difficulties of the critical philosophy. See XVIII, 633. See also *Kritik der praktischen Vernunft*, V, 6.

27. See V, 5, 51–58. Kant makes similar points in his marginal comments to his copy of the first *Kritik*. These marginalia were written at the beginning of the chapter on Noumena and Phenomena, and are *Reflexionen* CIV and CVII from the *Selbständige Reflexionen im Handexemplar der KrV*, XXIII, 34. Kant emended his copy of the first *Kritik* in several places to stress these points. See A 147, 247, 251, 259, 286.

28. For a vigorous defense of Kant's concept of noumenal causality, see Kenneth Westphal, 'Noumenal Causality Reconsidered: Affection, Agency, and Meaning in Kant,' *Canadian Journal of Philosophy* 27 (1997), 209–245.

29. This is the thrust of Kant's argument in the Appendix to the *Prolegomena*. See the important passage at IV, 375.

30. This third point does not correspond to Berkeley's own reasoning. In his *De Motu* Berkeley indeed criticizes the idea of an absolute space as illusory, but he does not draw the conclusion that this proves the unreality of the bodies within it. Rather, he holds that the idea of space is only relative, arising from the distances between specific things. See *De Motu* §§53, 58.

31. Berkeley, *Principles of Human Knowledge* §§34–40.

32. Ibid., §90.

33. On just these grounds, Joseph contends that there is little difference between Kant's and Berkeley's idealism. See his 'A Comparison,' pp. 221, 227.

34. See Berkeley's *Principles of Human Knowledge*, §§30, 33, 36.

35. For a defense of Kant along these lines, see Justin, 'On Kant's Analysis of Berkeley,' esp. 29–30; and Ralph Walker, 'Idealism: Kant and Berkeley,' pp. 114–117.

36. It is indeed on just this score that Kant is closer to common speech and experience than Berkeley. This is the one qualification I would make to Margaret Wil-

son's contrast between Kant and Berkeley. She argues that Kant attempts to uphold a scientific realism as opposed to Berkeley's more commonsense realism. See her 'The Phenomenalisms of Berkeley and Kant,' pp. 157–173.

37. See Metaphysik L1 from the 1770s: "Dogmatic egoism and idealism must be banished from philosophy because it has no utility" (XXVIII, 207). See also Metaphysik Herder, XXVIII, 43.

38. See Metaphysik Herder, XVIII, 42. Compare Metaphysik L1, XXVIII, 207.

39. See Metaphysik Herder, XVIII, 43. Compare Metaphysik K2, XXVIII, 770, 793.

40. Arthur Warda, *Immanuel Kants Bücher* (Berlin: Breslauer, 1922), p. 46. This edition is entitled *Philososophische Werke, Erster Theil* (Leipzig, 1781).

41. Eschenbach published together a translation of both Berkeley's *Dialogues* and Arthur Collier's *Clavis Universalis* under the title *Sammlung der vornehmsten Schriftsteller die die Wirklichkeit ihres eignen Körpers und der ganzen Körperwelt leugnen* (Rostock: Anton Ferdinand, 1756). The preface contains a critical discussion of idealism.

42. In his 'Kant's Critique of Berkeley,' p. 61, Allison argues on the basis of a passage from the *Vorarbeit* to the *Prolegomena* that Kant must have read the Eschenbach translation. The passage states: "Berkeley found nothing constant, and so could find nothing which the understanding conceives according to a priori principles. He therefore had to look for another intuition, namely the mystical one of God's ideas, which required a two-fold understanding, one which connected appearances in experience and another which knows things-in-themselves" (XXIII, 58). It is very difficult to understand, however, how this passage refers to anything in the *Dialogues,* where Berkeley still keeps to his general empiricism and does not claim a direct and mystical intuition of God's ideas. Indeed, Berkeley is very critical of the "enthusiasm of Malebranche." See *Philosophical Writings,* p. 177.

43. In his 'Kant's Conception of Berkeley's Idealism,' *Kant-Studien* 74 (1983), 161–175, G. J. Mattey holds that "until the last decade of his life, Kant maintained an active interest in Berkeley's work and continually availed himself of primary sources of it" (p. 163). The historical evidence he cites does not warrent such a confident assumption, however. Like Allison, Mattey maintains that Kant must have read the Eschenbach translation, though he too is skeptical of Allison's reasoning (explained above, note 42). Mattey thinks that Kant's attribution of illusionism to Berkeley is explicable from the peculiarities of the Eschenbach translation, which interprets Berkeley's denial of matter as a denial of the reality of things (p. 164). Still, this does not establish that Kant read Eschenbach, because there were other sources for such an interpretation, which was a commonplace of the German reception of Berkeley.

44. See Turbayne, 'Kant's Refutation,' pp. 242–243; Allison, 'Kant's Critique of Berkeley,' pp. 44, 59; Miller, 'Kant and Berkeley,' p. 322; Wilson, 'Dogmatic Idealism,' pp. 467n, 470n; and Mattey, 'Kant's Conception,' p. 173.

45. For an explanation of Kant's attribution of this argument to Berkeley, see Michael Ayers, 'Berkeley's Immaterialism and Kant's Transcendendental Idealism,'

in *Idealism Past and Present,* ed. Godfrey Vesey (Cambridge: Cambridge University Press, 1982), pp. 51–70.

46. In 1922 Ernst Cassirer maintained that Kant knew of Berkeley mainly from his *Siris.* See his *Das Erkenntnisproblem in der Philosophie und Wissenschaft der neueren Zeit* (Berlin: Cassirer, 1922), II, 327n. Cassirer cites both the French and German translations. He notes that the German translations did not cover the philosophical but only the medical portions of the work; the French translation, however, seems to have been complete. Cassirer's thesis has been questioned, however, by Stäbler, *Berkeley's Auffassung,* pp. 39–56, esp. 56–58, 64. But Stäbler's objection to Cassirer is rather weak: he reasons that if Kant really knew the work, he would have gone into more detail about it, and that Herder would have noted it. There is no compelling reason for these assumptions.

47. See Kemp Smith, *Commentary,* p. 156; Erdmann, *Kant's Kriticismus,* pp. 16, 191; and Stäbler, *Berkeley's Auffassung,* p. 58. The view is perfectly epitomized by G. Dawes Hickes: "Kant's Berkeley is largely an imaginary being—the product of very imperfect knowledge of Berkeley's speculation, obtained from indirect and unreliable sources." See his *Berkeley* (Bristol: Thoemmes, 1992), p. 268.

48. See the *Principles of Human Knowledge* §1. Berkeley's early empiricism is especially evident in the *Commonplace Book* §§740, 823.

49. On the early reception of *Siris,* see A. A. Luce, *The Life of George Berkeley, Bishop of Cloyne* (London: Thomas Nelson, 1949), pp. 200–203.

50. This is the thesis of Bracken, who argues that the early works were far from neglected. See *Reception,* pp. 1–38.

51. See *Siris* §§253, 264, 293–295, 297. On Berkeley's general sympathies for Platonism, see §§266, 304, 335–337. It is important to note that Berkeley's Platonism is consistent with his earlier nominalism because Berkeley does not interpret Plato's ideas as abstract concepts but as the ultimate causes of things. See §335. Allison, 'Kant's Critique of Berkeley,' p. 59, assumes that Kant could have learned of some of Berkeley's Platonic tendencies from *De Motu.* Berkeley does indeed show some sympathy with Platonism in this work; see §§32, 42, 69, 71–72. Yet the more likely source of Kant's Platonic understanding of Berkeley is the work he cites: *Siris.*

52. See *Siris* §§313, 330, 370.

53. See *Principles of Human Knowledge* §§27, 89, 140.

54. Thus Turbayne, 'Kant's Refutation,' p. 244.

55. Thus Wilkerson holds: "Transcendental Idealism is essentially a mixture of certain rationalist doctrines and Berkeleian idealism, expressed in an elaborate psychological vocabulary." See *Kant's Critique of Pure Reason,* p. 27.

6. The Second Edition Refutation of Problematic Idealism

1. Bennet, *Kant's Analytic,* p. 202.

2. See below, 1.6.8, note 49.

3. See Metaphysik Dohna, XXVIII, 680–682, and Metaphysik K2, XXVIII, 770–772.

4. The controversy is indeed very old. It began with Schopenhauer's declaration that the Refutation of Idealism was a betrayal of the transcendental idealism of the first edition of the *Kritik*. See his *Die Welt als Wille und Vorstellung*, in *Sämtliche Werke*, ed. Arthur Hubscher (Leipzig: Brockhaus, 1938), II, 514–517, 526–527. It was given new impulse in the 1880s after the publication of Kuno Fischer's *Immanuel Kant und seine Lehre* (Heidelberg: Winter, 1898), I, 603–620, which defended Schopenhauer's position. As early as 1884 Vaihinger gave a long bibliography of the *status controversiae*. See his 'Zu Kants Widerlegung des Idealismus,' *Strassburger Abhandlungen zur Philosophie* (Freiburg: Mohr, 1884), pp. 87–88.

5. In addition to Schopenhauer and Fischer, we can place in this tradition Erdmann, *Kants Kriticismus*, pp. 202–203; Vaihinger, 'Zu Kants Widerlegung,' 128–138; Kemp Smith, *Commentary*, pp. 298–321; Prichard, *Kant's Theory of Knowledge*, pp. 319–324; Erling Skorpen, 'Kants Refutation of Idealism,' *Journal of the History of Philosophy* 6 (1962) 23–34; and most recently Paul Guyer, 'Kant's Intentions in the Refutation of Idealism,' *Philosophical Review* 92 (1983), 329–383, and *Kant and the Claims of Knowledge*, pp. 279–332.

6. See, for example, Margaret Wilson, 'On Kant and the Refutation of Subjectivism,' pp. 597–606.

7. See, for example, Stroud, 'Transcendental Arguments,' *Journal of Philosophy* 65 (1968), pp. 241–256, reprinted in R. C. S. Walker, *Kant on Pure Reason* (Oxford: Oxford University Press, 1982), 117–131; and Wilkerson, *Kant's Critique*, p. 57.

8. See, for example, Strawson, *The Bounds of Sense*, pp. 124–128; and Bennet, *Kant's Analytic*, pp. 202–214. Though both Strawson and Bennet make interesting points on Kantian themes, their relevance to Kant's own doctrine is questionable. Because of its obscurity, Bennet says that if we take the argument seriously at all, we have *to speculate* about its meaning (p. 202). The idea that the argument could be read in a broader context does not seem to have occurred to him. For some telling criticisms of Strawson's and Bennet's interpretation, see Richard Aquila, 'Personal Identity and Kant's "Refutation of Idealism,"' *Kant-Studien* 70 (1979), 259–278.

9. This dilemma was first stated by H. A. Pistorius in his review of the second edition of the *Kritik*, which appeared in the *Allgemeine deutsche Bibliothek* 81/2 (1788), 343–354, esp. 349–352.

10. This statement from the Fourth Paralogism shows that Kant had this conception already in mind in the first edition of the *Kritik*. See A 493. Kant gives this doctrine more emphasis in the second edition Postulates (B 272).

11. See, for example, Wilkerson, *Kant's Critique of Pure Reason*, p. 81.

12. In Metaphysik K2, XXVIII, 770, Kant also defines idealism in general as the doctrine that we cannot prove the existence of objects outside us.

13. Indeed, Kant is sometimes so careless in stressing simply having a representation of spatial things, and in underplaying the role of coherence, that he writes: "All external perception therefore immediately proves something real in space, or it is rather the real itself" (A 375). He immediately corrects himself, however, when he notes that some representations might be illusory (376). To deal with

the problem of illusion, he applies the criteria of experience: that the actual is what coheres with a perception according to empirical laws. But as if to demote the role of these criteria in his case against idealism, Kant then quickly adds that simply having external perceptions is sufficient to refute the idealist (A 376–377). As Ameriks points out, *Kant's Theory of Mind*, p. 114, Kant's stress on the immediate perception of the outer, and his claim that the reality of outer things is indicated by sensation (A 374), suggest a strong form of subjectivism which it was Kant's intention to overthrow.

14. This was by no means a new doctrine for Kant; rather, he was simply stressing points he had made explicitly many years earlier. Many *Reflexionen* from the 1770s emphasize the role of coherence in refuting idealism. See R 4285 (XVII, 496), R 4536 (XVIII, 586), R 5400 (XVIII, 172), R 5461 (XVIII, 189), R 5563 (XVIII, 234), R 5636 (XVIII, 268), and R 5642 (XVIII, 280).

15. The idea of an *appearance in itself* was first formulated by Hans Vaihinger in his 'Zu Kants Widerlegung des Idealismus,' pp. 85–164, esp. 145n2, 156–157. Vaihinger maintained that Kant himself first used the phrase in his *Opus postumum*. The idea was then developed by Erich Adickes in his *Kants Lehre von der doppelten Affektion unseres Ich*, pp. 22–23. Although Adickes does not explicitly discuss the Refutation in this work, his general interpretation of Kant's idealism makes the object of experience ontologically and numerically distinct from the empirical subject. Kemp Smith applied Adickes theory to the Refutation in his *Commentary*, p. 614. Myron Gochnauer, 'Kant's Refutation of Idealism,' *Journal of the History of Philosophy* 12 (1974), 195–206, dismisses Kemp Smith's interpretation on the grounds that "an appearance by its very nature cannot be something which is different or distinct from the mental state which is a representation" (p. 199). Similarly, see Skoren, 'Kant's Refutation,' pp. 25–28. However, this ignores the broader context of Kemp Smith's views, which is set by the theory of double affection. An appearance in itself is indeed distinct from our empirical consciousness but not our transcendental activity.

16. See, for example, H. J. Paton, *Kant's Metaphysics of Experience*, II, 375–386, esp. 383; Gerhard Lehman, 'Kants Widerlegung des Idealismus,' *Kant-Studien* 50 (1958–1959), 348–363; Wolfgang Müller-Lauter, 'Kants Widerlegung des materialien Idealismus,' *Archiv für Geschichte der Philosophie* 46 (1964), 60–82; James Stuart, 'Kant's Two Refutations of Idealism,' *Southwestern Journal of Philosophy* 6 (1975), 29–46; Douglas Langston, 'The Supposed Incompatibility between Kant's Two Refutations of Idealism,' *Southern Journal of Philosophy* 17 (1979), 359–369; and Eckhart Förster, 'Kants Refutation of Idealism,' in *Philosophy, Its History and Historiography*, ed. A. J. Holland (Dordrecht: Reidel, 1983), pp. 287–303.

The early critics of transcendental idealism also read the Refutation along just these lines. They argued that the Refutation did not alter or add anything new to the subjectivism Kant had already outlined in the first edition of the *Kritik*. But, in their view, such consistency was more a flaw than a merit, for it showed how persistent and thoroughgoing was Kant's nihilism: even in attempting to refute idealism he presupposed it! See, for example, G. E. Schulze, *Aenesidemus,* pp. 202–206, 295–296; H. A. Pistorius, 'Kritik der reinen Vernunft,' *Allgemeine deutsche Bibliothek* 81 (1788), 343–354, esp. 349–352; Eberhard, *Philosophisches Magazin* I/3 (1788–1789), 243ff.

17. For these authors, see notes 4 and 5 above.
18. This is the position of Prichard, *Kant's Theory,* pp. 319–324. Prichard holds that the Refutation *implies* that things-in-themselves are in space and time and knowable. This is also the interpretation of Strawson, *The Bounds of Sense,* pp. 261–262.
19. Thus Fischer, *Kant,* pp. 603–620; Erdmann, *Kants Kriticismus,* pp. 202–203; and Guyer, *Kant and the Claims of Knowledge,* pp. 282, 291, and 'Kant's Intentions,' pp. 377–378.
20. Thus Vaihinger, Adickes, and Kemp Smith. See note 15 above.
21. Thus Guyer, 'Kant's Intentions,' pp. 377–378, and *Kant and the Claims of Knowledge,* pp. 282, 289.
22. Thus Vaihinger, 'Kant's Widerlegung,' pp. 134–138.
23. This is the view of Guyer, *Kant and the Claims of Knowledge,* pp. 11–38, 279–295.
24. See Kemp Smith, *Commentary,* p. 313. In employing this tactic Kemp Smith follows Vaihinger, 'Kants Widerlegung,' p. 131.
25. *Pace* Strawson, *The Bounds of Sense,* pp. 261–262.
26. This kind of weakness has been pointed out by many, most famously by Stroud, 'Transcendental Arguments,' pp. 121–122. See also Gardner, *Kant,* pp. 185–188; and Ralph Walker, *Kant,* pp. 122–135.
27. Here I take issue with Guyer. See note 21 above.
28. This point is made by Müller-Lauter, 'Kant's Widerlegung,' pp. 79–80.
29. This is the position of Stuart, 'Kant's Two Refutations,' pp. 41–44.
30. See KrV, B 12, 218, 161, 196. See also *Prolegomena* §21 Remark and §20.
31. See, for example, XXI, 89, 99; XXII, 40, 400, 405, 408, 447–448, 465, 474, 479.
32. The same point is clear from *Prolegomena* §49, where Kant is explicit that proving the *existence* of something outside us does not require showing a connection among things-in-themselves but only the conformity of appearances to the laws of experience (IV, 336–337).
33. Strawson, *The Bounds of Sense,* p. 122, states that the Refutation of Idealism is not very strategically placed in the Postulates; and Bennet, *Kant's Analytic,* p. 166, thinks that Kant put it in the middle of the Postulates for "a silly reason." But both the intention and the content of the argument confirm Kant's explicit remark that this is its appropriate place (B 274). The significance of the Postulates is stressed by Sellars, 'Kant's Transcendental Idealism,' in *Proceedings of the Ottawa Congress on Kant,* ed. Pierre Laberge, François Duchesneau, and Bryan Morrisey (Ottawa: University of Ottawa Press, 1976), 165–181; and Friedrich Kaulbach, 'Kants Beweis des "Daseins der Gegenstände im Raum Ausser Mir,"' *Kant-Studien* 50 (1958–1959), 323–347. See also the article by Reinhard Brandt cited note 49. Langston, 'Supposed Incompatibility,' pp. 365–368, sees a complete refutation in the Postulates, though this is squeezing the texts rather hard.

34. According to Kemp Smith, the transcendental object appears only in the first edition of the *Kritik,* and is a residue of his precritical years. See his *Commentary,* p. 204. But this claim is simply false. The concept reappears not only in the *Reflexionen* of the 1790s but also in the *Opus postumum.* See below 1.10.8. For an illuminating analysis of this concept, see Henry Allison, 'Kant's Concept of the Transcendental Object,' *Kant-Studien* 59 (1968), 165–186.

35. More precisely, there are two stages to the argument. The first stage consists in the first five sentences; the second stage in the next two. Kant supplements the argument with the two sentences because the first stage is not explicit that I have an immediate *consciousness* of something permanent outside me. It states only the necessary condition of my consciousness in time—that there is something permanent outside me—but it does not state that I am conscious of that necessary condition. It does state that I have a perception of the permanent; but it does not claim that I am conscious of it *as* the permanent outside me. Kant wants the conclusion, however, that the consciousness of my own existence involves the *immediate* consciousness of the existence of something outside me.

   This hiatus is rectified by the second stage, which consists in the following two steps:

   1. Consciousness in time is necessarily joined with the consciousness of the possibility of this time-determination.

   2. It is therefore also connected with the existence of things outside me as the conditions of this time-determination.

   Therefore, consciousness of my own existence is at the same time an immediate consciousness of the existence of other things outside me.

36. It is important to note that this involves a claim only to my having an experience now, at a specific moment of time, and so need not require any memory claims about my having experiences in the past. Such claims would make the premise vulnerable to skeptical doubt. Here I take issue with Bennet, *Kant's Analytic,* p. 118, 124, 208; and Gochnauer, 'Kant's Refutation,' pp. 200–202.

37. Aquila argues that the central concern of the Refutation is with the conditions of reference to oneself as a particular individual. See his 'Personal Identity and Kant's "Refutation of Idealism,"' pp. 262, 269, 274. There is, however, insufficient textual evidence for this view. Kant's primary concern is with determining the objective time of my experience, whoever I am, and not with determining who I am, whenever I have any experience. This interpretation also does not fit the context of Kant's argument: to determine who I am as a specific individual would involve appeal to memory claims, which are easily subject to skeptical doubt.

38. That the Refutation restates the argument of the Deduction is the view of Strawson, *The Bounds of Sense,* p. 259; and Bennet, *Kant's Analytic,* p. 202. For an appraisal of their views, see Aquila, 'Personal Identity,' pp. 260–261; and Allison, *Kant's Transcendental Idealism,* pp. 294–297.

39. *Pace* Bennet, *Kant's Analytic,* pp. 202–203.

40. These arguments seem plausible enough if we construe the permanent in rela-

tive terms. It does not follow, however, that the framework itself must be permanent: it could be changing with respect to some higher framework, of which it is only a part. But, of course, Kant could admit this, and then ask how we measure the time within the higher framework. This would require yet another framework, and so on, until we arrive at the one single time in which all change is measured.

41. In this respect I think that Bennet's interpretation is accurate. See *Kant's Analytic,* pp. 124, 208. See also Gochnauer, 'Kant's Refutation of Idealism,' pp. 196–206, esp. 200–202, who has a similar analysis of Kant's argument.

42. Kant equates the form of appearance with relations at KrV, A 21/B 35.

43. Accounting for relations was a serious problem for Berkeley's idealism. On this aspect of the Refutation and its relation to Berkeley, see the neglected but valuable study by A. H. Smith, *Kantian Studies* (Oxford: Clarendon Press, 1947), pp. 22–25.

44. See, for example, Strawson, *The Bounds of Sense,* pp. 51, 127; and Allison, *Kant's Transcendental Idealism,* pp. 298–299.

45. The importance of this change has been explained by Michael Washburn, 'The Second Edition of the Critique: Toward an Understanding of its Nature and Genesis,' *Kant-Studien* 66 (1975), 277–290.

46. On the close connection between the Refutation and the doctrines of the *Anfangsgründe,* see Michael Friedman, *Kant and the Exact Sciences* (Cambridge: Harvard University Press, 1992), pp. 130–135.

47. In his September 25, 1790 letter to A. W. Rehberg, Kant states the relevance of spatial measurement of temporal magnitudes for the Refutation of Idealism. See *Schriften,* XI, 210.

48. Here I take issue with Washburn, 'The Second Edition of the Critique,' p. 282.

49. There are several other relevant fragments: R 5709, XVIII, 332, which was composed some time in the late 1780s; and R 6323, XVIII, 643, which was written between April and August 1793. Also important is the newly discovered fragment 'Vom inneren Sinne.' For the text and commentary, see Reinhardt Brandt, 'Eine neu aufgefundene Reflexion Kants "Vom inneren Sinne" (Loses Blatt Leninggrad 1),' in *Neue Autographen und Dokumente zu Kants Leben, Schriften und Vorlesungen,* ed. Reinhardt Brandt and Werner Stark (Hamburg: Meiner, 1987) (Kant Forschungen, Band 1), pp. 1–30. The text has been translated by Hoke Robinson, 'A New Fragment of Immanuel Kant: "On Inner Sense,"' *International Philosophical Quarterly* 29 (1989), 251–261. See also in the same place the commentaries by Hoke Robinson, 'Inner Sense and the Leningrad Reflexion,' pp. 271–279; and Guenter Zoeller, 'Making Sense out of Inner Sense,' pp. 263–270.

50. See especially the argument in R 6312, XVIII, 612, 6–13; and R 6313, XVIII, 614, 11–30.

51. See below, 1.10.4.

52. On the rejection of transcendental realism, see R 6317, 627, 17ff.; R 6315, 618, 29; R 6313, 614–615, 31–38; and R 6314, 616, 20–21.

53. See R 5653, 309, 31, 33, and 310, 7–12, 11–19; R 56654, 313, 1–6; R 6311, 611, 20ff.; and R 6315, 618, 14–21, and 620–621, 28–4.
54. See R 5653, 307, 21–24, and 310, 22–28; R 6313, 613–614, 26–2; and R 6316, 622–623, 21–3.
55. See Guyer, 'Kant's Intentions,' pp. 340–343, and *Kant and the Claims of Knowledge*, pp. 290–292. See also Sassen, 'Critical Idealism,' pp. 421–455.
56. See Sassen, 'Critical Idealism,' pp. 446–455.
57. See R 6319, XVIII, 633, which was written around 1790.

7. Kant and the Way of Ideas

1. See Descartes, AT, VII, 181, 185. Descartes' usage of the term is, of course, much more complicated than the phrases cited above suggest. For an illuminating attempt to sort out the complexities and confusions, see Nicholas Jolley, *The Light of the Soul, Theories of Ideas in Leibniz, Malebranche, and Descartes* (Oxford: Oxford University Press, 1990), pp. 12–31. On Descartes' historical role in the development of the theory of ideas, see Robert McRae, '"Idea" as a Philosophical Term in the Seventeenth Century,' *Journal of the History of Ideas* 26 (1965), pp. 175–190.
2. Locke defines an idea as "Whatsoever is the object of thinking when a man thinks," *Essay concerning human Understanding*, Introduction §8. Leibniz accepts this account in *New Essays*, II, 1, 2, 109. Malebranche defines idea as "that which is the immediate object, or that which is nearest to the mind when it perceives something," *Recherche de la vérité*, Book III, Part 2, chap. i. Berkeley simply says that ideas are "objects of human knowledge," *Principles* §1. Hume, of course, uses the term in a more narrow sense to refer to the "faint images" of sense impressions. See *Treatise of human Nature*, Book I, Part I, section i, p. 1 (Selby-Bigge edition). Apart from this minor variation in usage, however, Hume does follow the fundamental tenets of the theory of ideas. He makes impressions the ultimate objects of consciousness and the basic units of meaning. "An object appears to the sense" and "an impression becomes present to the mind" are equivalent expressions for him. See Book I, Part I, section vii, p. 19.
3. Arnauld, *The Art of Thinking*, trans. James Dickoff and Patricia James (Indianapolis: Bobbs-Merrill, 1964), p. 31.
4. That Descartes and Locke held that ideas are entities between our perception of the world and the world itself has been questioned by John Yolton in his 'Ideas and Knowledge in Seventeenth Century Philosophy,' *Journal of the History of Philosophy* 13 (1975), 145–165. Though Yolton makes a plausible case, it is not necessary to defend the more traditional view here. It is only important that Kant and his contemporaries *read* Descartes and Locke in this manner. As already noted, their reading of Descartes and Locke was deeply influenced by Reid.
5. See Descartes, *Meditations*, AT, VII, 37–39. In the *Optics* and *Treatise on Light*, however, Descartes would question whether sense perceptions resemble their objects (XI, 3–6; VI, 113–114). In the *Essay* Locke assumes that the ideas of primary

qualities are objective because they resemble their objects (II, viii, 15). Leibniz thinks that ideas are "expressions" of their objects, where the relations in the idea are isomorphic to those in the object; he is explicit, however, that such an isomorphism does not require complete similarity. See his 'What is an Idea?' L, 207–208, and his October 9, 1687, letter to Arnauld, p. 339.

6. Berkeley, *Principles* §90.

7. Both Leibniz and Wolff took representation as basic, the phenomenon from which all other aspects of the soul are to be explained. See, for example, Leibniz's *Monadology* §60: "The nature of the monad is to represent"; and Wolff's *Vernünftige Gedanken von Gott, der Welt, und der Seele des Menschen* §784, 11th ed. (Halle, 1751): "We meet in the soul nothing but the power to represent the world." *Gesammelte Werke,* I/2, 488–489.

8. See also A 189–190.

9. See, for example, A 52/B 76; A 50/B 74; A 19/B 33; A 494; B 522; and B 1–2.

10. That Kant had completely transformed the account of representation was a point seen very clearly centuries ago by Solomon Maimon. See his *Briefe an Aenesidemus, Werke,* V, 377–378; see too IV, 217–218. That Kant breaks with the traditional account of representation has been well recognized in Kant scholarship. See, for example, Ernst Cassirer, *Das Erkenntnisproblem in der Philosophie und Wissenschaft der neueren Zeit* (Berlin: Cassirer, 1922), III, 87–89; Gerold Prauss, *Erscheinung bei Kant* (Berlin: de Gruyter, 1971), pp. 58–81; and Robert Paul Wolff, *Kant's Theory of Mental Activity* (Cambridge: Harvard University Press, 1963), pp. 105, 109–111, 263–264.

11. It is noteworthy that Kant does not want to deny but to explain the common view that truth consists in the correspondence of a representation with its object. See A 82; and *Logik,* IX, 49–50.

12. For an analysis of Kant's epistemology as a theory of representation, see especially Richard Alquila, 'Things in Themselves and Appearances: Intentionality and Reality in Kant,' *Archiv für Geschichte der Philosophie* 61 (1979), 293–308, and his *Representational Mind: A Study of Kant's Theory of Knowledge* (Bloomington: Indiana University Press, 1983).

13. That the categories cannot be representations was seen as early as 1796 by Sigismund Beck in his *Erläuternder Auszug aus den critischen Schriften des Herrn Prof. Kant* (Riga: Hartknoch, 1796), III, 140, 177–179. Beck argues that the categories cannot be attributes of objects—not even pure or abstract ones—because they determine the very conditions under which properties are attributed to objects.

14. This claim is explicit enough in the first edition of the *Kritik,* especially in the Critique of the Fourth Paralogism. See A 379, 386.

15. See A 23, and 357, and again the Critique of the Fourth Paralogism, A 379, 385.

16. This distinction is very old. Some of the first to make it were Fichte, in the *Zweite Einleitung in die Wissenschaftslehre, Werke,* I, 482; and Beck, in the *Erläuternder Auszug,* III, 3–7, 345–347.

17. See *Prolegomena* §24, IV, 306, and §26, IV, 309.

18. For a more detailed analysis of the role of sensation in Kant's theory, see Rolf George, 'Kant's Sensationism,' *Synthese* 47 (1981), 229–255; and Robert Pippin, *Kant's Theory of Form* (New Haven: Yale University Press, 1982), pp. 26–53.

19. See Locke, *Essay concerning Human Understanding*, Book II, chap. 1, sec. 4; Baumgarten, *Metaphysica* §535; Hutcheson, *An Essay on the Nature and Conduct of the Passions and Affections* (London, 1725), pp. xi, 4–5, and *Inquiry into the Originals of our Ideas of Beauty and Virtue* (London, 1725), v–vi; and Tetens, *Philosophische Versuche über die menschliche Natur und ihre Entwicklung* (Leipzig: Weidmann, 1777) (reissued in *Neudrucke seltener philosophischer Werke*, ed. Kantgesellschaft, Band IV), pp. 45–49.

The influence of Tetens theory of inner sense upon Kant has been the subject of some dispute. T. D. Weldon argued that Tetens' theory is the main source of Kant's, and more specifically that Kant followed Tetens' doctrine that all awareness involves a later act of self-awareness. See his *Kant's Critique of Pure Reason* (Oxford: Clarendon Press, 1958), pp. 256–270. Weldon's thesis has been acutely criticized by Allison, *Kant's Transcendental Idealism*, p. 260. If Tetens' theory had any special influence on Kant, it probably lies in a different place than that found by Weldon. Namely, Tetens anticipates Kant's theory of self-affection by stressing the active role of inner sense. Before Kant, Tetens explains that in inner sense we perceive changes in ourselves that are a result of our own activity. We have a feeling of our own thoughts that arises from the effects of our activity. See *Versuche*, pp. 45–49.

20. In the *Anthropologie* Kant gives a somewhat different account. He explains that outer sense occurs when the body is affected by physical things, and that inner sense occurs when the body is affected by the mind (§15, VII, 151).

21. See A 20 and 68. See also Kant's *Logik* §1, IX, 91.

22. Kant states that inner sense is "the mode in which the mind is affected through its own activity, and so is affected by itself" (B 68). But this is more a consequence of the activity of inner sense, of its becoming self-conscious of itself in time, than a formal definition.

23. Thus Kant writes in the *Anthropologie* that apperception is an awareness of my activity, whereas inner sense is an awareness of myself in experience. See §24, VII, 151. See also §7, VII, 142.

24. This is not to deny, of course, that to locate something in inner sense I ultimately presuppose the frame of reference of outer sense. That this is the case is the argument of the Refutation of Idealism in the second edition of the *Kritik*.

25. See, for example, Strawson, *The Bounds of Sense*, pp. 56–57. For an another antisubjectivist reading of inner sense, similar in spirit to that given here, see Hoke Robinson, 'The Priority of Inner Sense,' *Kant-Studien* 79 (1988), 165–182. Robinson's critique of the subjectivist interpretation assumes, however, the second edition doctrine of the priority of outer sense. My analysis here focuses on the first edition alone.

26. See Descartes, *Meditations*, VII, 23–34.

27. See Berkeley's *Three Dialogues*, where he affirms both that he has an immediate

knowledge of spirit and that he knows it through reflection, *Philosophical Writings*, pp. 195–196.

28. See letter to Sophia Charlotte, 1702, L, 549. See also *Demonstrationes catholicae:* "[M]ind is immediate to itself when it perceives itself thinking," p. 113. It must be said, however, that Leibniz's position was more complicated. Thus he criticized Descartes for thinking that knowledge of myself as an individual was complete and self-illuminating. See his July 14, 1686 letter to Arnauld, p. 334.

29. See, for example, A 38, 385, 539. In A 38 Kant comes closest to affirming its importance for his idealism as a whole, but gives it no emphasis.

30. See H. A. Pistorius, *Allgemeine deutsche Bibliothek* 59 (1784), 322–356.

31. These are subsection II of §6 of the Transcendental Aesthetic, B 66–69; and the second part of §24 of the second edition's Deduction, B 152–156. That Kant had a high opinion of Pistorius, and was concerned about his objections to the critical philosophy, is clear from the second *Kritik*, V, 8; the *Opus postumum*, XXI, 416; and Daniel Jenisch's May 14, 1787 letter to Kant, *Schriften*, X, 486.

8. The Transcendental Subject

1. This extreme position is represented by Collins, *Possible Experience*, pp. 1–25.

2. This is especially true of the first edition; but it also appears in the second edition. See, for example, B 45, 59, 164, 235–236, 519, 527, 591.

3. It is misleading and tendentious if one defines empirical idealism as "the doctrine that the mind can only have immediate access to its own ideas or representations." See Allison, *Kant's Transcendental Idealism*, pp. 6, 7, 15. If this is taken as empirical idealism, then it seems as if Kant is completely rejecting the general subjectivist principle. Kant defines empirical idealism much more narrowly: as either doubt about or denial of the reality of objects in space outside us.

4. This argument also appears in the second edition; see, for example, B 235.

5. See Berkeley, *Principles* §8; and *Commonplace Book* §5.

6. As we have already seen above, 1.5.3, this does not mean that Kant accepts Berkeley's *esse est percipi* dictum. Kant thinks that this dictum holds only for objects of experience, but not for objects in general.

7. See, for example, Allison, 'Two Aspect View,' p. 157.

8. See Kemp Smith, *Commentary*, pp. 261–262, 273–274, 277–280. Ironically, Kemp Smith insists on this point to distinguish Kant's transcendental idealism from Hegel's absolute idealism. But his concept of Hegel's absolute idealism rests on an implausible subjectivist interpretation of the Hegelian concept of *Geist*. In truth, his argument brings Kant *closer* to the objective idealists.

9. See Patricia Kitcher, *Kant's Transcendental Psychology* (Oxford: Oxford University Press, 1990), pp. 105, 121–122.

10. See Andrew Brook, *Kant and the Mind* (Cambridge: Cambridge University Press, 1994), pp. 44, 240.

11. In the *Anthropologie* Kant defines reflection as the representation of the spontaneous activity by which a thought becomes possible for us (§4, VII, 134n). Kant

virtually equates reflection and apperception, defining reflection as "consciousness of the understanding, pure apperception." This shows that Kant regards the 'I think' as an act of reflection.

12. *Pace* Kitcher, *Kant's Transcendental Psychology*, p. 253n.

13. Thus Kitcher, 'Kant's Real Self,' in *Self and Nature*, ed. Allen Wood (Ithaca: Cornell University Press, 1984), pp. 113–147, esp. p. 121.

14. For an argument along similar lines, see Robert Pippin, 'Kant on the Spontaneity of the Mind,' *Canadian Journal of Philosophy* 17 (1987), 449–475.

15. This is the contention of Brook, *Kant and the Mind*, pp. 239–240.

16. See also *Über den Gebrauch teleologischer Prinzipien in der Philosophie*, VIII, 181–182; and *Metaphysische Anfangsgründe der Naturwissenschaften*, IV, 543–545.

17. See, for example, Kitcher, *Kant's Transcendental Psychology*, p. 121; and Brook, *Kant and the Mind*, pp. 14–23.

9. The Status of the Transcendental

1. The chief exponent of the purely logical interpretation of Kant's transcendental discourse is Strawson, who insists that the more acceptable side of Kant's philosophy is a form of conceptual analysis. See *The Bounds of Sense*, pp. 15, 31–32, 257.

2. For the interpretation of the categories as epistemic conditions, see Allison, *Kant's Transcendental Idealism*, pp. 10–13, 65, 86, 87, 109, and his 'Two Aspect View,' pp. 156–157.

3. See Part 1, introduction, notes 2 and 4.

4. See, for example, Kitcher, *Kant's Transcendental Psychology*, pp. 21–29; Walker, *Kant*, pp. 122–135; and H. E. Matthews, 'Strawson on Transcendental Idealism,' *Philosophical Quarterly* 19 (1969), 204–220.

5. See Strawson, *The Bounds of Sense*, pp. 16, 19, 21.

6. For some sources, see Part 1, introduction, notes 2–4.

7. See his *Commentary*, pp. 274–275. A more recent exponent is Ralph Walker, 'Synthesis and Transcendental Idealism,' *Kant-Studien* 76 (1985), 14–27.

8. See, for example, B 678, where Kant explicitly rejects the merely hypothetical and heuristic status of the principles of the systematicity of nature, and expressly affirms that we must assume there *is* some systematic order in nature, so that the concept of the unity of nature is "inherent in objects" (*den Objekten selbst anhängend*). Kant then blurs his distinction between the regulative and constitutive, and indeed between reason and understanding, by suggesting that the assumption of systematicity is necessary for the application of the categories themselves. Without the idea of systematic unity, he writes, there would not be "coherent employment of the understanding" and not even "a sufficient criterion of empirical truth." See B 679. On these issues, see below, 3.1.6 and 4.3.5.

9. See Brook, *Kant and the Mind*, pp. 12–14; Kitcher, *Kant's Transcendental Psychology*, pp. 21, 25, 26; Wilfred Sellars, 'This I or He or It (the Thing) which Thinks . . . ,' in *Essays in Philosophy and Its History* (Dordrecht: Reidel 1974), pp. 62–90; and

Ralf Meerbote, 'Kant's Functionalism,' in *Historical Foundations of Cognitive Science,* ed. J. C. Smith (Dordrecht: Reidel, 1989), pp. 161–187.

10. As Kitcher admits, *Kant's Transcendental Psychology,* p. 25.

11. Ibid., p. 18. Although Kitcher too thinks that Kant is not guilty of psychologism (p. 9), her explanation of transcendental necessity makes him vulnerable to just such a charge. "For Kant, something is necessary if it is true in all situations that we can experience, constituted as we are" (p. 18). She understands this necessity along the lines of the Transcendental Aesthetic where the necessity of some truth depends upon our human constitution (pp. 18, 9n41).

12. See §27 of the B Deduction, B 167–168. See also the *Prolegomena, IV*, 258. As Beck has argued, Kant's recognition of this point was one of his fundamental differences with Tetens. See his *Early German Philosophy,* pp. 421–425.

13. This point was first made in 1794 by Solomon Maimon in his reply against G. E. Schulze's *Aenesidemus.* See his *Briefe Philalethes an Aenesidemus,* in *Streifereien im Gebiete der Philosophie, Werke,* ed. Valerio Verra (Hildesheim: Olms, 1965), V, 404–406, 412–413.

14. One could make just this objection to Allison's account of the transcendental in terms of "epistemic conditions." According to Allison, these conditions involve an idealistic commitment since they contain a "reference to the mind and its cognitive apparatus," and they reflect "the structure and operations of the human mind." See 'The Two Aspect View,' pp. 156–157. It is unclear, though, how Allison's account of epistemic conditions differs from the psychologistic interpretation. In general, the concept of an epistemic condition is too vague to do the explanatory work that Allison claims for it; rather than a solution, it is simply a vague word for the problem. The term suggests a mixture of the psychological and logical; but the problem is to explain in just what this mixture consists and how it is possible.

15. As W. H. Walsh has argued. See his 'Philosophy and Psychology in Kant's Critique,' *Kant-Studien* 56 (1966), 186–198.

16. This kind of interpretation appears in Strawson, *The Bounds of Sense,* pp. 15, 31–32, 44.

17. On this whole issue, see the important article by Dieter Henrich, 'Kant's Notion of a Deduction and the Methodological Background of the First *Critique,*' in *Kant's Transcendental Deductions,* ed. Eckhart Förster (Stanford: Stanford University Press, 1992), pp. 29–46. While Henrich's historical account of the concept of a deduction is illuminating, some aspects of his account of its formal features are troubling. Henrich maintains that although we can reconstruct the Deduction as a deductive argument, this does not by itself constitute what is distinctive of a deduction (p. 39). What is characteristic of a deduction, its general structure, is that "a particular operation cannot be carried out unless another and more fundamental operation comes into play" (pp. 43–44). But this just conflates the subjective with the objective deduction, or reduces the latter down to the former, completely contrary to Kant's order of priorities, which gave precedence to the objective deduction. Furthermore, if the transcendental deduction is in-

tended to be a reply to a skeptic, as Henrich also insists (p. 37), then such a deductive argument should be an essential feature of it, since nothing less would satisfy a skeptic. It is unclear how, from Henrich's account of its general structure, a deduction would constitute a reply to the skeptic. Simply showing that the operation of one faculty depends on the operation of another basic faculty does not shows us that this basic faculty gives us knowledge. The skeptic would ask whether this more basic faculty is anything more than a habit or psychological necessity of our human nature. The question would still remain whether such a habit or necessity were true of experience. Given Kant's insistence that appeals to the subjective necessity of our nature cannot prove their objective validity, it is clear that he would have rejected any such argument as insufficient.

18. This objection was first made by G. E. Schulze in his notorious *Aenesidemus*, which was first published anonymously and *sine loco* in 1793. See the Kantgesellschaft edition, ed. A. Liebert (Berlin: Ruether and Reichard, 1912), pp. 94–105, 135–136.

19. See, for example, Kitcher, *Kant's Transcendental Psychology*, p. 22.

20. For a more detailed account of the relations between transcendental and empirical psychology, see Gary Hatfield, *The Natural and the Normative* (Cambridge: MIT Press, 1990), pp. 77–87, 98–101.

21. Kant himself seems to suggest this dual aspect interpretation of his transcendental discourse when he states that the faculties of sense, imagination, and apperception have both an empirical and transcendental use (A 94); he states explicitly that these faculties can be *considered* both empirically and transcendentally: empirically in reference to experience, and transcendentally in reference to a priori knowledge (A 115). The difference between the transcendental and the empirical, he further explains, belongs only to the critique of cognitions and not to their relation to their object (A 56–57).

22. The point was made long ago by William James in his defense of pragmatism. James insisted that knowledge cannot be understood apart from the *process* or *activity* of cognition. See his *The Meaning of Truth* (New York: Longmans, Green, 1911), pp. 45–46, 141–143, 152–153.

23. This point is admitted even by such critics of transcendental idealism as Strawson, who states that transcendental idealism follows of necessity from transcendental psychology. This is indeed the main reason he rejects transcendental psychology. See *The Bounds of Sense*, pp. 39, 86, 112, 115, 251. He contends that Kant pushes the argument to the point of incoherence since he can no longer claim that objects affect our sensibility in any ordinary sense. Yet this very old criticism simply ignores Kant's distinction between thinking and knowing an object according to the categories.

24. Strawson, *The Bounds of Sense*, p. 15.

25. Ibid., p. 257.

26. Ibid., pp. 96, 244–245.

27. Another element of Strawson's interpretation is his attempt to excise the concept of synthesis from his reading of the Deduction. But this is a mere sleight of

hand, which revolves around an ambiguity in the term "synthesis" (noted by Strawson himself, p. 96). If this term refers to an *activity*, then Strawson indeed succeeds in removing it from Kant's argument; but, as Strawson himself notes (p. 95), Kant does not think that we have a special awareness of the self's synthesizing activity, so that such an activity should not play a role in any reconstruction of his argument. If, however, this term refers to the *product* of synthesis, specifically synthetic a priori principles establishing universal and necessary connections between distinct perceptions, then Strawson cannot succeed in removing it, since any such principles are involved in the "objective connections" he thinks are central to the conclusion of the Deduction. If a reconstruction of the Deduction does not invoke synthesis in this limited sense, it deprives it of all philosophical interest.

10. Kant's Idealism in the *Opus postumum*

1. That Kant remained true to his formal idealism in the *Opus postumum* is the thesis of Vitorrio Mathieu, *Kants Opus postumum* (Frankfurt: Klostermann, 1989), pp. 185–188; Kurt Hübner, 'Leib und Erfahrung in Kants Opus Postumum,' *Zeitschrift für philosophische Forschung* 7 (1953), 204–219; Hansgeorg Hoppe, *Kants Theorie der Physik* (Frankfurt: Klostermann, 1969), pp. 69–141; and Paul Guyer, 'The Unity of Nature and Freedom: Kant's Conception of the System of Philosophy,' in *The Reception of the Critical Philosophy,* ed. Sally Sedgwick (Cambridge: Cambridge University Press, 2000), pp. 19–53.

2. That Kant broke with his formal idealism and developed a more radical idealism like that of Schelling and Hegel is an old thesis. See, for example, Arthur Drews, *Kants Naturphilosophie als Grundlage seines Systems* (Berlin: Mitscher and Röstell, 1894), pp. 467–470; Nicholas Lehmann, *Beiträge zur Geschichte und Interpretation der Philosophie Kants* (Berlin: de Gruyter, 1969), pp. 364–365; Joachim Kopper, 'Kants Lehre vom Übergang als die Vollendung des Selbstbewusstseins der Transzendentalphilosophie,' *Kant-Studien* 55 (1964), 37–68; and Richard Kroner, *Von Kant bis Hegel* (Tübingen: Mohr, 1921), I, pp. 81–82. More recently, this position has been argued by Burkhard Tuschling in a stimulating and provocative series of articles. See his 'Apperception and Ether: On the Idea of a Transcendental Deduction of Matter in Kant's *Opus postumum*,' in *Kant's Transcendental Deductions,* ed. Eckart Förster (Stanford: Stanford University Press), pp. 193–216; 'The Concept of Transcendental Idealism in Kant's *Opus postumum*,' in *Kant and Critique: New Essays in Honor of W. H. Werkmeister,* ed. R. M. Dancy (Dordrecht: Kluwer, 1993), pp. 151–167; and in his 'Die Idee des transzendentalen Idealismus im späten Opus postumum,' in *Übergang: Zum Spätwerk Immanuel Kants* ed. Forum für Philosophie Bad Homburg (Frankfurt: Klostermann, 1991), pp. 105–145. In defense of Tuschling, see Kenneth Westphal, 'Kant's Dynamical Constructions,' *Journal of Philosophical Research* 20 (1995), 381–429; and Jeffrey Edwards, 'Spinozism, Freedom, and Transcendental Dynamics in Kant's Final System of Transcendental Idealism,' in Sedgwick, *Reception,* pp. 54–77, and *Substance, Force,*

634   Notes to Pages 183–185

and the Possibility of Knowledge (Berkeley: University of California Press, 2000), pp. 147–192.

3. See J. G. Kiesewetter to Kant, June 8, 1795, *Schriften,* XII, 23. Here Kiesewetter reminds Kant that "for some years now" he had promised to write such a work. This promise most probably goes back to Kiesewetter's visit to Königsberg in the autumn of 1790. For a more detailed argument for this dating, see Eckart Förster, 'Is there "A Gap" in Kant's Critical System?' *Journal of the History of Philosophy* 25 (1987), 533–555, esp. 536–537. Förster argues that it is necessary to distinguish between Kant's idea for a transition project and his discovery of a gap in the critical system, which came only much later in the earliest notes of the *Opus postumum.* However, his arguments rest on a very narrow conception of the gap, and on very circumstantial historical evidence. Simply because Kant explicitly refers to a gap only in 1798 does not mean that he had discovered it only then. The main issue behind the gap is clear from the first *Kritik,* though Kant later gave it new formulations. It is noteworthy that Kant already refers to a "gap" (*Lücke*) in the preface to the *Kritik der Urteilskraft* (V, 175). Though this explicitly refers to the gap between the realm of freedom and nature, it also involves for Kant the issue of the relationship between the general principles of the understanding and the multiplicity of empirical laws.

4. Here I take issue with Henry Allison, 'Is the *Critique of Judgment* Post-Critical?' in Sedgwick, *Reception,* pp. 78–92, who contends that there is a clear line between how systematicity and the categories are conditions of experience. Allison claims that systematicity "conditions experience in a different way and at a different level than the categories and principles of the understanding" (82). Namely, systematicity does not provide conditions of objectivity, like the categories, but determines only "the connectability, and hence the coherence, of the first-order empirical claims regarding objects falling under these conditions." But this clear line does not agree with Kant's statements at B 679, 682. Moreover, Allison's own attempt to draw the line fails, because he makes systematicity a condition of judgments of experience (p. 85), which are the paradigmatic expression of objectivity.

5. In explaining the transition project Kant usually emphasizes that experience cannot provide a sufficient foundation for the systematic unity of physics. Yet he is also explicit that the metaphysical principles cannot provide such a foundation. The same problem that holds between the categories and specific laws of experience described in the *Kritik der Urtheilskraft* (V, 179–180) also applies to the general laws of motion of the *Anfangsgründe* and the specific laws of physics: "The transition to physics cannot lie in the metaphysical first principles (attraction and repulsion), for they do not give any specifically determinate properties and one cannot think of any specific properties from which one could know that they are in nature or even whether they exist" (XXII, 282).

6. See Friedman, *Kant and the Exact Sciences,* p. 239.

7. Kant insists that the moving powers are known only through experience: XXI, 291, 295, 396, 508, 621, 623; XXII, 253.

8. Kant experimented with several different ways of organizing the variables of force according to the categories. On this topic, see Eckart Förster, 'Die Idee des Übergangs,' in *Übergang,* pp. 28–48.

9. Edwards has argued, persuasively, that the idea of the material a priori is already implicit in the Third Analogy of the first *Kritik.* See *Substance, Force, and the Possibility of Knowledge,* pp. 11–60. Kant only fully articulates the idea, however, in the *Opus postumum.*

10. According to Hoppe, *Kants Theorie der Physik,* pp. 96, 100, there is no extension of the a priori involved in Kant's transition program, and there are "no material conditions of experience." He maintains that the transition gives a priori status only to the form of physics, which consists in the *relations* between the moving powers, and that the moving powers themselves are only empirical (p. 89). Although the a priori status of the moving powers indeed rests upon the relations, the question remains what status we bestow on them. They are not equivalent to the categories themselves because they determine the specific variables of matter itself; they are also not simply empirical instantiations of the categories because Kant frequently states that experience cannot be conceived without them. Hoppe's reading runs into special difficulties in trying to explain the status of the ether. He concedes that Kant wants to understand the ether as a material condition of the possibility of experience (pp. 104, 110), yet argues that Kant *ought* not to mean this because the ether proof is transcendent and so incompatible with the principles of his criticism (pp. 106–109). We shall deal with this point below. But it should be clear that Hoppe's interpretation has passed beyond the boundaries of what Kant *did* say or think.

11. On the relation of the ether theory to late-eighteenth-century science, see Friedman, *Kant and the Exact Sciences,* pp. 264–290.

12. That Kant drops these strictures is the thesis of Mathieu, *Opus postumum,* pp. 42–44. Förster has criticized Mathieu's suggestion that Kant's dissatisfaction with the regulative constraints was one reason for his developing the transition program. See his 'Die Idee des Übergangs,' in *Übergang,* pp. 28–31. Yet, whatever Kant's motives for embarking on his program, its implications for the doctrine of the third *Kritik* are clear.

13. In his 'Kants Nachlaßwerk und die Kritik der Urteilskraft,' *Beiträge,* pp. 295–373, Lehmann has argued that Kant's transition project stands under the regulative constraints of the third *Kritik,* and that this alone prevents it from relapsing into the dogmatism of the old rationalism (p. 299). Hence Lehmann denies that the system of forces has a constitutive status. Yet he fails to bring forward satisfactory textual evidence for this thesis, and much of his argument only confuses Kant's architechtonic. He fails to observe Kant's sharp distinction between organic and inorganic nature (though he notes on p. 327 that Kant rejected hylozism, he does not realize its implications for his general thesis). Simply because Kant thinks that the dynamic forces of matter form a system does not mean, as Lehmann implies (p. 334), that they are organic; though the concept of the organic is indeed systematic, the converse does not necessarily hold. Al-

though Kant also states that the system of dynamic forces *can* be treated as if they form an organism (Lehmann, pp. 325–326), this does not mean that they *must* be so, so again there is no reason to think that the regulative constraints apply. Since Lehmann himself admits that the system of dynamic forces anticipates perception and even creates a second order of appearances (p. 341), it is not clear in the end what his claim about the persistence of regulative constraints amounts to.

14. *Pace* Tuschling, 'Apperception and Ether,' p. 213.

15. This criticism of Kant was made by Drews, *Kant's Naturphilosophie*, p. 485. More recently, the same point has been made by Hoppe, *Kants Theorie der Physik*, pp. 106–109.

16. Partly on these grounds I resist Jeffrey Edwards' thesis that there is a move toward transcendental realism in the *Opus postumum*. See his 'Spinozism, Freedom, and Transcendental Dynamics,' in Sedgwick, *Reception*, pp. 63–70. Edwards argues that the concept of the ether means that space is "in some sense, transcendentally real," because the ether is "the subject independent basis of all outer perception" (p. 66). Yet the question remains: Is this the empirical or transcendental subject? Is the ether real only in an empirical or also in a transcendental sense? The texts Edwards cites are ambiguous. He just assumes that all matter in experience, anything more determinate than the universal a priori forms of the understanding and sensibility, must have a reality independent of the subject; but this is hard to reconcile with Kant's other claims that the self-positing subject posits itself through not only the forms but also the matter of experience. In short, why cannot Kant's extension of the concept of the transcendental be seen as a widening of his original transcendental idealism rather than as a commitment to some form of transcendental realism?

17. See, for example, Drews, *Naturphilosophie*, pp. 470–471, 476–477; Kemp Smith, *Commentary*, pp. 618, 623–624; and Lehmann, *Beiträge*, pp. 284, 388.

18. See Gerhard Lehmann, 'Kants Widerlegung des Idealismus,' *Kant-Studien* 50 (1958–1959), pp. 359, 362.

19. *Theätet oder über das menschliche Wissen. Ein Beytrag zur Vernunftkritik* (Frankfurt: Varrentrapp and Wenner, 1794), pp. 16–19. Tiedemann was one of the first reviewers of the *Kritik*. His 1785 review 'Über die Natur der Metaphysik,' which appeared in the *Hessische Beyträge zur Gelehrsamkeit und Kunst*, I, 17–30, was dismissed by Kant. See Kant to Johann Bering, April 7, 1786, *Schriften*, X, 440.

20. On the connection between the ether proofs and third analogy, see Edwards, 'Der Ätherbeweis des Opus postumum und Kants 3. Analogie der Erfahrung,' in *Übergang*, pp. 77–104.

21. See Adickes, *Kants Opus postumum*, pp. 664, 668–669. Lehmann follows Adickes, *Beiträge*, p. 358. In a similar vein, see H. J. de Vleeschauwer, *The Development of Kantian Thought* (London: Nelson, 1962), p. 189.

22. As Förster has pointed out, 'Kants *Selbstsetzungslehre*,' in *Kant's Transcendental Deductions*, pp. 217–218.

23. See, for example, J. S. Beck to Kant, June 20, 1797, *Schriften*, XII, 162.

24. See, for example, XXI, 76, where he uses Reinhold's and Schiller's jargon of a *Trieb nach Form* and a *Trieb nach Stoff;* and XXII, 43, 58, 73, 77, 92, where he adopts Reinhold's term of a *Vorstellungsvermögen.* In the tenth Convolut Kant uses Fichtean terminology in describing the unity of apperception as the principle '*Ich bin*' (XII, 413); and in the first Convolut he even adopts Fichte's characteristic term '*Wissenschaftslehre,*' XXI, 155, 156.

25. That Kant had not studied Fichte's writings is clear from his December 1797 letter to Fichte (XII, 221) and his April 5, 1798 letter to Tieftrunk (XII, 240–241). Kant told Tieftrunk that he had no time to read Fichte, but that he had formed some idea of his work from a review in the *Allgemeine Literatur Zeitung.* This comprehensive review of four of Fichte's early writings, which was written by Reinhold, appeared in January 1798, Nr. 5–9 (I, 33–69, 4–8 January) (reprinted in *J. G. Fichte in zeitgenössischen Rezensionen,* ed. Erich Fuchs *et al.* (Stuttgart–Bad Cannstatt: Fromann, 1995), I, 286–322). In the review Reinhold explains that pure reason constitutes itself only through an act of freedom, which is thinkable only as "*bloßes Setzen durch sich selber, durch bloßes Setzen*" (p. 47).

26. This point is made by Adickes himself, *Kants Opus postumum,* p. 664. Yet Adickes fails to see the deeper differences between Kant and Fichte, and the extent to which Fichte's concept of the self-positing self contradicts some of Kant's fundamental doctrines, such as the qualitative distinction between the understanding and sensibility and the unknowability of the noumenal self. These differences will be explored more thoroughly below, 2.5.4–2.5.6.

27. Adickes claimed that the *Selbstsetzungslehre* did not involve "eine wirkliche Bereicherung oder glückliche Fortbildung des kantischen Systems," *Kants Opus postumum,* p. 668. Lehmann holds it to be central to the new transcendental deduction and development of Kant's idealism after 1790. See his *Beiträge,* pp. 357–363, 380. According to Förster, the doctrine is crucial to filling a real gap in Kant's system, though it does not involve a new transcendental deduction. See his 'Kants *Selbstsetzungslehre,*' pp. 217–238.

28. This is the thesis of Tuschling, 'Apperception and Ether,' pp. 213, 215, and 'Die Idee des Transzendentalen Idealismus,' pp. 112–117; Lehmann, *Beiträge,* pp. 357–363; and Edwards, 'Spinozism, Freedom and Transcendental Dynamics,' pp. 60–70, and *Substance, Force, and the Possibility of Knowledge,* pp. 167–192.

29. XXII, 287, 306, 309–310, 319, 323, 331, 343.

30. That all perception is only a form of self-affection in the *Opus postumum* has been stressed by Lehman, *Beiträge,* pp. 359, 364, 368, 388.

31. The radical idealist reading of the *Opus postumum* insists, of course, that the thing-in-itself is the mere product of the understanding; but we will see below, 1.10.8, that this interpretation is mistaken.

32. See also XXII, 39, 85, 446.

33. Though it does not appear as such, this passage was a reasonably accurate citation from Brief XIX of Schiller's *Über die Aesthetische Erziehung des Menschen.* See *Schillers Werke, Nationalausgabe,* ed. Benno von Wiese et al. (Weimar: Böhlaus, 1962), XX, 371. The source was first identified by Karl Vorländer, 'Ein bisher

noch unentdecker Zusammenhang Kants mit Schiller' *Philosophische Monatshefte* 30 (1894), 57–62. It must be added that, in citing Schiller, Kant was effectively echoing himself, since Schiller was reaffirming Kant's doctrine of the finitude of all knowledge.

34. See XXI, 293, 486; XXII, 308, 310–311, 313, 316, 319, 404, 458.

35. See XXII, 348, 362, 371, 391–392, 397, 400, 404, 455, 493, 502, 504.

36. The close connection in Kant between self-positing and self-affection in Kant was first recognized by Adickes, *Kants Opus postumum*, pp. 657, 660. He cites a wealth of passages that show their similarity in meaning, pp. 655–659.

37. See XXII, 320, 327, 339–340, 343, 346, 367, 373.

38. Adickes, *Kants Opus postumum*, pp. 294, 303.

39. Mathieu, *Kants Opus postumum*, pp. 144–145.

40. According to Vaihinger, Kemp Smith, and Adickes, Kant's empirical realism in the *Opus postumum* attributes not only a formal but also a material existence to objects independent of the empirical subject. See above, 1.2.5.

41. Vaihinger, 'Zu Kants Widerlegung des Idealismus,' pp. 145n, 156–159; Adickes, *Kants Opus postumum*, pp. 293–304; and Kemp Smith, *Commentary*, pp. 607, 641, esp. 621–622n.

42. See, Lehmann, *Beiträge*, pp. 374–391, 357–371.

43. See Hübner, 'Leib und Erfahrung,' pp. 210–213; and Mathieu, *Kants Opus postumum*, pp. 137–161. See also Lehmann, *Beiträg*, pp. 374–391.

44. On appearance of appearances, see XXII, 318–320, 333, 357, 367, 371, 373, 404; and on appearance, see XXII, 346, 352, 404.

45. See especially XXII, 286, 290–291, 295, 315, 322, 331, 339, 570. The close connection between the amphibolies and the appearance of appearances emerges from this passage of the tenth Convolut: "The amphiboly of concepts of reflection: to take that which is valid in appearances as true of things-in-themselves and conversely; in physics the distinction between direct and indirect phenomena" (339).

46. See Lehmann, *Beiträge*, p. 390. This is Lehmann's critique of Hübner.

47. See Vaihinger, 'Zu Kants Widerlegung des Idealismus,' pp. 145n2, 156–159; Drews, *Kants Naturphilosophie*, pp. 466, 473–474; Kemp Smith, *Commentary*, pp. 621–622n; and Adickes, *Kants Opus postumum*, pp. 293–304. Here I simplify Adickes' much more nuanced and complicated discussion, which distinguishes several senses of appearance of appearance in the *Opus postumum*. Still, Adickes thinks that the main sense of the doctrine should be interpreted as above (pp. 294–295). In his general explanation he describes appearances of appearances as "die subjektive Art und Weise, wie unser empirisches Ich das Rohmaterial der Erscheinungen vereinheitlicht, auffaßt, verarbeitet" (295).

In his 'Erscheinungsstufen und Realitätsproblem,' Lehmann sharply criticizes the interpretation of Adickes, especially the doctrine of double affection (Beiträge, pp. 375, 379, 387). Yet Lehmann himself understands appearance of appearance in a similar manner to Adickes, defining it in terms of the empirical subject's representation of appearances. See pp. 383, 389.

48. According to Adickes (pp. 300–301), there are three passages that favor reading

appearance of appearance in terms of empirical representation of appearances: (1) "Die subjective Erfahrung, durch Afficirung der Organe eine Erscheinung der Erscheinung im Gantzen des empirischen Bewußtseins welches vor dem objectiven vorhergeht als Erscheinung" (XXII, 350, 19–21); (2) "Erscheinung von der Erscheinung da das Subject vom Object afficirt wird und sich selbst afficirt" (XXII, 321, 17–18); and (3) "die Einnehmung aber des Raums ist selbst nichts weiter als Erscheinung ihrer [die bewegenden Kräfte] Koexistenz und da diese Aufsammelung des im Raum Aggregierten reale Beziehung auf den Körper durch Einwirkung auf dessen Organ ist Erscheinung von der Erscheinung" (XXII, 334, 24–27). Closely read in context, only the first gives unequivocal support for this reading by pairing subjective experience with appearances of appearances and objective experience with appearances themselves. But, as Adickes notes, the passage is exceptional.

Adickes himself admits that Kant rarely uses the term to refer to the *sensations* or *perceptions* from the standpoint of the physicist, and maintains that he usually uses it to designate "die subjektive Art und Weise, wie unser empirisches Ich das ihm gegebene Erscheinungsmaterial verarbeitet und vereinheitlicht, d.h. wie es vermöge seiner apriorischen formalen Gesetzmäßigkeit die Empfindungen zu Wahrnhmungsgegenständen und diese zur Einheit des Erfahrungssystems verknüpft" (p. 301). What is remarkable here is that Adickes attributes the function of unifying the manifold to the *empirical* ego. There is no textual evidence for this reading—Kant does not use the phrase 'empirical ego'—and it is simply the result of Adickes' allegiance to the double affection doctrine, which he persistently reads into Kant's texts. It is a consequence of Adickes' doctrine that it replicates the problem of knowledge on the empirical level, and so makes it necessary to attribute many transcendental cognitive functions to the empirical level. See above, 1.2.5, where this criticism is made in more detail.

49. See the passages in note 48 above.
50. Vaihinger cites this passage in 'Zu Kants Widerlegung des Idealismus,' p. 156.
51. That appearances of appearances are the result of self-affection in contrast to appearances arising from affection of sensibility, see XXII, 321, 326, 340, 367, 371, 373.
52. See XXII, 4, 27, 31–32, 37, 414, 417, 420–421.
53. For the first view, see Hans Vahinger, *Die Philosophie des Als Ob*, 9th ed. (Leipzig: Meiner, 1927), pp. 721–724; Drews, *Kants Naturphilosophie*, pp. 472–476; and Lehmann, *Beiträge*, pp. 361, 376. For the second view, see Adickes, *Kants Opus postumum*, pp. 669–718; and Mathieu, *Kants Opus postumum*, pp. 189–211.
54. Thus Lehmann, *Beiträge*, pp. 361, 376.
55. Adickes, *Kants Opus postumum*, p. 675, points out a multitude of passages where this equation is either stated or implied: B 63, 236, 333, 344, 506, 566, 568, 593, 726; and A 37, 358, 361, 366, 393.
56. See B xxvi, 55, 60, 69, 566. See also *Prolegomena* §13, Anm. II, IV, 289.
57. This was the explanation of Adickes, *Kants Opus postumum*, pp. 712–713, which is essentially correct.
58. This is indeed not surprising, given that Kant had essentially reaffirmed his posi-

tion as late as December 11, 1792, in his letter to Tieftrunk. See *Schriften*, XII, 223–224.

Part II. Introduction

1. In the English-speaking world this interpretation gained wide currency from Josiah Royce, *The Spirit of Modern Philosophy* (Cambridge: Houghton Mifflin, 1892), pp. 158–160, 165. It became the textbook version of Fichte's idealism in Frederick Copleston, *The History of Philosophy* (New York: Doubleday, 1965), VII, 72, 79. The interpretation has been frequently reaffirmed by several recent scholars. See, for example, John Lachs, 'Fichte's Idealism,' *American Philosophical Quarterly* 9 (1972), 311–318; Robert C. Solomon, *In the Spirit of Hegel* (Oxford: Oxford University Press, 1983), pp. 85–96; the preface to Peter Heath's and John Lach's translation of Fichte's 1794 *Grundlage der gesamten Wissenschaftslehre, The Science of Knowledge* (Cambridge: Cambridge University Press, 1982); and Patrick Gardiner, 'Fichte's Idealism,' in *Idealism Past and Present*, ed. Godfrey Vesey (Cambridge: Cambridge University Press, 1982), pp. 111–126. This interpretation has been recently revived by Manfred Frank, *Unendliche Annäherung: die Anfänge der philosophischen Frühromantik* (Frankfurt: Suhrkamp, 1997), pp. 133–151. Not that this interpretation has lacked critics. For some sound criticisms of it, see Ernst Cassirer, *Das Erkenntnisproblem in der Philosophie und Wissenschaft der neueren Zeit*, Band 3: *Die nachkantische Systeme* (Darmstadt: Wissenschaftliche Buchgesellschaft, 1974), pp. 126–216; and Alexis Philonenko, *La Liberté humaine dans la Philosophie de Fichte* (Paris: Vrin, 1980), pp. 25–26, 74–75.

2. See, for example, Manfred Buhr, *Revolution und Philosophie: Die Ursprüngliche Philosophie Johann Gottlieb Fichte und die französische Revolution* (Berlin: Akademie, 1965), pp. 106, 111, 126; and Georg Lukács, *Der junge Hegel* (Frankfurt: Suhrkamp, 1969), II, 409–445.

3. I have already put forward such an interpretation in Chapter 2 of my *Enlightenment, Revolution and Romanticism* (Cambridge: Harvard University Press, 1992), pp. 57–83. The content and argument of the present section differs substantially from my earlier treatment.

   For a spirited defense of a pragmatic interpretation similar to my own, see A. J. Mandt, 'Fichte's Idealism in Theory and Practice,' *Idealistic Studies* 14 (1984), 127–147. Mandt's interpretation has been severely criticized by John Lach, 'Is There an Absolute Self,' *The Philosophical Forum* 19 (1987–1988), pp. 169–182. Both Mandt and I have been criticized by Daniel Breazeale, 'The Theory of Practice and the Practice of Theory: Fichte and "the Primacy of Practical Reason,"' *International Philosophical Quarterly* 36 (1996), 47–64.

4. In stressing Fichte's pragmatism I oppose the foundationalist interpretation of his philosophy, which sees it as the culmination of the tradition of *philosophia prima* inaugurated by Descartes. This interpetation is still actively promoted by Reinhard Lauth and the so-called Munich School. See Lauth, 'Die Bedeutung der Fichteschen Philosophie für die Gegenwart,' *Philosophisches Jahrbuch* 70

(1962–1963), 252–270, and his 'The Transcendental philosophy of the Munich School,' *Idealistic Studies* 11 (1981), 8–39, esp. 22–25. Lauth's views represent a much older tradition that has interpreted Fichte's epistemology as a form of first philosophy. See, for example, Fritz Medicus, *J. G. Fichte: Dreizehn Vorlesungen* (Berlin: Reuther and Reichard, 1905); Heinz Heimsoeth, *Fichte: Leben und Lehre* (Munich: Ernst Reinhardt, 1923); and Max Wundt, *Johann Gottlieb Fichte* (Stuttgart: Fromann, 1927). For some recent criticisms of the foundationalist interpretation, see Tom Rockmore, 'Fichtean Epistemology and the Idea of Philosophy,' in *Der transzendentale Gedanke*, ed. Klaus Hammacher (Hamburg: Meiner, 1981), 485–497; and Wayne Martin, *Idealism and Objectivity: Understanding Fichte's Jena Project* (Stanford: Standford University Press, 1997), pp. 55–77.

5. This point was not appreciated by Dewey, who claimed that the dualism between theory and practice, thinking and doing, infected post-Kantian idealism, since the idealist understood thinking as an inner activity, "some occult internal operation." See his *The Quest for Certainty* (New York: Capricorn, 1960), pp. 22–23, 172, 289. Dewey's critique does not apply to Fichte, however, who sees cognition in concrete practical terms. In stressing the unity of thinking and doing, and in criticizing the traditional contemplative model of knowledge, Dewey simply follows in Fichte's footsteps.

6. Here I take issue with Robert Pippin, 'Fichte's Alleged Subjective, Psychological, One-Sided Idealism,' in Sedgwick, *Reception*, pp. 141–171. A similar thesis has been defended by Wayne Martin, *Idealism and Objectivity*, pp. 30–54, and Paul Franks, 'Subjectivity without Subjectivism: Fichte's Philosophy Today,' *Cambridge Companion to Fichte*, ed. Günter Zöller (Cambridge: Cambridge University Press, forthcoming).

7. See Günter Zöller, *Fichte's Transcendental Philosophy: The Original Duplicity of Intelligence and Will* (Cambridge: Cambridge University Press, 1998), p. 6. Zöller's exposition of the Jena *Wissenschaftslehre* is based upon the 1797–1798 lecture transcripts. For a fuller account of these issues see my review of Zöller in *Mind* 109 (2000), 668–676.

8. The Halle transcript most probably covers the winter semester 1797–1798, while the Krause transcript the winter semester 1798–1799. On the philological issues surrounding the transcripts of the *Wissenschaftslehre novo methodo*, see Daniel Breazeale, *Fichte: Foundations of Transcendental Philosophy* (Ithaca: Cornell University Press, 1992), pp. 1–54, and Erich Fuchs, *Wissenschaftslehre novo methodo* (Hamburg: Meiner, 1994), pp. ix–xxxiv.

1. Fichte and the Subjectivist Tradition

1. Fichte makes his debt to skepticism especially clear in the opening statement of the *Aenesidemus* review, *Werke*, I, 3, and in the early fragment 'Wer Hume, Aenesidemus wo er Recht hat, u. Maimon noch nicht verstanden hat,' AA, II/3, 389–390. Fichte read Hume and did not rely on secondary sources. In his August 3, 1795, letter to Gottlieb Hufeland he reports that he had a revelation

while studying Hume: he now fully understands what Kant saw as the purpose of his work, and why in the second and third *Kritiken* he was compelled to go much further than the first. See AA, III/2, 359.

Fichte had received a copy of Schulze's *Aenesidemus* in May 1793. See Fichte to C. G. Schütz, May 25, 1793, AA, III/1, 409. By early November 1793 he reported to his friend L. W. Wloemer that Schulze's work had led him "to abandon his previous system." See AA, III/2, 14. Fichte worked on his famous review of the work from November 1793 to January 1794.

Fichte was acquainted with Maimon's skepticism by late 1793. See the reference to Maimon in *Eigenen Meditationen zur Elementarphilosophilosophie,* AA, II/3, 23, a work written almost simultaneously with the Schulze review. See the foreword by R. Lauth and H. Gliwitzky to AA, II/3, 7–8.

Fichte's knowledge of Platner's *Aphorismen* also dates back to the Autumn of 1793. See Fichte to Voigt, November 18/19, 1793, AA, III/2, 212. Althought Fichte respected Platner less than Maimon and Schulze, he still took him seriously. Since 1794–1795, Fichte's lectures on logic and metaphysics used Platner's work as a textbook. See R. Lauth and H. Gliwitzky, AA, II/4, 3–35.

2. I use the term 'nihilism' in its original sense, as defined by Jacobi in his 1799 *Brief an Fichte,* where it means doubt about the existence of anything beyond one's immediate representations. See Jacobi, *Werke,* III, 22–23, 44.

3. It is important to recognize that we can explain *much* but not *everything.* It has been argued, rightly, that Fichte developed some of the fundamental strategies of his later *Wissenschaftslehre* before formulating his reply to Schulze's skepticism and as a result of his early dispute with Reinhold about how to demonstrate the reality of freedom. See Alessandro Lazarri, 'Fichtes Entwicklung von der zweiten Auflage der Offenbarungskritik bis zur Rezeption von Schulzes *Aenesidemus,*' *Fichte-Studien* 9 (1997), 181–196, esp. 192–193. The importance of Fichte's early concern with the reality of freedom has also been pointed out by Frederick Neuhouser, *Fichte's Theory of Subjectivity* (Cambridge: Cambridge University Press, 1990), pp. 24–25, 35–38. Yet, as we shall see in Chapter 5, Fichte's early concern with demonstrating the reality of freedom became an essential element of his response to skepticism.

4. Kant was impressed by the manuscript of Maimon's *Versuch über die Transcendentalphilosohie.* After a cursory reading he reported to Marcus Herz, May 26, 1789: "very few could claims so much penetration and subtlety of mind in profound inquiries of this sort." Kant did not write, however, a detailed reply to Maimon, and his response is confined to the letter to Herz. It is clear from *obiter dicta* in the *Opus postumum* that Kant was aware of Schulze's *Aenesidemus.* See *Schriften,* XXI, 23, 31 and XXII, 99, 104.

5. This formulation is in Fichte's early polemical writing 'Vergleichung des vom Herrn Prof. Schmid aufgestellten Systems mit der Wissenschaftslehre,' *Werke,* II, 440; see also 435.

6. See *Wissenschaftslehre nova methodo,* ed. Erich Fuchs (Hamburg: Meiner, 1994), p. 4.

7. See *Erste Einleitung in die Wissenschaftslehre, Werke,* I, 422–423.

8. Fichte's Jena project is completely misunderstood if one does not keep in mind the specific form of the skeptical problem. It is false to argue that because Fichte is not troubled with Cartesian skepticism—with the possibility that our representations do not correspond with things-in-themselves—that he is not concerned with skepticism at all. See Martin, *Idealism and Objectivity,* pp. 15–21. Martin fails to see that the problem of skepticism for Fichte arises within a Kantian context and concerns the neo-Humean problem of the application of universal and necessary laws to perception. For further details, see my review of his work in *Mind* 109 (2000), 672–676.

9. See Eduard Spranger's 'Geleitwort' to his edition of Fichte's *Bestimmung des Menschen* (Hamburg: Meiner, 1962), pp. 176–187; and Max Wundt, *Fichte-Forschungen* (Stuttgart: Fromann, 1929), pp. 147ff.

10. The charge of nihilism against Kant was first made by J. H. Obereit in his *Der Wiederkommende Lebensgesit der verzweifelten Metaphysik* (Berlin: Decker, 1787). Obereit's use of the term is somewhat vague and unsystematic, but he uses it to denote the apparent subjectivist consequences of Kant's epistemology. See pp. 56–59. On Obereit's role in the *Goethezeit,* see Hermann Timm, *Gott und die Freiheit: Studien zur Religionsphilosophie der Goethezeit* (Frankfurt: Klostermann, 1974), pp. 348–359. On his role in the development of nihilism, see Stephen Wagner Cho, *The Historical Origins of Nihilism before Nietzsche* (Lewiston: Mellin Press, 1995), chap. 2. There can be little doubt that Fichte knew about Obereit's position. Obereit was a well-known and much loved Jena personality; Goethe, Wieland, and Schiller attempted to support him. Fichte too was very fond of Obereit, conversed frequently with him, and attempted to find him work and home. See Fichte to his wife, September 2, 1795, AA, III/2, 394. In September 1795 Obereit sent Fichte a letter filled with queries about his position, though, unfortunately, it has been lost. See AA, III/2, 406. Fichte was very impatient with some of Obereit's objections. See Fichte to his wife, September 27, 1795, AA, III/2, 409. He called Obereit's *"letzter Aufsatz" "kraßer Unverstand."* See Fichte to his wife, Summer 1795, AA, III/2, 399–400. This is probably a reference to the manuscript of Obereit's *Finale-Vernunftkritik für das gerade Herz* (Nürnberg, 1796).

11. On Fichte's reply to Jacobi's criticisms, see Fichte to Jacobi, April 22, 1799, AA, III/3, 334–337, and Fichte to Reinhold, April 22, 1799, AA, III/3, 325–333, and September 8, 1800, AA, III/4, 178–184.

12. Fichte makes this point in the *Zweite Einleitung in die Wissenschaftslehre, Werke,* I, 483n. See too Fichte's July 4, 1797, letter to Reinhold, AA, III/3, 70.

13. See below, 2.2.5 and 2.3.4.

14. See, for example, the *Grundlage der gesamten Wissenschaftslehre, Werke,* I, 147, 155, 172, 178, 281.

15. See, especially, *Zweite Einleitung in die Wissenschaftslehre,* I, 455n, 482n, 490.

16. See Fichte's comment on Berkeley in the *Erste Einleitung in die Wissenschaftslehre, Werke,* I, 438.

17. See, for example, *Grundlage, Werke,* I, 155–156, 173, 175, 178, 186. See too *Wissenschaftslehre novo methodo,* IV/2, 33, 55, 129, 139.

18. On the origin of Fichte's terms '*Tatsache*' and '*Tathandlung*,' see Paul Franks, 'Freedom, *Tatsache* and *Tathandlung* in the Development of Fichte's Jena *Wissenschaftslehre, Archiv für Geschichte der Philosophie* 79 (1997), 310–323, esp. 317–319.

19. Fichte's preface to the second edition has the postscript *Zur Jubilate-Messe 1793*. Since this was the final week of April, the date of composition was probably even earlier.

20. These kinds of objections had a venerable ancestry, going back to the pietist battle against the rationalism of Wolff's theory of the *vis representativae*. On the early history of this controversy, see L. W. Beck, *Early German Philosophy* (Cambridge: Harvard University Press, 1969), pp. 300, 401.

21. Kant, *Kritik der praktischen Vernunft*, V, 5.

22. Reinhold, *Versuch einer neuen Theorie des menschlichen Vorstellungsvermögens* (Prague: Widtmann and Mauke, 1789), 'Grundlinien der Theorie des Begehrungsvermögens,' pp. 560–579.

23. See Kant, *Schriften*, V, 134–142.

24. See Part III of *Über den Begriff der Wissenschaftslehre,* which appeared only in the first edition of this work. See AA, I/1, 150–152.

25. In his *Wissenschaftslehre novo methodo* Fichte argued explicitly that Kant's doctrine of moral postulates should be extended along these lines. All consciousness could be explained on the basis of the postulates, and not only the beliefs in the existence of God and immortality. See AA, IV/2, 139.

26. See his later 1798 essay 'Über den Grund unseres Glaubens an eine göttliche Weltregierung,' *Werke*, V, 185.

27. On the systematic form of reason, see KrV, A xiii, B xx, 673, 861–862; on the unity of theoretical and practical reason, see *Kritik der praktischen Vernunft*, V, 91.

28. See *Kritik der Vrteilskraft,* 171, 174–175. Kant is explicit: "Only in the practical sphere can reason legislate; with regard to theoretical cognition (of nature), all it can do . . . is to use given laws to infer consequences from them."

29. This reading of Kant's postulates is most apparent in Fichte's *Vorlesungen über die Bestimmung des Gelehrten, Werke*, VI, 299–300, 310.

30. KrV, B xviii.

31. Fichte, *Werke*, II, 263.

32. It is misleading, therefore, to see Fichte as the ancestor of Nietzsche. This is the suggestion of Daniel Breazeale in his 'The Theory of Practice and the Practice of Theory: Fichte and the Primacy of Practical Reason,' *International Philosophical Quarterly* 36 (1996), 47–64. For similar reasons I also part company with the portrait of Fichte in Isaiah Berlin's 'The Romantic Revolution,' in *The Sense of Reality: Studies in Ideas and their History* (New York: Farrar, Straus and Giroux, 1996), pp. 179–184. Because Fichte conceived the categorical imperative as a universally binding constraint, he would not have accepted the stronger forms of individualism characteristic of romanticism.

33. See, for example, *Versuch einer Kritik aller Offenbarung, Werke*, V, 121; and *Rückerinnerungen, Antworten, Fragen*, V, 348.

34. This is most apparent in Fichte's later *System der Sittenlehre, Werke,* IV, 208–210. Although Fichte makes conscience the ultimate criterion for the rightness of conduct, he insists that such a criterion functions only from a practical point of view. The feelings of conscience had to be grounded more deeply on the law of reason.

35. These writings are the *Über den Begriff der Wissenschaftslehre, Werke,* I, 129–181, and the *Erste Einleitung in die Wissenschaftslehre, Werke,* I, 419–449.

36. See Fichte's formulation in *Erste Einleitung in die Wissenschaftslehre, Werke,* I, 442.

37. Fichte is explicit about this point in a footnote to the first edition of *Über den Begriff der Wissenschaftslehre, Werke,* I, 64.

38. Ibid., I, 443.

39. See Fichte to K. A. Böttiger, February 4, 1794, AA, III/2, 55; to J. F. Flatt, November–December 1793, AA, III/2, 18; to Heinrich Stephani, mid-December 1793, AA, III/2, 28; and to F. V. Reinhard, January 15, 1794, AA, III/2, 39–40. See also the first preface to *Über den Begriff der Wissenschaftslehre, Werke,* I, 29.

40. See the *Zweite Einleitung in die Wissenschafslehre, Werke,* I, 489–490.

41. *Werke,* I, 156, 177, 211, 218, 248.

42. Ibid., I, 104.

43. Ibid., I, 156, 177, 211, 218, 248.

44. See, for example, Fichte's *Erste Einleitung in die Wissenschaftslehre, Werke,* §7, I, 440–449; *Annalen des philosophischen Tons, Werke,* II, 471; and his 1801 *Sonnenklarer Bericht, Werke,* II, 353–354.

45. See, for example, *Erste Einleitung, Werke,* I, 429–435; and *System der Sittenlehre, Werke,* IV, 45–46, 52–53, 133; and the *Wissenschaftslehre novo methodo,* AA, IV/2, 26, 124–125.

46. See *Wissenschaftslehre novo methodo,* AA, IV/2, 28–20; and *Eigene Meditationen,* AA, II/3, 26.

47. See Tom Rockmore, 'Fichtean Epistemolgy and Contemporary Philosophy,' *Philosophical Forum* 19 (1987–1988), 156–168; 'Antifoundationalism, Circularity, and the Spirit of Fichte,' in *Fichte: Historical Contexts/Contemorary Controversies,* ed. Tom Rockmore and D. Breazeale (Atlantic Highlands, N.J.: Humanities Press, 1994), pp. 96–112; and the articles cited in Introduction, note 4.

48. Fichte is perfectly explicit about this point in his *Über den Begriff der Wissenschaftslehre, Werke,* I, 43. Although Fichte does not think that his first principle is demonstrable, as Rockmore points out, he also holds that it must have an immediate certainty or self-evidence, which it does not acquire from the system that it grounds. See ibid., I, 40–41, 43.

2. The Battle against Skepticism

1. AA, III/1, 372–374.

2. J. F. Schultz, *Erläuterung über des Herrn Professor Kants Kritik der reinen Vernunft* (Königsberg: Dengel, 1784); and *Prüfung der kantischen Critik der reinen Vernunft* (Königsberg: Hartung, 1789 and 1792). Schultz's *Erläuterung* has been translated

by James C. Morrison as *Exposition of Kant's Critique of Pure Reason* (Ottawa: University of Ottawa Press, 1995).

3. See Kant's 'Erklärung,' May 29, 1797, in *Schriften*, XII, 367.

4. See the *Zweite Einleitung in die Wissenschaftslehre, Werke*, I, 473.

5. The review originally appeared in the *Königsbergische Gelehrte und Politische Zeitungen*, Stück 94 and 95, November 22 and 25, 1771, pp. 369–371, 373–375. The text has been edited by Reinhardt Brandt in *Beiträge zur Kritik der reinen Vernunft*, ed. Ingeborg Heidemann and Wolfgang Ritzel (Berlin: Walter de Gruyter, 1981), pp. 59–66. There is a translation in Morrison, *Exposition*, pp. 163–170. It is striking that in the second part of his review Schultz appears to anticipate Fichte by defending the possibility of an *intuitus intellectualium*. However, he gives this concept a very different meaning from the later Fichte since, for Schultz, I am passive in intellectual intuition, being affected by given inner objects.

6. See Schultz, *Erläuterung*, pp. 195–202.

7. According to Hamann, Schultz's Ulrich review upset Kant, who had a special meeting with Schultz to talk about it. See Hamann to Jacobi, April 9, 1786, in Hamann, *Briefwechsel*, ed. W. Ziesemer and A. Henkel (Wiesbaden: Insel, 1955–1957), VI, 349. The reason Fichte probably does not reveal his interlocuter in his letter to Reinhard was probably to protect Schultz's relationship with Kant. Fichte is indeed cagey about the issue and tells Reinhard that he will be able to identify his interlocuter only later.

8. See *Allgemeine Literatur Zeitung* 295 (December 13, 1785), 297–299. I have dealt in more detail with the context and content of Schultz's review in *The Fate of Reason*, pp. 206–207.

9. Kant's response appeared in an important footnote to his *Metaphysische Anfangsgründe der Naturwissenschaften*, Kant, *Schriften*, IV, 474n.

10. See Platner, *Aphorismen* §699 (1793 edition), and Maimon, *Werke*, IV, 72–73, II, 186–187, V, 477–479, and VII, 55–59. See too Schulze *Aenesidemus*, pp. 94–105, whose argument is similar but different. Kant begs the question against Hume, Schulze argues, because transcendental philosophy has to presuppose the category of causality to investigate the origins and conditions of knowledge. In his letter to Reinhard Fichte refers to "the indisputably refuted Humean skepticism"; but he evidently soon changed his assessment of Hume, probably under the influence of Schulze and Maimon. See his early fragment 'Wer Hume, Aenesidemus u. Maimon nicht gelesen hat,' AA, II/3, 389–390, and his August 3, 1795 letter to Hufeland, AA, III/3, 359.

11. The association was a very personal one: Schulze married Feder's daughter. See Feder to Reinhold, July 23, 1794, in Ernst Reihold, *K. L. Reinhold's Leben und literarisches Wirken* (Jena: Fromann, 1825), p. 380.

12. AA, III/2, 18.

13. See Fichte's November 1793 letter to L. W. Wloemer, AA, III/2, 14; his mid-December 1793 letter to Heinrich Stephani, AA, III/2, 28; and his January 15, 1794 letter to F. V. Reinhard, AA, III/2, 39.

14. See Fichte to C. G. Schütz, December 1793, AA, III/2, 26.
15. See Xavier Léon, *Fichte et son temps* (Paris: Armand Colin, 1954), I, 249–254; Fritz Medicus, *Fichte's Leben* (Leipzig: Meiner, 1922), p. 65; and Daniel Breazeale, 'Fichte's *Aenesidemus* Review and the Transformation of German Idealism,' *Review of Metaphysics* 34 (1981), 545–581.
16. See Fichte to Reinhard, January 15, 1794, AA, III/2, 39.
17. G. E. Schulze, *Aenesidemus oder über die Fundamente der von dem Herrn Prof. Reinhold in Jena gelieferten Elementarphilosophie*, ed. A. Liebert, (Berlin: Reuther and Reichard, 1912), pp. 202–206, 295–296. The original edition appeared anonymously in 1792, without indicating the publisher or place of publication.
18. Ibid., pp. 94–105, 135–136.
19. Ibid., pp. 133–134.
20. Ibid., p. 307.
21. Ibid., pp. 116–130.
22. See, for example, the preface to the first edition of *Über den Begriff der Wissenschaftslehre, Werke,* I, 29, and the footnote in the *Grundlage der gesamten Wissenschaftslehre, Werke,* I, 121n.
23. See the *Grundlage der gesamten Wissenschaftslehre, Werke,* I, 227. Though Fichte does not mention Maimon by name here, he later does so in a very similar context. See *Grundriß des Eigenthümlichen der Wissenschaftslehre, Werke,* I, 387.
24. See, for example, the preface to the first edition of *Über den Begriff der Wissenschaftslehre, Werke,* I, 29.
25. See *Grundlage der gesammten Wissenschaftslehre, Werke* I, 120n. See also the fragment 'Wer Hume, Anesidemus u. Maimon nicht gelesen hat,' in AA, II/3, 389–390.
26. AA, III/2, 282.
27. See Maimon's *Versuch über die Transcendentalphilosophie, Werke,* II, 62–65, 182–183, 362–364.
28. Ibid., II, 187–188, 370–373; and his *Versuch einer neuen Logik, Werke,* V, 489–490.
29. See Maimon, *Werke,* V, 191–192.
30. See Maimon's *Briefe Philalethes an Aenesidemus, Werke,* V, 358–359.
31. This point has been rightly stressed by Cassirer, *Erkenntnisproblem,* III, 89–96. In his 'Fichte on Skepticism,' *Journal of the History of Philosophy* 29 (1991), 427–453, Daniel Breazeale provides an account of Fichte's reply to Schulze and Maimon that fails to see the fundamental difference between Maimon's and Schulze's skepticism. He completely misses, therefore, the purport of Fichte's reply to Maimon. The same failure vitiates Martin's account of Fichte's Jena project in his *Idealism and Objectivity,* pp. 17–18. To claim that Fichte is not concerned with problems of skepticism because he does not attempt to demonstrate the existence of objects outside us in the sense of transcendental realism is to fail to see the challenge Maimon's skepticism posed for Fichte.
32. See Maimon, *Sreifereien im Gebiete der Philosophie, Werke,* IV, 38.
33. See Fichte, *Werke,* I, 99, 227, 387–389.
34. On the theme of finitude, see *Grundlage, Werke,* I, 253, 270, 275, 354–355; and

on the critique of dogmatic idealism, see ibid., I, 155–156, 173, 175, 178, 186; and the *Wissenschaftslehre novo methodo*, AA, IV/2, 33–34, 55, 128, 141.

35. See *Grundlage, Werke*, I, 297–301, 313–314; and the 'Vorrede zur ersten Ausgabe' of *Über den Begriff der Wissenschaftslehre, Werke*, I, 29n.

36. *Grundlage, Werke*, I, 215.

37. See the *Zweite Einleitung in die Wissenschaftslehre, Werke*, I, 476–477, 489.

38. There is a reference to Maimon in the *Eigene Meditationen*, AA, II/3, 23–24n. It has been argued, however, that this is really a slip of the pen because the source of the views under discussion is Schulze rather than Maimon. See Willy Kabitz, *Studien zur Entwicklungsgechichte der Fichteschen Wissenschaftslehre aus der kantischen Philosophie* (Berlin: Reuther and Reichard, 1912), p. 62n2; Kabitz's views have been endorsed by Jürgen Stolzenberg, *Fichtes Begriff der intellektuellen Anschauung* (Stuttgart: Klett-Cotta, 1986), p. 16. Yet Maimon was concerned with substantially the same issue that is under consideration in these passages: How does the transcendental philosopher know that his propositions are true of consciounsess itself? This was indeed the central thrust of Maimon's critique of Reinhold, which appeared in his *Streifereien im Gebiete der Philosophie*. See the detailed reference in AA, II/3, 23n1. For the details of Maimon's dispute with Reinhold, see my *The Fate of Reason*, pp. 317–320.

39. See *Werke*, III, 186–187, 193.

40. See again Maimon's *Wörterbuch, Werke*, III, 200–201.

41. See Fichte's critique of traditional epistemology in the *Wissenschaftslehre novo methodo*, AA, IV/2, 49.

42. On Bacon's response to skepticism, see *The New Organon*, ed. F. H. Anderson (Indianapolis: Bobbs Merrill, 1960), Book I, nos. 21, 37, 50, 67, and especially 'The Great Instauration,' pp. 7–29.

3. Criticism versus Dogmatism

1. See *Werke*, I, 422–429. See also *Wissenschaftslehre novo methodo*, AA, IV/2, 20–27.

2. See *Grundlage der gesamten Wissenschaftslehre, Werke*, I, 100–101, 120–121, 255, and the *Zweite Einleitung in die Wissenschaftslehre, Werke*, I, 513–514.

3. See Kant's original formulation of his problem in his February 2, 1772 letter to Marcus Herz, *Schriften*, X, 124–126; and the first *Kritik*, B xvii, 124–125.

4. See KrV, B 571.

5. Thus Kant wrote in the second *Kritik*: "if the ideality of space and time is not assumed, only Spinozism remains, which holds space and time to be essential attributes of the first being itself and the things dependent upon it (ourselves included) not to be substances but merely accidents inhering in it" (V, 101–102).

6. But, as we shall see below, Fichte's account in the *Erste Einleitung* is simplistic. See below, 2.3.4 and 2.5.2.

7. See the *Erste Einleitung in die Wissenschaftslehre* §5, *Werke*, I, 431: "A consistent dogmatist is also necessarily a materialist."

8. See Fichte's formulation of his problem in the introduction to the *Sittenlehre, Werke*, IV, 1–2, and in his *Streitschrift gegen Schmid, Werke*, II, 434–436.

9. See Fichte's July 2, 1795 letter to Reinhold, AA, III/2, 345, and his *Grundlage der gesamten Wissenschaftslehre, Werke*, I, 114.

10. In his 'Fichte's Anti-Dogmatism,' *Ratio* 2 (1992), 129–146, Wayne Martin argues that dogmatism is for Fichte not "a general ontological view" but a naturalistic account of consciousness. Although Martin is correct in stressing the naturalism involved in dogmatism, it is also important to recognize its ontological dimension, which is apparent from the Spinozistic concepts Fichte uses to characterize it.

11. See again Fichte's formulation of his problem in his July 2, 1795 letter to K. L. Reinhold, AA, III/2, 345.

12. The fourth question is discussed in detail below, 2.4.3 and 2.6.2–3.

13. On just these grounds Fichte has been criticized for limiting the options for the explanation of experience. See John Lachs, 'Fichte's Idealism,' *American Philosophical Quarterly* 9 (1972), 311–318, esp. 314–315.

14. KrV, A 385, 389–391.

15. See, for example, Fichte's *Zweite Einleitung in die Wissenschaftslehre, Werke*, I, 484–485; and Schelling's *Ideen zu einer Philsophie der Natur, Werke*, II, 16–18, 20–21, and *Erläuterung zur Idealismus der Wissenschaftslehre, Werke*, II, 377–379.

16. See the *Erste Einleitung in die Wissenschaftslehre, Werke*, I, 431.

17. See Fichte's account of the principle of sufficient reason in the *Grundlage der gesamten Wissenschaftslehre, Werke*, I, 118–121.

18. See Fichte, *System der Sittenlehre, Werke*, IV, 174, 228.

19. This is Fichte's own analogy in his *Annalen des philosophischen Tons, Werke*, II, 475.

20. This is at odds, however, with Fichte's view, expressed elsewhere, that there are natural laws to explain organisms that are not mechanical in nature. See, for example, his *System der Sittenlehre, Werke*, IV, 120.

21. Fichte articulates just this assumption in his *Grundlage der gesamten Wissenschaftslehre:* "A lifeless body has no causality except outside itself" (I, 293); and in his *System der Sittenlehre:* "A power of inertia *(vis inertiae)* is to be ascribed to nature in general or as such" (IV, 199).

22. In his *Kant and the Fate of Autonomy*, p. 181, Karl Ameriks oversimplifies Fichte's position by claiming that he entirely dispenses with the thing-in-itself when he rejects the existence of the unthinkable.

23. See the *Zweite Einleitung in die Wissenschaftslehre, Werke*, I, 481–486.

24. Kant writes in A 372: "We can indeed admit that something, which may be (in the transcendental sense) outside us, is the cause of our outer intuitions, but this is not the object of which are thinking in the representations of matter and of corporeal things; for these are merely appearances . . . The transcendental object is equally unknown in respect to inner and to outer intuitions. But it is not of this that we are here speaking but of the empirical object."

25. Fichte defines the noumenon as "something . . . we merely *think of* in addition to appearances," "something produced only by our own thinking" or "something that exists only *for our own thinking*." See the *Zweite Einleitung in die Wissenschaftslehre, Werke*, I, 482–483 (Fichte's emphasis).

26. See the footnote to the first introduction to *Über den Begriff der Wissenschaftslehre,*

Werke, I, 29. See also the footnote to Fichte's essay 'Von der Sprachfähigkeit und dem Ursprunge der Sprache,' VIII, 321n. Here Fichte insists what is felt is only the object of *belief;* here he does not refer explicitly, however, to the thing-in-it-self but only to "things outside us" (*Dinge ausser uns*).

4. Freedom and Subjectivity

1. See Fichte's famous spring 1795 letter to Jens Baggesen, AA, III/2, 298.
2. See Fichte's statement in the 'Zweite Einleitung' to the *Wissenschaftslehre novo methodo,* AA, IV/2, 23: "Kant speaks of the interest of speculative reason and that of practical reason, and opposes them; this is correct from his standpoint, but not in itself, for reason is always one and has only one interest. Its interest is faith in independence and freedom."
3. *System der Sittenlehre, Werke,* IV, 79.
4. See especially §3, and §§13–14.
5. On Kant's two concepts of the will, see Allen Wood, 'Kant's Compatibilism,' in *Self and Nature in Kant's Philosophy* (Ithaca: Cornell University Press, 1984), pp. 73–102; and Henry Allison, *Kant's Theory of Freedom* (Cambridge: Cambridge University Press, 1990), pp. 129–136.
6. *Wissenschaftslehre novo methodo,* AA, IV/2, 135.
7. Ibid., AA, IV/2, 136, 155–156.
8. Spinoza, *Ethica,* Pars I, def. 7.
9. See *System der Sittenlehre, Werke,* IV, 35–38, 45, 134–135; and *Wissenschaftslehre novo methodo,* AA, IV/2, 150.
10. The parallel is sometimes uncanny. See Fichte's comments in the *Wissenschaftslehre novo methodo* regarding the distinction between my wanting to move my hand and my hand moving. AA, IV/2, 182, 227. Fichte maintains that this is a distinction between different standpoints, two different ways of explaining one and the same thing.
11. See, for example, Fichte's argument in the second lecture of the *Bestimmung des Gelehrten, Werke,* VI, 304–305, and in the *Erste Einleitung in die Wissenschaftslehre, Werke,* I, 436–437.
12. See *Wissenschaftslehre novo methodo,* AA IV/2, 44, 48; and *System der Sittenlehre, Werke,* IV, 36.
13. See *System der Sittenlehre, Werke,* IV, 35–36, 50–51, 157–159; and *Wissenschaftslehre novo methodo,* AA, IV/2, 43–47.
14. The connection has been largely unexplored; at least the *J. G. Fichte Bibliographie (1968–1992/93)* (Amsterdam: Rodopoi, 1993) lists no article or monograph on the topic. Two older and still useful studies on Sartre's relation to Fichte are Louis Phillip Ricard, 'La Philosophie de Fichte et l'existentialisme,' in *Proceedings of the Tenth International Congress of Philosophy* (Amsterdam, 1948), II, 1174–1176; and Kurt Hübner, 'Fichte, Sartre und der Nihilismus,' in *Zeitschrift für philosophische Forschung* X (1956), 29–43.
15. See *System der Sittenlehre, Werke,* IV, 222; see also 38, 50. This is indeed much of

what Fichte means with the first principle of the *Wissenschaftslehre:* "The absolute subject is that whose being (essence) consists merely in what it posits itself to be." See too *Grundlage der gesamten Wissenschaftslehre, Werke,* I, 97.

16. See *System der Sittenlehre, Werke,* IV, 213; *Vorlesungen über die Bestimmung des Gelehrten, Werke,* VI, 297–298.

17. This is very clear from the first lecture of the *Vorlesungen über die Bestimmung des Gelehrten,* in *Werke,* VI, 296–297.

18. For a more detailed treatment of the subject, see Frederick Neuhouser, *Fichte's Theory of Subjectivity* (Cambridge: Cambridge University Press, 1990).

19. See *Wissenschaftslehre novo methodo,* AA, IV/2, 31, 46; *Versuch einer neuen Darstellung der Wissenschaftslehre, Werke,* I, 529; *Grundlage der gesamten Wissenschaftslehre, Werke,* I, 98n; *System der Sittenlehre, Werke,* IV, 42; *Vergleichung des vom Herrn Prof. Schmid aufgestellten Systems mit der Wissenschaftslehre, Werke,* II, 442.

20. See Kant, *Grundlegung zur Metaphysik der Sitten,* IV, 412.

21. See the *Zweite Einleitung in die Wissenschaftslehre, Werke,* I, 475–477, 501.

22. See *Wissenschaftslehre novo methodo* §§3–4, AA, IV/2, 43–49; *Grundlage der gesamten Wissenschaftslehre, Werke,* I, 296–297, 300–309, 312–313; and *System der Sittenlehre, Werke,* IV, 73–74, 84–85; virtually all of §§1–3, IV, 18–62, is relevant.

23. See *System der Sittenlehre, Werke,* IV, 85.

24. Ibid., *Werke,* IV, 29, 39–40.

25. This is the implication of Fichte's argument throughout §§4–9. I analyze this argument in detail below.

26. See AA, IV/2, 45, 48.

27. See *Wissenschaftslehre novo methodo,* AA, IV/2, 44, 48; and *System der Sittenlehre* §2, *Werke,* V, 36.

28. *System der Sittenlehre, Werke,* IV, 133–134, 137.

29. Ibid., *Werke,* IV, 38.

30. Fichte's explicit target seems to have been Ernst Platner, whose views are in many respects representative of the rationalist tradition. See Fichte's comment in *Wissenschaftslehre novo methodo,* AA, IV/2, 31; 32. See also Fichte's comments on Platner's *Philosophische Aphorismen* in AA, IV/1, 225.

31. In *Essay,* II, xxvii, 17, Locke defines the self as "that conscious thinking thing, (whatever Substance, made up of whether Spiritual, or Material, Simple, or Compounded, it matters not) which is sensible, conscious of Pleasure and Pain, capable of Happiness or Misery, and so is concern'd for it *self,* as far as that consciousness extends." After forcefully criticizing any account of personal identity in terms of substance, Locke admits at §25 that "the more probable Opinion is, that this consciousness is annexed to, and the Affection of one individual immaterial Substance."

32. Fichte is clear about this point, which is central to his rejection of classical metaphysics. See, for example, his *Sonnenklarer Bericht, Werke,* II, 331–332, and his April 22, 1799 letter to Reinhold, AA, III/2, 337, 331.

33. See, for example, *Zweite Einleitung in die Wissenschaftslehre, Werke,* I, 471–472.

34. See Fichte's critical comment on mysticism in *System der Sittenlehre, Werke,* IV, 151.

35. See, for example, *Grundlage der gesammten Wissenschaftslehre, Werke,* I, 313; *System der Sittenlehre, Werke,* IV, 102; and *Wissenschaftslehre novo methodo,* AA, IV/2, 34, 60.

36. This point has been questioned, however. See Alexis Philonenko, *La Liberté humaine dans la Philosophie de Fichte,* pp. 77–94, and his 'Die intellektuelle Anschauung bei Fichte,' *Der transcendentale Gedanke: Die gegewärtige Darstellung der Philosophie Fichtes,* ed. K. Hamacher (Hamburg: Meiner, 1981), pp. 91–106. Also see T. P. Hohler, *Imagination and Reflection: Intersubjectivity. Fichte's* Grundlage *of 1794* (The Hague: Martinus Nijhoff, 1982), pp. 93–115. According to Philonenko and Hohler, it is anachronistic to read the self-positing ego of the *Grundlage* in terms of intellectual intuition, and hence along the lines of Fichte's later distinction in the *Zweite Einleitung.* They stress that Fichte does not employ the concept of intellectual intuition in the *Grundlage,* and that he developed it only in the later *Wissenschaftslehre novo methodo.* While the later *Wissenschaftslehre* indeed begins with intellectual intuition, the earlier *Grundlage* only leads up to that point. Supposedly, this follows from Fichte's own account of the differences between these works, where he says that the earlier *Grundlage* begins with the theoretical and ends with the practical, while the later *Wissenschaftslehre novo methodo* begins with the practical and ends with the theoretical. Furthermore, the first principles of the *Grundlage* have only a regulative meaning, which is scarcely compatible with an intellectual intuition. These are not purely scholastic points, it is argued, because they invalidate Hegel's famous criticisms of Fichte, which are based on the assumption that his philosophy begins with intellectual intuition.

    Whatever the merits of Hegel's criticisms, there are several serious problems with this reading. First, Fichte had already developed the theory of intellectual intuition in the *Eigene Meditationen,* where it has the same function as in the *Grundlage,* so that reading intellectual intuition into the *Grundlage* cannot be regarded as anachronistic. Second, whatever differences there otherwise might be between the starting points of the *Grundlage* and *Wissenschaftslehre novo methodo,* both works begin with the self-positing ego. Since Fichte describes the self-positing ego in the *Wissenschaftslehre novo methodo* in terms of intellectual intuition, there is no reason to say that it is excluded in principle from the *Grundlage.* Third, while the first principle of the *Grundlage* does have a regulative meaning, this is not undermined by ascribing an intellectual intuition to it. Everything depends on the specific meaning of this principle, which describes both the 'I' that begins and the 'I' that ends the *Wissenschaftslehre.* While the 'I' that begins the *Wissenschaftslehre* is an intellectual intuition, that which ends it is merely a regulative idea.

37. See, for example, John Lachs, 'Is There an Absolute Self?' *Philosophical Forum* 19 (1987–1988), 169–182.

38. See, for example, Neuhouser, *Fichte's Theory of Subjectivity,* pp. 44–45, 52.

5. Knowledge of Freedom

1. See *Werke*, V, 117–118, 132, 136.
2. See, for example, the *System der Sittenlehre, Werke*, IV, 45.
3. See the important *Entwürfe zur Recension Gebhard*, AA, II/2, 253–280.
4. See *Grundlage der gesamten Wissenschaftslehre, Werke*, I, 264. Indeed, in his *System der Sittenlehre* Fichte engaged in this strategy in attempting to establish the applicability of the moral law. See *Werke*, IV, 63–75.
5. There are striking Kantian precedents for this position. In his 'Theory-Practice' essay, Kant maintains that, although we can never be completely sure of the motives of our actions, we can be aware of "the maxim of striving towards moral purity." See Kant, *Schriften*, VIII, 285.
6. See KrV, A 346, 350, 365, A 402, B 422.
7. These arguments will be explained below, 2.5.7.
8. See Dieter Henrich, *Fichtes ursprüngliche Einsicht* (Franfurt: Klostermann, 1967).
9. See Robert Pippin, 'Fichte's Contribution,' *Philosophical Forum* 19 (1987–1988), 74–96; and Neuhouser, *Fichte's Theory of Subjectivity*, pp. 68–86. Both Pippin (pp. 80–84) and Neuhouser (pp. 69, 73–74) are rightly critical of Henrich for ignoring the specific context of Fichte's theory, more specifically his concern with the unity of apperception.
10. For a detailed study of the evolution of Fichte's concept from this context, see Jürgen Stolzenberg, *Fichtes Begriff der intellektuellen Anschauung* (Stuttgart: Klett-Cotta, 1986), pp. 1–174.
11. It might seem that Fichte restores just such a subject when he insists that subject–object identity or immediate consciousness cannot be the object of consciousness. See, for example, the *Wissenschaftslehre novo methodo*, AA, IV/2, 31, 38, and *System der Sittenlehre, Werke*, IV, 6, 42. It is important to see, however, that it cannot be an object of consciousness *for consciousness* itself. It can, however, be an object for philosophical reflection. Indeed, in the *Wissenschaftslehre novo methodo* Fichte clearly rejects the conclusion that immediate consciousness is unknowable because it is the condition of all consciousness (AA, IV/2, 31, 35, 37). He explains that the philosopher has an immediate consciousness of such immediate consciousness, an intellectual intuition of intellectual intuition.
12. KrV, B 158n. Kant does not refer explicitly to intellectual intuition in this passage, but that he has it in mind is clear by comparison with other passages. See also B 135, 139.
13. Hence Fichte's metaphor for an intellectual intuition as *self-reverting* activity (*zurückkehrendes Handeln*) (I, 462).
14. See KrV, B 93, and *Logik*, XI, 1, §1.
15. KrV, B 135, 139.
16. See the *Zweite Einleitung in die Wissenschaftslehre, Werke*, I, 471–472.
17. In the *Zweite Einleitung* Fichte refers to Kant's polemical essay *Von einem neuerdings vornehmen Ton in der Philosophie*, where Kant's use of the term 'intellectual intuition' is exactly as Fichte portrays it. See Kant, VIII, 391.

18. Fichte could have read this in the first *Kritik*. See B 68, 135, 138–139, 159. In the second *Kritik* Kant implies that only an intellectual intuition would give me knowledge of my spontaneity or freedom. See IV, 31, 32.

19. In his 'Intellectual Intuition: The Continuity Thesis,' *Journal of the History of Ideas* 42 (1981), 287–304, Moltke Gram argues that it is idle to think that the post-Kantian idealists are opposed to Kant on the issue of intellectual intuition because Kant, Fichte, and Schelling all use these terms in different senses and for different reasons. While this is often the case, it is not always so. His claim that Kant implicitly sanctions Fichte's intellectual intuition (p. 299) ignores how Fichte affirms a form of knowledge neither conceptual nor empirical.

20. See Fichte's discussion in the *Zweite Einleitung in die Wissenschaftslehre, Werke*, I, 472–479.

21. Of course, this represents only one line of thinking in the *Kritik*, because Kant also states that the 'I think' is "an indeterminate empirical perception" (B 422n). But this position brings Kant further from Fichte; for, in calling the 'I think' an empirical proposition, Kant stresses that it must have some given matter for reflection (B 423n).

22. AA, IV/2, 30. See also AA, IV/2, 115.

23. See Fichte's September 28, 1799 letter to Reinhold, where his criticism becomes even disrespectful. He now writes that Kant is a "*Dreiviertelskopf,*" AA, III/4, 93.

24. Kant stresses this circularity at B 422, A 346, 366, 402.

25. See KrV, B 67–69, 152–156, A 343, B 406–407.

26. This, of course, is for the sake of convenience. Fichte himself does not use these terms; I apply them here only as an aid to analyze his argument.

27. AA, IV/2, 29–33.

28. See *Werke*, IV, 25–26, 46–47, 53–54, 135–136.

6. Critical Idealism

1. AA, I/1, 151–152.

2. AA, IV/2, 67.

3. See, for example, Copleston, *History*, pp. 72, 79; and Zöller, *Fichte's Transcendental Philosophy*, pp. 49–50, 51.

4. See Fichte's comments on mysticism in the *System der Sittenlehre, Werke*, IV, 151.

5. See Fichte's own account of the primacy of practical reason in *Grundlage, Werke*, I, 126, 144, 156, 177, 264; and his *Über den Begriff der Wissenschaftslehre, Werke*, I, 65.

6. See especially *Werke*, I, 155–156, 173, 175, 178, 186. On Fichte's concept of critical idealism, see also the *Wissenschaftslehre novo methodo*, AA, IV/2, 33–34, 55, 128, 141.

7. This discrepancy has raised much discussion. Tom Rockmore has argued, rightly, that Fichte's critical idealism is a synthesis of idealism and realism, and he has seen Fichte's rejection of realism as essentially rhetorical. See his 'Fichte's Idealism and Marx's Materialism,' *Man and World* 8 (1975), 189–206, and 'Activity in

Fichte and Marx,' *Idealistic Studies* 6 (1976), 191–214. His views have been criticized by Douglas Raab, who insists that Fichte rejects any form of realism, and who denies that Fichte's talk about a synthesis is his considered view. See his 'Is Critical Idealism Idealism?' *Idealistic Studies* 9 (1979), 131–139. Raab's view that Fichte's talk about a synthesis is only provisional and exploratory does not agree with much of the text, especially *Grundlage,* I, 154–156, where Fichte speaks of the synthesis as the best vantage point for a view of his whole system. Furthermore, Fichte continues to describe his idealism as a synthesis in the *Wissenschaftslehre novo methodo,* AA, IV/2, 55.

Wayne Martin has proposed a middle path between these positions by contending that, for Fichte, dogmatism does not mean realism as much as naturalism. Hence the rejection of dogmatism need not be seen as a critique of realism, so that the texts are consistent after all. See his 'Fichte's Anti-Dogmatism,' *Ratio* 2 (1992), 129–146, and his *Idealism and Objectivity,* pp. 30–54. Unfortunately, this irenic effort does not work. The problem is that the descriptions of dogmatic idealism and realism in the *Grundlage* correspond too closely to those of criticism and dogmatism in the *Einleitung,* insofar as both give one-sided monistic explanations of experience. Furthermore, dogmatism is not only a species of naturalism but also a form of realism insofar as it is a transcendental form of Spinozism, which locates the condition of experience outside the subject in the single universal substance. Hence Fichte identifies dogmatism with Spinozism (I, 120), and he sees Spinozism as a form of realism (I, 155).

There is another *apparent* explanation for the discrepancy: that Fichte intends only to establish an *empirical* realism in the *Grundlage,* while what he opposes in the *Einleitung* is only a species of *transcendental* idealism. But this too fails, mainly because it does not agree with the text of the *Grundlage,* where Fichte makes it clear that his realism is not only formal but also material, that is, he holds that the realm of experience consists not only in conformity with universal and necessary rules but in appearances *of* the thing-in-itself. It seems to me that the only way to avoid the contradiction is to consider the purposes and audiences of the texts. The sharp contrast between criticism and dogmatism appears mainly in the *Erste Einleitung,* which is intended for "readers who do not already have a philosophical system." Fichte was simplifying, indeed oversimplifying. He was discussing idealism and realism *en abstracto* and in their general principles without attempting to provide a more nuanced and balanced account of how these principles must be qualified in attempting to explain experience.

8. See *Werke,* I, 155, 172, 281. See also the *Wissenschaftslehre novo methodo* where Fichte defines "transcendent idealism" as the doctrine that states the existence of objects is only delusion (AA, IV/2, 139).
9. See *Werke,* I, 175, 298.
10. Fichte describes his idealism as a synthesis of realism and idealism at *Werke,* I, 156, 281.
11. See, for example, ibid., I, 248, 279–280.
12. Ibid., I, 187, 279–280, 298.

13. Ibid., I, 209–210, 227–228, 248–250, 275, 279.
14. Ibid., I, 209–210, 227–228.
15. Ibid., I, 281; see also I, 156, 178, 186.
16. Fichte himself notes this at I, 110.
17. See Hegel, *Geschichte der Philosophie, Werke,* XX, 404.
18. Virtually all of the first part of section 4 is relevant, *Werke,* I, 125–217.
19. See *Grundlage, Werke,* I, 156, 281.
20. See also the important footnote to the preface of the first edition of *Über den Begriff der Wissenschaftslehre, Werke,* I, 29. Here Fichte explains that things are represented as appearances but felt as things-in-themselves.

7. The Refutation of Idealism

1. The essential texts are sections 4–8 of the Second Main Section (*Zweite Hauptstück*) of the *System der Sittenlehre, Werke,* IV, 75–122, and sections 1–4 of the First Main section (*Erstes Hauptstück*) of the *Grundlage des Naturrechts, Werke,* III, 17–55. The first text is the main subject of interpretation in this chapter; the second text, though it is interpreted extensively in this chapter, is analyzed in more detail in chapter 8.
2. For a fuller account of the meaning of positing and its role in Fichte's early philosophy, see Daniel Breazeale, 'The Spirit of the *Wissenschaftslehre,*' in Sedgwick, *Reception,* pp. 171–198.
3. Fichte explains his argument in just such terms in the *Zweite Einleitung in die Wissenschaftslehre, Werke,* I, 457–458.
4. *System der Sittenlehre, Werke,* IV, 21, 29.
5. In this respect Fichte follows Kant. See KrV, B 505.
6. See *Versuch einer neuen Darstellung der Wissenschaftslehre, Werke,* I, 523.
7. See *Grundlage der gesamten Wissenschaftslehre, Werke,* I, 101–105; *Wissenschaftslehre novo methodo,* AA, IV/2, 33–40.
8. Compare Fichte's analysis of space in the *Wissenschaftslehre novo methodo,* §11, AA IV/2, 109–110, 113, and §12, 120–122.
9. Thus Fichte concludes the section devoted to Proposition 5: "The result of the present investigation is consequently the following: as certain as I exist, I must ascribe causality to nature; for I can posit myself only as its product"(IV, 121–122).

8. The Structure of Intersubjectivity

1. With good reason this aspect of Fichte's philosophy has been receiving increasing attention. See, for example, Georg Mohr, 'Freedom and the Self: From Introspection to Intersubjectivity,' in *The Modern Subject,* ed. K. Ameriks and D. Sturma (Albany: SUNY Press, 1995), pp. 31–46; Robert Williams, *Recognition: Fichte and Hegel on the Other* (Albany: SUNY Press, 1992), 'The Question of the Other in Fichte's Thought,' in D. Breazeale and T. Rockmore, *Fichte: Historical Context and Contemporary Controversies* (Atlantic City: Humanities Press, 1992),

pp. 142–157; and Paul Franks, 'The Discovery of the Other: Cavell, Fichte, and Skepticism,' *Common Knowledge* 5 (1996), 72–105.

2. See his *Grundlage des Naturrechts, Werke,* III, 80.

3. See Fichte's August 29, 1795 letter to Reinhold, AA, III/2, 386.

4. See *Wissenschaftslehre novo methodo,* AA, IV/2, 142; see also *Grundlage des Naturrechts, Werke,* III, 37.

5. For the sake of simplicity, I shall ignore here Kant's second edition remark that the 'I think' is an indeterminate empirical proposition. See B 422n, 428. On Kant's reasons for reformulating the status of this principle, see Erdmann, *Kants Kriticismus,* pp. 217–223.

6. Fichte himself saw his argument in such a light. See Fichte to Reinhold, August 29, 1795, AA, III/2, 385–386. To achieve universal agreement among rational beings, he explained, we must first know whether and under what conditions such beings exist.

7. See especially the second lecture, 'Ueber die Bestimmung des Menschen in der Gesellschaft,' *Werke,* VI, 301–311.

8. In his later *Wissenschaftslehre novo methodo* Fichte attempted to find something in appearances that would justify the inference to other minds. See AA, IV/2, 248, §19. In both the *Rechtslehre* and *Sittenlehre,* however, he had excluded the possibility of any such proof. See *Werke,* III, 36–37, and IV, 223. This raises questions of consistency that go beyond the limits of the present discussion.

9. The relevant sections are §§1–4 of the Erstes Hauptstück, 'Deduktion des Begriffes vom Rechte,' *Werke,* III, 17–55.

10. See also *Wissenschaftslehre novo methodo,* AA, IV/2, 172, §16, where Fichte maintains that all our knowledge of the external world begins with other minds.

11. The account given here is based on Fichte's formulation of his argument in the *Rechtslehre* and its reformulation in the *Sittenlehre.* See *Sittenlehre, Werke,* IV, 219–220, and *Rechtslehre Werke,* III, 32–33.

12. See too *Wissenschaftslehre novo methodo,* AA, IV/2, 251, §19.

1. Absolute Idealism: General Introduction

1. The first to coin the term appears to have been Friedrich Schlegel, who uses it frequently in his notebooks. See his *Philosophische Lehrjahre,* KA, XVIII, 33 (no. 151), 65 (no. 449), 80 (no. 606), 85 (no. 658), 90 (no. 736), 282 (no. 1046), 396 (no. 908). On Schelling's use of the term, see *Fernere Darstellungen, Werke,* IV, 404; 'Ueber das Verhältniß der Naturphilosophie zur Philosophie überhaupt,' V, 112; the 'Zusatz zur Einleitung' to the *Ideen zu einer Philosophie der Natur,* II, 67, 68; and *Bruno,* IV, 257, 322. On Hegel's use of the term, see Hegel, *Enzyklopädie der philosophischen Wissenschaften* §§160Z, 32Z and 45Z, and his *Wissenschaft der Logik,* V, 172. In his *Differenzschrift* Hegel uses the term 'idealism' but distinguishes his position from 'subjective idealism,' *Werke,* II, 55–56. This term was not used by Hölderlin, nor by Hardenberg, who preferred his term 'syncriticism' or 'magical idealism.'

2. In his *Unendliche Annäherung: Die Anfänge der philosophischen Frühromantik*

(Frankfurt: Suhrkamp, 1997), pp. 27, 65–66, 662, Manfred Frank makes a sharp distinction between the philosophy of early romanticism and absolute idealism. Frank uses the term 'absolute idealism' to designate the doctrine that "the basic facts of our reality are mental (even ideal) entities" (p. 27). In this sense it is certainly correct to claim that the early romantics were not absolute idealists. However, it is important to see that the romantics themselves did not use the term in this sense, and that they did sometimes espouse a doctrine they called "idealism" (see the citations in the preceding note). Furthermore, it is misleading to place the romantics outside the idealist tradition entirely, as Frank would like (p. 27), because they still adhere to some of its central principles, even while reinterpreting and transforming them. Thus Schelling and Hegel would claim to represent the "spirit" of Kant's and Fichte's philosophy—the principle of subject–object identity—even though for them it no longer refers to the self-consciousness of the transcendental subject but the unity of nature itself.

In placing the romantics within the tradition of absolute idealism, I follow an older tradition of scholarship. Perhaps the founder of this tradition was Rudolf Haym, who, in his magisterial *Die romantische Schule* (Berlin: Gaertner, 1870), p. 657, saw Schelling's absolute idealism as the epitome of romantic philosophy. For some more recent examples of this tradition, see Ernst Behler, *Frühromantik* (Berlin: de Gruyter, 1992), pp. 151–157, and Hans Dierkes, 'Philosophie der Romantik,' *Romantik-Handbuch,* ed. Helmut Schanze (Tübingen: Kroner, 1994), pp. 427–477. However, insofar as some scholars in this tradition have understood absolute idealism simply as a radical form of Kant's or Fichte's idealism, I part company with them. In this respect, Frank's distinction between early romanticism and absolute idealism is perfectly understandable, and he is surely right to protest against any conflation of the romantic views with the Kantian–Fichtean tradition.

3. On Sinclair, see Hannelore Hegel, 'Reflexion und Einheit: Sinclair und der Bund der Geister," *Hegel-Studien, Beiheft* 9 (1973), 91–106, and *Isaak von Sinclair zwischen Fichte, Hölderlin und Hegel* (Frankfurt: Klostermann, 1971), which contains an edition of his 'Philosophische Raisonnements.' See also Christoph Jamme, 'Isaak von Sinclairs Philosophische Raisonnements,' *Hegel-Studien* 18 (1983), 240–244; and Ursula Brauer, *Isaac von Sinclair: Eine Biographie* (Stuttgart: Klett-Cotta, 1993). On Zwilling, see Ludwig Strauß, 'Jacob Zwilling und sein Nachlass,' *Euphorion* 29 (1928), 368–396; and Dieter Henrich and Christoph Jamme, *Jakob Zwillings Nachlass: Eine Rekonstruktion, Hegel-Studien, Beiheft* 28 (1986).

4. The most important member of this circle for the history of idealism was Hülsen. On Hülsen and his writings, see Karl Obenauer, *August Ludwig Hülsen* (Erlangen: Junge and Sohn, 1910). Since they published little, the views of other members of the circle are not well known. On this circle, see Willy Flitner, *August Ludwig Hülsen und der Bund der Freien Männer* (Jena: Eugen Diederichs, 1913). According to Flitner (p. 17), the whole circle adopted pantheistic views around 1796. For a glimpse into the life of the circle, see Erich Fuchs, 'Reinhold und Fichte im

Briefwechsel zweier Jenenser Studenten 1793/94,' and 'Aus dem Tagebuch von Johann Smidt,' *Fichte-Studien* 7 (1995), 143–193.

5. On the chronology of the term '*Frühromantik*,' see Behler, *Frühromantik*, pp. 9–35; and Paul Kluckhohn, *Das Ideengut der deutschen Romantik*, 3rd ed. (Tübingen: Niemeyer, 1953), pp. 8–9.

6. On the intellectual atmosphere of Jena in the 1790s, see Theodore Ziolkowski, *Das Wunderjahr in Jena* (Stuttgart: Klett-Cotta, 1998); and the rich anthology *Evolution des Geistes: Jena um 1800*, ed. Friedrich Strack (Stuttgart: Klett-Cotta, 1994).

7. This has been the claim of Dieter Henrich, who sees Hölderlin as the turning point in the battle against Fichte's subjective idealism. See his *Der Grund im Bewußtsein: Untersuchungen zu Hölderlins Denken (1794–1795)* (Stuttgart: Klett-Cotta, 1992), pp. 125, 127. (See also the literature cited 3.1.1, note 1). The grand claims Henrich makes for Hölderlin, and the remarkable lengths he goes in examining the formation of his views, contrast markedly with his own insistence that the history of philosophy should move away from leading figures and focus more on the details of intellectual context. See his *Konstellationen: Probleme und Debatten am Ursprung der idealistischen Philosophie (1789–1795)* (Stuttgart: Klett-Cotta, 1991), pp. 27–46. The more we examine this context, the less Hölderlin appears to be a solitary or singular figure.

8. On this dating, see below, 3.2.3.

9. On Hülsen's early pantheism, see Flinter, *Hülsen*, p. 21.

10. As Haym wisely remarks about this period: "In an epoch so rich in ideas, who would want to be so pedantic as to determine the ancestry of individual thoughts or the property rights of individual minds?" See *Die romantische Schule*, p. 264.

11. See Schelling, *Werke*, VI, 148, §7.

12. It is noteworthy that the same meaning can be found in Kant, who used the term in a similar but adjectival sense. In the first *Kritik* he wrote that one of the common meanings of the term in his day was "merely to indicate that something is true of a thing considered *in itself*, and therefore of its *inward* nature" (B, 381).

13. *Ethica*, Pars I, def. 3.

14. I use the term 'vitalism' here warily and only for lack of suitable synonyms. Unfortunately, the term sometimes designates a doctrine that postulates the existence of some supernatural substance or agent existing within nature. But none of the romantics were vitalists in this sense; their vitalism was limited to the belief that the structure of an organism is distinctive from mechanism. Their thesis is about the characteristic *structure* or *form* of life, not about the existence of some special kind of *substance* or *agent*. To dub this thesis as "functionalism," a very hard-worked contemporary term, would be no less misleading.

15. See Schelling's statements in 'Über das Verhältniß der Naturphilosophie zur Philosophie überhaupt,' *Werke*, V, 112, *Bruno*, IV, 257, 332, and the *Fernere Darstellungen*, *Werke*, IV, 404.

16. See Schelling, 'Zusatz zu Einleitung,' II, 67, *Fernere Darstellungen, Werke*, IV, 408; and Hegel, *Enzyklopädie* §45Z.

17. See Schelling's statement in *Bruno*, IV, 257; and Hegel's statement in the *Wissenschaft der Logik*, V, 172.

18. On this use of 'real,' see Schelling's *Bruno*, IV, 301.

19. See Frank, *Unendliche Annäherung*, p. 663.

20. See ibid., pp. 717–718, 825–826; and Henrich, *Grund im Bewußtsein*, pp. 43, 108, 112.

21. I have developed my criticisms of the Henrich–Frank interpretation of *Frühromantik* in more detail in my '*Frühromantik* and the Platonic Tradition,' *Journal of the History of Ideas* (forthcoming).

22. The role of intellectual intuition is a difficulty for Henrich's and Frank's interpretation. While Henrich says little about it, Frank virtually admits that it does not fit well with his interpretation by claiming that it is inconsistent with the general romantic position. See *Unendliche Annäherung*, pp. 718, 826–830. It would be more accurate, however, to claim that intellectual intuition is only a problem for *his* interpretation.

23. See, for example, Plato, *The Republic*, Book VI, 508–509; and Plotinus, *Enneads*, I, vi, 9.

24. This becomes especially clear from Schelling's dispute with Fichte. See below, 3.1.4.

25. Hence Schelling and Hegel reject decisively the view that the absolute has reality only outside us. See the 'Über das Verhältnis der Naturphilosophie zur Philosophie überhaupt,' Schelling, *Werke*, V, 108–115.

26. See, for example, Novalis' *Allgemeine Brouillon*, III, 429 (no. 820), and *Vorarbeiten*, II, 551 (no. 118). See also Schelling's and Hegel's *Fernere Darstellung aus dem System der Philosophie* in Schelling, *Werke*, IV, 356–361; and, again, their 'Über das Verhältniß der Naturphilosophie zur Philosophie überhaupt' in Schelling, *Werke*, V, 108–115.

27. See below, 3.3.6 and 4.3.3–4.3.4.

28. This interpretation is still common even among the most scrupulous scholars. See, for example, Karl Ameriks' account of Hegel in *Kant and the Fate of Autonomy*, pp. 278–279, 308.

29. We will examine these arguments in more detail below, 3.2.3 and 3.3.2. The importance of these arguments has been rightly stressed by Henrich, *Grund im Bewusstsein*, pp. 425–591, and *Konstellationen*, pp. 47–80; and by Frank, *Unendliche Annäherung*, pp. 735–534, 802–861, and *Eine Einführung in Schellings Philosophie* (Frankfurt: Suhrkamp, 1985), pp. 48–71.

30. Spinoza, *The Emendation of the Intellect, Works*, I, 20.

31. See Schlegel's *Athenaeumsfragment*, KA, II, 170 (no. 28); Novalis, *Allgemeine Brouillon*, NS, III, 333, 419 (nos. 457, 778); and Schelling's *Briefe über Dogmatismus und Kritizismus, Werke*, I, 301–302, where he refers to the standpoint of the absolute as "criticism."

32. See Schelling's and Hegel's *Fernere Darstellungen aus dem System der Philosophie* in

Schelling, *Werke*, IV, 356–361; and, once again, their 'Über das Verhältniß der Naturphilosophie zur Philosophie überhaupt,' in Schelling, *Werke*, V, 108–115.

33. See especially the first chapter of Hölderlin's *Hyperions Jugend*, GSA, III, 199; and Hegel's *Glauben und Wissen*, *Werke*, II, 417–430.

34. See Schelling, *Briefe über Dogmatismus und Kriticismus*, *Werke*, I, 286.

35. The *locus classicus* for this view is the young Schlegel's review of Jacobi's *Woldemar*, KA, II, 57–77. See below, 3.4.5.

36. Jacobi, *Werke*, IV/2, 54.

37. Such were the symbols written in Hegel's *Stammbuch* in 1791.

38. The single exception to this is Schelling, who mimicked Spinoza's method in his 1801 *Darstellung meines Systems* and in his 1804 *System der gesammten Philosophie*.

39. The crucial edition of his writings was *Vermischten philosophischen Schriften des Herrn Hemsterhuis* (Leipzig, 1797). The translator is unknown. The edition was revied by Julius Hilß and reissued as *Philosophische Schriften* (Karlsruhe: Dreililien Verlag, 1912). All references will be to this later edition.

40. On the importance of Hemsterhuis for the romantics, see Erwin Kirchner, *Philosophie der Romantik* (Jena: Diederichs, 1906), pp. 8–34.

41. The significance of Platonism for Romanticism has long been recognized. See, for example, Oskar Walzel, *German Romanticism* (New York: Putnam, 1932), pp. 5–8, who maintains that the romantic *Weltanschauung* derives from Neo-Platonism.

42. The antirationalist interpretation of romanticism is commonplace. See, for example, Carl Schmitt, *Politische Romantik*, 2nd ed. (Munich: Duncker and Humblot, 1925), pp. 79–84; Jacques Droz, *Le Romantisme allemand et l'état* (Paris: Payot, 1966), pp. 19–49; and Isaiah Berlin, *The Roots of Romanticism* (Princeton: Princeton University Press, 1999), pp. 93–117.

43. This is overlooked by Frank's interpretation, which sees the heart of early romanticism as its commitment to the existence of some suprarational ground of being. See, for example, *Unendliche Annäherung*, p. 751 (though also see his qualification of this position, pp. 718–719). While this ground of being is indeed supradiscursive, this does not mean that it is suprarational, for in the Platonic tradition rational insight transcends discursivity.

44. On the history of Platonism in eighteenth-century Germany, see Max Wundt, 'Die Wiederentdeckung Platons im 18. Jahrhundert,' *Blätter für deutsche Philosophie* 15 (1941), 149–158; and Michael Franz, *Schellings Tübinger Platon-Studien* (Göttingen: Vandenhoeck and Ruprecht, 1996) (Neue Studien zur Philosophie, Band 11), pp. 45–98.

45. See Leibniz's *Specimen Dynamicum*, in Gerhardt, VI, 234.

46. On its importance for freemasonry, see Margaret C. Jacob, *The Radical Enlightenment* (London: George, Allen and Unwin, 1981), pp. 20–27, 87–108, 215–255.

47. On some of these developments, see Thomas Hankins, *Science and the Enlightenment* (Cambridge: Cambridge University Press, 1985), pp. 50–57.

48. C. F. Kielmeyer, *Über die Verhältnisse der organischen Kräfte untereinander in der Reihe der verschiedenen Organisation, die Gesetze und Folgen dieser Verhältnisse*. The

speech was first given February 11, 1793. It has been reprinted in *Sudhoffs Archiv für Geschichte der Medizin* 23 (1930), pp. 247–267. Kielmeyer was best known for his lectures, notes of which were disseminated in many parts of Germany. On his influence, see the accompanying essays in *Sudhoffs Archiv* by Felix Buttersack, pp. 237–246 and Henrich Balss, pp. 268–287. See also Manfred Durner, 'Die Naturphilosophie im 18. Jahrhundert und der naturwissenschaftlichen Unterricht in Tübingen,' *Archiv für Geschichte der Philosophie* 73 (1991), 72–103, esp. 95–99.

49. On Spinoza's conception of substance as power, see *Ethica*, Pars I, Prop. XXXIV; on his banishment of final causes, see Pars I, Appendix.

50. Schelling, *Werke*, II, 56.

51. The *locus classicus* for this claim is Hegel's argument in the *Differenzschrift* that the speculative principle of subject–object identity is implicit in Kant's transcendental deduction. See Hegel, *Werke*, II, 11. But Hegel was not alone in advancing this claim. Schlegel too held that all his criticisms of Fichte's philosophy in the end amounted to developing its basic principle. See *Philosophische Lehrjahre*, KA, XVIII, 348 (no. 324). Hölderlin, Sinclair, and Hülsen also formed their philosophy by developing the implications of Fichte's principle of subject–object identity.

52. This point has not been fully appreciated by Kant's defenders. The monistic aspirations of post-Kantian philosophy arose from an *internal* critique of Kant and not from any alien agenda. Here I take issue with Karl Ameriks, 'The Practical Foundation of Philosophy in Kant, Fichte, and After,' in Sedgwick, *Reception*, pp. 109–129, esp. 118–119; and Paul Guyer, 'Absolute Idealism and the Rejection of Kantian Dualism,' in Ameriks, *Cambridge Companion to German Idealism*, pp. 37–56.

53. See, for example, Hamann's 'Metakritik zur Purismum der reinen Vernunft,' *Werke*, III, 286; Maimon, *Versuch über die Transcendentalphilosophie, Werke*, II, 62–65; Jacobi, *Über das Unternehmen des Kriticismus, die Vernunft zu Verstande zu bringen*, in *Werke*, III, 85–91; and Platner, *Aphorismen* §§697–700.

54. Seeing Hegel's strategy in the early 1800s in this same light avoids the dilemma that makes his philosophy either a relapse into a rationalist metaphysics or a mere doctrine of categories. If the former approach is too metaphysical, ignoring the extent to which Hegel attempted to respond to Kant's challenge, the latter approach is not metaphysical enough, reducing Hegel's system down to neopositivistic standards. For my views on this latter approach, see my 'Hegel, A Non-Metaphysician!', in the *Bulletin of the Hegel Society of Great Britian* (1995). *Pace* most Hegel scholars, however, I do not think that Hegel's attempt to provide such a transcendental justification of his metaphysics is unique to him; rather, it reflects the strategy of the romantic generation as a whole.

55. *Blüthenstaub*, NS, II, 413 (no. 1). The point of the aphorism rests on an untranslatable pun. The German term '*Unbedingte*' means both what is not a thing and what is not conditioned. The aphorism could also be translated as 'We seek everywhere what is not a thing and always find only things.' Novalis' point here is

indebted to Schelling's argument in *Vom Ich als Princip der Philosophie*, *Werke*, I, 87–94, §§2–3.

56. See *Vorlesungen über Transcendentalphilosophie*, KA, XII, 105.

57. This argument for the dependence of the sciences on the idea of synthetic unity, and of synthetic unity on the aesthetic, appears quite explicitly in Schlegel's *Gespräch über die Poesie*, KA, II, 324–325, in Hölderlin's *Hyperion*, GSA, III, 81–84, and in Schelling's *System des transcendentalen Idealismus*, *Werke*, III, 612–629.

2. Hölderlin and Absolute Idealism

1. Hölderlin's role in the development of German idealism has long been recognized. It was pointed out by Karl Rosenkranz as early as 1844 in his *G. W. F. Hegels Leben* (Berlin: Duncker and Humblot, 1844). Eager to trump any Schellingian claim to originality in the development of absolute idealism, Rosenkranz stated that Hölderlin was the prophet who first declared "den Sturm und Drang des Geistes nach Allheit und Einheit" (p. xi). Rosenkranz's view was reaffirmed by Haym, *Die romantische Schule*, pp. 305–306, and stressed by Dilthey, *Das Erlebnis und die Dichtung*, 2nd ed. (Leipzig: Tuebner, 1907), pp. 342, 346–347, 355. It was later defended and developed by Ernst Cassirer, 'Hölderlin und der deutsche Idealismus,' in *Idee und Gestalt* (Berlin: Cassirer, 1924), pp. 113–155. Hölderlin's relation to philosophy first received detailed treatment in Wilhelm Böhm's massive two-volume biography, *Hölderlin* (Halle-Saale: Niemeyer, 1928). It then became the subject of controversy after the work of Kurt Hildebrandt, *Hölderlin, Dichtung und Philosophie* (Stuttgart: Kohlhammer, 1939), who made excessive claims for Hölderlin's "philosophical genius—even in the sense of a systematic thinker" (p. v). Hildebrandt was duly criticized by two works of the 1940s: Johannes Hoffmeister, *Hölderlin und die Philosophie* (Leipzig: Felix Meiner, 1942); and Ernst Müller, *Hölderlin: Studien zur Geschichte seines Geistes* (Stuttgart: Kohlhammer, 1944). Both Hoffmeister and Müller stressed Hölderlin's poetic calling and limitations as a philosopher. That Hölderlin was a provider of metaphysical insights was, for Müller, "ein bloßer Wunschtraum" (p. 5).

These works were all written before the publication in 1961 by Friedrich Beißner of Hölderlin's important manuscript 'Urtheil und Seyn,' which has greatly increased his stature as a philosopher. Since its publication, the most important work on Hölderlin's early philosophy has been that of Dieter Henrich. See the works listed in 3.1.1n7.

2. It is not possible to determine accurately how long Schelling and Hegel had been out of touch with one another. Schelling's last surviving letter to Hegel before their Jena years was written June 20, 1796. In his November 2, 1800 letter to Schelling, Hegel refers to "eine Trennung mehrerer Jahre." See *Briefe von und an Hegel*, ed. J. Hoffmeister (Hamburg: Meiner, 1952), I, 58.

3. See Hölderlin to Immanuel Niethammer, February 24, 1796, GSA, VI/1, 203. For a detailed reconstruction of the themes discussed by Schelling and Hölderlin

around this time, see Müller, *Hölderlin*, pp. 146–173. All references to Hölderlin's writings are to the *Sämtliche Werke, Grosse Stuttgarter Ausgabe,* ed. Friedrich Beißner (Stuttgart: Cotta Nachfolger, 1946), abbreviated as GSA.

4. See the story by Gustave Shwab, Hölderlin's first biographer, in GSA, VI/2, 833. Some of these discussions were recorded in verse form by Hölderlin's friend Isaak von Sinclair, *Gedichte von Crisalin* (Frankfurt: Hermann'sche Buchhandlung, 1812), II, 188 ff. On Sinclair's role as a transmitter of Hölderlin's views to Hegel, see Hannelore Hegel, 'Reflexion und Einheit: Sinclair und der "Bund der Geister"—Frankfurt 1795–1800,' *Hegel-Studien* 9 (1973), 91–106.
5. GSA, VII/2, 47.
6. Hartmut Buchner has argued that it is wrong to assume that Schelling and Hegel saw themselves as the only possible contributors to their journal. See his 'Hegel und das Kritische Journal der Philosophie,' *Hegel-Studien* 3 (1965), 110–111. It is also noteworthy that Hölderlin wanted Schelling to be a contributor to his journal *Iduna.* See his July 1799 letter to Schelling, GSA, VI/1, 345–349. The goals of Hölderlin's journal already anticipate the antidualistic motives of the *Kritisches Journal.* See Hölderlin's letter to Friedrich Steinkopf, June 18, 179, GSA, VI/1, 335.
7. Hegel, *Briefe,* I, 71.
8. Hölderlin makes his loyalties very plain in two important letters. See his letter to Neuffer, November 12, 1798, GSA VI/1, 289; and his letter to his mother, January 1799, GSA VI/1, 311.
9. See letter to his brother, October 13, 1796, GSA, VI/1, 218.
10. On these plans, see Henrich, *Grund,* pp. 31–40.
11. See letter to Neuffer, November 12, 1798, GSA, VI/1, 289.
12. See 'Zu Jakobis Briefen über die Lehre des Spinoza,' GSA, IV/1, 207–210.
13. Jacobi, *Werke,* IV/2, 57.
14. Ibid., IV/2, 61.
15. See the 'Vorrede' to the 'Vorletzte Fassung' of *Hyperion,* GSA, III, 236.
16. The *En kai pan* symbols inscribed next to Hölderlin's entry in Hegel's *Stammbuch* have been attributed to Hölderlin himself. The entry can be dated to February 1791. See Rosenkranz, *Hegels Leben,* p. 40. But the symbols were written with a different hand and ink, and were probably added later. Still, H. S. Harris argues that they reflect Hölderlin's thinking around this time. See his *Hegel's Development: Toward the Sunlight* (Oxford: Clarendon Press, 1972), pp. 97–106. Henrich, *Grund,* p. 162, is more cautious, pointing out that even the hymns can be interpreted in a Platonic fashion and do not imply that Hölderlin had yet embraced Lessing's credo.
17. Henrich, *Konstellationen,* pp. 155–158, and *Grund* pp. 164–166, sees Kantian terminology already evident in the fragment on Jacobi, though the evidence is not compelling. The 'Hymne an die Schönheit,' which was published in 1791, GSA, IV/2, 152, bears an inscription from the *Kritik der Urteilskraft.* It is unclear, however, how thoroughly Hölderlin had read Kant by this date. Böhm, *Hölderlin,* I,

60, maintains that the poem could have been written as much against as for the inscription; and Paul Böckmann has argued that Hölderlin took this citation from Jacobi's *Allwill* rather than directly from Kant. See his 'Das Späte in Hölderlins Spätlyrik,' *Hölderlin Jahrbuch* 12 (1961–1962), 205–222, esp. 209–211. In her *Hölderlins Spinoza-Rezeption* (Tübingen: Niemeyer, 1990), p. 12, Margarethe Wegenast points out that the Jacobian argument of Hölderlin's February 1791 letter is scarcely compatible with Henrich's assumption that Hölderlin was already a mature Kantian.

18. In May 1793 Hölderlin wrote his friend Neuffer that he was "now once again in Herr Kant's school" (VI/1, 83). The interest in Kant only grew, so that in May 1794 he wrote his brother: "Almost my only reading now is Kant. More and more this spendid spirit reveals himself to me" (VI/1, 119).

19. See April 13, 1795, GSA, VI/1, 164; see also his August 21, 1794, letter to his brother, ibid., VI/1, 131, where he stresses the "unshakable maxim" to recognize no authority in judging the correctness of assertions and actions.

20. This has been suggested by Cassirer, 'Hölderlin und der deutsche Idealismus,' pp. 119–120.

21. Böhm sees the clear influence of Herder on Hölderlin's early hymns. See his *Hölderlin*, I, 79. He maintains that the influence of Herder was so pervasive that it is hardly necessary to point to the reading of any specific text (I, 84). He also finds it obvious that Hölderlin would probably have discussed Herder's *Gott* during his visits to the household of Charlotte von Kalb (I, 141). Henrich, *Grund*, p. 172, points out that Jacobi criticizes Herder's work in the second edition of his *Briefe*, so that Hölderlin must have had at least some secondhand knowledge of it.

22. Hölderlin wrote Neuffer, November 8, 1790: "Leibniz und mein Hymnus auf die Wahrheit [the earlier title for the poem] haußen seit Tagen ganz in m. Capitolium. Jener hat Einfluß auf diesen." GSA VI/1, 56. According to Müller, *Hölderlin* p. 74, Hölderlin was influenced in this regard by his teacher F. A. Boek, who was a Leibnizian. The chief thesis of one of his tracts defending Leibniz was *"nihil sterile, nihil mortuum, nihil incultum datur in universo."*

23. Schiller, *Werke* XX, 123–4.

24. See letter to Neuffer, May 1793, GSA, VI/1, 84; and to his brother-in-law Breulin, June 8, 1794.

25. Thus Rosenkranz reports that "sicheren Nachrichten zufolge" Hegel and Hölderlin had read Plato along with Kant and Jacobi. See *Hegels Leben*, p. 40. Furthermore, in September 1792 Hölderlin had borrowed two volumes of Plato from the *Stiftsbibliothek*. See Ulrich Gaier, *Hölderlin* (Tübingen: Francke Verlag, 1993), p. 73.

26. See Böhm, *Hölderlin*, I, 144. Böhm cites this passage, but offers no proof for why Hölderlin would have it in mind. In his interesting article '"Platons frommer Garten." Hölderlins Platonlektüre von Tübingen bis Jena,' *Hölderlin Jahrbuch* 28 (1992–1993), 111–127, Michael Franz suggests that Hölderlin has in mind 250b,

where beauty is more important than justice and wisdom in reminding us of the eternal perception of the forms. This too is plausible; Böhm's reading and Franz's are indeed compatible and come from a single paragraph.

27. The case for Jacobi's influence has been made in great detail by Henrich, *Grund,* pp. 48–92.

28. In the second edition of his *Briefe über die Lehre von Spinoza* (Breslau: Löwe, 1789), p. xv, Jacobi wrote that one cannot place the *sum* after the *cogito.* This formulation for the priority of being goes back to Hamann, who wrote to Jacobi on June 1, 1785: "Not *cogito ergo sum,* but conversely, or more Hebraically *Est ergo cogito;* and with the inversion of so simple a proposition the whole system takes on a different language and direction." See Hamann, *Briefwechsel,* V, 448. See also letters to Jacobi, December 12, 1785, and January 15, 1786, *Briefwechsel,* VI, 201, 230.

29. See *Briefe,* 2nd ed., pp. 61, 398. This interpretation of Spinoza appears only in the second edition, and it was not reprinted in Jacobi's *Werke.*

30. See his November 17, 1794 letter to his mother, GSA, VI, 142.

31. This is clear from Schiller's October 28, 1794 letter to Goethe, who reported that Fichte had "strong enemies in his own camp," who would not hesitate to say loud and clear that his system reduces down to "subjective Spinozism." Of these enemies Schiller mentions only Weißhuhn by name. See Schiller, *Werke,* XXVII, 75. See also Schiller's October 26, 1794 letter to J. B. Erhard, ibid., XXVII, 72.

32. On the influence of the Niethammer circle on Hölderlin, see Frank, *Unendliche Annäherung,* pp. 422, 526, 530–531, 599–604, 622; and Henrich, *Konstellationen,* pp. 137–170.

33. See Hölderlin to Schiller, September 4, 1795, GSA, VI, 180–181, and to Niethammer, February 24, 1796, ibid., VI, 202–203.

34. On the dating of 'Urtheil und Seyn,' see Beißner, GSA, IV, 402–403; and Henrich, *Konstellationen,* pp. 49–80, and *Grund,* pp. 238–239. Henrich and Beißner both put the date of composition as sometime in early 1795; Henrich argues that it was most probably written in April of that year.

35. Müller, *Hölderlin* pp. 125–127, sees evidence for Hölderlin's lack of philosophical acumen in this letter. He maintains that Hölderlin is distorting Fichte by interpreting him in Spinozist terms. Müller fails to see, however, that Hölderlin is making an immanent critique of Fichte.

36. See, for example, the *Wissenschaftslehre novo methodo,* AA, IV/1, 39, 44–45.

37. *Pace* Henrich, *Konstellationen,* pp. 73–75, who maintains that Hölderlin was not willing to move beyond Kant in his letter to Hegel. Henrich further contends, *Grund,* pp. 274–275, that going beyond the Kantian limits means simply that Hölderlin intends to deny Kant's sharp distinction between reason and sensibility; it does not imply a claim to metaphysical knowledge of the unconditioned. Yet Hölderlin certainly does intend to go beyond the Kantian limits in another sense not considered by Henrich: he postulates the objective existence of the aesthetic ideas. Being does not have a strictly regulative status for Hölderlin, as we shall see in the next section.

38. See Henrich, *Grund*, pp. 48–73.
39. See Jacobi, *Werke*, IV/1, 67.
40. This is clear from the preface to the *Fragment von Hyperion*, GSA, III, 163, and the preface to the penultimate version, ibid., III, 236–237. This argument will be developed below, 2.2.6.
41. See the *Wissenschaftslehre novo methodo*, AA, IV/2, 30.
42. The quote considerably alters Kant's text. The passage is from Kant, *Schriften*, V, 301, lines 4 and 5. According to Böckmann, Hölderlin took this quote from Jacobi's *Allwill* and not directly from Kant. See note 17 above.
43. See also 'Hymne an die Schönheit,' I, 154.
44. See Hölderlin to Neuffer, October 10, 1794, GSA, VI, 137; to Schiller, September 4, 1795, VI, 181; to Niethammer, February 24, 1796, VI, 202–203; to his brother, June 2, 1796, VI, 208–209; the fragment 'Hermokrates an Cephalus,' IV, 213; and the passages in *Hyperion*, VI, 81–83.
45. See Henrich, *Konstellationen*, pp. 71, 74–75, and *Grund*, pp. 43, 108, 112. Henrich draws this conclusion because he tacitly equates knowledge with judgment, which implies the very discursive model of knowledge Hölderlin questions. Cassirer is much more accurate when he writes: "Im Grunde bleibt ihm [Hölderlin] doch das Unendliche selbst noch ein Faßbares und Fühlbares." See *Form und Gestalt*, p. 123.
46. On the dating of this fragment, see Beißner in GSA, IV/2, 401–402, who places it in early 1795.
47. See especially Schiller's February 8, 1793 letter to Körner, NA, XXVI, 179–180, 183.
48. This is clear from Hölderlin's belief in the value of Kantian criticism. See note 9 above. It is a complete misconception of Hölderlin to think that he utterly disaowed Kantian criticism for the sake of an irrationalist metaphysics. This is the view of Hildebrandt, *Hölderlin*, pp. 52–54, who insists that Kantian criticism was for Hölderlin only "*eine Wüste*" in comparison with the metaphysical views of Leibniz and Herder. Henrich is certainly right to maintain, *Grund*, pp. 112–113, 233–234, 274–275, that Hölderlin intends to avoid any relapse into pre-Kantian dogmatism. However, Henrich pushes Hölderlin too far in the direction of Kant by making him deny all knowledge of the absolute.
49. On Hölderlin's relationship to skepticism, see Violetta Waibel, *Hölderlin und Fichte 1794–1800* (Paderborn: Schöningh, 2000), pp. 83–116.
50. On the dangers of conceptualizing, see the early essay 'Parallele zwischen Salomons Sprüchwörtern und Hesiods Werken und Tagen,' GSA, IV, 183–184, and *Hyperion*, III, 10; on the necessity of conceptualizing, see 'Reflexion,' IV, 235, the November 12, 1798 letter to Neuffer, VI, 290, and the August, 1797, letter to Schiller, VI, 249.
51. This point was stressed long ago by Dilthey, *Erlebnis und Dichtung*, pp. 346–347, 355.
52. Spinoza, *Ethica*, Par. I, def. IV.
53. *Pace* Henrich, *Grund*, p. 187, who states that fundamental philosophical issues

have an only "indirect relation" to Hölderlin's novel. It is necessary to take more seriously Hölderlin's claims about the philosophical relevance of literature.

54. Hölderlin wrote his mother November 17, 1794: "Fichte's philosophy now occupies me entirely. I hear only him and otherwise no one" (VI, 142). Concerning the dates of composition of the various fragments, see Beißner's discussion in GSA, III, 296–311.

55. See especially the preface to the penultimate version, GSA, III, 236; the preface to the *Fragment von Hyperion,* III, 163; and the final version, III, 38.

56. See Hölderlin's April 13, 1794 letter to his brother, where he describes Fichte's concept of striving in very positive terms. GSA, VI/1, 162–164.

57. See especially the early 1793 poem 'Dem Genius der Kühnheit,' GSA, I/1, 176–177, and the later 1793 'Das Schicksal,' I/1, 184–186.

58. Plato, *Symposium,* 203c–204c.

59. See the first chapter of *Hyperions Jugend,* esp. GSA, III, 199.

60. Fichte is explicit about this in his 1794 *Vorlesungen über die Bestimmung des Gelehrten,* which Schiller and Hölderlin read. Fichte says that the purpose of culture is "to repress and eradicate" (*zu unterdrücken und auszutilgen*) inclinations" (*Werke,* VI, 298). Though Schiller praises Fichte's work in his *Ästhetische Briefe,* he also makes some implicit critical allusions to this passage. See NA, XX, 315–318.

61. Compare Kant's 'Mutmaßlicher Anfang der Menschengeschichte,' *Schriften,* VIII, 107–124, and Schiller, 'Etwas über die erste Menschengesellschaft nach dem Leitfaden der mosaische Urkunde,' NA, XVIII, 398–413.

62. On Hölderlin's metaphor of the "eccentric orbit," see Wolfgang Schadewaldt, 'Das Bild der Exzentrischen Bahn bei Hölderlin,' *Hölderlin Jahrbuch* (1952), 1–16 (no volume number).

3. Novalis' Magical Idealism

1. See Novalis to Friedrich Schlegel, July 8, 1796, IV, 188. All references to Novalis works will be to the second edition of *Novalis Schriften,* ed. Richard Samuel, Hans Joachim Mähl, and Gerhard Schulz (Stuttgart: Kohlhammer, 1960–1988). Since the fragment collections are divided into numbered notes, which are sometimes longer and sometimes shorter than a page, all references will include note number, followed by volume (marked by Roman numeral) and page numbers.

2. Little is known about the meeting. It seems that there was some discussion about religion. Niethammer's diary for that occasion records: "Much spoken about religion and revelation and that here many questions remain open for philosophy." See Novalis, *Schriften,* IV, 588.

3. On the dating of Novalis' early notebooks, see Frank, *Unendliche Annäherung,* pp. 781–801. According to Hans Joachim Mähl, the editor of the *Fichte-Studien* for the critical edition, (see *Schriften,* II, 43), the composition most probably began in September 1795. Frank further argues against Henrich (pp. 800–801) that Novalis could have come to many of his central ideas around the same time

as Hölderlin (early winter 1795) because many ideas were in gestation before the composition of the notebooks.

4. For a useful review of the early reception of Novalis' philosophical work, see Herbert Uerling, *Friedrich von Hardenberg, Werk und Forschung* (Stuttgart: J. B. Metzler, 1991), pp. 105–114.

5. Thus Haym, *Die romantische Schule*, pp. 325–390.

6. Theodor Haering, *Novalis als Philosoph* (Stuttgart: Kohlhammer, 1954).

7. On the recent literature, see again Uerling, *Hardenberg*, pp. 105–146.

8. This has been the case for not only Haering, but also the earlier studies by Nicolai Hartmann, *Die Philosophie des deutschen Idealismus* (Berlin: Walter de Gruyter, 1954), I, 220–233; and Heinrich Simon, *Der magische Idealismus. Studien zur Philosophie des Novalis* (Heidelberg: Winters, 1906).

9. See Frank, *Unendliche Annäherung*, pp. 821, 825; 'Die Philosophie des sogenannten "magischen Idealismus,"' *Euphorion* 63 (1969), pp. 88–116, and 'Philosophical Foundations of Early Romanticism,' in *The Modern Subject*, ed. Karl Ameriks and Dieter Sturma (Albany: SUNY Press, 1995), pp. 65–86, esp. pp. 74, 76.

10. See W. O'Brian, *Novalis* (Durham: Duke University Press, 1995), pp. 79, 87, 106.

11. In the sense of absolute idealism defined in 3.1.2.

12. Novalis insisted on this point even in his later years, despite the growing neo-Platonic influence on him. See the *Allgemeine Brouillon* no. 342: "The unknown and mysterious is the *result* . . . and the *beginning* of everything . . . Knowledge is only a means to attain *ignorance* . . . Nature is inconceivable in itself" (III, 302). These passages are the stumbling block of Haering's proto-Hegelian reading of Novalis.

13. *Pace* O'Brian, *Novalis*, pp. 106–107.

14. This is the case even in the early *Fichte-Studien*, where Novalis' critique of philosophy is most extreme. See, for example, no. 130; II, 154. In his later work Novalis continued to believe in the value of regulative principles. See *Allgemeine Brouillon* no. 640; II, 385.

15. The role of Plotinus in Novalis' mature thought has been painstakingly investigated by Hans Joachim Mähl, 'Novalis und Plotin,' *Jahrbuch des freien deutschen Hochstifts* (1963), pp. 139–250.

16. See Novalis to his brother Erasmus, November 12, 1795, IV, 159.

17. Manfred Frank, *Einführung in die frühromantische Ästhetik* (Frankfurt: Suhrkamp, 1989), p. 248.

18. *Pace* Friedrich Hiebel, *Novalis* (Bern: Francke, 1972), p. 124.

19. See the 'Tagebuchnotizen aus der Zeit der Fichte-Studien,' in the Hanser edition of Novalis' *Werke*, ed. Richard Samuel (Munich: Hanser Verlag, 1978), I, 451; in the critical edition this appears in the *Fichte-Studien* no. 484; II, 457.

20. See Novalis to his brother Erasmus, February 27, 1796, IV, 172; and to Caroline Just, April 10, 1795, IV, 180–181; on these letters, see the interpretation of Mähl, IV, 32–33.

21. For a more detailed treatment of the context and structure of Novalis' theory of self-consciousness in the *Fichte-Studien,* see Manfred Frank, *Das Problem «Zeit» in der deutschen Romantik* (Paderborn: Schöningh, 1990), pp. 130–155.

22. For a more detailed treatment of this theme, see Frank, *Unendliche Annäherung,* pp. 802–830. On the general importance of this theme in early romanticism, see Manfred Frank and Gerhard Kurz, 'Ordo inversus. Zu einer Reflexionsfigur bei Novalis, Hölderlin, Kleist und Kafka,' in *Geist und Zeichen. Festschrift für Arthur Henkel,* ed. H. Anton, B. Gajek, and P. Pfaff (Heidelberg: Winter, 1977), pp. 75–97.

23. On Novalis' sources, see Frank, *Unendliche Annäherung,* pp. 808–809.

24. Frank, *Einführung,* p. 248.

25. It is indeed striking how all the passages Frank cites for his reading refer to later works. See *Einführung,* pp. 255–256. In his *Novalis' "Fichte Studies"* (The Hague: Mouton, 1970), p. 111, Gezá von Molnár writes, much more accurately, that in the notebooks Novalis is "a stranger" to a doctrine that simply declares the supremacy of the aesthetic.

26. Von Molnár maintains (*Fichte Studies,* p. 29) that Novalis' concern in the notebooks is only to interpret rather than to criticize Fichte, and argues that these passages imply a rejection of not Fichte's *concept* of the absolute ego but only his *terminology* (pp. 35–37). But Novalis' point is also *conceptual:* that the absolute, which transcends all opposition, cannot be described in terms of some opposition, such as the subjective and objective. While Molnár is right to point out how Novalis sometimes continues to equate the absolute with the ego (nos. 8, 567; II, 107–108, 270), there are other passages (cited above) where he clearly resists such an equation (see above). Here again Novalis' text reveals its ambivalence. That Novalis is also departing from Fichte is also clear from his July 8, 1796 letter to Friedrich Schlegel.

27. It is possible, of course, to claim that an idea is only regulative and an object of belief. To hold that an idea is regulative might mean only that there is not sufficient evidence to believe in its existence, and that one does not therefore *know* that it exists, which makes it still possible to *believe* in its existence. This is not Novalis' position, however. He contends that belief in the reality of pure being is a *fiction,* implying that it would be false to assume that it exists; and he makes the idea of the unconditioned into *a goal of action* rather than *an object of belief* in some of the later fragments. See, for example, no. 566; II, 270.

28. See Novalis to A. C. Just, March 29, 1797, IV, 214.

29. See Haym, *Die romantische Schule,* pp. 332, 354–365. Haym's account is the basis for the interpretation of H. A. Korff in his standard work *Geist der Goethe Zeit* (Leipzig: Koehler and Amelang, 1964), III, 246–252. In *Der magische Idealismus* Simon quarreled with some of the details of Haym's interpretation (pp. 22–23); nevertheless, he still assumed the Fichtean sources of Novalis' magical idealism, stressing that Novalis' achievement consisted in making the purely "logical" and formal Fichtean ego more aesthetic and concrete (pp. 8, 17–18, 20–21). True to Haym's tradition, Nicolai Hartmann provided an essentially Fichtean interpreta-

tion of magical idealism in his *Die Philosophie des deutschen Idealismus*, I, 220–233, esp. 221, 224, 226, 228.

30. The problems with this interpretation were first made clear by Haering, who rightly stressed that Novalis' philosophy is a synthesis of idealism and realism. See *Novalis als Philosoph*, pp. 163–165, 364–365. The Fichtean reading of Novalis' idealism was also criticized by Manfred Dick, *Die Entwicklung des Gedankens der Poesie in den Fragmenten des Novalis* (Bonn: Bouvier, 1967) (Mainzer Philosophische Forschungen, Band 7), pp. 15–48. Although I agree with aspects of Dick's interpretation, I cannot accept his arguments, which ignore crucial passages and are based on a superficial interpretation of Fichte. The Fichtean interpretation has been challenged more successfully, on far more straightforward grounds, by John Neubauer, *Novalis* (Boston: Twayne, 1980), pp. 26–29, 60–62.

31. See Novalis to F. I. Niethammer, April 16, 1791, IV, 85.

32. See *Allgemeine Brouillon* nos. 75, 634, 820; III, 252, 382, 429. See also his 1799 *Fragmente und Studien*, where Novalis virtually identified true idealism with Spinozism: "The true philosophy is completely realistic idealism—or Spinozism" (no. 611; III, 671).

33. See Friedrich Schlegel to A. W. Schlegel, January 1792, IV, 572.

34. See Haym, *Die romantische Schule*, pp. 355–356.

35. See Novalis to K. L. Reinhold, October 5, 1791, IV, 93–94.

36. See *Allgemeine Brouillon* nos. 399, 638, 642, 826; III, 315, 384–385, 430. See also *Vorarbeiten* nos. 111, 112, 115, 117–120, 125, 233, 235, 247–249, 256, 273; II, 546–547, 548–552, 554, 576, 583–584, 587, 589.

37. See *Teplitzer Fragmente* no. 375; II, 605.

38. See Hans-Jaochim Mähl, *Die Idee des goldene Zeitalters im Werk des Novalis* (Heidelberg: Winter, 1965) (Studien zur deutschen Literatur, No. 7), pp. 306–307n, 343n.

39. See Haering, *Novalis als Philosoph*, pp. 364–365; and Uerling, *Hardenberg*, pp. 106–111.

40. The tension has been widely felt: see Mähl, *Zeitalter*, pp. 306–307n; and John Neubauer, *Bifocal Vision: Novalis Philosophy of Nature and Disease* (Chapel Hill: University of North Carolina Press, 1971) (Studies in Germanic Languages and Literature No. 68), p. 155n1.

41. See esp. nos. 111–112, 235, 247; II, 546–548, 577–578, 583.

42. Fichte, *Werke*, VI, 299–300.

43. *Pace* Hartmann, *Philosophie des deutschen Idealismus*, I, 229; and Korff, *Geist der Goethe Zeit*, III, 247.

44. Hence in the *Fichte-Studien* Novalis states that "If one only wills then one can also" (no. 420; II, 235–236), and that "We can find our being only in the will" (no. 83; II, 146).

45. On Novalis' formulas for romanticism, see the *Vorarbeiten* no. 105; II, 545, and the *Allgemeine Brouillon* nos. 234, 237; II, 280, 281.

46. This is not to say, of course, that Novalis' doctrine is essentially Schillerian. Where Novalis goes beyond Schiller is in extending the range and results of aes-

thetic education, so that it affects not only moral conduct but also the world we live in.

47. On Brown's physiology and its importance for Novalis' idealism, see John Neubauer, *Bifocal Vision*, pp. 31–75, and his 'Dr. John Brown and Early German Romanticism,' *Journal of the History of Ideas* 28 (1967), 367–382.

48. On Novalis' critique of Werner, see Neubauer, *Bifocal Vision*, pp. 80–83.

49. See the *Allgemeine Brouillon* nos. 240, 702; III, 282, 403.

50. This distinction is explained in detail by Haering, *Novalis als Philosoph*, pp. 367–377.

51. See KrV, B xvii.

52. On the earlier use of the term, see Hans-Joachim Mähl's note, *Schriften*, IV, 908–909.

53. See his descriptions of his meeting with Schelling in his December 25, 1797 letter to A. W. Schlegel, and his December 26, 1797 letter to Friedrich Schlegel, IV, 240, 242.

54. See Novalis' diary entry, June 29, 1797, IV, 47.

55. *Pace* Ernst Behler, who maintains that Schelling was the chief source of Novalis' absolute idealism. See his *German Romantic Literary Theory* (Cambridge: Cambridge University Press, 1993), p. 196.

56. See the *Allgemeine Brouillon* nos. 60–61; III, 250. See also *Fragmente und Studien*, where Novalis complains about Schelling's "limited concept of nature" (III, 666).

57. See *Materialien zu Schellings philosophischen Anfängen* (Frankfurt: Suhrkamp, 1975), pp. 145–153. On the background to this work see H. Kunz, *Schellings Gedichte und dichterische Pläne* (Zurich: Jüris, 1955).

58. On the influence of Hemsterhuis, see Neubauer, *Bifocal Vision*, pp. 88–90. Neubauer's discussion of Hemsterhuis in this regard is warranted by Novalis himself. On the influence of Paracelsus, see Mähl's note in IV, 852, 909.

59. See no. 481; II, 650. This note was written around late summer 1798, about the same time as Novalis' letter to Schlegel. It continues the association with Hemsterhuis stated in the letter.

60. See *Allgemeine Brouillon* no. 143; III, 268.

61. See ibid., no. 137; III, 266. Concerning Novalis' understanding of this neo-Platonic doctrine, see Mähl, 'Novalis und Plotin,' pp. 166–170.

62. See also *Fichte-Studien* no. 568; II 274, and the *Allgemeine Brouillion* no. 820; III, 430.

63. On the important idea of "variation," see the 'Dialogen,' II, 665.

64. 'Novalis' meant newly cleared ground. According to Haym, the name is nothing more than a translation of his family name, since 'Hardenberg' once meant unplowed virgin land. See his *Die romantische Schule*, p. 325.

4. Friedrich Schlegel's Absolute Idealism

1. This is the view of Ernst Behler in his introduction to volume 18 of the *Kritische Friedrich Schlegel Ausgabe*, ed. Ernst Behler, Jean-Jacques Anstett, and Hans

Eichner (Paderborn: Ferdinand Schöningh, 1958f), XXVIII, ix; and of Josef Körner in his introduction to *Friedrich Schlegel. Neue Philosophische Schriften* (Frankfurt: Verlag Gerhard Schulte-Bulmke, 1935), pp. 3–4.

2. See *Aus F. H. Jacobis Nachlaß*, ed. R. Zoeppritz (Leipzig: Engelmann, 1869), II, 104.

3. All references in parentheses are to the *Kritische Ausgabe*, cited in note 1 above, and abbreviated as 'KA.' Paragraph numbers are given first, followed by Roman numerals that refer to volume numbers and arabic numerals to page numbers.

4. This was the opinion of both Wilhelm Dilthey and Rudolf Haym. See Dilthey, *Leben Schleiermachers*, ed. Martin Redeker (Göttingen: Vandenhoeck & Ruprecht, 1970), p. 249; and Haym, *Die romantische Schule*, p. 213.

5. The importance of Schlegel's epistemology for his aesthetics was first stressed by Walter Benjamin in his *Der Begriff der Kunstkritik in der deutschen Romantik* (Bern: Francke, 1920). Though Benjamin's work is still of value, it is somewhat anti-quated. He did not have access to many of Schlegel's notebooks, nor to his lectures on transcendental philosophy. As a result, his analysis of Schlegel's idealism is still essentially Fichtean, and his account of Schlegel's epistemology ignores its antifoundationalism.

6. Schlegel finished his Jena lectures on transcendental idealism in March 1801; Schelling's *Darstellung meines Systems der Philosophie* did not appear until May of that year.

7. In his review of Schiller's *Musenalmanach für das Jahr 1796*, Schlegel refused to judge Schiller according to the same standards as "einen Neuffer oder Hölderlin," who were also contributors (II, 154). In this work Hölderlin had published his 'Der Gott der Jugend.' Later, Schlegel seemed to have become an admirer of Hölderlin. See Isaak von Sinclair's May 30, 1807 letter to Hegel in *Briefe von und an Hegel*, I, 165. For his part, Hölderlin did not seem to have a high opinion of Schlegel, because he wanted his own journal *Iduna* to be an antidote to the *Athenäum*.

8. On Schlegel's relationship to Schelling, see Ernst Behler's introduction to KA, VIII, xxxvii–liii.

9. On Schlegel's influence on Schleiermacher, see Dilthey, *Leben Schleiermachers*, 253–259, and Haym, *Die romantische Schule*, pp. 244–246. There has been some controversy about Schlegel's influence on Hegel, who allegedly attended his 1801 lectures on transcendental philosophy. On this whole question, see Behler, 'Friedrich Schlegel und Hegel,' *Hegel-Studien* 2 (1963), 203–250, esp. 234–240; and Körner, *Neue Philosophische Schriften*, pp. 88–92.

10. Schlegel's best statement of his historicist methodology appears in the preface to his 1804 *Lessings Gedanken und Meinungen*, KA, XII, 46–102, especially 51–60.

11. Dilthey acknowledges Schlegel's importance in this regard in *Leben Schleiermachers*, pp. 249–252, though he thinks that Schlegel was too undisciplined to make a clear methodology out of his historicism.

12. See his letter to August Wilhelm, December 23, 1795, KA, XXIII, 263.

13. Novalis and Schlegel seemed to have come to Fichte independently, Novalis from his encounter with Fichte in Jena and Schlegel from his reading of Fichte

in Dresden. Novalis' July 8, 1796 letter to Schlegel, written after a long lapse in their correspondence, ascribes his study of philosophy directly to Fichte himself. See KA, XXIII, 319.

14. See *Über das Studium der griechischen Poesie*, KA, I, 358. See also Schlegel's 1804–1805 *Die Entwicklung der Philosophie in Zwölf Büchern*, KA, XII, 291.

15. *Athenäumsfragment* no. 216; KA, II, 198.

16. See Schlegel's 'Literatur,' in his *Europa*, KA, I, 41–63, III, 3–16.

17. See Schlegel's May 27, 1796 letter to his brother, where he confesses that republicanism is now closer to his heart than criticism. KA, XXIII, 304–305.

18. The first edition was published in *Deutschland*, KA, III (1796), 10–41; VII, 11–25.

19. For a more detailed account of Schlegel's Fichtean phase, see Frank, *Unendliche Annäherung*, pp. 578–589, and Ernst Behler, 'Friedrich Schlegel's Theory of an Alternating Principle Prior to his Arrival in Jena (6 August 1796), *Revue Internationale de Philosophie* 50 (1996), 383–402.

20. On Schlegel's early ties with the Niethammer circle, see Frank, *Unendliche Annäherung*, pp. 569–593, 862–886.

21. The first number (or set of numbers) designates the fragment, the second number (or set) after the semicolon the corresponding volume and page number of the *Kritische Ausgabe*. Because there are three collections of fragments, which are not consecutively numbered, it is necessary to cite both fragment and page number here.

22. As Frank has observed, *Unendliche Annäherung*, p. 578.

23. See Schlegel to Körner, September 21 and 30, 1796, KA, XXIII, 333.

24. See Schlegel's letter to J. F. Cotta, April 7, 1897, KA, XVIII, 356, and his March 10, 1797, letter to Novalis, XXIII, 350. Though Schlegel implies that the essay is complete, he had only sketched some of his ideas. These are in the *Philosophische Lehrjahre*, KA, XVIII, 31–39, nos. 126–227.

25. Schlegel does not explain these points in any detail, but this reading can be supported from his later 1804 Cologne Lectures, KA, XII, 293.

26. See the collection entitled 'Zur Wissenschaftslehre 1796,' nos. 1–121, KA, XVIII, 3–15; 'Philosophische Fragmente 1796,' Beilage I, KA, XVIII, 505–516; and 'Zur Logik und Philosophie,' Beilage II, KA, XVIII, 517–521. The more finished form of the second collection suggests that Schlegel had publication in mind; whether as part of 'Geist der Wissenschaftslehre' is uncertain.

27. The influence of Schleiermacher is most apparent in Schlegel's *Ideen*, KA, II, 267 (no. 112), 269 (no. 125), 271 (no. 151). Schlegel had noted Schleiermacher's Spinozism much earlier, See *Philosophische Lehrjahre*, KA, XVIII, 38 (no. 211).

28. See Schlegel to C. G. Körner, January 30, 1797, KA, XVIII, 345.

29. Ibid. See also Schlegel to Novalis, January 2, 1797, XXIII, 341. Schlegel's review of Niethammer's *Philosophische Journal*, which he was writing around this time, states his views about Schelling's work. See KA, VIII, 24–25.

30. See Novalis to Schlegel, June 14, 1797, Novalis, *Schriften*, IV, 230.

31. In his still valuable introduction to *Neue Philosophische Schriften*, p. 20, Josef Körner maintains that Schelling was a model for Schlegel in the attempt to

move beyond Fichte, though this hardly jibes with Schelling's continuing allegiance to the principles of the *Wissenschaftslehre* in the winter of 1798 when Schlegel wrote the notes for his 'Geist der Wissenschaftslehre.' Körner is more accurate when he says (p. 53) that, though Schlegel found some confirmation in Schelling, he would have probably found his way without him.

32. See Ernst Behler in his 'Einleitung' to the *Philosophische Lehrjahre*, KA, XVIII, xxvi. Behler ascribes the "realistische Wendung Schlegels" to the idea of the "Religion des Universums" that he develops with Schleiermacher.

33. Schlegel's first reference to Hülsen appears in his March 10, 1793 letter to Novalis, where he writes of the prize essay and the first article in the *Philosophisches Journal*. See KA, XXIII, 349–350. Schlegel's doubts about Hülsen's position appear in the *Philosophisches Lehrjahre*, KA, XVIII, 38 (no. 211) and 41 (no. 236).

34. See the October 4, 1791 letter to his brother, KA, XXIII, 24; his mid-July 1798 letter to Schleiermacher, XXIV, 148; and the *Blüthenstaub* fragment no. 26, which is ascribed to Schlegel. The importance of these influences upon Schlegel was emphasized long ago by Körner, *Neue Philosophische Schriften*, pp. 16–17.

35. See Friedrich's later October 16, 1793 letter to his brother, KA, XXIII, 143–144, which further clarifies the meaning of the ideal.

36. See *Philosophische Lehrjahre*, KA, XVIII, 250–251 (no. 682). See also no. 839; XVIII, 264 and no. 41; XVIII, 509.

37. Both of these points follow from Schlegel's claim that every proposition and proof is infinitely perfectible. See *Philosophische Lehrjahre*, KA, XVIII, 506 (no. 12) and 50 (no. 15).

38. Schlegel makes this point most clearly in his later lectures on *Transcendentalphilosophie*, KA, XII, 96.

39. On Schlegel's complex attitude toward systematicity, see also his August 28, 1793 letter to his brother, KA, XXIII, 125–126.

40. On the context of Schlegel's coherence theory, see Manfred Frank, "'Alle Wahrheit ist Relativ, Alles Wissen Symbolisch,'" in *Revue Internationale de Philosophie* 50 (1996), 403–436.

41. Also important for Schlegel's early aesthetic are two drafts for a deduction of beauty, "Von der Schönheit in der Dichtkunst III,' XVI, 3–14, and the similarly titled 'Von der Schönheit in der Dichtkunst,' XVI, 15–31. These drafts attempt to provide a universal standard of criticism and follow a Fichtean precedent.

42. Here I take issue with Haym, *Die romantische Schule*, pp. 256–261. Though Haym is certainly correct to pinpoint the Fichtean elements of Schlegel's aesthetic, he overstates his case, saying that irony, for example, is "Nichts anderes als die Anwendung dieses von Fichte systematisch durchgeführten Gedankens auf die ästhetische Welt" (260). Such an exaggeration is the result of Haym's belief that Schlegel is not an original philosopher but a dilettante.

43. See Schlegel's April 7, 1797 letter to J. F. Cotta, where he states that he plans to write an essay provisionally entitled '*Charakteristik der sokratische Ironie.*' KA, XXIII, 356.

44. As Schlegel put this point in his notebooks: "*Knowing* means conditioned cognition. The unknowability of the absolute is therefore a tautologous triviality" (no. 62; II, 511).

45. See *Athenäumsfragment* no. 51; II, 172–173.

46. Here I take issue with Frank, *Unendliche Annäherung*, p. 866, and *Das Problem «Zeit» in der deutschen Romantik*, pp. 22–28.

47. See *Athenäumsfragmente* no. 270, 274, 301, 450.

48. See the essay 'Über Lessing,' KA, II, 100–125 (first published in the *Lyceum der schönen Künste* I [1797], 76–128). Schlegel developed these themes in a later essay 'Lessings Gedanken und Meinungen,' KA, III, 46–102, which was published as an introduction for *Lessings Gedanken und Meinungen aus dessen Schriften zusammengestellt und erläutert* (Leipzig: Junius, 1804), pp. 3–18.

49. See 'Jacobis Woldemar,' KA, II, 57–77 (first published *Deutschland* III [1796], 185–213), and 'Der Deutsche Orpheus,' VIII, 3–11 (first published *Deutschland* IV [1796], 49–66) and the review of J. G. Schlossers *Schreiben an einen jungen Mann, der die Kritische Philosophie studiren wollte*, KA, VIII, 33–37 (first published *Philosophisches Journal* V [1797], 184–192). The Schlosser reviews should be seen in the context of Kant's debate with Schlosser. Kant's contributions to the debate are his essays 'Von einem neuerdings erhobenen vornehmen Ton in der Philosophie' and 'Verkündigung des nahen Abschlusses eines Tractats zum ewigen Frieden in der Philosophie,' in *Schriften*, VIII, 387–406, 413–422. In this dispute Schlegel defends Kant against Schlosser. According to Behler, *Friedrich Schlegel* (Hamburg: Rowohlt, 1966), p. 53, Kant was apparently delighted by Schlegel's caustic and damning review.

50. See Schlegel to Novalis, December 1, 1796, KA, XXIII, 339–340. The notes are in *Philosophische Lehrjahre*, KA, XVIII, 3–23.

51. They were first published by Körner in 1935 in *Neue Philosophische Schriften*, pp. 115–220. See note 1 above. On the context, manuscript remains, and the identity of the author, see Körner's introduction, pp. 45–50; and Ernst Behler, 'Friedrich Schlegels Vorlesungen über Transzendentalphilosophie Jena 1800–01,' in *Transzendentalphilosophie und Spekulation. Der Streit um die Gestalt einer Ersten Philosophie (1799–1807)*, ed. Walter Jaeschke (Hamburg: Meiner, 1993), pp. 52–71. The text has been reproduced in KA, XII, 3–105. All references in parentheses are to this later edition.

52. These theses are reproduced in KA, XVIII, xxxvi.

53. The enduring importance of Plato for Schlegel's thinking around 1800 is apparent from a notebook entry from the time of the lectures: "Plato contains properly wisdom, the whole spirit of philosophy is in him. He knew *everything*, namely the whole, that upon which everything rests. His praise of being against becoming is not in dispute with idealism" (no. 624; XVIII, 372).

54. Schlegel makes his skeptical views about ideal systems perfectly clear in some entries to his notebooks written at the same time as his lectures: "*Axiom*. Every system is only an approximation of its ideal. Skepticism is eternal" (no. 1149; XVIII, 417).

55. See the notebook entry no. 1089; XVIII, 412: "All ideas are only one idea; hence it is a task for every philosopher to multiply the multiplicity of his ideas *ad infinitum* and still to make them one . . . The order of ideas remains completely arbitrary and individual."
56. See *Philosophische Lehrjahre,* KA, XVIII, 412 (no. 1095) and 413 (nos. 1107–1108).
57. The aesthetic dimension of his idealism becomes even more evident when he declares *"the correspondence of idealism and art is perfect"* (29; his emphasis).
58. See also the notebook entry no. 1064; XVIII, 409.
59. See also notebook entry no. 296; XVIII, 148: "The philosophy of physics contains nothing more than a characteristic of nature as an infinite animal, an infinite plant and an infinite mineral."
60. He did not always hold this view. See, for example, the notebooks no. 975; XVIII, 401–402, where idealism is opposed to the realism of religion.
61. See the notebooks no. 672; XVIII, 249: "Schelling's physics is a dangerous false tendency."
62. Schlegel himself endorses such implications in the lectures when he says that the true concept of religion involves the proposition "everything is divine" (XII, 75).
63. See also the lectures, XII, 39, 53; and the notebooks nos. 447, 459, 462; XVIII, 358, 358, 359.
64. See also the lectures XII, 53, and notebooks no. 1222; XVIII, 421.
65. Notebooks no. 1277; XVIII, 301 and no. 74; XVIII, 330. This is not, however, Fichte's doctrine of the purely regulative status of God, because Schlegel thinks that there is an infinite, though incomplete and evolving, universe of which our actions are only a part.

Part IV. Introduction

1. The honorable exceptions are Andrew Bowie, *Schelling and Modern Philosophy* (London: Routledge, 1993); Dale Snow, *Schelling and the End of Idealism* (Albany: SUNY Press, 1996); Alan White, *Schelling: Introduction to the System of Freedom* (New Haven: Yale University Press, 1983); and Thomas O'Meara, *Romantic Idealism and Roman Catholicism: Schelling and the Theologians* (Notre Dame: Notre Dame Press, 1982).
2. It is a sign of Schelling's declining stature that there is not a single article on him in Jaegwon Kim's and Ernest Sosa's *A Companion to Metaphysics* (Oxford: Blackwell, 1995). There is a ten-page article by Jean-Francois Courtine on Schelling in Simon Blackburn's *A Companion to Continental Philosophy* (Oxford: Blackwell, 1998), pp. 83–92; but Courtine's exposition, like most recent scholars, focuses on Schelling's later philosophy at the expense of his earlier doctrines. A more balanced exposition, though lamentably short, is Dale Snow's article in *The Columbia History of Western Philosophy,* ed. Richard Popkin (New York: Columbia University Press, 1999), pp. 528–533.

3. The main exception is Xavier Tilliette's magisterial *Schelling: Un Philosophie en Devenir*, 2 vols. (Paris: Vrin, 1970).

4. Karl Rosenkranz, *Schelling. Vorlesungen gehalten im Sommer 1842* (Danzig: 1842), p. xxiii.

5. Hegel, *Vorlesungen über die Geschichte der Philosophie, Werke*, XX, 420–454.

6. See, for example, Bowie, *Schelling and Modern European Philosophy;* Alan White, *Schelling;* Manfred Frank, *Der unendliche Mangel an Sein* (Frankfurt: Suhrkamp, 1975); Karl Jaspers, *Schelling, Grösse und Verhängnis* (Munich: Piper, 1955); Walter Schulz, *Die Vollendung des deutschen Idealismus in der späten Philosophie Schellings* (Pfulligen: Neske, 1955); and Martin Heidegger, *Schellings Abhandlung über das Wesen der menschichen Freiheit*, ed. Hildegard Fleck (Tübingen: Niemeyer, 1971).

7. Although commentators rarely spend much time on it, the *System der gesammten Philosophie* is the only complete exposition of Schelling's absolute idealism. Kuno Fischer ignores it in his otherwise extremely thorough *Schellings Leben, Werke und Lehre* (Heidelberg: Winters, 1923), and Henrich Knittermeyer hastily devotes only a few pages to it in his *Schelling und die romantische Schule* (Munich: Reinhardt, 1929), pp. 421–422. The common but mistaken belief that Schelling never completed his system, and that he never developed its "ideal" half, that dealing with history and politics, is a sad tribute to the neglect of this important work.

1. The Path toward Absolute Idealism

1. See F. W. J. Schelling, *Briefe und Dokumente*, ed. Horst Fuhrmanns (Bonn: Bouvier, 1962–1975), II, 51–52.

2. See Schelling's explanation in the preface, *Werke*, I, 87–88.

3. Schelling wrote Hegel that he had received the *Grundlage* in December 1795. See *Briefe von und an Hegel*, I, 15.

4. Schelling knew of the philosophical developments in Jena from Hölderlin, who visited him in the summer and winter of 1795. On their conversations, see Hölderlin to Niethammer, December 22, 1795, in Hölderlin, GSA, VI/1, 191; February 24, 1796, ibid., VI/1, 203. For the interpretation of these passages, see Frank, *Unendliche Annäherung*, pp. 731–733. In a review of Schelling's *Vom Ich als Princip* Erhard had also strongly criticized Schelling for his foundationalism and subjectivist concept of the absolute. See *Allgemeine Literatur Zeitung* 319 (October 11, 1796), 89–91. Schelling wrote a scorching counterreview, 'Einiges aus Gelegenheit der Rez. Meiner Schrift *Vom Ich* . . . ,' which appeared in the *Intelligenzblatt* of the *Allgemeine Literatur Zeitung* 165 (December 10, 1796), 1405–1408.

5. The story of their later battles has been told by Xavier Léon, 'Fichte contra Schelling,' *Revue de Metaphysique et de Morale* (1904), pp. 949–976.

6. The story has, of course, been told before. See especially Xavier Léon, *Fichte et son temps* (Paris: Armand Colin, 1924), II, 332–371; Xavier Tilliette, *Schelling, Une*

Philosophie en Devenir (Paris: Vrin, 1970), I, 265–293; Reinhard Lauth, *Die Entstehung von Schellings Identitätsphilosophie in der Auseinandersetzung mit Fichtes Wissenschaftslehre* (Freiburg: Verlag Karl Alber, 1975); Richard Kroner, *Von Kant bis Hegel* (Tübingen: Mohr, 1921), II, 129–141; and Furhmanns, *Schelling, Briefe und Dokumente*, I, 217–230.

7. All references in parentheses are to Schelling, *Sämtliche Werke*, ed. K. F. A. Schelling (Stuttgart: Cotta, 1856–1861). Roman numerals refer to volume numbers, arabic numerals to page numbers.

8. See Schelling to Hegel, February 4, 1795, *Briefe von und an Hegel*, I, 22.

9. See Schelling to Hegel, February 4, 1795, in *Briefe und Dokumente*, II, 65.

10. The political significance of the new philosophy for Schelling is apparent from his January 6, and February 4, 1795 letters to Hegel. See *Materialien zu Schellings philosophischen Anfängen*, ed. Manfred Frank and Gerhard Kurz (Frankfurt: Suhrkamp, 1975), pp. 117–120, 125–128.

11. Schelling's hesitation and equivocation on this score has been pointed out by Manfred Frank, *Eine Einführung in Schellings Philosophie* (Frankfurt: Suhrkamp, 1985), pp. 57–60.

12. See Fuhrmanns, 'Schelling im Tübinger Stift Herbst 1790-Herbst 1795,' in *Briefe und Dokumente* I, 9–39. Concerning Schelling's knowledge of the *Grundlage der gesamten Wissenschaftslehre*, see his January 22 and March 23, 1796 letters to Niethammer, where he confesses that he still has not been able to read the third part of the work. See *Briefe und Dokumente*, I, 59–62, 66–68.

13. See, for example, Lauth, *Die Entstehung von Schellings Identitätsphilosophie*, pp. 19, 23, 198; and Philonenko, *La Liberté humaine dans la Philosophie de Fichte*, pp. 74–75, 83–94.

14. The first four letters appeared November 1795 in Band II, Heft 3, 177–203, and the next six appeared in April 1796 in Band III, Heft 3, 173–239. Citations will be to the *Werke* edition.

15. See also Hölderlin to Niethammer, February 24, 1796: "He [Schelling] has gone a better path with his new convictions, even before he came to the end of the bad old one" (GSA VI/1, 203). Hölderlin is again referring to the Fichteanism of the earlier work.

16. In her editorial report to the *Historisch-Kritische Ausgabe* of the *Briefe*, Annemarie Pieper contends that Schelling's correspondent most probably does not refer to any historical person but simply to a fictional character. See *Werke*, III, 34. She notes that the views of the correspondent do not exactly coincide with those of either Hegel or Hölderlin. While this might be the case, it does not exclude the possibility that Schelling is replying to many of Hölderlin's views.

17. See Fichte to Reinhold, July 2, 1795, AA, III/2, 347.

18. This early dispute between Fichte and Schelling has been studied in detail, first by Léon, *Fichte et son temps*, I, 415–422, and then by Reinhart Lauth, 'Die erste philosophische Auseinandersetzung zwischen Fichte und Schelling 1795-1797,' *Zeitschrift für philosophischen Forschung* 21 (1967), 341–367.

19. This is clear from Fichte's May 31–August 7, 1801 letter to Schelling, where he explained that he had once "gently contradicted" his thesis in the *Briefe* that idealism and realism are two systems that can stand beside one another. See *Briefe und Dokumente*, II, 339; AA III/5, 43, no. 605. That Fichte contradicted him specifically in the *Einleitungen* becomes clear from the context of this work.

20. Significantly, in the *Einleitungen* Fichte did not repeat the doctrine, already advanced in section 5 of the *Grundlage*, that the critical idealism of the *Wissenschaftslehre* does admit the *existence* of the thing-in-itself after all. As we have already seen (2.6.2), Fichte's more precise position is that, though the *essence* or all the *properties* of the non-ego are posited by the ego, and so are only valid from the empirical standpoint, its *existence* still remains indeterminable and utterly opposed to the ego, and so holds even from the transcendental standpoint. The reason Fichte does not mention this qualification of his position in the *Zweite Einleitung* was probably only forensic, deriving from his unwillingness to make any concessions to dogmatism and his need to distinguish his position from it. Still, even when this qualification in Fichte's position is taken into account, it does not diminish the main source of friction with Schelling. For Schelling was affirming, and Fichte was denying, the transcendental reality of things *as we perceive them*. While Fichte was willing to admit the existence of the thing-in-itself, he still refused, as a critical idealist, to equate appearances with things-in-themselves. This was just the equation, however, that Schelling wished to sanction in stressing the coordinate status of idealism and realism.

21. Compare Daniel Breazeale, 'How to Make an Idealist: Fichte's "Refutation of Dogmatism" and the Problem of the Starting Point of the *Wissenschaftslehre*,' *Philosophical Forum* 19 (1987–1988), 97–123. Breazeale argues that Fichte's position can be made consistent because his claim that the decision between dogmatism and criticism depends on the person means not that there cannot be any refutation of dogmatism, but only that *the ability to understand and see the truth of idealism* depends on having a certain character and experience—namely, the sense of one's own freedom (pp. 109–110, 111). Although Fichte indeed stresses the importance of having an experience of freedom for making sense of idealism, this does not mean that the arguments against dogmatism are perfectly unproblematic and that it is only a question of the dogmatist acquiring the appropriate experience. Such a reading does not do full justice to Fichte's doctrine about the limits of theoretical reason, in both the *Grundlage* and *Einleitungen*.

22. Fichte is explicit in the *Erste Einleitung*: "Every consistent dogmatist is necessarily a fatalist" (I, 430).

2. The Development of *Naturphilosophie*

1. Compare *Ideen*, *Werke*, II, 213–223, and *Weltseele*, *Werke*, II, 396.

2. See sections 1 and 2 of Schelling's *Abhandlungen zur Idealismus der Wissenschaftslehre*, *Werke*, I, 355–357, 368–369.

3. See *Abhandlungen zur Idealismus der Wissenschaftslehre*, *Werke*, I, 380.

3. Schelling's Break with Fichte

1. See Fichte to Schelling, October 3, 1800, in *Briefe und Dokumente*, II, 263; see also Fichte, AA, III/4, 322–323. All references to Fichte's correspondence will be to the Akademie edition, designated 'AA.'

2. Fichte knew all too well why Schelling was not available to discuss philosophy. See Fichte to Schelling, October 3, 1800, *Briefe und Dokumente*, II, 264; AA, III/4, 323: "I especially looked forward to your company during my journey to Jena. But I could never find it in your home; for you were never there, and I had looked for you too often in vain. I could not, and would not, look for you where you were usually staying."

3. This is evident from Schelling's November 19, 1800 and May 15, 1801 letters to Fichte, where Schelling writes of his philosophy as an "extension" (*Erweiterung*) of Fichte's principles. See *Briefe und Dokumente*, II, 298, 324.

4. *Briefe und Dokumente*, II, 222–223; AA, III/4, 242–244.

5. Since Schelling's letter has been lost, the precise nature of these rumors is unknown. They can be inferred from Fichte's October 3, 1800 reply.

6. This is the suggestion of Fuhrmanns. See his reconstruction of the events, *Briefe und Dokumente*, II, 262n1. The intrigues of the Schlegel brothers in starting their own journal independent of Fichte are clear from the letters between A. W. Schlegel and Schleiermacher in late summer 1800. See especially A. W. Schlegel to Schleiermacher, August 20, 1800; Schleiermacher to A. W. Schlegel, August 29, 1800; and A. W. Schlegel to Schleiermacher, September 8, 1800, in *Fichte im Gespräch*, II, 379–381, 384–388, 390–392.

7. See Schelling to Fichte, October 31, 1800, *Briefe und Dokumente*, II, 283.

8. This is Fuhrmanns' reconstruction of a lost letter, which he assumes was written around the end of September 1800. See *Briefe und Dokumente*, II, 262n1.

9. See *Briefe und Dokumente*, II, 262–270, 275–280; AA, III/4, 322–328, 339–343.

10. Ibid., II, 282–284; AA, III/4, 345.

11. *Briefe und Dokumente*, II, 289–292.

12. See 'Bemerkungen bei der Lektüre von Schellings transcendental Idealismus,' *Werke*, XI, 367–370. AA, II/5, 413–415. Fichte probably wrote these remarks in early November of 1800, shortly before sending his November 15, 1800 letter to Schelling.

13. See *Werke*, II, 362–367; AA, II/5, 421–430. This manuscript was probably written toward the end of 1800, shortly before or after Fichte's November 15 letter.

14. This became especially clear in the draft of Fichte's December 27 letter to Schelling: "the subjective in its subjective = objective nature still cannot be anything other than *the projected analogy of our self-determination* (nature as *noumenon*) [read into appearances] by thought as (indisputably our) creation of imagination. Now I cannot conversely explain the ego from that which is otherwise completely explained by it" (*Briefe und Dokumente*, II, 304; AA, III/4, 404–405; Fichte's emphasis).

15. *Werke*, II, 386; AA, I/7, 239. According to Lauth, this remark is directed against

Schelling's essay 'Anhang zu dem Aufsatz des Herrn Eschenmeyer betreffend den wahren Begriff der Naturphilosophie, und die richtige Art ihre Probleme aufzulösen.' Though Fichte is indeed reacting to Schelling, it cannot be to this essay, which did not appear until January 1801. It is much more likely that Fichte is reacting to Schelling's November 19, 1800 letter.

16. See Fichte, *Werke*, II, 398–400; AA, I/7, 249–250. As we shall soon see (4.5.2), however, Schelling himself warned against confusing the dynamic construction of nature with something temporal.

17. See Fichte, *Werke*, II, 410–420, esp. 419; AA, I/7, 259–268, esp. 267.

18. See Schelling to Fichte, October 3, 1801, AA, III/5, 89–90.

19. *Briefe und Dokumente*, II, 294–300; AA, III/4, 362–369.

20. *Briefe und Dokumente*, II, 305; AA, III/4, 404–407.

21. Schelling's marginal comment on Fichte's statement about the individual is telling: "I said the *Ego*, which makes a difference." See *Briefe und Dokumente*, II, 305n4, and AA, III/4, 406.

22. According to Lauth, when Fichte wrote of an extension of principles he meant according to *Schelling's* conception of the *Wissenschaftslehre* but not according to his own; at most Fichte envisaged a shift in the *derived* or subsidiary principles of his philosophy, and Schelling misread this as a change in fundamentals. See his *Die Entstehung*, pp. 143–144. But this does not agree with with the content of the December 27 letters, in either its draft or final version, as explained above. Lauth exaggerates the consistency in Fichte's transcendental philosophy and underplays the important change in his position involved in the *Bestimmung des Menschen*.

23. See Fichte, *Werke*, II, 303, 316.

24. See [*Ankündigung:*] *Seit Sechs Jahren*, in AA, I/7, 153–164.

25. See AA, III/5, 88, 19n. In his October 3, 1801 letter to Fichte Schelling complained that the ambiguities of the announcement had only encouraged their enemies. See AA, III/5, 88–89.

26. Schelling's stated his reaction to Fichte's announcement in a lost letter to Karoline Schlegel, which was written around February 1801. Its contents may be inferred from Karoline's February [?] 1801 letter to Schelling, *Fichte im Gespräch*, III, 12 (no. 1188), and Schelling's October 3, 1801 letter to Fichte, *Briefe und Dokumente*, II, 355; AA, III/5, 88–89.

27. See Karoline Schlegel to Schelling, February [?] 1801 and March 1, 1801, in *Fichte im Gespräch*, III, 12–13 (no. 1188), and 14–15 (no. 1190).

28. *Briefe und Dokumente* II, 323–325; AA, III/5, 35–36.

29. *Briefe und Dokumente* II, 325–329; AA, III/5, 39–42.

30. See *J. G. Fichtes Antwortschreiben an Herrn Professor Reinhold*, *Werke*, II, 506, 508, 513, 517.

31. See Schelling to Goethe, May 25, 1801, *Fichte im Gespräch*, III, 46 (no. 1232).

32. This is clear from Karoline Schlegel's June 29, 1801 letter to A. W. Schlegel. This is how she described Schelling's mood before he knew Fichte's response to his May 24 letter: "Sch. is in a valiant mood. He hopes he is on the right side and is

still full of respect for the holy strength of his enemy. If the two really are to confront one another publicly, it will take place in an honest and dignified manner and everyone else will have to stand back." See *Fichte im Gespräch,* III, 56 (no. 1245). Because Schelling seemed prepared for the worst, it is somewhat inaccurate to describe Fichte's May 25 letter as a severe blow and disappointment for Schelling, as Fuhrmanns does. See *Briefe und Dokumente,* I, 226.

33. See Schleiermacher to Ehrenfried von Willich, June 25, 1801: "I fear the two men [Fichte and Schelling] will give the world the scandal of a public dispute, and if they only conduct it with dignity and moderation!" In *Schelling im Spiegel seiner Zeitgenossen,* ed. Xavier Tilliete (Torino: Bottega d' Erasmo, 1974), p. 59, no. 87.

34. It is not clear whether Schelling knew of Fichte's negative reaction before receiving his letter. Although Karoline Schlegel's letter to August Wilhelm of June 29, 1801 writes of Schelling fearing the worst, she also swears not to reveal the contents of *der große Brief* to him if Schlegel insisted on secrecy. See *Fichte im Gespräch* III, 56 (no. 1245). Unfortunately, A. W. Schlegel's letters to Karoline during this period are lost.

35. This is apparent from Fichte's *Sonnenklarer Bericht,* II, 219, 235.

36. Fichte reaffirmed these limits on our knowledge in the *Sonnenklarer Bericht,* II, 333–334.

37. This point has been emphasized by Lauth, *Die Entstehung,* pp. 120–121. He overlooks, however, the extent to which Fichte still insists on a mechanical model of explanation.

38. *Briefe und Dokumente,* II, 348–356; AA, III/5, 80–90, no. 613.

39. This is not to say that the correspondence ended with Schelling's October 3 letter. Though Fichte too abandoned all hope of collaboration, he continued to write Schelling to explain the main points at issue between them. His letters of October 15, 1801, and January 15, 1802 contain important objections to Schelling's position, which we will consider below.

4. Problems, Methods, and Concepts of *Naturphilosophie*

1. On Schelling's use of the term, see *Fernere Darstellungen,* IV, 404; 'Über das Verhältniß der Naturphilosophie zur Philosophie überhaupt,' V, 112; the 'Zusatz zur Einleitung' to the *Ideen zu einer Philosophie der Natur,* II, 67, 68; and *Bruno,* IV, 257, 322.

2. This was the view of Justus Liebig, 'Über das Studium der Naturwissenschaften und über der Zustand der Chemie in Preußen,' in *Reden und Abhandlungen* (Heidelberg: Winter, 1874), p. 24.

3. It is necessary to mention here the pioneering efforts of Rudolf Haym and Kuno Fischer, who were the first to recognize the historical significance of *Naturphilosophie.* In *Die romantische Schule,* pp. 552–660, Haym devoted a substantial chapter to Schelling's *Naturphilosophie,* placing it in the context of the literature and philosophy of his day. Shortly after Haym's work, Fischer published

his *Schelling's Leben, Werke und Lehre* (Heidelberg: Winter, 1872), which contains a much more substantial treatment of Schelling's *Naturphilosophie*. Though it is nearly forgotten, Fischer's work remains the most thorough examination of all phases of Schelling's work.

4. See, for example, Andrew Cunningham and Nicholas Jardine, eds., *Romanticism and the Sciences* (Cambridge: Cambridge University Press, 1990); S. Poggi and M. Bossi, eds., *Romanticism in Science* (Dordrecht: Kluwer, 1994) (Boston Studies in the Philosophy of Science, No. 152); L. Hassler, ed., *Schelling. Seine Bedeutung für eine Philosophie der Natur und der Geschichte* (Stuttgart: Fromann, 1981); G. Biedermann and E. Lange, eds., *Die Philosophie des jungen Schelling* (Wiemar: Böhlaus, 1977); R. Heckmann, H. Krings, and R. W. Meyer, eds. *Zur Auseinandersetzung mit der Naturphilosophie des jungen Schelling* (Stuttgart: Fromann, 1985); H. Sandkühler, ed. *Natur und geschichtlicher Prozeß* (Frankfurt: Suhrkamp, 1984); Karen Gloy and Paul Burger, eds., *Die Naturphilosophie im Deutschen Idealismus* (Stuttgart: Fromann, 1994); and Stephen Houlgate, ed., *Hegel and the Philosophy of Nature* (Albany: SUNY Press, 1998).

5. On Schelling, see especially the supplementary volume to the *Historisch-Kritische Ausgabe, Wissenschaftlicher Bericht zu Schellings Naturphilosphischen Schriften 1797–1800* (Stuttgart: Fromann, 1994); and on Hegel, see the three-volume edition by M. J. Petry, *Philosophy of Nature* (London: George, Allen and Unwin, 1970).

6. But modern advocates of Schelling are not lacking. For an attempt to defend his continuing relevance to the modern sciences, see Marie-Luise Heuser-Kessler, 'Schellings Organismusbegriff und seine Kritik des Mechanismus und Vitalismus,' *Allgemeine Zeitschrift für Philosophie* 14 (1989), and *Die Produktivität der Natur: Schellings Naturphilosophie und das neue Paradigma der Selbstorganisation in den Naturwissenschaften* (Berlin: Duncker and Humblot, 1986). For a sharp critique of her approach, see Bernd-Olaf Küppers, *Natur als Organismus. Schellings frühe Naturphilosophie und ihre Bedeutung für die modern Biologie* (Frankfurt: Klostermann, 1992) (Philosophische Abhandlungen, Band 58).

7. See, for example, Timothy Lenoir, 'Kant, Blumenbach, and Vital Materialism in German Biology,' *Isis* 71 (1980), 77–108; 'The Göttingen School and the Development of Transcendental Naturphilosophie in the Romantic Era,' *Studies in the History of Biology* V (1981), 111–205; and *The Strategy of Life: Teleology and Mechanics in Nineteenth-Century German Biology* (Chicago: University of Chicago Press, 1989), pp. 1–53. Lenoir's strategy is to free late-eighteenth- and early-nineteenth-century German physiology from the associations of *Naturphilosophie* by showing the impact of Kant on such physiologists as Blumenbach, Kielmeyer, Treviranus, and Humboldt, who he thinks were responsive to Kant's criticisms of teleology and vitalism. For a more detailed criticism of Lenoir's views along the lines suggested above, see K. L. Caneva, 'Teleology with Regrets,' *Annals of Science* 47 (1990), 291–300; and Robert Richards, *Romantic Biology* (Chicago: University of Chicago Press, forthcoming), chap. 4.

8. See James Larson, 'Vital Forces: Regulative Principles or Constitutive Agents? A Strategy in German Physiology, 1786–1802,' *Isis* 70 (1979), 235–249.

9. This image of *Naturphilosophie* has been remarkably persistent. See, for example, H. A. M. Snelders, 'Romanticism and Naturphilosophie and the Inorganic Natural Sciences 1797–1840: An Introductory Survey,' *Studies in Romanticism* 9 (1970), 193–215, esp. 195–196, 199. This image lies behind much of Lenoir's argument in the texts cited above, note 7.

10. This point has been made by Walter Wetzels, 'Aspects of Natural Science in German Romanticism,' *Studies in Romanticism* 10 (1971), 44–59.

11. This tendency is especially apparent in the work of Robert Pippin, *Hegel's Idealism* (Cambridge: Cambridge University Press, 1992); Alan White, *Absolute Knowledge: Hegel and the Problem of Metaphysics* (Athens: University of Ohio Press, 1983); Terry Pinkard, *Hegel's Dialectic* (Philadelphia: Temple University Press, 1988); Klaus Hartmann, 'Hegel: A Non-Metaphysical View,' in *Hegel: A Collection of Critical Essays*, ed. A. MacIntyre (New York: Doubleday, 1972); and the work of the Hartmann school. See especially the *Festschrift* for Hartmann, *Rediscovering Hegel*, ed. Terry Pinkard (The Hague: Dordrecht, 1995). I have criticized the interpretive assumptions of the Hartmann school in 'Hegel, A Non-Metaphysician? A Polemic,' *Bulletin of the Hegel Society of Great Britian* 32 (Autumn/Winter 1995), 1–12.

12. See, for example, Werner Hartkopf, 'Denken und Naturentwicklung: Zur Aktualität der Philosophie des jungen Schelling,' in *Natur und geschichtlicher Prozeß*, ed. H. J. Sandkühler (Frankfurt: Suhrkamp, 1984), 83–126, esp. 99–101. This common view of Schelling's *Naturphilosophie* has been questioned by Wolfgang Wieland in his insightful article 'Die Anfänge der Philosophie Schellings und die Frage nach der Natur,' in *Materialien zu Schellings philosophischen Anfängen*, ed. M. Frank and G. Kurz (Frankfurt: Suhrkamp, 1975), pp. 237–279, esp. pp. 238, 256–257, 274.

13. See, for example, the view of Schelling espoused by Erhard Lange and Georg Biedermann, 'Die Philosophie des jungen Schelling, sein aufrichtiger Jugendgedanke,' in *Philosophie des jungen Schelling*, ed. Erhard Lange (Weimar: Böhlaus Nachfolger, 1977), pp. 10, 25, 27–29, 37, 41.

14. On the nineteenth-century reaction against Schelling's *Naturphilosophie*, see Herbert Schnädelbach, *Philosophy in Germany 1831–1933* (Cambridge: Cambridge University Press, 1984), pp. 76–108.

15. See, for example, the introduction to the *System des transcendentalen Idealismus*, *Werke*, II, 339–342. Here Schelling explains that transcendental philosophy and the philosophy of nature provide complementary proofs of the principle of subject–object identity. While transcendental philosophy begins from the subject and derives the object, the philosophy of nature starts from the object and derives the subject.

16. Unlike modern versions of naturalist epistemology, Schelling did not deny the normative and a priori; his naturalism derives the mental rather than the normative.

17. It is already implicit in Schelling's 1797 *Ideen zu einer Philosophie der Natur*, but its status is somewhat ambivalent. In this work Schelling conceives of a unifying

explanation of the mental and physical world, but he also is wary of a naturalistic explanation of the mind. See *Werke*, II, 26, 48. He has still not broken the association of naturalism with materialism. This he will be able to do only after the development of his organic concept of nature in *Von der Weltseele*.

18. See *Principia philosophiae*, Pars II, §4, 11–12, in AT, VIII, 42, 46–47.

19. Ibid., Par II, §37, VIII, 62–63.

20. Ibid., Par IV, §187, VIII, 314–315.

21. Ibid., Par II, §64, VIII, 78–79.

22. Although these philosophers were mechanists they were also atomists, and so not entirely true to Descartes, who had rejected the possibility of indivisibility. See his *Principia*, §20, VIII, 51–52. On Descartes' critique of atomism, see Daniel Garber, *Descartes' Metaphysical Physics* (Chicago: University of Chicago Press, 1992), pp. 117–155.

23. Friedrich Albert Gren, *Grundriß der Chemie* (Halle, 1796–1797), viii, as cited by Manfred Durner, *Wissenschaftshistorischer Bericht*, p. 37.

24. Schelling explicitly criticized Le Sage in Part Two, chapter 3, of the *Ideen*, *Werke*, II, 200–212. It is unlikely, however, that Schelling directly knew Le Sage's main work, *Essai de chymie méchanique* (1758), which was only privately published. See *Wissenschaftlicher Bericht*, p. 21, n59. He bases his discussion mainly on the work of his disciple Pierre Prevost, *De l'origine des forces magnétiques* (Geneva: Barde, Manget, 1788). It is noteworthy that Schelling's physics teacher in Tübingen, C. F. Pfleiderer (1736–1821), was a disciple of Le Sage. On the importance of Schelling's Tübingen years for his *Naturphilosophie*, see Manfred Durner, 'Die Naturphilosophie im 18. Jahrhundert und der naturwissenschaftliche Unterricht im Tübingen,' *Archiv für Geschichte der Philosophie* 73 (1991), 71–103.

25. See *Metaphysische Anfangsgründe der Naturwissenschaften*, Hauptstück 2, Lehrsatz 1 and 2, *Schriften*, IV, 496–497, 499.

26. Erklärung 2 and Zusatz, IV, 498–499.

27. Lehrsatz 5, Beweis, IV, 508–509.

28. Lehrsatz 6, Beweis, IV, 510–511.

29. See the following works. (1) A. C. A. Eschenmayer, *Säze aus Natur-Metaphysik auf chemische und medicinische Gegenstände angewandt* (Tübingen: Heerbrandt, 1797). This developed the ideas of his dissertation *Principia quaedam disciplinae naturali, imprimis chemiae ex metaphysica naturae substernenda* (Tübingen, 1796). Schelling praised Eschenmayer's dissertation in the *Ideen*, *Werke*, II, 313. (2) C. F. Kielmeyer, *Vorlesungen über die Chemie*, in *Gesammelte Schriften* ed. F. H. Holler (Berlin, 1938). Kielmeyer's lectures were first given in 1792–1793. (3) H. F. Link, *Über einige Grundlehren der Physik und Chemie* (Rostock: Stiller 1795), and *Beiträge zur Philosophie der Physik und Chemie* (Rostock: Stiller, 1797). (4) A. N. Scherer, *Grundzüge der neuern chemischen Theorie* (Jena, 1795).

For a useful summary of these works, see Manfred Durer, 'Theorien der Chemie,' in *Wissenschaftlicher Bericht*, pp. 44–56.

30. Concerning the influence of Eschenmayer and Kielmeyer, see Manfred Durner,

'Die Naturphilosophie im 18 Jahrhundert,' pp. 95–99, 99–102. In his later years Schelling gave Eschenmayer credit for being the first among his contemporaries for developing a dynamic physics. See *Werke*, IV, 82.

31. The *Ideen* is not so critical of Kant in this regard, but Schelling becomes much more so in his later *Entwurf eines Systems der Naturphilosophie*. Here he argues that Kant simply analyzes the concept matter but does not explain its possibility itself. See *Werke*, III, 101.

32. In the *Anfangsgründe* Kant is explicit that the forces of attraction and repulsion are basic and incapable of further deduction. See Zweiter Hauptstück, Lehrsatz 7, Anmerkung 1, *Schriften*, IV, 513.

33. See the introduction to the *Ideen zu einer Philosophie der Natur*, *Werke*, II, 41–43; *Von der Weltseele*, *Werke*, II, 519–520; and chapter V of the *System des transcendentalen Idealismus*, *Werke*, III, 607–611, esp. 609.

34. See, for example, Schelling's statement in *Von der Weltseele*, *Werke*, II, 384, 386.

35. See *Kritik der Urteilskraft*, 'Einleitung,' §V, V, 181–186, and §61, V, 360–361. See too Kant's argument in *Über den Gebrauch teleologischer Prinzipien in der Philosophie*, VIII, 181–182.

36. See *Erste Einleitung in die Kritik der Urteilskraft*: "We put final causes into things and do not, as it were, lift them from perception." See *Schriften*, XX, 221n.

37. See 'Metaphysische Anfangsgründe der Mechanik,' Lehrsatz 3 and Anmerkung, IV, 543–544.

38. Concerning Kant's equivocation, see Paul Guyer, 'Reason and Reflective Judgment: Kant on the Significance of Systematicity,' *Nous* 24 (1990), 17–43, and 'Kant's Conception of Empirical Law,' *Proceedings of the Aristotelian Society*, Supp. vol. 64 (199), 221–242.

39. See KrV, B 679, 681–682, 685, 688.

40. Ibid., B 679.

41. See especially §V, V, 185.

42. The most important places are 'Einige allgemeine Betrachtungen' and 'Einzelne Bemerkungen' from the *Zeitschrift für spekulative Physik*, *Werke*, IV, 527–34, and sections 1–6 of the *Einleitungen zu dem Entwurf eines Systems der Naturphilosophie*. Also relevant are the prefaces to the *Ideen zu einer Philosophie der Natur* and *Von der Weltseele*.

43. See Schelling's statement in *Von der Weltseele*: "I hate nothing more than that mindless attempt to destroy the multiplicity of natural causes through invented identities" (II, 348). See too the preface to *Ideen zu einer Philosophie der Natur*: "my goal is not to apply philosophy to the doctrine of nature . . . I cannot think of anymore miserable business than such an application of abstract principles upon an already given empirical science" (II, 6). See also *Entwurf*, *Werke*, III, 28. These statements are noteworthy in view of Hegel's later charge of formalism against Schelling.

44. See, for example, Schelling's discussion of the concept of affinity in Part Two, section 7 of *Ideen*, *Werke*, II, 259–263.

45. See, for example, *Von der Weltseele, Werke*, II, 384, 386, the *Entwurf eines Systems, Werke*, III, 23n, the *Einleitung zu dem Entwurf, Werke*, III, 293, and the *Ideen, Werke*, II, 129, 161, 194.

46. See the preface to the *Ideen, Werke*, II, 5.

47. We will examine Schelling's critique of vitalism below, 4.5.3–4.5.4.

48. See, for example, *Allgemeine Deduktion des dynamischen Prozesses, Werke*, IV, 27, and *Ideen, Werke*, II, 49.

49. See *Einleitung, Werke*, III, 273–274.

50. For Schelling's critique of Le Sage, see *Ideen, Werke*, II, 200–212, and 'Einige Allgemeine Betrachtungen,' *Werke*, IV, 528–530.

51. Kant himself criticized mechanical physics on these grounds. See the 'Allgemeine Anmerkung zur Dynamik' in his *Metaphysische Anfangsgründe der Naturwissenschaften, Schriften*, IV, 524, 533.

52. We will consider Schelling's method of construction in some detail below, 4.8.6.

53. See also 'Einzelne Bemerkungen': "Experience would indeed be very good, if one could always immediately determine *what* it actually says. This can happen only through theory," *Werke*, IV, 534.

54. See below, 4.8.6. *Contra* Kant in the first *Kritik*, Schelling thinks that a method of construction is possible in philosophy and not just in mathematics. It is striking, however, that in the *Anfangsgründe* Kant himself uses the method of construction, contrary to his prohibition against it in the first *Kritik*.

55. On this conflict in Schelling's views, see Hans Poser, 'Spekulative Physik und Erfahrung. Zum Verhältniß von Experiment und Theorie in Schellings Naturphilosophie,' in Hasler, *Schelling*, pp. 129–138.

5. Theory of Life and Matter

1. Spinoza, *Ethica*, Par I, Prop. XXXIV.

2. For Schelling's later critique of Kant's dynamics, see *Erster Entwurf, Werke*, III, 20–27, 101–103, and *Einleitung zu dem Entwurf, Werke*, III, 281, 293–297.

3. See the *System des transcendentalen Idealismus, Werke*, III, 440–450, and the *Entwurf eines Systems der Naturphilosophie, Werke*, III, 192–220.

4. See *Allgemeine Deduktion* §§30–31; *Werke*, IV, 25–28, and *System des transcendentalen Idealismus, Werke*, III, 444.

5. On this aspect of eighteenth-century biology, see Giulio Barsanti, 'Lamarck and the Birth of Biology, 1740–1810,' in *Romanticism in Science*, pp. 47–74; and Lenoir, 'The Göttingen School and the Development of Transcendental Naturphilosophie in the Romantic Era, *Studies in the History of Biology* 5 (1981), 111–205.

6. See *Von der Weltseele, Werke*, II, 521, and *Ideen zu einer Philosophie der Natur, Werke*, II, 40–41.

7. See, for example, *Einleitung zu dem Entwurf, Werke*, III, 289.

8. See *Von der Weltseele, Werke*, II, 386: "It is a first principle of the doctrine of nature not to regard any principle as absolute, and to accept a *material* principle as the

vehicle of every power." Schelling states that this material principle will explain things empirically, according to the interaction between its material elements.

9. For a detailed account of these concepts, see Jörg Jantzen, 'Theorien der Irritabilität und Sensibilität,' in *Wissenschaftlicher Bericht*, pp. 375–498.

10. On Brown's physiology, see Jantzen, *Wissenschaftlicher Bericht*, pp. 466–470. See also 3.3.4, note 47.

11. This was deliberate on Brown's part, who renounced speculation about the source of irritability itself. See his *Elements of Medicine* (London, 1795), p. 7: "We know not what excitability is, or in what manner it is affected by the exciting powers."

12. In the *Allgemeine Deduktion des dynamischen Prozesses* Schelling makes galvanism rather than sensibility the central concept of organic life (§§59–61; IV, 72–75). There he maintains that galvanism is the unity-in-difference of magnetism, electricity, and the chemical process. On Schelling's relationship with galvanism, see Fischer, *Schelling's Leben, Werke und Lehre*, pp. 347–348, 416–418, 446–447.

13. On the debates surrounding irritability, see Thomas Hankins, *Science and the Enlightenment* (Cambridge: Cambridge University Press, 1985), pp. 119–130.

14. It is interesting to note that Bordeu was the protagonist of Diderot's famous *La Rêve de D'Alembert* (1769), which anticipates Schelling's position in remarkable respects.

15. See *Einleitung, Werke*, III, 325–326, and *Allgemeine Deduktion*, §§3, 43; IV, 4, 47.

16. On Schelling's interesting and complex relationship to Leibniz, see Hans Heinz Holz, 'Der Begriff der Natur in Schellings spekulativem System. Zum Einfluß von Leibniz auf Schelling,' in *Natur und geschichtlicher Prozeß*, pp. 202–226.

6. Schelling's Absolute Idealism

1. The *Darstellung meines Systems* should be read in conjunction with the *Vorlesungsnachschriften* of I. P. V. Troxler, who wrote down Schelling's lectures based on this text. See *Schellings und Hegels erste absolute Metaphysik (1801–02)*, ed. Klaus Düsing (Cologne: Dinter Verlag, 1988), pp. 27–62. These notes sometimes provide illuminating comments and additions to the often schematic and abstract exposition of the published text.

2. That Schelling was still hoping for Fichte's agreement with his new principles is apparent from his May 24, 1801 letter to Fichte, *Briefe und Dokumente*, II, 325–326.

3. The title was Schelling's reaction to Fichte's *Ankündkigung*. See *Briefe und Dokumente*, II, 223–224, and above, 4.3.5.

4. See his July 30, 1805 letter to Eschenmeyer, in *Briefe und Dokumente*, III, 222.

5. See his *Philosophische Einleitung in die Philosophie der Mythologie*, II/1, 371. The reference is to the second book of this work, which has been dated between 1847 and 1852.

6. Of all Schelling's contemporaries, Friedrich Schlegel alone had attempted to give some systematic form to his visions when he gave his lectures on transcendental

philosophy in 1800; yet his method of exposition was much too loose to make any claim to logical rigor. Such indeed was Schelling's reaction to Schlegel's lectures. See Schelling to Fichte, October 31, 1800, in *Briefe und Dokumente*, II, 283, where he criticizes Schlegel for his "poetische und philosophische Dilletantismus."

7. See, for example, Schelling's critical reference to Schleiermacher in *Vorlesungen über die Methode des akademischen Studiums, Werke*, V, 278–279.

8. Schelling's sympathy for Spinoza is especially apparent in the Troxler *Nachschriften*, where he equates his absolute standpoint with Spinoza's substance; though Spinoza emphasizes more the objective side of absolute identity, he still means the unity of the subjective and objective. See Düsing, *Metaphysik*, pp. 39–40. See also Schelling's *Fernere Darstellungen aus dem System der Philosophie, Werke*, IV, 372–373. See Schelling's more critical later account of Spinozism in the *Propädeutik der Philosophie, Werke*, VI, 93–104. Here Schelling demotes Spinzoism to expressing the realistic and naturalistic side of the philosophy of identity.

9. See especially Schelling's, 'Über das Verhältniß der Naturphilosophie zur Philosophie überhaupt,' *Werke*, V, 108–115; and his May 24, 1801 letter to Fichte, *Briefe und Dokumente*, II, 327.

10. See, for example, *Bruno, Werke*, IV, 322–326, and the 'Zusatz zur Einleitung' to the *Ideen zu einer Philosophie der Natur, Werke*, II, 65.

11. Schelling explains these differing manifestations appearances of the absolute in much detail in later works. See especially *Fernere Darstellungen, Werke*, IV, 412–423, 'Zusatz zur Einleitung' to *Ideen, Werke*, II, 63–68, and the *Aphorismen zur Einleitung in die Naturphilosophie, Werke*, VII, 159–174, §81–161.

12. See 'Zusatz zur Einleitung' to *Ideen, Werke*, II, 58, 67; *Vorlesungen über die Methode des akademischen Studiums, Werke*, V, 253; and the *Philosophie der Kunst, Werke*, V, 368, 371.

13. In his later years Schelling demoted the position of the *Naturphilosophie* within the *Identitätsystem*. He stressed that it was only one side of the system. See his *Philosophie der Mythologie, Werke*, II/1, 372. But he also admitted that it was the foundation of the idealism of the system, only to emphasize that the foundation is only that and its culmination is idealism. See his *Geschichte der Philosophie, Werke*, X, 107. In downplaying the role of the *Naturphilosophie* in the *Identitätssystem* Schelling was only reinterpreting his past in the light of his later views, much as he did in the preface to the *Darstellung meines Systems*. On no account should Schelling be regarded as the authoritative expositor of his own intellectual development.

14. See 'Über das Verhältniß der Naturphilosophie zur Philosophie überhaupt,' *Werke*, V, 112, and 'Zusatz zur Einleitung' to *Ideen, Werke*, II, 68.

15. See Schelling, *Fernere Darstellungen, Werke*, IV, 404.

16. See Pippin, *Hegel's Idealism*, pp. 60–88, who applies his neo-Kantian interpretation even to Hegel's early Jena period.

17. See, for example, the *Philosophie der Kunst* §8, *Werke*, V, 378, and *System der gesammten Philosophie* §42, *Werke*, VI, 192.

18. See 'Über das Verhältniß der Naturphilosophie zur Philosophie überhaupt,' *Werke*, V, 112, and 'Zusatz zur Einleitung' to *Ideen*, *Werke*, II, 68.

19. Compare the *Allgemeine Deduktion des dynamischen Prozesses* §63, *Werke*, IV, 76, with the final section of Schelling's 1804 *System der gesamten Philosophie*, which realizes his original program in great detail. See §§260–291, *Werke*, VI, 425–524.

20. See *Bruno*, *Werke*, IV, 288.

21. See, for example, Schelling's *Fernere Darstellungen*, *Werke*, IV, 372–373, and Schelling to Fichte, October 3, 1801, *Briefe und Dokumente*, II, 351. See Hegel's statements in the *Differenzschrift*, *Werke*, II, 106, 116.

22. Schelling's neologism for these opposing movements, which sounds as barbarous in German as in its literal English translation, is *Ein-bildungen*. He chose this term to stress the unity of the absolute and the inseparability of the subjective and objective in each of its appearances.

23. See Schelling's *Propädeutik der Philosophie*, VI, 93–98.

24. See Spinoza, *Ethica*, Part I, Prop. XXXIX.

25. See Schelling's *System der gesammten Philosophie* §59: "The absolute is beyond all potency, or it is potencyless" (VI, 212). In the *Darstellung meines Systems* Schelling seems to give more status to the concept of power: "The essence of absolute identity, insofar as it is the immediate ground of reality, is *power (Kraft)*" (§52; IV, 145). This is, however, to grant the concept of power a merely relative status as the source of the real or natural side of the absolute.

26. See *Darstellung meines Systems* §§142–145, *Werke*, IV, 202–204.

27. See, for example, *Bruno*, *Werke*, IV, 239–257, and 'Zusatz zur Einleitung' to *Ideen*, *Werke*, II, 60–63.

28. See Schelling's reference to Plato in *Vom Ich als Princip*, *Werke*, I, 216. Of course, Schelling's study of, and fondness for, Plato go back to his early days in the *Tübinger Stift*. On Schelling's early Plato studies, see Michael Franz, *Schellings Tübinger Platon Studien* (Göttingen: Vandenhoeck and Ruprecht, 1996), pp. 157–282; and Manfred Baum, 'The Beginnings of Schelling's Philosophy of Nature,' in Sedgwick, *Reception*, pp. 195–215. Schelling's early commentary on the *Timeaus* is generally seen as an important source of his *Naturphilosophie*. See Hermann Krings essay introducing the commentary, 'Genesis und Materie—Zur Bedeutung der Timaeus Handschrift für Schellings Naturphilosophie,' in *Historsich-Kritische Ausgabe*, I/5, 115–155. On Schelling's Neo-Platonism, see Harold Holz, 'Die Beziehungen zwischen Schellings Naturphilosophie und dem Identitätssystem in den Jahren 1801/02,' *Philosophisches Jahrbuch* 78 (1971), 260–294. Holz dates Schelling's study of Neo-Platonism to 1798, so that it is not far-fetched to find implicit Platonic motives in the earliest version of the *Identitätssystem*.

7. The Dark Night of the Absolute

1. All references to Schelling's *Darstellung meines Systems* will cite both the paragraph number (indicated by '§'), and the page number in volume IV of the *Werke* edition. 'Z' indicates *Zusatz*, an explanatory addition to a theorem.

2. See the phrase added to proposition §17: "[d.h. ein Attribut der absoluten Identität selbst"], *Werke*, III, 122.

3. There is a passage from the Troxler *Nachschriften*, which is based on the *Darstellung meines Systems*, that criticizes those philosophers whose concept of the infinite excludes the finite. See Düsing, *Metaphysik*, p. 34. Assuming these notes are accurate, then Schelling already had the view of *Bruno*.

4. This line of reasoning, implicit in *Bruno*, becomes more explicit in the *Aphorismen zur Einleitung in die Naturphilosophie, Werke*, VII, 171, §§148–149.

5. It could well be that this was under Hegel's influence. The *Fernere Darstellung* was indeed co-authored, at least officially. On the whole question of Hegel's influence on Schelling during these years, see Klaus Düsing, 'Spekulation und Reflexion: Zur Zusammenarbeit Schellings und Hegels in Jena', *Hegel-Studien* 5 (1969), 95–128; and H. Buchner, 'Hegel und das Kritische Journal der Philosophie', *Hegel-Studien* 3 (1965), 95–156.

6. According to Rosenkranz, Hegel criticized Schelling in his 1805–1806 lectures on the history of philosophy for not including qualitative differences within the absolute. See his *G. W. F. Hegels Leben* (Berlin, 1844), p. 201.

7. See Carl Eschenmeyer, *Die Philosophie in ihrem Übergang zur Nichtphilosophie* (Erlangen: Walther, 1803), p. 70. Schelling cites this passage in *Philosophie und Religion, Werke*, VI, 31–32.

8. According to Rosenkranz, Hegel rejected Schelling's theory of the fall because it did not recognize the necessity of negation within the absolute. See *Hegels Leben*, p. 188.

8. Absolute Knowledge

1. See 'Über das Wesen der philosophischen Kritik überhaupt, und ihr Verhältniß zum gegenwärtigen Zustand der Philosophie insbesondere,' in Schelling, *Werke*, V, 3–17, esp. 16.

2. See especially section IV of the *Fernere Darstellungen*, IV, *Werke*, 391–411, and lectures one, four, and six of the *Vorlesungen über die Methode des akademischen Studiums, Werke*, V, 212–222, 248–256, 266–275.

3. See *Fernere Darstellungen*, IV, *Werke*, 350–351; *Vorlesungen, Werke*, V, 272; and 'Über das Wesen der philosophischen Kritik,' *Werke*, V, 10.

4. See *Fernere Darstellungen, Werke*, IV, 349; and *Vorlesungen, Werke*, IV, 299–300.

5. See *Vorlesungen, Werke*, V, 270.

6. The charge of mysticism and irrationalism is common. See, for example, Rudolf Haym, *Die romantische Schule*, pp. 655–656; and Lukács, *Der junge Hegel*, p. 657. The thesis of Lukács' *Die Zerstörung der Vernunft* (Berlin: Aufbau, 1955), pp. 103–124, is that Schelling's concept of intellectual intuition is nothing less than the birthplace of modern irrationalism. The best antidote to these interpretations is offered by Ernst Cassirer, *Das Erkenntnisproblem in der Philosophie und Wissenschaft der neueren Zeit*, III, 253–274.

7. See, for example, 'Über das Wesen der philosophischen Kritik,' *Werke*, V, 8–10;

Schelling's critical allusions to Schleiermacher's intuition of the universe in the *Vorlesungen*, *Werke*, V, 278–279; and Hegel's similar references in the *Differenzschrift* and *Glauben und Wissen*, Hegel, *Werke*, II, 32, 391–393.

8. See *Fernere Darstellungen*, *Werke*, IV, 362.

9. Schelling adheres to Leibniz's principle of the identity of indiscernibles (see his *Aphorismen zur Einleitung in die Naturphilosophie* §220, *Werke*, VI, 188), so that if objects are stripped of all their properties, all those determinate features by virtue of which they relate to one another, they become identical.

10. It is crucial that one understand these differences. It is a complete misinterpretation of Schelling's and Hegel's position to hold that "The indifference point from which speculative philosophy starts is the self that intuits its own spontaneity" or that "The indifference point as unity is the rationally self-conscious individual." See Harris' introduction to his and Walter Cerf's translation of Hegel, *The Difference between Fichte's and Schelling's Systems of Philosophy* (Albany: CUNY, 1977), p. 42. Such an interpretation of Schelling and Hegel reads their concept of intellectual intuition in Fichtean terms, and makes nonsense of their polemic against Fichte.

11. See Spinoza, *Ethica*, Part V, Prop. xv, xxx.

12. See *System der gesammten Philosophie* §§310–315, *Werke*, VI, 556–568.

13. See *Philosophische Briefe über Dogmatismus und Kriticismus*, I, 319.

14. Thus Haym, *Die romantische Schule*, p. 650; Knittermeyer, *Schelling und die romantische Schule* (Munich: Reinhardt, 1929), p. 232; and Fackenheim, *The God Within* (Toronto: University of Toronto Press, 1996), p. 51.

15. See Schelling's explanation in the *Fernere Darstellungen*, *Werke*, IV, 345–348; the *Vorlesungen*, *Werke*, V, 248–256; and 'Über die Construktion in der Philosophie,' *Werke*, V, 125–151.

16. See 'Über die Construktion in der Philosophie,' *Werke*, V, 128.

17. *Werke*, V, 125–134.

18. See 'Über den wahren Begriff der Naturphilosophie,' *Werke*, IV, 87–88.

19. The importance of this argument for Schelling is plain from the many works in which he elaborated it. See *Bruno*, *Werke*, IV, 252–257; *Vorlesungen*, *Werke*, V, 215–222; 'Über den wahren Begriff der Naturphilosophie,' *Werke*, IV, 90–91; 'Zusatz zur Einleitung' to the later 1802 edition of the *Ideen zu einer Philosophie der Natur*, *Werke*, II, 61; 'Über das Verhältniß der Naturphilosophie zur Philosophie überhaupt,' *Werke*, V, 110–111; and especially the *System der gesammten Philosophie*, *Werke*, VI, 142–145.

20. See *Aphorismen zur Einleitung in die Naturphilosophie* §44; *Werke*, VII, 148.

21. See Schelling, *Fernere Darstellungen*, *Werke*, IV, 361–372; *System der gesammten Philosophie* §§1, 4, *Werke*, VI, 140, 143; and *Aphorismen zur Einleitung in die Naturphilosophie* §§42–54, *Werke*, VII, 148–150.

22. See *Aphorismen zur Einleitung in die Naturphilosophie* §43, *Werke*, VI, 148. See also *System der gesammten Philosophie* §§1, 4; *Werke*, VI, 140, 143.

23. *Aphorismen zur Einleitung in die Naturphilosophie* §44, *Werke*, VI, 46; *System der gesammten Philosophie*, *Werke*, VI, 149–150.

24. See, for example, the passage in the *Vorlesungen, Werke,* V, 217.
25. *System der gesammten Philosophie* §§1, 4, *Werke,* VI, 140, 143.
26. Schelling denies that it is possible to have a dialectic leading to a positive knowledge of the absolute. See his *Vorlesungen, Werke,* V, 268–270, and his *Aphorismen zur Einleitung in die Naturphilosophie* §51, *Werke,* VII, 150.

Bibliography

Primary Sources

Arnauld, A. *The Art of Thinking*, trans. J. Dickoff and P. James. Indianapolis: Bobbs-Merrill, 1964.

Bacon, F. *The New Organon*, ed. F. Anderson. Indianapolis: Bobbs-Merrill, 1960.

Beck, J. S. *Einzig möglicher Standpunkt, aus welchem die kritische Philosophie beurteilt werden muss*. Vol. 3 of *Erläuternden Auszugs aus den kritischen Schriften des Herrn Prof. Kant*. Riga: Hartknoch, 1796.

Berkeley, G. *The Works of George Berkeley*, eds. A. A. Luce and T. E. Jessop. 9 vols. Edinburgh: Nelson, 1948–1957.

——— *Philosophical Writings*, ed. D. Armstrong. New York: Collier, 1965.

Blumenbach, J. F. *Über den Bildungstrieb*. 2nd ed. Göttingen: Dietrich, 1791.

Descartes, R. *Oeuvres de Descartes*, ed. C. Adam and P. Tannery. Paris: Vrin, 1964–1976.

Eberhard, J. A. *Philosophisches Magazin*. 4 vols. Halle: Gebauer, 1788–1792.

——— *Philosophisches Archiv*. 2 vols. Berlin: Matzdorf, 1792–1795.

Eschenmeyer, Carl. *Säze aus Natur-Metaphysik auf chemische und medicinische Gegenstände angewandt*. Tübingen, 1797.

——— *Die Philosophie in ihren Uebergang zur Nichtphilosophie*. Erlangen: Walter, 1803.

——— 'Spontaneität-Weltseele, oder das Höchste Princip der Naturphilosophie,' *Zeitschrift für spekulative Physik* 2 (1801), 1–68.

Feder, J. G. H. 'Kritik der reinen Vernunft.' *Zugabe zu den Göttinger gelehrte Anzeige* 1 (19 January 1782), 40–48.

——— *Über Raum und Causalität*. Frankfurt: Dietrich, 1788.

——— *J. G. H. Feders Leben, Natur und Grundsätze*. Leipzig: Schwickert, 1825.

Fichte, J. G. *Johann Gottlieb Fichtes nachgelassene Werke*, ed. I. H. Fichte. 3 vols. Bonn: Adolph-Marcus, 1834–1835.

——— *Johann Gottlieb Fichtes sämtliche Werke*, ed. I. H. Fichte. 8 vols. Berlin: Veit, 1845–1846.

——— *Die Bestimmung des Menschen*, ed. F. Medicus. Hamburg: Meiner, 1962.

——— *Das System der Sittenlehre*, ed. F. Medicus. Hamburg: Meiner, 1963.

——— *J. G. Fichte: Gesamtausgabe der Bayerischen Akademie der Wissenschaften*, ed. R. Lauth, H. Jacob, and H. Gliwitsky. Stuttgart–Bad Cannstatt: Fromann, 1964–.

695

────── *Grundlage der gesamten Wissenschaftslehre,* ed. W. Jacobs. Hamburg: Meiner, 1970.

────── *Grundriß des Eigentümlichen der Wissenschaftslehre* (1795), ed. W. Jacobs. Hamburg: Meiner, 1975.

────── *Versuch einer neuen Darstellung der Wissenschaftslehre (1797–1798),* ed. P. Baumanns. Hamburg: Meiner, 1975.

────── *Fichte im Gespräch,* ed. E. Fuchs. 6 vols. Stuttgart–Bad Cannstadt: Friedrich Fromann, 1978.

────── *The Science of Knowledge,* ed. P. Hearth and J. Lachs. Cambridge: Cambridge University Press, 1982.

────── *Wissenschaftslehre novo methodo,* ed. E. Fuchs. Hamburg: Meiner, 1982.

────── *Early Philosophical Writings,* ed. D. Breazeale. Ithaca: Cornell University Press, 1988.

────── *Foundations of Transcendental Philosophy: Wissenschaftslehre novo methodo,* ed. D. Breazeale. Ithaca: Cornell University Press, 1992.

────── *Introduction to the Wissenschaftslehre,* ed. D. Breazeale. Indianapolis: Hackett, 1992.

────── *J. G. Fichte in zeitgenössischen Rezensionen,* ed. E. Fuchs et al. Stuttgart–Bad Cannstatt: Fromann, 1995.

────── *Züricher Vorlesungen über den Begriff der Wissenschaftslehre Februar 1794,* ed. E. Fuchs. Neuried: Ars Una, 1996.

Garve, C. 'Kritik der reinen Vernunft.' *Allgemeine deutsche Bibliothek.* Anhang zu 37–52 (1783), 838–862.

Hamann, J. G. *Sämtliche Werke, Historisch-Kritische Ausgabe,* ed. J. Nadler. 6 vols. Vienna: Herder, 1949–1957.

────── *Briefwechsel,* ed. W. Ziesemer and A. Henkel. Wiesbaden: Insel, 1955–1957.

Hardenberg, F. von. *Novalis Schriften,* ed. R. Samuel, H. J. Mähl, and G. Schulz. Stuttgart: Kohlhammer, 1960–1988.

Hausius, K. G. *Materialien zur Geschichte der critischen Philosophie.* Leipzig: Breitkopf, 1793.

Hegel, G. W. F. *Briefe von und an Hegel,* ed. J. Hoffmeister. Hamburg: Meiner, 1952.

────── *Werke in zwanzig Bänden, Studien Ausgabe,* ed. E. Moldenhauer and K. Michel. Frankfurt: Suhrkamp, 1971.

Hemsterhuis, Franz. *Philosophische Schriften,* ed. J. Hilß. Karlsruhe: Dreililien Verlag, 1912.

Herder, J. G. *Sämtliche Werke,* ed. B. Suphan. 33 vols. Berlin: Weidmann, 1881–1913.

Hölderlin, F. *Sämtliche Werke. Grosse Stuttgarter Ausgabe,* ed. F. Beißner and A. Beck. Stuttgart: Cottanachfolger, 1943–1985.

Hume, D. *A Treatise of Human Nature,* ed. L. A. Selby-Bigge. Oxford: Oxford University Press, 1958.

────── *An Enquiry concerning human Understanding,* ed. T. Beauchamp. Oxford: Oxford University Press, 1999.

Jacobi, F. H., *Werke,* ed. F. Roth and F. Köppen. 6 vols. Leipzig: Fleischer, 1812.

———— *Über die Lehre des Spinoza in Briefen an den Herrn Moses Mendelssohn.* 2nd ed. Leipzig: Löwe, 1789.

———— *Aus F. H. Jacobis Nachlaß,* ed. R. Zoeppritz. Leipzig: Engelmann, 1869.

Kant, I. *Vorlesungen über die Metaphysik,* ed. K. H. Pölitz. Erfurt: Keyserischen Buchhandlung, 1821.

———— *Nachträge zu Kants Kritik der reinen Vernunft,* ed. B. Erdmann. Kiel: Lipsius and Tischler, 1881.

———— *Reflexionen Kants zur Kritische Philosophie,* ed. B. Erdmann. Leipzig: Feuss, 1882.

———— *Gesammelte Schriften,* ed. Preußischen Akademie der Wissenschaften. Berlin: de Gruyter, 1902–.

———— *Kritik der reinen Vernunft,* ed. R. Schmidt. Hamburg: Meiner, 1956.

———— *Die Philosophischen Hauptvorlesungen Immanuel Kants,* ed. A. Kowalewski. Hildesheim: Olms, 1965.

———— *Prolegomena zu einer jeden künftigen Metaphysik,* ed. K. Vorländer. Hamburg: Meiner, 1969.

———— *Critique of Pure Reason,* trans. P. Guyer and A. Wood. Cambridge: Cambridge University Press, 1998.

Kielmeyer, C. F. *Über die Verhältnisse der organischen Kräfte untereinander in der Reihe der verschiedenen Organisaton, die Gesetze und Folgen dieser Verhältnisse,* in *Sudhoffs Archiv für Geschichte der Medicin* 23 (1930), pp. 247–267.

Leibniz, G. W. *Die philosophischen Schriften,* ed. C. Gerhardt. 7 vols. Hildesheim: Olms, 1960.

———— *Philosophical Papers and Letters,* ed. L. Loemker. 2nd ed. Dordrecht: Reidel, 1969.

———— *New Essays on Human Understanding,* ed. J. Bennet and P. Remnant. Cambridge: Cambridge University Press, 1981.

Locke, J. *An Essay concerning human Understanding,* ed. A. C. Fraser. 2 Vols. New York: Dover, 1959.

Maimon, S. *Gesammelte Werke,* ed. V. Verra. 5 vols. Hildesheim: Olms, 1965.

Mendelssohn, Moses. *Gesammelte Schriften, Jubiläumsausgabe,* ed. A. Altmann et al. Stuttgart–Bad Cannstatt: Holzboog, 1971–.

Obereit, J. H. *Die verzweifelte Metaphysik zwischen Kant und Wizenmann.* No place or publisher, 1787.

———— *Die wiederkommende Lebensgeist der verzweifelte Metaphysik.* Berlin: Decker, 1787.

———— *Beobachtungen über die Quelle der Metaphysik von alten Zuschauern, veranlasst durch Kants Kritik der reinen Vernunft.* Meiningen: Hanisch, 1791.

Reinhold, Karl Leonhard. *Versuch einer neuen Theorie des menschlichen Vorstellungsvermögens.* Jena: Widtmann and Mauke, 1789.

———— *Beyträge zur Berichtigung bisheriger Missverständnisse der Philosophen.* Jena: Widtmann and Mauke, 1790–1794.

———— *Über das Fundament des philosophischen Wissens.* Jena: Widtmann and Mauke, 1791.

———— *Korrespondenz,* ed. R. Lauth, E. Heller, and K. Hiller. Stuttgart–Bad Cannstatt: Fromann, 1983–.

Schelling, F. W. J. *Sämtliche Werke,* ed. K. F. A. Schelling. 14 vols. Stuttgart: Cotta, 1856–1861.

———— *Aus Schellings Leben. In Briefen,* ed. G. I. Plitt. 3 vols. Leipzig: Hirzel, 1869–1870.

———— *Briefe und Dokumente,* ed. H. Fuhrmanns. 3 vols. Bonn: Bouvier, 1962–1975.

———— *Schelling im Spiegel seiner Zeitgenossen,* ed. X. Tilliete. 3 vols. Torino: Bottega, 1974–1988.

———— *Werke. Historisch-Kritische Ausgabe,* ed. H. M. Baumgartner, W. G. Jacobs, and H. Krings. Stuttgart–Bad Cannstatt: Fromann, 1976–.

———— *Schelling Rariora,* ed. L. Payerson. Torino: Erasmus Bottega, 1977.

———— *Materialien zu Schellings philosophischen Anfängen,* ed. M. Frank and G. Kurz. Frankfurt: Suhrkamp, 1975.

———— *Schellings und Hegels erste absolute Metaphysik. Zusammenfassende Vorlesungs-nachschriften von I. P. V. Troxler,* ed. K. Düsing. Cologne: Dinter Verlag, 1988.

———— *Schelling: Timaeus (1974),* ed. H. Buchner. Stuttgart–Bad Cannstatt: Fromann, 1994.

Schiller, F. *Briefwechsel zwischen Schiller und Goethe,* ed. H. Graf and A. Leitzmann. 3 vols. Leipzig: Insel, 1912.

———— *Werke. Nationalausgabe,* ed. J. Peterson, L. Blumenthal, and B. von Wiese. 42 vols. Weimar: Böhlau, 1943–.

Schlegel, F. *Friedrich Schlegel. Neue Philosophische Schriften,* ed. J. Körner. Frankfurt: Verlag Gerhard Schulte-Bulmke, 1935.

———— *Kritische Friedrich Schlegel Ausgabe,* ed. E. Behler, Jean-Jacques Anstett, and H. Eichner. Paderborn: Ferdinand Schöningh, 1958–.

Schultz, J. *Erläuterung des Herrn Prof. Kants Kritik der reinen Vernunft.* Königsberg: Dengel, 1784.

———— 'Institutiones logicae et metaphysicae,' *Allgemeine Literatur Zeitung* 295 (13 December 1785), 297–299.

———— *Prüfung der kantischen Critik der reinen Vernunft.* Königsberg: Nicolovius, 1789–1792.

———— *Exposition of Kant's Critique of Pure Reason,* ed. and trans. J. Morrison. Ottawa: University of Ottawa Press, 1995. Philosophica Series No. 47.

Schulze, G. E. *Aenesidemus oder über die Fundamente der von dem Herrn Prof. Reinhold in Jena gelieferten Elementar-Philosophie.* No place or publisher, 1792. Reprint: ed. A. Liebert. Berlin: Reuther and Reichard, 1912. Kantgesellschaft edition.

Sinclair, I. von. *Gedichte von Crisalin.* Frankfurt: Hermann'sche Buchhandlung, 1812.

Tetens, J. *Über die allgemeine speculativische Philosophie.* Butzow: Berger and Boedner, 1775. Reprint: *Neudrucke seltener philosophischer Werke,* Band IV. Berlin: Reuther and Reichardt, 1913.

———— *Philosophsche Versuche über die menschliche Natur und ihre Entwicklung.* Leipzig: Weidmann, 1777. Reprint: *Neudrucke seltener philosophischer Werke,* Band IV. Berlin: Reuther and Reichardt, 1913.

Secondary Sources

German Idealism in General

Ameriks, K. *Kant and the Fate of Autonomy.* Cambridge: Cambridge University Press, 2000.

Ameriks, K. ed. *The Cambridge Companion to German Idealism.* Cambridge: Cambridge University Press, 2001.

Ameriks, K., and D. Sturma, eds. *The Modern Subject: Conceptions of the Self in Classical German Philosophy.* Albany: SUNY Press, 1995.

Baumgartner, H. M., ed. *"Frankfurt aber ist der Nabel dieser Erde": Das Schicksal einer Generation der Goethezeit.* Stuttgart: Klett-Cotta, 1983.

Baur, M., and Dahlstrom, eds. *The Emergence of German Idealism.* Washington, D.C.: Catholic University Press, 1999.

Beck, L. W. *Early German Philosophy.* Cambridge, Mass: Harvard University Press, 1969.

Beiser, F. *The Fate of Reason: German Philosophy Between Kant and Fichte.* Cambridge, Mass: Harvard University Press, 1987.

——— *Enlightenment, Revolution and Romanticism: The Genesis of Modern German Political Thought, 1790–1800.* Cambridge, Mass: Harvard University Press, 1992.

Brunschwig, H. *Enlightenment and Romanticism in Eighteenth Century Prussia,* trans. F. Jellinek. Chicago: University of Chicago Press, 1974.

Cassirer, E. *Die Nachkantischen Systeme.* Vol. 3 of *Das Erkenntnisproblem in der Philosophie und Wissenschaft der neueren Zeit.* 2nd ed. Berlin: Cassirer, 1923.

Copleston, F. *From the Post-Kantian Idealists to Marx, Kierkegaard, and Nietzsche.* Vol. 7 of *A History of Philosophy.* New York: Doubleday, 1965.

Erdmann, J. *Die Entwicklung der deutschen Spekulation seit Kant.* Vol. 5 of *Versuch einer wissenschaftlichen Darstellung der Geschichte der Philosophie.* Stuttgart: Holzboog, 1977.

Fackenheim, E. *The God Within: Kant, Schelling, and Historicity.* Toronto: University of Toronto Press, 1996.

Hartmann, N. *Die Philosophie des deutschen Idealismus.* 2 vols. Berlin: de Gruyter, 1923.

Henrich, Dieter. *Konstellationen: Probleme und Debatten am Ursprung der idealistischen Philosophie (1789–1795).* Stuttgart: Klett-Cotta, 1991.

Horstmann, R-P. *Die Grenzen der Vernunft: Eine Untersuchung zu Zielen und Motiven des Deutschen Idealismus.* Frankfurt: Hain, 1991.

Jacob, Margaret. *The Radical Enlightenment.* London: George, Allen and Unwin, 1981.

Jaescke, Walter, ed. *Transzendentalphilosophie und Spekulation. Der Streit um die Gestalt einer Ersten Philosophie (1799–1807).* Hamburg: Meiner, 1993. Philosophisch-literarische Streitsachen 2.

Jamme, C., and Hans-Jürgen Gawoll, eds. *Idealismus mit Folgen: Die Epochenschwelle um 1800 in Kunst und Geisteswissenschaften.* Munich: Fink Verlag, 1994.

Kelly, G. A. *Idealism, Politics and History.* Cambridge: Cambridge University Press, 1969.

Klemm, D., and G. Zöller, eds. *Figuring the Self: Subject, Absolute, and Others in Classical German Philosophy*. Albany: SUNY Press, 1997.

Köhnke, K. C. *The Rise of Neo-Kantianism*. Cambridge: Cambridge University Press, 1991.

Korff, H. A. *Geist der Goethe Zeit*. 4 vols. Leipzig: Köhler and Amelang, 1964.

Kronenberg, M. *Geschichte des deutschen Idealismus*. Munich: Beck, 1909.

Kroner, R. *Von Kant bis Hegel*. 2 vols. Tübingen: Mohr, 1921.

Mell, D., T., Braum, and L. Palmer, eds. *Man, God, and Nature in the Enlightenment*. East Lansing, Mich: Colleagues Press, 1988.

Pippin, R. *Idealism as Modernism*. Cambridge: Cambridge University Press, 1997.

Rosenkranz, K. *Geschichte der Kant'schen Philosophie*, ed. S. Dietzsch. Berlin: Akademie Verlag, 1987.

Royce, J. *The Spirit of Modern Philosophy*. Boston: Houghton, Mifflin, 1892.

———— *Lectures on Modern Idealism*. New Haven: Yale University Press, 1919.

Solomon, R. *Continental Philosophy since 1750: The Rise and Fall of the Self*. Oxford: Oxford University Press, 1988.

Solomon, R., and K. Higgens, eds. *The Age of German Idealism*. Routledge: London, 1993.

Strack, F. *Evolution des Geistes: Jena um 1800*. Stuttgart: Klett-Cotta, 1994.

Taylor, C. *Hegel*. Cambridge: Cambridge University Press, 1975.

Timm, H. *Gott und die Freiheit: Studien zur Religionsphilosophie der Goethezeit*. Frankfurt: Klostermann, 1974.

Weiser, C. F. *Shaftesbury und das deutsche Geistesleben*. Leipzig: Teubner, 1916.

Wundt, M. *Die Philosophie an der Universität Jena in ihrem Geschichtlichen Verlaufe Dargestellt* (Jena: Gustav Fischer, 1932). Beiträge zur Geschichte der Universität Jena, Heft 4.

———— *Die deutsche Schulphilosophie im Zeitalter der Aufklärung*. Tübingen: Mohr, 1945.

Ziolkowski, T. *Das Wunderjahr in Jena*. Stuttgart: Klett-Cotta, 1998.

Kant

ANTHOLOGIES

Beck, L. W., ed. *Kant Studies Today*. LaSalle, Ill.: Open Court, 1967.

———— *Proceedings of the Third International Kant Congress*. Dordrecht: Reidel, 1970.

Blasche, S., et al. *Übergang: Untersuchungen zum Spätwerk Immanuel Kants*. Frankfurt: Klostermann, 1989.

Brandt, R., and W. Stark, eds. *Neue Autographen und Dokumente zu Kants Leben, Schriften und Vorlesungen*. Hamburg: Meiner, 1987. Kant Forschungen, Band 1.

Cicovacki, P., ed. *Kant's Legacy: Essays in Honor of Lewis White Beck*. Rochester: University of Rochester Press, 2001.

Dancy, R. M., ed. *Kant and Critique: New Essays in Honor of W. H. Werkmeister*. Dordrecht: Kluwer, 1993.

Förster, E., ed. *Kant's Transcendental Deductions.* Stanford: Stanford University Press, 1989.

Gram, M., ed. *Kant: Disputed Questions.* Chicago: Quadrangle, 1967.

—— *Interpreting Kant.* Iowa City: University of Iowa Press, 1982.

Guyer, P., ed. *The Cambridge Companion to Kant.* Cambridge: Cambridge University Press, 1992.

Harper, W., and R. Meerbote, eds. *Kant on Causality, Freedom, and Objectivity.* Minneapolis: University of Minnesota Press, 1984.

Heimsoeth, H., et al. *Studien zu Kants philosophischer Entwicklung.* Hildesheim: Olms, 1967. Studien und Materialien zur Geschichte der Philosophie, Band 6.

Kennington, R., ed., *The Philosophy of Immanuel Kant.* Washington, D.C.: Catholic University Press, 1985. Studies in Philosophy and the History of Philosophy, Vol. 12.

Kitcher, P., ed., *Kant's Critique of Pure Reason.* Lanham, Md: Rowan and Littlefield, 1998.

Mohanty, J. N., and R. Shahan, eds. *Essays on Kant's Critique of Pure Reason,* Norman: Oklahoma University Press, 1982.

Ouden, B., and M. Moen, eds. *New Essays on Kant.* New York: Lang, 1987.

Penelhum, T., and J. J. MacIntosh, eds. *The First Critique.* Belmont, Cal: Wadsworth, 1969.

Ross, G., and T. McWalter, eds. *Kant and His Influence.* Bristol: Thoemmes, 1990.

Schaper, E., and W. Vossenkuhl, eds. *Reading Kant.* Oxford: Blackwell, 1989.

Sedgwick, S., ed., *The Reception of Kant's Critical Philosophy.* Cambridge: Cambridge University Press, 2000.

Walker, R., ed. *Kant on Pure Reason.* Oxford: Oxford University Press, 1982.

—— *The Real in the Ideal: Berkeley's Relation to Kant.* Garland: New York, 1988.

Watkins, E., ed. *Kant and the Sciences.* Oxford: Oxford University Press, 2001.

Werkmeister, W. H., ed. *Reflections on Kant's Philosophy.* Gainesville: University Presses of Florida, 1975.

Wolff, R. P., ed. *Kant: A Collection of Critical Essays.* London: Macmillan, 1968.

Wood, A., ed. *Self and Nature in Kant's Philosophy.* Ithaca: Cornell University Press, 1984.

ARTICLES AND MONOGRAPHS

Adams, G. 'Berkeley and Kant,' in *George Berkeley,* ed. S. C. Pepper, K. Aschenbrenner, and B. Mates. *University of California Publications in Philosophy* 29 (1957), 189–206.

Adickes, E. *Kants Opus postumum.* Berlin: Reuther and Reichard, 1920. *Kant-Studien Ergänzungsheft* No. 50.

—— *Kant als Naturforscher.* Berlin: de Gruyter, 1924.

—— *Kants Lehre von der Doppelten Affektion unseres Ich als Schlüssel zu seiner Erkenntnistheorie.* Tübingen: Mohr, 1929.

——— *Kant und das Ding an sich*. Berlin: Pan Verlag, 1924. Reprint: Hildesheim: Olms, 1977.

——— *German Kantian Bibliography*. New York: Burt Franklin, 1970.

Albrecht, W. 'Die sogenannte Neue Deduktion in Kants Opus Postumum,' *Archiv für Philosophie* 5 (1954–1956), 57–65.

Al-Azm, S. *The Origins of Kant's Arguments in the Antinomies*. Oxford: Clarendon Press, 1972.

Allison, H. 'Kant's Concept of the Transcendental Object,' *Kant-Studien* 59 (1968), 165–186.

——— 'Transcendental Idealism and Descriptive Metaphysics,' *Kant-Studien* 60 (1969), 216–233.

——— 'Kant's Critique of Berkeley,' *Journal of the History of Philosophy* 11 (1973), 43–63.

——— *The Kant–Eberhard Controversy*. Baltimore: Johns Hopkins University Press, 1973.

——— 'Kant's Refutation of Realism,' *Dialectica* 30 (1976), 223–253.

——— 'The Non-spatiality of Things in Themselves for Kant,' *Journal of the History of Philosophy* 14 (1976), 313–321.

——— *Kant's Transcendental Idealism: An Interpretation and Defense*. New Haven: Yale University Press, 1983.

——— 'Reflections on the B Deduction,' *Southern Journal of Philosophy* 25 Supplement (1986), 1–15.

——— 'Transcendental Idealism: The Two Aspect View,' in Ouden and Moen, *New Essays on Kant*, pp. 155–178.

——— 'Kant's Refutation of Materialism,' *Monist* 72 (1989), 190–208.

——— *Idealism and Freedom*. Cambridge: Cambridge University Press, 1996.

——— 'Is the *Critique of Judgment* Post-Critical?', in Sedgwick, *Reception*, pp. 78–92.

Ameriks, K. 'Kant's Transcendental Deduction as a Regressive Argument,' *Kant-Studien* 69 (1978), 273–287.

——— 'Recent Work on Kant's Theoretical Philosophy,' *American Philosophical Quarterly* 19 (1982), 6–11.

——— *Kant's Theory of Mind*. Oxford: Clarendon Press, 1982.

——— 'Kant, Fichte, and Short Arguments to Idealism,' *Archiv für Geschichte der Philosophie* 72 (1990), 63–85.

——— 'Kantian Idealism Today,' *History of Philosophy Quarterly* 9 (1992), 329–340.

——— *Kant and the Fate of Autonomy*. Cambridge: Cambridge University Press, 2000.

Aquila, R. 'Kant's Phenomenalism,' *Idealistic Studies* 5 (1975), 108–126.

——— 'Things in Themselves and Appearances: Intentionality and Reality in Kant,' *Archiv für Geschichte der Philosophie* 61 (1979), 293–308.

——— 'Personal Identity and Kant's Refutation of Idealism' *Kant-Studien* 70 (1979), 259–277.

——— 'Intentional Objects and Kantian Appearances,' in Mohanty and Shahan, *Essays on Kant's Critique of Pure Reason*, pp. 9–37.

———— 'Is Sensation the Matter of Appearances,' in Gram, *Interpreting Kant,* pp. 11–29.

———— *Representational Mind: A Study of Kant's Theory of Knowledge.* Bloomington: Indiana University Press, 1983.

Arnoldt, E. *Kants Prolegomena nicht doppelt redigiert. Widerlegung der Benno Erdmannschen Hypothese.* Berlin: Leipmannsohn, 1879.

———— *Kritische Exkurse im Gebiete der Kant Forschung.* Vol. 4 of *Gesammelete Schriften.* Berlin: Cassirer, 1908.

Ayers, M. 'Berkeley's Immaterialism and Kant's Transcendental Idealism,' in *Idealism Past and Present,* ed. G. Vesey, pp. 51–70. Cambridge: Cambridge University Press, 1982.

Barker, S. 'Appearing and Appearances in Kant,' *Monist,* 51 (1967), 426–441.

Beck, L. W. A Commentary on Kant's Critique of Practical Reason. Chicago: University of Chicago Press, 1960.

———— *Studies in the Philosophy of Kant.* Indianapolis: Bobbs-Merrill, 1965.

———— *Early German Philosophy.* Cambridge, Mass: Harvard University Press, 1969.

———— *Essays on Hume and Kant.* New Haven: Yale University Press, 1978.

Bennet, J. *Kant's Analytic.* Cambridge: Cambridge University Press, 1966.

———— *Kant's Dialectic.* Cambridge: Cambridge University Press, 1974.

Bird, G. *Kant's Theory of Knowledge: An Outline of One Central Argument in the* Critique of Pure Reason. New York: Humanities Press, 1962.

———— 'Kant's Transcendental Idealism,' in *Idealism Past and Present,* ed. G. Vesey, pp. 71–92. Cambridge: Cambridge University Press, 1982.

———— 'Kant's Transcendental Arguments,' in Schaper and Vossenkuhl, *Reading Kant,* pp. 21–40.

Bracken, H. *The Early Reception of Berkeley's Immaterialism: 1710–1733.* The Hague: Nijhoff, 1959.

Brandt, R. 'Feder und Kant,' *Kant-Studien* 80 (1980), 249–263.

———— 'Eine neu aufgefundene Reflexion Kants "Vom inneren Sinne,"' in Brandt and Stark, *Neue Autographen und Dokumente,* pp. 1–30.

Buchdahl, G. *Metaphysics and the Philosophy of Science: The Classical Origins Descartes to Kant.* Oxford: Blackwell, 1969.

———— *Kant and the Dynamics of Reason.* Oxford: Blackwell, 1992.

Caird, E. *The Critical Philosophy of Immanuel Kant.* 2 vols. Glasgow: Maclehose and Sons, 1889.

Carl, W. *Der schweigende Kant: Die Entwürfe zu einer Deduktion der Kategorien vor 1781.* Göttingen: Vandenhoeck and Ruprecht, 1989.

———— 'Kant's First Drafts of the Deduction of the Categories,' in Förster, *Kants Transcendental Deductions,* pp. 3–20.

Cassirer, E. *Kants Leben und Lehre.* 2nd ed. Berlin: Cassirer, 1921.

———— *Substanzbegriff und Funktionsbegriff.* Berlin: Cassirer, 1921.

———— *Das Erkenntnisproblem in der Philosophie und Wissenschaft der neueren Zeit.* Vol. 3, *Die Nachkantischen Systeme.* Berlin: Cassirer, 1922.

———— 'Paul Natorp,' *Kant-Studien* 30 (1925), 273–298.

—— 'Hermann Cohen, 1842–1918,' *Social Research* 10 (1943), 219–232.

—— 'Kant and the Problem of Metaphysics,' in Gram, *Disputed Questions,* pp. 131–157.

Cohen, H. *Kants Theorie der Erfahrung.* 2nd ed. Berlin: Dümmler, 1885.

Collins, A. *Possible Experience: Understanding Kant's* Critique of Pure Reason. Berkeley: University of California Press, 1999.

De Pierris, G. 'Kant and Innatism,' *Pacific Philosophical Quarterly* 68 (1987), 285–305.

Drews, A. *Kants Naturphilosophie als Grundlage seines Systems.* Berlin: Mitscher and Röstell, 1894.

Edwards, J. 'Der Ätherbeweis des Opus postumum und Kants 3. Analogie der Erfahrung,' in Blasche et al., *Übergang,* pp. 77–104.

—— 'Spinozism, Freedom, and Transcendental Dynamics in Kant's Final System of Transcendental Idealism,' in Sedgwick, *Reception,* pp. 54–77.

—— *Substance, Force, and the Possibilty of Knowledge: On Kant's Philosophy of Material Nature.* Berkeley: University of California Press, 2000.

Engstrom, S. 'The Transcendental Deduction and Skepticism,' *Journal of the History of Philosophy* 32 (1994), 359–380.

Erdmann, B. *Martin Knutzen und seine Zeit.* Leipzig: Voss, 1876.

—— *Kants Kriticismus in der ersten und in der zweiten Auflage der Kritik der reinen Vernunft.* Leipzig: Voss, 1878.

—— 'Einleitung' to *Kants Prolegomena zu einer jeden künftigen Metaphysik,* pp. x–cxvi. Leipzig: Voss, 1878.

—— *Nachträge zu Kants Kritik der reinen Vernunft.* Kiel: Lipsius and Tischler, 1881.

—— 'Kant und Hume um 1762,' *Archiv für Geschichte der Philosophie* 1 (1888), 62–77, 216–230.

—— *Historische Untersuchungen über Kants Prolegomena.* Halle: Max Niemeyer, 1904. Reprint: Hildesheim: Gerstenberg, 1975.

Ewing, A. C. *A Short Commentary on Kant's Critique of Pure Reason.* Chicago: University of Chicago Press, 1938.

Falkenstein, L. 'Kant's Argument for the Non-Spatio-Temporality of Things-in-themselves, *Kant-Studien* 80 (1989), 265–83.

—— 'Was Kant a Nativist,' *Journal of the History of Ideas* 50 (1990), 573–597.

—— 'Kant, Mendelssohn, Lambert and the Subjectivity of Time,' *Journal of the History of Philosophy* 19 (1991), 227–251.

—— 'The Great Light of 1769—A Humean Awakening?' *Archiv für Geschichte der Philosophie* 77 (1995), 63–79.

—— *Kant's Intuitionism: A Commentary on the Transcendental Aesthetic.* Toronto: University of Toronto Press, 1995.

Fischer, K. *Immanuel Kant und seine Lehre.* Heidelberg: Winter, 1898.

Förster, E. 'Kant's Refutation of Idealism,' in *Philosophy, Its History and Historiography,* ed. A. J. Holland, pp. 287–303. Dordrecht: Riedel, 1983.

—— 'Is there "A Gap" in Kant's Critical System?', *Journal of the History of Philosophy* 25 (1987), 533–555.

—— 'How Are Transcendental Arguments Possible,' in Schaper and Vossenkuhl, *Reading Kant,* pp. 3–21.

—— 'Die Idee des Übergangs,' in Blasche et al., *Übergang*, pp. 28–48.

—— 'Kant's Notion of Philosophy,' *Monist* 72 (1989), 285–304.

—— 'Kants *Selbstsetzungslehre*,' in Förster, *Kants Transcendental Deductions*, pp. 217–238.

—— 'Fichte, Beck and Schelling in Kant's *Opus Postumum*,' in Ross, *Kant and His Influence*.

—— *Kant's Final Synthesis*. Cambridge, Mass.: Harvard University Press, 2000.

Friedman, M. 'Causal Laws and the Foundations of Natural Science,' in Guyer, *The Cambridge Companion to Kant*, pp. 161–199.

—— *Kant and the Exact Sciences*. Cambridge, Mass: Harvard University Press, 1992.

Gardner, S. *Kant and the Critique of Pure Reason*. London: Routledge, 1999.

Garnett, C. *The Kantian Philosophy of Space*. New York: Columbia University Press, 1939.

George, R. 'Kant's Sensationism,' *Synthese* 47 (1981), 229–255.

Gochnauer, M. 'Kant's Refutation of Idealism,' *Journal of the History of Philosophy*, 12 (1974), 195–206.

Gram, M. 'Intellectual Intuition: The Continuity Thesis,' *Journal of the History of Ideas* 42 (1981), 287–304.

—— 'What Kant Really Did to Idealism,' in Mohanty and Shahan, *Essays on Kant's Critique of Pure Reason*, pp. 127–155.

—— *The Transcendental Turn*. Gainsville: University of Florida Press, 1984.

Groos, K. 'Hat Kant Hume's Treatise gelesen?,' *Kant-Studien* 5 (1901), 177–181.

Guyer, P. 'Kant on Apperception and A Priori Synthesis,' *American Philosophical Quarterly* 17 (1980), 205–212.

—— 'Kant's Intentions in the Refutation of Idealism,' *Philosophical Review* 92 (1983), 329–383.

—— *Kant and the Claims of Knowledge*. Cambridge: Cambridge University Press, 1987.

—— 'The Rehabilitation of Transcendental Idealism?,' in Schaper and Vossenkuhl, *Reading Kant*, pp. 140–168.

—— 'The Unity of Reason: Pure Reason as Practical Reason in Kant's Early Conception of the Transcendental Dialectic,' *Monist* 72 (1989), 139–167.

—— 'Kant's Conception of Empirical Law,' *Proceedings of the Aristotelian Society*, 64 supplement (1990), 221–242.

—— 'Reason and Reflective Judgment: Kant on the Significance of Systematicity,' *Nous* 24 (1990), 17–43.

—— 'The Unity of Nature and Freedom: Kant's Conception of the System of Philosophy,' in Sedgwick, *Reception*, pp. 19–53.

Harper, W. 'Kant's Empirical Realism and the Second Analogy of Experience,' *Synthese* 47 (1981), 465–480.

—— 'Kant on Space, Empirical Realism and the Foundations of Geometry,' *Topoi* 3 (1984), 143–161.

—— 'Kant's Empirical Realism and the Distinction between Subjective and Objective Succession,' in Harper and Meerbote, *Kant on Causality, Freedom, and Objectivity*, pp. 108–137.

Hatfield, G. *The Natural and the Normative: Theories of Perception from Kant to Helmholtz.* Cambridge, Mass: MIT Press, 1990.

Heidegger, M. *Kant und das Problem der Metaphysik.* Frankfurt: Klostermann, 1951.

Heidemann, D. *Kant und das Problem des metaphysischen Idealismus.* Berlin: de Gruyter, 1988. *Kant-Studien Ergänzungsheft* 131.

Henrich, D. 'Kant's Notion of a Deduction and the Methodological Background of the First *Critique*,' in Förster, *Kant's Transcendental Deductions,* pp. 29–46.

——— *The Unity of Reason,* ed. R. Velkley. Cambridge, Mass: Harvard University Press, 1994.

Herring, H. *Das Problem der Affektion bei Kant.* Cologne: Kölner Universitäts-Verlag, 1953. *Kant-Studien Ergänzungsheft* 67.

Hinske, N. 'Kants Begriff der Antinomie und die Etappen seiner Ausarbeitung,' *Kant-Studien* 55 (1966), 485–496.

Hoppe, H. G. *Kants Theorie der Physik.* Frankfurt: Klostermann, 1969.

Hübner, K. 'Leib und Erfahrung in Kants Opus Postumum,' *Zeitschrift für philosophische Forschung* 7 (1953), 204–219.

Humphrey, T. 'The Historical and Conceptual Relations between Kant's Metaphysics of Space and Philosophy of Geometry,' *Journal of the History of Philosophy* 11 (1973), 483–512.

Joseph, H. W. B. 'A Comparison of Kant's Idealism with that of Berkeley,' *Proceedings of the British Academy* (1929), 213–234.

Justin, G. 'On Kant's Analysis of Berkeley,' *Journal of the History of Philosophy* 11 (1973), 43–63.

——— 'Re-Relating Kant and Berkeley,' *Kant-Studien* 68 (1977), 77–89.

Kalter, A. *Kants vierter Paralogismus.* Meisenheim am Glan: Verlag Anton Hain, 1975. Monographien zur philosophischen Forschung 142.

Kaulbach, F. 'Kants Beweis des Daseins der Gegenstände Ausser Mir,' *Kant-Studien* 50 (1958–1959), 323–347.

——— 'Leibbewusstsein und Wleterfahrung bein frühen und späten Kant,' *Kant-Studien* 54 (1963), 464–490.

Kitcher, P. 'Kant on Self-Identity,' *Philosophical Review* 91 (1982), 41–72.

——— 'Kant's Paralogisms,' *Philosophical Review* 91 (1982), 515–547.

——— 'Kant's Real Self,' in Wood, *Self and Nature in Kant's Philosophy,* pp. 113–147.

——— *Kant's Transcendental Psychology.* Oxford: Oxford University Press, 1990.

Klotz, C. *Kants Widerlegung des Problematischen Idealismus.* Göttingen: Vandenhoeck and Ruprecht, 1993. Neue Studien zur Philosophie 6.

Kopper, J. 'Kants Lehre vom Übergang als die Vollendung des Selbstbewusstseins der Transzendentalphilosophie,' *Kant-Studien* 55 (1964), 37–68.

Kreimendahl, L. *Hume in der deutschen Idealismus: Umrisse einer Rezeptionsgeschichte.* Stuttgart–Bad Canstaat: Fromann-Holzboog, 1987. Forschungen und Materialien zur deutschen Aufklärung, Part 2, vol. 4.

——— *Kant—der Durchbruch von 1769.* Cologne: Dinter, 1990.

Kuehn, M. 'Kant's Conception of Hume's Problem,' *Journal of the History of Philosophy* 21 (1983), 176–193.

—— *Scottish Common Sense in German, 1760–1800.* Montreal: McGill–Queens University Press, 1986. McGill–Queen's Studies in the History of Ideas, No. 11.

—— 'Kant and the Refutations of Idealism in the Eighteenth Century,' in *Mind, God, and Nature in the Enlightenment,* ed. D. Mell, T. Braum, and L. Palmer, pp. 25–35. East Lansing, Mich.: Colleagues Press, 1988.

Langton, R. *Kantian Humility: Our Ignorance of Things-in-Themselves.* Oxford: Oxford University Press, 1998.

Laywine, A. *Kant's Early Metaphysics and the Origins of the Critical Philosophy.* Atascadero: Ridgeview, 1993. North American Kant Society Studies in Philosophy, vol. 3.

Lehmann, G. 'Kant's Widerlegung des Idealismus,' *Kant-Studien* 50 (1958–1959), 348–363.

—— *Beiträge zur Geschichte und Interpretation der Philosophie Kants.* Berlin: de Gruyter, 1969.

Mathieu, V. 'Äther und Organismus in Kants Opus Postumum,' in *Studien zur Kants Philosophischer Entwicklung,* ed. H. Meimsoeth, D. Henrich, and G. Tonelli, pp. 184–191. Hildesheim: Olms Verlag, 1967.

—— 'Erfinderische Vernunft in Kants *Opus postumum,* in Blasche et al., *Übergang,* pp. 65–76.

—— *Kants Opus postumum.* Frankfurt: Klostermann, 1989.

Mattey, G. J. 'Kant's Conception of Berkeley's Idealism,' *Kant-Studien* 74 (1983), 161–175.

Matthews, H. E. 'Strawson on Transcendental Idealism,' in Walker, *Kant on Pure Reason,* pp. 132–149.

McRae, R. '"Idea" as a Philosophical Term in the Seventeenth Century,' *Journal of the History of Ideas* 26 (1965) 175–190.

Meerbote, R. 'The Unknowability of Things in Themselves,' *Proceedings of the Third International Kant Congress,* ed. L. W. Beck, pp. 415–423. Dordrecht: Reidel, 1972.

—— 'Kant's Refutation of Problematic Material Idealism,' in Ouden and Moen, *New Essays on Kant,* pp. 111–138.

—— 'Kant's Functionalism,' in *Historical Foundations of Cognitive Science,* ed. J.-C. Smith. Dordrecht: Kluwer, 1990. Philosophical Studies Series 46.

Melnick, A. *Kant's Analogies of Experience.* Chicago: University of Chicago Press, 1973.

Miller, G. 'Kant's First Edition Refutation of Dogmatic Idealism,' *Kant-Studien* 62 (1971), 298–317.

—— 'Kant and Berkeley,' *Kant-Studien* 64 (1973), 315–335.

Moore, G. E. 'Kant's Idealism,' *Proceedings of the Aristotelian Society* 4 (1904), 127–140.

Mossner, E. 'The Continental Reception of Hume's *Treatise,* 1739–1741,' *Mind* 56 (1947), 31–43.

Müller-Lauter, W. 'Kants Widerlegung des materialen Idealismus,' *Archiv für Geschichte der Philosophie* 46 (1964), 60–82.

Nagel, G. *The Structure of Experience: Kant's System of Principles.* Chicago: University of Chicago Press, 1983.

Neiman, S. *The Unity of Reason. Rereading Kant.* Oxford: Oxford University Press, 1994.

Park, D. 'Kant and Berkeley's Idealism,' *Studi Internazionali de Filosofia* 2 (1969–1970), 3–10.

Paton, H. J. 'Kant on the Errors of Leibniz,' in Beck, *Kant Studies Today,* 160–180.

—— *Kant's Metaphysic of Experience.* London: George Allen and Unwin, 1970.

Pippin, R. *Kant's Theory of Form.* New Haven: Yale University Press, 1982.

—— 'Kant on the Spontaneity of the Mind,' *Canadian Journal of Philosophy* 17 (1987), 449–476.

Prauss, G. *Erscheinung bei Kant.* Berlin: de Gruyter, 1974.

—— *Kant und das Problem der Dinge an sich.* Bonn: Bouvier, 1974.

Prichard, H. A. *Kant's Theory of Knowledge.* Oxford: Clarendon Press, 1909.

Riehl, A. *Der philosophische Kriticismus und seine Bedeutung für die Positive Wissenschaft.* Leipzig: Engelmann, 1876–1887.

Ritzel, W. 'Die Stellung des Opus Postumum in Kants Gesamtwerk,' *Kant-Studien* 61 (1970), 112–125.

Robinson, H. 'Incongruent Counterparts and the Refutation of Idealism,' *Kant-Studien* 72 (1981), 391–397.

—— 'The Priority of Inner Sense,' *Kant-Studien* 79 (1988), 165–182.

—— 'A New Fragment of Immanuel Kant: "On Inner Sense," *International Philosophical Quarterly* 29 (1989), 25–261.

—— 'Two Perspectives on Kant's Appearances and Things-in-Themselves,' *Journal of the History of Philosophy* 33 (1994), 411–441.

Sassen, B. 'Critical Idealism in the Eyes of Kant's Contemporaries,' *Journal of the History of Philosophy* 35 (1997), 421–455.

Schönfeld, M. *The Philosophy of the Young Kant.* Oxford: Oxford University Press, 2000.

Schrader, G. 'The Thing in Itself in Kantian Philosophy,' *Review of Metaphysics* 2 (1949), 30–44.

—— 'The Transcendental Ideality and Empirical Reality of Kant's Space and Time,' *Review of Metaphysics* 4 (1951), 507–536.

—— 'The Status of Teleological Judgment in the Critical Philosophy,' *Kant-Studien* 45 (1953), 204–235.

—— 'Kant's Theory of Concepts,' *Kant-Studien* 49 (1957), 264–278.

Sellars, W. 'Kant's Views on Sensibility and Understanding,' in Beck, *Kant Studies Today,* pp. 181–209.

—— 'Some Remarks on Kant's Theory of Experience,' *Journal of Philosophy* 64 (1967), 633–645.

—— 'Kant's Transcendental Idealism,' *Proceedings of the Ottawa Congress on Kant,* ed. P. Laberge, F. Duchesneau, and B. Morrisey, pp. 165–181. Ottawa: University of Ottawa Press, 1974.

—— 'This I or He or It (the Thing) which Thinks . . . ,' in *Essays in Philosophy and Its History,* pp. 62–90. Dordrecht: Reidel, 1974. Philosophical Studies, vol. 12.

Sherover, C. 'Kant's Evaluation of his Relationship to Leibniz,' in Kennington, *The Philosophy of Immanuel Kant*, pp. 201–228.

Skorpen, E. 'Kant's Refutation of Idealism,' *Journal of the History of Philosophy* 6 (1962), 23–34.

Smith, A. H. *Kantian Studies*. Oxford: Clarendon Press, 1947.

Smith, N. K. *A Commentary to Kant's* Critique of Pure Reason. 2nd ed. London: Macmillan, 1923.

Stroud, B. 'Transcendental Arguments,' *The Journal of Philosophy* 65 (1968), 241–256.

Stäbler, E. *Berkeley's Auffassung und Wirkung in der deutsche Philosophie*. Tübingen: Sporn, 1935.

Stuart, J. 'Kant's Two Refutations of Idealism,' *Southwestern Journal of Philosophy* 6 (1975), 29–46.

Tonelli, G. 'Die Umwälzung von 1769 bei Kant,' *Kant-Studien* 54 (1963), 369–375.

Turbayne, C. 'Kant's Refutation of Dogmatic Idealism,' *Philosophical Quarterly* 5 (1955), 225–244.

Tuschling, B. *Metaphysische und transzendentale Dynamik in Kants Opus postumum*. Berlin: de Gruyter, 1971.

—— 'Apperception and Ether: On the Idea of a Transcendental Deduction of Matter in Kant's *Opus postumum*,' in Förster, *Kant's Transcendental Deductions*, pp. 193–216.

—— 'Die Idee des transzendentalen Idealismus im späten Opus postumum,' in Blasche et al., *Übergang*, pp. 105–145.

—— 'The System of Transcendental Idealism: Questions Raised and Left Unanswered in the *Kritik der Urteilskraft*,' *The Southern Journal of Philosophy* 30, supplement (1990), 109–127.

—— 'The Concept of Transcendental Idealism in Kant's *Opus Postumum*,' in Dancy, *Kant and Critique*, pp. 151–167.

Vaihinger, H. 'Die Erdmann-Arnoldt'sche Controverse über Kants Prolegomena,' *Philosophische Monatshefte* 16 (1880), 44–71.

—— 'Zu Kants Widerlegung des Idealismus,' *Strassberger Abhandlungen zur Philosophie*, pp. 88–164. Freiburg: Mohr, 1884.

—— 'Die transcendentale Deduktion der Kategorien in der Erste Ausgabe der Kritik der reinen Vernunft,' in *Philosophische Abhandlungen*, pp. 24–98. Halle: Niemeyer, 1902.

—— *Commentar zu Kants Kritik der reinen Vernunft*. 2 vols. Stuttgart: Deutsche Verlags Anstalt, 1922.

—— *Die Philosophie des Als Ob*. 9th ed. Leipzig: Meiner, 1927.

Van Cleve, J. *Problems from Kant*. Oxford: Oxford University Press, 1999.

Vleeschauwer, H. J. *The Development of Kantian Thought*. London: Nelson, 1962.

Vorländer, K. *Immanuel Kant, der Mann und das Werk*. 2 vols. Hamburg: Meiner, 1977.

Walker, R. *Kant*. London: Routledge, 1978.

—— 'Idealism: Kant and Berkeley,' in *Essays on Berkeley*, ed. John Foster and Howard Robinson. Oxford: Oxford University Press, 1985.

—— 'Synthesis and Transcendental Idealism,' *Kant-Studien* 76 (1985), 14–27.

Walsh, W. H. 'Philosophy and Psychology in Kant's Critique,' *Kant-Studien* 57 (1966), 186–198.

—— *Kant's Criticism of Metaphysics*. Edinburgh: Edinburgh University Press, 1975.

—— 'Kant's Transcendental Idealism,' in Harper and Meerbote, *Kant on Causality, Freedom and Objectivity,* pp. 83–96.

Warda, A. *Immanuel Kants Bücher.* Berlin: Breslauer, 1922.

Washburn, M. 'The Second Edition of the *Critique:* Toward an Understanding of its Nature and Genesis,' *Kant-Studien* 66 (1975), 277–290.

Watkins, E. 'The Development of Physical Influx in Early Eighteenth Century Germany: Gottsched, Knutzen, and Crusius,' *Review of Metaphysics* 49 (1995), 295–339.

—— 'Kant's Theory of Physical Influx,' *Archiv für Geschichte der Philosophie* 77 (1995), 285–324.

—— 'From Pre-Established Harmony to Physical Influx: Leibniz's Reception in Eighteenth Century Germany,' *Perspectives on Science* 6 (1998), 136–203.

Waxman, W. *Kant's Model of the Mind.* Oxford: Oxford University Press, 1991.

Weldon, T. D. *Kant's Critique of Pure Reason.* Oxford: Clarendon Press, 1958.

Werkmeister, W. H. *Kant, The Architechtonic of His Philosophy.* La Salle: Open Court, 1980.

Westphal, K. 'Kant's Dynamic Constructions.' *Journal of Philosophical Research* 20 (1995), 382–429.

—— 'Noumenal Causality Reconsidered: Affection, Agency and Meaning in Kant,' *Canadian Journal of Philosophy* 27 (1997), 209–245.

Wilkerson, T. E. *Kant's Critique of Pure Reason.* Oxford: Oxford University Press, 1976.

Wilson, C. 'Confused Perceptions, Darkened Concepts: Some Features of Kant's Leibniz-Critique,' in Ross and McWalter, *Kant and His Influence,* pp. 73–103.

Wilson, M. 'Kant and the Refutation of Subjectivism,' in Beck, *Proceedings of the Third International Kant Congress,* pp. 597–605.

—— 'Kant and "The Dogmatic Idealism of Berkeley,"' *Journal of the History of Philosophy* 9 (1971), 459–475.

—— 'The Phenomenalisms of Kant and Berkeley,' in Wood, *Self and Nature in Kant's Philosophy,* pp. 157–173.

—— *Ideas and Mechanism.* Princeton: Princeton University Press, 1999.

—— 'The Phenomenalisms of Leibniz and Berkeley,' in *Ideas and Mechanism,* pp. 306–321.

Wolff, R. P. 'Kant's Debt to Hume via Beattie,' *Journal of the History of Ideas* 21 (1960), 117–123.

—— *Kant's Theory of Mental Activity.* Cambridge, Mass: Harvard University Press, 1963.

Yolton, J. 'Ideas and Knowledge in Seventeenth Century Philosophy,' *Journal of the History of Philosophy* 13 (1975), 145–165.

Fichte

Ameriks, K. 'Kant, Fichte, and Short Arguments to Idealism,' *Archiv für Geschichte der Philosophie* 72 (1990), 63–85.

Baumanns, P. *Fichtes ursprüngliches System. Sein Standort zwichen Kant und Hegel.* Stuttgart–Bad Cannstatt: Holzboog, 1972.

—— *Fichtes Wissenschaftslehre: Probleme ihres Anfangs.* Bonn: Bouvier, 1974.

Breazeale, D. 'Fichte's *Aenesidemus* Review and the Transformation of German Idealism,' *Review of Metaphysics* 34 (1981), 545–568.

—— 'Between Kant and Fichte: Karl Leonhard Reinhold's "Elementary Philosophy," ' *Review of Metaphysics* 35 (1982), 785–821.

—— 'How to Make an Idealist: Fichte's "Refutation of Dogmatism" and the Problem of the Starting Point of the *Wissenschaftslehre*,' *Philosophical Forum* 19 (1987–1988), 97–123.

—— 'The "Standpoint of Life" and the "Standpoint of Philosophy" in the Context of the "Jena *Wissenschaftslehre*" (1794–1801)' in *Transzendentalphilosophie als System: Die Auseinandersetzung zwischen 1794 und 1806,* ed. A. Mues, pp. 81–104. Hamburg: Meiner, 1989.

—— 'Fichte on Skepticism,' *Journal of the History of Philosophy* 29 (1991), 77–102.

—— 'Why Fichte Now?' *Journal of Philosophy* 88 (1991), 524–531.

—— 'Kant, Fichte and "The Interests of Reason," ' *Revista de Filosofia* 9 (1994), 81–98.

—— 'Check or Checkmate? On the Finitude of the Fichtean Self,' in *The Modern Subject: Conceptions of the Self in Classical German Philosophy,* ed. K. Ameriks and D. Sturma, pp. 87–114. Albany: SUNY Press, 1996.

—— 'The Theory of Practice and the Practice of Theory: Fichte and the "Primacy of Practical Reason," ' *International Philosophical Quarterly* 36 (1996), 47–64.

—— ed. *New Perspectives on Fichte.* Atlantic Highlands, N.J.: Humanities Press, 1996.

Breazeale, D., and Tom Rockmore, eds. *Fichte: Historical Contexts/Contemporary Controversies.* Atlantic Highlands, N.J.: Humanities Press, 1994.

Buhr, M. *Revolution und Philosophie: Die Ursprüngliche Philosophie Johann Gottlieb Fichte und die französische Revolution.* Berlin: Akademie Verlag, 1965.

Dewey, J. *The Quest for Certainty.* New York: Capricorn, 1960.

Flach, W. 'Fichte über Kritizismus und Dogmatismus,' *Zeitschrift für philosophische Forschung* 18 (1964), 585–596.

Franks, P. 'The Discovery of the Other: Cavell, Fichte, and Skepticism,' in *Common Knowledge* 5 (1996), 72–105.

—— 'Freedom, *Tatsache* and *Tathandlung* in the Development of Fichte's Jena *Wissenschaftslehre*,' *Archiv für Geschichte der Philosophie* 79 (1997), 310–323.

—— 'Subjectivity without Subjectivism: Fichte's Philosophy Today,' in *The Cam-*

bridge Companion to Fichte, ed. Günter Zöller (Cambridge: Cambridge University Press, forthcoming).

Fuchs, E. 'Einleitung' to *Wissenschaftslehre novo methodo,* pp. ix–xxxiv. (Hamburg: Meiner, 1994).

———— 'Reinhold und Fichte in Briefwechsel zweier Jenenser Studenten,' *Fichte-Studien* 7 (1995), 143–172.

Gardiner, P. 'Fichte and German Idealism,' in *Idealism Past and Present,* ed. G. Vesey, pp. 111–126. Cambridge: Cambridge University Press, 1982.

Griswold, C. 'Fichte's Modification of Kant's Transcendental Idealism in the *Wissenschaftslehre* of 1794 and the Introductions of 1797,' *Auslegung* 4 (1977), 131–151.

Gueroult, M. *L'evolution et structure de la doctrine de la science chez Fichte.* 2 vols. Paris: Belles Lettres, 1930.

Heimsoeth, H. *Fichte.* Munich: Reinhardt,1923.

Henrich, D. *Fichtes ursprüngliche Einsicht.* Frankfurt: Klostermann, 1967.

Hohler, T. 'Intellectual Intuition and the Beginning of Fichte's Philosophy: A New Interpretation.' *Tijdscrit voor Filosofie* 37 (1975), 52–73.

———— *Imagination and Reflection: Intersubjectivity: Fichte's Grundlage of 1794.* The Hague: Martinus Nijhoff, 1982.

Holz, H. 'Die Struktur der Dialektik in den Frühschriften von Fichte und Schelling,' *Archiv für Geschichte der Philosophie* 52 (1970), 71–90.

Hübner, K. 'Fichte, Sartre und der Nihilismus,' *Zeitschrift für philosophische Forschung* 10 (1956), 29–43.

Jacobs, W. *Johann Gottlieb Fichte.* Hamburg: Rowohlt, 1984.

Jalloh, C. *Fichte's Kant-Interpretation and the Doctrine of Science.* Washington, D.C.: University Press of America, 1988.

———— 'Fichte: Foundationalism, Anitfoundationalism, and the New Nihilism,' *The Journal of Philosophy* 88 (1991), 542–543.

Kabitz, W. *Studien zur Entwicklungsgeschichte der Fichteschen Wissenschaftslehre aus der kantischen Philosophie.* Berlin: Reuther and Reichard, 1902.

Lachs, J. 'Fichte's Idealism,' *American Philosophical Quarterly* 9 (1972), 311–318.

———— 'Preface' to *Fichte. The Science of Knowledge,* vii–xviii. Cambridge: Cambridge University Press, 1982.

———— 'Is There an Absolute Self," *Philosophical Forum* 19 (1988), 169–181.

Lauth, R. 'Die Bedeutung der Fichteschen Philosophie für die Gegenwart,' *Philosophisches Jahrbuch* 70 (1962–1963), 252–270.

———— 'J. G. Fichtes Gesamtidee der Philosophie,' *Philosophisches Jahrbuch* 71 (1964), 253–285.

———— *Die Entstehung von Schellings Identitätsphilosophie in der Auseinandersetzung mit Fichtes "Wissenschaftslehre" (1795–1801).* Freiburg: Alber, 1975.

———— 'The Transcendental Philosophy of the Munich School,' *Idealistic Studies* 11 (1981), 8–39.

———— *Vernünftige Durchdringung der Wirklichkeit: Fichte und sein Umkreis.* Neuried: Ars Una, 1994.

Lazzari, A. 'Fichtes Entwicklung von der zweiten Auflage der Offenbarungskritik bis zur Rezeption von Schulzes *Anesidemus,' Fichte-Studien* 9 (1997), 181–196.

Léon, X. *Fichte et son temps.* 2 vols. Paris: Colin, 1922–1927.

Mandt, A. J. 'Fichte's Idealism in Theory and Practice,' *Idealistic Studies* 14 (1984), 127–147.

Martin, W. 'Fichte's Anti-Dogmatism,' *Ratio* 2 (1992), 129–146.

———— '"Without a Striving No Object Is Possible": Fichte's Striving Doctrine and the Primacy of Practice,' in *New Perspectives on Fichte,* ed. D. Breazeale and T. Rockmore, pp. 19–33. Atlantic Highlands, N.J.: Humanities Press, 1996.

———— *Idealism and Objectivity: Understanding Fichte's Jena Project.* Stanford: Stanford University Press, 1997.

Medicus, F. *J. G. Fichte: Dreizehn Vorlesungen.* Berlin: Reuther and Reichard, 1905.

Naylor, J. 'Interpretations of Fichte,' *Idealistic Studies* 11 (1981), 125–141.

Neuhouser, F. *Fichte's Theory of Subjectivity.* Cambridge: Cambridge University Press, 1990.

Philonenko, A. *La Liberté humaine dans la philosophie de Fichte.* Paris: Vrin, 1980.

———— 'Die intellektuelle Anschauung bei Fichte,' in *Der transcendentale Gedanke: Die gegenwärtige Darstellung der Philosophie Fichtes,* ed. Klaus Hammacher, pp. 91–106. Hamburg: Meiner, 1981.

———— 'Fichte and the Critique of Metaphysics,' *Philosophical Forum* 19 (1988), 124–139.

Pippin, R. 'Fichte's Contribution,' *Philosophical Forum* 19 (1988), 74–96.

———— 'Fichte's Alleged Subjective, Psychological, One-Sided Idealism,' in Sedgwick, S., ed., *The Reception of Kant's Critical Philosophy,* pp. 141–171. Cambridge: Cambridge University Press, 2000.

Raab, D. 'Lachs on Fichte.' *Dialogue* 12 (1975), 480–485.

———— 'J. G. Fichte: Three Arguments for Idealism,' *Idealistic Studies* 6 (1976), 169–177.

———— 'Is Critical Idealism Idealism?', *Idealistic Studies* 9 (1979), 131–137.

Ricard, L. 'La Philosophie de Fichte et L'Existentialisme,' *Proceedings of the Tenth International Congress of Philosophy,* 2:1174–1176. Amsterdam, 1948.

Rockmore, T. 'Fichte's Idealism and Marx's Materialism,' *Man and World* 8 (1975), 189–206.

———— 'Activity in Fichte and Marx,' *Idealistic Studies* 6 (1976), 191–214.

———— 'Fichtean Epistemology and the Idea of Philosophy,' in *Der transcendentale Gedanke: Die gegenwärtige Darstellung der Philosophie Fichtes,* ed. K. Hammacher, pp. 485–497. Hamburg: Meiner, 1981.

———— 'Fichtean Epistemology and Contemporary Philosophy,' *Philosophical Forum* 19 (1987), 156–168.

———— 'Antifoundationalism, Circularity and the Spirit of Fichte,' in Breazeale and Rockmore, *Fichte: Historical Contexts Contemporary Controversies,* pp. 96–112.

Rohs, P. *Johann Gottlieb Fichte*. Munich: Beck, 1991.

Schussler, I. *Die Auseinandersetzung von Idealismus und Realismus in Fichtes Wissenschaftslehre 1794/5, zweite Darstellung der Wissenschaftslehre 1804*. Frankfurt: Klostermann, 1972.

Stolzenberg, J. *Fichtes Begriff der intellektuellen Anschauung*. Stuttgart: Klett, 1986.

Verweyen, H. 'New Perspectives on J. G. Fichte,' *Idealistic Studies* 6 (1976), 118–159.

Wood, A. 'Fichte's Philosophical Revolution,' *Philosophical Topics* 19 (1992), 1–28.

—————— 'The "I" as Principle of Practical Philosophy,' in Sedgwick, *Reception*, pp. 93–108.

Wundt, M. *J. G. Fichte*. Stuttgart: Fromann, 1927.

—————— *Fichte Forschungenen*. Stuttgart: Fromann, 1929.

Zöller, G. *Fichte's Transcendental Philosophy: The Original Duplicity of Intelligence and Will*. Cambridge: Cambridge University Press, 1998.

Zöller, G., ed. *The Cambridge Companion to Fichte*. Cambridge: Cambridge University Press, forthcoming.

Romantics

Ayrault, R. *La Genèse du romantisme allemand*. 3 vols. Paris: Aubier, 1961.

Baum, W. 'Der Klagenfurter Herbert-Kreis zwischen Aufklärung und Romantik,' *Revue Internationale de Philosophie* 50 (1996), 483–514.

Baumgardt, D. 'Spinoza und der deutsche Spinozismus,' *Kant-Studien* 32 (1927), 182–192.

Behler, E. 'Friedrich Schlegels Vorlesungen über Transzendentalphilosophie Jena 1800–01,' in *Transzendentalphilosophie und Spekulation. Der Streit um die Gestalt einer Ersten Philosophie (1799–1807)*, ed. Walter Jaeschke. Hamburg: Meiner, 1953.

—————— Friedrich Schlegels Theorie der Universalpoesie,' *Jahrbuch der deutschen Schillergesellschaft* 1 (1957), 211–252.

—————— 'Friedrich Schlegel's Theory of an Alternating Principle Prior to his Arrival in Jena (6 August 1796),' *Revue Internationale de Philosophie* 50 (1996), 383–402.

—————— 'Einleitung' to *Philosophische Lehrjahre*. Vol. 8 of *Friedrich Schlegel Kritische Ausgabe*, ed. E. Behler, J-J. Anstett, and H. Eichner. Paderborn: Schöningh, 1958.

—————— 'Schlegels Frühe Position in der Ausbildung der idealistischen Philosophie,' in the 'Einleitung' to vol. 8 of the *Friedrich Schlegel Kritische Ausgabe*, pp. xxi–lxxxvii.

—————— 'Friedrich Schlegel und Hegel,' *Hegel-Studien* 2 (1963), 203–250.

—————— *Friedrich Schlegel*. Hamburg: Rowohlt, 1966.

—————— *Studien zur Romantik und zur idealistischen Philosophie*. Paderborn: Schöningh, 1988.

—————— *Frühromantik*. Berlin: de Gruyter, 1992.

—————— *German Romantic Literary Theory*. Cambridge: Cambridge University Press, 1993.

Behler, E., ed. *Die Aktualität der Frühromantik*. Paderborn: Schöningh, 1987.

Benjamin, W. *Der Begriff der Kunstkritik in der deutschen Romantik.* Bern: Francke, 1920.

Berlin, I. 'The Romantic Revolution: A Crisis in the History of Modern Thought,' in *The Sense of Reality,* ed. Henry Hardy. New York: Farrar, Straus and Giroux, 1996.

—— *The Roots of Romanticism.* Princeton: Princeton University Press, 1999.

Böckmann, P. 'Das Späte in Hölderlins Spätlyrik,' *Hölderlin Jahrbuch* 12 (1961–1962), 205–222.

Böhm, W. *Hölderlin.* 2 vols. Halle-Saale: Niemeyer, 1928.

Brauer, U. *Isaak von Sinclair.* Stuttgart: Klett-Cotta, 1993.

Brecht, M. 'Hölderlin und das Tübinger Stift,' *Hölderlin Jahrbuch* 18 (1973), 20–48.

Cassirer, E. 'Hölderlin und der deutsche Idealismus,' in *Idee und Gestalt,* pp. 113–155. Berlin: Cassirer, 1924.

Dick, M. *Die Entwicklung des Gedankens der Poesie in den Fragmenten des Novalis.* Bonn: Bouvier, 1967. Mainzer Philosophische Forschungen, Band 7.

Dilthey, W. *Leben Schleiermachers,* ed. M. Redeker. Göttingen: Vandenhoeck and Ruprecht, 1970.

—— *Das Erlebnis und die Dichtung.* Leipzig: Tuebner, 1907.

Droz, J. *La Romantisme allemand et l' état.* Paris: Payot, 1966.

Flitner, W. *August Ludwig Hülsen und der Bund der Freien Männer.* Jena: Eugen Diederichs, 1913.

Frank, M. 'Die Philosophie des sogenannten "magischen Idealismus,"' *Euphorion* 63 (1969), 88–116.

—— 'Ordo inversus. Zu einer Reflexionsfigur bei Novalis, Hölderlin, Kleist und Kafka, in *Geist und Zeichen. Festschrift für Arthur Henkel,* ed. H. Anton, B. Gajek, and P. Pfaff. Heidelberg: Winter, 1977.

—— *Eine Einführung in Schellings Philosophie.* Frankfurt: Suhrkamp, 1985.

—— *Einführung in die frühromantische Ästhetik.* Frankfurt: Suhrkamp, 1989.

—— *Das Problem «Zeit» in der deutschen Romantik.* Paderborn: Schöningh, 1990.

—— '"Alle Wahrheit ist Relativ, Alles Wissen Symbolisch,"' *Revue Internationale de Philosophie* 50 (1996), 403–436.

—— 'Philosophical Foundations of Early Romanticism,' in *The Modern Subject,* ed. K. Ameriks and D. Sturma. Albany: SUNY Press, 1995.

—— *Unendliche Annäherung: Die Anfänge der philosophischen Frühromantik.* Frankfurt: Suhrkamp, 1997.

Franz, M. '"Platons frommer Garten." Hölderlins Platonlektüre von Tübingen bis Jena,' *Hölderlin Jahrbuch* 28 (1992–1993), 111–127.

Gaier, U. *Hölderlin.* Tübingen: Francke Verlag, 1993.

Harris, H. S. *Hegel's Development: Toward the Sunlight.* Oxford: Clarendon Press, 1972.

Haym, R. *Die romantische Schule.* Berlin: Gaertner, 1882.

Haering, T. *Novalis als Philosoph.* Stuttgart: Kohlhammer, 1954.

Heine, H. *Die romantische Schule.* Stuttgart: Reclam, 1976.

Henrich, D. 'Jakob Zwillings Nachlass: Eine Rekonstruktion,' *Hegel-Studien Beiheft* 28 (1986).

———— *Der Grund im Bewußtsein: Untersuchungen zu Hölderlins Denken (1794–1795).* Stuttgart: Klett-Cotta, 1992.

Hegel, H. *Isaak von Sinclair zwischen Fichte, Hölderlin und Hegel.* Frankfurt: Klostermann, 1971.

———— 'Reflexion und Einheit: Sinclair und der Bund der Geister,' *Hegel-Studien Beiheft* 9 (1973), 91–106.

Hiebel, F. *Novalis.* Bern: Francke, 1972.

Hildebrandt, K. *Hölderlin, Dichtung und Philosophie.* Stuttgart: Kohlhammer, 1939.

Hoffmeister, J. *Hölderlin und die Philosophie.* Leipzig: Meiner, 1942.

Huch, R. *Die Romantik.* Leipzig: Haessel, 1924.

Jamme, C. *«Ein Ungelehrtes Buch» Die philosophische Gemeinschaft zwischen Hölderlin und Hegel in Frankfurt 1797.* Bonn: Bouvier, 1983.

———— 'Isaak von Sinclairs Philosophische Raisonnements,' *Hegel-Studien* 18 (1983), 240–244.

Kirchner, E. *Philosophie der Romantik.* Jena: Diederischs, 1906.

Kluckhohn, P. *Das Ideengut der deutschen Romantik.* 3rd ed. Tübingen: Niemeyer, 1953.

Lacoue-Labarthe, P., and J-L. Nancy. *The Literary Absolute,* trans. Phillip Barnard and Cheryl Lester. Albany: SUNY Press, 1988.

Mähl, H-J. 'Novalis und Plotin,' *Jahrbuch des freien deutschen Hochstifts* (1963), 139–250.

———— *Die Idee des goldene Zeitlaters im Werk des Novalis.* Heidelberg: Winter, 1965.

Molnár, G. *Novalis' "Fichte Studies."* The Hague: Mouton, 1970.

Müller, E. *Hölderlin: Studien zur Geschichte seines Geistes.* Stuttgart: Kohlhammer, 1944.

Neubauer, J. *Novalis.* Boston: Twayne, 1980.

Neubauer, J. 'Dr. John Brown and Early German Romanticism,' *Journal of the History of Ideas* 28 (1967), 367–382.

———— *Bifocal Vision: Novalis Philosophy of Nature and Disease.* Chapel Hill: University of North Carolina Press, 1971. Studies in Germanic Languages and Literature, No. 68.

Obenauer, K. *August Ludwig Hülsen.* Erlangen: Junge and Sohn, 1910.

O'Brian, W. *Novalis.* Durham: Duke University Press, 1995.

Pikulik, L. *Frühromantik.* Munich: Beck, 1992.

Pippin, R., *Hegel's Idealism.* Cambridge: Cambridge University Press, 1989.

Prang, H., ed. *Begriffsbestimmung der Romantik.* Darmstadt: Wissenschaftliche Buchgesellschaft, 1968.

Prawer, S., ed. *The Romantic Period in Germany.* New York: Schocken, 1970.

Schadewaldt, W. 'Das Bild der Exzentischen Bahn bei Hölderlin,' *Hölderlin Jahrbuch* (1952), 1–16

Schanze, H., ed. *Romantik-Handbuch.* Tübingen: Kröner, 1994.

Schmitt, C. *Politische Romantik.* Munich: Duncker and Humblot, 1925.

Seyhan, A. *Representation and Its Discontents: The Critical Legacy of German Romanticism.* Berkeley: University of California Press, 1992.

Silz, W. *Early German Romanticism.* Cambridge: Harvard University Press, 1929.

Simon, H. *Der magische Idealismus. Studien zur Philosophie des Novalis.* Heidelberg: Winter, 1906.

Strauß, L. 'Jakob Zwilling und sein Nachlass,' *Euphorion* 29 (1928), 368–369.

Uerling, H. *Friedrich von Hardenberg. Werk und Forschung.* Stuttgart: J. B. Metzlar, 1991.

Waibel, V. *Hölderlin und Fichte 1794–1800.* Paderborn: Schöningh, 2000.

Walzel, O. *German Romanticism.* New York: Putnam, 1932.

Wegengast, M. *Hölderlins Spinoza Rezeption.* Tübingen: Niemeyer, 1990.

Wild, R. 'Freidenker in Deutschland,' *Zeitschrift für historische Forschung* 6 (1979), 253–285.

Wundt, M. 'Die Wiederentdeckung Platons im 18. Jahrhundert,' *Blätter für deutsche Philosophie* 15 (1941), 149–158.

Ziolkowski, T. *German Romanticism and Its Institutions.* Princeton: Princeton University Press, 1990.

Schelling

Balss, H. 'Kielmeyer als Biologe,' *Sudhoffs Archiv für Geschichte der Medizin* 23 (1930), 268–289.

Barsanti, G. 'Lamarck and the Birth of Biology, 1740–1810,' in Poggi and Bossi, *Romanticism in Science,* pp. 47–74.

Baumgartner, H. M., and H. Korten. *Friedrich Wilhelm Joseph Schelling.* Munich: Beck, 1996.

Bowie, A. *Schelling and Modern European Philosophy: An Introduction.* London: Routledge, 1993.

Buchner, H. 'Hegel und das Kritische Journal der Philosophie,' *Hegel-Studien* 3 (1965), 95–156.

Büttersack, F. 'Karl Friedrich Kielmeyer,' *Sudhoffs Archiv für Geschichte der Medizin* 23 (1930), 236–246.

Caneva, K. L. 'Teleology with Regrets,' *Annals of Science* 47 (1990), 291–300.

Cunningham, A., and N. Jardine, eds. *Romanticism and the Sciences.* Cambridge: Cambridge University Press, 1990.

Durner, M. 'Schellings Begegnung mit den Naturwissenschaften in Leipzig,' *Archiv für Geschichte der Philosophie* 72 (1990), 220–236.

——— 'Die Naturphilosophie im 18. Jahrhundert und der naturwissenschaftliche Unterricht im Tübingen,' *Archiv für Geschichte der Philosophie* 73 (1991), 71–103.

Düsing, K. 'Spekulation und Reflexion: Zur Zusammenarbeit Schellings und Hegels in Jena,' *Hegel-Studien* 5 (1969), 95–128.

——— 'Ein Brief von Schelling an Steffens über Naturphilosophie,' *Hegel-Studien* 9 (1974), 39–42.

——— *Schellings und Hegels erste absolute Metaphysik (1801–1802)* Cologne: Jürgen Dinter Verlag für Philosophie, 1988.

——— 'Die Entstehung des spekulativen Idealismus: Schellings und Hegels Wandlungen zwischen 1800 und 1801,' in *Transzendentalphilosophie und*

Spekulation: Der Streit um die Gestalt einer Ersten Philosophie (1799–1807), ed. W. Jaeschke. Hamburg: Meiner, 1993.

Esposito, J. *Schelling's Idealism and Philosophy of Nature.* Cranbury, N.J.: Associated University Presses, 1977.

Fischer, K. *Schellings Leben, Werke und Lehre.* Heidelberg: Winter, 1872.

Frank, M. *Eine Einführung in Schellings Philosophie.* Frankfurt: Suhrkamp, 1985.

Frank, M., ed. *Materialien zu Schellings philosophischen Anfängen.* Frankfurt: Suhrkamp, 1975.

Franz, M. *Schellings Tübinger Platon-Studien.* Göttingen: Vandenhoeck and Ruprecht, 1996.

Fuhrmanns, H. 'Schelling im Tübinger Stift Herbst 1790–1795,' in *Briefe und Dokumente.* 2 vols. Bonn: Bouvier, 1962–1975.

Gloy, K., and P. Burger, eds. *Die Naturphilosophie im Deutschen Idealismus.* Stuttgart: Fromann, 1994.

Gram, M. 'Intellectual Intuition: The Continuity Thesis,' *Journal of the History of Ideas* 42 (1981), 287–304.

Hankins, T. *Science and the Enlightenment.* Cambridge: Cambridge University Press, 1985.

Hartkopf, W. 'Denken und Naturentwicklung: Zur Aktualität der Philosophie des jungen Schelling,' in Sandkühler, *Natur und geschichtlicher Prozeß,* pp. 83–126.

Hasler, L. *Schelling, Seine Bedeutung für eine Philosophie der Natur und der Geschichte.* Stuttgart: Fromann-Holzboog, 1981.

Heckmann, R., and H. Krings, eds. *Zur Auseinandersetzung mit der Naturphilosophie des jungen Schelling.* Stuttgart: Fromann, 1985.

Henckmann, W. 'Solgers Schellingstudium in Jena 1801/02,' *Hegel-Studien* 13 (1978), 53–74.

Heuser-Kessler, M-L. *Die Produktivität der Natur: Schellings Naturphilosophie und das neue Paradigma der Selbstorganisation in den Naturwissenschaften.* Berlin: Duncker and Humblot, 1986.

——— 'Schellings Organismusbegriff und seine Kritik des Mechanismus und Vitalismus,' *Allgemeine Zeitschrift für Philosophie* 14 (1989), 17–36.

Holz, H. 'Der Begriff der Natur in Schellings spekulativem System. Zum Einfluß von Leibniz auf Schelling,' in Sandkühler, *Natur und geschichtlicher Prozeß,* pp. 202–226.

Holz, H. 'Die Beziehungen zwischen Schellings Naturphilosophie und dem Identitätssystem in den Jahren 1801/02,' *Philosophisches Journal des Görresgesellschaft* 8 (1971), 270–294.

Jacobs, W. *Zwischen Revolution und Orthodoxie?: Schelling und seine Freunde im Stift und an der Universität Tübingen. Texte und Untersuchungen.* Stuttgart–Bad Cannstatt: Fromann-Holzboog, 1989. Spekulation und Erfahrung: Abt. 2, Untersuchungen, Band 12.

Jantzen, J. 'Theorien der Irritabilität und Sensibilität,' in *Wissenschaftlicher Bericht zu Schellings Naturphilosophischen Schriften 1797–1800,* pp. 375–498. Stuttgart: Fromann, 1994.

Jaspers, K. *Schelling, Grösse und Verhängnis.* Munich: Piper, 1955.

Kirchhoff, J. *Schelling.* Hamburg: Rowohlt, 1982.

Knight, D. M. 'The Physical Sciences and the Romantic Movement,' *History of Science* 9 (1970), 54–75.

Knittermeyer, H. *Schelling und die romantische Schule.* Munich: Reinhardt, 1929.

Krings, H.'Genesis und Materie—Zur Bedeutung der Timaeus Handschrift für Schellings Naturphilosophie,' in *Historisch-Kritische Ausgabe* I/5, 115–155.

Kuhlmann, H. *Schellings Früher Idealismus.* Stuttgart: Metzler, 1993.

Küppers, B-O. *Natur als Organismus. Schellings frühe Naturphilosophie und ihre Bedeutung für die moderne Biologie.* Frankfurt: Klostermann, 1972. Philosophsiche Abhandlungen, Band 58.

Lange, E., and G. Biedermann. *Die Philosophie des jungen Schelling.* Weimar: Böhlaus Nachfolger, 1977.

Larson, J. 'Vital Forces: Regulative Principles or Constitutive Agents? A Strategy in German Physiology, 1786–1802,' *Isis* 70 (1979), 235–249.

—— *Interpreting Nature: The Science of Living Form from Linnaeus to Kant.* Baltimore: Johns Hopkins, 1994.

Lauth, R. 'Die erste philosophische Auseinandersetzung zwischen Fichte und Schelling 1795–1797,' *Zeitschrift für philosophische forschung* 21 (1967), 341–367.

—— *Die Entstehung von Schellings Identitätsphilosophie in der Auseinandersetzung mit Fichtes Wissenschaftslehre.* Freiburg: Alber, 1975.

Lenoir, T. 'Generational Factors in the Origin of *Romantische Naturphilosophie*,' *Journal of the History of Biology* 11 (1978), 57–100.

—— 'Kant, Blumenbach, and Vital Materialism in German Biology,' *Isis* 71 (1980), 77–108.

—— 'The Göttingen School and the Deveopment of Transcendental Naturphilosophie in the Romantic Era,' *Studies in the History of Biology* 5 (1981), 111–205.

—— *The Strategy of Life: Teleology and Mechanics in Nineteenth Century Biology,* pp. 1–53. Chicago: University Chicago Press, 1989).

Léon, X. 'Fichte contre Schelling,' *Revue de Metaphysique et de Morale,* 1904, 949–976.

Lukács, G. *Die Zerstörung der Vernunft.* Berlin: Aufbau, 1955.

Morgan, S. R. *The Palingenesis of Ancient Wisdom and the Kingdom of God: An Historical Interpretation of Schelling's Earliest Philosophy.* Ph.D. diss., Cambridge University, 1995.

Nauen, F. *Revolution, Idealism and Human Freedom: Schelling, Hölderlin, and Hegel, and the Crisis of Early German Idealism.* The Hague: Nijhoff, 1971.

Poggi, S., and M. Bossi, eds. *Romanticism in Science.* Dordrecht: Kluwer, 1994.

Richards, R. *The Romantic Conception of Life: Poetry and the Organic in the Age of Goethe.* Chicago: University of Chicago Press, 2001.

Roger, J. *The Life-Sciences in Eighteenth Century French Thought.* Stanford: Stanford University Press, 1997. First published as *Les Sciences de la vie dans la pensée francaise au XVIIIe siécle.* Paris: Armand Colin, 1963.

Rosenkranz, K. *Schelling. Vorlesungen gehalten im Sommer 1842.* Danzig, 1842.

Sandkühler, H. J. *Friedrich Wilhelm Joseph Schelling*. Stuttgart: Metzler, 1970.

Sandkühler, H. J., ed. *Natur und geschichtlicher Prozeß*. Frankfurt: Suhrkamp, 1984.

Snelders, H. A. M. 'Romanticism and Naturphilosophie and the Inorganic Natural Sciences 1797–1840: An Introductory Survey,' *Studies in Romanticism* 9 (1970), 193–215.

Snow, D. *Schelling and the End of Idealism*. Albany: SUNY Press, 1996.

Steffens, H. *Was ich erlebte*. 10 vols. Breslau: J. Max, 1841.

Tilliette, X. *Schelling: Une Philosophie en Devenir*. 2 vols. Paris: Vrin: 1970.

Wetzels, W. 'Aspects of Natural Science in German Romanticism,' *Studies in Romanticism* 19 (1971), 44–59.

White, A. *Schelling: An Introduction to the System of Freedom*. New Haven: Yale University Press, 1983.

Wieland, W. 'Die Anfänge der Philosophie Schellings und die Frage nach der Natur,' in Frank, *Materialien zu Schellings philosophischen Anfängen*, pp. 237–279.

Index

726   **Index**